THE SIXTEEN DOCUMENTS
OF VATICAN II

THE SIXTEEN DOCUMENTS OF VATICAN II

Introductions by
Douglas G. Bushman, S.T.L.

General Editor
Marianne Lorraine Trouvé, FSP

Pauline
BOOKS & MEDIA
BOSTON

Nihil Obstat (for the introductions)
Rev. Paul E. Ritt, S.T.D.

Imprimatur
†Bernard Cardinal Law

Library of Congress Cataloging-in-Publication Data

Vatican Council (2nd : 1962–1965)
    [Documents of Vatican II]
    The sixteen documents of Vatican II / introductions by Douglas G.
Bushman ; general editor, Marianne Lorraine Trouvé ;   [N.C.W.C.
translation].
     p. cm.
    Includes bibliographical references and index.
    ISBN 0-8198-7018-8
    1. Vatican Council (2nd : 1962–1965) 2. Catholic Church—
Doctrines. I. Trouvé, Marianne Lorraine. II. Title.
BX830 1962.A3G3 1999
262'.52—dc21   · 99-29519
                                             CIP

N.C.W.C. Translation

The Appendix to *Lumen Gentium* from the Acts of the Council was reprinted
from: *The Pope Speaks,* Vol. 10, No. 4. Summer-Autumn, 1965, 400–402.

Cover Design: Helen Rita Lane, FSP

Printed and published in the U.S.A. by Pauline Books & Media, 50 Saint
Pauls Avenue, Boston, MA 02130-3491.

www.pauline.org

Pauline Books & Media is the publishing house of the Daughters of St. Paul,
an international congregation of women religious serving the Church with the
communications media.

1 2 3 4 5 6   04 03 02 01 00 99

CONTENTS

DECREE ON THE CATHOLIC CHURCHES OF THE EASTERN RITE
Orientalium Ecclesiarum

DECREE ON ECUMENISM
Unitatis Redintegratio

DECREE ON THE PASTORAL OFFICE OF BISHOPS IN THE CHURCH
Christus Dominus

DECREE ON THE ADAPTATION AND RENEWAL OF RELIGIOUS LIFE
Perfectae Caritatis

DECREE ON PRIESTLY TRAINING
Optatam Totius

DECLARATION ON CHRISTIAN EDUCATION
Gravissimum Educationis

DECLARATION ON THE RELATION OF THE CHURCH TO NON-CHRISTIAN RELIGIONS
Nostra Aetate

DOGMATIC CONSTITUTION ON DIVINE REVELATION
Dei Verbum

DECREE ON THE APOSTOLATE OF THE LAITY
Apostolicam Actuositatem

DECLARATION ON RELIGIOUS FREEDOM
Dignitatis Humanae

DECREE ON THE MISSION ACTIVITY OF THE CHURCH
Ad Gentes

DECREE ON THE MINISTRY AND LIFE OF PRIESTS
Presbyterorum Ordinis

PASTORAL CONSTITUTION ON THE CHURCH IN THE MODERN WORLD
Gaudium et Spes

ABOUT THE AUTHOR
OF THE INTRODUCTIONS

Douglas Bushman has taught theology at the parish, diocesan, undergraduate and graduate levels. Currently he is the Director of the Institute for Religious and Pastoral Studies at the University of Dallas in Irving, Texas, where he teaches courses on Vatican II, the writings of Pope John Paul II, ecclesiology and spirituality. He holds a Licentiate in sacred theology granted by the Pontifical Faculty of the University of Fribourg, Switzerland.

Professor Bushman is the author of the *In His Image Program of Renewal Through Education* and has contributed to the *In His Image* religion textbook series, both published by Ignatius Press. He has written numerous articles for Catholic journals and magazines, has appeared on Catholic television and radio programs, and gives lectures and retreats on a wide range of doctrinal, pastoral and spiritual subjects. He and his wife, JoAnn, home-school their six children.

EDITOR'S NOTE

The conciliar documents in this volume appear in the order in which they were promulgated.

There are four constitutions, nine decrees and three declarations. The constitutions are the most weighty and formal documents, dealing with substantive matters, usually of a doctrinal nature. The decrees and declarations are less solemn than the constitutions. A decree is a statement that may be of a doctrinal or pastoral nature, and often gives guidelines for appropriate updating. A declaration deals with topics of current interest, especially insofar as they raise pastoral concerns.

The official text of the documents of Vatican II is in Latin and can be found in *Sacrosanctum Oecumenicum Concilium Vaticanum II: Constitutiones, Decreta, Declarationes* (Vatican, 1966). Although various English translations have been published, there is no "official" English translation of these documents. The translation used in this edition is that of the N.C.W.C. (National Catholic Welfare Conference, the precursor of the National Council of Catholic Bishops).

GENERAL INTRODUCTION

The Universal Call to Holiness

To sum up the intention, content and pastoral orientation of the Second Vatican Council, one could well choose the following statement: "The saints have always been the source and origin of renewal in the most difficult moments in the Church's history."[1]

The *Constitution on the Sacred Liturgy,* the first document the Council promulgated, states that the Council's first and most general goal was "to impart an ever increasing vigor to the Christian life of the faithful" (*SC* 1). This reflects the inspiration and intention of Pope John XXIII, who convoked the Council. It was called to "strengthen spiritual energies" so that the Church "will become greater in spiritual riches."[2]

The Popes to follow him, Paul VI, John Paul I and John Paul II, would look at the Council no differently. For Paul VI the Council desired to see "the unique interest which the life of Christ deserves reawakened, not so much for the sake of elaborating new theories as for generating new energies. They should be used for acquiring that sanctity which Christ teaches" (*ES* 41). With several years retrospective view, he would write: "This strong invitation to holiness could be regarded as the most characteristic element in the whole magisterium of the Council, and so to say, its ultimate purpose."[3]

As Pope John Paul II put it, the "Vatican Council has significantly spoken on the universal call to holiness. It is possible to say that this call

---

1. Pope John Paul II, *Christifideles Laici,* 16; quoted in the *Catechism of the Catholic Church,* 828.

2. Opening Speech of the Council, October 11, 1962.

3. Motu Proprio *Sanctitatis Clarior* (March 19, 1969): *AAS* 61 (1969), p. 149.

to holiness is precisely the basic charge entrusted to all the sons and daughters of the Church by a Council which intended to bring a renewal of Christian life based on the Gospel" (*CL* 16).

This explains why he also wrote: "The best preparation for the new millennium, therefore, can only be expressed in a renewed commitment to apply, as faithfully as possible, the teachings of Vatican II to the life of every individual and of the whole Church" (*TMA* 20). His vision for the Church of the third millennium—a vision which includes Christian reunification, a new evangelization, justice based on human dignity and a preferential love for the poor—calls for the work of saints. That is to say, only God can accomplish it, and God is present and active in the world through his saints.

Holiness in the Plan of Renewal

Ecclesiam Suam, the first encyclical of Pope Paul VI, articulates renewal in a systematic and comprehensive way. Its three-point outline of the renewal process reinforces the call to holiness as the key concept of the Council. The importance of *Ecclesiam Suam* does not derive only from the fact that Paul VI wrote it during the Council to communicate his thoughts to his brother bishops assembled in Rome, in order to promote unity in vision and purpose. It also has great importance because Pope John Paul II has made its three-point outline of renewal a fundamental principle of his own understanding of the Council and his efforts to implement it.[4]

For Paul VI, renewal begins with awareness. This means that "the Church should deepen its consciousness of itself" (*ES* 9). Awareness is the fruit of listening to the word of God so that the Church can more precisely understand God's will. Vatican II asked: what does the word of God say to today's Church about itself? The starting point of renewal is to turn to the sources of revelation expecting to be challenged by God's word, which always comes to us anew. While all the Council's teaching reflects this effort, *Dei Verbum* stands out as directly related to the theme of awareness.

After awareness comes renewal proper. Renewal begins with the judgment that a gap exists between God's word and our reality. The

---

4. This is very clear in his first encyclical, *Redemptor Hominis,* 4, and his synthesis of the Council, before becoming Pope, in *Sources of Renewal.*

same light of faith that brings a greater awareness of God's will also illumines all that diverges from it. "The actual image of the Church is never as perfect, as lovely, as holy or as brilliant as that formative divine idea would wish it to be" (*ES* 10). The *Decree on Ecumenism* succinctly describes the essence of renewal: "Every renewal of the Church is essentially grounded in an increase of fidelity to her own calling" (*UR* 6).

According to the gospel principle that more will be asked from the one who has received more, an increased awareness of God's will calls us to conversion. Renewal encompasses all the efforts to bridge the distance between God's vision for the Church and the present reality of the Church. Renewal is nothing other than conversion, for the Church always needs reform, following the path of penance and renewal.

The word "dialogue" captures the final step of renewal. Dialogue relates to the manner in which the Church carries out its mission of salvation in the world, following the pattern of the dialogue of salvation between God and his people in divine revelation.

The relationship between renewal and dialogue is the key to grasping the centrality of the call to holiness in Vatican II's teaching. For the conversion process of renewal results in a deepening of the Church's life in Christ, and in him, in the life of God. This divine life is the supreme and infinite Good that embraces all goodness. Its nature is to communicate itself to others, since good diffuses itself.[5] The Trinity is a mystery of this diffusion of the good, and it is the key to the mysteries of creation and redemption as well. In less philosophical language, God is love, and through the holiness that flows from conversion the Church enters ever more deeply into the fullness of God's life of love.

The Church is missionary by its very nature, since love is missionary, and love is the essence of the Church's life of holiness. Holiness places the Church in relation both to God and to the world. Holiness is, first of all, participation in God's own life, which is a life of love. For this reason, holiness also places the Church in relation to all human beings who need divine love.

Here we discover the fundamental principle and inspiration of the renewal Vatican II called for: the actions of a renewed Church—the ex-

---

5. The role of this principle *(bonum diffusivum sui)* in the thought of John Paul can be seen in the way he used it in *Sign of Contradiction* (New York: Seabury Press, 1979), p. 22, and *Dominum et Vivificantem,* 37.

ercise of the prophetic, priestly and kingly offices of Christ—must be grounded in and flow from the Church's communion with God. To use another principle: action follows upon being *(operatio sequitur esse)*. The Church must first strengthen its life in Christ, which means to pursue holiness. When the Church's members can say with St. Paul, "It is no longer I who live, but it is Christ who lives in me" (Gal 2:20), then the Church makes Christ present and active in the world through its actions. Through renewal in the holiness of God's own life, Vatican II hoped to make the Church a transparent witness to Christ. As the Extraordinary Synod of 1985 put it: "The Church makes herself more credible if she speaks less of herself and ever more preaches Christ crucified (cf. 1 Cor 2:2) and witnesses with her own life.... The whole importance of the Church derives from her connection with Christ."[6]

In this light, the place of the *Constitution on the Sacred Liturgy* becomes clear. The liturgy communicates God's life to us, and dialogue, the ultimate fruit of renewal, depends on our sharing in this life. The liturgical renewal aims to make possible the "full, conscious and active participation" of the faithful in the liturgy. This is the means to a full, active and conscious participation in God's life and thus in all the activities of the Church.

These reflections allow us to perceive the relationships among the Council's four constitutions. The *Dogmatic Constitution on Divine Revelation* and the *Constitution on the Sacred Liturgy* promote the more effective utilization of the gifts of God's word and the liturgy. Thus they establish the foundation of renewal: God's truth and grace, by which we participate in divine life. The *Dogmatic Constitution on the Church* shows what the Church, grounded and renewed in God's word and shar-

---

6. The Christocentric character of Vatican II is well known. Twenty times the Council speaks of "the mystery of Christ." If the expressions "Paschal Mystery" and "mystery of salvation" are taken as synonyms, then the number is increased many fold. One text speaks of developing "a personal relationship with Christ," and though that exact expression is not found elsewhere, the idea abounds in the texts.

The four constitutions exhibit this Christocentric quality: the very titles of *Lumen Gentium* and *Dei Verbum* are references to Christ. In *Dei Verbum,* Christ is the perfection and fullness of revelation, and ignorance of Scripture is ignorance of Christ. In *Lumen Gentium,* the messianic People of God continue the mission of Christ the prophet, priest and king. *Sacrosanctum Concilium* grounds all liturgy in his Paschal Mystery, and *Gaudium et Spes* presents Christ as the center of history and the definitive answer to all human questions and searching.

ing in God's life through the liturgy, looks like. Finally, the *Pastoral Constitution on the Church in the Modern World* outlines that dialogue with the world that is the fruit of increased holiness.

The remaining conciliar texts fall in order in light of this schema. The decrees on the laity, religious, bishops, priests and priestly formation all develop related chapters in the *Dogmatic Constitution on the Church*. Their interior structure reproduces the foundational role of God's word and the liturgy as principles of holiness. Then, each decree develops the specific mission which flows from the holiness proper to each group: laity, religious, bishops, priests. For Vatican II, the actions of the members of the Church are never separated from their being in Christ, that is, holiness.

Vatican II As a Gift of the Holy Spirit

In 1959, Pope John XXIII stunned the cardinals in Rome when he announced his decision to convoke the Second Vatican Ecumenical Council. He stated that he decided this in fidelity to an inspiration from God. In its origin, then, Vatican II must be understood as the Church's response to an initiative of the Holy Spirit.

In the texts themselves the council fathers understood that they were responding to the signs of the times which the Holy Spirit pointed out. The texts of Vatican II are the fruit of a dialogue between God and his Church. The theme of dialogue figures prominently in the conciliar texts, but this theme is rooted in Paul VI's first encyclical, *Ecclesiam Suam*. There it is used to describe the dialogue of salvation between God and his people. In this dialogue God takes the initiative out of love, respecting human free will. God gives the grace people need in order to respond freely in faith (cf. *DV* 5).

The Council itself needs to be situated within this dialogical framework. Theologically and canonically, an ecumenical council is a solemn exercise of the college of bishops' pastoral office in the universal Church when the council is convoked, presided over and confirmed by the Bishop of Rome (cf. *LG* 22). It is an act of the successors to the apostles in communion with the Successor of Peter, in order to exercise pastoral solicitude for the welfare of the Church. Ecumenical councils take up questions that were not asked or answered directly by the Lord himself. In them the Spirit of truth Christ promised is present and active so that the directives of a council are the joint work of the Spirit and of the bishops. In this way the teaching of a council can be preceded by the formula of the Council of Jerusalem: "It has seemed good to the Holy Spirit and to us..." (Acts 15:28).

The Second Vatican Council was first and foremost this kind of supernatural "solemn celebration of the union of Christ and his Church"[7] in the Holy Spirit. Vatican II was convoked to answer the question: "What does it mean to be a believer, to be a Christian, to be in the Church and also in the modern world?"[8] To the eyes of faith, the Council's teachings are much more than a merely human attempt to bring the Church up to date. They are the word of the Spirit and a gift of God to the Church of today, containing "precisely all that the Spirit says to the churches (cf. Rv 2:29; 3:6; 13:22) with regard to the present phase of the history of salvation" (*DViv* 26).

This is why the Pope can write that "Through the whole experience of the Council we have contracted a debt toward the Holy Spirit, the Spirit of Christ who speaks to the churches (cf. Rv 2:7)."[9] There is a great need for the Catholic faithful to cultivate this attitude toward the Council, especially since there is little evidence that the majority of the faithful have read these texts, let alone studied them.[10] Thirty-five years after the Council, its texts largely remain unopened gifts. One thinks of entrusted talents being buried in the ground (cf. Mt 25:24–30).

Pope John Paul II's consistent reference to Vatican II as a gift of the Holy Spirit, linking it with preparation for the third millennium, is perhaps rooted in the lesson of the parable of the rich man and Lazarus (cf. Lk 16:19-31). Abraham ends the parable by saying that if the rich man's brothers will not listen to Moses and the prophets, they will not listen even if someone should rise from the dead. John Paul seems to be saying that the grace of our time has already been given, and our first focus should be to implore Providence for the graces required to implement the Council. Vatican II was intended to prepare the Church for the third

---

7. Pope John XXIII, Opening Speech of the Council.

8. Karol Cardinal Wojtyla (Pope John Paul II), *Sources of Renewal. On the Implementation of Vatican II* (San Francisco: Harper & Row, 1979), p. 420.

9. *Sources of Renewal*, pp. 9–10.

10. What Henri Cardinal de Lubac has said about *Lumen Gentium* applies to the entire Council: "Much has been said and written about this constitution *[Lumen Gentium]*; a thousand and one attempts have been made to extract its 'spirit.' But I have noticed more and more that those who have actually read it all the way through are rare, and that those who have studied it (closely and as a whole) are extremely rare" (Henri de Lubac: *A Theologian Speaks*, Los Angeles: Twin Circle Publishing Co., 1985, p. 8).

millennium, as Moses and the prophets were intended to prepare God's people for Jesus Christ. The disposition of faith to recognize and appropriate those future graces calls for the Council to be gratefully received and enthusiastically implemented.

The Holy Spirit has taken the initiative, which has been observed and acknowledged as one of the "signs of the times." Through the texts of Vatican II the apostolic Church desires to respond to God's lead. The Council is an exercise of that responsibility of the Church's shepherds to make judgments about the movements and gifts of the Holy Spirit, "not to extinguish the Spirit but to test all things and hold for what is good (cf. 1 Thes 5:12, 19, 21)" (*AA* 3). Fidelity to God requires discerning his will through the signs of the times.

Vatican II and the Principle of Integration

All the popes of conciliar renewal have clearly articulated the renewal that Vatican II called for. They have stressed a balance between adaptation of non-essential and historically and culturally conditioned elements of the Church's life with fidelity to all that is essential by reason of divine institution.

For Pope John XXIII, "The greatest concern of the Ecumenical Council is this: that the sacred deposit of Christian doctrine should be guarded and taught more efficaciously." For doctrine to yield its full potential "to influence the numerous fields of human activity...it is necessary first of all that the Church should never depart from the sacred patrimony of truth received from the Fathers." From a "pure and integral" transmission of doctrine "without any attenuation or distortion" Pope John expected a "doctrinal penetration and a formation of consciousness in faithful and perfect conformity to the authentic doctrine" that would allow the Church to speak more effectively to contemporary people. "The substance of the ancient doctrine of the deposit of faith is one thing, and the way in which it is presented is another."[11]

Pope Paul VI developed in terms of dialogue the same concern for renewal and fidelity to what God has determined. The Church's missionary dialogue with the world must take as its pattern God's dialogue in revelation. In fidelity to the eternal truth which he himself is, God revealed himself in a manner "adapted to the spiritual needs and disposi-

---

11. Opening Speech of the Council.

tions of the recipients" (*ES* 75). Similarly, the Church should carry on "a dialogue adapted to the nature of the interlocutor and to factual circumstances" (*ES* 78) of the group or individual. The renewal of the Church "cannot concern either the essential conception of the Church or its basic structure" (*ES* 46). He went on to state: "We should rather always wish to lead her [the Church] back to her perfect form corresponding, on the one hand, to her original design and on the other fully consistent with the necessary development which like a seed grown into a tree has given to the Church her legitimate and concrete form in history" (*ES* 47).

Paul VI here states an important point about renewal. What is essential to the Church and to the Catholic faith is permanent but not static. Development means that this permanent element remains throughout the changes it undergoes. The Pope's comparison with a tree is an excellent image because it brings out that the form of the Church is not merely something external and incidental, but dynamically related to its inner reality. What is essential to the faith is related to the form in which that essence is expressed not just in an extrinsic and accidental way, but more organically.

The missionary dialogue envisioned by Paul VI requires two attitudes. The first is fidelity to God, and the second is love of neighbor. No tension exists between the two once it is realized that authentic love must be based on the truth about God and his Church. In fidelity to the authority of God and the content of revelation, the development of sacred Tradition involves a growth in our understanding of it. The pastoral renewal of Vatican II does not mean revising the essential nature of the Church or of divine truth, but of renewing those human structures and institutions which serve the Church's mission. While love for neighbor requires "forcing our reasoning process out of the worn paths and by obliging it to deepen its research, to find fresh expressions," fidelity to God assures that this will not result in a compromise of divine truth. Love requires that the dialogue "does not bind itself to ineffectual theories and does not cling to hard and fast forms when these have lost their power to speak to men and move them" (*ES* 83, 85), while fidelity to God knows the limits of adaptation.

Pope John Paul II has placed his own stamp on the theme of "fidelity to tradition and openness to legitimate development."[12] He has ex-

---

12. *Vicesimus Quintus Annus,* 4.

pressed it most frequently in terms of "the old and the new," comparing the Church to the wise scribe of Matthew 13:52 who "brings out of his treasure what is new and what is old" (cf. *RH* 4).

> The Second Vatican Council is often considered as the beginning of a new era in the life of the Church. This is true, but at the same time it is difficult to overlook the fact that the Council drew much from the experiences and reflections of the immediate past, especially from the intellectual legacy left by Pius XII. In the history of the Church, the "old" and the "new" are always closely interwoven. The "new" grows out of the "old," and the "old" finds a fuller expression in the "new." Thus it was for the Second Vatican Council... (*TMA* 18).

While still Cardinal-Archbishop of Cracow, John Paul wrote that "First and foremost, all that Vatican II has said must be subjected to the principle of the integration of faith." This means seeing that the teaching of the Council is expressed in such a way that:

> ...on the one hand we can rediscover and, as it were, reread the magisterium of the last Council in the whole previous magisterium of the Church, while on the other we can rediscover and reread the whole preceding magisterium in that of the last Council. It would seem that the principle of integration, thus conceived and applied, is indirectly the principle of the Church's identity.[13]

The Popes of conciliar renewal have seen the essential continuity in the life of the Church as it develops through time. Vatican II is the most recent solemn expression of that life. In faith they are confident that the Holy Spirit guides the Church today as he has from the beginning, so that the Church holds faithfully to the apostolic teaching even as new insights into it develop.

Vatican II As a Pastoral Council

Vatican II was a pastoral council, not a doctrinal council in the same way that previous councils had been. John XXIII was well aware of this when he stated: "The salient point of this Council is not, therefore, a discussion of one article or another of the fundamental doctrine of the Church." Vatican II would not respond to errors about particular points of doctrine; instead, it would presuppose the entirety of the "sacred pat-

---

13. *Sources of Renewal*, p. 40.

rimony of truth" and seek "a doctrinal penetration and formation of consciousness in faithful and perfect conformity to the authentic doctrine."[14] Vatican II would simply express the perennial faith of the Church in a manner appropriate to modern times.

One theologian used an image drawn from medicine to describe the pastoral intuition of John XXIII. He wrote that previous councils had almost always been the Church's response to a doctrinal crisis, applying a remedy well after the infection had taken its toll. John XXIII had the inspiration to practice preventive medicine, desiring to fortify the body of Christ against the potential threats to its health that would arise in our time. Inoculations can disrupt the body, causing a fever and stimulating antibodies. So, too, the body of Christ has experienced some turmoil in these years since the Council, but hopefully this will only strengthen it to meet current challenges.[15]

For John XXIII, Vatican II's pastoral aim was to release the Church's pent-up spiritual energies through a deepening of faith, the renewal of Christian life and a revision of the Church's law. Paul VI would specify that these spiritual energies are to be released for an openness to that holiness by which the life of Christ more fully pulsates through the veins of the Mystical Body. John Paul II would stress the enrichment of faith that makes it possible for the faithful to live in constant reference to God in the obedience of faith. Referring to *Dei Verbum* (n. 5) regarding the self-commitment or self-entrusting to God which faith involves, he wrote: "In speaking of the attitude of self-commitment to God, Vatican II touches on the most vital and vivifying point relating to the whole process of the enrichment of faith."[16] "The implementation of the Council consists first and foremost in enriching that faith."[17] This self-entrusting to God in faith "is at the very center of the teaching of Vatican II and contains in a certain manner all that the Council wished to say about the Church, mankind and the world."[18]

---

14. Opening Address of the Council.

15. Gerard Philips, *L'Eglise et son mystère au deuxième Concile du Vatican. Histoire, texte et commentaire de la Constitution* Lumen Gentium (Paris: Desclee, 1967), vol. I, pp. 7–8.

16. *Sources of Renewal*, p. 206.

17. *Ibid.*, p. 420.

18. *Ibid.*, p. 225.

The goal of the enrichment of faith made Vatican II a pastoral council: "Thus it is in the light of the purpose of Vatican II as preeminently a pastoral council that we should consider the postulate of an enrichment of faith as the basis of any realization of the Council and any renewal of the Church." [19]

> If we study the conciliar magisterium as a whole, we find that the pastors of the Church were not so much concerned to answer questions like "What should men believe?" and so on, but rather to answer the more complex question: "What does it mean to be a believer, a Catholic and a member of the Church?" They endeavored to answer this question in the broad context of today's world, as indeed the complexity of the question itself requires.
>
> The question "What does it mean to be a believing member of the Church?" is indeed difficult and complex, because it not only presupposes the truth of faith and pure doctrine, but also calls for that truth to be situated in the human consciousness and calls for a definition of the attitude, or rather the many attitudes, that go to make the individual a believing member of the Church. This would seem to be the main respect in which the conciliar magisterium has a pastoral character, corresponding to the pastoral purpose for which it was called. A "purely" doctrinal council would have concentrated on defining the precise meaning of the truths of faith, whereas a pastoral council proclaims, recalls or clarifies truths for the primary purpose of giving Christians a lifestyle, a way of thinking and acting. In our efforts to put the Council into practice, this is the style we must keep before our minds.[20]

Very importantly, the Holy Father stresses the unity of doctrinal content and pastoral orientation:

> The doctrine of faith and morals...is the content of the teaching of the pastors of the Church, so that on the one hand doctrinal acts of the magisterium have a pastoral sense, while on the other pastoral acts have a doctrinal significance, deeply rooted as they are in faith and morals. These pastoral acts contain the doctrine that the Church proclaims; they often make it clearer and more precise....[21]

Doctrinal and pastoral orientations are complementary because the pastoral aspect is concerned with living out the content of the Church's

---

19. *Ibid.,* p. 16.
20. *Ibid.,* pp. 17–18.
21. *Ibid.,* p. 17

faith. Interrelating the doctrinal and pastoral was one of the Council's great achievements, and for this it was indebted to the great work of the theologians who had returned to the sources of the Church's faith.[22] "The Council is pastoral in its fusion of truth and love, 'doctrine' and pastoral solicitude; it wished to reach beyond the dichotomy between pragmatism and doctrinalism, back to the biblical unity in which practice and doctrine are one, a unity grounded in Christ."[23] As a pastoral council, Vatican II is not less than doctrinal, but more than doctrinal, going beyond the simple declaration of what the Catholic faith holds, to considering its implications for the inner life of the Church and for the Church's relationship with the world.

These two elements of pastoral concern permeate the conciliar texts. The first, implications for the Church's inner life, especially focuses on holiness, which self-entrusting to God expresses. It also attempts to translate the Church's deepened self-understanding into more adequate practical and canonical organization of ecclesial life.

The second element of the Council's pastoral concern regards the Church's relationship with the world. This too is directly related to the enrichment of faith and holiness, as the Church's own life in Christ compels it to engage in a dynamic dialogue with the various groups of people to whom the Church is related: non-Catholic Christians, Jews and other non-Christians, non-believers, and the entire world.

The Implementation of Vatican II

In fidelity to the Church's tradition, Vatican II represents a new consciousness of the Church about itself. This is seen in the vocabulary it introduced which was new to the majority of the faithful at the time, but is no longer novel. The Council has given us some new concepts and has given a new emphasis to other ideas which have developed the Church's self-awareness. Some of these are: collegiality, renewal, dialogue, ecumenism, the People of God, the Church as sacrament, religious liberty.

---

22. Cf. Marcellino D'Ambrosio, "Resourcement Theology, Aggiornamento, and the Hermeneutics of Tradition," *Communio* 18 (winter 1991): 530–555.

23. Joseph Ratzinger, *Commentary on the Documents of Vatican II,* ed. Herbert Voɪ.rimler (New York: Herder and Herder, 1967), vol. I, p. 299.

No doubt, Vatican II has directly reached the greatest number of faithful in the shortest period of time following it than any other council in the Church's history. This is due to the tremendous advances in the availability of education, especially in the West, and the means of communication. While this was certainly a desire of the Council, it has brought some difficulties. At times confusion has arisen due to the quite understandable phenomenon of people reading their own understanding of terms into the texts. This tendency to project our own understanding upon the words used by another is a common experience. It can even be seen in the Scriptures when, for example, on the day of the Lord's ascension into heaven, the apostles asked if he was going to restore the reign to Israel. Peter's remonstration with the Lord over his predicted passion shows that Peter had a different definition of "Messiah" than the Lord did.

The implementation of Vatican II will require, first, the commitment to read the texts and to study them, in an effort to understand the meaning the council fathers intended to convey. This will require reading them in the light of the preceding development of the Church's living tradition in order to discover their essential continuity with that tradition. For what is distinctive can only be determined in light of what is common.

Second, for this reading and implementation to attain the objective truth of the texts, humility is indispensable. According to St. Thomas Aquinas, humility is the disposition of being ready to defer to what is of God in another. As we have seen, the texts of Vatican II are a gift from God. Humility approaches these texts with the disposition that Paul VI described for the Church: readiness to break out of one's limited understanding in order to embrace a truth which is greater than the reader and has a claim upon him or her. Humility helps us recognize that we are all conditioned by our culture and personal history, and that we must apply a critical self-examination every time we attempt to discover the meaning of a text. The prerequisite for reading the texts of Vatican II is the readiness to undertake the renewal through conversion which the Council made the vocation of the Church today.

LIST OF ABBREVIATIONS

1. Documents of Vatican II

AA   *Apostolicam Actuositatem* (Decree on the Apostolate of the Laity)

AG   *Ad Gentes* (Decree on the Mission Activity of the Church)

CD   *Christus Dominus* (Decree on the Pastoral Office of Bishops in the Church)

DH   *Dignitatis Humanae* (Declaration on Religious Freedom)

DV   *Dei Verbum* (Dogmatic Constitution on Divine Revelation)

GE   *Gravissimum Educationis* (Declaration on Christian Education)

GS   *Gaudium et Spes* (Pastoral Constitution on the Church in the Modern World)

IM   *Inter Mirifica* (Decree on the Media of Social Communication)

LG   *Lumen Gentium* (Dogmatic Constitution on the Church)

NA   *Nostra Aetate* (Declaration on the Relation of the Church to Non-Christian Religions)

OE   *Orientalium Ecclesiarum* (Decree on the Catholic Churches of the Eastern Rite)

OT   *Optatam Totius* (Decree on Priestly Training)

PC   *Perfectae Caritatis* (Decree on the Adaptation and Renewal of Religious Life)

PO   *Presbyterorum Ordinis* (Decree on the Ministry and Life of Priests)

SC   *Sacrosanctum Concilium* (Constitution on the Sacred Liturgy)

UR   *Unitatis Redintegratio* (Decree on Ecumenism)

2. Other documents and sources

AAS	*Acta Apostolicae Sedis*
CCC	Catechism of the Catholic Church
CIC	*Codex Iuris Canonici* (Code of Canon Law)
CL	*Christifideles Laici* (The Lay Members of Christ's Faithful People)
CSEL	*Corpus Scriptorum Ecclesiasticorum Latinorum* (Collection of writings of Latin Fathers of the Church)
DC	*Dominicae Cenae* (On the Mystery and Worship of the Eucharist)
Denz.	H. Denzinger, *Enchiridion Symbolorum* (Collection of Church documents)
DS	*Denzinger-Schönmetzer* (New edition of Denzinger)
DViv	*Dominum et Vivificantem* (On the Holy Spirit)
EN	*Evangelii Nuntiandi* (On Evangelization in the Modern World)
ES	*Ecclesiam Suam* (Paths of the Church)
GCS	*Die Grieschischen Christlichen Schriftsteller der ersten drei Jahrhunderte* (Collection of early Greek Christian writings)
OL	*Orientale Lumen* (Light of the East)
PDV	*Pastores Dabo Vobis* (I Will Give You Shepherds)
PG	*Patrologia Graeca* (Collection of writings of Greek Fathers of the Church)
PL	*Patrologia Latina* (Collection of writings of Latin Fathers of the Church)
RH	*Redemptor Hominis* (The Redeemer of Man)
ST	*Summa Theologiae* (of St. Thomas Aquinas)
TMA	*Tertio Millennio Adveniente* (As the Third Millennium Draws Near)
VC	*Vita Consecrata* (Consecrated Life)
VQA	*Vicesimus Quintus Annus* (On the 25th Anniversary of *Sacrosanctum Concilium*)

CONSTITUTION ON THE SACRED LITURGY

Sacrosanctum Concilium

Promulgated by
His Holiness Pope Paul VI
On December 4, 1963

INTRODUCTION

The *Constitution on the Sacred Liturgy (SC)* was the first document the Council promulgated. Its opening statement sets forth the pastoral goals of the Council: spiritual renewal, necessary adaptation, ecumenism, evangelization and mission.

Each document of the Council contributes in its own way to all of these goals, though some apply more directly to one or another of them. *SC* most directly concerns the goals of spiritual renewal and adaptation, since the liturgy is the source and summit of the entire life of the Church. For this reason, no other dimension of the conciliar renewal has had such a powerful impact as liturgical renewal. As Pope John Paul II has noted: "A very close and organic bond exists between the renewal of the liturgy and the renewal of the whole life of the Church. The Church not only acts but also expresses herself in the liturgy and draws from the liturgy the strength for her life" (*DC* 13).

Also for this reason, the liturgical renewal undertaken by the Council is related to the goals of ecumenism and mission. The ecumenism adopted by Vatican II is a "spiritual ecumenism" of conversion (cf. *UR* 8). Based on faith, conversion is both an essential preparation for and a fruit of this celebration, since the grace of the sacraments leads to holiness. Regarding mission, *SC* considers the celebration of the liturgy in missionary territories. But even more importantly, it sees the liturgy, as the source and summit of the Church's life (cf. *SC* 10), as a principle of a renewed commitment to evangelization. God's life is one of love and spurs the Christian to bring it to others. The liturgy draws the faithful "into the compelling love of Christ" and sets them afire with this love (cf. *SC* 10).

The constitution concerns the *entire liturgy* of the Church. Besides the Mass and the sacraments, this includes the Divine Office (or Liturgy of the Hours) and the sacramentals. These are all public acts in which the Church prays, and they are distinguished from devotional prayer or popular piety. The constitution also concerns the liturgy of the *entire Church,* giving general principles intended for all the Catholic liturgical rites as well as practical norms for the Roman rite (cf. *SC* 3). Significantly, *SC* recognizes that all the lawfully acknowledged rites are "equal in right and dignity" (*SC* 4).

The Council saw the need for a special commission to direct *SC's* implementation. In January 1964 Paul VI established the Consilium for this purpose. Since 1975 the Sacred Congregation for Sacraments and Divine Worship has continued this work. Of all the Council documents, *SC* has given rise to the greatest number of post-conciliar documents and directives.

As is the case for the Council as a whole, the pastoral goal of *SC* is most broadly understood as the Church's response to the working of the Holy Spirit (cf. *SC* 43). This response concerns those matters in which God has given the Church a responsibility to adapt for the good of its mission. It is not a question of changing those essential elements of divine institution which the Church has received from the Lord. In addition, the adaptation which *SC* envisions is principled and disciplined. It requires a careful study of the liturgical sources and must be an organic development of existing forms (cf. *SC* 23).

The most general principle to guide the liturgical renewal is that the "Church earnestly desires that all the faithful should be led to that full, conscious and active participation in liturgical celebrations which is demanded by the very nature of the liturgy." This principle "is the aim to be considered above all else" (*SC* 14) and the constitution repeatedly stresses it.

The liturgy requires active participation, for through and in the liturgy, "the work of our redemption is accomplished" (*SC* 2). People are sanctified, the Church is built up, and public worship is given to God (cf. *SC* 7, 59). The liturgy is an exercise of the priestly office of Christ in which he is present and his saving mysteries are reactualized. In this, he "associates the Church with himself" so that the liturgy is "an action of Christ the priest and of his body which is the Church" (*SC* 7).

The active participation of the faithful is first and foremost the participation of faith, for the liturgy presupposes a faith disposed to cooperate with God (cf. *SC* 11). It nourishes, strengthens and expresses faith and thereby "effectively disposes the faithful to receive this grace" (*SC* 59). By such faith God's people exercise their common or baptismal priesthood and offer their spiritual sacrifices (cf. *LG* 10, 34), that is, their very selves (cf. *SC* 48) with Christ in the Eucharist.

Such cooperating faith is marvelously portrayed in the healing of the woman with a hemorrhage (cf. Lk 8:42–48). A picture of this episode introduces the section of the *Catechism of the Catholic Church* on the celebration of the Christian mystery. The faith of this woman who discerned the saving presence of God in Jesus Christ serves as a model of the faith by which his saving presence is discerned in the liturgy today. Responding to the signs of his miracles and the message of his teaching, the woman came in faith bringing her need to Jesus. Like her, the People of God today assembled in faith respond to his word and the signs in which he is present. Finally, by faith a saving touch occurred, a touch of faith on the woman's part. She opened herself to the divine power in Jesus offered to all out of love. Similarly, in the sacraments Christ continues to touch people of faith with healing and saving power, so that truly through them he effects the sanctification of others (cf. *SC* 7).

SC states of Christ: "His humanity, united with the person of the Word, was the instrument of our salvation." The sacraments are actions of Christ the high priest. Jesus said that the woman's faith had healed her, but faith disposed her to be open to Jesus' power. Faith is the condition for receiving grace, but not its cause, for grace comes from God. Applied to the sacraments, the constitution teaches that "in order that the liturgy may be able to produce its full effects, it is necessary that the faithful come to it with proper dispositions" (*SC* 11).

The faith of the woman healed from a hemorrhage illustrates the kind of active faith required for participation in the liturgy: her every action was motivated by faith. Active participation in the liturgy does not mean that the faithful must constantly be doing something, since the constitution explicitly mentions reverent silence as a form of active participation (cf. *SC* 30). It does mean, however, that all actions and gestures should be motivated by faith. Significantly, the account of the healing of the woman who in faith touched Jesus' robe mentions many others who came into contact with him. They crowded close to him and some even touched him, but Jesus' saving power flowed out to the one among them who touched him in faith.

An anthropological foundation for this principle of active participation can help us understand how the liturgy is worship of God: "Only in freedom can man direct himself toward goodness" (*GS* 19). Paul VI emphasized God's respect for our free will in the dialogue of salvation, and this respect is the basis of the Church's teaching on religious freedom (see introduction to *Dignitatis Humanae*). As St. Augustine concisely phrased it: "God, who created us without our cooperation, will not save us without our cooperation."

In this light, the liturgy and the sacraments in particular appear as a continuation of the dialogue of salvation between God and humanity. Though the constitution does not use the word "dialogue" with respect to the liturgy, the *Catechism of the Catholic Church* does (cf. *CCC* 1153). The notion of dialogue structured the teaching of *Dei Verbum*. The call that a more prominent role be assigned to Sacred Scripture in the liturgy (cf. *SC* 24, 35) could hardly help but shape *SC* with this dialogical understanding. Here we see the close connection between *Dei Verbum* and *SC*. The former beautifully states: "The Church has always venerated the divine Scriptures just as she venerates the body of the Lord, since, especially in the sacred liturgy, she unceasingly receives and offers to the faithful the bread of life from the table both of God's word and of Christ's body" (*DV* 21). Since *SC* aimed at establishing "an intimate connection between words and rites" (*SC* 35), familiarity with God's inspired word greatly contributes to liturgical participation.

Liturgy as dialogue is implicitly present in one of the fundamental principles of liturgical renewal, that of making the sacramental signs easier to understand (cf. *SC* 21, 59). Out of pastoral concern for the faithful, the Council calls for a "purification" of the liturgy by eliminating things which in themselves obscure the relation between the sign and the spiritual reality which it signifies. The signs of the liturgy are a means of communication between God and his people. They are instruments of the dialogue of salvation. For the faithful to enter this dialogue in a full, conscious and active manner, the signs must be made as clear as possible to instruct, nourish and strengthen faith (cf. *SC* 59). This is to be accomplished through a "noble simplicity" characterized by making the rites "short, clear, and unencumbered by useless repetitions" so that they are "within the people's powers of comprehension" and do "not require much explanation" (*SC* 34). In addition, the Council asks that "anything out of harmony with the inner nature of the liturgy or...unsuited to it" be eliminated (*SC* 21). This is Vatican II's version of what

Pope St. Pius X called "clearing away the marks of old age" in liturgical practice.

This corresponds to Pope Paul VI's call to the Church in *Ecclesiam Suam* to break out of "worn paths...to find new expressions." He urged that the Church should not cling to "ineffectual theories" or "hard and fast norms when these have lost their power to speak to men and move them" (*ES* 83, 85). This must be accomplished, however, with the strictest fidelity to the essential nature of the Church. Similarly, in the case of the liturgy, the elements of divine institution must be carefully preserved, while those deriving from cultural and historical factors can and must be revised (cf. *SC* 21).

The constitution indicates that the competent ecclesiastical authority should oversee this revision. Because the liturgy is an action of Christ and of his Church, and because the Church experiences its unity and holiness in the most perfect manner in the liturgy (cf. *SC* 2, 10, 41), its regulation "depends solely on the authority of the Church, that is, on the Apostolic See, and as laws may determine, on the bishop." Importantly, "no other person, even if he be a priest, may add, remove or change anything in the liturgy on his own authority" (*SC* 22).

SC balances the principle of clarifying the liturgical signs with a call for a serious program of liturgical education. The constitution indicates that pastors "must promote the liturgical instruction of the faithful" (*SC* 19). Referring to the "noble simplicity" the Council envisioned, John Paul II has said that "this desired simplicity must not degenerate into an impoverishment of the signs" (*VQA* 10). The constitution also calls for an education program for liturgical ministers (cf. *SC* 14), that they may help the faithful to a full, conscious and active participation (cf. *SC* 19, 33, 35, 56). In addition, catechesis is required for the faithful to understand the meaning of the liturgical signs.

Fifteen years after the Council, Pope John Paul II reechoed the importance of this educational program: "It is therefore necessary and urgent to actuate a new and intensive education in order to discover all the riches contained in the liturgy" (*DC* 9). In 1988 he called for "an ever deeper grasp of the liturgy of the Church, celebrated according to the current books and lived above all as a reality in the spiritual order" (*VQA* 14).

In its desire to make the liturgical signs easily understood (cf. *SC* 21, 59), the Council approved the use of the vernacular in the liturgy (cf. *SC*

36). Lengthy and sometimes passionate debate accompanied this issue at the Council, and it has continued since. Mindful of the great variety of pastoral situations throughout the Church, the Council left it to episcopal conferences to determine the extent of the vernacular's use.

While the Council did not envision that the vernacular would completely replace Latin in the liturgy, it did establish certain principles and procedures which, in retrospect, paved the way. First, the extent of the use of the vernacular, as well as translations, had to be approved by the Apostolic See. Thus, the same apostolic authority responsible for *SC* has overseen the expanded use of the vernacular. The Council's understanding of renewal was not limited to making final decisions followed by practical implementation. Rather, unlike the Council itself, renewal is ongoing, as is the guidance of the Holy Spirit.[1]

Second, the Council desired a more extensive use of the Word of God in the liturgy. *DV* called upon bishops to provide accurate translations of the Bible to facilitate the dialogue between God and his people. During the Council's debate, the Melchite Patriarch Maximos Saigh pointed out that "Christ spoke to his contemporaries in their own language" and "the apostles and disciples acted likewise." Then he quoted 1 Cor 14:16–19 where St. Paul elaborates on the difficulty of speaking in tongues which are not comprehensible to "outsiders," thus making it impossible for them to participate by saying "Amen."[2]

However, Sacred Scripture contains another important principle that balances the preceding considerations. Though the New Testament was written in Greek, it has certain non-Greek expressions. Jesus' use of "Abba" (cf. Mk 14:36) is a prime example. Words such as this can link the Christians who never knew Jesus in the flesh to the origins of the tradition which they inherited in faith. The Latin liturgy incorporated the Greek *Kyrie eleison,* providing a similar link to the preceding tradition. The call for the faithful to be prepared to say or sing their parts of the Mass in Latin (cf. *SC* 54) would assure a vital link to the liturgical tradition.

---

1. See the very balanced remarks of Joseph Cardinal Ratzinger on this, in *Principles of Catholic Theology: Building Stones for a Fundamental Theology* (San Francisco: Ignatius Press, 1987), pp. 367–393.

2. Quoted by Joseph Ratzinger in *Theological Highlights of Vatican II* (New York: Paulist Press, Deus Books, 1966), pp. 17–18).

The constitution centers the Church's liturgy on the central event of salvation history, the Paschal Mystery of Jesus Christ—his passing over to the Father through his death, resurrection and ascension. Through this mystery Jesus glorified God and accomplished human redemption (cf. *SC* 5). The Paschal Mystery is celebrated both through reading the Holy Spirit's inspired witness to it in Sacred Scripture and by celebrating it in the Eucharist (cf. *SC* 6, 106). The Paschal Mystery is the font of power of all the sacraments and sacramentals (cf. *SC* 61), and is celebrated in the veneration of the saints (cf. *SC* 104). Sunday is the "foundation and kernel of the whole liturgical year" (*SC* 106). The Easter Triduum, the most solemn celebration of the Paschal Mystery, is "the culmination of the entire liturgical year"[3] and the "feast of feasts" (*VQA* 6).

The liturgy is the continuing accomplishment or reactualization of the Paschal Mystery. Its purpose is God's glory and human salvation and sanctification, for the two are inseparable. According to St. Thomas Aquinas, the end of divine worship is that we "may give glory to God, and submit to him in mind and body" (*ST* II–II, 93, 2). "The worship [cultus] of God is receiving and giving divine gifts" (*ST* III, 63, 2). The understanding of worship in the sacraments is found in the relationship between these two statements. In the first, St. Thomas tells us that the human person glorifies God by becoming everything he or she is called to be. This is Thomas' version of St. Irenaeus's famous saying, "The glory of God is the human person fully alive." Just as a work of art is the glory of the artist, so the Church in its saints, especially the Virgin Mother of God, is the glory of the divine artist. God's infinite power, wisdom and love can be seen in his works, the greatest of which is Christ and all those who are made new creatures in him.

We cannot make ourselves into this reflection of the divine artist's virtue, but need grace for this. This is why St. Thomas could say that the worship of God is in receiving and giving divine gifts, that is, grace. This grace comes most efficaciously through the sacraments (cf. *SC* 7), which, to carry the analogy, are the actions of the divine artist working on his subject. The faithful are called to an active participation in this work of God. This is accomplished in the freedom of faith (cf. *DV* 5) by which the Church cooperates with God in his act of transforming love. Thus, the role of the liturgy in worship of God is not confined to the

---

3. General Norms for the Liturgical Year and the Calendar (March 21, 1969), 18.

actual celebrations, but extends to all those actions which are performed by the faithful and animated by the graces received through liturgical celebrations.

In this way, the full, conscious and active participation in the liturgy which *SC* calls for is the foundation for the overall goal of the Council. This can be described as the full, conscious, free and active participation of the People of God in the life and mission of Christ and of the Church.

TOPICAL OUTLINE

1. Introduction: nature of the liturgy, and its reform (1–4)

2. General principles for the restoration and promotion of the sacred liturgy

   A. The nature of the liturgy and its importance in the Church's life

      1. The mission of Jesus Christ and his Paschal Mystery (5)

      2. The mission of the apostles; the sacraments (6)

      3. The liturgy and the priestly office of Jesus Christ (7)

      4. Foretaste of the heavenly liturgy (8)

      5. The liturgy and other activity of the Church (9–11)

      6. Extra-liturgical prayer and popular devotions (12–13)

   B. Promotion of liturgical instruction and active participation (14–20)

   C. Reform of the sacred liturgy (21)

      1. General norms (22–25)

      2. Norms drawn from the hierarchic and communal nature of the liturgy (26–32)

      3. Norms based on the didactic and pastoral nature of the liturgy (33–36)

      4. Norms for adapting the liturgy to cultures (37–40)

   D. Promotion of liturgical life in the diocese and parish (41–42)

   E. Promotion of pastoral-liturgical action (43–46)

3. The sacred mystery of the Eucharist

A. The Eucharistic mystery (47)

B. Principles for renewal of the Eucharistic liturgy

    1. Active participation of the faithful (48–49)

    2. Simplification of rites (50)

    3. Greater use of Scripture (51)

    4. The homily and prayer of the faithful (52–53)

    5. The use of the vernacular (54)

    6. Communion (55)

    7. Unity of the liturgy of the word and the Eucharistic liturgy (56)

    8. Concelebration (57–58)

4. The other sacraments and sacramentals

A. Purpose of the sacraments and sacramentals (59–61)

B. Necessary revisions (62)

    1. Use of the vernacular and revision of ritual books (63)

    2. Restoration of the catechumenate (64–65)

    3. Baptism (66–70)

    4. Confirmation (71)

    5. Penance (72)

    6. Anointing of the Sick (73–75)

    7. Orders (76)

    8. Matrimony (77–78)

    9. Sacramentals (79)

    10. Religious profession (80)

    11. Christian burial (81–82)

5. The divine office

A. Prayer of Christ and the Church (83–85)

B. Importance of this prayer (86)

C. Particular directives for its revision (87–101)

6. The liturgical year

A. The liturgical year unfolds the mysteries of redemption

    1. Centrality of the mystery of Christ (102)

    2. The Blessed Virgin Mary (103)

    3. The saints (104)

B. Revision of the liturgical year

    1. Importance of Sunday (106)

    2. Sacred seasons (107–108)

      a. Lent (109–110)

      b. Feasts of saints (111)

7. Sacred music

    A. Importance of sacred music (112)

    B. Various directives (113–121)

8. Sacred art and furnishings (122–130)

9. Appendix: the liturgical calendar

CONSTITUTION ON THE SACRED LITURGY

Sacrosanctum Concilium

INTRODUCTION

1. This sacred Council has several aims in view: it desires to impart an ever increasing vigor to the Christian life of the faithful; to adapt more suitably to the needs of our own times those institutions which are subject to change; to foster whatever can promote union among all who believe in Christ; to strengthen whatever can help to call the whole of mankind into the household of the Church. The Council, therefore, sees particularly cogent reasons for undertaking the reform and promotion of the liturgy.

2. For the liturgy, "through which the work of our redemption is accomplished,"[1] most of all in the divine sacrifice of the Eucharist, is the outstanding means whereby the faithful may express in their lives and manifest to others the mystery of Christ and the real nature of the true Church. It is of the essence of the Church that she be both human and divine, visible and yet invisibly equipped, eager to act and yet intent on contemplation, present in this world and yet not at home in it; and she is all these things in such wise that in her the human is directed and subordinated to the divine, the visible likewise to the invisible, action to contemplation, and this present world to that city yet to come, which we

---

1. Secret prayer of the ninth Sunday after Pentecost.

seek (cf. Heb 13:14). While the liturgy daily builds up those who are within into a holy temple of the Lord, into a dwelling place for God in the Spirit (cf. Eph 2:21–22), to the mature measure of the fullness of Christ (cf. Eph 4:13), at the same time it marvelously strengthens their power to preach Christ, and thus shows forth the Church to those who are outside as a sign lifted up among the nations (cf. Is 11:12) under which the scattered children of God may be gathered together (cf. Jn 11:52), until there is one sheepfold and one shepherd (cf. Jn 10:16).

3. Wherefore, the sacred Council judges that the following principles concerning the promotion and reform of the liturgy should be called to mind, and that practical norms should be established.

Among these principles and norms there are some which can and should be applied both to the Roman rite and also to all the other rites. The practical norms which follow, however, should be taken as applying only to the Roman rite, except for those which, in the very nature of things, affect other rites as well.

4. Lastly, in faithful obedience to tradition, the sacred Council declares that holy mother Church holds all lawfully acknowledged rites to be of equal right and dignity, that she wishes to preserve them in the future and to foster them in every way. The Council also desires that, where necessary, the rites be revised carefully in the light of sound tradition, and that they be given new vigor to meet the circumstances and needs of modern times.

GENERAL PRINCIPLES FOR THE RESTORATION AND PROMOTION OF THE SACRED LITURGY

1. The Nature of the Sacred Liturgy and Its Importance in the Church's Life

5. God who "wills that all men be saved and come to the knowledge of the truth" (1 Tm 2:4), "who in many and various ways spoke in times past to the fathers by the prophets" (Heb 1:1), when the fullness of time had come sent his Son, the Word made flesh, anointed by the Holy Spirit, to preach the Gospel to the poor, to heal the contrite of heart (cf. Is 61:1; Lk 4:18), to be a "bodily and spiritual medicine,"[2] the Mediator between God and man (cf. 1 Tm 2:5). For his humanity, united with the person of the Word, was the instrument of our salvation. Therefore, in Christ "the perfect achievement of our reconciliation came forth, and the fullness of divine worship was given to us."[3]

The wonderful works of God among the people of the Old Testament were but a prelude to the work of Christ the Lord in redeeming mankind and giving perfect glory to God. He achieved his task principally by the Paschal Mystery of his blessed passion, resurrection from the dead and the glorious ascension, whereby "dying, he destroyed our death, and rising he restored our life."[4] For it was from the side of Christ as he slept the sleep of death upon the cross that there came forth "the wondrous sacrament of the whole Church."[5]

6. Just as Christ was sent by the Father, so also he sent the apostles, filled with the Holy Spirit. This he did that, by preaching the Gospel to

---

2. St. Ignatius of Antioch, *To the Ephesians* 7, 2.

3. *Sacramentarium Veronese,* ed. L. C. Mohlberg (Rome: 1956), n. 1265; cf. also n. 1241, 1248.

4. Easter preface of the Roman Missal.

5. Prayer before the second lesson for Holy Saturday, as it was in the Roman Missal before the restoration of Holy Week.

every creature (cf. Mk16:15), they might proclaim that the Son of God, by his death and resurrection, had freed us from the power of Satan (cf. Acts 26:18) and from death, and brought us into the kingdom of his Father. His purpose also was that they might accomplish the work of salvation which they had proclaimed, by means of sacrifice and sacraments, around which the entire liturgical life revolves. Thus, by Baptism men are plunged into the Paschal Mystery of Christ: they die with him, are buried with him and rise with him;[6] they receive the spirit of adoption as sons "in which we cry: Abba, Father" (Rm 8:15), and thus become true adorers whom the Father seeks (cf. Jn 4:23). In like manner, as often as they eat the supper of the Lord they proclaim the death of the Lord until he comes (cf. 1 Cor 11:26). For that reason, on the very day of Pentecost, when the Church appeared before the world, "those who received the word" of·Peter "were baptized." And "they continued steadfastly in the teaching of the apostles and in the communion of the breaking of bread and in prayers...praising God and being in favor with all the people" (Acts 2:41–47). From that time onward the Church has never failed to come together to celebrate the Paschal Mystery: reading those things "which were in all the Scriptures concerning him" (Lk 24:27), celebrating the Eucharist in which "the victory and triumph of his death are again made present,"[7] and at the same time giving thanks "to God for his unspeakable gift" (2 Cor 9:15) in Christ Jesus, "in praise of his glory" (Eph 1:12), through the power of the Holy Spirit.

7. To accomplish so great a work, Christ is always present in his Church, especially in her liturgical celebrations. He is present in the sacrifice of the Mass, not only in the person of his minister, "the same now offering, through the ministry of priests, who formerly offered himself on the cross,"[8] but especially under the Eucharistic species. By his power he is present in the sacraments, so that when a man baptizes it is really Christ himself who baptizes.[9] He is present in his Word, since it is he himself who speaks when the holy Scriptures are read in the Church. He is present, lastly, when the Church prays and sings, for he promised:

---

6. Cf. Rm 6:4; Eph 2:6; Col 3:1; 2 Tm 2:11.

7. Council of Trent, Session 13, *Decree on the Holy Eucharist,* ch. 5.

8. Council of Trent, Session 22, *Doctrine on the Holy Sacrifice of the Mass,* ch. 2.

9. Cf. St. Augustine, *Tractatus in Ioannem* 6, 7.

"Where two or three are gathered together in my name, there am I in the midst of them" (Mt 18:20).

Christ indeed always associates the Church with himself in this great work wherein God is perfectly glorified and men are sanctified. The Church is his beloved Bride who calls to her Lord, and through him offers worship to the Eternal Father.

Rightly, then, the liturgy is considered as an exercise of the priestly office of Jesus Christ. In the liturgy the sanctification of the man is signified by signs perceptible to the senses, and is effected in a way which corresponds with each of these signs; in the liturgy the whole public worship is performed by the Mystical Body of Jesus Christ, that is, by the head and his members.

From this it follows that every liturgical celebration, because it is an action of Christ the priest and of his body which is the Church, is a sacred action surpassing all others; no other action of the Church can equal its efficacy by the same title and to the same degree.

8. In the earthly liturgy we take part in a foretaste of that heavenly liturgy which is celebrated in the holy city of Jerusalem toward which we journey as pilgrims, where Christ is sitting at the right hand of God, a minister of the holies and of the true tabernacle (cf. Rv 21:2; Col 3:1; Heb 8:2); we sing a hymn to the Lord's glory with all the warriors of the heavenly army; venerating the memory of the saints, we hope for some part and fellowship with them; we eagerly await the Savior, our Lord Jesus Christ, until he, our life, shall appear and we too will appear with him in glory (cf. Phil 3:20; Col 3:4).

9. The sacred liturgy does not exhaust the entire activity of the Church. Before men can come to the liturgy, they must be called to faith and to conversion: "How then are they to call upon him in whom they have not yet believed? But how are they to believe him whom they have not heard? And how are they to hear if no one preaches? And how are men to preach unless they be sent?" (Rm 10:14–15).

Therefore, the Church announces the good tidings of salvation to those who do not believe, so that all men may know the true God and Jesus Christ whom he has sent, and may be converted from their ways, doing penance (cf. Jn 17:3; Lk 24:27; Acts 2:38). To believers also the Church must ever preach faith and penance; she must prepare them for the sacraments, teach them to observe all that Christ has commanded (cf. Mt 28:20), and invite them to all the works of charity, piety and the apostolate. For all these works make it clear that Christ's faithful, though not of this world, are to be the light of the world and to glorify the Father before men.

10. Nevertheless, the liturgy is the summit toward which the activity of the Church is directed; at the same time it is the font from which all her power flows. For the aim and object of apostolic works is that all who are made sons of God by faith and Baptism should come together to praise God in the midst of his Church, to take part in the sacrifice and to eat the Lord's Supper.

The liturgy in its turn moves the faithful, filled with "the paschal sacraments," to be "one in holiness";[10] it prays that "they may hold fast in their lives to what they have grasped by their faith";[11] the renewal in the Eucharist of the covenant between the Lord and man draws the faithful into the compelling love of Christ and sets them on fire. From the liturgy, therefore, and especially from the Eucharist, as from a font, grace is poured forth upon us, and the sanctification of men in Christ and the glorification of God, to which all other activities of the Church are directed as toward their end, is achieved in the most efficacious possible way.

11. But in order that the liturgy may be able to produce its full effects, it is necessary that the faithful come to it with proper dispositions, that their minds should be attuned to their voices, and that they should cooperate with divine grace lest they receive it in vain (cf. 2 Cor 6:1). Pastors of souls must therefore realize that when the liturgy is celebrated, something more is required than the mere observation of the laws governing valid and licit celebration; it is their duty also to ensure that the faithful take part fully aware of what they are doing, actively engaged in the rite and enriched by its effects.

12. The spiritual life, however, is not limited solely to participation in the liturgy. The Christian is indeed called to pray with his brethren, but he must also enter into his chamber to pray to the Father in secret (cf. Mt 6:6); yet more, according to the teaching of the Apostle, he should pray without ceasing (cf. 1 Thes 5:17). We learn from the same Apostle that we must always bear about in our body the dying of Jesus, so that

---

10. Postcommunion for both Masses of Easter Sunday.
11. Collect of the Mass for Tuesday of Easter Week.

the life also of Jesus may be made manifest in our bodily frame (cf. 2 Cor 4:10–11). This is why we ask the Lord in the sacrifice of the Mass that, "receiving the offering of the spiritual victim," he may fashion us for himself "as an eternal gift."[12]

13. Popular devotions of the Christian people are to be highly commended, provided they accord with the laws and norms of the Church, above all when they are ordered by the Apostolic See.

Devotions proper to individual churches also have a special dignity if they are undertaken by mandate of the bishops according to customs or books lawfully approved.

But these devotions should be so drawn up that they harmonize with the liturgical seasons, accord with the sacred liturgy, are in some fashion derived from it and lead the people to it, since, in fact, the liturgy by its very nature far surpasses any of them.

2. The Promotion of Liturgical Instruction and Active Participation

14. Mother Church earnestly desires that all the faithful should be led to that full, conscious and active participation in liturgical celebrations which is demanded by the very nature of the liturgy. Such participation by the Christian people as "a chosen race, a royal priesthood, a holy nation, a redeemed people" (1 Pt 2:9; cf. 2:4–5), is their right and duty by reason of their Baptism.

In the restoration and promotion of the sacred liturgy, this full and active participation by all the people is the aim to be considered before all else; for it is the primary and indispensable source from which the faithful are to derive the true Christian spirit, and therefore, pastors of souls must zealously strive to achieve it, by means of the necessary instruction, in all their pastoral work.

Yet it would be futile to entertain any hopes of realizing this unless the pastors themselves, in the first place, become thoroughly imbued with the spirit and power of the liturgy, and undertake to give instruction about it. A prime need, therefore, is that attention be directed, first of all, to the liturgical instruction of the clergy. Wherefore, the sacred Council has decided to enact as follows:

---

12. Secret prayer for Monday of Pentecost Week.

15. Professors who are appointed to teach liturgy in seminaries, religious houses of study and theological faculties must be properly trained for their work in institutes which specialize in this subject.

16. The study of sacred liturgy is to be ranked among the compulsory and major courses in seminaries and religious houses of studies; in theological faculties it is to rank among the principal courses. It is to be taught under its theological, historical, spiritual, pastoral and juridical aspects. Moreover, other professors, while striving to expound the mystery of Christ and the history of salvation from the angle proper to each of their own subjects, must nevertheless do so in a way which will clearly bring out the connection between their subjects and the liturgy, as also the unity which underlies all priestly training. This consideration is especially important for professors of dogmatic, spiritual and pastoral theology and for those of holy Scripture.

17. In seminaries and houses of religious, clerics shall be given a liturgical formation in their spiritual life. For this they will need proper direction, so that they may be able to understand the sacred rites and take part in them wholeheartedly, and they will also need personally to celebrate the sacred mysteries, as well as popular devotions which are imbued with the spirit of the liturgy. In addition, they must learn how to observe the liturgical laws, so that life in seminaries and houses of religious may be thoroughly influenced by the spirit of the liturgy.

18. Priests, both secular and religious, who are already working in the Lord's vineyard are to be helped by every suitable means to understand ever more fully what it is that they are doing when they perform sacred rites; they are to be aided to live the liturgical life and to share it with the faithful entrusted to their care.

19. With zeal and patience, pastors of souls must promote the liturgical instruction of the faithful and also their active participation in the liturgy, both internally and externally, taking into account their age and condition, their way of life and standard of religious culture. By so doing, pastors will be fulfilling one of the chief duties of a faithful dispenser of the mysteries of God, and in this matter they must lead their flock not only in word but also by example.

20. Transmissions of the sacred rites by radio and television shall be done with discretion and dignity, under the leadership and direction of a suitable person appointed for this office by the bishops. This is especially important when the service to be broadcast is the Mass.

3. The Reform of the Sacred Liturgy

21. In order that the Christian people may more certainly derive an abundance of graces from the sacred liturgy, holy mother Church desires to undertake with great care a general restoration of the liturgy itself. For the liturgy is made up of immutable elements divinely instituted, and of elements subject to change. These not only may but ought to be changed with the passage of time if they have suffered from the intrusion of anything out of harmony with the inner nature of the liturgy or have become unsuited to it.

In this restoration, both texts and rites should be drawn up so that they express more clearly the holy things which they signify; the Christian people, so far as possible, should be enabled to understand them with ease and to take part in them fully, actively and as befits a community.

Wherefore, the sacred Council establishes the following general norms:

A) General Norms

22. § 1. Regulation of the sacred liturgy depends solely on the authority of the Church, that is, on the Apostolic See, and as laws may determine, on the bishop.

§ 2. In virtue of power conceded by the law, the regulation of the liturgy within certain defined limits belongs also to various kinds of competent territorial bodies of bishops legitimately established.

§ 3. Therefore, no other person, even if he be a priest, may add, remove or change anything in the liturgy on his own authority.

23. That sound tradition may be retained, and yet the way remain open to legitimate progress, a careful investigation is always to be made into each part of the liturgy which is to be revised. This investigation should be theological, historical and pastoral. Also the general laws governing the structure and meaning of the liturgy must be studied in conjunction with the experience derived from recent liturgical reforms and from the indults conceded to various places. Finally, there must be no innovations unless the good of the Church genuinely and certainly requires them, and care must be taken that any new forms adopted should in some way grow organically from forms already existing.

As far as possible, notable differences between the rites used in adjacent regions must be carefully avoided.

24. Sacred Scripture is of the greatest importance in the celebration of the liturgy. For it is from Scripture that lessons are read and explained in the homily, and psalms are sung; the prayers, collects and liturgical songs are scriptural in their inspiration and their force, and it is from the Scriptures that actions and signs derive their meaning. Thus, to achieve the restoration, progress and adaptation of the sacred liturgy, it is essential to promote that warm and living love for Scripture to which the venerable tradition of both Eastern and Western rites gives testimony.

25. The liturgical books are to be revised as soon as possible; experts are to be employed on the task, and bishops are to be consulted, from various parts of the world.

B) Norms Drawn from the Hierarchic and Communal Nature of the Liturgy

26. Liturgical services are not private functions but are celebrations of the Church, which is the "sacrament of unity," namely, the holy people united and ordered under their bishops.[13]

Therefore, liturgical services pertain to the whole body of the Church; they manifest it and have effects upon it, but they concern the individual members of the Church in different ways, according to their differing rank, office and actual participation.

27. It is to be stressed that whenever rites, according to their specific nature, make provision for communal celebration involving the presence and active participation of the faithful, this way of celebrating them is to be preferred, so far as possible, to a celebration that is individual and quasi-private.

This applies with especial force to the celebration of Mass and the administration of the sacraments, even though every Mass has of itself a public and social nature.

28. In liturgical celebrations each person, minister or layman, who has an office to perform, should do all of but only those parts which pertain to his office by the nature of the rite and the principles of liturgy.

29. Servers, lectors, commentators and members of the choir also exercise a genuine liturgical function. They ought, therefore, to discharge their office with the sincere piety and decorum demanded by so exalted a ministry and rightly expected of them by God's people.

---

13. St. Cyprian, *On the Unity of the Catholic Church* 7; cf. *Letter 66*, 8, 3.

Consequently, they must all be deeply imbued with the spirit of the liturgy, each in his own measure, and they must be trained to perform their functions in a correct and orderly manner.

30. To promote active participation, the people should be encouraged to take part by means of acclamations, responses, psalmody, antiphons and songs, as well as by actions, gestures and bodily attitudes. And at the proper times, all should observe a reverent silence.

31. The revision of the liturgical books must carefully attend to the provision of rubrics, also for the people's parts.

32. The liturgy makes distinctions between persons according to their liturgical function and sacred Orders, and there are liturgical laws providing for due honors to be given to civil authorities. Apart from these instances, no special honors are to be paid in the liturgy to any private persons or classes of persons, whether in the ceremonies or by external display.

C) Norms Based upon the Didactic and Pastoral Nature of the Liturgy

33. Although the sacred liturgy is above all things the worship of the divine majesty, it likewise contains much instruction for the faithful.[14] For in the liturgy God speaks to his people and Christ is still proclaiming his Gospel. And the people reply to God both by song and prayer.

Moreover, the prayers addressed to God by the priest who presides over the assembly in the person of Christ are said in the name of the entire holy people and of all present. And the visible signs used by the liturgy to signify invisible divine things have been chosen by Christ or the Church. Thus, not only when things are read "which were written for our instruction" (Rm 15:4), but also when the Church prays or sings or acts, the faith of those taking part is nourished and their minds are raised to God, so that they may offer him their rational service and more abundantly receive his grace.

Wherefore, in the revision of the liturgy, the following general norms should be observed:

34. The rites should be distinguished by a noble simplicity; they should be short, clear and unencumbered by useless repetitions; they

---

14. Cf. Council of Trent, Session 22, *Doctrine on the Holy Sacrifice of the Mass,* ch. 8.

should be within the people's powers of comprehension, and normally should not require much explanation.

35. That the intimate connection between words and rites may be apparent in the liturgy:

1) In sacred celebrations there is to be more reading from holy Scripture, and it is to be more varied and suitable.

2) Because the sermon is part of the liturgical service, the best place for it is to be indicated even in the rubrics, as far as the nature of the rite will allow; the ministry of preaching is to be fulfilled with exactitude and fidelity. The sermon, moreover, should draw its content mainly from scriptural and liturgical sources, and its character should be that of a proclamation of God's wonderful works in the history of salvation, the mystery of Christ, ever made present and active within us, especially in the celebration of the liturgy.

3) Instruction which is more explicitly liturgical should also be given in a variety of ways; if necessary, short directives to be spoken by the priest or proper minister should be provided within the rites themselves. But they should occur only at the more suitable moments and be in prescribed or similar words.

4) Bible services should be encouraged, especially on the vigils of the more solemn feasts, on some weekdays in Advent and Lent, and on Sundays and feast days. They are particularly to be commended in places where no priest is available; when this is so, a deacon or some other person authorized by the bishop should preside over the celebration.

36. § 1. Particular law remaining in force, the use of the Latin language is to be preserved in the Latin rites.

§ 2. But since the use of the mother tongue, whether in the Mass, the administration of the sacraments or other parts of the liturgy, frequently may be of great advantage to the people, the limits of its employment may be extended. This will apply in the first place to the readings and directives, and to some of the prayers and chants, according to the regulations on this matter to be laid down separately in subsequent chapters.

§ 3. These norms being observed, it is for the competent territorial ecclesiastical authority mentioned in Art. 22, § 2, to decide whether and to what extent the vernacular language is to be used; their decrees are to be approved, that is, confirmed, by the Apostolic See. And whenever it seems to be called for, this authority is to consult with bishops of neighboring regions which have the same language.

§ 4. Translations from the Latin text into the mother tongue intended for use in the liturgy must be approved by the competent territorial ecclesiastical authority mentioned above.

D) Norms for Adapting the Liturgy to the Culture and Traditions of Peoples

37. Even in the liturgy, the Church has no wish to impose a rigid uniformity in matters which do not implicate the faith or the good of the whole community; rather does she respect and foster the genius and talents of the various races and peoples. Anything in these peoples' way of life which is not indissolubly bound up with superstition and error, she studies with sympathy, and if possible, preserves intact. Sometimes in fact she admits such things into the liturgy itself, so long as they harmonize with its true and authentic spirit.

38. Provisions shall also be made when revising the liturgical books for legitimate variations and adaptations to different groups, regions and peoples, especially in mission lands, provided that the substantial unity of the Roman rite is preserved, and this should be borne in mind when drawing up the rites and devising rubrics.

39. Within the limits set by the typical editions of the liturgical books, it shall be for the competent territorial ecclesiastical authority mentioned in Art. 22, § 2, to specify adaptations, especially in the case of the administration of the sacraments, the sacramentals, processions, liturgical language, sacred music and the arts, but according to the fundamental norms laid down in this Constitution.

40. In some places and circumstances, however, an even more radical adaptation of the liturgy is needed, and this entails greater difficulties.

Wherefore:

1) The competent territorial ecclesiastical authority mentioned in Art. 22, § 2, must, in this matter, carefully and prudently consider which elements from the traditions and culture of individual peoples might appropriately be admitted into divine worship. Adaptations which are judged to be useful or necessary should then be submitted to the Apostolic See, by whose consent they may be introduced.

2) To ensure that adaptations may be made with all the circumspection which they demand, the Apostolic See will grant power to this same territorial ecclesiastical authority to permit and to direct, as the case re-

quires, the necessary preliminary experiments over a determined period of time among certain groups suited for the purpose.

3) Because liturgical laws often involve special difficulties with respect to adaptation, particularly in mission lands, men who are experts in these matters must be employed to formulate them.

4. Promotion of Liturgical Life in Diocese and Parish

41. The bishop is to be considered as the high priest of his flock, from whom the life in Christ of his faithful is in some way derived and dependent.

Therefore, all should hold in great esteem the liturgical life of the diocese centered around the bishop, especially in his cathedral church; they must be convinced that the preeminent manifestation of the Church consists in the full, active participation of all God's holy people in these liturgical celebrations, especially in the same Eucharist, in a single prayer, at one altar, at which there presides the bishop surrounded by his college of priests and by his ministers.[15]

42. But because it is impossible for the bishop always and everywhere to preside over the whole flock in his Church, he cannot do other than establish lesser groupings of the faithful. Among these the parishes set up locally under a pastor who takes the place of the bishop are the most important, for in some manner they represent the visible Church constituted throughout the world.

And therefore, the liturgical life of the parish and its relationship to the bishop must be fostered theoretically and practically among the faithful and clergy; efforts also must be made to encourage a sense of community within the parish, above all in the common celebration of the Sunday Mass.

5. The Promotion of Pastoral-Liturgical Action

43. Zeal for the promotion and restoration of the liturgy is rightly held to be a sign of the providential dispositions of God in our time, as a movement of the Holy Spirit in his Church. It is today a distinguishing mark of the Church's life, indeed of the whole tenor of contemporary religious thought and action.

---

15. Cf. St. Ignatius of Antioch, *To the Smyrnians* 8; *To the Magnesians* 7; *To the Philadelphians* 4.

So that this pastoral-liturgical action may become even more vigorous in the Church, the sacred Council decrees:

44. It is desirable that the competent territorial ecclesiastical authority mentioned in Art. 22, § 2, set up a liturgical commission, to be assisted by experts in liturgical science, sacred music, art and pastoral practice. So far as possible, the commission should be aided by some kind of institute for pastoral liturgy, consisting of persons who are eminent in these matters, and including laymen as circumstances suggest. Under the direction of the above-mentioned territorial ecclesiastical authority, the commission is to regulate pastoral-liturgical action throughout the territory, and to promote studies and necessary experiments whenever there is question of adaptations to be proposed to the Apostolic See.

45. For the same reason, every diocese is to have a commission on the sacred liturgy under the direction of the bishop for promoting the liturgical apostolate.

Sometimes it may be expedient that several dioceses should form between them one single commission which will be able to promote the liturgy by common consultation.

46. Besides the commission on the sacred liturgy, every diocese, as far as possible, should have commissions for sacred music and sacred art.

These three commissions must work in closest collaboration; indeed it will often be best to fuse the three of them into one single commission.

CHAPTER II

THE MOST SACRED MYSTERY
OF THE EUCHARIST

47. At the Last Supper, on the night when he was betrayed, our Savior instituted the Eucharistic Sacrifice of his Body and Blood. He did this in order to perpetuate the sacrifice of the cross throughout the centuries until he should come again, and so to entrust to his beloved spouse, the Church, a memorial of his death and resurrection: a sacrament of love, a sign of unity, a bond of charity,[16] a paschal banquet in which Christ is eaten, the mind is filled with grace, and a pledge of future glory is given to us.[17]

48. The Church, therefore, earnestly desires that Christ's faithful, when present at this mystery of faith, should not be there as strangers or silent spectators; on the contrary, through a good understanding of the rites and prayers, they should take part in the sacred action conscious of what they are doing, with devotion and full collaboration. They should be instructed by God's Word and be nourished at the table of the Lord's Body; they should give thanks to God; by offering the Immaculate Victim, not only through the hands of the priest but also with him, they should learn also to offer themselves; through Christ the Mediator,[18] they should be drawn day by day into ever more perfect union with God and with each other, so that finally God may be all in all.

49. For this reason, the sacred Council, having in mind those Masses which are celebrated with the assistance of the faithful, especially on Sundays and feasts of obligation, has made the following decrees in or-

---

16. Cf. St. Augustine, *Tractatus in Ioannem* 6, 13.

17. *Roman Breviary,* Feast of Corpus Christi, Second Vespers, antiphon to the Magnificat.

18. Cf. St. Cyril of Alexandria, *Commentary on the Gospel of John* 11, 11–12: *PG* 74, 557–564.

der that the sacrifice of the Mass, even in the ritual forms of its celebration, may become pastorally efficacious to the fullest degree.

50. The rite of the Mass is to be revised in such a way that the intrinsic nature and purpose of its several parts, as also the connection between them, may be more clearly manifested, and that devout and active participation by the faithful may be more easily achieved.

For this purpose, the rites are to be simplified, due care being taken to preserve their substance; elements which with the passage of time came to be duplicated, or were added with but little advantage, are now to be discarded; other elements which have suffered injury through accidents of history are now to be restored to the vigor which they had in the days of the holy Fathers, as may seem useful or necessary.

51. The treasures of the Bible are to be opened up more lavishly, so that richer fare may be provided for the faithful at the table of God's Word. In this way a more representative portion of the holy Scriptures will be read to the people in the course of a prescribed number of years.

52. By means of the homily, the mysteries of the faith and the guiding principles of the Christian life are expounded from the sacred text during the course of the liturgical year; the homily, therefore, is to be highly esteemed as part of the liturgy itself; in fact, at those Masses which are celebrated with the assistance of the people on Sundays and feasts of obligation, it should not be omitted except for a serious reason.

53. Especially on Sundays and feasts of obligation, there is to be restored, after the Gospel and the homily, "the common prayer" or "the prayer of the faithful." By this prayer, in which the people are to take part, intercession will be made for holy Church, for the civil authorities, for those oppressed by various needs, for all mankind and for the salvation of the entire world (cf. 1 Tm 2:1–2).

54. In Masses which are celebrated with the people, a suitable place may be allotted to their mother tongue. This is to apply in the first place to the readings and "the common prayer," but also, as local conditions may warrant, to those parts which pertain to the people, according to the norm laid down in Art. 36 of this Constitution.

Nevertheless, steps should be taken so that the faithful may also be able to say or to sing together in Latin those parts of the ordinary of the Mass which pertain to them.

And wherever a more extended use of the mother tongue within the

Mass appears desirable, the regulation laid down in Art. 40 of this Constitution is to be observed.

55. That more perfect form of participation in the Mass, whereby the faithful, after the priest's Communion, receive the Lord's Body from the same sacrifice, is strongly commended.

The dogmatic principles which were laid down by the Council of Trent remaining intact,[19] Communion under both kinds may be granted when the bishops think fit, not only to clerics and religious but also to the laity, in cases to be determined by the Apostolic See, as, for instance, to the newly ordained in the Mass of their sacred ordination, to the newly professed in the Mass of their religious profession, and to the newly baptized in the Mass which follows their baptism.

56. The two parts which in a certain sense go to make up the Mass, namely, the liturgy of the Word and the Eucharistic liturgy, are so closely connected with each other that they form but one single act of worship. Accordingly, this sacred synod strongly urges pastors of souls that, when instructing the faithful, they insistently teach them to take their part in the entire Mass, especially on Sundays and feasts of obligation.

57. § 1. Concelebration, whereby the unity of the priesthood is appropriately manifested, has remained in use to this day in the Church both in the East and in the West. For this reason, it has seemed good to the Council to extend permission for concelebration to the following cases:

1. a) on the Thursday of the Lord's Supper, not only at the Mass of the Chrism but also at the evening Mass;

    b) at Masses during councils, bishops' conferences, and synods;

    c) at the Mass for the blessing of an abbot.

2. Also, with permission of the ordinary, to whom it belongs to decide whether concelebration is opportune:

    a) at conventual Mass, and at the principal Mass in churches when the needs of the faithful do not require that all priests available should celebrate individually;

    b) at Masses celebrated at any kind of priests' meetings, whether the priests be secular clergy or religious.

---

19. Council of Trent, Session 21, *Doctrine on Communion under Both Species,* ch. 1–3.

§ 2. 1. The regulation, however, of the discipline of concelebration in the diocese pertains to the bishop.

2. Nevertheless, each priest shall always retain his right to celebrate Mass individually, though not at the same time in the same church as a concelebrated Mass, nor on Thursday of the Lord's Supper.

58. A new rite for concelebration is to be drawn up and inserted into the Pontifical and into the Roman Missal.

CHAPTER III

THE OTHER SACRAMENTS AND THE SACRAMENTALS

59. The purpose of the sacraments is to sanctify men, to build up the body of Christ and finally, to give worship to God; because they are signs, they also instruct. They not only presuppose faith, but by words and objects they also nourish, strengthen and express it; that is why they are called "sacraments of faith." They do indeed impart grace, but in addition the very act of celebrating them most effectively disposes the faithful to receive this grace in a fruitful manner, to worship God duly and to practice charity.

It is therefore of the highest importance that the faithful should easily understand the sacramental signs, and should frequent with great eagerness those sacraments which were instituted to nourish the Christian life.

60. Holy mother Church has, moreover, instituted sacramentals. These are sacred signs which bear a resemblance to the sacraments; they signify effects, particularly of a spiritual kind, which are obtained through the Church's intercession. By them men are disposed to receive the chief effect of the sacraments, and various occasions in life are rendered holy.

61. Thus, for well-disposed members of the faithful, the liturgy of the sacraments and sacramentals sanctifies almost every event in their lives; they are given access to the stream of divine grace which flows from the Paschal Mystery of the passion, death, the resurrection of Christ, the font from which all sacraments and sacramentals draw their power. There is hardly any proper use of material things which cannot thus be directed toward the sanctification of men and the praise of God.

62. With the passage of time, however, there have crept into the rites of the sacraments and sacramentals certain features which have rendered their nature and purpose far from clear to the people of today; hence, some changes have become necessary to adapt them to the needs

of our own times. For this reason, the sacred Council decrees as follows concerning their revision:

63. Because the use of the mother tongue in the administration of the sacraments and sacramentals can often be of considerable help to the people, this use is to be extended according to the following norms:

a) The vernacular language may be used in administering the sacraments and sacramentals, according to the norm of Art. 36.

b) In harmony with the new edition of the Roman Ritual, particular rituals shall be prepared without delay by the competent territorial ecclesiastical authority mentioned in Art. 22, § 2, of this constitution. These rituals, which are to be adapted, also as regards the language employed, to the needs of the different regions, are to be reviewed by the Apostolic See and then introduced into the regions for which they have been prepared. But in drawing up these rituals or particular collections of rites, the instructions prefixed to the individual rites the Roman Ritual, whether they be pastoral and rubrical or whether they have special social import, shall not be omitted.

64. The catechumenate for adults, comprising several distinct steps, is to be restored and to be taken into use at the discretion of the local ordinary. By this means the time of the catechumenate, which is intended as a period of suitable instruction, may be sanctified by sacred rites to be celebrated at successive intervals of time.

65. In mission lands it is found that some of the peoples already make use of initiation rites. Elements from these, when capable of being adapted to Christian ritual, may be admitted along with those already found in Christian tradition, according to the norm laid down in Art. 37–40 of this Constitution.

66. Both the rites for the Baptism of adults are to be revised, not only the simpler rite but also the more solemn one, which must take into account the restored catechumenate. A special Mass "for the conferring of Baptism" is to be inserted into the Roman Missal.

67. The rite for the Baptism of infants is to be revised, and it should be adapted to the circumstance that those to be baptized are, in fact, infants. The roles of parents and godparents, and also their duties, should be brought out more clearly in the rite itself.

68. The baptismal rite should contain variants, to be used at the discretion of the local ordinary, for occasions when a very large number are to be baptized together. Moreover, a shorter rite is to be drawn up, espe-

cially for mission lands, to be used by catechists, but also by the faithful in general when there is danger of death and neither priest nor deacon is available.

69. In place of the rite called the "Order of Supplying What Was Omitted in the Baptism of an Infant," a new rite is to be drawn up. This should manifest more fittingly and clearly that the infant baptized by the short rite has already been received into the Church.

And a new rite is to be drawn up for converts who have already been validly baptized; it should indicate that they are now admitted to communion with the Church.

70. Except during Eastertide, baptismal water may be blessed within the rite of Baptism itself by an approved shorter formula.

71. The rite of Confirmation is to be revised and the intimate connection which this sacrament has with the whole of Christian initiation is to be more clearly set forth; for this reason, it is fitting for candidates to renew their baptismal promises just before they are confirmed.

Confirmation may be given within the Mass when convenient; when it is given outside the Mass, the rite that is used should be introduced by a formula to be drawn up for this purpose.

72. The rite and formulas for the sacrament of Penance are to be revised so that they more clearly express both the nature and effect of the sacrament.

73. "Extreme Unction," which may also and more fittingly be called "Anointing of the Sick," is not a sacrament for those only who are at the point of death. Hence, as soon as any one of the faithful begins to be in danger of death from sickness or old age, the fitting time for him to receive this sacrament has certainly already arrived.

74. In addition to the separate rites for Anointing of the Sick and for Viaticum, a continuous rite shall be prepared according to which the sick man is anointed after he has made his confession and before he receives Viaticum.

75. The number of the anointings is to be adapted to the occasion, and the prayers which belong to the rite of Anointing are to be revised so as to correspond with the varying conditions of the sick who receive the sacrament.

76. Both the ceremonies and texts of the ordination rites are to be revised. The address given by the bishop at the beginning of each ordination or consecration may be in the mother tongue.

When a bishop is consecrated, the laying of hands may be done by all the bishops present.

77. The marriage rite now found in the Roman Ritual is to be revised and enriched in such a way that the grace of the sacrament is more clearly signified and the duties of the spouses are taught.

"If any regions are wont to use other praiseworthy customs and ceremonies when celebrating the sacrament of Matrimony, the sacred synod earnestly desires that these by all means be retained."[20]

Moreover, the competent territorial ecclesiastical authority mentioned in Art. 22, § 2, of this Constitution is free to draw up its own rite suited to the usages of place and people, according to the provision of Art. 63. But the rite must always conform to the law that the priest assisting at the marriage must ask for and obtain the consent of the contracting parties.

78. Matrimony is normally to be celebrated within the Mass, after the reading of the Gospel and the homily and before "the prayer of the faithful." The prayer for the bride, duly amended to remind both spouses of their equal obligation to remain faithful to each other, may be said in the mother tongue.

But if the sacrament of Matrimony is celebrated apart from Mass, the epistle and Gospel from the nuptial Mass are to be read at the beginning of the rite, and the blessing should always be given to the spouses.

79. The sacramentals are to undergo a revision which takes into account the primary principle of enabling the faithful to participate intelligently, actively and easily; the circumstances of our own days must also be considered. When rituals are revised, as laid down in Art. 63, new sacramentals may also be added as the need for these becomes apparent.

Reserved blessings shall be very few; reservations shall be in favor of bishops or ordinaries.

Let provision be made that some sacramentals, at least in special circumstances and at the discretion of the ordinary, may be administered by qualified lay persons.

80. The rite for the consecration of virgins at present found in the Roman Pontifical is to be revised.

Moreover, a rite of religious profession and renewal of vows shall be

---

20. Council of Trent, Session 24, *On Reform,* ch. 1; cf. *Roman Ritual,* title 8, ch. 2, n. 6.

drawn up in order to achieve greater unity, sobriety and dignity. Apart from exceptions in particular law, this rite should be adopted by those who make their profession or renewal of vows within the Mass.

Religious profession should preferably be made within the Mass.

81. The rite for the burial of the dead should express more clearly the paschal character of Christian death, and should correspond more closely to the circumstances and traditions found in various regions. This holds good also for the liturgical color to be used.

82. The rite for the burial of infants is to be revised, and a special Mass for the occasion should be provided.

CHAPTER IV

THE DIVINE OFFICE

83. Christ Jesus, high priest of the new and eternal covenant, taking human nature, introduced into this earthly exile that hymn which is sung throughout all ages in the halls of heaven. He joins the entire community of mankind to himself, associating it with his own singing of this canticle of divine praise.

For he continues his priestly work through the agency of his Church, which is ceaselessly engaged in praising the Lord and interceding for the salvation of the whole world. She does this not only by celebrating the Eucharist, but also in other ways, especially by praying the divine office.

84. By tradition going back to early Christian times, the divine office is devised so that the whole course of the day and night is made holy by the praises of God. Therefore, when this wonderful song of praise is rightly performed by priests and others who are deputed for this purpose by the Church's ordinance, or by the faithful praying together with the priest in the approved form, then it is truly the voice of the bride addressed to her bridegroom; it is the very prayer which Christ himself, together with his body, addresses to the Father.

85. Hence, all who render this service are not only fulfilling a duty of the Church, but also are sharing in the greatest honor of Christ's spouse, for by offering these praises to God, they are standing before God's throne in the name of the Church their mother.

86. Priests who are engaged in the sacred pastoral ministry will offer the praises of the hours with greater fervor the more vividly they realize that they must heed St. Paul's exhortation: "Pray without ceasing" (1 Thes 5:17). For the work in which they labor will effect nothing and bring forth no fruit except by the power of the Lord who said: "Without me you can do nothing" (Jn 15:5). That is why the apostles, instituting deacons, said: "We will devote ourselves to prayer and to the ministry of the word" (Acts 6:4).

87. In order that the divine office may be better and more perfectly prayed in existing circumstances, whether by priests or by other members of the Church, the sacred Council, carrying further the restoration already so happily begun by the Apostolic See, has seen fit to decree as follows concerning the office of the Roman rite:

88. Because the purpose of the office is to sanctify the day, the traditional sequence of the hours is to be restored so that once again they may be genuinely related to the time of the day when they are prayed, as far as this may be possible. Moreover, it will be necessary to take into account the modern conditions in which daily life has to be lived, especially by those who are called to labor in apostolic works.

89. Therefore, when the office is revised, these norms are to be observed:

a) By the venerable tradition of the universal Church, Lauds as morning prayer and Vespers as evening prayer are the two hinges on which the daily office turns; hence, they are to be considered as the chief hours and are to be celebrated as such.

b) Compline is to be drawn up so that it will be a suitable prayer for the end of the day.

c) The hour known as Matins, although it should retain the character of nocturnal praise when celebrated in choir, shall be adapted so that it may be recited at any hour of the day; it shall be made up of fewer psalms and longer readings.

d) The hour of Prime is to be suppressed.

e) In choir the hours of Terce, Sext and None are to be observed. But outside choir it will be lawful to select any one of these three, according to the respective time of the day.

90. The divine office, because it is the public prayer of the Church, is a source of piety and nourishment for personal prayer. And therefore, priests and all others who take part in the divine office are earnestly exhorted in the Lord to attune their minds to their voices when praying it. The better to achieve this, let them take steps to improve their understanding of the liturgy and of the Bible, especially of the psalms.

In revising the Roman office, its ancient and venerable treasures are to be so adapted that all those to whom they are handed on may more extensively and easily draw profit from them.

91. So that it may really be possible in practice to observe the course of the hours proposed in Art. 89, the psalms are no longer to be distributed throughout one week, but through some longer period of time.

The work of revising the psalter, already happily begun, is to be finished as soon as possible and is to take into account the style of Christian Latin, the liturgical use of psalms—also when sung—and the entire tradition of the Latin Church.

92. As regards the readings, the following shall be observed:

a) Readings from Sacred Scripture shall be arranged so that the riches of God's word may be easily accessible in more abundant measure.

b) Readings excerpted from the works of the Fathers, doctors and ecclesiastical writers shall be better selected.

c) The accounts of martyrdom or the lives of the saints are to accord with the facts of history.

93. To whatever extent may seem desirable, the hymns are to be restored to their original form, and whatever smacks of mythology or ill accords with Christian piety is to be removed or changed. Also, as occasion may arise, let other selections from the treasury of hymns be incorporated.

94. That the day may be truly sanctified and that the hours themselves may be recited with spiritual advantage, it is best that each of them be prayed at a time which most closely corresponds with its true canonical time.

95. Communities obliged to choral office are bound to celebrate the office in choir every day in addition to the conventual Mass. In particular:

a) Orders of canons, of monks and of nuns, and of other regulars bound by law or constitutions to choral office must celebrate the entire office.

b) Cathedral or collegiate chapters are bound to recite those parts of the office imposed on them by general or particular law.

c) All members of the above communities who are in major orders or who are solemnly professed, except for lay brothers, are bound to recite individually those canonical hours which they do not pray in choir.

96. Clerics not bound to office in choir, if they are in major orders, are bound to pray the entire office every day, either in common or individually, as laid down in Art. 89.

97. Appropriate instances are to be defined by the rubrics in which a liturgical service may be substituted for the divine office.

In particular cases and for a just reason, ordinaries can dispense their subjects wholly or in part from the obligation of reciting the divine office, or may commute the obligation.

98. Members of any institute dedicated to acquiring perfection who, according to their constitutions, are to recite any parts of the divine office, are thereby performing the public prayer of the Church.

They too perform the public prayer of the Church, who in virtue of their constitutions, recite any short office, provided this is drawn up after the pattern of the divine office and is duly approved.·

99. Since the divine office is the voice of the Church, that is, of the whole Mystical Body publicly praising God, those clerics who are not obliged to office in choir, especially priests who live together or who assemble for any purpose, are urged to pray at least some part of the divine office in common.

All who pray the divine office, whether in choir or in common, should fulfill the task entrusted to them as perfectly as possible; this refers not only to the internal devotion of their minds but also to their external manner of celebration.

It is, moreover, fitting that the office, both in choir and in common, be sung when possible.

100. Pastors of souls should see to it that the chief hours, especially Vespers, are celebrated in common in church on Sundays and the more solemn feasts. And the laity, too, are encouraged to recite the divine office, either with the priests, or among themselves, or even individually.

101. § 1. In accordance with the centuries-old tradition of the Latin rite, the Latin language is to be retained by clerics in reciting the divine office. But in individual cases the ordinary has the power of granting the use of a vernacular translation to those clerics for whom the use of Latin constitutes a grave obstacle to their praying the office properly. The vernacular version, however, must be one that is drawn up according to the provision of Art. 36.

§ 2. The competent superior has the power to grant the use of the vernacular in the celebration of the divine office, even in choir, to nuns and to members of institutes dedicated to acquiring perfection, both men who are not clerics and women. The version, however, must be one that is approved.

§ 3. Any cleric bound to the divine office fulfills his obligation if he prays the office in the vernacular together with a group of the faithful or with those mentioned in § 2 above provided that the text of the translation is approved.

CHAPTER V

THE LITURGICAL YEAR

102. Holy mother Church is conscious that she must celebrate the saving work of her divine spouse by devoutly recalling it on certain days throughout the course of the year. Every week, on the day which she has called the Lord's day, she keeps the memory of the Lord's resurrection, which she also celebrates once in the year, together with his blessed passion, in the most solemn festival of Easter.

Within the cycle of a year, moreover, she unfolds the whole mystery of Christ, from the Incarnation and birth until the ascension, the day of Pentecost and the expectation of blessed hope and of the coming of the Lord.

Recalling thus the mysteries of redemption, the Church opens to the faithful the riches of her Lord's powers and merits, so that these are in some way made present for all time, and the faithful are enabled to lay hold upon them and become filled with saving grace.

103. In celebrating this annual cycle of Christ's mysteries, holy Church honors with especial love the Blessed Mary, Mother of God, who is joined by an inseparable bond to the saving work of her Son. In her the Church holds up and admires the most excellent fruit of the redemption and joyfully contemplates, as in a faultless image, that which she herself desires and hopes wholly to be.

104. The Church has also included in the annual cycle days devoted to the memory of the martyrs and the other saints. Raised up to perfection by the manifold grace of God and already in possession of eternal salvation, they sing God's perfect praise in heaven and offer prayers for us. By celebrating the passage of these saints from earth to heaven, the Church proclaims the Paschal Mystery achieved in the saints who have suffered and been glorified with Christ; she proposes them to the faithful as examples drawing all to the Father through Christ, and through their merits she pleads for God's favors.

105. Finally, in the various seasons of the year and according to her traditional discipline, the Church completes the formation of the faithful by means of pious practices for soul and body, by instruction, prayer and works of penance and of mercy.

Accordingly, the sacred Council has seen fit to decree as follows:

106. By a tradition handed down from the apostles which took its origin from the very day of Christ's resurrection, the Church celebrates the Paschal Mystery every eighth day; with good reason this, then, bears the name of the Lord's day or Sunday. For on this day Christ's faithful are bound to come together into one place so that by hearing the Word of God and taking part in the Eucharist, they may call to mind the passion, the resurrection and the glorification of the Lord Jesus, and may thank God who "has begotten them again, through the resurrection of Jesus Christ from the dead, unto a living hope" (1 Pt 1:3). Hence, the Lord's day is the original feast day, and it should be proposed to the piety of the faithful and taught to them so that it may become in fact a day of joy and of freedom from work. Other celebrations, unless they be truly of greatest importance, shall not have precedence over the Sunday which is the foundation and kernel of the whole liturgical year.

107. The liturgical year is to be revised so that the traditional customs and discipline of the sacred seasons shall be preserved or restored to suit the conditions of modern times; their specific character is to be retained, so that they duly nourish the piety of the faithful who celebrate the mysteries of Christian redemption, and above all the Paschal Mystery. If certain adaptations are considered necessary on account of local conditions, they are to be made in accordance with the provisions of Art. 39 and 40.

108. The minds of the faithful must be directed primarily toward the feasts of the Lord whereby the mysteries of salvation are celebrated in the course of the year. Therefore, the proper of the time shall be given the preference which is its due over the feasts of the saints, so that the entire cycle of the mysteries of salvation may be suitably recalled.

109. The season of Lent has a twofold character; primarily by recalling or preparing for Baptism and by Penance, it disposes the faithful, who more diligently hear the Word of God and devote themselves to prayer, to celebrate the Paschal Mystery. This twofold character is to be brought into greater prominence both in the liturgy and by liturgical catechesis. Hence:

a) More use is to be made of the baptismal features proper to the Lenten liturgy; some of them, which used to flourish in bygone days, are to be restored as may seem good.

b) The same is to apply to the penitential elements. As regards instruction it is important to impress on the minds of the faithful not only the social consequences of sin but also that essence of the virtue of penance which leads to the detestation of sin as an offense against God; the role of the Church in penitential practices is not to be passed over, and the people must be exhorted to pray for sinners.

110. During Lent penance should not be only internal and individual, but also external and social. The practice of penance should be fostered in ways that are possible in our own times and in different regions and according to the circumstances of the faithful; it should be encouraged by the authorities mentioned in Art. 22.

Nevertheless, let the paschal fast be kept sacred. Let it be celebrated everywhere on Good Friday and, where possible, prolonged throughout Holy Saturday, so that the joys of the Sunday of the resurrection may be attained with uplifted and clear mind.

111. The saints have been traditionally honored in the Church and their authentic relics and images held in veneration. For the feasts of the saints proclaim the wonderful works of Christ in his servants, and display to the faithful fitting examples for their imitation.

Lest the feasts of the saints should take precedence over the feasts which commemorate the very mysteries of salvation, many of them should be left to be celebrated by a particular Church or nation or family of religious; only those should be extended to the universal Church which commemorate saints who are truly of universal importance.

CHAPTER VI

SACRED MUSIC

112. The musical tradition of the universal Church is a treasure of inestimable value, greater even than that of any other art. The main reason for this preeminence is that, as sacred song united to the words, it forms a necessary or integral part of the solemn liturgy.

Holy Scripture, indeed, has bestowed praise upon sacred song (cf. Eph 5:19; Col 3:16), and the same may be said of the Fathers of the Church and of the Roman Pontiffs who in recent times, led by St. Pius X, have explained more precisely the ministerial function supplied by sacred music in the service of the Lord.

Therefore, sacred music is to be considered the more holy in proportion as it is more closely connected with the liturgical action, whether it adds delight to prayer, fosters unity of minds or confers greater solemnity upon the sacred rites. But the Church approves of all forms of true art having the needed qualities and admits them into divine worship.

Accordingly, the sacred Council, keeping to the norms and precepts of ecclesiastical tradition and discipline, and having regard to the purpose of sacred music, which is the glory of God and the sanctification of the faithful, decrees as follows:

113. Liturgical worship is given a more noble form when the divine offices are celebrated solemnly in song, with the assistance of sacred ministers and the active participation of the people.

As regards the language to be used, the provisions of Art. 36 are to be observed; for the Mass, Art. 54; for the sacraments, Art. 63; for the divine office, Art. 101.

114. The treasure of sacred music is to be preserved and fostered with great care. Choirs must be diligently promoted, especially in cathedral churches, but bishops and other pastors of souls must be at pains to ensure that whenever the sacred action is to be celebrated with song, the

whole body of the faithful may be able to contribute that active participation which is rightly theirs, as laid down in Art. 28 and 30.

115. Great importance is to be attached to the teaching and practice of music in seminaries, in the novitiates and houses of study of religious of both sexes and also in other Catholic institutions and schools. To impart this instruction, teachers are to be carefully trained and put in charge of the teaching of sacred music.

It is desirable also to found higher institutes of sacred music whenever this can be done.

Composers and singers, especially boys, must also be given a genuine liturgical training.

116. The Church acknowledges Gregorian chant as specially suited to the Roman liturgy; therefore, other things being equal, it should be given pride of place in liturgical services.

But other kinds of sacred music, especially polyphony, are by no means excluded from liturgical celebrations so long as they accord with the spirit of the liturgical action, as laid down in Art. 30.

117. The typical edition of the books of Gregorian chant is to be completed, and a more critical edition is to be prepared of those books already published since the restoration by St. Pius X.

It is desirable also that an edition be prepared containing simpler melodies for use in small churches.

118. Religious singing by the people is to be intelligently fostered so that in devotions and sacred exercises, as also during liturgical services, the voices of the faithful may ring out according to the norms and requirements of the rubrics.

119. In certain parts of the world, especially mission lands, there are peoples who have their own musical traditions, and these play a great part in their religious and social life. For this reason, due importance is to be attached to their music, and a suitable place is to be given to it, not only in forming their attitude toward religion but also in adapting worship to their native genius, as indicated in Art. 39 and 40.

Therefore, when missionaries are being given training in music, every effort should be made to see that they become competent in promoting the traditional music of these peoples, both in schools and in sacred services, as far as may be practicable.

120. In the Latin Church the pipe organ is to be held in high esteem, for it is the traditional musical instrument which adds a wonderful

splendor to the Church's ceremonies and powerfully lifts up man's mind to God and to higher things.

But other instruments also may be admitted for use in divine worship with the knowledge and consent of the competent territorial authority, as laid down in Art. 22, § 2, 37 and 40. This may be done, however, only on condition that the instruments are suitable or can be made suitable for sacred use, accord with the dignity of the temple and truly contribute to the edification of the faithful.

121. Composers, filled with the Christian spirit, should feel that their vocation is to cultivate sacred music and increase its store of treasures.

Let them produce compositions which have the qualities proper to genuine sacred music, not confining themselves to works which can be sung only by large choirs, but providing also for the needs of small choirs and for the active participation of the entire assembly of the faithful.

The texts intended to be sung must always be in conformity with Catholic doctrine; indeed, they should be drawn chiefly from holy Scripture and from liturgical sources.

CHAPTER VII

SACRED ART AND
SACRED FURNISHINGS

122. Very rightly the fine arts are considered to rank among the noblest activities of man's genius, and this applies especially to religious art and to its highest achievement, which is sacred art. These arts, by their very nature, are oriented toward the infinite beauty of God which they attempt in some way to portray by the work of human hands; they achieve their purpose of redounding to God's praise and glory in proportion as they are directed the more exclusively to the single aim of turning men's minds devoutly toward God.

Holy mother Church has therefore always been the friend of the fine arts and has ever sought their noble help, with the special aim that all things set apart for use in divine worship should be truly worthy, becoming and beautiful, signs and symbols of the supernatural world, and for this purpose she has trained artists. In fact, the Church has with good reason always reserved to herself the right to pass judgment upon the arts, deciding which of the works of artists are in accordance with faith, piety and cherished traditional laws, and thereby fitted for sacred use.

The Church has been particularly careful to see that sacred furnishings should worthily and beautifully serve the dignity of worship, and has admitted changes in materials, style or ornamentation prompted by the progress of the technical arts with the passage of time.

Wherefore, it has pleased the fathers to issue the following decrees on these matters:

123. The Church has not adopted any particular style of art as her very own; she has admitted styles from every period according to the natural talents and circumstances of peoples, and the needs of the various rites. Thus, in the course of the centuries, she has brought into being a treasury of art which must be very carefully preserved. The art of our own days, coming from every race and region, shall also be given free scope in the Church, provided that it adorns the sacred buildings and

holy rites with due reverence and honor; thereby, it is enabled to contribute its own voice to that wonderful chorus of praise in honor of the Catholic faith sung by great men in times gone by.

124. Ordinaries, by the encouragement and favor they show to art which is truly sacred, should strive after noble beauty rather than mere sumptuous display. This principle is to apply also in the matter of sacred vestments and ornaments.

Let bishops carefully remove from the house of God and from other sacred places those works of artists which are repugnant to faith, morals and Christian piety, and which offend true religious sense either by depraved forms or by lack of artistic worth, mediocrity and pretense.

And when churches are to be built, let great care be taken that they be suitable for the celebration of liturgical services and for the active participation of the faithful.

125. The practice of placing sacred images in churches so that they may be venerated by the faithful is to be maintained. Nevertheless, their number should be moderate and their relative positions should reflect right order. For otherwise they may create confusion among the Christian people and foster devotion of doubtful orthodoxy.

126. When passing judgment on works of art, local ordinaries shall give a hearing to the diocesan commission on sacred art, and if needed, also to others who are especially expert, and to the commissions referred to in Art. 44, 45 and 46.

Ordinaries must be very careful to see that sacred furnishings and works of value are not disposed of or dispersed; for they are the ornaments of the house of God.

127. Bishops should have a special concern for artists, so as to imbue them with the spirit of sacred art and of the sacred liturgy. This they may do in person or through suitable priests who are gifted with a knowledge and love of art.

It is also desirable that schools or academies of sacred art should be founded in those parts of the world where they would be useful, so that artists may be trained.

All artists who, prompted by their talents, desire to serve God's glory in holy Church, should ever bear in mind that they are engaged in a kind of sacred imitation of God the Creator, and are concerned with works destined to be used in Catholic worship, to edify the faithful and to foster their piety and their religious formation.

128. Along with the revision of the liturgical books, as laid down in Art. 25, there is to be an early revision of the canons and ecclesiastical statutes which govern the provision of material things involved in sacred worship. These laws refer especially to the worthy and well planned construction of sacred buildings, the shape and construction of altars, the nobility, placing, and safety of the Eucharistic tabernacle, the dignity and suitability of the baptistry, the proper ordering of sacred images, embellishments and vestments. Laws which seem less suited to the reformed liturgy are to be brought into harmony with it or else abolished, and any which are helpful are to be retained if already in use, or introduced where they are lacking.

According to the norm of Art. 22 of this Constitution, the territorial bodies of bishops are empowered to adapt such things to the needs and customs of their different regions; this applies especially to the materials and form of sacred furnishings and vestments.

129. During their philosophical and theological studies, clerics are to be taught about the history and development of sacred art, and about the sound principles governing the production of its works. In consequence, they will be able to appreciate and preserve the Church's venerable monuments, and be in a position to aid by good advice artists who are engaged in producing works of art.

130. It is fitting that the use of pontificals be reserved to those ecclesiastical persons who have episcopal rank or some particular jurisdiction.

APPENDIX

A Declaration of the Second Ecumenical Council of the Vatican on Revision of the Calendar

The Second Ecumenical Sacred Council of the Vatican, recognizing the importance of the wishes expressed by many concerning the assignment of the feast of Easter to a fixed Sunday and concerning an unchanging calendar, having carefully considered the effects which could result from the introduction of a new calendar, declares as follows:

1. The sacred Council would not object if the feast of Easter were assigned to a particular Sunday of the Gregorian calendar, provided that those whom it may concern, especially the brethren who are not in communion with the Apostolic See, give their assent.

2. The sacred Council likewise declares that it does not oppose efforts designed to introduce a perpetual calendar into civil society.

But among the various systems which are being suggested to stabilize a perpetual calendar and to introduce it into civil life, the Church has no objection only in the case of those systems which retain and safeguard a seven-day week with Sunday, without the introduction of any days outside the week, so that the succession of weeks may be left intact, unless there is question of the most serious reasons. Concerning these the Apostolic See shall judge.

Given in Rome at St. Peter's, December 4, 1963

DECREE ON THE MEDIA OF SOCIAL COMMUNICATION

Inter Mirifica

Promulgated by
His Holiness Pope Paul VI
On December 4, 1963

INTRODUCTION

A council so vividly conscious that one of the signs of the times is the heightened sense of the unity of all people (cf. *LG* 1; *GS* 26; *NA* 1), could hardly overlook the role of the media in this development. Promulgated on December 4, 1963, along with the *Constitution on the Sacred Liturgy,* the *Decree on the Media of Social Communication (IM)* was one of the first two documents the Council completed. All comparisons between the two end there. Because its subject matter was perceived as being somewhat peripheral to the Council's focus, and because of factors related to the internal working and progression of the Council, *IM* benefited the least from the process of dialogue and maturation that is so evident in later texts. This accounts for the observation of some commentators that *IM* is conspicuous for the absence of certain themes which developed with the Council itself, for the Council was a dynamic event. Since all the documents are products of the same Council and unified by its goals, what might be lacking in *IM* when viewed in light of the whole conciliar work can be provided through a search for complementary themes in the conciliar teaching.

As an example, the preface and introductory statement of *Gaudium et Spes* more amply develops the theme set forth in the introduction to *IM,* which begins by situating the media "among the wonderful technological discoveries." It goes on to state that their importance lies in their ability to "reach and influence" individuals, large groups "and the whole of human society." Its main theme is that moral principles must direct the use of the media. This is introduced by stating that the media can be either a service or a disservice to humanity, depending on whether they are used in accordance with or contrary to the Creator's plan. The introduction also uses the term "media of social communication" to indicate that the Church's interest is in the whole process of human communication. It is not narrowly focused on technical means but considers communication as a profound process of human interaction.

Only later does the decree touch on the questions which the media raise (cf. *IM* 5–7). Unfortunately, this is not presented in such a way that it is clearly seen that these questions concern everyone. *Gaudium et Spes* accomplishes this by placing the moral order at the center of the Church's dialogue with the world, and by tying it to human dignity, responsibility and the fundamental questions which people today are asking. Because the Church is solicitous about the human person, it listens to the questions that life in the modern world presents, believing that this is a point of contact with the world.

In the words of *Gaudium et Spes,* the development of mass media certainly deserves to be counted among the "profound and rapid changes" that are "triggered by the intelligence and creative energies of man," but which can have a recoil effect. This effect is not always for the better, as man "does not always succeed in subjecting [his accomplishments] to his own welfare" (*GS* 4).

The media are one of those advances which cause wonder and hope along with anxiety (cf. *GS* 3, 4). In response to the awareness "that it is his responsibility to guide aright the forces which he has unleashed and which can enslave him or minister to him," the human person asks fundamental questions (cf. *GS* 10). These questions go to the heart of what it means to be a human being, endowed with freedom and responsibility, and called to communion with God.

In particular, the fact that the media can be used either to serve people or to harm them, to promote or to diminish human dignity, naturally raises the question of the definition of human dignity, and thus of the nature of the person. The Church believes that in Jesus Christ the full truth about the human person has been revealed (cf. *GS* 22), which can answer the fundamental questions that are raised, explicitly or implicitly, by the progress of the modern world.

The Church does not offer technical advice or directives regarding the use of the media. But it does discuss how the media affect human life, and from this the Church derives moral limits and corresponding rights and duties with regard to their content and use. The main assertion of *IM's* first chapter is that the media should be used according to God's design (cf. *IM* 3) and be guided by "the norms of morality" (cf. *IM* 4). "It is, however, especially necessary that all parties concerned should adopt for themselves a proper moral outlook on the use of these media" (*IM* 5).

In *IM* 6 the same principle is repeated: "The Council proclaims that all must hold to the absolute primacy of the objective moral order," further stating that this primacy means:

> this [moral] order by itself surpasses and fittingly coordinates all other spheres of human affairs.... For man, who is endowed by God with the gift of reason and summoned to pursue a lofty destiny, is alone affected by the moral order in his entire being. And likewise, if man resolutely and faithfully upholds this order, he will be brought to the attainment of complete perfection and happiness (*IM* 6).

Later the decree mentions the necessity of a proper formation of conscience so that the media can be used in a way consistent with the moral code and thus without harm to human dignity (cf. *IM* 9). This is reinforced by what the Council teaches elsewhere about conscience (cf. *GS* 8, 16, 43, 76; *DH* 3).

IM elaborates this principle by stating that art is to be guided by the rule of morality (cf. *IM* 6). It also mentions the importance of moral norms when it is a question of "the narration, description or portrayal of moral evil" (*IM* 7). The Church's understanding of human nature and dignity and the moral norms relating to them results in a twofold judgment concerning the actual use of the media in concrete circumstances. They can either promote human dignity and development, or detract from them. Two attitudes toward the media correspond to these fundamental criteria: a positive attitude and a defensive attitude. The Church adopts a positive attitude toward the media and embraces what is good in them. It is essential to understand this in order to appreciate the teaching of *IM*.

In line with this positive attitude, *IM* acknowledges the usefulness of the media in communicating truthful news and information. This promotes the common good, establishes relationships and provides a sound basis for making decisions (*IM* 5). This corresponds to the right that people have to the information they require to effectively contribute to society by making decisions based on the truth. In addition, the Church claims the right to use the media as a useful means to realizing her mission. The decree calls for instruction and guidance from pastors so that the media can be incorporated into this mission (cf. *IM* 3).

The decree also warns against harmful ways of using the media.

Even when the content complies with good morality, the way in which information is conveyed can itself offend morality (*IM* 5). The opposite of communicating the truth occurs when the information is purposefully not true or incomplete. When this occurs the media can become a means of manipulation.

IM shows a pastoral solicitude for young people, mentioning them six times in this short document. This manifests the council fathers' awareness of the far-reaching influence of the media. *IM* states that young people in particular should "endeavor to deepen their understanding of what they see, hear or read. They should discuss these matters with their teachers and experts, and learn to pass sound judgment on them" (*IM* 10). So that the media can contribute to the authentic human and thus moral development of the young, the decree calls for "the production and showing of films that have value as decent entertainment, humane culture or art" designed for young people (cf. *IM* 14, 11). Though parents are called upon to be vigilant in discerning what is appropriate in light of moral norms, they are mentioned only once and unfortunately their role is not further elaborated. Catholic schools are called to contribute to this education (cf. *IM* 16).

The decree discusses the various groups of people who must be guided by the moral norms concerning the media. Two general groups are the laity and the clergy. While the primary responsibility for teaching the moral principles lies with the clergy, the presumption is that lay people will be engaged in the various activities involving the media. All members of the Church—priests, religious and laity—are called to adapt the media to the goals of the Church's mission.

Significantly, *IM* recognizes the value of technical expertise as a dimension of the apostolate of the laity who are involved in the media, presumably by profession or livelihood. They are called to bear witness to Christ "first of all by carrying out their individual duties or office expertly and with an apostolic spirit," and when the occasion presents itself, "by being of direct help in the pastoral activity of the Church" (*IM* 13).

Chapter two, on the pastoral activity of the Church, essentially calls for three things: education and formation, the establishment and support of organizations, and the establishment of ecclesial institutions. Two significant developments here are the call for a world day of communication to be celebrated every year, and for the formation of the Pontifical Council for Social Communication (cf. *IM* 18, 19).

IM 23 calls for a pastoral instruction for the implementation of its principles and norms. This resulted in *Communio et Progressio,* the *Pastoral Instruction on the Means of Social Communication,* which the Pontifical Council for Social Communication issued on January 29, 1971.

This pastoral instruction is an important elaboration and clarification of the fundamental points of *IM,* incorporating the fully mature thought and themes of the Council. This document takes a very positive attitude toward the media of social communication. Its first part presents a theological basis for a Christian view of communication. Then it goes on to discuss how communication has vitally contributed to human progress.

Communio et Progressio situates *IM's* teaching on the moral principles that must guide the use of the media in the context of a better developed anthropology. This Christian view of the human person includes the understanding that the great struggle between good and evil which marks human history is found also in the way the media are used. Human communication presents a great challenge, as does the good use of the media. An evaluation of media from the perspective of Christian faith requires assessing their contribution to the genuine unity, or communion, of humanity. The text is clear that such communion must be based on an accurate understanding of the human person, concern for human dignity, freedom and responsibility, and the necessity of moral norms for the common good.

The pastoral instruction also provides a well developed theological understanding of the means of social communication. They indicate the human capacity and call to be good stewards of the earth. They fall within the vast range of human work by which people become co-creators with God by applying their minds to discover the Creator's order of wisdom and by using created goods to serve humanity. In this way, the text emphasizes the dignity of working with the media.

In many respects the instruction shows the influence of *Gaudium et Spes,* referring to *GS* 36 which sets forth the Council's understanding of the autonomy of temporal or earthly affairs. It means that "created things and societies themselves enjoy their own laws and values which must be gradually deciphered, put to use, and regulated by men." People must respect the "stability, truth, goodness, proper laws and order" of creation and when they do, they are "being led by the hand of God," whether or not they realize it.

Since the Christian vision of history sees Christ at its center, the instruction defines communication from the perspective of its fullest realization in Christ, who is described as the "perfect communicator." This leads to a truly Christocentric definition of communication as "the giving of self in love." Such an approach helps create a point of contact between the Church and the modern world concerning the vital role of the media. What is at stake is nothing less than the human person's ability to "find himself...through a sincere gift of himself" (*GS* 24). The moral principles which direct the proper use of the media can be seen as the truth which sets persons free to use the media in a way which makes authentic communion possible.

For the 20th anniversary of *Communio et Progressio,* the Pontifical Council for Social Communication issued a second pastoral instruction entitled *Aetatis Novae.* This document discusses technological changes that have taken place in social communication, and emphasizes the need for pastoral planning in their regard.

TOPICAL OUTLINE

1. Introduction (1–2)

2. Church teaching concerning social communication

    A. The Church, evangelization and the media (3)

    B. The media and the norms of morality

        1. Circumstances and nature of the medium (4)

        2. Information and news reporting (5)

        3. Art and morality (6)

        4. Portrayal of moral evil (7)

    C. Responsibilities regarding the media

        1. Forming public opinion (8)

        2. Responsibilities of those who use the media (9–10)

        3. Responsibilities of media professionals (11)

        4. Public authority and the media (12)

3. Pastoral Activity of the Church

    A. Pastors and the laity (13)

    B. Catholic activities regarding the press, film, radio and TV (14)

    C. Formation and training (15–16)

    D. Financial support (17)

    E. Various means of promoting the media

        1. World day of communication (18)

        2. Pontifical council for communication (19)

DECREE ON THE MEDIA OF SOCIAL COMMUNICATION

Inter Mirifica

INTRODUCTION

1. Among the wonderful technological discoveries which men of talent, especially in the present era, have made with God's help, the Church welcomes and promotes with special interest those which have a most direct relation to men's minds and which have uncovered new avenues of communicating most readily news, views and teachings of every sort. The most important of these inventions are those media which, such as the press, movies, radio, television and the like, can, of their very nature, reach and influence not only individuals, but the very masses and the whole of human society, and thus can rightly be called the media of social communication.

2. The Church recognizes that these media, if properly utilized, can be of great service to mankind, since they greatly contribute to men's entertainment and instruction as well as to the spread and support of the kingdom of God. The Church recognizes, too, that men can employ these media contrary to the plan of the Creator and to their own loss. Indeed, the Church experiences maternal grief at the harm all too often done to society by their evil use.

Hence, this sacred synod, attentive to the watchful concern manifested by the supreme Pontiffs and bishops in a matter of such great importance, judges it to be its duty to treat of the principal questions linked with the media of social communication. It trusts, moreover, that the teaching and regulations it thus sets forth will serve to promote not only the eternal welfare of Christian, but also the progress of all mankind.

CHAPTER I

ON THE TEACHING OF THE CHURCH

3. The Catholic Church, since it was founded by Christ our Lord to bear salvation to all men and thus is obliged to preach the Gospel, considers it one of its duties to announce the Good News of salvation also with the help of the media of social communication and to instruct men in their proper use.

It is, therefore, an inherent right of the Church to have at its disposal and to employ any of these media insofar as they are necessary or useful for the instruction of Christians and all its efforts for the welfare of souls. It is the duty of pastors to instruct and guide the faithful so that they, with the help of these same media, may further the salvation and perfection of themselves and of the entire human family.

In addition, the laity especially must strive to instill a human and Christian spirit into these media, so that they may fully measure up to the great expectations of mankind and to God's design.

4. For the proper use of these media it is most necessary that all who employ them be acquainted with the norms of morality and conscientiously put them into practice in this area. They must look, then, to the nature of what is communicated, given the special character of each of these media. At the same time they must take into consideration the entire situation or circumstances, namely, the persons, place, time and other conditions under which communication takes place and which can affect or totally change its propriety. Among these circumstances to be considered is the precise manner in which a given medium achieves its effect. For its influence can be so great that men, especially if they are unprepared, can scarcely become aware of it, govern its impact, or, if necessary, reject it.

5. It is, however, especially necessary that all parties concerned should adopt for themselves a proper moral outlook on the use of these

media, especially with respect to certain questions that have been vigorously aired in our day.

The first question has to do with "information," as it is called, or the search for and reporting of the news. Now clearly this has become most useful and very often necessary for the progress of contemporary society and for achieving closer links among men. The prompt publication of affairs and events provides every individual with a fuller, continuing acquaintance with them, and thus all can contribute more effectively to the common good and more readily promote and advance the welfare of the entire civil society. Therefore, in society men have a right to information, in accord with the circumstances in each case, about matters concerning individuals or the community. The proper exercise of this right demands, however, that the news itself that is communicated should always be true and complete, within the bounds of justice and charity. In addition, the manner in which the news is communicated should be proper and decent. This means that in both the search for news and in reporting it, there must be full respect for the laws of morality and for the legitimate rights and dignity of the individual. For not all knowledge is helpful, but "it is charity that edifies" (1 Cor 8:1).

6. The second question deals with the relationship between the rights, as they are called, of art and the norms of morality. Since the mounting controversies in this area frequently take their rise from false teachings about ethics and aesthetics, the Council proclaims that all must hold to the absolute primacy of the objective moral order, that is, this order by itself surpasses and fittingly coordinates all other spheres of human affairs—the arts not excepted—even though they be endowed with notable dignity. For man, who is endowed by God with the gift of reason and summoned to pursue a lofty destiny, is alone affected by the moral order in his entire being. And likewise, if man resolutely and faithfully upholds this order, he will be brought to the attainment of complete perfection and happiness.

7. Finally, the narration, description or portrayal of moral evil, even through the media of social communication, can indeed serve to bring about a deeper knowledge and study of humanity and, with the aid of appropriately heightened dramatic effects, can reveal and glorify the grand dimensions of truth and goodness. Nevertheless, such presentations ought always to be subject to moral restraint, lest they work to the harm rather than the benefit of souls, particularly when there is question

of treating matters which deserve reverent handling or which, given the baneful effect of original sin in men, could quite readily arouse base desires in them.

8. Since public opinion exercises the greatest power and authority today in every sphere of life, both private and public, every member of society must fulfill the demands of justice and charity in this area. As a result, all must strive, through these media as well, to form and spread sound public opinion.

9. All who, of their own free choice, make use of these media of communication as readers, viewers or listeners have special obligations. For a proper choice demands that they fully favor those presentations that are outstanding for their moral goodness, their knowledge and their artistic or technical merit. They ought, however, to avoid those that may be a cause or occasion of spiritual harm to themselves, or that can lead others into danger through base example, or that hinder desirable presentations and promote those that are evil. To patronize such presentations, in most instances, would merely reward those who use these media only for profit.

In order that those who make use of these media may fulfill the moral code, they ought not to neglect to inform themselves in time about judgments passed by authorities competent in these matters. They ought also to follow such judgments according to the norms of an upright conscience. So that they may more easily resist improper inducements and rather encourage those that are desirable, let them take care to guide and instruct their consciences with suitable aids.

10. Those who make use of the media of communication, especially the young, should take steps to accustom themselves to moderation and self-control in their regard. They should, moreover, endeavor to deepen their understanding of what they see, hear or read. They should discuss these matters with their teachers and experts, and learn to pass sound judgments on them. Parents should remember that they have a most serious duty to guard carefully lest shows, publications and other things of this sort, which may be morally harmful, enter their homes or affect their children under other circumstances.

11. The principal moral responsibility for the proper use of the media of social communication falls on newsmen, writers, actors, designers, producers, displayers, distributors, operators and sellers, as well as critics and all others who play any part in the production and trans-

mission of mass presentations. It is quite evident what gravely important responsibilities they have in the present day when they are in a position to lead the human race to good or to evil by informing or arousing mankind.

Thus, they must adjust their economic, political or artistic and technical aspects so as never to oppose the common good. For the purpose of better achieving this goal, they are to be commended when they join professional associations, which—even under a code, if necessary, of sound moral practice—oblige their members to show respect for morality in the duties and tasks of their craft.

They ought always to be mindful, however, that a great many of their readers and audiences are young people, who need a press and entertainment that offer them decent amusement and cultural uplift. In addition, they should see to it that communications or presentations concerning religious matters are entrusted to worthy and experienced hands and are carried out with fitting reverence.

12. The public authority, in these matters, is bound by special responsibilities in view of the common good, to which these media are ordered. The same authority has, in virtue of its office, the duty of protecting and safeguarding true and just freedom of information, a freedom that is totally necessary for the welfare of contemporary society, especially when it is a question of freedom of the press. It ought also to encourage spiritual values, culture and the fine arts and guarantee the rights of those who wish to use the media. Moreover, public authority has the duty of helping those projects which, though they are certainly most beneficial for young people, cannot otherwise be undertaken.

Lastly, the same public authority, which legitimately concerns itself with the health of the citizenry, is obliged, through the promulgation and careful enforcement of laws, to exercise a fitting and careful watch lest grave damage befall public morals and the welfare of society through the base use of these media. Such vigilance in no wise restricts the freedom of individuals or groups, especially where there is a lack of adequate precaution on the part of those who are professionally engaged in using these media.

Special care should be taken to safeguard young people from printed matter and performances which may be harmful at their age.

CHAPTER II

ON THE PASTORAL
ACTIVITY OF THE CHURCH

13. All the children of the Church should join without delay and with the greatest effort in a common work to make effective use of the media of social communication in various apostolic endeavors, as circumstances and conditions demand. They should anticipate harmful developments, especially in regions where more urgent efforts to advance morality and religion are needed.

Pastors should hasten, therefore, to fulfill their duty in this respect, one which is intimately linked with their ordinary preaching responsibility. The laity, too, who have something to do with the use of these media, should endeavor to bear witness to Christ, first of all by carrying out their individual duties or office expertly and with an apostolic spirit, and, further, by being of direct help in the pastoral activity of the Church—to the best of their ability—through their technical, economic, cultural and artistic talents.

14. First, a good press should be fostered. To instill a fully Christian spirit into readers, a truly Catholic press should be set up and encouraged. Such a press—whether immediately fostered and directed by ecclesiastical authorities or by Catholic laymen—should be edited with the clear purpose of forming, supporting and advancing public opinion in accord with natural law and Catholic teaching and precepts. It should disseminate and properly explain news concerning the life of the Church. Moreover, the faithful ought to be advised of the necessity both to spread and read the Catholic press to formulate Christian judgments for themselves on all events.

The production and showing of films that have value as decent entertainment, humane culture or art, especially when they are designed for young people, ought to be encouraged and assured by every effective means. This can be done particularly by supporting and joining in projects and enterprises for the production and distribution of decent films, by encouraging worthwhile films through critical approval and awards, by patronizing or jointly sponsoring theaters operated by Catholic and responsible managers.

Similarly, effective support should be given to good radio and television programs, above all those that are suitable for families. Catholic programs should be promoted, in which listeners and viewers can be brought to share in the life of the Church and learn religious truths. An effort should also be made, where it may be necessary, to set up Catholic stations. In such instances, however, care must be taken that their programs are outstanding for their standards of excellence and achievement.

In addition, there should be an effort to see that the noble and ancient art of the drama, which now is diffused everywhere by the media of social communication, serves the cultural and moral betterment of audiences.

15. To provide for the needs just set forth, priests, religious and laymen who are equipped with the proper skills for adapting these media to the objectives of the apostolate should be appointed promptly.

Importantly, laymen ought to be afforded technical, doctrinal and moral training. For this purpose, the number of school faculties and institutes should be increased, where newsmen, writers for screen, radio and television and all other interested parties can obtain a sound training that is imbued with the Christian spirit, especially with respect to the social teaching of the Church.

Finally, care must be taken to prepare literary, film, radio, television and other critics, who will be equipped with the best skills in their own crafts and trained and encouraged to render judgments which always put moral issues in their proper light.

16. Since the proper use of the media of social communication, which are available to audiences of different cultural backgrounds and ages, calls for instruction proper to their needs, programs which are suitable for the purpose—especially where they are designed for young people—should be encouraged, increased in numbers and organized according to Christian moral principles. This should be done in Catholic schools at every level, in seminaries and in lay apostolate groups. To speed this along catechetical manuals should present and explain Catholic teaching and regulations on this matter.

17. It is quite unbecoming for the Church's children idly to permit

the message of salvation to be thwarted or impeded by the technical delays or expenses, however vast, which are encountered by the very nature of these media. Therefore, this sacred synod advises them of the obligation they have to maintain and assist Catholic newspapers, periodicals and film projects, radio and television programs and stations, whose principal objective is to spread and defend the truth and foster Christian influence in human society. At the same time, the synod earnestly invites those organizations and individuals who possess financial and technical ability to support these media freely and generously with their resources and their skills, inasmuch as they contribute to genuine culture and the apostolate.

18. Moreover, that the varied apostolates of the Church with respect to the media of social communication may be strengthened effectively, each year in every diocese of the world, by the determination of the bishops, there should be celebrated a day on which the faithful are instructed in their responsibilities in this regard. They should be invited to pray and contribute funds for this cause. Such funds are to be expended exclusively on the promotion, maintenance and development of institutes and undertakings of the Church in this area, according to the needs of the whole Catholic world.

19. In fulfilling his supreme pastoral charge with respect to the media of social communication, the Sovereign Pontiff has at hand a special office of the Holy See.[1]

20. It will be the task of the bishops, however, to watch over such works and undertakings in their own dioceses, to promote them and, as far as the public apostolate is concerned, to guide them, not excluding those that are under the direction of exempt religious.

21. Since an effective apostolate on a national scale calls for unity of planning and resources, this sacred synod decrees and orders that national offices for affairs of the press, films, radio and television be established everywhere and given every aid. It will be the special task of these offices to see to it that the consciences of the faithful are properly

---

1. Moreover, the Fathers of the Council, freely acceding to the wish of the "Secretariat for the Supervision of Publications and Entertainment," reverently request that the Sovereign Pontiff extend the duties and competence of this office to include all media of social communication, including the press, and that experts from various countries be named to it, including laymen.

instructed with respect to these media. Likewise, they should foster and guide whatever is done by Catholics in these areas.

In each country the direction of such offices should be entrusted to a special committee of bishops, or to a single bishop. Moreover, laymen who are experts in Catholic teaching and in these arts or techniques should have a role in these offices.

22. Since the effectiveness of these media reaches beyond national boundaries and has an impact on individual members of the whole human family, national offices should cooperate among themselves on an international plane. The offices spoken of in Number 21 should assiduously work together with their own international Catholic associations. These Catholic international associations are legitimately approved by the Holy See alone and depend on it.

APPENDICES

23. So that the general principles and norms of this sacred synod with respect to the media of social communication may be put into effect, by the express will of the Council, the office of the Holy See mentioned in Number 19 should undertake, with the assistance of experts from various countries, to issue a pastoral instruction.

24. As for the rest, this sacred synod is confident that its issuance of these instructions and norms will be gladly accepted and religiously kept by all the Church's children. By using these helps they will experience no harm and, like salt and light, they will give savor to the earth and brighten the world. Moreover, the synod invites all men of good will, especially those who have charge of these media, to strive to turn them solely to the good of society, whose fate depends more and more on their proper use. Thus, as was the case with ancient works of art, the name of the Lord may be glorified by these new discoveries in accordance with those words of the Apostle: "Jesus Christ, yesterday and today, and the same forever" (Heb 13:8).

DOGMATIC CONSTITUTION ON THE CHURCH

Lumen Gentium

Promulgated by
His Holiness Pope Paul VI
On November 21, 1964

INTRODUCTION

The central place of the *Dogmatic Constitution on the Church (LG)* among the sixteen documents of Vatican II is the result of the Council making the Church its unifying subject. Two great figures of the Council, Cardinals Suenens and Montini (who would become Pope Paul VI), were instrumental in giving Vatican II this ecclesiological focus. The Council would answer the question: "Church, what do you say of yourself?"

Such a focus on the Church can surprise, consternate, even alienate. Isn't this exactly the problem with Catholicism, its preoccupation with itself rather than with God? What about the concern for ecumenism? Surely, if any issue divides Christians, isn't it the role of the Church, the nature and limits of apostolic authority and the primacy of the Bishop of Rome?

Significantly, the first sentence of *LG* makes a statement about Jesus Christ, not the Church: "Jesus Christ is the light of nations." The Church can understand itself only through the light of Christ. Twenty years after the close of the Council, the Extraordinary Synod of Bishops would put it this way: "The Church makes herself more credible if she speaks less of herself and ever more preaches Christ crucified (cf. 1 Cor 2:2) and witnesses with her own life.... The whole importance of the Church derives from her connection with Christ."

Speaking of the Church must be motivated by giving God glory and making known his will concerning the Church. St. Paul provides an example. Though he stated that he only wanted to talk of Christ crucified (cf. 1 Cor 2:2), Paul wrote much about himself in his letters. His vocation was rooted in the mystery of Christ, so Paul spoke of it in proclaiming the Gospel. Similarly, the Church can and must speak of itself, but must first proclaim Christ.

"The Church is in Christ like a sacrament or as a sign and instrument both of a very closely knit union with God and of the unity of the whole human race" (*LG* 1). The Church understands itself to be the place where the abiding presence of God in Jesus Christ can be discerned and experienced. The Church is everything it is because of its relation to Christ, and through him, its relation to the Blessed Trinity.

Vatican II used the fundamental theme of communion to reflect on the mystery of the Church. "The ecclesiology of communion is a central and fundamental concept in the conciliar documents" (Extraordinary Synod). The Church understands itself through relationships, and the foundational relationship is with the Trinity who, through the missions of the Son and Spirit, established the Church (cf. *LG* 2–4). The Council moved away from seeing the Church mainly in juridical terms and used rich biblical images to express the Church's self-understanding. This leads to a less static and more dynamic view of the Church, now seen through the lens of salvation history. The Father, Son and Holy Spirit are considered from the perspective of God's self-revelation in salvation history. The Father conceived the entire loving plan to communicate divine life to the human race, and the first great act of this communication, creation. The Son was sent to fulfill this plan so that through his sacrificial death, sin and its effect of rupturing communion between God and humanity might be overcome. The Holy Spirit completes the work of God through all the gifts by which people are sanctified and the Church is established.

The Church did not originate through human plans, nor can it be understood as the accidental result of merely historical events. The Father planned it, Christ established it, and the Holy Spirit manifested and brought it to life. The essential being and mission of the Church are received from God. While remaining faithful to this divine gift, the Church develops dynamically through the centuries, always seeking to better fulfill this mission. This dynamic development entails a continuing effort at adaptation and renewal. Such pastoral concerns would be taken up in the documents that depend on the various chapters of *LG* as follows:

LG chapter two (on the People of God):
   Orientalium Ecclesiarum (Eastern Churches)
   Ad Gentes (Missions)

Unitatis Redintegratio (Ecumenism)
Nostra Aetate (Non-Christian Religions)

LG chapter three (on the hierarchical structure of the Church):
Christus Dominus (Bishops)
Presbyterorum Ordinis (Priests)
Optatam Totius (Seminarians)

LG chapter four (on the laity):
Apostolicam Actuositatem (Laity)
Gaudium et Spes (Church in the World)
Inter Mirifica (Media)

LG chapter six (on religious):
Perfectae Caritatis (Renewal and Adaptation of Religious Life)

LG stresses the fundamental importance of another kind of pastoral concern. In this second sense, pastoral means spiritual. *LG* gives great attention to a pastoral-spiritual implication of the Church knowing itself as the sacrament of salvation and unity *because of its relation to Christ.* To be faithful to itself and to become ever more perfectly what it is called to be, it must remain firmly united to Christ and deepen its bonds with him in faith, hope and charity. This is why chapter five on the universal call to holiness in the Church is so important, as is the theme of the Church following the path of renewal and penance. This is precisely the vision Paul VI sketched in *Ecclesiam Suam.*

The Church's concern to deepen its bond with Christ through holiness is motivated by a desire to respond as generously as possible to its own vocation. The Church is called to reflect the light which is Christ, so that as many as possible can experience communion in God's love. *LG* understands the connection between mission and holiness in terms of the relation between action and being: action follows upon being *(operatio sequitur esse).* The necessary starting point for the Church's mission is her being in Christ.

An important aspect of this which the Council chose to underscore is the Church as a sign or sacrament of salvation. The Church is a sign of the presence of God. Understanding the Church as a sacrament situates the Church in the flow of time between its full manifestation on Pentecost and the culmination of all God's work in the kingdom of heaven. The "age of the Church" spans that period between the ascension of

Christ and the outpouring of the Holy Spirit, and Christ's glorious return. This period must be called the "fullness of time" because God has filled it with all the gifts he has planned to give until the "end of time" when Christ will return (cf. *LG* 48).

The Church is the sacrament or instrument through which the missions of Christ and the Holy Spirit are continued until the end of time. By pursuing this vocation, always united with Christ, the Church plays a vital role in the salvation and sanctification of humanity and in glorifying God.

LG often focuses on giving glory to God, and it recognizes that this is accomplished through the transformation of people's lives brought about by God's love. "The glory of God is the human person fully alive" (St. Irenaeus), and Christ is the true life of the person. While "embracing in its bosom sinners" (*LG* 8), through the holiness of its members the Church is a sign of the power of God's transforming love.

The Church knows no other way to glorify God than to grow in that holiness which is most perfectly realized in Mary, Mother of the Lord. The Church desires to draw the attention of its sons and daughters to the saints in heaven, who reached holiness only by the grace of God (cf. *LG* chapter 7). Mary and the saints do not detract from God's glory, but give evidence of it. In their union with Christ, they play a role in extending God's glory through their intercession and the effect their examples have on those still on earth. Thus, the Council's teaching about the role of the saints in the life of the Church is directed to the increase of charity among the Church's members (cf. *LG* 51) for the greater glory of God (cf. *LG* 69).

The Christ-centered self-understanding of the Church as the sacrament of unity and salvation is especially developed in chapters two through four. Chapter two establishes the unifying theme that the Church is the messianic People of God. It is not just the People of God, but the people made one by the mission of the Christ, the Anointed One, the Messiah. Not only are they united *by* him, they are united *in* him by sharing in his anointing. They are thus constituted a priestly, prophetic and kingly people. By this anointing the messianic People of God is commissioned to continue the mission of the Messiah, participating in the three messianic offices of Jesus Christ.

Chapter three presents the role of apostolic authority as a divine gift whose purpose is to serve the Church by communicating saving truth and grace, and by shepherding God's people. They serve by making Christ present and active as head of the Church. Chapter four then develops the role of the laity in the Church, showing how they exercise the messianic offices in the realm of secular affairs. Chapter five speaks of the universal call to holiness. The role of religious in the Church, who seek holiness through the practice of the evangelical counsels, is developed in chapter six.

This holiness is best exemplified in the saints. Chapter seven discusses the role of the communion of saints, once again emphasizing the theme of *communio*. The document concludes with a chapter on the role of the Blessed Virgin Mary in the Church. The Council's decision to incorporate its treatment of Mary in the document on the Church places Mary in an ecclesial context. This clarifies her role both in relation to Christ and to the Church, and brings Marian theology into a more unified context.

This structure shows how the Council departed from a catechetical structure based on the Creed. The unifying order of *LG* is not taken from the profession of faith in the Church as one, holy, catholic and apostolic, even though these four notes of the Church can be found in *LG*. Unity is developed in chapter one, holiness in chapter five, catholicity in chapter two, and apostolicity in chapter three.

The teaching of *LG* shows why it is a dogmatic constitution. Though as a whole Vatican II must be considered a pastoral council, *LG* contains many "firsts" of a doctrinal nature. It is the first time a council has expressly developed the role of the lay faithful in the Church. It is the first instance of a conciliar text calling the Church a sacrament, and treating the eschatological nature of the Church in a systematic way. *LG* also innovated by teaching that the fullness of the sacrament of orders is conferred by episcopal consecration. An important new emphasis surfaced in the theme of the collegiality of the body of bishops. This was a necessary complement to Vatican I's teaching on the papal primacy. *LG* also called for the restoration of the permanent diaconate.

Notwithstanding its dogmatic character, the general pastoral orientation of the Council is evident in *LG,* especially the concern to overcome the split between faith and life (cf. *GS* 43). This means developing what might be called an "ecclesial consciousness" that pervades all of one's life, making the Church a reality daily lived and experienced. This is accomplished in several ways. For example, *LG* 11 outlines the ecclesial dimension of the sacraments. The sacraments are more than a private, personal encounter with the Lord. They are that, but the Church is active and present in the sacraments as well, and the sacramental grace that each confers is an ecclesial reality. Noteworthy here is the emphasis that the sacrament of Penance brings reconciliation with the Church which is wounded by sin, and the exhortation to those who receive Anointing of the Sick to exercise the graces they receive for the good of the ecclesial community. Importantly, the family is called the domestic church which evangelizes and nurtures vocations (cf. *LG* 11).

Ecclesial consciousness is also a central element of chapter four on the laity. They receive the messianic anointing of the Holy Spirit in Baptism and Confirmation. This gives their existence, life and activities an ecclesial dimension such that they make the "Church present and operative in those places and circumstances where only through them can it become the salt of the earth. Thus every layman, in virtue of the very gifts bestowed upon him, is at the same time a witness and a living instrument of the mission of the Church itself, 'according to the measure of Christ's bestowal' (Eph 4:7)" (*LG* 33). It is expected that the lay faithful be and experience the Church in all that they do. For even as by sanctifying grace they participate in the life of God, they also participate in the life and mission of the Church in and through their secular activities.

Also indicating the pastoral orientation is the link between the description of the Church in article eight and the description of full incorporation in article fourteen. The teaching on the mystery of the Church in chapter one ends with an affirmation that the Church of Christ subsists in the Catholic Church which has the Successor of Peter as its visible head on earth (cf. *LG* 8). The Church is not an abstraction, but a concrete reality, yet it cannot be reduced to that which is visible. The Church is an interpersonal, spiritual communion of persons united in grace, faith, hope and charity, yet it is a visible and hierarchically structured society in which the visible and invisible, human and divine, interpersonal and institutional "form one complex reality" (*LG* 8).

An order exists among these elements. That which is visible, human and institutional is at the service of that which is invisible, divine and eschatological (cf. *SC* 2). This is the mystery of the Church's sacramental reality. That which is time-bound bears the eternal; the human is united with the divine; the institutional and structural serve the interpersonal. Nothing short of a fully catechized faith is required to see all of this in the Church.

When *LG* describes full incorporation into the Church, it coordinates objective, visible and institutional elements with the divine element of grace and interpersonal communion. The document states:

> They are fully incorporated in the society of the Church who, possessing the Spirit of Christ, accept her entire system and all the means of salvation given to her, and are united with her as part of her visible bodily structure and through her with Christ, who rules her through the Supreme Pontiff and the bishops. The bonds which bind men to the Church in a visible way are profession of faith, the sacraments, and ecclesiastical government and communion (*LG* 14).

Significantly, the objective, institutional criteria are complemented by the invisible, grace-filled, divine dimension of the Church. This is done in three ways. *LG* states that the first criterion for full incorporation into the Church is that one must possess the Spirit of Christ. Second, *LG* draws out the implications of this by comparing a member of the Church who lacks grace and charity to a lifeless or paralyzed limb of a body. Although physically attached to the body, such a limb cannot function. The text then confronts Catholics with the principle of accountability according to knowledge. From the one to whom more is given, more will be demanded (cf. Lk 12:48). Catholics have a serious responsibility to respond in thought, word and deed to the grace of God which is offered in the Church.

The third way is discerned in the very structure of *LG* 14. It concerns the presentation of the teaching that "the Church...is necessary for salvation." The text states that anyone who, "knowing that the Catholic Church was made necessary by Christ, would refuse to enter it or to remain in it, could not be saved" (*LG* 14). The Council clearly means here those who are outside the Church through their own fault. It is not suggesting that non-Catholics cannot be saved, for it is presumed they have good will. The description of faith in *DV* 5 can be helpful for illuminating this teaching. Through faith a person freely entrusts himself to God, gives God the full obedience of intellect and will, and assents to what God has revealed. The acceptance and surrender are grounded in recognizing God's prerogatives. The profession of faith becomes the concrete expression of fidelity to God himself and of one's personal communion with him.

The formulation of *LG* links this kind of personal faith in Christ with knowing that the Church is necessary for salvation. It is possible for people to be in error about this through no fault of their own. It is possible for people to know who Jesus is, and to know a great deal about his life and teaching, and yet not arrive at knowing that Christ established the necessity of the Church. The implications of this are drawn out in *LG* 15, where a further distinction is made. It is possible that people could know that the Church was made necessary by Christ, and yet not know the full truth about the nature of that Church, and in particular the role of the Successor of Peter. Although such persons are not fully incorporated into the Church, they are linked with it in various ways. *LG* states: "The Church recognizes that in many ways she is linked with those who, being baptized, are honored with the name of Christian, though they do not profess the faith in its entirety or do not preserve unity of communion with the Successor of Peter" (*LG* 15).

In this light, one of the challenges that *LG* sets before Catholics is to see that their faith regarding the Church is grounded in entrusting oneself through faith to God himself. Adherence to the Church is the concrete expression of an unconditional "yes" to Christ in faith. This communion with Christ is the basis for communion with the other members of the Church. The Council made *communio,* or the ecclesiology of communion, a central focus of its teaching. This communion is a gift of God, and highlights the Church as a mystery. This fundamental theme found in *LG* can illuminate the other council documents as well.

TOPICAL OUTLINE

1. The Mystery of the Church

   A. Introduction: the Church as a sacrament (1)

   B. The Church in God's plan of salvation
      1. Work of Christ (3)
      2. The Holy Spirit (4)

   C. The Church and the kingdom of God (5)

   D. Various images of the Church (6)

   E. The Church as the body of Christ (7)

   F. The mystery of the Church, visible and invisible (8)

2. The People of God

   A. The messianic People of God (9)

   B. Common priesthood of the faithful (10)

   C. Sacramental life (11)

   D. Prophetic mission and charismatic graces (12)

   E. Catholicity (13)

   F. Membership in the Church
      1. The Catholic faithful (14)
      2. Other Christians (15)
      3. Those who have not yet received the Gospel (16)

G. The need for evangelization (17)

3. The hierarchical structure of the Church

    A. The primacy of the Roman Pontiff (18)

    B. The apostolic college united with Peter (19)

    C. Bishops as successors to the apostles (20)

    D. Nature of the episcopal office (21)

    E. The role of the episcopal college (22)

    F. The relation of bishops to the whole Church (23)

    G. Mission of the bishop (24)

    H. Teaching office and infallibility (25)

    I. Sacramental office (26)

    J. Pastoral office (27)

    K. Role of priests (28)

    L. Role of deacons (29)

4. The laity

    A. Importance of the laity (30)

    B. Vocation of the laity in temporal affairs (31)

    C. Diversity of roles in the Church (32)

    D. Apostolic vocation of the laity (33)

    E. Spiritual sharing in Christ's priesthood (34)

    F. Sharing in the prophetic office of Christ (35)

    G. Sharing in the kingly office of Christ (36)

    H. Relation of laity and pastors; witness of life (37–38)

5. The universal call to holiness in the Church

    A. The Church is indefectibly holy (39)

    B. All the faithful are called to holiness (40)

C. Holiness as lived by various groups in the Church (41)

D. Love as the basis of holiness (42)

6. Religious

A. The evangelical counsels as a state of life (43)

B. Consecrated life and its relation to the Church (44)

C. Relation to the hierarchy (45)

D. Witness of religious (46–47)

7. Eschatological nature of the pilgrim Church and its union with the Church in heaven

A. The eschatological goal of the Church (48)

B. The communion of saints (49)

C. Veneration of the saints (50–51)

8. The Blessed Virgin Mary, Mother of God, in the mystery of Christ and the Church

A. Introduction: reverence for the Blessed Virgin (52–54)

B. The role of the Blessed Mother in the economy of salvation

1. Testimony of Scripture (55)

2. Mary's role in the Incarnation (56)

3. Mary's union with Jesus in the work of salvation

a. During Jesus' infancy and childhood (57)

b. During Jesus' public life (58)

4. Pentecost and the Assumption (59)

C. The Blessed Virgin and the Church

1. The unique mediation of Christ (60)

2. Mary is our mother in the order of grace (61)

3. Mary's maternal intercession (62)

4. Mary in the mystery of the Church (63)

5. The Church as virgin and mother (64)

6. Mary as a model of virtues (65)

D. Devotion to the Blessed Virgin

    1. Veneration of Mary (66)

    2. Balanced devotion (67)

E. Mary as a sign of hope

    1. Mary gives hope to and consoles the People of God on earth (68)

    2. Mary intercedes for the Church (69)

DOGMATIC CONSTITUTION ON THE CHURCH

Lumen Gentium

1. Christ is the Light of nations. Because this is so, this sacred synod gathered together in the Holy Spirit eagerly desires, by proclaiming the Gospel to every creature (cf. Mk 16:15), to bring the light of Christ to all men, a light brightly visible on the countenance of the Church. Since the Church is in Christ like a sacrament or as a sign and instrument both of a very closely knit union with God and of the unity of the whole human race, it desires now to unfold more fully to the faithful of the Church and to the whole world its own inner nature and universal mission. This it intends to do following faithfully the teaching of previous councils. The present-day conditions of the world add greater urgency to this work of the Church so that all men, joined more closely today by various social, technical and cultural ties, might also attain fuller unity in Christ.

CHAPTER I

THE MYSTERY OF THE CHURCH

2. The eternal Father, by a free and hidden plan of his own wisdom and goodness, created the whole world. His plan was to raise men to a participation of the divine life. Fallen in Adam, God the Father did not leave men to themselves, but ceaselessly offered helps to salvation, in view of Christ the Redeemer, "who is the image of the invisible God, the firstborn of every creature" (Col 1:15). All the elect, before time began, the Father "foreknew and predestined to become conformed to the image of his Son, that he should be the firstborn among many brethren" (Rm 8:29). He planned to assemble in the holy Church all those who would believe in Christ. Already from the beginning of the world the foreshadowing of the Church took place. It was prepared in a remarkable way throughout the history of the people of Israel and by means of the Old Covenant.[1] In the present era of time the Church was constituted, and by the outpouring of the Spirit, was made manifest. At the end of time it will gloriously achieve completion, when, as is read in the Fathers, all the just, from Adam and "from Abel, the just one, to the last of the elect,"[2] will be gathered together with the Father in the universal Church.

3. The Son, therefore, came, sent by the Father. It was in him, before the foundation of the world, that the Father chose us and predestined us to become adopted sons, for in him it pleased the Father to reestablish all things (cf. Eph 1:4–5, 10). To carry out the will of the Father, Christ inaugurated the kingdom of heaven on earth and revealed to us the mys-

---

1. Cf. St. Cyprian, *Epist.* 64, 4: *PL* 3, 1017, *CSEL,* Hartel, III B, 720; St. Hilary, *In Mt.* 23, 6: *PL* 9, 1047; St. Augustine, *passim;* St. Cyril of Alexandria, *Glaph in Gen.* 2, 10: *PG* 69, 110 A.

2. Cf. St. Gregory the Great, *Hom in Evang.* 19, 1: *PL* 76, 1154 B; St. Augustine, *Serm. 341,* 9, 11: *PL* 39, 1499 f.; St. John Damascene, *Adv. Iconocl.* 11: *PG* 96, 1357.

tery of that kingdom. By his obedience he brought about redemption. The Church, or in other words, the kingdom of Christ now present in mystery, grows visibly through the power of God in the world. This inauguration and this growth are both symbolized by the blood and water which flowed from the open side of a crucified Jesus (cf. Jn 19:34), and are foretold in the words of the Lord referring to his death on the cross: "And I, if I be lifted up from the earth, will draw all things to myself" (Jn 12:32). As often as the sacrifice of the cross in which Christ our Passover was sacrificed (1 Cor 5:7) is celebrated on the altar, the work of our redemption is carried on, and in the sacrament of the Eucharistic bread, the unity of all believers who form one body in Christ (cf. 1 Cor 10:17) is both expressed and brought about. All men are called to this union with Christ, who is the light of the world, from whom we go forth, through whom we live, and toward whom our whole life strains.

4. When the work which the Father gave the Son to do on earth (cf. Jn 17:4) was accomplished, the Holy Spirit was sent on the day of Pentecost in order that he might continually sanctify the Church, and thus, all those who believe would have access through Christ in one Spirit to the Father (cf. Eph 2:18). He is the Spirit of Life, a fountain of water springing up to life eternal (cf. Jn 4:14; 7:38–39). To men, dead in sin, the Father gives life through him, until in Christ he brings to life their mortal bodies (cf. Rm 8:10–11). The Spirit dwells in the Church and in the hearts of the faithful, as in a temple (cf. 1 Cor 3:16; 6:19). In them he prays on their behalf and bears witness to the fact that they are adopted sons (cf. Gal 4:6; Rm 8:15–16, 26). The Church, which the Spirit guides in way of all truth (cf. Jn 16:13) and which he unifies in communion and in works of ministry, he both equips and directs with hierarchical and charismatic gifts and adorns with his fruits (cf. Eph 4:11–12; 1 Cor 12:4; Gal 5:22). By the power of the Gospel he makes the Church keep the freshness of youth. Uninterruptedly he renews it and leads it to perfect union with its Spouse.[3] The Spirit and the Bride both say to Jesus the Lord, "Come!" (cf. Rv 22:17).

Thus, the Church has been seen as "a people made one with the unity of the Father, the Son and the Holy Spirit."[4]

---

3. Cf. St. Irenaeus, *Against Heretics* III 24, 1: *PG* 7, 966 B, Harvey 2, 131, ed. Sagnard, *Sources Chr.,* 398.

4. St. Cyprian, *De Orat Dom.* 23: *PL* 4, 553, Hartel, III A, 285; St. Augustine, *Serm. 71,* 20, 33: *PL* 38, 463 f.; St. John Damascene, *Adv. Iconocl.* 12: *PG* 96, 1358 D.

5. The mystery of the holy Church is manifest in its very foundation. The Lord Jesus set it on its course by preaching the Good News, that is, the coming of the kingdom of God, which for centuries had been promised in the Scriptures: "The time is fulfilled, and the kingdom of God is at hand" (Mk 1:15; cf. Mt 4:17). In the word, in the works, and in the presence of Christ, this kingdom was clearly open to the view of men. The Word of the Lord is compared to a seed which is sown in a field (Mk 4:14); those who hear the Word with faith and become part of the little flock of Christ (Lk 12:32) have received the kingdom itself. Then, by its own power the seed sprouts and grows until harvest time (cf. Mk 4:26–29). The miracles of Jesus also confirm that the kingdom has already arrived on earth: "If I cast out devils by the finger of God, then the kingdom of God has come upon you" (Lk 11:20; cf. Mt 12:28). Before all things, however, the kingdom is clearly visible in the very Person of Christ, the Son of God and the Son of Man, who came "to serve and to give his life as a ransom for many" (Mk 10:45).

When Jesus, who had suffered the death of the cross for mankind, had risen, he appeared as the one constituted as Lord, Christ and eternal priest (cf. Acts 2:36; Heb 5:6; 7:17–21), and he poured out on his disciples the Spirit promised by the Father (cf. Acts 2:33). From this source the Church, equipped with the gifts of its Founder and faithfully guarding his precepts of charity, humility and self-sacrifice, receives the mission to proclaim and to spread among all peoples the kingdom of Christ and of God and to be on earth the initial budding forth of that kingdom. While it slowly grows, the Church strains toward the completed kingdom, and with all its strength, hopes and desires to be united in glory with its king.

6. In the Old Testament the revelation of the kingdom is often conveyed by means of metaphors. In the same way the inner nature of the Church is now made known to us in different images taken either from tending sheep or cultivating the land, from building or even from family life and betrothals; the images receive preparatory shaping in the books of the prophets.

The Church is a sheepfold whose one and indispensable door is Christ (Jn 10:1–10). It is a flock of which God himself foretold he would be the shepherd (cf. Is 40:11; Ex 34:11 f.), and whose sheep, although ruled by human shepherds, are nevertheless continuously led and nourished by Christ himself, the good shepherd and the prince of the shepherds (cf. Jn 10:11; 1 Pt 5:4), who gave his life for the sheep (cf. Jn 10:11–15).

The Church is a piece of land to be cultivated, the village of God (1 Cor 3:9). On that land the ancient olive tree grows whose holy roots were the prophets and in which the reconciliation of Jews and Gentiles has been brought about and will be brought about (Rm 11:13–26). That land, like a choice vineyard, has been planted by the heavenly husbandman (Mt 21:33–43; cf. Is 5:1 f.). The true vine is Christ who gives life and the power to bear abundant fruit to the branches, that is, to us, who through the Church remain in Christ without whom we can do nothing (Jn 15:1–5).

Often the Church has also been called the building of God (1 Cor 3:9). The Lord himself compared himself to the stone which the builders rejected, but which was made into the cornerstone (Mt 21:42; cf. Acts 4:11; 1 Pt 2:7; Ps 117:22). On this foundation the Church is built by the apostles (cf. 1 Cor 3:11), and from it the Church receives durability and consolidation. This edifice has many names to describe it: the house of God (1 Tm 3:15) in which dwells his family, the household of God in the Spirit (Eph 2:19–22), the dwelling place of God among men (Rv 21:3), and especially the holy temple. This temple, symbolized in places of worship built out of stone, is praised by the Holy Fathers, and not without reason is compared in the liturgy to the Holy City, the New Jerusalem.[5] As living stones we here on earth are built into it (1 Pt 2:5). John contemplates this holy city coming down from heaven at the renewal of the world as a bride made ready and adorned for her husband (Rv 21:1 f.).

The Church, further, "that Jerusalem which is above" is also called "our mother" (Gal 4:26; cf. Rv 12:17). It is described as the spotless spouse of the spotless Lamb (Rv 19:7; 21:2; 9:22, 17), whom Christ "loved and for whom he delivered himself up that he might sanctify her" (Eph 5:26), whom he unites to himself by an unbreakable covenant, and whom he unceasingly "nourishes and cherishes" (Eph 5:29), and whom,

---

5. Cf. Origen, *In Matth.* 16, 21: *PG* 13, 1443 C; Tertullian *Adv. Marc.* 3, 7: *PL* 2, 357 C, *CSEL* 47, 3, p. 386. For liturgical documents cf. *Sacramentarium Gregorianum: PL* 78, 160 B; L. C. Mohlberg, *Liber Sacramentorum Romanae Ecclesiae* (Rome: 1950), 111, XC: "*Deus, qui ex omni coaptacione sanctorum aeternum tibi condis habitaculum....*" The hymn *Urbs Ierusalem beata* in the monastic breviary and *Coelestis urbs Ierusalem* in the Roman breviary.

once purified, he willed to be cleansed and joined to himself, subject to him in love and fidelity (cf. Eph 5:24), and whom, finally, he filled with heavenly gifts for all eternity, in order that we may know the love of God and of Christ for us, a love which surpasses all knowledge (cf. Eph 3:19). The Church, while on earth it journeys in a foreign land away from the Lord (cf. 2 Cor 5:6), is like an exile. It seeks and experiences those things which are above, where Christ is seated at the right hand of God, where the life of the Church is hidden with Christ in God until it appears in glory with its spouse (cf. Col 3:1–4).

7. In the human nature united to himself the Son of God, by overcoming death through his own death and resurrection, redeemed man and remolded him into a new creation (cf. Gal 6:15; 2 Cor 5:17). By communicating his Spirit, Christ made his brothers, called together from all nations, mystically the components of his own body.

In that body the life of Christ is poured into the believers who, through the sacraments, are united in a hidden and real way to Christ who suffered and was glorified.[6] Through Baptism we are formed in the likeness of Christ: "For in one Spirit we were all baptized into one body" (1 Cor 12:13). In this sacred rite a oneness with Christ's death and resurrection is both symbolized and brought about: "For we were buried with him by means of Baptism into death," and if "we have been united with him in the likeness of his death, we shall be so in the likeness of his resurrection also" (Rm 6:4–5). Really partaking of the body of the Lord in the breaking of the Eucharistic bread, we are taken up into communion with him and with one another. "Because the bread is one, we though many, are one body, all of us who partake of the one bread" (1 Cor 10:17). In this way all of us are made members of his Body (cf. 1 Cor 12:27), "but severally members one of another" (Rm 12:5).

As all the members of the human body, though they are many, form one body, so also are the faithful in Christ (cf. 1 Cor 12:12). Also, in the building up of Christ's body, various members and functions have their part to play. There is only one Spirit who, according to his own richness and the needs of the ministries, gives his different gifts for the welfare of the Church (cf. 1 Cor 12:1–11). What has a special place among these gifts is the grace of the apostles, to whose authority the Spirit himself subjected even those who were endowed with charisms (cf. 1 Cor 14).

---

6. Cf. St. Thomas, *Summa Theol.,* III, q. 62, a. 5, *ad* 1.

Giving the body unity through himself and through his power and inner joining of the members, this same Spirit produces and urges love among the believers. From all this it follows that if one member endures anything, all the members coendure it, and if one member is honored, all the members together rejoice (cf. 1 Cor 12:26).

The head of this body is Christ. He is the image of the invisible God and in him all things came into being. He is before all creatures and in him all things hold together. He is the head of the body which is the Church. He is the beginning, the firstborn from the dead, that in all things he might have the first place (cf. Col 1:15–18). By the greatness of his power he rules the things in heaven and the things on earth, and with his all-surpassing perfection and way of acting he fills the whole body with the riches of his glory (cf. Eph 1:18–23).[7]

All the members ought to be molded in the likeness of him, until Christ be formed in them (cf. Gal 4:19). For this reason we, who have been made to conform with him, who have died with him and risen with him, are taken up into the mysteries of his life, until we will reign together with him (cf. Phil 3:21; 2 Tm 2:11; Eph 2:6; Col 2:12, etc.). On earth, still as pilgrims in a strange land, tracing in trial and in oppression the paths he trod, we are made one with his sufferings like the body is one with the head, suffering with him, that with him we may be glorified (cf. Rm 8:17).

From him, "the whole body, supplied and built up by joints and ligaments, attains a growth that is of God" (Col 2:19). He continually distributes in his body, that is, in the Church, gifts of ministries in which, by his own power, we serve each other unto salvation so that, carrying out the truth in love, we might through all things grow unto him who is our head (cf. Eph 4:11–16).

In order that we might be unceasingly renewed in him (cf. Eph 4:23), he has shared with us his Spirit who, existing as one and the same being in the head and in the members, gives life to, unifies and moves through the whole body. This he does in such a way that his work could be compared by the holy Fathers with the function which the principle of life, that is, the soul, fulfills in the human body.[8]

---

7. Cf. Pius XII, Encyclical Letter *Mystici Corporis* (June 29, 1943): *AAS* 35 (1943), 208.

8. Cf. Leo XIII, Encyclical Epistle *Divinum Illud* (May 9, 1897): *AAS* 29 (1896–97), 650; Pius XII, Encyclical Letter *Mystici Corporis* (June 29, 1943): *AAS* 35 (1943), 219–

Christ loves the Church as his bride, having become the model of a man loving his wife as his body (cf. Eph 5:25–28); the Church, indeed, is subject to its head (Eph 5:23–24). "Because in him dwells all the fullness of the Godhead bodily" (Col 2:9), he fills the Church, which is his body and his fullness, with his divine gifts (cf. Eph 1:22–23) so that it may expand and reach all the fullness of God (cf. Eph 3:19).

8. Christ, the one Mediator, established and continually sustains here on earth his holy Church, the community of faith, hope and charity, as an entity with visible delineation[9] through which he communicates truth and grace to all. But the society structured with hierarchical organs and the Mystical Body of Christ are not to be considered as two realities, nor are the visible assembly and the spiritual community, nor the earthly Church and the Church enriched with heavenly things; rather they form one complex reality which coalesces from a divine and a human element.[10] For this reason, by no weak analogy, it is compared to the mystery of the incarnate Word. As the assumed nature inseparably united to him serves the divine Word as a living organ of salvation, so, in a similar way, does the visible social structure of the Church serve the Spirit of Christ, who vivifies it, in the building up of the body (cf. Eph 4:16).[11]

This is the one Church of Christ which in the Creed is professed as one, holy, catholic and apostolic,[12] which our Savior, after his resurrection, commissioned Peter to shepherd (Jn 21:17), and him and the other apostles to extend and direct with authority (cf. Mt 28:18 f.), which he erected for all ages as "the pillar and mainstay of the truth" (1 Tm 3:15). This Church constituted and organized in the world as a society, subsists

---

220, Denz. 2288 (3808); St. Augustine, *Serm. 268*, 2: *PL* 38, 1232, and in other works; St. John Chrysostom, *In Eph.*, Hom. 9, 3: *PG* 62, 72; Didymus of Alex., *Trin.* 2, 1: *PG* 39, 449; St. Thomas, *In Col.* 1, 18 lect. 5, ed. Marietti, II, n. 46: *"Sicut constituitur unum corpus ex unitate animae, ita Ecclesia ex unitate Spiritus...."* ("As the body is made one by the unity of the soul, so is the Church by the unity of the Spirit....")

9. Leo XIII, Encyclical Letter *Sapientiae Christianae* (Jan. 10, 1890): *AAS* 22 (1889–90), 392; Leo XIII, Encyclical Epistle *Satis Cognitum* (Jan. 29, 1896): *AAS* 28 (1895–96), 710 and 724 ff.; Pius XII, Encyclical Letter *Mystici Corporis* (June 29, 1943): *AAS* 35 (1943), 199–200.

10. Cf. Pius XII, Encyclical Letter *Mystici Corporis* (June 29, 1943): *AAS* 35 (1943), 221ff.; Pius XII, Encyclical Letter *Humani Generis* (Aug. 12, 1950): *AAS* 42 (1950), 571.

11. Leo XIII, Encyclical Epistle *Satis Cognitum* (Jan. 29, 1896): *AAS* 28 (1895–96), 713.

12. Cf. Apostles' Creed, Denz. 6–9 (10–13); Nicene-Const. Creed, Denz. 86 (150), coll. *Tridentine Profession of Faith*, Denz. 994, 999 (1862 and 1868).

in the Catholic Church, which is governed by the Successor of Peter and by the bishops in communion with him,[13] although many elements of sanctification and of truth are found outside of its visible structure. These elements, as gifts belonging to the Church of Christ, are forces impelling toward catholic unity.

Just as Christ carried out the work of redemption in poverty and persecution, so the Church is called to follow the same route that it might communicate the fruits of salvation to men. Christ Jesus, "though he was by nature God...emptied himself, taking the nature of a slave" (Phil 2:6), and "being rich, became poor" (2 Cor 8:9) for our sakes. Thus, the Church, although it needs human resources to carry out its mission, is not set up to seek earthly glory, but to proclaim, even by its own example, humility and self-sacrifice. Christ was sent by the Father "to bring good news to the poor, to heal the contrite of heart" (Lk 4:18), "to seek and to save what was lost" (Lk 19:10). Similarly, the Church encompasses with love all who are afflicted with human suffering and in the poor and afflicted sees the image of its poor and suffering Founder. It does all it can to relieve their need and in them it strives to serve Christ. While Christ, holy, innocent and undefiled (Heb 7:26) knew nothing of sin (2 Cor 5:21), but came to expiate only the sins of the people (cf. Heb 2:17), the Church, embracing in its bosom sinners, at the same time holy and always in need of being purified, always follows the way of penance and renewal. The Church, "like a stranger in a foreign land, presses forward amid the persecutions of the world and the consolations of God,"[14] announcing the cross and death of the Lord until he comes (cf. 1 Cor 11:26). By the power of the risen Lord it is given strength that it might, in patience and in love, overcome its sorrows and its challenges, both within itself and from without, and that it might reveal to the world, faithfully though darkly, the mystery of its Lord until, in the end, it will be manifested in full light.

---

13. It is called: *Sancta (catholica apostolica) Romana Ecclesia* in the *Tridentine Profession of Faith, loc. cit.* and First Vatican Ecumenical Council, Session III, Constitution *Dei Filius,* Denz. 1782 (3001).

14. St. Augustine, *City of God* XVIII, 51, 2: *PL* 41, 614.

CHAPTER II

ON THE PEOPLE OF GOD

9. At all times and in every race God has given welcome to whoever fears him and does what is right (cf. Acts 10:35). God, however, does not make men holy and save them merely as individuals, without bond or link between one another. Rather has it pleased him to bring men together as one people, a people which acknowledges him in truth and serves him in holiness. He therefore chose the race of Israel as a people unto himself. With it he set up a covenant. Step by step he taught and prepared this people, making known in its history both himself and the decree of his will and making it holy unto himself. All these things, however, were done by way of preparation and as a figure of that new and perfect covenant, which was to be ratified in Christ, and of that fuller revelation which was to be given through the Word of God himself made flesh. "Behold the days shall come says the Lord, and I will make a new covenant with the House of Israel, and with the house of Judah.... I will give my law in their bowels, and I will write it in their heart, and I will be their God, and they shall be my people.... For all of them shall know me, from the least of them even to the greatest, says the Lord" (Jer 31:31–34). Christ instituted this New Covenant, the New Testament, that is to say, in his Blood (cf. 1 Cor 11:25), calling together a people made up of Jew and Gentile, making them one, not according to the flesh but in the Spirit. This was to be the new People of God. For those who believe in Christ, who are reborn not from a perishable but from an imperishable seed through the word of the living God (cf. 1 Pt 1:23), not from the flesh but from water and the Holy Spirit (cf. Jn 3:5–6), are finally established as "a chosen race, a royal priesthood, a holy nation, a purchased people...who in times past were not a people, but are now the People of God" (1 Pt 2:9–10).

That messianic people has Christ for its head, "who was delivered up for our sins, and rose again for our justification" (Rm 4:25), and now, having won a name which is above all names, reigns in glory in heaven. The state of this people is that of the dignity and freedom of the sons of God, in whose hearts the Holy Spirit dwells as in his temple. Its law is the new commandment to love as Christ loved us (cf. Jn 13:34). Its end is the kingdom of God, which has been begun by God himself on earth, and which is to be further extended until it is brought to perfection by him at the end of time, when Christ our life (cf. Col 3:4) shall appear, and "creation itself will be delivered from its slavery to corruption into the freedom of the glory of the sons of God" (Rm 8:21). So it is that that messianic people, although it does not actually include all men, and at times may look like a small flock, is nonetheless a lasting and sure seed of unity, hope and salvation for the whole human race. Established by Christ as a communion of life, charity and truth, it is also used by him as an instrument for the redemption of all, and is sent forth into the whole world as the light of the world and the salt of the earth (cf. Mt 5:13–16).

Israel according to the flesh, which wandered as an exile in the desert, was already called the Church of God (2 Esdr 13:1; cf. Dt 23:1 ff.; Nm 20.4). So likewise the new Israel, which while living in this present age goes in search of a future and abiding city (cf. Heb 13:14), is called the Church of Christ (cf. Mt 16:18). For he has bought it for himself with his blood (cf. Acts 20:28), has filled it with his Spirit and provided it with those means which befit it as a visible and social union. God gathered together as one all those who in faith look upon Jesus as the author of salvation and the source of unity and peace, and established them as the Church that for each and all it may be the visible sacrament of this saving unity.[1] While it transcends all limits of time and confines of race, the Church is destined to extend to all regions of the earth and so enters into the history of mankind. Moving forward through trial and tribulation, the Church is strengthened by the power of God's grace, which was promised to her by the Lord, so that in the weakness of the flesh she may not waver from perfect fidelity, but remain a bride worthy of her Lord, and moved by the Holy Spirit may never cease to renew herself, until through the cross she arrives at the light which knows no setting.

---

1. Cf. St. Cyprian, *Epist.* 69, 6: *PL* 3, 1142 B, Hartel 3 B, 754: *"inseparabile unitatis sacramentum..."* ("the inseparable sacrament of unity.")

10. Christ the Lord, high priest taken from among men (cf. Heb 5:1–5), made the new people "a kingdom and priests to God the Father" (cf. Rv 1:6; cf. 5:9–10). The baptized, by regeneration and the anointing of the Holy Spirit, are consecrated as a spiritual house and a holy priesthood, in order that through all those works which are those of the Christian man they may offer spiritual sacrifices and proclaim the power of him who has called them out of darkness into his marvelous light (cf. 1 Pt 2:4–10). Therefore all the disciples of Christ, persevering in prayer and praising God (cf. Acts 2:42, 47), should present themselves as a living sacrifice, holy and pleasing to God (cf. Rm 12:1). Everywhere on earth they must bear witness to Christ and give an answer to those who seek an account of that hope of eternal life which is in them (cf. 1 Pt 3:15).

Though they differ from one another in essence and not only in degree, the common priesthood of the faithful and the ministerial or hierarchical priesthood are nonetheless interrelated: each of them in its own special way is a participation in the one priesthood of Christ.[2] The ministerial priest, by the sacred power he enjoys, teaches and rules the priestly people; acting in the person of Christ, he makes present the Eucharistic Sacrifice, and offers it to God in the name of all the people. But the faithful, in virtue of their royal priesthood, join in the offering of the Eucharist.[3] They likewise exercise that priesthood in receiving the sacraments, in prayer and thanksgiving, in the witness of a holy life, and by self-denial and active charity.

11. It is through the sacraments and the exercise of the virtues that the sacred nature and organic structure of the priestly community is brought into operation. Incorporated in the Church through Baptism, the faithful are destined by the baptismal character for the worship of the Christian religion; reborn as sons of God they must confess before men the faith which they have received from God through the Church.[4] They are more perfectly bound to the Church by the sacrament of Confirmation, and the Holy Spirit endows them with special strength so that they are more strictly obliged to spread and defend the faith, both by

---

2. Cf. Pius XII, *Allocution Magnificate Dominum* (Nov. 2, 1954): *AAS* 46 (1954), 669; Encyclical Letter *Mediator Dei* (Nov. 20, 1947): *AAS* 39 (1947), 555.

3. Cf. Pius XI, Encyclical Letter *Miserentissimus Redemptor* (May 8, 1928): *AAS* 20 (1928), 171; Pius XII *Allocution Vous Nous Avez* (Sept. 22, 1956): *AAS* 48 (1956), 714.

4. Cf. St. Thomas, *Summa Theol.*, III, q. 63, a. 2.

word and by deed, as true witnesses of Christ.[5] Taking part in the Eucharistic Sacrifice, which is the fount and apex of the whole Christian life, they offer the divine victim to God, and offer themselves along with It.[6] Thus both by reason of the offering and through Holy Communion all take part in this liturgical service, not indeed, all in the same way but each in that way which is proper to himself. Strengthened in Holy Communion by the Body of Christ, they then manifest in a concrete way that unity of the People of God which is suitably signified and wondrously brought about by this most august sacrament.

Those who approach the sacrament of Penance obtain pardon from the mercy of God for the offense committed against him and are at the same time reconciled with the Church, which they have wounded by their sins, and which by charity, example and prayer seeks their conversion. By the sacred Anointing of the Sick and the prayer of her priests the whole Church commends the sick to the suffering and glorified Lord, asking that he may lighten their suffering and save them (cf. Jas 5:14–16); she exhorts them, moreover, to contribute to the welfare of the whole People of God by associating themselves freely with the passion and death of Christ (cf. Rm 8:17; Col 1:24; 2 Tm 2:11–12; 1 Pt 4:13). Those of the faithful who are consecrated by Holy Orders are appointed to feed the Church in Christ's name with the word and the grace of God. Finally, Christian spouses, in virtue of the sacrament of Matrimony, whereby they signify and partake of the mystery of that unity and fruitful love which exists between Christ and his Church (cf. Eph 5:32), help each other to attain to holiness in their married life and in the rearing and education of their children. By reason of their state and rank in life they have their own special gift among the People of God (cf. 1 Cor 7:7).[7] From the wedlock of Christians there comes the family, in which new citizens of human society are born, who by the grace of the Holy Spirit received in Baptism are made children of God, thus perpetuating the

---

5. Cf. St. Cyril of Jerusalem, *Catech.* 17, *De Spiritu Sancto,* II, 35–37: *PG* 33, 1009–1012; Nic. Cabasilas, *De Vita in Christo,* bk. III, *De Utilitate Chrismatis: PG* 150, 569–580; St. Thomas, *Summa Theol.,* III, q. 65, a. 3 and q. 72, a. 1 and 5.

6. Cf. Pius XII, Encyclical Letter *Mediator Dei* (Nov. 20, 1947): *AAS* 39 (1947), especially 552 ff.

7. 1 Cor 7:7: "Each one has his own gift from God, one this kind and another that." Cf. St. Augustine, *De Dono Persev.* 14, 37: *PL* 45, 1015 ff. "Not only continence is a gift of God; so also is the chastity of the married."

People of God through the centuries. The family is, so to speak, the domestic church. In it parents should, by their word and example, be the first preachers of the faith to their children; they should encourage them in the vocation which is proper to each of them, fostering with special care the vocation to a sacred state.

Fortified by so many and such powerful means of salvation, all the faithful, whatever their condition or state, are called by the Lord, each in his own way, to that perfect holiness whereby the Father himself is perfect.

12. The holy People of God shares also in Christ's prophetic office; it spreads abroad a living witness to him, especially by means of a life of faith and charity and by offering to God a sacrifice of praise, the tribute of lips which give praise to his name (cf. Heb 13:15). The entire body of the faithful, anointed as they are by the Holy One (cf. Jn 2:20, 27), cannot err in matters of belief. They manifest this special property by means of the whole people's supernatural discernment in matters of faith when "from the bishops down to the last of the lay faithful"[8] they show universal agreement in matters of faith and morals. That discernment in matters of faith is aroused and sustained by the Spirit of truth. It is exercised under the guidance of the sacred teaching authority, in faithful and respectful obedience to which the People of God accepts that which is not just the word of men but truly the Word of God (cf. 1 Thes 2:13). Through it, the People of God adheres unwaveringly to the faith given once and for all to the saints (cf. Jude 3), penetrates it more deeply with right thinking, and applies it more fully in its life.

It is not only through the sacraments and the ministries of the Church that the Holy Spirit sanctifies and leads the People of God and enriches it with virtues, but, "allotting his gifts to everyone according as he wills" (1 Cor 12:11), he distributes special graces among the faithful of every rank. By these gifts he makes them fit and ready to undertake the various tasks and offices which contribute toward the renewal and building up of the Church, according to the words of the Apostle: "The manifestation of the Spirit is given to everyone for profit" (1 Cor 12:7). These charisms, whether they be the more outstanding or the more simple and widely diffused, are to be received with thanksgiving and consolation, for they are perfectly suited to and useful for the needs of the Church. Extraordinary gifts are not to be sought after, nor are the

---

8. Cf. St. Augustine, *De Praed. Sanct.* 14, 27: *PL* 44, 980.

fruits of apostolic labor to be presumptuously expected from their use, but judgment as to their genuinity and proper use belongs to those who are appointed leaders in the Church, to whose special competence it belongs, not indeed to extinguish the Spirit, but to test all things and hold fast to that which is good (cf. 1 Thes 5:12; 19–21).

13. All men are called to belong to the new People of God. Wherefore this people, while remaining one and only one, is to be spread throughout the whole world and must exist in all ages, so that the decree of God's will may be fulfilled. In the beginning God made human nature one and decreed that all his children, scattered as they were, would finally be gathered together as one (cf. Jn 11:52). It was for this purpose that God sent his Son, whom he appointed heir of all things (cf. Heb 1:2), that he might be teacher, king and priest of all, the head of the new and universal people of the sons of God. For this too God sent the Spirit of his Son as Lord and Life-giver. He it is who brings together the whole Church and each and every one of those who believe, and who is the wellspring of their unity in the teaching of the apostles and in fellowship, in the breaking of bread and in prayers (cf. Acts 2:42).

It follows that though there are many nations there is but one People of God, which takes its citizens from every race, making them citizens of a kingdom which is of a heavenly rather than of an earthly nature. All the faithful, scattered though they be throughout the world, are in communion with each other in the Holy Spirit, and so, "he who dwells in Rome knows that the people of India are his members."[9] Since the kingdom of Christ is not of this world (cf. Jn 18:36), the Church or People of God in establishing that kingdom takes nothing away from the temporal welfare of any people. On the contrary, it fosters and takes to itself, insofar as they are good, the ability, riches and customs in which the genius of each people expresses itself. Taking them to itself, it purifies, strengthens, elevates and ennobles them. The Church in this is mindful that she must bring together the nations for that king to whom they were given as an inheritance (cf. Ps 2:8), and to whose city they bring gifts and offerings (cf. Ps 72:10; Is 60:4–7; Rv 21:24). This characteristic of universality which adorns the People of God is a gift from the Lord himself. By reason of it, the Catholic Church strives constantly and with due

9. Cf. St. John Chrysostom, *On John,* Hom. 65, 1: *PG* 59, 361.

effect to bring all humanity and all its possessions back to its source in Christ, with him as its head and united in his Spirit.[10]

In virtue of this catholicity, each individual part contributes through its special gifts to the good of the other parts and of the whole Church. Through the common sharing of gifts and through the common effort to attain fullness in unity, the whole and each of the parts receive increase. Not only, then, is the People of God made up of different peoples, but in its inner structure also it is composed of various ranks. This diversity among its members arises either by reason of their duties, as is the case with those who exercise the sacred ministry for the good of their brethren, or by reason of their condition and state of life, as is the case with those many who enter the religious state, and tending toward holiness by a narrower path, stimulate their brethren by their example. Moreover, within the Church particular churches hold a rightful place; these churches retain their own traditions, without in any way opposing the primacy of the Chair of Peter, which presides over the whole assembly of charity[11] and protects legitimate differences, while at the same time assuring that such differences do not hinder unity but rather contribute toward it. Between all the parts of the Church there remains a bond of close communion whereby they share spiritual riches, apostolic workers and temporal resources. For the members of the People of God are called to share these goods in common, and of each of the churches the words of the Apostle hold good: "According to the gift that each has received, administer it to one another as good stewards of the manifold grace of God" (1 Pt 4:10).

All men are called to be part of this catholic unity of the People of God which in promoting universal peace presages it. And there belong to or are related to it in various ways, the Catholic faithful, all who believe in Christ, and indeed the whole of mankind, for all men are called by the grace of God to salvation.

14. This sacred Council wishes to turn its attention firstly to the Catholic faithful. Basing itself upon Sacred Scripture and Tradition, it teaches that the Church, now sojourning on earth as an exile, is neces-

---

10. Cf. St. Irenaeus, *Against Heretics* III, 16, 6; III, 22, 1–3: *PG* 7, 925 C–926 A and 955 C–958 A, Harvey 2, 87 ff. and 120–123; ed. Sagnard, ed. *Sources Chr.,* 290–292 and 372 ff.

11. Cf. St. Ignatius Martyr, *Ad Rom.,* Praef.: ed. F. X. Funk, I, 252.

sary for salvation. Christ, present to us in his body, which is the Church, is the one Mediator and the unique way of salvation. In explicit terms he himself affirmed the necessity of faith and Baptism (cf. Mk 16:16; Jn 3:5) and thereby affirmed also the necessity of the Church, for through Baptism as through a door men enter the Church. Whosoever, therefore, knowing that the Catholic Church was made necessary by Christ, would refuse to enter or to remain in it, could not be saved.

They are fully incorporated in the society of the Church who, possessing the Spirit of Christ, accept her entire system and all the means of salvation given to her, and are united with her as part of her visible bodily structure and through her with Christ, who rules her through the Supreme Pontiff and the bishops. The bonds which bind men to the Church in a visible way are profession of faith, the sacraments, and ecclesiastical government and communion. He is not saved, however, who, though part of the body of the Church, does not persevere in charity. He remains indeed in the bosom of the Church, but, as it were, only in a "bodily" manner and not "in his heart."[12] All the Church's children should remember that their exalted status is to be attributed not to their own merits but to the special grace of Christ. If they fail, moreover, to respond to that grace in thought, word and deed, not only shall they not be saved but they will be the more severely judged.[13]

Catechumens who, moved by the Holy Spirit, seek with explicit intention to be incorporated into the Church are by that very intention joined with her. With love and solicitude, mother Church already embraces them as her own.

15. The Church recognizes that in many ways she is linked with those who, being baptized, are honored with the name of Christian, though they do not profess the faith in its entirety or do not preserve unity of communion with the Successor of Peter.[14] For there are many who honor Sacred Scripture, taking it as a norm of belief and a pattern

---

12. Cf. St. Augustine, *Bapt. c. Donat.* V, 28, 39; *PL* 43, 197: *"Certe manifestum est, id quod dicitur, in Ecclesia intus et foris, in corde, non in corpore cogitandum."* ("Surely it is obvious that what is said, inside the Church and outside, is to be understood according to the heart, and not according to the body.") Cf. *ibid.,* III, 19, 26: col. 152; V, 18, 24: col. 189; *In Io. Tr.* 61, 2: *PL* 35, 1800, and often elsewhere.

13. Cf. Lk 12:48: "Of everyone to whom much has been given, much will be required." Cf. also Mt 5:19–20; 7:21–22; 25:41–46; Jas 2:14.

14. Cf. Leo XIII, Apostolic Letter *Praeclara Gratulationis* (June 20, 1894): *AAS* 26 (1893–94), 707.

of life, and who show a sincere zeal. They lovingly believe in God the Father Almighty and in Christ, the Son of God and Savior.[15] They are consecrated by baptism, in which they are united with Christ. They also recognize and accept other sacraments within their own Churches or ecclesiastical communities. Many of them rejoice in the episcopate, celebrate the Holy Eucharist and cultivate devotion toward the Virgin Mother of God.[16] They also share with us in prayer and other spiritual benefits. Likewise we can say that in some real way they are joined with us in the Holy Spirit, for to them too he gives his gifts and graces whereby he is operative among them with his sanctifying power. Some indeed he has strengthened to the extent of the shedding of their blood. In all of Christ's disciples the Spirit arouses the desire to be peacefully united, in the manner determined by Christ, as one flock under one shepherd, and he prompts them to pursue this end.[17] Mother Church never ceases to pray, hope and work that this may come about. She exhorts her children to purification and renewal so that the sign of Christ may shine more brightly over the face of the earth.

16. Finally, those who have not yet received the Gospel are related in various ways to the People of God.[18] In the first place we must recall the people to whom the testament and the promises were given and from whom Christ was born according to the flesh (cf. Rm 9:4–5). On account of their fathers this people remains most dear to God, for God does not repent of the gifts he makes nor of the calls he issues (cf. Rm 11:28–29). But the plan of salvation also includes those who acknowledge the Creator. In the first place amongst these there are the Mohamedans, who, professing to hold the faith of Abraham, along with us adore the one and merciful God, who on the last day will judge mankind. Nor is God far distant from those who in shadows and images seek the unknown God, for it is he who gives to all men life and breath and all things (cf. Acts 17:25–28), and as Savior wills that all men be saved (cf.

---

15. Cf. Leo XIII, Encyclical Epistle *Satis Cognitum* (Jan. 29, 1896): *AAS* 28 (1895–96), 738; Encyclical Epistle *Caritatis Studium* (July 25, 1898): *AAS* 31 (1898–99), 11; Pius XII, Radio Message *Nell'alba* (Dec. 24, 1941): *AAS* 34 (1942), 21.

16. Cf. Pius XI, Encyclical Letter *Rerum Orientalium* (Sept. 8, 1928): *AAS* 20 (1928), 287; Pius XII, Encyclical Letter *Orientalis Ecclesiae* (April 9, 1944): *AAS* 36 (1944), 137.

17. Cf. Instruction of the Holy Office (Dec. 20, 1949): *AAS* 42 (1950), 142.

18. Cf. St. Thomas, *Summa Theol.*, III, q. 8, a. 3, ad 1.

1 Tm 2:4). Those also can attain to salvation who through no fault of their own do not know the Gospel of Christ or his Church, yet sincerely seek God and moved by grace, strive by their deeds to do his will as it is known to them through the dictates of conscience.[19] Nor does divine Providence deny the helps necessary for salvation to those who, without blame on their part, have not yet arrived at an explicit knowledge of God and with his grace strive to live a good life. Whatever good or truth is found amongst them is looked upon by the Church as a preparation for the Gospel.[20] She knows that it is given by him who enlightens all men so that they may finally have life. But often men, deceived by the Evil One, have become vain in their reasonings and have exchanged the truth of God for a lie, serving the creature rather than the Creator (cf. Rm 1:21, 25). Or some there are who, living and dying in this world without God, are exposed to final despair. Wherefore to promote the glory of God and procure the salvation of all of these, and mindful of the command of the Lord, "Preach the Gospel to every creature" (Mk 16:16), the Church fosters the missions with care and attention.

17. As the Son was sent by the Father (cf. Jn 20:21), so he too sent the apostles, saying: "Go, therefore, make disciples of all nations, baptizing them in the name of the Father and of the Son and of the Holy Spirit, teaching them to observe all things whatsoever I have commanded you. And behold I am with you all days even to the consummation of the world" (Mt 21:18–20). The Church has received this solemn mandate of Christ to proclaim the saving truth from the apostles and must carry it out to the very ends of the earth (cf. Acts 1:8). Wherefore she makes the words of the Apostle her own: "Woe to me, if I do not preach the Gospel" (1 Cor 9:16), and continues unceasingly to send heralds of the Gospel until such time as the infant churches are fully established and can themselves continue the work of evangelizing. For the Church is compelled by the Holy Spirit to do her part that God's plan may be fully realized, whereby he has constituted Christ as the source of salvation for the whole world. By the proclamation of the Gospel she prepares her hearers to receive and profess the faith. She gives them the dispositions necessary for Baptism, snatches them from the slavery of error and of idols and incorporates them in Christ so that through charity

---

19. Cf. *Letter of the Holy Office to the Archbishop of Boston:* Denz. 3869–72.
20. Cf. Eusebius of Caesarea, *Praeparatio Evangelica* 1, 1: *PG* 21, 28 AB.

they may grow up into full maturity in Christ. Through her work, whatever good is in the minds and hearts of men, whatever good lies latent in the religious practices and cultures of diverse peoples, is not only saved from destruction but is also cleansed, raised up and perfected unto the glory of God, the confusion of the devil and the happiness of man. The obligation of spreading the faith is imposed on every disciple of Christ, according to his state.[21] Although, however, all the faithful can baptize, the priest alone can complete the building up of the body in the Eucharistic Sacrifice. Thus are fulfilled the words of God, spoken through his prophet: "From the rising of the sun until the going down thereof my name is great among the Gentiles, and in every place a clean oblation is sacrificed and offered up in my name" (Mal 1:11).[22] In this way the Church both prays and labors in order that the entire world may become the People of God, the body of the Lord and the temple of the Holy Spirit, and that in Christ, the head of all, all honor and glory may be rendered to the Creator and Father of the universe.

---

21. Cf. Benedictus XV, Apostolic Letter *Maximum Illud: AAS* 11 (1919), 440, especially p. 451ff.; Pius XI, Encyclical Letter *Rerum Ecclesiae: AAS* 18 (1926), 68–69; Pius XII, Encyclical Letter *Fidei Donum* (April 21, 1957): *AAS* 49 (1957), 236–237.

22. Cf. *Didache,* 14: ed. F. X. Funk, I, 32; St. Justin, *Dial.* 41: *PG* 6, 564; St. Irenaeus, *Against Heretics* IV, 17, 5; *PG* 7, 1023, Harvey, 2, 199 f.; Council of Trent, Session 22, ca. 1; Denz. 939 (1742).

CHAPTER III

ON THE HIERARCHICAL STRUCTURE OF THE CHURCH AND IN PARTICULAR ON THE EPISCOPATE

18. For the nurturing and constant growth of the People of God, Christ the Lord instituted in his Church a variety of ministries, which work for the good of the whole body. For those ministers, who are endowed with sacred power, serve their brethren, so that all who are of the People of God, and therefore enjoy a true Christian dignity, working toward a common goal freely and in an orderly way, may arrive at salvation.

This sacred Council, following closely in the footsteps of the First Vatican Council, with that Council teaches and declares that Jesus Christ, the eternal shepherd, established his holy Church, having sent forth the apostles as he himself had been sent by the Father (Jn 20:21), and he willed that their successors, namely the bishops, should be shepherds in his Church even to the consummation of the world. And in order that the episcopate itself might be one and undivided, he placed Blessed Peter over the other apostles, and instituted in him a permanent and visible source and foundation of unity of faith and communion.[1] And all this teaching about the institution, the perpetuity, the meaning and reason for the sacred primacy of the Roman Pontiff and of his infallible magisterium, this sacred Council again proposes to be firmly believed by all the faithful. Continuing in that same undertaking, this Council is resolved to declare and proclaim before all men the doctrine concerning bishops, the successors of the apostles, who together with the Successor of Peter, the Vicar of Christ,[2] the visible head of the whole Church, govern the house of the living God.

---

1. Cf. First Vatican Ecumenical Council, Session 4, Constitution *Pastor Aeternus,* Denz. 1821 (3050 f.).

2. Cf. Council of Florence, *Decretum pro Graecis,* Denz. 694 (1307) and First Vatican Ecumenical Council, *ibid.:* Denz. 1826 (3059).

19. The Lord Jesus, after praying to the Father, calling to himself those whom he desired, appointed twelve to be with him, and whom he would send to preach the kingdom of God (Mk 3:13–19; Mt 10:1–42), and these apostles (cf. Lk 6:13) he formed after the manner of a college or a stable group, over which he placed Peter, chosen from among them (cf. Jn 21:15–17). He sent them first to the children of Israel and then to all nations (Rm 1:16), so that as sharers in his power they might make all peoples his disciples, and sanctify and govern them (cf. Mt 28:16–20; Mk 16:15; Lk 24:45–48; Jn 20:21–23), and thus spread his Church, and by ministering to it under the guidance of the Lord, direct it all days even to the consummation of the world (cf. Mt 28:20). And in this mission they were fully confirmed on the day of Pentecost (cf. Acts 2:1–26) in accordance with the Lord's promise: "You shall receive power when the Holy Spirit comes upon you, and you shall be witnesses for me in Jerusalem, and in all Judea and in Samaria, and even to the very ends of the earth" (Acts 1:8). And the apostles, by preaching the Gospel everywhere (cf. Mk 16:20), and it being accepted by their hearers under the influence of the Holy Spirit, gather together the universal Church, which the Lord established on the apostles and built upon Blessed Peter, their chief, Christ Jesus himself being the supreme cornerstone (cf. Rv 21:14; Mt 16:18; Eph 2:20).[3]

20. That divine mission, entrusted by Christ to the apostles, will last until the end of the world (cf. Mt 28:20), since the Gospel they are to teach is for all time the source of all life for the Church. And for this reason the apostles, appointed as rulers in this society, took care to appoint successors.

For they not only had helpers in their ministry[4] but also, in order that the mission assigned to them might continue after their death, they passed on to their immediate cooperators, as it were, in the form of a testament, the duty of confirming and finishing the work begun by them-

---

3. Cf. *Liber Sacramentorum,* St. Gregory, *Praefatio in Cathedra St. Petri, in Natali St. Mathiae et St. Thomas: PL* 78, 50, 51 and 152; cf. Cod. Vat. lat. 3548, f. 18; St. Hilary, *In Ps.* 67, 10: *PL* 9, 450; *CSEL* 22, 286; St. Jerome, *Adv. Iovin.* 1, 26: *PL* 23, 247 A; St. Augustine, *In Ps.* 86, 4: *PL* 37, 1103; St. Gregory the Great, *Mor. in Job,* XXVIII, V: *PL* 76, 455–456; Primasius, *Comm. in Apoc.,* V: *PL* 68, 924 B, C; Paschasius Radbertus, *In Matth.* Bk. VIII, ch. 16: *PL* 120, 561 C; cf. Leo XIII, Epistle *Et Sane* (Dec. 17, 1888): *AAS* 21 (1888), 321.

4. Cf. Acts 6:2–6; 11:30; 13:1, 14:23; 20:17; 1 Thes 5:12–13; Phil 1:1; Col 4:11 and *passim.*

selves,[5] recommending to them that they attend to the whole flock in which the Holy Spirit placed them to shepherd the Church of God (cf. Acts 20:28). They therefore appointed such men, and gave them the order that, when they should have died, other approved men would take up their ministry.[6] Among those various ministries which, according to tradition, were exercised in the Church from the earliest times, the chief place belongs to the office of those who, appointed to the episcopate, by a succession running from the beginning[7] are passers-on of the apostolic seed.[8] Thus, as St. Irenaeus testifies, through those who were appointed bishops by the apostles, and through their successors down in our own time, the apostolic tradition is manifested[9] and preserved.[10]

Bishops, therefore, with their helpers, the priests and deacons, have taken up the service of the community,[11] presiding in place of God over the flock[12] whose shepherds they are, as teachers for doctrine, priests for sacred worship, and ministers for governing.[13] And just as the office granted individually to Peter, the first among the apostles, is permanent and is to be transmitted to his successors, so also the apostles' office of nurturing the Church is permanent, and is to be exercised without interruption by the sacred order of bishops.[14] Therefore, the sacred Council teaches that bishops by divine institution have succeeded to the place of the apostles,[15] as shepherds of the Church, and he who hears them, hears

---

5. Cf. Acts 20:25–27; 2 Tm 4:6 f. together with 1 Tm 5:22; 2 Tm 2:2; Ti 1:5; St. Clement of Rome, *Ad Cor.* 44, 3; ed. F. X. Funk, I, 156.

6. St. Clement of Rome, *Ad Cor.* 44, 2; ed. F. X. Funk, I, 154 f.

7. Cf. Tertullian, *Praescr. Haer.* 32: *PL* 2, 52 f.; St. Ignatius Martyr, *passim.*

8. Cf. Tertullian, *Praescr. Haer.* 32: *PL* 2, 53.

9. Cf. St. Irenaeus, *Against Heretics* III, 3, 1: *PG* 7, 848 A, Harvey 2, 8, ed. Sagnard, 100 f., *"manifestatam."*

10. Cf. St. Irenaeus, *Against Heretics* III, 2, 2: *PG* 7, 847, Harvey 2, 7, ed. Sagnard, 100, *"custoditur";* cf. *ibid.* IV, 26, 2; col. 1053, Harvey 2, 236 and IV, 33, 8; col. 1077; Harvey 2, 262.

11. St. Ignatius Martyr, *Philad.* Praef.; ed. F. X. Funk, I, 264.

12. St. Ignatius Martyr, *Philad.* 1, 1; *Magn.* 6, 1; ed. F. X. Funk, I, 264 and 234.

13. St. Clement of Rome, l. c., 42, 3–4; 44, 3–4; 57, 1–2; ed. F. X. Funk, I, 152, 156, 171f.; St. Ignatius Martyr, *Philad.* 2; *Smyrn.* 8; *Magn.* 3; *Trall.* 7; ed. F. X. Funk, I, 265 f., 282; 232, 246 f. etc.; St. Justin, *Apol.* 1, 65: *PG* 6, 428; St. Cyprian, *Epist., passim.*

14. Cf. Leo XIII, Encyclical Epistle *Satis Cognitum* (Jan. 29, 1896): *AAS* 28 (1895–96), 732.

15. Cf. Council of Trent, Session 23, Decree *De Sacr. Ordinis,* ca. 4; Denz. 960 (1768); First Vatican Ecumenical Council, Session 4, Dogmatic Constitution *De Ecclesia Christi,* ca. 3: Denz. 1828 (3061); Pius XII, Encyclical Letter *Mystici Corporis* (June 29, 1943): *AAS* 35 (1943), 209 and 212; *Code of Canon Law,* c. 329 § 1.

Christ, and he who rejects them, rejects Christ and him who sent Christ (cf. Lk 10:16).[16]

21. In the bishops, therefore, for whom priests are assistants, our Lord Jesus Christ, the supreme high priest, is present in the midst of those who believe. For sitting at the right hand of God the Father, he is not absent from the gathering of his high priests[17] but above all through their excellent service he is preaching the Word of God to all nations, and constantly administering the sacraments of faith to those who believe; by their paternal functioning (cf. 1 Cor 4:15) he incorporates new members in his body by a heavenly regeneration, and finally by their wisdom and prudence he directs and guides the People of the New Testament in their pilgrimage toward eternal happiness. These pastors, chosen to shepherd the Lord's flock of the elect, are servants of Christ and stewards of the mysteries of God (cf. 1 Cor 4:1), to whom has been assigned the bearing of witness to the Gospel of the grace of God (cf. Rm 15:16; Acts 20:24), and the ministration of the Spirit and of justice in glory (cf. 2 Cor 3:8–9).

For the discharging of such great duties, the apostles were enriched by Christ with a special outpouring of the Holy Spirit coming upon them (cf. Acts 1:8; 2:4; Jn 20:22–23), and they passed on this spiritual gift to their helpers by the imposition of hands (cf. 1 Tm 4:14; 2 Tm 1:6–7), and it has been transmitted down to us in episcopal consecration.[18] And the sacred Council teaches that by episcopal consecration the fullness of the sacrament of Orders is conferred, that fullness of power, namely, which both in the Church's liturgical practice and in the language of the Fathers of the Church is called the high priesthood, the supreme power of the sacred ministry.[19] But episcopal consecration, together with the office of sanctifying, also confers the office of teaching and of governing, which, however, of its very nature, can be exercised only in hierar-

---

16. Cf. Leo XIII, Epistle *Et Sane* (Dec. 17, 1888): *AAS* 21 (1888), 321 f.

17. St. Leo the Great, *Serm.* 5, 3: *PL* 54, 154.

18. Council of Trent, Session 23, c. 3, cites the words of 2 Tm 1: 6–7, to show that Orders is a true sacrament: Denz. 959 (1766).

19. In the *Apostolic Tradition,* 3, ed. Botte, *Sources Chr.,* 27–30, "to the bishop is attributed 'primacy of priesthood.'" Cf. *Sacramentarium Leonianum,* ed. L. C. Mohlberg, *Sacramentarium Veronens,* (Rome: 1955), 119: "To the ministry of high priesthood.... Fulfill in your priests the fullness of the mystery." *Idem, Liber Sacramentorum Romanae Ecclesiae* (Rome: 1960), 121–122: "Grant them, Lord, the bishop's throne to rule your Church and all people." Cf. *PL* 78, 224.

chical communion with the head and the members of the college. For from the tradition, which is expressed especially in liturgical rites and in the practice of both the Church of the East and of the West, it is clear that, by means of the imposition of hands and the words of consecration, the grace of the Holy Spirit is so conferred[20] and the sacred character so impressed[21] that bishops in an eminent and visible way sustain the roles of Christ himself as teacher, shepherd and high priest, and that they act in his person.[22] Therefore it pertains to the bishops to admit newly elected members into the episcopal body by means of the sacrament of Orders.

22. Just as in the Gospel, the Lord so disposing, St. Peter and the other apostles constitute one apostolic college, so in a similar way the Roman Pontiff, the Successor of Peter, and the bishops, the successors of the apostles, are joined together. Indeed, the very ancient practice whereby bishops duly established in all parts of the world were in communion with one another and with the Bishop of Rome in a bond of unity, charity and peace,[23] and also the councils assembled together[24] in which more profound issues were settled in common,[25] the opinion of the many having been prudently considered,[26] both of these factors are already an indication of the collegiate character and aspect of the episcopal order, and the ecumenical councils held in the course of centuries are also manifest proof of that same character. And it is intimated also in the practice, introduced in ancient times, of summoning several bishops

---

20. *Apostolic Tradition,* 2, ed. Botte, 27.

21. Council of Trent, Session 23, c. 4, teaches that the sacrament of Orders imprints an indelible character: Denz. 960 (1767). Cf. John XXIII, *Allocution Jubilate Deo* (May 8, 1960): *AAS* 52 (1960), 466; Paul VI, *Homily* in St. Peter's Basilica (Oct. 20, 1963): *AAS* 55 (1963), 1014.

22. St. Cyprian, *Epist.* 63, 14: *PL* 4, 386; Hartel, III B, 713: "The priest truly acts in the place of Christ"; St. John Chrysostom, *In 2 Tm,* Hom. 2, 4: *PG* 62, 612: "The priest is a 'symbolon' of Christ." St. Ambrose, *In Ps.* 38, 25–26: *PL* 14, 105, 1–52: *CSEL* 64, 203–204; Ambrosiaster, *In 1 Tm* 5, 19: *PL* 17, 479C and *In Eph.* 4:11–12: col. 387 C; Theodore of Mopsuestia, *Hom. Catech.* XV, 21 and 24: ed. Tonneau, 497 and 503; Hesychius of Jerusalem, *In Lev.* L. 2, 9, 23: *PG* 93, 894 B.

23. Cf. Eusebius, *Hist. Eccl.,* V, 24, 10: GCS II, 1, 495; ed. Bardy, *Sources Chr.* II, 69; Dionysius, as given in Eusebius, *ibid.* VII 5, 2: GCS 11, 2, 638 f.; Bardy, II, 168 f.

24. For the ancient councils, cf. Eusebius, *Hist. Eccl.,* V, 23–24: *GCS* 11, 1, 488 ff.; Bardy, 11, 66 ff. and *passim.* Council of Nicea, can. 5: *Conc. Oec. Decr.* 7.

25. Tertullian, *De Ieiunio* 13: *PL* 2, 972 B; *CSEL* 20, 292, lin. 13–16.

26. St. Cyprian, *Epist.* 56, 3: Hartel, III B, 650; Bayard, 154.

to take part in the elevation of the newly elected to the ministry of the high priesthood. Hence, one is constituted a member of the episcopal body in virtue of sacramental consecration and hierarchical communion with the head and members of the body.

But the college or body of bishops has no authority unless it is understood together with the Roman Pontiff, the Successor of Peter, as its head. The Pope's power of primacy over all, both pastors and faithful, remains whole and intact. In virtue of his office, that is as Vicar of Christ and pastor of the whole Church, the Roman Pontiff has full, supreme and universal power over the Church. And he is always free to exercise this power. The order of bishops, which succeeds to the college of apostles and gives this apostolic body continued existence, is also the subject of supreme and full power over the universal Church, provided we understand this body together with its head the Roman Pontiff and never without this head.[27] This power can be exercised only with the consent of the Roman Pontiff. For our Lord placed Simon alone as the rock and the bearer of the keys of the Church (cf. Mt 16:18–19), and made him shepherd of the whole flock (cf. Jn 21:15 ff.); it is evident, however, that the power of binding and loosing, which was given to Peter (Mt 16:19), was granted also to the college of apostles, joined with their head (Mt 18:18; 28:16–20).[28] This college, insofar as it is composed of many, expresses the variety and universality of the People of God, but insofar as it is assembled under one head, it expresses the unity of the flock of Christ. In it, the bishops, faithfully recognizing the primacy and preeminence of their head, exercise their own authority for the good of their own faithful, and indeed of the whole Church, the Holy Spirit supporting its organic structure and harmony with moderation. The supreme power in the universal Church, which this college enjoys, is exercised in a solemn way in an ecumenical council. A council is never ecumenical unless it is confirmed or at least accepted as such by the Successor of Peter, and it is the prerogative of the Roman Pontiff to

---

27. Cf. Zinelli, *Relatio officialis,* on First Vatican Ecumenical Council: Mansi 52, 1109 C.

28. Cf. First Vatican Ecumenical Council, *Schema* on the Dogmatic Constitution II, *De Ecclesia Christi,* c. 4: Mansi 53, 310. Cf. Kleutgen's account of the reformed schema: Mansi 53, 321 B–322 B and Zinelli's *Declaratio:* Mansi 52, 1110 A. Cf. also St. Leo the Great, *Serm.* 4, 3: *PL* 54, 151 A.

convoke these councils, to preside over them and to confirm them.[29] This same collegiate power can be exercised together with the Pope by the bishops living in all parts of the world, provided that the head of the college calls them to collegiate action, or at least approves of or freely accepts the united action of the scattered bishops, so that it is thereby made a collegiate act.

23. This collegial union is apparent also in the mutual relations of the individual bishops with particular churches and with the universal Church. The Roman Pontiff, as the Successor of Peter, is the perpetual and visible principle and foundation of unity of both the bishops and of the faithful.[30] The individual bishops, however, are the visible principle and foundation of unity in their particular churches,[31] fashioned after the model of the universal Church, in and from which churches comes into being the one and only Catholic Church.[32] For this reason the individual bishops represent each his own church, but all of them together and with the Pope represent the entire Church in the bond of peace, love and unity.

The individual bishops, who are placed in charge of particular churches, exercise their pastoral government over the portion of the People of God committed to their care, and not over other churches nor over the universal Church. But each of them, as a member of the episcopal college and legitimate successor of the apostles, is obliged by Christ's institution and command to be solicitous for the whole Church,[33] and this solicitude, though it is not exercised by an act of jurisdiction, contributes greatly to the advantage of the universal Church. For it is the duty of all bishops to promote and to safeguard the unity of faith and the discipline common to the whole Church, to instruct the faithful to love for the whole Mystical Body of Christ, especially for its poor and sorrowing members and for those who are suffering persecution for justice's sake (cf. Mt 5:10), and finally to promote every activity

---

29. Cf. *Code of Canon Law,* c. 227.

30. Cf. First Vatican Ecumenical Council, Constitution *Pastor Aeternus:* Denz. 1821 (3050 f.).

31. Cf. St. Cyprian, *Epist.* 66, 8: Hartel III, 2, 733: "The bishop is in the Church and the Church in the bishop."

32. Cf. St. Cyprian, *Epist.* 55, 24: Hartel, 642, line. 13: "One Church throughout the whole world divided into many members." *Epist.* 36, 4: Hartel, 575, lin. 20–21.

33. Cf. Pius XII, Encyclical Letter *Fidei Donum* (April 21, 1957): *AAS* 49 (1957), 237.

that is of interest to the whole Church, especially that the faith may take increase and the light of full truth appear to all men. And this also is important, that by governing well their own church as a portion of the universal Church, they themselves are effectively contributing to the welfare of the whole Mystical Body, which is also the body of the churches.[34]

The task of proclaiming the Gospel everywhere on earth pertains to the body of pastors, to all of whom in common Christ gave his command, thereby imposing upon them a common duty, as Pope Celestine in his time recommended to the Fathers of the Council of Ephesus.[35] From this it follows that the individual bishops, insofar as their own discharge of their duty permits, are obliged to enter into a community of work among themselves and with the Successor of Peter, upon whom was imposed in a special way the great duty of spreading the Christian name.[36] With all their energy, therefore, they must supply to the missions both workers for the harvest and also spiritual and material aid, both directly and on their own account, as well as by arousing the ardent cooperation of the faithful. And finally, the bishops, in a universal fellowship of charity, should gladly extend their fraternal aid to other churches, especially to neighboring and more needy dioceses in accordance with the venerable example of antiquity.

By divine Providence it has come about that various churches, established in various places by the apostles and their successors, have in the course of time coalesced into several groups organically united, which preserving the unity of faith and the unique divine constitution of the universal Church, enjoy their own discipline, their own liturgical usage, and their own theological and spiritual heritage. Some of these churches, notably the ancient patriarchal churches, as parent-stocks of the faith, so to speak, have begotten others as daughter churches, with which they are connected down to our own time by a close bond of char-

---

34. Cf. St. Hilary of Poitiers, *In Ps.* 14, 3: *PL* 9, 206; *CSEL* 22, 86; St. Gregory the Great, *Moral.,* IV, 7, 12: *PL* 75, 643 C; Pseudo Basil, *In Is.* 15, 296: *PG* 30, 637 C.

35. St. Celestine, *Epist.* 18, 1–2, to the Council of Ephesus: *PL* 50, 505 AB, Schwartz, *Acta Conc. Oec.* I, 1, 1, 22; cf. Benedict XV, Apostolic Letter *Maximum Illud: AAS* 11 (1919), 440; Pius XI, Encyclical Letter *Rerum Ecclesiae* (Feb. 28, 1926): *AAS* 18 (1926), 69; Pius XII, Encyclical Letter *Fidei Donum* (April 21, 1957): *AAS* 49 (1957), 237.

36. Leo XIII, Encyclical Letter *Grande Munus* (Sept. 30, 1880): *AAS* 13 (1880), 145; cf. *Code of Canon Law,* c. 1327; c. 1350 par. 2.

ity in their sacramental life and in their mutual respect for their rights and duties.[37] This variety of local churches with one common aspiration is splendid evidence of the catholicity of the undivided Church. In like manner the episcopal bodies of today are in a position to render a manifold and fruitful assistance, so that this collegiate feeling may be put into practical application.

24. Bishops, as successors of the apostles, receive from the Lord, to whom was given all power in heaven and on earth, the mission to teach all nations and to preach the Gospel to every creature, so that all men may attain to salvation by faith, Baptism and the fulfillment of the commandments (cf. Mt 28:18; Mk 16:15–16; Acts 26:17 ff.). To fulfill this mission, Christ the Lord promised the Holy Spirit to the apostles, and on Pentecost day sent the Spirit from heaven, by whose power they would be witnesses to him before the nations and peoples and kings even to the ends of the earth (cf. Acts 1:8; 2:1 ff.; 9:15). And that duty, which the Lord committed to the shepherds of his people, is a true service, which in sacred literature is significantly called "diakonia" or ministry (cf. Acts 1:17, 25; 21:19; Rm 11:13; 1 Tm 1:12).

The canonical mission of bishops can come about by legitimate customs that have not been revoked by the supreme and universal authority of the Church, or by laws made or recognized by that same authority, or directly through the Successor of Peter himself, and if the latter refuses or denies apostolic communion, such bishops cannot assume any office.[38]

25. Among the principal duties of bishops the preaching of the Gospel occupies an eminent place.[39] For bishops are preachers of the faith, who lead new disciples to Christ, and they are authentic teachers, that is, teachers endowed with the authority of Christ, who preach to the people committed to them the faith they must believe and put into practice, and by the light of the Holy Spirit illustrate that faith. They bring forth from

---

37. On the rights of patriarchal Sees, cf. Council of Nicea, can. 6 on Alexandria and Antioch, and can. 7 on Jerusalem: *Conc. Oec. Decr.,* 8; Fourth Lateran Council (1215), Constit. V: *De Dignitate Patriarcharum: ibid.,* 212; Council of Ferrara-Florence: *ibid.,* 504.

38. Cf. *Code of Canon Law for the Eastern Churches,* c. 216–314: regarding patriarchs; c. 324–399: on major archbishops; c. 362–391: regarding other dignitaries, in particular, c. 238 13; 216; 240; 251; 255: regarding bishops to be named by patriarchs.

39. Cf. Council of Trent, Session 5, *Decr. de Reform.,* c. 2, n. 9; and Session 24, can. 4; *Conc. Oec. Decr.,* 645 and 739.

the treasury of revelation new things and old (cf. Mt 13:52), making it bear fruit and vigilantly warding off any errors that threaten their flock (cf. 2 Tm 4:1–4). Bishops, teaching in communion with the Roman Pontiff, are to be respected by all as witnesses to divine and Catholic truth. In matters of faith and morals, the bishops speak in the name of Christ and the faithful are to accept their teaching and adhere to it with a religious assent. This religious submission of mind and will must be shown in a special way to the authentic magisterium of the Roman Pontiff, even when he is not speaking *ex cathedra;* that is, it must be shown in such a way that his supreme magisterium is acknowledged with reverence, the judgments made by him are sincerely adhered to, according to his manifest mind and will. His mind and will in the matter may be known either from the character of the documents, from his frequent repetition of the same doctrine, or from his manner of speaking.

Although the individual bishops do not enjoy the prerogative of infallibility, they nevertheless proclaim Christ's doctrine infallibly whenever, even though dispersed through the world, but still maintaining the bond of communion among themselves and with the Successor of Peter, and authentically teaching matters of faith and morals, they are in agreement on one position as definitively to be held.[40] This is even more clearly verified when, gathered together in an ecumenical council, they are teachers and judges of faith and morals for the universal Church, whose definitions must be adhered to with the submission of faith.[41]

And this infallibility with which the divine Redeemer willed his Church to be endowed in defining doctrine of faith and morals extends as far as the deposit of revelation extends, which must be religiously guarded and faithfully expounded. And this is the infallibility which the Roman Pontiff, the head of the college of bishops, enjoys in virtue of his office, when as the supreme shepherd and teacher of all the faithful, who confirms his brethren in their faith (cf. Lk 22:32), by a definitive act he proclaims a doctrine of faith or morals.[42] And therefore his definitions,

---

40. Cf. First Vatican Ecumenical Council, Session III, Constitution *Dei Filius,* Denz. 1712 (3011). Cf. the note added to Schema I *De Ecclesia* (taken from St. Robert Bellarmine): Mansi 51, I 579; cf. also the revised Schema of Const. II *De Ecclesia Christi,* with the commentary by Kleutgen: Mansi 53, 313 AB; Pius IX, Letter *Tuas Libenter:* Denz. 1683 (2879).

41. Cf. *Code of Canon Law,* c. 1322–1323.

42. Cf. First Vatican Ecumenical Council, Constitution *Pastor Aeternus:* Denz. 1839 (3074).

of themselves, and not from the consent of the Church, are justly styled irreformable, since they are pronounced with the assistance of the Holy Spirit, promised to him in Blessed Peter, and therefore they need no approval of others, nor do they allow an appeal to any other judgment. For then the Roman Pontiff is not pronouncing judgment as a private person, but as the supreme teacher of the universal Church, in whom the charism of infallibility of the Church itself is individually present, he is expounding or defending a doctrine of Catholic faith.[43] The infallibility promised to the Church resides also in the body of bishops, when that body exercises the supreme magisterium with the Successor of Peter. To these definitions the assent of the Church can never be wanting, on account of the activity of that same Holy Spirit, by which the whole flock of Christ is preserved and progresses in unity of faith.[44]

But when either the Roman Pontiff or the body of bishops together with him defines a judgment, they pronounce it in accordance with revelation itself, which all are obliged to abide by and be in conformity with, that is, the revelation which as written or orally handed down is transmitted in its entirety through the legitimate succession of bishops and especially in care of the Roman Pontiff himself, and which under the guiding light of the Spirit of truth is religiously preserved and faithfully expounded in the Church.[45] The Roman Pontiff and the bishops, in view of their office and the importance of the matter, by fitting means diligently strive to inquire properly into that revelation and to give apt expression to its contents,[46] but a new public revelation they do not accept as pertaining to the divine deposit of faith.[47]

26. A bishop, marked with the fullness of the sacrament of Orders, is "the steward of the grace of the supreme priesthood,"[48] especially in the Eucharist, which he offers or causes to be offered[49] and by which the Church continually lives and grows. This Church of Christ is truly

---

43. Cf. the explanation by Gasser of First Vatican Ecumenical Council: Mansi 52, 1213 AC.

44. Gasser, *ibid.:* Mansi 1214 A.

45. Gasser, *ibid.:* Mansi 1215 CD, 1216–1217 A.

46. Gasser, *ibid.:* Mansi 1213.

47. First Vatican Ecumenical Council, Constitution *Pastor Aeternus:* Denz. 1836 (3070) no. 26.

48. Prayer of episcopal consecration in the Byzantine rite: *Euchologion to mega,* Rome, 1873, 139.

49. Cf. St. Ignatius Martyr, *Smyrn.* 8, 1: ed. F. X. Funk, I, 282.

present in all legitimate local congregations of the faithful which, united with their pastors, are themselves called churches in the New Testament.[50] For in their locality these are the new people called by God, in the Holy Spirit and in much fullness (cf. 1 Thes 1:5). In them the faithful are gathered together by the preaching of the Gospel of Christ, and the mystery of the Lord's Supper is celebrated, that by the food and Blood of the Lord's Body the whole brotherhood may be joined together.[51] In any community of the altar, under the sacred ministry of the bishop[52] there is exhibited a symbol of that charity and "unity of the Mystical Body, without which there can be no salvation."[53] In these communities, though frequently small and poor, or living in the Diaspora, Christ is present, and in virtue of his presence there is brought together one, holy, catholic and apostolic Church.[54] For "the partaking of the Body and Blood of Christ does nothing other than make us be transformed into that which we consume."[55]

Every legitimate celebration of the Eucharist is regulated by the bishop, to whom is committed the office of offering the worship of Christian religion to the divine majesty and of administering it in accordance with the Lord's commandments and the Church's laws, as further defined by his particular judgment for his diocese.

Bishops, thus, by praying and laboring for the people, make outpourings in many ways and in great abundance from the fullness of Christ's holiness. By the ministry of the Word they communicate God's power to those who believe unto salvation (cf. Rm 1:16), and through the sacraments, the regular and fruitful distribution of which they regulate by their authority,[56] they sanctify the faithful. They direct the conferring of Baptism, by which a sharing in the kingly priesthood of Christ is granted. They are the original ministers of Confirmation, dispensers of sacred Orders and the moderators of penitential discipline, and they earnestly exhort and instruct their people to carry out with faith and rever-

---

50. Cf. Acts 8:1; 14:22–23; 20:17, and *passim*.
51. Mozarabic prayer: *PL* 96, 759 B.
52. Cf. St. Ignatius Martyr, *Smyrn.* 8, 1: ed. F. X. Funk, I, 282.
53. St. Thomas, *Summa Theol.*, III, q. 73, a. 3.
54. Cf. St. Augustine, *C. Faustum* 12, 20: *PL* 42, 265; *Serm.* 57, 7: *PL* 38, 389, etc.
55. St. Leo the Great, *Serm.* 63, 7: *PL* 54, 357 C.
56. *Apostolic Tradition* of Hippolytus, 2–3: ed. Botte, 26–30.

ence their part in the liturgy and especially in the holy sacrifice of the Mass. And lastly, by the example of their way of life they must be an influence for good to those over whom they preside, refraining from all evil, and as far as they are able with God's help, exchanging evil for good, so that together with the flock committed to their care they may arrive at eternal life.[57]

27. Bishops, as vicars and ambassadors of Christ, govern the particular churches entrusted to them[58] by their counsel, exhortations, example and even by their authority and sacred power, which indeed they use only for the edification of their flock in truth and holiness, remembering that he who is greater should become as the lesser and he who is the chief become as the servant (cf. Lk 22:26–27). This power, which they personally exercise in Christ's name, is proper, ordinary and immediate, although its exercise is ultimately regulated by the supreme authority of the Church, and can be circumscribed by certain limits, for the advantage of the Church or of the faithful. In virtue of this power, bishops have the sacred right and the duty before the Lord to make laws for their subjects, to pass judgment on them and to moderate everything pertaining to the ordering of worship and the apostolate.

The pastoral office or the habitual and daily care of their sheep is entrusted to them completely; nor are they to be regarded as vicars of the Roman Pontiffs, for they exercise an authority that is proper to them, and are quite correctly called "prelates," heads of the people whom they govern.[59] Their power, therefore, is not destroyed by the supreme and universal power, but on the contrary, it is affirmed, strengthened and vindicated by it[60] since the Holy Spirit unfailingly preserves the form of government established by Christ the Lord in his Church.

---

57. Cf. the text of the *examen* at the beginning of the consecration of a bishop, and the prayer at the end of the Mass of the same consecration, after the *Te Deum*.

58. Benedict XIV, Brief *Romana Ecclesia* (Oct. 5, 1752), 1: *Bullarium Benedicti XIV,* t. IV, Rome, 1758, 21: "The bishop represents Christ, and acts by his authority"; Pius XII, Encyclical Letter *Mystici Corporis* (June 29, 1943): *AAS* 35 (1943), 211: "Each of them, in the name of Christ, feeds and rules the particular flock assigned to him."

59. Leo XIII, Encyclical Epistle *Satis Cognitum* (Jan. 29, 1896): *AAS* 28 (1895–96), 732; Leo XIII, Letter *Officio Sanctissimo* (Dec. 22, 1887): *AAS* 20 (1887), 264; Pius IX, Apostolic Letter to the bishops of Germany (March 12, 1875) and his Consistorial Allocution (March 15, 1875): Denz. 3112–3117, only in the new edition.

60. First Vatican Ecumenical Council, Constitution *Pastor Aeternus,* 3: Denz. 1828 (3061); cf. Zinelli, *Relatio,* Mansi 52, 1114 D.

A bishop, since he is sent by the Father to govern his family, must keep before his eyes the example of the good shepherd, who came not to be ministered unto but to minister (cf. Mt 20:28; Mk 10:45), and to lay down his life for his sheep (cf. Jn 10:11). Being taken from among men, and himself beset with weakness, he is able to have compassion on the ignorant and erring (cf. Heb 5:1–2). Let him not refuse to listen to his subjects, whom he cherishes as his true sons and exhorts to cooperate readily with him. As having one day to render an account for their souls (cf. Heb 13:17), he takes care of them by his prayer, preaching and all the works of charity, and not only of them but also of those who are not yet of the one flock, who also are commended to him in the Lord. Since, like Paul the Apostle, he is debtor to all men, let him be ready to preach the Gospel to all (cf. Rm 1:14–15), and to urge his faithful to apostolic and missionary activity. But the faithful must cling to their bishop, as the Church does to Christ, and Jesus Christ to the Father, so that all may be of one mind through unity[61] and abound to the glory of God (cf. 2 Cor 4:15).

28. Christ, whom the Father has sanctified and sent into the world, (Jn 10:36), has through his apostles, made their successors, the bishops, partakers of his consecration and his mission.[62] They have legitimately handed on to different individuals in the Church various degrees of participation in this ministry. Thus the divinely established ecclesiastical ministry is exercised on different levels by those who from antiquity have been called bishops, priests and deacons.[63] Priests, although they do not possess the highest degree of the priesthood, and although they are dependent on the bishops in the exercise of their power, nevertheless are united with the bishops in sacerdotal dignity.[64] By the power of the sacrament of Orders,[65] in the image of Christ the eternal high priest (Heb 5:1–10; 7:24; 9:11–28), they are consecrated to preach the Gospel and

---

61. Cf. St. Ignatius Martyr, *Ad Ephes.* 5, 1: ed. F. X. Funk, I, 216.

62. Cf. St. Ignatius Martyr, *Ad Ephes.* 6, 1: ed. F. X. Funk, I, 218.

63. Cf. Council of Trent, Session 23, *De Sacr. Ordinis,* ca. 2: Denz. 958 (1765), and can. 6: Denz. 966 (1776).

64. Cf. Innocent I, *Epist. ad Decentium: PL* 20, 554 A, Mansi 3, 1029; Denz. 98 (215): "Presbyters, although they are priests of the second rank, do not possess the high degree of the pontificate."; St. Cyprian, *Epist.* 61, 3: ed. Hartel, 696.

65. Cf. Council of Trent, *loc. cit.,* Denz. 956a–968 (1763–1778), and in particular can. 7: Denz. 967 (1777); Pius XII, Apostolic Constitution *Sacramentum Ordinis:* Denz. 2301 (3857–61).

shepherd the faithful and to celebrate divine worship, so that they are true priests of the New Testament.[66] Partakers of the function of Christ the sole Mediator (1 Tm 2:5), on their level of ministry, they announce the divine word to all. They exercise their sacred function especially in the Eucharistic worship or the celebration of the Mass by which, acting in the person of Christ[67] and proclaiming his mystery, they unite the prayers of the faithful with the sacrifice of their head and renew and apply[68] in the sacrifice of the Mass until the coming of the Lord (cf. 1 Cor 11:26) the only sacrifice of the New Testament, namely that of Christ offering himself once for all a spotless victim to the Father (cf. Heb 9:11–28). For the sick and the sinners among the faithful, they exercise the ministry of alleviation and reconciliation, and they present the needs and the prayers of the faithful to God the Father (Heb 5:1–4). Exercising within the limits of their authority the function of Christ as shepherd and head,[69] they gather together God's family as a brotherhood all of one mind[70] and lead them in the Spirit, through Christ, to God the Father. In the midst of the flock they adore him in spirit and in truth (Jn 4:24). Finally, they labor in word and doctrine (cf. 1 Tm 5:17), believing what they have read and meditated upon in the law of God, teaching what they have believed, and putting in practice in their own lives what they have taught.[71]

Priests, prudent cooperators with the episcopal order,[72] its aid and instrument, called to serve the People of God, constitute one priesthood[73] with their bishop, although bound by a diversity of duties. Associated with their bishop in a spirit of trust and generosity, they make him present in a certain sense in the individual local congregations, and take

---

66. Cf. Innocent I, *loc. cit.;* St. Gregory of Nazianzen, *Apol.* II, 22: *PG* 35, 432 B; Pseudo Dionysius, *Eccl. Hier.,* 1, 2: *PG* 3, 372 D.

67. Cf. Council of Trent, Session 22: Denz. 940 (1743); Pius XII, Encyclical Letter *Mediator Dei* (Nov. 20, 1947): *AAS* 39 (1947), 553; Denz. 2300 (3850).

68. Cf. Council of Trent, Session 22: Denz. 938 (1739–40). Second Vatican Ecumenical Council, *Constitution on the Liturgy,* nn. 7, 47.

69. Cf. Pius XII, Encyclical Letter *Mediator Dei* (Nov. 20, 1947): *AAS* 39 (1947): *AAS* 39 (1947), 553.

70. Cf. St. Cyprian, *Epist.* 11, 3: *PL* 4, 242 B; Hartel, II, 2, 497.

71. *Order of Priestly Consecration,* at the giving of the vestments.

72. *Order of Priestly Consecration,* Preface.

73. Cf. St. Ignatius Martyr, *Philad.* 4: ed. F. X. Funk, I, 266; St. Cornelius I, as given in St. Cyprian, *Epist.* 48, 2: Hartel, III, 2, 610.

upon themselves, as far as they are able, his duties and the burden of his care, and discharge them with a daily interest. And as they sanctify and govern under the bishop's authority that part of the Lord's flock entrusted to them, they make the universal Church visible in their own locality and bring an efficacious assistance to the building up of the whole body of Christ (cf. Eph 4:12). Intent always upon the welfare of God's children, they must strive to lend their effort to the pastoral work of the whole diocese, and even of the entire Church. On account of this sharing in their priesthood and mission, let priests sincerely look upon the bishop as their father and reverently obey him. And let the bishop regard his priests as his co-workers and as sons and friends, just as Christ called his disciples now not servants but friends (cf. Jn 15:15). All priests, both diocesan and religious, by reason of Orders and ministry, fit into this body of bishops and priests, and serve the good of the whole Church according to their vocation and the grace given to them.

In virtue of their common sacred ordination and mission, all priests are bound together in intimate brotherhood, which naturally and freely manifests itself in mutual aid, spiritual as well as material, pastoral as well as personal, in their meetings and in communion of life, of labor and charity.

Let them, as fathers in Christ, take care of the faithful whom they have begotten by Baptism and their teaching (cf. 1 Cor 4:15; 1 Pt 1:23). Becoming from the heart a pattern to the flock (1 Pt 5:3), let them so lead and serve their local community that it may worthily be called by that name, by which the one and entire People of God is signed, namely, the Church of God (cf. 1 Cor 1:2; 2 Cor 1:1). Let them remember that by their daily life and interests they are showing the face of a truly sacerdotal and pastoral ministry to the faithful and the infidel, to Catholics and non-Catholics, and that to all they bear witness to the truth and life, and as good shepherds go after those also (cf. Lk 15:4–7) who, though baptized in the Catholic Church, have fallen away from the use of the sacraments, or even from the faith.

Because the human race today is joining more and more into a civic, economic and social unity, it is that much the more necessary that priests, by combined effort and aid, under the leadership of the bishops and the Supreme Pontiff, wipe out every kind of separateness, so that the whole human race may be brought into the unity of the family of God.

29. At a lower level of the hierarchy are deacons, upon whom hands are imposed "not unto the priesthood, but unto a ministry of service."[74] For strengthened by sacramental grace, in communion with the bishop and his group of priests they serve in the diaconate of the liturgy, of the Word, and of charity to the People of God. It is the duty of the deacon, according as it shall have been assigned to him by competent authority, to administer Baptism solemnly, to be custodian and dispenser of the Eucharist, to assist at and bless marriages in the name of the Church, to bring Viaticum to the dying, to read the Sacred Scripture to the faithful, to instruct and exhort the people, to preside over the worship and prayer of the faithful, to administer sacramentals, and to officiate at funeral and burial services. Dedicated to duties of charity and of administration, let deacons be mindful of the admonition of Blessed Polycarp: "Be merciful, diligent, walking according to the truth of the Lord, who became the servant of all."[75]

Since these duties, so very necessary to the life of the Church, can be fulfilled only with difficulty in many regions in accordance with the discipline of the Latin Church as it exists today, the diaconate can in the future be restored as a proper and permanent rank of the hierarchy. It pertains to the competent territorial bodies of bishops, of one kind or another, with the approval of the Supreme Pontiff, to decide whether and where it is opportune for such deacons to be established for the care of souls. With the consent of the Roman Pontiff, this diaconate can, in the future, be conferred upon men of more mature age, even upon those living in the married state. It may also be conferred upon suitable young men, for whom the law of celibacy must remain intact.

---

74. Constitutions of the Egyptian Church, III, 2: ed. F. X. Funk, *Didascalia,* II, 103, *Statuta Eccl. Ant.* 371: Mansi 3, 954.

75. St. Polycarp, *Ad Phil.* 5, 2: ed. F. X. Funk, I, 300: "It is said that Christ became the deacon of all." Cf. *Didache,* 15, 1: *ibid.,* 32; St. Ignatius Martyr, *Trall.* 2, 3: *ibid.,* 242; *Constitutiones Apostolorum* 8, 28, 4: ed. F. X. Funk, *Didascalia,* I, 530.

Chapter IV

THE LAITY

30. Having set forth the functions of the hierarchy, the sacred Council gladly turns its attention to the state of those faithful called the laity. Everything that has been said above concerning the People of God is intended for the laity, religious and clergy alike. But there are certain things which pertain in a special way to the laity, both men and women, by reason of their condition and mission. Due to the special circumstances of our time the foundations of this doctrine must be more thoroughly examined. For their pastors know how much the laity contribute to the welfare of the entire Church. They also know that they were not ordained by Christ to take upon themselves alone the entire salvific mission of the Church toward the world. On the contrary, they understand that it is their noble duty to shepherd the faithful and to recognize their ministries and charisms, so that all according to their proper roles may cooperate in this common undertaking with one mind. For we must all "practice the truth in love, and so grow up in all things in him who is head, Christ. For from him the whole body, being closely joined and knit together through every joint of the system, according to the functioning in due measure of each single part, derives its increase to the building up of itself in love" (Eph 4:15–16).

31. The term "laity" is here understood to mean all the faithful except those in Holy Orders and those in the state of religious life specially approved by the Church. These faithful are by Baptism made one body with Christ and are constituted among the People of God; they are in their own way made sharers in the priestly, prophetical and kingly functions of Christ, and they carry out for their own part the mission of the whole Christian people in the Church and in the world.

What specifically characterizes the laity is their secular nature. It is true that those in Holy Orders can at times be engaged in secular activities, and even have a secular profession. But they are by reason of their particular vocation especially and professedly ordained to the sacred ministry. Similarly, by their state in life, religious give splendid and striking testimony that the world cannot be transformed and offered to God without the spirit of the beatitudes. But the laity, by their very vocation, seek the kingdom of God by engaging in temporal affairs and by ordering them according to the plan of God. They live in the world, that is, in each and in all of the secular professions and occupations. They live in the ordinary circumstances of family and social life, from which the very web of their existence is woven. They are called there by God that by exercising their proper function and led by the spirit of the Gospel, they may work for the sanctification of the world from within as a leaven. In this way they may make Christ known to others, especially by the testimony of a life resplendent in faith, hope and charity. Therefore, since they are tightly bound up in all types of temporal affairs it is their special task to order and to throw light upon these affairs in such a way that they may come into being and then continually increase according to Christ to the praise of the Creator and the Redeemer.

32. By divine institution, holy Church is ordered and governed with a wonderful diversity. "For just as in one body we have many members, yet all the members have not the same function, so we, the many, are one body in Christ, but severally members one of another" (Rm 12:4–5). Therefore, the chosen People of God is one: "one Lord, one faith, one Baptism" (cf. Eph 4:5), sharing a common dignity as members from their regeneration in Christ, having the same filial grace and the same vocation to perfection, possessing in common one salvation, one hope and one undivided charity. There is, therefore, in Christ and in the Church no inequality on the basis of race or nationality, social condition or sex, because "there is neither Jew nor Greek; there is neither bond nor free; there is neither male nor female. For you are all 'one' in Christ Jesus" (Gal 3:28; cf. Col 3:11).

If therefore in the Church everyone does not proceed by the same path, nevertheless all are called to sanctity and have received an equal privilege of faith through the justice of God (cf. 2 Pt 1:1). And if by the will of Christ some are made teachers, pastors and dispensers of mysteries on behalf of others, yet all share a true equality with regard to the dignity and to the activity common to all the faithful for the building up of the body of Christ. For the distinction which the Lord made between sacred ministers and the rest of the People of God bears within it a certain union, since pastors and the other faithful are bound to each other by a mutual need. Pastors of the Church, following the example of the Lord, should minister to one another and to the other faithful. These in their turn should enthusiastically lend their joint assistance to their pastors and teachers. Thus in their diversity all bear witness to the wonderful unity in the body of Christ. This very diversity of graces, ministries and works gathers the children of God into one, because "all these things are the work of one and the same Spirit" (1 Cor 12:11).

Therefore, from divine choice the laity have Christ for their brother, who though he is the Lord of all, came not to be served but to serve (cf. Mt 20:28). They also have for their brothers those in the sacred ministry who by teaching, by sanctifying and by ruling with the authority of Christ feed the family of God, so that the new commandment of charity may be fulfilled by all. St. Augustine puts this very beautifully when he says: "What I am for you terrifies me; what I am with you consoles me. For you I am a bishop; but with you I am a Christian. The former is a duty; the latter a grace. The former is a danger; the latter, salvation."[1]

33. The laity are gathered together in the People of God and make up the body of Christ under one head. Whoever they are, they are called upon, as living members, to expend all their energy for the growth of the Church and its continuous sanctification, since this very energy is a gift of the Creator and a blessing of the Redeemer.

The lay apostolate, however, is a participation in the salvific mission of the Church itself. Through their Baptism and Confirmation all are commissioned to that apostolate by the Lord himself. Moreover, by the sacraments, especially the Holy Eucharist, that charity toward God and man which is the soul of the apostolate is communicated and nourished. Now the laity are called in a special way to make the Church present and operative in those places and circumstances where only through them can it become the salt of the earth.[2] Thus every layman, in virtue of the very gifts bestowed upon him, is at the same time a witness and a living instrument of the mission of the Church itself, "according to the measure of Christ's bestowal" (Eph 4:7).

Besides this apostolate, which certainly pertains to all Christians, the laity can also be called in various ways to a more direct form of co-

---

1. St. Augustine, *Serm.* 340, 1: *PL* 38, 1483.

2. Cf. Pius XI, Encyclical Letter *Quadragesimo Anno* (May 15, 1931): *AAS* 23 (1931), 121f.; Pius XII, *Allocution De Quelle Consolation* (Oct. 14, 1951): *AAS* 43 (1951), 790 f.

operation in the apostolate of the hierarchy.[3] This was the way certain men and women assisted Paul the Apostle in the Gospel, laboring much in the Lord (cf. Phil 4:3; Rm 16:3 ff.). Further, they have the capacity to assume from the hierarchy certain ecclesiastical functions, which are to be performed for a spiritual purpose.

Upon all the laity, therefore, rests the noble duty of working to extend the divine plan of salvation to all men of each epoch and in every land. Consequently, may every opportunity be given them so that, according to their abilities and the needs of the times, they may zealously participate in the saving work of the Church.

34. The supreme and eternal priest, Christ Jesus, since he wills to continue his witness and service also through the laity, vivifies them in this Spirit and increasingly urges them on to every good and perfect work.

For besides intimately linking them to his life and his mission, he also gives them a sharing in his priestly function of offering spiritual worship for the glory of God and the salvation of men. For this reason, the laity, dedicated to Christ and anointed by the Holy Spirit, are marvelously called and wonderfully prepared so that ever more abundant fruits of the Spirit may be produced in them. For all their works, prayers and apostolic endeavors, their ordinary married and family life, their daily occupations, their physical and mental relaxation, if carried out in the Spirit, and even the hardships of life, if patiently borne—all these become "spiritual sacrifices acceptable to God through Jesus Christ" (1 Pt 2:5). Together with the offering of the Lord's body, they are most fittingly offered in the celebration of the Eucharist. Thus, as those everywhere who adore in holy activity, the laity consecrate the world itself to God.

35. Christ, the great prophet, who proclaimed the kingdom of his Father both by the testimony of his life and the power of his words, continually fulfills his prophetic office until the complete manifestation of glory. He does this not only through the hierarchy who teach in his name and with his authority, but also through the laity whom he made his witnesses and to whom he gave understanding of the faith *(sensus fidei)* and an attractiveness in speech (cf. Acts 2:17–18; Rv 19:10), so that the power of the Gospel might shine forth in their daily social and family

---

3. Cf. Pius XII, *Allocution Six Ans Sont Écoulés* (Oct. 5, 1957): *AAS* 49 (1957), 927; concerning the "mandate" and canonical mission, cf. *Decretum De Apostolatu Laicorum,* ca. IV, n. 16, with notes 12 and 15.

life. They conduct themselves as children of the promise, and thus, strong in faith and in hope, they make the most of the present (cf. Eph 5:16; Col 4:5), and with patience await the glory that is to come (cf. Rm 8:25). Let them not, then, hide this hope in the depths of their hearts, but even in the program of their secular life let them express it by a continual conversion and by wrestling "against the world-rulers of this darkness, against the spiritual forces of wickedness" (Eph 6:12).

Just as the sacraments of the New Law, by which the life and the apostolate of the faithful are nourished, prefigure a new heaven and a new earth (cf. Rv 21:1), so too the laity go forth as powerful proclaimers of a faith in things to be hoped for (cf. Heb 11:1), when they courageously join to their profession of faith a life springing from faith. This evangelization, that is, this announcing of Christ by a living testimony as well as by the spoken word, takes on a specific quality and a special force in that it is carried out in the ordinary surroundings of the world.

In connection with the prophetic function, that state of life which is sanctified by a special sacrament is obviously of great importance, namely, married and family life. For where Christianity pervades the entire mode of family life, and gradually transforms it, one will find there both the practice and an excellent school of the lay apostolate. In such a home husbands and wives find their proper vocation in being witnesses of the faith and love of Christ to one another and to their children. The Christian family loudly proclaims both the present virtues of the kingdom of God and the hope of a blessed life to come. Thus by its example and its witness it accuses the world of sin and enlightens those who seek the truth.

Consequently, even when preoccupied with temporal cares, the laity can and must perform a work of great value for the evangelization of the world. For even if some of them have to fulfill their religious duties on their own, when there are no sacred ministers or in times of persecution, and even if many of them devote all their energies to apostolic work, still it remains for each one of them to cooperate in the external spread and the dynamic growth of the kingdom of Christ in the world. Therefore, let the laity devotedly strive to acquire a more profound grasp of revealed truth, and let them insistently beg of God the gift of wisdom.

36. Christ, becoming obedient even unto death and because of this exalted by the Father (cf. Phil 2:8–9), entered into the glory of his kingdom. To him all things are made subject until he subjects himself and all created things to the Father that God may be all in all (cf. 1 Cor

15:27–28). Now Christ has communicated this royal power to his disciples that they might be constituted in royal freedom and that by true penance and a holy life they might conquer the reign of sin in themselves (cf. Rm 6:12). Further, he has shared this power so that serving Christ in their fellow men they might by humility and patience lead their brethren to that king for whom to serve is to reign. But the Lord wishes to spread his kingdom also by means of the laity, namely, a kingdom of truth and life, a kingdom of holiness and grace, a kingdom of justice, love and peace.[4] In this kingdom creation itself will be delivered from its slavery to corruption into the freedom of the glory of the sons of God (cf. Rm 8:21). Clearly then a great promise and a great trust is committed to the disciples: "All things are yours, and you are Christ's, and Christ is God's" (1 Cor 3:23).

The faithful, therefore, must learn the deepest meaning and the value of all creation, as well as its role in the harmonious praise of God. They must assist each other to live holier lives even in their daily occupations. In this way the world may be permeated by the spirit of Christ and it may more effectively fulfill its purpose in justice, charity and peace. The laity have the principal role in the overall fulfillment of this duty. Therefore, by their competence in secular training and by their activity, elevated from within by the grace of Christ, let them vigorously contribute their effort, so that created goods may be perfected by human labor, technical skill and civic culture for the benefit of all men according to the design of the Creator and the light of his Word. May the goods of this world be more equitably distributed among all men, and may they in their own way be conducive to universal progress in human and Christian freedom. In this manner, through the members of the Church, will Christ progressively illumine the whole of human society with his saving light.

Moreover, let the laity also by their combined efforts remedy the customs and conditions of the world, if they are an inducement to sin, so that they all may be conformed to the norms of justice and may favor the practice of virtue rather than hinder it. By so doing they will imbue culture and human activity with genuine moral values; they will better prepare the field of the world for the seed of the Word of God, and at the

---

4. From the *Preface* of the feast of Christ the King.

same time they will open wider the doors of the Church by which the message of peace may enter the world.

Because of the very economy of salvation the faithful should learn how to distinguish carefully between those rights and duties which are theirs as members of the Church, and those which they have as members of human society. Let them strive to reconcile the two, remembering that in every temporal affair they must be guided by a Christian conscience, since even in secular business there is no human activity which can be withdrawn from God's dominion. In our own time, however, it is most urgent that this distinction and also this harmony should shine forth more clearly than ever in the lives of the faithful, so that the mission of the Church may correspond more fully to the special conditions of the world today. For it must be admitted that the temporal sphere is governed by its own principles, since it is rightly concerned with the interests of this world. But that ominous doctrine which attempts to build a society with no regard whatever for religion, and which attacks and destroys the religious liberty of its citizens, is rightly to be rejected.[5]

37. The laity have the right, as do all Christians, to receive in abundance from their spiritual shepherds the spiritual goods of the Church, especially the assistance of the Word of God and of the sacraments.[6] They should openly reveal to them their needs and desires with that freedom and confidence which is fitting for children of God and brothers in Christ. They are, by reason of the knowledge, competence or outstanding ability which they may enjoy, permitted and sometimes even obliged to express their opinion on those things which concern the good of the Church.[7] When occasions arise, let this be done through the organs erected by the Church for this purpose. Let it always be done in truth, in courage and in prudence, with reverence and charity toward those who by reason of their sacred office represent the person of Christ.

---

5. Cf. Leo XIII, Encyclical Epistle *Immortale Dei* (Nov. 1, 1885): *AAS* 18 (1885), 166 ff.; Leo XIII Encyclical Letter *Sapientiae Christianae* (Jan. 10, 1890): *AAS* 22 (1889–90), 397 ff.; Pius XII, *Allocution Alla Vostra Filiale* (March 23, 1958): *AAS* 50 (1958), 220: *"la legittima sana laicita dello Stato"* (the legitimate and healthy laicity of the State).

6. *Code of Canon Law,* can. 682.

7. Cf. Pius XII, *Allocution De Quelle Consolation* (Oct. 14, 1951): *AAS* 43 (1951), 789: "Dans les batailles décisives, c'est parfois du front que partent les plus heureuses initiatives...." ("In decisive battles, it is sometimes at the front that the happiest initiatives originate."); *Allocution L'importance de la Presse Catholique* (Feb. 17, 1950): *AAS* 42 (1950), 256.

The laity should, as all Christians, promptly accept in Christian obedience decisions of their spiritual shepherds, since they are representatives of Christ as well as teachers and rulers in the Church. Let them follow the example of Christ, who by his obedience even unto death, opened to all men the blessed way of the liberty of the children of God. Nor should they omit to pray for those placed over them, for they keep watch as having to render an account of their souls, so that they may do this with joy and not with grief (cf. Heb 13:17).

Let the spiritual shepherds recognize and promote the dignity as well as the responsibility of the laity in the Church. Let them willingly employ their prudent advice. Let them confidently assign duties to them in the service of the Church, allowing them freedom and room for action. Further, let them encourage lay people so that they may undertake tasks on their own initiative. Attentively in Christ, let them consider with fatherly love the projects, suggestions and desires proposed by the laity.[8] However, let the shepherds respectfully acknowledge that just freedom which belongs to everyone in this earthly city.

A great many wonderful things are to be hoped for from this familiar dialogue between the laity and their spiritual leaders: in the laity a strengthened sense of personal responsibility, a renewed enthusiasm, a more ready application of their talents to the projects of their spiritual leaders. The latter, on the other hand, aided by the experience of the laity, can more clearly and more incisively come to decisions regarding both spiritual and temporal matters. In this way, the whole Church, strengthened by each one of its members, may more effectively fulfill its mission for the life of the world.

38. Each individual layman must stand before the world as a witness to the resurrection and life of the Lord Jesus and a symbol of the living God. All the laity as a community and each one according to his ability must nourish the world with spiritual fruits (cf. Gal 5:22). They must diffuse in the world that spirit which animates the poor, the meek, the peace makers—whom the Lord in the Gospel proclaimed as blessed (cf. Mt 5:3–9). In a word, "Christians must be to the world what the soul is to the body."[9]

---

8. Cf. 1 Thes 5:19 and 1 Jn 4:1.

9. *Epist. ad Diognetum,* 6: ed. F. X. Funk, I, 400; cf. St. John Chrysostom, *In Matth. Hom.* 46 (47) 2: *PG* 58, 78, on the leaven in the dough.

CHAPTER V

THE UNIVERSAL CALL
TO HOLINESS IN THE CHURCH

39. The Church, whose mystery is being set forth by this sacred synod, is believed to be indefectibly holy. Indeed, Christ, the Son of God, who with the Father and the Spirit is praised as "uniquely holy,"[1] loved the Church as his bride, delivering himself up for her. He did this that he might sanctify her (cf. Eph 5:25–26). He united her to himself as his own body and brought it to perfection by the gift of the Holy Spirit for God's glory. Therefore in the Church, everyone whether belonging to the hierarchy, or being cared for by it, is called to holiness, according to the saying of the Apostle: "For this is the will of God, your sanctification" (1 Thes 4:3; Eph 1:4). However, this holiness of the Church is unceasingly manifested, and must be manifested, in the fruits of grace which the Spirit produces in the faithful; it is expressed in many ways in individuals, who in their walk of life, tend toward the perfection of charity, thus causing the edification of others; in a very special way this (holiness) appears in the practice of the counsels, customarily called "evangelical." This practice of the counsels, under the impulsion of the Holy Spirit, undertaken by many Christians, either privately or in a Church-approved condition or state of life, gives and must give in the world an outstanding witness and example of this same holiness.

40. The Lord Jesus, the divine teacher and model of all perfection, preached holiness of life to each and every one of his disciples of every condition. He himself stands as the author and consummator of this holiness of life: "Be you therefore perfect, even as your heavenly Father is perfect" (Mt 5:48).[2] Indeed, he sent the Holy Spirit upon all men that he

---

1. The Roman Missal, *Gloria in excelsis.* Cf. Lk 1:35, 4:34; Mk 1:24; Jn 6:69 *(ho hagios tou theou);* Acts 3:14; 4:27, 30; Heb 7:26; 1 Jn 2:20; Rv 3:7.

2. Cf. Origen, *Comm. Rm* 7, 7: *PG* 14, 1122 B; Pseudo-Macarius, *De Oratione,* 11: *PG* 34, 861 AB; St. Thomas, *Summa Theol.,* II–II, q. 184, a. 3.

might move them inwardly to love God with their whole heart and their whole soul, with all their mind and all their strength (cf. Mk 12:30) and that they might love each other as Christ loves them (cf. Jn 13:34; 15:12). The followers of Christ are called by God, not because of their works, but according to his own purpose and grace. They are justified in the Lord Jesus, because in the Baptism of faith they truly become sons of God and sharers in the divine nature. In this way, they are really made holy. Then too, by God's gift, they must hold onto and complete in their lives this holiness they have received. They are warned by the Apostle to live "as becomes saints" (Eph 5:3), and to put on "as God's chosen ones, holy and beloved, a heart of mercy, kindness, humility, meekness, patience" (Col 3:12), and to possess the fruit of the Spirit in holiness (cf. Gal 5:22; Rm 6:22). Since truly we all offend in many things (cf. Jas 3:2), we all need God's mercies continually and we all must daily pray: "Forgive us our debts" (Mt 6:12).[3]

Thus it is evident to everyone that all the faithful of Christ, of whatever rank or status, are called to the fullness of the Christian life and to the perfection of charity;[4] by this holiness as such a more human manner of living is promoted in this earthly society. In order that the faithful may reach this perfection, they must use their strength accordingly as they have received it, as a gift from Christ. They must follow in his footsteps and conform themselves to his image, seeking the will of the Father in all things. They must devote themselves with all their being to the glory of God and the service of their neighbor. In this way, the holiness of the People of God will grow into an abundant harvest of good, as is admirably shown by the life of so many saints in Church history.

41. The classes and duties of life are many, but holiness is one—that sanctity which is cultivated by all who are moved by the Spirit of God, and who obey the voice of the Father and worship God the Father in spirit and in truth. These people follow the poor Christ, the humble and cross-bearing Christ in order to be worthy of being sharers in his glory. Ev-

---

3. Cf. St. Augustine, *Retract.* II, 18: *PL* 32, 637 f.; Pius XII, Encyclical Letter *Mystici Corporis* (June 29, 1943): *AAS* 35 (1943), 225.

4. Cf. Pius XI, Encyclical Letter *Rerum Omnium* (Jan. 26, 1923): *AAS* 15 (1923), 50 and 59–60; Encyclical Letter *Casti Connubii* (Dec. 31, 1930): *AAS* 22 (1930), 548; Pius XII, Apostolic Constitution *Provida Mater* (Feb. 2, 1947): *AAS* 39 (1947), 117; Allocution *Annus Sacer* (Dec. 8, 1950): *AAS* 43 (1951), 27–28; *Allocution Nel Darvi* (July 1, 1956): *AAS* 48 (1956), 574 f.

ery person must walk unhesitatingly according to his own personal gifts and duties in the path of living faith, which arouses hope and works through charity.

In the first place, the shepherds of Christ's flock must holily and eagerly, humbly and courageously carry out their ministry, in imitation of the eternal high priest, the shepherd and guardian of our souls. They ought to fulfill this duty in such a way that it will be the principal means also of their own sanctification. Those chosen for the fullness of the priesthood are granted the ability of exercising the perfect duty of pastoral charity by the grace of the sacrament of Orders. This perfect duty of pastoral charity[5] is exercised in every form of episcopal care and service, prayer, sacrifice and preaching. By this same sacramental grace, they are given the courage necessary to lay down their lives for their sheep, and the ability of promoting greater holiness in the Church by their daily example, having become a pattern for their flock (cf. 1 Pt 5:3).

Priests, who resemble bishops to a certain degree in their participation of the sacrament of Orders, form the spiritual crown of the bishops.[6] They participate in the grace of their office and they should grow daily in their love of God and their neighbor by the exercise of their office through Christ, the eternal and unique Mediator. They should preserve the bond of priestly communion, and they should abound in every spiritual good and thus present to all men a living witness to God.[7] All this they should do in emulation of those priests, who often down through the course of the centuries, left an outstanding example of the holiness of humble and hidden service. Their praise lives on in the Church of God. By their very office of praying and offering sacrifice for their own people and the entire People of God, they should rise to greater holiness. Keeping in mind what they are doing and imitating what they are handling,[8] these priests, in their apostolic labors, rather than being ensnared by perils and hardships, should rather rise to greater holiness through

5. Cf. St. Thomas, *Summa Theol.*, II–II, q. 184, a. 5 and 6; *De Perf. Vitae Spir.*, c. 18; Origen, *In Is.* Hom. 6, 1: *PG* 13, 239.

6. Cf. St. Ignatius Martyr, *Magn.* 13, 1: ed. F. X. Funk, I, 241.

7. Cf. St. Pius X, Exhortation *Haerent Animo* (Aug. 4, 1908): *AAS* 41 (1908), 560 f.; *Code of Canon Law,* can. 124; Pius XI, Encyclical Letter *Ad Catholici Sacerdotii* (Dec. 20, 1935): *AAS* 28 (1936), 22 f.

8. *Order of priestly consecration,* introductory exhortation.

these perils and hardships. They should ever nourish and strengthen their action from an abundance of contemplation, doing all this for the comfort of the entire Church of God. All priests, and especially those who are called "diocesan priests," due to the special title of their ordination, should keep continually before their minds the fact that their faithful loyalty toward and their generous cooperation with their bishop is of the greatest value in their growth in holiness.

Ministers of lesser rank are also sharers in the mission and grace of the supreme priest. In the first place among these ministers are deacons, who inasmuch as they are dispensers of Christ's mysteries and servants of the Church,[9] should keep themselves free from every vice and stand before men as personifications of goodness and friends of God (cf. 1 Tm 3:8–10, 12–13). Clerics, who are called by the Lord and are set aside as his portion in order to prepare themselves for the various ministerial offices under the watchful eye of spiritual shepherds, are bound to bring their hearts and minds into accord with this special election (which is theirs). They will accomplish this by their constancy in prayer, by their burning love, and by their unremitting recollection of whatever is true, just and of good repute. They will accomplish all this for the glory and honor of God. Besides these already named, there are also laymen, chosen of God and called by the bishop. These laymen spend themselves completely in apostolic labors, working in the Lord's field with much success.[10]

Furthermore, married couples and Christian parents should follow their own proper path (to holiness) by faithful love. They should sustain one another in grace throughout the entire length of their lives. They should imbue their offspring, lovingly welcomed as God's gift, with Christian doctrine and the evangelical virtues. In this manner, they offer all men the example of unwearying and generous love; in this way they build up the brotherhood of charity; in so doing, they stand as the witnesses and cooperators in the fruitfulness of holy mother Church; by such lives, they are a sign and a participation in that very love with which Christ loved his bride and for which he delivered himself up for

---

9. Cf. St. Ignatius Martyr, *Trall.* 2, 3: ed. F. X. Funk, I, 244.

10. Cf. Pius XII, *Allocution Sous la Maternelle Protection* (Dec. 9, 1957): *AAS* 50 (1958), 36.

her.[11] A like example, but one given in a different way, is that offered by widows and single people, who are able to make great contributions toward holiness and apostolic endeavor in the Church. Finally, those who engage in labor—and frequently it is of a heavy nature—should better themselves by their human labors. They should aid their fellow citizens. They should raise all of society, and even creation itself, to a better mode of existence. Indeed, they should imitate by their lively charity, in their joyous hope and by their voluntary sharing of each other's burdens, the very Christ who plied his hands with carpenter's tools and who, in union with his Father, is continually working for the salvation of all men. In this, then, their daily work they should climb to the heights of holiness and apostolic activity.

May all those who are weighed down with poverty, infirmity and sickness, as well as those who must bear various hardships or who suffer persecution for justice sake—may they all know they are united with the suffering Christ in a special way for the salvation of the world. The Lord called them blessed in his Gospel, and they are those whom "the God of all graces, who has called us unto his eternal glory in Christ Jesus, will himself, after we have suffered a little while, perfect, strengthen and establish" (1 Pt 5:10).

Finally all Christ's faithful, whatever be the conditions, duties and circumstances of their lives—and indeed through all these—will daily increase in holiness, if they receive all things with faith from the hand of their heavenly Father and if they cooperate with the divine will. In this temporal service, they will manifest to all men the love with which God loved the world.

42. "God is love, and he who abides in love, abides in God and God in him" (1 Jn 4:16). But God pours out his love into our hearts through the Holy Spirit, who has been given to us (cf. Rm 5:5); thus the first and most necessary gift is love, by which we love God above all things and our neighbor because of God. Indeed, in order that love, as good seed may grow and bring forth fruit in the soul, each one of the faithful must willingly hear the Word of God and accept his will, and must complete by their own actions what God has begun, with the help of God's grace.

---

11. Pius XI, Encyclical Letter *Casti Connubii* (Dec. 31, 1930): *AAS* 22 (1930), 548 f.; cf. St. John Chrysostom, *In Ephes.* Hom. 20, 2: *PG* 62, 136 ff.

These actions consist in the use of the sacraments and in a special way the Eucharist, frequent participation in the sacred action of the liturgy, application of oneself to prayer, self-abnegation, lively fraternal service and the constant exercise of all the virtues. For charity, as the bond of perfection and the fullness of the law (cf. Col 3:14; Rm 13:10), rules over all the means of attaining holiness and gives life to these same means.[12] It is charity which guides us to our final end. It is the love of God and the love of one's neighbor which point out the true disciple of Christ.

Since Jesus, the Son of God, manifested his charity by laying down his life for us, so too no one has greater love than he who lays down his life for Christ and his brothers (cf. 1 Jn 3:16; Jn 15:13). From the earliest times, then, some Christians have been called upon—and some will always be called upon—to give the supreme testimony of this love to all men, but especially to persecutors. The Church, then, considers martyrdom as an exceptional gift and as the fullest proof of love. By martyrdom a disciple is transformed into an image of his Master by freely accepting death for the salvation of the world—as well as his conformity to Christ in the shedding of his blood. Though few are presented such an opportunity, nevertheless all must be prepared to confess Christ before men. They must be prepared to make this profession of faith even in the midst of persecutions, which will never be lacking to the Church, in following the way of the cross.

Likewise, the holiness of the Church is fostered in a special way by the observance of the counsels proposed in the Gospel by our Lord to his disciples.[13] An eminent position among these is held by virginity or the celibate state (cf. 1 Cor 7:32–34). This is a precious gift of divine grace given by the Father to certain souls (cf. Mt 19:11; 1 Cor 7:7), whereby they may devote themselves to God alone the more easily, due to an undivided heart.[14] This perfect continency, out of desire for the kingdom of

---

12. Cf. St. Augustine, *Enchir.* 121, 32: *PL* 40, 288; St. Thomas, *Summa Theol.,* II–II, q. 184, a. 1; Pius XII, Apostolic Exhortation *Menti Nostrae* (Sept. 23, 1950): *AAS* 42 (1950), 660.

13. On the counsels in general, cf. Origen, *Comm. Rm* X, 14: *PG* 14 1275 B; St. Augustine, *De S. Virginitate* 15, 15: *PL* 40, 403; St. Thomas, *Summa Theol.,* I–II, q. 100, a. 2 C (end); II–II, q. 44, a. 4 *ad* 3.

14. On the excellence of holy virginity, cf. Tertullian, *Exhort. Cast.* 10: *PL* 2, 925 C; St. Cyprian, *Hab. Virg.* 3 and 22: *PL* 4, 443 B and 461 A f.; St. Athanasius (?), *De Virg.: PG* 28, 252 ff.; St. John Chrysostom, *De Virg.: PG* 48, 533 ff.

heaven, has always been held in particular honor in the Church. The reason for this was and is that perfect continency for the love of God is an incentive to charity, and is certainly a particular source of spiritual fecundity in the world.

The Church continually keeps before it the warning of the Apostle, which moved the faithful to charity, exhorting them to experience personally what Christ Jesus had known within himself. This was the same Christ Jesus, who "emptied himself, taking the nature of a slave...becoming obedient to death" (Phil 2:7–8), and because of us, "being rich, he became poor" (2 Cor 8:9). Because the disciples must always offer an imitation of and a testimony to the charity and humility of Christ, mother Church rejoices at finding within her bosom men and women who very closely follow their Savior, who debased himself to our comprehension. There are some who, in their freedom as sons of God, renounce their own wills and take upon themselves the state of poverty. Still further, some become subject of their own accord to another man, in the matter of perfection for love of God. This is beyond the measure of the commandments, but is done in order to become more fully like the obedient Christ.[15]

Therefore, all the faithful of Christ are invited to strive for the holiness and perfection of their own proper state. Indeed, they have an obligation to so strive. Let all then have care that they guide aright their own deepest sentiments of soul. Let neither the use of the things of this world nor attachment to riches, which is against the spirit of evangelical poverty, hinder them in their quest for perfect love. Let them heed the admonition of the Apostle to those who use this world; let them not come to terms with this world, for this world, as we see it, is passing away (cf. 1 Cor 7:31 ff.).[16]

---

15. On spiritual *poverty*, cf. Mt 5:3; 19:21; Mk 10:21; Lk 18:22; on *obedience*, Christ's example is given in Jn 4:34; 6:38; Phil 2:8–10; Heb 10:5–7. There are many texts on this from the Fathers and founders of orders.

16. On the effective practice of the counsels which is not imposed on all, cf. St. John Chrysostom, *In Matth.* Hom. 7, 7: *PG* 57, 81 f.; St. Ambrose, *De Viduis* 4, 23: *PL* 16, 241 f.

CHAPTER VI

RELIGIOUS

43. The evangelical counsels of chastity dedicated to God, poverty and obedience are based upon the words and examples of the Lord. They were further commanded by the apostles and Fathers of the Church, as well as by the doctors and pastors of souls. The counsels are a divine gift which the Church received from its Lord and which it always safeguards with the help of his grace. Church authority has the duty, under the inspiration of the Holy Spirit, of interpreting these evangelical counsels, of regulating their practice and finally to build on them stable forms of living. Thus, it has come about, that, as if on a tree which has grown in the field of the Lord, various forms of solidarity and community life, as well as various religious families, have branched out in a marvelous and multiple way from this divinely given seed. Such a multiple and miraculous growth augments both the progress of the members of these various religious families themselves and the welfare of the entire body of Christ.[1] These religious families give their members the support of a more firm stability in their way of life and a proven doctrine of acquiring perfection. They further offer their members the support of fraternal association in the militia of Christ and of liberty strengthened by obedience. Thus these religious are able to tranquilly fulfill and faithfully observe their religious profession and so, spiritually rejoicing, make progress on the road of charity.[2]

From the point of view of the divine and hierarchical structure of the Church, the religious state of life is not an intermediate state between

---

1. Cf. Rosweydus, *Vitae Patrum*, Antwerp 1628; *Apophtegmata Patrum: PG* 65; Palladius, *Historia Lausiaca: PG* 34, 995 ff.; ed. C. Butler, Cambridge 1898 (1904); Pius XI, Apostolic Constitution *Umbratilem* (July 8, 1924): *AAS* 16 (1924), 386–387; Pius XII, *Allocution Nous Sommes Heureux* (April 11, 1958): *AAS* 50 (1958), 283.

2. Paul VI, *Allocution Magno Gaudio* (May 23, 1964): *AAS* 56 (1964), 566.

the clerical and lay states. But, rather, the faithful of Christ are called by God from both these states of life so that they might enjoy this particular gift in the life of the Church and thus, each in one's own way, may be of some advantage to the salvific mission of the Church.[3]

44. The faithful of Christ bind themselves to the three aforesaid counsels either by vows or by other sacred bonds, which are like vows in their purpose. By such a bond, a person is totally dedicated to God, loved beyond all things. In this way, that person is ordained to the honor and service of God under a new and special title. Indeed through Baptism a person dies to sin and is consecrated to God. However, in order that he may be capable of deriving more abundant fruit from this baptismal grace, he intends, by the profession of the evangelical counsels in the Church, to free himself from those obstacles which might draw him away from the fervor of charity and the perfection of divine worship. By his profession of the evangelical counsels, then, he is more intimately consecrated to divine service.[4] This consecration will be the more perfect, inasmuch as the indissoluble bond of the union of Christ and his bride, the Church, is represented by firm and more stable bonds.

The evangelical counsels which lead to charity[5] join their followers to the Church and its mystery in a special way. Since this is so, the spiritual life of these people should then be devoted to the welfare of the whole Church. From this arises their duty of working to implant and strengthen the kingdom of Christ in souls and to extend that kingdom to every clime. This duty is to be undertaken to the extent of their capacities and in keeping with the proper type of their own vocation. This can be realized through prayer or active works of the apostolate. It is for this reason that the Church preserves and fosters the special character of her various religious institutes.

The profession of the evangelical counsels, then, appears as a sign which can and ought to attract all the members of the Church to an effective and prompt fulfillment of the duties of their Christian vocation.

---

3. Cf. *Code of Canon Law,* can. 487 and 488, par 4; Pius XII, *Allocution Annus Sacer* (Dec. 8, 1950): *AAS* 43 (1951), 27 f.; Pius XII, Apostolic Constitution *Provida Mater* (Feb. 2, 1947): *AAS* 39 (1947), 120 ff.

4. Paul VI, *Allocution Magno Gaudio* (May 23, 1964): *AAS* 56 (1964), 567.

5. Cf. St. Thomas, *Summa Theol.,* II–II, q. 184, a. 3 and q. 188, a. 2; St. Bonaventure, *Opusc. X, Apologia Pauperum,* c. 3, 3: ed. Opera, Quaracchi, vol. 8, 1898, 245 a.

The People of God have no lasting city here below, but look forward to one that is to come. Since this is so, the religious state, whose purpose is to free its members from earthly cares, more fully manifests to all believers the presence of heavenly goods already possessed here below. Furthermore, it not only witnesses to the fact of a new and eternal life acquired by the redemption of Christ, but it foretells the future resurrection and the glory of the heavenly kingdom. Christ proposed to his disciples this form of life, which he, as the Son of God, accepted in entering this world to do the will of the Father. This same state of life is accurately exemplified and perpetually made present in the Church. The religious state clearly manifests that the kingdom of God and its needs, in a very special way, are raised above all earthly considerations. Finally, it clearly shows all men both the unsurpassed breadth of the strength of Christ the king and the infinite power of the Holy Spirit marvelously working in the Church.

Thus, the state which is constituted by the profession of the evangelical counsels, though it does not belong to the hierarchical structure of the Church, nevertheless, undeniably belongs to its life and holiness.

45. It is the duty of the ecclesiastical hierarchy to regulate the practice of the evangelical counsels by law, since it is the duty of the same hierarchy to care for the People of God and to lead them to most fruitful pastures (Ez 34:14). The importance of the profession of the evangelical counsels is seen in the fact that it fosters the perfection of love of God and love of neighbor in an outstanding manner, and that this profession is strengthened by vows.[6] Furthermore, the hierarchy, following with docility the prompting of the Holy Spirit, accepts the rules presented by outstanding men and women and authentically approves these rules after further adjustments. It also aids by its vigilant and safeguarding authority those institutes variously established for the building up of Christ's body, in order that these same institutes may grow and flourish according to the spirit of the founders.

Any institute of perfection and its individual members may be removed from the jurisdiction of the local ordinaries by the Supreme Pon-

---

6. Cf. First Vatican Ecumenical Council, Schema *De Ecclesia Christi,* ca. XV, and annotation 48: Mansi 51, 549 f. and 619 f.; Leo XIII, Letter *Au Milieu des Consolations* (Dec. 23, 1900): *AAS* 33 (1900–01), 361; Pius XII, Apostolic Constitution *Provida Mater* (Feb. 2, 1947): *AAS* 39 (1947), 114 f.

tiff and subjected to himself alone. This is done in virtue of his primacy over the entire Church, in order to more fully provide for the necessities of the entire flock of the Lord and in consideration of the common good.[7] In like manner, these institutes may be left or committed to the charge of the proper patriarchical authority. The members of these institutes, in fulfilling their obligation to the Church due to their particular form of life, ought to show reverence and obedience to bishops according to the sacred canons. The bishops are owed this respect because of their pastoral authority in their own churches and because of the need of unity and harmony in the apostolate.[8]

The Church not only raises the religious profession to the dignity of a canonical state by her approval, but even manifests that this profession is a state consecrated to God, by the liturgical setting of that profession. The Church itself, by the authority given to it by God, accepts the vows of the newly professed. It begs aid and grace from God for them by its public prayer. It commends them to God, imparts a spiritual blessing on them and accompanies their self-offering by the Eucharistic Sacrifice.

46. Religious should carefully keep before their minds the fact that the Church presents Christ to believers and non-believers alike in a striking manner daily through them. The Church thus portrays Christ in contemplation on the mountain, in his proclamation of the kingdom of God to the multitudes, in his healing of the sick and maimed, in his work of converting sinners to a better life, in his solicitude for youth and his goodness to all men, always obedient to the will of the Father who sent him.[9]

All men should take note that the profession of the evangelical counsels, though entailing the renunciation of certain values which are to be undoubtedly esteemed, does not detract from a genuine development of the human person, but rather by its very nature is most beneficial to that development. Indeed, the counsels, voluntarily undertaken according to each one's personal vocation, contribute a great deal

---

7. Cf. Leo XIII, Constitution *Romanos Pontifices* (May 8, 1881): *AAS* 13 (1880–81), 483; Pius XII, *Allocution Annus Sacer* (Dec. 8, 1950): *AAS* 43 (1951), 28 f.

8. Cf. Pius XII, *Allocution Annus Sacer* (Dec. 8, 1950): *AAS* 43 (1951), 28; Pius XII, Apostolic Constitution *Sedes Sapientiae* (May 31, 1956): *AAS* 48 (1956), 355; Paul VI, *Allocution Magno Gaudio* (May 23, 1964): *AAS* 56 (1964), 570–571.

9. Cf. Pius XII, Encyclical Letter *Mystici Corporis* (June 19, 1943): *AAS* 35 (1943), 214 f.

to the purification of heart and spiritual liberty. They continually stir up the fervor of charity. But especially they are able to more fully mold the Christian man to that type of chaste and detached life which Christ the Lord chose for himself and which his Mother also embraced. This is clearly proven by the example of so many holy founders. Let no one think that religious have become strangers to their fellowmen or useless citizens of this earthly city by their consecration. For even though it sometimes happens that religious do not directly mingle with their contemporaries, yet in a more profound sense these same religious are united with them in the heart of Christ and spiritually cooperate with them. In this way the building up of the earthly city may have its foundation in the Lord and may tend toward him, lest perhaps those who build this city shall have labored in vain.[10]

Therefore, this sacred synod encourages and praises the men and women, brothers and sisters, who in monasteries, or in schools and hospitals, or in the missions, adorn the bride of Christ by their unswerving and humble faithfulness in their chosen consecration and render generous services of all kinds to mankind.

47. Let each of the faithful called to the profession of the evangelical counsels, therefore, carefully see to it that he persevere and ever grow in that vocation God has given him. Let him do this for the increased holiness of the Church, for the greater glory of the one and undivided Trinity, which in and through Christ is the fount and the source of all holiness.

---

10. Cf. Pius XII, *Allocution Annus Sacer* (Dec. 8, 1950): *AAS* 43 (1951), 30; *Allocution Sous la Maternelle Protection* (Dec. 9, 1957): *AAS* 50 (1958), 39 f.

CHAPTER VII

THE ESCHATOLOGICAL NATURE
OF THE PILGRIM CHURCH AND ITS
UNION WITH THE CHURCH IN HEAVEN

48. The Church, to which we are all called in Christ Jesus, and in which we acquire sanctity through the grace of God, will attain its full perfection only in the glory of heaven, when there will come the time of the restoration of all things (Acts 3:21). At that time the human race, as well as the entire world, which is intimately related to man and attains to its end through him, will be perfectly reestablished in Christ (cf. Eph 1:10; Col 1:20; 2 Pt 3:10–13).

Christ, having been lifted up from the earth, has drawn all to himself (cf. Jn 12:32). Rising from the dead (cf. Rm 6:9), he sent his life-giving Spirit upon his disciples and through him has established his body, which is the Church, as the universal sacrament of salvation. Sitting at the right hand of the Father, he is continually active in the world, that he might lead men to the Church and through it join them to himself, and that he might make them partakers of his glorious life by nourishing them with his own Body and Blood. Therefore the promised restoration which we are awaiting has already begun in Christ, is carried forward in the mission of the Holy Spirit and through him continues in the Church, in which we learn the meaning of our terrestrial life through our faith, while we perform with hope in the future the work committed to us in this world by the Father, and thus work out our salvation (cf. Phil 2:12).

Already the final age of the world has come upon us (cf. 1 Cor 10:11) and the renovation of the world is irrevocably decreed and is already anticipated in some kind of a real way, for the Church already on this earth is signed with a sanctity which is real although imperfect. However, until there shall be new heavens and a new earth in which justice dwells (cf. 2 Pt 3:13), the pilgrim Church in her sacraments and institutions, which pertain to this present time, has the appearance of this world which is passing, and she herself dwells among creatures who groan and travail in pain until now and await the revelation of the sons of God (cf. Rm 8:19–22).

Joined with Christ in the Church and signed with the Holy Spirit, "who is the pledge of our inheritance" (Eph 1:14), truly we are called and we are sons of God (cf. 1 Jn 3:1), but we have not yet appeared with Christ in glory (cf. Col 3:4), in which we shall be like to God, since we shall see him as he is (cf. 1 Jn 3:2). And therefore "while we are in the body, we are exiled from the Lord" (2 Cor 5:6), and having the first-fruits of the Spirit we groan within ourselves (cf. Rm 8:23) and we desire to be with Christ (cf. Phil 1:23). By that same charity, however, we are urged to live more for him, who died for us and rose again (cf. 2 Cor 5:15). We strive, therefore, to please God in all things (cf. 2 Cor 5:9) and we put on the armor of God, that we may be able to stand against the wiles of the devil and resist in the evil day (cf. Eph 6:11–13). Since, however, we know not the day nor the hour, on our Lord's advice we must be constantly vigilant so that, having finished the course of our earthly life (cf. Heb 9:27), we may merit to enter into the marriage feast with him and to be numbered among the blessed (cf. Mt 25:31–46), and that we may not be ordered to go into eternal fire (cf. Mt 25:41) like the wicked and slothful servant (cf. Mt 25:26), into the exterior darkness where "there will be the weeping and the gnashing of teeth" (Mt 22:13; 25:30). For before we reign with Christ in glory, all of us will be made manifest "before the tribunal of Christ, so that each one may receive what he has won through the body, according to his works, whether good or evil" (2 Cor 5:10), and at the end of the world, "They who have done good shall come forth unto resurrection of life; but those who have done evil unto resurrection of judgment" (Jn 5:29; cf. Mt 25:46). Reckoning, therefore, that "the sufferings of the present time are not worthy to be compared with the glory to come that will be revealed in us" (Rm 8:18; cf. 2 Tm 2:11–12), strong in faith we look for the "blessed hope and the glorious coming of our great God and Savior, Jesus Christ" (Ti 2:13), "who will refashion the body of our lowliness, conforming it to the body of his glory" (Phil 3:21), and who will come "to be glorified in his saints and to be marveled at in all those who have believed" (2 Thes 1:10).

49. Until the Lord shall come in his majesty, and all the angels with him (cf. Mt 25:31) and death being destroyed, all things are subject to him (cf. 1 Cor 15:26–27), some of his disciples are exiles on earth, some

having died are purified, and others are in glory beholding "clearly God himself triune and one, as he is";[1] but all in various ways and degrees are in communion in the same charity of God and neighbor and all sing the same hymn of glory to our God. For all who are in Christ, having his Spirit, form one Church and cleave together in him (cf. Eph 4:16). Therefore the union of the wayfarers with the brethren who have gone to sleep in the peace of Christ is not in the least weakened or interrupted, but on the contrary, according to the perpetual faith of the Church, is strengthened by communication of spiritual goods.[2] For by reason of the fact that those in heaven are more closely united with Christ, they establish the whole Church more firmly in holiness, lend nobility to the worship which the Church offers to God here on earth and in many ways contribute to its greater edification (cf. 1 Cor 12:12–27).[3] For after they have been received into their heavenly home and are present to the Lord (cf. 2 Cor 5:8), through him and with him and in him they do not cease to intercede with the Father for us,[4] showing forth the merits which they won on earth through the one Mediator between God and man (cf. 1 Tm 2:5), serving God in all things and filling up in their flesh those things which are lacking of the sufferings of Christ for his body which is the Church (cf. Col 1:24).[5] Thus by their brotherly interest our weakness is greatly strengthened.

50. Fully conscious of this communion of the whole Mystical Body of Jesus Christ, the pilgrim Church from the very first ages of the Christian religion has cultivated with great piety the memory of the dead,[6] and "because it is a holy and wholesome thought to pray for the dead that they may be loosed from their sins" (2 Mc 12:46), also offers suffrages

---

1. Council of Florence, *Decretum pro Graecis,* Denz. 693, (1305).

2. Besides older documents against any kind of invocation of spirits, from the time of Alexander IV (Sept. 27, 1258), cf. the encyclical of the Holy Office, *De Magnetismi Abusu* (Aug. 4, 1856): *AAS* (1865), 177–178, Denz. 1653–1654 (2823–2825); reply of the Holy Office (April 24, 1917): *AAS* 9 (1917), 268, Denz. 218 (3642).

3. For a synthesis of this Pauline doctrine, cf. Pius XII, Encyclical Letter *Mystici Corporis* (June 19, 1943): *AAS* 35 (1943), 200 and *passim.*

4. Cf., among others, St. Augustine, *Enarr. in Ps.* 85, 24: *PL* 37, 1095; St. Jerome, *Liber Contra Vigilantium* 6: *PL* 23, 344; St. Thomas, *In 4 Sent.,* d. 45, q. 3, a. 2; St. Bonaventure, *In 4 Sent.,* d. 45, a. 3, q. 2; etc.

5. Cf. Pius XII, Encyclical Letter *Mystici Corporis* (June 19, 1943): *AAS* 35 (1943), 245.

6. Cf. many inscriptions in the Roman catacombs.

for them. The Church has always believed that the apostles and Christ's martyrs who had given the supreme witness of faith and charity by the shedding of their blood are closely joined with us in Christ, and she has always venerated them with special devotion, together with the Blessed Virgin Mary and the holy angels.[7] The Church has piously implored the aid of their intercession. To these were soon added also those who had more closely imitated Christ's virginity and poverty,[8] and finally others whom the outstanding practice of the Christian virtues[9] and the divine charisms recommended to the pious devotion and imitation of the faithful.[10]

When we look at the lives of those who have faithfully followed Christ, we are inspired with a new reason for seeking the city that is to come (cf. Heb 13:14; 11:10), and at the same time we are shown a most safe path by which among the vicissitudes of this world, in keeping with the state in life and condition proper to each of us, we will be able to arrive at perfect union with Christ, that is, perfect holiness.[11] In the lives of those who, sharing in our humanity, are, however, more perfectly transformed into the image of Christ (cf. 2 Cor 3:18), God vividly manifests his presence and his face to men. He speaks to us in them, and gives us a sign of his kingdom[12] to which we are strongly drawn, having so great a cloud of witnesses over us (cf. Heb 12:1) and such a witness to the truth of the Gospel.

Nor is it by the title of example only that we cherish the memory of those in heaven, but still more in order that the union of the whole Church may be strengthened in the Spirit by the practice of fraternal charity (cf. Eph 4:1–6). For just as Christian communion among wayfarers brings us closer to Christ, so our companionship with the saints joins

---

7. Cf. Gelasius I, the Decretal *De Libris Recipiendis* 3: *PL* 59, 160, Denz. 165 (353).

8. Cf. St. Methodius, *Symposium,* VII, 3: *GCS* (Bonwetsch), 74.

9. Cf. Benedict XV, *Decretum Approbationis Virtutum in Causa Beatificationis et Canonizationis Servi Dei Ioannis Nepomuceni Neumann: AAS* 14 (1922–23); many allocutions of Pius XI on the saints: *Inviti all'eroismo. Discorsi...* vol. I–III, Rome 1941–1942, *passim;* Pius XII, *Discourses and Radio Messages,* vol. 10, 1949, 37– 43.

10. Cf. Pius XII, Encyclical Letter *Mediator Dei* (Nov. 20, 1947): *AAS* 39 (1947): *AAS* 39 (1947), 581.

11. Cf. Heb 13:7; Eccl 44–50; Heb 2:3–40. Cf. also Pius XII, Encyclical Letter *Mediator Dei* (Nov. 20, 1947): *AAS* 39 (1947): *AAS* 39 (1947), 582–583.

12. Cf. First Vatican Ecumenical Council, Constitution *De Fide Catholica,* ca. 3, Denz. 1794 (3013).

us to Christ, from whom as from its fountain and head issues every grace and the very life of the People of God.[13] It is supremely fitting, therefore, that we love those friends and coheirs of Jesus Christ, who are also our brothers and extraordinary benefactors, that we render due thanks to God for them[14] and "suppliantly invoke them and have recourse to their prayers, their power and help in obtaining benefits from God through his Son, Jesus Christ, who is our Redeemer and Savior."[15] For every genuine testimony of love shown by us to those in heaven, by its very nature tends toward and terminates in Christ, who is the "crown of all saints,"[16] and through him, in God who is wonderful in his saints and is magnified in them.[17]

Our union with the Church in heaven is put into effect in its noblest manner especially in the sacred liturgy, wherein the power of the Holy Spirit acts upon us through sacramental signs. Then, with combined rejoicing we celebrate together the praise of the divine majesty;[18] then all those from every tribe and tongue and people and nation (cf. Rv 5:9) who have been redeemed by the blood of Christ and gathered together into one Church, with one song of praise magnify the one and triune God. Celebrating the Eucharistic Sacrifice, therefore, we are most closely united to the Church in heaven in communion with and venerating the memory first of all of the glorious ever virgin Mary, of Blessed Joseph and the blessed apostles and martyrs and of all the saints.[19]

51. This sacred Council accepts with great devotion this venerable faith of our ancestors regarding this vital fellowship with our brethren who are in heavenly glory or who having died are still being purified, and it proposes again the decrees of the Second Council of Nicea,[20] the Council of Florence[21] and the Council of Trent.[22] And at the same time,

---

13. Cf. Pius XII, Encyclical Letter *Mystici Corporis* (June 19, 1943): *AAS* 35 (1943), 216.

14. In regard to gratitude to the saints, cf. E. Diehl, *Inscriptiones Latinae Christianae Veteres*, 1, Berlin, 1925, nn. 2008, 2382 and *passim*.

15. Council of Trent, Session 25, *De invocatione...Sanctorum:* Denz. 984 (1821).

16. Roman Breviary, *Invitatory for the feast of All Saints*.

17. Cf. e.g., 2 Thes 1:10.

18. Second Vatican Ecumenical Council, Constitution on the Sacred Liturgy *Sacrosanctum Concilium*, ch. 5, n. 104.

19. Canon of the Roman Mass.

20. Second Council of Nicea, Act. VII: Denz. 302 (600).

21. Council of Florence, *Decretum pro Graecis,* Denz. 693 (1304).

22. Council of Trent, Session 35, *De Invocatione, Veneratione et Reliquiis Sanctorum*

in conformity with our own pastoral interests, we urge all concerned, if any abuses, excesses or defects have crept in here or there, to do what is in their power to remove or correct them, and to restore all things to a fuller praise of Christ and of God. Let them therefore teach the faithful that the authentic cult of the saints consists not so much in multiplying external acts, but rather in the greater intensity of our love, whereby, for our own greater good and that of the whole Church, we seek from the saints "example in their way of life, fellowship in their communion, and aid by their intercession."[23] On the other hand, let them teach the faithful that our communion with those in heaven, provided that it is understood in the fuller light of faith according to its genuine nature, in no way weakens, but conversely, more thoroughly enriches the latreutic worship we give to God the Father, through Christ, in the Spirit.[24]

For all of us, who are sons of God and constitute one family in Christ (cf. Heb 3:6) as long as we remain in communion with one another in mutual charity and in one praise of the most holy Trinity, are corresponding with the intimate vocation of the Church and partaking in foretaste the liturgy of consummate glory[25] For when Christ shall appear and the glorious resurrection of the dead will take place, the glory of God will light up the heavenly city and the Lamb will be the lamp thereof (cf. Rv 21:24). Then the whole Church of the saints in the supreme happiness of charity will adore God and "the Lamb who was slain" (Rv 5:12), proclaiming with one voice: "To him who sits upon the throne, and to the Lamb blessing, and honor and glory, and dominion forever and ever" (Rv 5:13–14).

---

et Sacris Imaginibus, Denz. 984–988 (1821–1824); Session 25, *Decretum de Purgatorio,* Denz. 983 (1820); Session 6, *Decretum de Iustificatione,* can. 30: Denz. 840 (1580).

23. From the preface granted to some dioceses.

24. Cf. St. Peter Canisius, *Catechismus Maior seu Summa Doctrinae Christianae,* ch. III, ed. crit. F. Streicher, par. I, pp. 15–16, n. 44 and pp. 100–101, n. 49.

25. Cf. Second Vatican Ecumenical Council, Constitution on the Sacred Liturgy *Sacrosanctum Concilium,* ch. 1, n. 8.

CHAPTER VIII

THE BLESSED VIRGIN MARY, MOTHER OF GOD IN THE MYSTERY OF CHRIST AND THE CHURCH

I. Introduction

52. Wishing in his supreme goodness and wisdom to effect the redemption of the world, "when the fullness of time came, God sent his Son, born of a woman...that we might receive the adoption of sons" (Gal 4:4–5). "He for us men, and for our salvation, came down from heaven, and was incarnate by the Holy Spirit from the Virgin Mary."[1] This divine mystery of salvation is revealed to us and continued in the Church, which the Lord established as his body. Joined to Christ the head and in the unity of fellowship with all his saints, the faithful must in the first place reverence the memory "of the glorious ever Virgin Mary, Mother of our God and Lord Jesus Christ."[2]

53. The Virgin Mary, who at the message of the angel received the Word of God in her heart and in her body and gave Life to the world, is acknowledged and honored as being truly the Mother of God and Mother of the Redeemer. Redeemed by reason of the merits of her Son and united to him by a close and indissoluble tie, she is endowed with the high office and dignity of being the Mother of the Son of God, by which account she is also the beloved daughter of the Father and the temple of the Holy Spirit. Because of this gift of sublime grace she far surpasses all creatures, both in heaven and on earth. At the same time, however, because she belongs to the offspring of Adam she is one with all those who are to be saved. She is "the mother of the members of Christ...having cooperated by charity that faithful might be born in the

---

1. Creed of the Roman Mass: Symbol of Constantinople: Mansi 3, 566; cf. Council of Ephesus, *ibid.* 4, 1130 (and *ibid.* 2, 665 and 4, 1071); Council of Chalcedon, *ibid.* 7, 111–116; Second Council of Constantinople, *ibid.* 9, 375–396.

2. Canon of the Roman Mass.

Church, who are members of that head."[3] Wherefore she is hailed as a preeminent and singular member of the Church, and as its type and excellent exemplar in faith and charity. The Catholic Church, taught by the Holy Spirit, honors her with filial affection and piety as a most beloved mother.

54. Wherefore this holy synod, in expounding the doctrine on the Church, in which the divine Redeemer works salvation, intends to describe with diligence both the role of the Blessed Virgin in the mystery of the Incarnate Word and the Mystical Body, and the duties of redeemed mankind toward the Mother of God, who is mother of Christ and mother of men, particularly of the faithful. It does not, however, have it in mind to give a complete doctrine on Mary, nor does it wish to decide those questions which the work of theologians has not yet fully clarified. Those opinions, therefore, may be lawfully retained which are propounded in Catholic schools concerning her, who occupies a place in the Church which is the highest after Christ and yet very close to us.[4]

II. The Role of the Blessed Mother in the Economy of Salvation

55. The Sacred Scriptures of both the Old and the New Testament, as well as ancient Tradition, show the role of the Mother of the Savior in the economy of salvation in an ever clearer light and draw attention to it. The books of the Old Testament describe the history of salvation, by which the coming of Christ into the world was slowly prepared. These earliest documents, as they are read in the Church and are understood in the light of a further and full revelation, bring the figure of the woman, Mother of the Redeemer, into a gradually clearer light. When it is looked at in this way, she is already prophetically foreshadowed in the promise of victory over the serpent, which was given to our first parents after their fall into sin (cf. Gn 3:15). Likewise she is the Virgin who shall conceive and bear a son, whose name will be called Emmanuel (cf. Is 7:14; cf. Mi 5:2–3; Mt 1:22–23). She stands out among the poor and humble of the Lord, who confidently hope for and receive salvation from him. With her, the exalted Daughter of Sion, and after a long ex-

---

3. St. Augustine, *De S. Virginitate* 6: *PL* 40, 399.
4. Cf. Paul VI, *Allocution to the Council* (Dec. 4, 1963): *AAS* 56 (1964), 37.

pectation of the promise, the times are fulfilled and the new economy established, when the Son of God took a human nature from her, that he might in the mysteries of his flesh free man from sin.

56. The Father of mercies willed that the Incarnation should be preceded by the acceptance of her who was predestined to be the mother of his Son, so that just as a woman contributed to death, so also a woman should contribute to life. That is true in outstanding fashion of the mother of Jesus, who gave to the world him who is Life itself and who renews all things, and who was enriched by God with the gifts which befit such a role. It is no wonder therefore that the usage prevailed among the Fathers whereby they called the mother of God entirely holy and free from all stain of sin, as though fashioned by the Holy Spirit and formed as a new creature.[5] Adorned from the first instant of her conception with the radiance of an entirely unique holiness, the Virgin of Nazareth is greeted, on God's command, by an angel messenger as "full of grace" (cf. Lk 1:28), and to the heavenly messenger she replies: "Behold the handmaid of the Lord, be it done unto me according to thy word" (Lk 1:38). Thus Mary, a daughter of Adam, consenting to the divine Word, became the mother of Jesus, the one and only Mediator. Embracing God's salvific will with a full heart and impeded by no sin, she devoted herself totally as a handmaid of the Lord to the person and work of her Son, under him and with him, by the grace of almighty God, serving the mystery of redemption. Rightly, therefore, the holy Fathers see her as used by God not merely in a passive way, but as freely cooperating in the work of human salvation through faith and obedience. For, as St. Irenaeus says, she "being obedient, became the cause of salvation for herself and for the whole human race."[6] Hence not a few of the early Fathers gladly assert in their preaching, "The knot of Eve's disobedience was untied by Mary's obedience; what the virgin Eve bound through her unbelief, the Virgin Mary loosened by her faith."[7] Comparing Mary with

---

5. Cf. St. Germanus of Constantinople, *Hom. in Annunt. Deiparae: PG* 98, 328 A; *In Dorm.* 2: col. 357; Anastasius of Antioch, *Serm. 2 de Annunt.,* 2: *PG* 89, 1377 AB; *Serm.* 3, 2: col. 1388 C; St. Andrew of Crete, *Can. in B. V. Nat.* 4: *PG* 97, 1321 B; *In B. V. Nat.,* 1: col. 812 A; *Hom. in Dorm.* 1: col. 1068 C; St. Sophronius, *Or. 2 in Annunt.,* 18: *PG* 87 (3), 3237 BD.

6. St. Irenaeus, *Against Heretics,* III, 22, 4: *PG* 7, 959 A; Harvey, 2, 123.

7. St. Irenaeus, *Against Heretics,* III, 22, 4: *PG* 7, 959 A; Harvey, 2, 124.

Eve, they call Mary "the Mother of the living,"[8] and still more often they say: "death through Eve, life through Mary."[9]

57. This union of the Mother with the Son in the work of salvation is made manifest from the time of Christ's virginal conception up to his death. It is shown first of all when Mary, arising in haste to go to visit Elizabeth, is greeted by her as blessed because of her belief in the promise of salvation and the precursor leaped with joy in the womb of his mother (cf. Lk 1:41–45). This union is manifest also at the birth of our Lord, who did not diminish his mother's virginal integrity but sanctified it[10] when the Mother of God joyfully showed her firstborn Son to the shepherds and Magi. When she presented him to the Lord in the temple, making the offering of the poor, she heard Simeon foretelling at the same time that her Son would be a sign of contradiction and that a sword would pierce the mother's soul, that out of many hearts thoughts might be revealed (cf. Lk 2:34–35). When the child Jesus was lost and they had sought him sorrowing, his parents found him in the temple, taken up with the things that were his Father's business, and they did not understand the word of their Son. His Mother indeed kept these things to be pondered over in her heart (cf. Lk 2:41–51).

58. In the public life of Jesus, Mary makes significant appearances. This is so even at the very beginning, when at the marriage feast of Cana, moved with pity, she brought about by her intercession the beginning of miracles of Jesus the Messiah (cf. Jn 2:1–11). In the course of her Son's preaching she received the words whereby, in extolling a kingdom beyond the calculations and bonds of flesh and blood, he declared blessed (cf. Mk 3:35; par. Lk 11:27–28) those who heard and kept the Word of God, as she was faithfully doing (cf. Lk 2:19, 51). After this manner the Blessed Virgin advanced in her pilgrimage of faith, and faithfully persevered in her union with her Son unto the cross, where she stood, in keeping with the divine plan (cf. Jn 19:25), grieving exceed-

---

8. St. Epiphanius, *Haer.* 78, 18: *PG* 42, 728 CD; 729 AB.

9. St. Jerome, *Epist.* 22, 21: *PL* 22, 408; cf. St. Augustine, *Serm.* 51, 2, 3: *PL* 38, 335; *Serm.* 232, 2: col. 1108; St. Cyril of Jerusalem, *Catech.* 12, 15: *PG* 33, 741 AB; St. John Chrysostom, *In Ps.* 44, 7: *PG* 55, 193; St. John Damascene, *Hom. 2 in Dorm. B.M.V.*, 3: *PG* 96, 728.

10. Cf. Council of Lateran, (649 AD), can. 3: Mansi 10, 1151; St. Leo the Great, *Epist. ad Flav.: PL* 54, 759; Council of Chalcedon: Mansi 7, 462; St. Ambrose, *De Inst. Virg.: PL* 16, 320.

ingly with her only begotten Son, uniting herself with a maternal heart with his sacrifice, and lovingly consenting to the immolation of this victim which she herself had brought forth. Finally, she was given by the same Christ Jesus dying on the cross as a mother to his disciple with these words: "Woman, behold thy son" (cf. Jn 19:26–27).[11]

59. But since it has pleased God not to manifest solemnly the mystery of the salvation of the human race before he would pour forth the Spirit promised by Christ, we see the apostles before the day of Pentecost "persevering with one mind in prayer with the women and Mary, the Mother of Jesus, and with his brethren" (Acts 1:14), and Mary by her prayers imploring the gift of the Spirit, who had already overshadowed her in the annunciation. Finally, the Immaculate Virgin, preserved free from all guilt of original sin,[12] on the completion of her earthly sojourn was taken up body and soul into heavenly glory[13] and exalted by the Lord as queen of the universe, that she might be the more fully conformed to her Son, the Lord of lords (cf. Rv 19:16) and the conqueror of sin and death.[14]

III. On the Blessed Virgin and the Church

60. There is but one Mediator, as we know from the words of the Apostle, "for there is one God and one mediator of God and men, the man Christ Jesus, who gave himself a redemption for all" (1 Tm 2:5–6). The maternal duty of Mary toward men in no wise obscures or diminishes this unique mediation of Christ, but rather shows his power. For all the salvific influence of the Blessed Virgin on men originates, not from some inner necessity, but from the divine pleasure. It flows forth from the superabundance of the merits of Christ, rests on his mediation, de-

11. Cf. Pius XII, Encyclical Letter *Mystici Corporis* (June 29, 1943): *AAS* 35 (1943), 247–248.

12. Cf. Pius IX, Bull *Ineffabilis* (Dec. 8, 1854): Acts of Pius IX, I, I, 616; Denz. 1641 (2803).

13. Cf. Pius XII, Apostolic Constitution *Munificentissimus* (Nov. 1, 1950): *AAS* 42 (1950): Denz. 2333 (3903); cf. St. John Damascene, *Enc. in Dorm. Dei Genitricis,* Hom. 2 and 3: *PG* 96, 721–761, especially col. 728 B; St. Germanus of Constantinople, *In St. Dei Gen. Dorm., Serm.* 1: *PG* 98 (6), 340–348; *Serm.* 3: col. 361; St. Modestus of Jerusalem, *In Dorm. SS. Deiparae: PG* 86 (2), 3277–3312.

14. Cf. Pius XII, Encyclical Letter *Ad Coeli Reginam* (Oct. 11, 1954): *AAS* 46 (1954), 633–636; Denz. 3913 ff.; cf. St. Andrew of Crete, *Hom. 3 in Dorm. SS. Deiparae: PG* 97, 1089–1109; St. John Damascene, *De Fide Orth.,* IV, 14: *PG* 94, 1153–1161.

pends entirely on it and draws all its power from it. In no way does it impede, but rather does it foster the immediate union of the faithful with Christ.

61. Predestined from eternity to be the Mother of God by that decree of divine providence which determined the Incarnation of the Word, the Blessed Virgin was on this earth the virgin Mother of the Redeemer, and above all others and in a singular way the generous associate and humble handmaid of the Lord. She conceived, brought forth and nourished Christ. She presented him to the Father in the temple, and was united with him by compassion as he died on the cross. In this singular way she cooperated by her obedience, faith, hope and burning charity in the work of the Savior in giving back supernatural life to souls. Wherefore she is our mother in the order of grace.

62. This maternity of Mary in the order of grace began with the consent which she gave in faith at the annunciation and which she sustained without wavering beneath the cross, and lasts until the eternal fulfillment of all the elect. Taken up to heaven she did not lay aside this salvific duty, but by her constant intercession continued to bring us the gifts of eternal salvation.[15] By her maternal charity, she cares for the brethren of her Son, who still journey on earth surrounded by dangers and difficulties, until they are led into the happiness of their true home. Therefore the Blessed Virgin is invoked by the Church under the titles of Advocate, Auxiliatrix, Adjutrix and Mediatrix.[16] This, however, is to be so understood that it neither takes away from nor adds anything to the dignity and efficaciousness of Christ the one Mediator.[17]

For no creature could ever be counted as equal with the incarnate Word and Redeemer. Just as the priesthood of Christ is shared in various ways both by the ministers and by the faithful, and as the one goodness of God is really communicated in different ways to his creatures, so also

---

15. Cf. Kleutgen, corrected text *De Mysterio Verbi Incarnati,* ch. IV: Mansi 53, 290; cf. St. Andrew of Crete, *In Nat. Mariae, Serm.* 4: *PG* 97, 865 A; St. Germanus of Constantinople, *In Annunt. Deiparae: PG* 98, 321 BC; *In Dorm. Deiparae,* III: col. 361 D; St. John Damascene, *In Dorm. B. V. Mariae,* Hom. 1, 8: *PG* 96, 712 BC–713 A.

16. Cf. Leo XIII, Encyclical Letter *Adiutricem Populi* (Sept. 5, 1895): *AAS* 15 (1895–96), 303; St. Pius X, Encyclical Letter *Ad Diem Illum* (Feb. 2, 1904): *Acta,* I, 154 Denz. 1978a (3370); Pius XI, Encyclical Letter *Miserentissimus* (May 8, 1928): *AAS* 20 (1928), 178; Pius XII, *Radio Message* (May 13, 1946): *AAS* 38 (1946), 266.

17. St. Ambrose, *Epist.* 63: *PL* 16, 1218.

the unique mediation of the Redeemer does not exclude but rather gives rise to a manifold cooperation which is but a sharing in this one source.

The Church does not hesitate to profess this subordinate role of Mary. It knows it through unfailing experience of it and commends it to the hearts of the faithful, so that encouraged by this maternal help they may the more intimately adhere to the Mediator and Redeemer.

63. By reason of the gift and role of divine maternity, by which she is united with her Son, the Redeemer, and with his singular graces and functions, the Blessed Virgin is also intimately united with the Church. As St. Ambrose taught, the Mother of God is a type of the Church in the order of faith, charity and perfect union with Christ.[18] For in the mystery of the Church, which is itself rightly called mother and virgin, the Blessed Virgin stands out in eminent and singular fashion as exemplar both of virgin and mother.[19] By her belief and obedience, not knowing man but overshadowed by the Holy Spirit, as the new Eve she brought forth on earth the very Son of the Father, showing an undefiled faith, not in the word of the ancient serpent, but in that of God's messenger. The Son whom she brought forth is he whom God placed as the first-born among many brethren (Rm 8:29), namely the faithful, in whose birth and education she cooperates with a maternal love.

64. The Church indeed, contemplating her hidden sanctity, imitating her charity and faithfully fulfilling the Father's will, by receiving the Word of God in faith becomes herself a mother. By her preaching she brings forth to a new and immortal life the sons who are born to her in baptism, conceived of the Holy Spirit and born of God. She herself is a virgin, who keeps whole and entire the faith given to her by her spouse. Imitating the mother of her Lord, and by the power of the Holy Spirit, she keeps with virginal purity an entire faith, a firm hope and a sincere charity.[20]

65. But while in the most holy Virgin the Church has already reached that perfection whereby she is without spot or wrinkle, the fol-

---

18. St. Ambrose, *Expos. Lc.* II, 7: *PL* 15, 1555.

19. Cf. Pseudo-Peter Damian, *Serm.* 63: *PL* 144, 861 AB; Godfrey of St. Victor, *In Nat. B. M.,* Ms. Paris, Mazarine, 1002, fol. 109; Gerhoch of Reichersberg, *De Gloria et Honore Filii Hominis,* 10: *PL* 194, 1105 AB.

20. St. Ambrose, *loc. cit.* and *Expos. Lc.* X, 24–25: *PL* 15, 1810; St. Augustine, *In Io. Tr.* 13, 12: *PL* 35, 1499; cf. *Serm.* 191, 2, 3: *PL* 38, 1010, etc.; cf. also Ven. Bede, *In Lc. Expos.* I, ca 2: *PL* 92, 330; Isaac of Stella, *Serm.* 51: *PL* 194, 1863 A.

lowers of Christ still strive to increase in holiness by conquering sin (cf. Eph 5:27). And so they turn their eyes to Mary, who shines forth to the whole community of the elect as the model of virtues. Piously meditating on her and contemplating her in the light of the Word made man, the Church with reverence enters more intimately into the great mystery of the Incarnation and becomes more and more like her spouse. For Mary, who since her entry into salvation history unites in herself and recchocs the greatest teachings of the faith as she is proclaimed and venerated, calls the faithful to her Son and his sacrifice and to the love of the Father. Seeking after the glory of Christ, the Church becomes more like her exalted type, and continually progresses in faith, hope and charity, seeking and doing the will of God in all things. Hence, the Church, in her apostolic work also, justly looks to her, who brought forth Christ, who was conceived of the Holy Spirit and born of the Virgin, that through the Church he may be born and may increase in the hearts of the faithful also. The Virgin in her own life lived an example of that maternal love, by which it behooves that all should be animated who cooperate in the apostolic mission of the Church for the regeneration of men

IV. The Cult of the Blessed Virgin in the Church

66. Placed by the grace of God, as God's Mother, next to her Son and exalted above all angels and men, Mary intervened in the mysteries of Christ and is justly honored by a special cult in the Church. Clearly, from earliest times the Blessed Virgin is honored under the title of Mother of God, under whose protection the faithful took refuge in all their dangers and necessities.[21] Hence, after the Synod of Ephesus the cult of the People of God toward Mary wonderfully increased in veneration and love, in invocation and imitation, according to her own prophetic words: "All generations shall call me blessed, because he that is mighty hath done great things to me" (Lk 1:48). This cult, as it always existed, although it is altogether singular, differs essentially from the cult of adoration which is offered to the incarnate Word, as well to the Father and the Holy Spirit, and it is most favorable to it. The various forms of piety toward the Mother of God, which the Church, within the limits of sound and orthodox doctrine, according to the conditions of

---

21. *Sub tuum praesidium.*

time and place, and the nature and ingenuity of the faithful, has approved, bring it about that while the Mother is honored, the Son, through whom all things have their being (cf. Col 1:15–16) and in whom it has pleased the Father that all fullness should dwell (Col 1:19), is rightly known, loved and glorified, and that all his commands are observed.

67. This most holy synod deliberately teaches this Catholic doctrine and at the same time admonishes all the sons of the Church that the cult, especially the liturgical cult, of the Blessed Virgin be generously fostered, and the practices and exercises of piety, recommended by the magisterium of the Church toward her in the course of centuries, be made of great moment, and those decrees, which have been given in the early days regarding the cult of images of Christ, the Blessed Virgin and the saints, be religiously observed.[22] But it exhorts theologians and preachers of the divine Word to abstain zealously both from all gross exaggerations as well as from petty narrow-mindedness in considering the singular dignity of the Mother of God.[23] Following the study of Sacred Scripture, the holy Fathers, the doctors and liturgy of the Church, and under the guidance of the Church's magisterium, let them rightly illustrate the duties and privileges of the Blessed Virgin which always look to Christ, the source of all truth, sanctity and piety. Let them assiduously keep away from whatever, either by word or deed, could lead separated brethren or any other into error regarding the true doctrine of the Church. Let the faithful remember moreover that true devotion consists neither in sterile or transitory affection, nor in a certain vain credulity, but proceeds from true faith, by which we are led to know the excellence of the Mother of God, and we are moved to a filial love toward our mother and to the imitation of her virtues.

V. Mary the Sign of Created Hope and Solace to the Wandering People of God

68. In the interim, just as the Mother of Jesus, glorified in body and soul in heaven, is the image and beginning of the Church as it is to be perfected in the world to come, so too does she shine forth on earth, until

---

22. Second Council of Nicea (787): Mansi 13, 378–379; Denz. 302 (600–601); Council of Trent, Session 25: Mansi 33, 171–172.

23. Cf. Pius XII, *Radio Message* (Oct. 24, 1954): *AAS* 46 (1954), 679; Encyclical Letter *Ad Coeli Reginam* (Oct. 11, 1954): *AAS* 46 (1954), 637.

the day of the Lord shall come (cf. 2 Pt 3:10), as a sign of sure hope and solace to the People of God during its sojourn on earth.

69. It gives great joy and comfort to this holy and general synod that even among the separated brethren there are some who give due honor to the Mother of our Lord and Savior, especially among the Orientals, who with devout mind and fervent impulse give honor to the Mother of God, ever virgin.[24] The entire body of the faithful pours forth urgent supplications to the Mother of God and Mother of men, that she, who aided the beginnings of the Church by her prayers, may now, exalted as she is above all the angels and saints, intercede before her Son in the fellowship of all the saints, until all families of people, whether they are honored with the title of Christian or whether they still do not know the Savior, may be happily gathered together in peace and harmony into one People of God, for the glory of the most holy and undivided Trinity.

Each and all these items which are set forth in this dogmatic Constitution have met with the approval of the Council fathers. And We by the apostolic power given Us by Christ, together with the venerable fathers in the Holy Spirit, approve, decree and establish it and command that what has thus been decided in the Council be promulgated for the glory of God.

Given in Rome at St. Peter's on November 21, 1964.

---

24. Cf. Pius XI, Encyclical Letter *Ecclesiam Dei* (Nov. 12, 1923): *AAS* 15 (1923) 581; Pius XII, Encyclical Letter *Fulgens Corona* (Sept. 8, 1953): *AAS* 45 (1953), 590–591.

APPENDIX
FROM THE ACTS OF THE COUNCIL

Notificationes

Given by the Secretary General of the Council at the 123rd General Congregation, November 16, 1964.

A question has arisen regarding the precise *theological note* which should be attached to the doctrine that is set forth in the Schema *De Ecclesia* and is being put to a vote.

The Theological Commission has given the following response regarding the *Modi* that have to do with Chapter III of the *De Ecclesia* Schema: "As is self-evident, the Council's text must always be interpreted in accordance with the general rules that are known to all."

On this occasion the Theological Commission makes reference to its Declaration of March 6, 1964, the text of which we transcribe here:

> Taking conciliar custom into consideration and also the pastoral purpose of the present Council, the sacred Council defines as binding on the Church only those things in matters of faith and morals which it shall openly declare to be binding. The rest of the things which the sacred Council sets forth, inasmuch as they are the teaching of the Church's supreme magisterium, ought to be accepted and embraced by each and every one of Christ's faithful according to the mind of the sacred Council. The mind of the Council becomes known either from the matter treated or from its manner of speaking, in accordance with the norms of theological interpretation.

The following was published as an appendix to the official Latin version of the Constitution on the Church.

A preliminary note of explanation is being given to the Council Fathers from higher authority, regarding the *Modi* bearing on Chapter III of the Schema *De Ecclesia;* the doctrine set forth in Chapter III ought to be explained and understood in accordance with the meaning and intent of this explanatory note.

Preliminary Note of Explanation

The Commission has decided to preface the assessment of the *Modi* with the following general observations.

1. "College" is not understood in a *strictly juridical* sense, that is as a group of equals who entrust their power to their president, but as a stable group whose structure and authority must be learned from revelation. For this reason, in reply to *Modus* 12 it is expressly said of the Twelve that the Lord set them up "as a college or *stable group*" (cf. also *Modus* 53, c).

For the same reason, the words *"ordo"* or *"corpus"* are used throughout with reference to the college of bishops. The parallel between Peter and the rest of the apostles on the one hand, and between the Supreme Pontiff and the bishops on the other hand, does not imply the transmission of the apostles' extraordinary power to their successors; nor does it imply, as is obvious, *equality* between the head of the college and its members, but only a *proportionality* between the first relationship (Peter—apostles) and the second (Pope—bishops). Thus the Commission decided to write *"pari ratione,"* not *"eadem ratione,"* in number 22 (cf. *Modus* 57).

2. A person becomes a *member of the college* by virtue of episcopal consecration and by hierarchical communion with the head of the college and with its members (cf. n. 22, end of par. 1).

In his *consecration* a person is given an *ontological* participation in the *sacred* functions *[munera];* this is absolutely clear from Tradition, liturgical tradition included. The word "functions *[munera]* " is used deliberately instead of the word "powers *[potestates]*," because the latter word could be understood as a power *fully ready to act.* But for this power to be fully ready to act, there must be a further *canonical* or *juridical determination* through the hierarchical authority. This determination of power can consist in the granting of a particular office or in the allotment of subjects, and it is done according to the *norms* approved by the supreme authority. An additional norm of this sort is required by the *very nature of the case,* because it involves functions *[munera]* which must be exercised *by many subjects* cooperating in a hierarchical manner in accordance with Christ's will. It is evident that this "communion" was applied in the Church's life according to the circumstances of the time, before it was codified as *law.*

For this reason it is clearly stated that *hierarchical* communion with the head and members of the Church is required. *Communion* is a notion which is held in high honor in the ancient Church (and also today, especially in the East). However, it is not understood as some kind of vague *disposition,* but as an *organic reality* which requires a juridical form and is animated by charity. Hence the Commission, almost unanimously, decided that this wording should be used: "in *hierarchical* communion" (cf. *Modus* 40 and the statements on canonical mission, n. 24).

The documents of recent Pontiffs regarding the jurisdiction of bishops must be interpreted in terms of this necessary determination of powers.

3. The college, which does not exist without the head, is said "to exist *also as the subject of supreme and full power* in the universal Church." This must be admitted of necessity so that the fullness of power belonging to the Roman Pontiff is not called into question. For the college, always and of necessity, includes its head, *because in the college he preserves unhindered his function as Christ's Vicar and as Pastor of the universal Church.* In other words, it is not a distinction between the Roman Pontiff and the bishops taken collectively, but a distinction between the Roman Pontiff taken separately and the Roman Pontiff together with the bishops. Since the Supreme Pontiff is *head* of the college, he alone is able to perform certain actions which are not at all within the competence of the bishops, e.g., convoking the college and directing it, approving norms of action, etc. (cf. *Modus* 81). It is up to the judgment of the Supreme Pontiff, to whose care Christ's whole flock has been entrusted, to determine, according to the needs of the Church as they change over the course of centuries, the way in which this care may best be exercised—whether in a personal or a collegial way. The Roman Pontiff, taking account of the Church's welfare, proceeds according to his own discretion in arranging, promoting and approving the exercise of collegial activity.

4. As supreme Pastor of the Church, the Supreme Pontiff can always exercise his power at will, as his very office demands. Though it is always in existence, the college is not as a result permanently engaged in *strictly* collegial activity; the Church's Tradition makes this clear. In other words, the college is not always "fully active *[in actu pleno]*";

rather, it acts as a college in the strict sense only from time to time and only *with the consent of its head.* The phrase "with the consent of its head" is used to avoid the idea of *dependence* on some kind of *outsider;* the term "consent" suggests rather *communion* between the head and the members, and implies the need for an *act* which belongs properly to the competence of the head. This is explicitly affirmed in number 22, paragraph 2, and is explained at the end of that section. The word *"only"* takes in all cases. It is evident from this that the *norms* approved by the supreme authority must always be observed (cf. *Modus* 84).

It is clear throughout that it is a question of the bishops acting in *conjunction with their head,* never of the bishops acting *independently* of the Pope. In the latter instance, without the action of the head, the bishops are not able to act as a college: this is clear from the concept of "college." This hierarchical communion of all the bishops with the Supreme Pontiff is certainly firmly established in Tradition.

N.B. Without hierarchical communion the ontologico-sacramental function *[munus],* which is to be distinguished from the juridico-canonical aspect, *cannot* be exercised. However, the Commission has decided that it should not enter into question of *liceity* and *validity.* These questions are left to theologians to discuss—specifically the question of the power exercised *de facto* among the separated Eastern Churches, about which there are various explanations.

†Pericle Felici
Titular Archbishop of Samosata
Secretary General of the
Second Vatican Ecumenical Council

DECREE ON THE CATHOLIC CHURCHES OF THE EASTERN RITE

Orientalium Ecclesiarum

Promulgated by
His Holiness Pope Paul VI
On November 21, 1964

INTRODUCTION

The fact that the modern world has brought people closer together greatly influenced the bishops at Vatican II. Advances in travel and the media have facilitated communication and interaction, leading to a heightened awareness of the unity of the human family (cf. *GS* 33; *LG* 1). In these circumstances the contemporary Church is even more conscious of the gift of catholic unity, in part because of this increased sense of solidarity among peoples. The Church has always been conscious of its own catholicity, that wonderful universality which embraces men and women of all cultures and conditions. Today, because "the Church herself knows how richly she has profited by the history and development of humanity" (*GS* 44), this consciousness has been deepened.

The *Decree on the Eastern Catholic Churches (OE)* is, in part, a product of this deepened consciousness, as well as of the Council's ecumenical commitment. The Catholic Churches of the Eastern rites have much in common with the separated Eastern Churches, and can play a special role in dialogue with them.

The pastoral nature of Vatican II is also evident in *OE's* concern to give practical and juridical expression to the doctrine of the Church about the Church, in this case, the full and equal ecclesial dignity and status of the Eastern Catholic Churches. This juridical concern is evident in articles 7–11 treating patriarchs and articles 12–23 treating norms regarding the sacraments and divine worship. This includes such matters as the date of Easter, the permanent diaconate, validity and liceity of marriages between Eastern Catholics and baptized Eastern non-Catholics, and the observance of Sunday.

Another example of the decree's pastoral character is its call for establishing parishes and a special hierarchy to serve the needs of the faithful who belong to one of the various rites of the Church (cf. *OE* 4).

This is the responsibility of bishops, who, according to *Christus Dominus,* are united with the Successor of Peter in solicitude for all the churches (cf. *CD* 2, 3). This solicitude requires that diocesan bishops should provide for the spiritual needs of the faithful of a different rite "either through priests or parishes of that rite or through an episcopal vicar endowed with the necessary faculties" (*CD* 23).

The pastoral aim of this directive is "the protection and advancement of all the individual churches" (*OE* 4). The overall intention of the decree is similarly stated: that the Eastern Churches "may flourish and with new apostolic vigor execute the task entrusted to them" (*OE* 1). In this decree Vatican II takes up a number of issues specific to the Eastern Churches concerning the general goal of the Council: the renewal of the Church and the advancement of its mission in the world.

This goal, in turn, is based on the Church's understanding of the place of the individual churches or rites in God's plan for the Church. Here we enter the domain of doctrine, the domain of the Church's self-understanding based on divine revelation and the experience of nearly 2000 years of living the mystery of Christ. This is where we discover that *OE* greatly depends on *Lumen Gentium,* especially article thirteen on catholic unity.

The description of the Church in *OE* probably does not correspond to the experience of many Catholics of the Latin Rite. They often do not think of themselves as belonging to a church or rite that, along with other churches, constitutes the Catholic Church. Lack of exposure to the various rites of the Church results in many Catholics of the Latin Rite being virtually unaware of the other churches or rites which are as fully Catholic as they, and equal in dignity (cf. *OE* 3). This is seen in the often experienced need for clarification of the term "Roman Catholic." All Catholics are not "Roman" if this is restricted to a synonym for one of the papal titles, "Patriarch of the West." However, all Catholics are "Roman" in the sense of belonging to the universal Church which Peter was commissioned to shepherd (cf. *LG* 8) and which, by the will of Christ, has been "entrusted to the pastoral government of the Roman Pontiff" (*OE* 3). This is because Christ willed that the Successor of Peter should be the "the perpetual and visible principle and foundation of unity of both the bishops and of the faithful" (*LG* 23) and "supreme shepherd and teacher of all the faithful" (*LG* 25).

Yet, the reality of the universal Church being present in and constituted by particular churches (cf. *LG* 23) is, at least implicitly, regularly experienced by the faithful of the Latin Rite. This occurs in the liturgy of the Eucharist which is celebrated in communion with the bishop of the particular church and the Pope, who are mentioned by name in the Eucharistic prayer.

OE closely parallels *LG* 14 in presenting the Church as the communion of all the faithful "who are organically united" (*OE* 2). The first principle of this communion is the Holy Spirit. The Church's unity is constituted above all by participation in the life of God through grace (cf. *LG* 4). This life is essentially one and the same in all believers. The Spirit has worked in diverse ways throughout the history of the Church. In conjunction with human and cultural factors, this has resulted in the richness of the various rites. The Eastern Churches or rites are constituted as a result of groups of Christians being unified from an early time according to a combination of these factors. *OE* recognizes the suitability of such churches or rites, since this is "more harmonious with the character of their faithful and more suited to the promotion of the good of souls" (*OE* 5).

The Catholic unity of the Church is a gift for which Christ prayed (cf. Jn 17:21) and offered himself in sacrifice to the Father. The Church's first and most fundamental attitude is gratitude for this gift, expressed in the Council's declaration of esteem and joy for the Eastern Churches and their living witness to the apostolic tradition (cf. *OE* 1, 30).

A second attitude is a sense of responsibility for this gift. The homogenization of culture poses the risk of losing elements of some cultures as the world changes. This is a particular concern for the Eastern Rite Churches, considering that in some cases half or more of their members live among Catholics of the Western Rite.

The Church, too, is concerned about losing the richness that contributes to its resplendent beauty. The fullness of grace in Jesus Christ cannot be completely expressed or realized by any one member or part of the Church. A diversity of gifts is required for the well-being of the whole Church. This wonderful diversity-in-unity within the Church has resulted from the diverse historical situations and challenges the Church has faced, combined with the various cultural goods of peoples.

Preserving the integrity of the Eastern Churches is not a matter of simply "making room" for groups that wish to retain their own customs and traditions. It is certainly not just a question of preserving ancient ways for their own sake. As already seen, the existence of these churches corresponds to the diverse characters of their faithful and promotes their good (cf. *OE* 5). For these reasons, "their legitimate liturgical rite and their established way of life...may not be altered except to obtain for themselves an organic improvement" (*OE* 6). It can happen that the institutional structures which are intended to express, preserve and develop God's gifts can begin to overshadow them. There is always a need to "return to the sources" in order to examine the present situation in the light of original and defining experiences. Vatican II called all members of the Church to do exactly that, to return to the sources of ecclesial life—the revealed Word of God, the sacraments, prayer—in order to deepen their life in Christ. In a manner similar to the call to religious orders to "return" to the charism of their founders (cf. *PC* 2), the decree calls upon the Eastern Churches "to return to their ancestral traditions" (*OE* 6).

The doctrinal foundation for *OE* is article thirteen of *Lumen Gentium* on the universality or catholicity of the one People of God. The first paragraph underscores the universality of the divine call. No one is excluded from the call to belong to the new People of God. The second paragraph teaches that although drawn from many nations and races, God's people and kingdom are one. Those who belong to the Church remain citizens of their nation and members of their race, yet they form a communion among themselves. The various participants bring into this communion all that is good in their cultural heritage, which is purified and strengthened. This second paragraph ends with a beautiful vision of the Church being the place where the various gifts of peoples are brought together to be offered to God.

This leads to the emphasis on the positive contribution each part of the Church makes. Each part enriches the whole through sharing its goods and exercising its gifts in communion. Because these gifts and goods come from God, the Church esteems them and welcomes them with generosity.

Particular churches are those churches in communion with the Catholic Church through communion with the Bishop of Rome and which possess a further, distinctive unity by reason of historical, liturgical and disciplinary factors. Such churches "hold a rightful place" and "retain their own traditions, without in any way opposing the primacy of the Chair of Peter" (*LG* 13). This diversity is not opposed to this primacy;

Lumen Gentium even specifies that the Bishop of Rome has a positive duty to see that the riches of God's gifts reflected in this legitimate diversity are protected. This protection is not an end in itself, but is meant to foster authentic catholic unity. The differences among the churches are to be protected to the extent that they "do not hinder unity but rather contribute toward it" (*LG* 13).

The pastoral nature of Vatican II and this decree is evident in its ecumenical concern. Thus, *OE* is also closely associated with the *Decree on Ecumenism*. Because of their closeness to those Eastern Christians separated from full communion with the Catholic Church, the Eastern Rite Churches have a special responsibility with regard to ecumenical dialogue with them. This recognition of responsibility itself expresses the equality in dignity among the churches united in the universal Church. To assume responsibility supposes possessing the requisite gifts. As authentic churches, they possess precisely what the universal Church itself, which exists in them, possesses. *OE* summarizes the ecumenical means put forward in the *Decree on Ecumenism:* prayer, example, fidelity to the ancient traditions of the East, greater knowledge of one another, collaboration and mutual respect (*OE* 24).

The full Catholic communion which exists in the Eastern Catholic Churches has ecumenical value of itself. It indicates the rich catholic unity of the Church and shows the possibility of maintaining distinct traditions of ecclesiastical order and liturgical celebration. The separated Eastern Churches can see in them to what a degree their precious heritage is valued and protected in full Catholic communion.

The Council's understanding of the varying degrees of communion as stated in the *Decree on Ecumenism* is concretely applied in *OE*. First, it requires a close reading of the text. Although it refers primarily to the Eastern Catholic Churches, at times the Orthodox Churches are also meant. For example, articles five and six also refer to the Orthodox Churches due to the rich heritage they have in common with the Catholic Eastern Churches.

A second application concerns admittance of separated Eastern Christians to the sacraments of Penance, Eucharist and Anointing of the Sick (cf. *OE* 27). *OE* establishes "a mild policy" guided by "the needs of the salvation of souls and their spiritual good" (*OE* 26) which allows Eastern Christians separated from the Catholic Church to receive these sacraments "if they ask of their own accord and have the right dispositions" (*OE* 27). Reciprocally, on the condition that access to a Catholic priest is not possible, Catholics may seek these sacraments from ordained ministers of the separated Eastern Churches.

The pastoral concerns for ecumenism and for the juridical life of the Church converge in the conclusion which states that the decree's canonical directives are normative "till such time as the Catholic Church and the separated Easters Churches come together into complete unity" (*OE* 30). In 1995 Pope John Paul II issued the apostolic letter *Orientale Lumen,* which incorporates the theme of the new evangelization. Using the "question-answer" dynamic of *Gaudium et Spes,* the document stresses that "the cry of men and women today seeking meaning for their lives reaches all the churches of the East and of the West" (*OL* 4). Together the churches of East and West can give a unified "harmonious, illuminating, life-giving response to the world's expectations and sufferings" and thus "truly contribute to a more effective proclamation of the Gospel among the people of our time" (*OL* 4).

The Pope echoes the Council to the effect that division among Christians "openly contradicts the will of Christ, scandalizes the world, and damages the holy cause of preaching the Gospel to every creature" (*UR* 1). "Christ cries out but man finds it hard to hear his voice because we fail to speak with one accord." Thus, the world is "deprived of a joint witness" because "the words of the West need the words of the East, so that God's word may ever more clearly reveal its unfathomable riches" (*OL* 28).

What could make it clearer that the unity sought by ecumenism, while being an end in itself, has a sign value in bringing the Good News to the world? More is at stake than simply unity. The urgency of evangelization is a compelling ecumenical force. The power of evangelical love can, it is hoped, contribute to healthy sorrow over the realization that by "our sins and mutual misunderstanding...we have deprived the world of a joint witness that could, perhaps, have avoided so many tragedies and even changed the course of history" (*OL* 28). The power of love for others is capable of raising people to great and heroic heights.

TOPICAL OUTLINE

1. Introduction: esteem for the Eastern Churches (1)

2. The individual churches or rites

    A. Variety of rites manifests unity (2)

    B. Equal dignity of the rites (3)

    C. Means to foster the various rites (4)

3. Preservation of the spiritual heritage of the Eastern Churches

    A. Regard for the Eastern heritage (5)

    B. Preservation of the Eastern rites (6)

4. Eastern rite patriarchs

    A. Jurisdiction of patriarchs (7)

    B. Patriarchates equal in dignity (8)

    C. Rights and privileges (9–11)

5. Discipline of the sacraments

    A. Approval of ancient discipline (12)

    B. Confirmation (13)

    C. Baptism (14)

    D. Sunday liturgy and divine office (15)

    E. Reconciliation (16)

    F. Permanent diaconate (17)

G. Matrimony (18)

6. Divine worship

    A. Feast days and Easter in particular (19–20)

    B. Other directives (21–23)

7. Relations with the brethren of the separated Churches

    A. Promoting unity (24)

    B. Eastern Christians who join the unity of the Catholic Church (25)

    C. Worship in common (26)

    D. Participation in the sacraments (27–29)

8. Conclusion (30)

DECREE ON THE CATHOLIC CHURCHES OF THE EASTERN RITE

Orientalium Ecclesiarum

PREAMBLE

1. The Catholic Church holds in high esteem the institutions, liturgical rites, ecclesiastical traditions and the established standards of the Christian life of the Eastern Churches; for in them, distinguished as they are for their venerable antiquity, there remains conspicuous the tradition that has been handed down from the apostles through the Fathers[1] and that forms part of the divinely revealed and undivided heritage of the universal Church. This sacred ecumenical Council, therefore, in its care for the Eastern Churches which bear living witness to this Tradition, in order that they may flourish and with new apostolic vigor execute the task entrusted to them, has determined to lay down a number of principles in addition to those which refer to the universal Church; all else is remitted to the care of the Eastern synods and of the Holy See.

---

1. Leo XIII, Apostolic Letter *Orientalium Dignitas* (Nov. 30, 1894): Acts of Leo XIII, vol. 14, pp. 201–202.

THE INDIVIDUAL CHURCHES OR RITES

2. The holy Catholic Church, which is the Mystical Body of Christ, is made up of the faithful who are organically united in the Holy Spirit by the same faith, the same sacraments and the same government and who, combining together into various groups which are held together by a hierarchy, form separate churches or rites. Between these there exists an admirable bond of union, such that the variety within the Church in no way harms its unity; rather it manifests it, for it is the mind of the Catholic Church that each individual church or rite should retain its traditions whole and entire, and likewise that it should adapt its way of life to the different needs of time and place.[2]

3. These individual churches, whether of the East or the West, although they differ somewhat among themselves in rite (to use the current phrase), that is, in liturgy, ecclesiastical discipline and spiritual heritage, are nevertheless each as much as the others, entrusted to the pastoral government of the Roman Pontiff, the divinely appointed Successor of St. Peter in primacy over the universal Church. They are consequently of equal dignity, so that none of them is superior to the others as regards rite and they enjoy the same rights and are under the same

---

2. St. Leo IX, Letter *In Terra Pax* (1053); *Ut Enim;* Innocent III, Fourth Lateran Council (1215): ch. IV: *Licet Graecos;* Letter *Inter Quattuor* (Aug. 2, 1206): *Postulasti Postmodum;* Innocent IV, Letter *Cum de Cetero* (Aug. 27, 1247); Letter *Sub Catholicae* (March 6, 1254), proem.; Nicholas III, Instruction *Istud Est Memoriale* (Oct. 9, 1278); Leo X, Apostolic Letter *Accepimus Nuper* (May 18, 1521); Paul III, Apostolic Letter *Dudum* (Dec. 23, 1534); Pius IV, Constitution *Romanus Pontifex* (Feb. 16, 1564), n. 5; Clement VIII, Constitution *Magnus Dominus* (Dec. 23, 1595), n. 10; Paul V, Constitution *Suprema* (Jan. 6, 1848), n. 3; Apostolic Letter *Ecclesiam Christi* (Nov. 26, 1853); Constitution *Romani Pontificis* (Jan. 6, 1862); Leo XIII, Apostolic Letter *Praeclara Gratulationis* (June 20, 1894), n. 7; Apostolic Letter *Orientalium Dignitas* (Nov. 30, 1894), proem.; etc.

obligations, also in respect of preaching the Gospel to the whole world (cf. Mk 16:15) under the guidance of the Roman Pontiff.

4. Means should be taken, therefore, in every part of the world for the protection and advancement of all the individual churches, and to this end there should be established parishes and a special hierarchy where the spiritual good of the faithful demands it. The hierarchs of the different individual churches with jurisdiction in one and the same territory should, by taking common counsel in regular meetings, strive to promote unity of action and with common endeavor to sustain common tasks, so as better to further the good of religion and to safeguard more effectively the ordered way of life of the clergy.[3]

All clerics and those aspiring to sacred Orders should be instructed in the rites and especially in the practical norms that must be applied in interritual questions. The laity, too, should be taught as part of its catechetical education about rites and their rules.

Finally, each and every Catholic, as also the baptized of every non-Catholic church or denomination who enters into the fullness of the Catholic communion, must retain his own rite wherever he is, must cherish it and observe it to the best of his ability,[4] without prejudice to the right in special cases of persons, communities or areas, of recourse to the Apostolic See, which as the supreme judge of interchurch relations, will, acting itself or through other authorities, meet the needs of the occasion in an ecumenical spirit by the issuance of opportune directives, decrees or rescripts.

---

3. Pius XII, Motu Proprio *Cleri Sanctitati* (June 2, 1957), can. 4.

4. Pius XII, Motu Proprio *Cleri Sanctitati* (June 2, 1957), can. 8: "sine licentia Sedis Apostolicae," following the practice of preceding centuries; similarly with regard to baptized non-Catholics, canon 11 states: "ritum quem maluerint amplecti possunt"; in the text proposed there is a positive ruling on the observance of rite for all persons everywhere.

PRESERVATION OF THE SPIRITUAL
HERITAGE OF THE EASTERN CHURCHES

5. History, tradition and abundant ecclesiastical institutions bear outstanding witness to the great merit owing to the Eastern Churches by the universal Church.[5] The sacred Council, therefore, not only accords to this ecclesiastical and spiritual heritage the high regard which is its due and rightful praise, but also unhesitatingly looks on it as the heritage of the universal Church. For this reason, it solemnly declares that the churches of the East, as much as those of the West, have a full right and are in duty bound to rule themselves, each in accordance with its own established disciplines, since all these are praiseworthy by reason of their venerable antiquity, more harmonious with the character of their faithful and more suited to the promotion of the good of souls.

6. All members of the Eastern rite should know and be convinced that they can and should always preserve their legitimate liturgical rite and their established way of life, and that these may not be altered except to obtain for themselves an organic improvement. All these, then, must be observed by the members of the Eastern rites themselves. Besides, they should attain to an ever greater knowledge and a more exact use of them, and if in their regard they have fallen short owing to contingencies of times and persons, they should take steps to return to their ancestral traditions.

Those who by reason of their office or apostolic ministries are in frequent communication with the Eastern Churches or their faithful, should be instructed according as their office demands in the knowledge and veneration of the rites, discipline, doctrine, history and character of

---

5. Cf. Leo XIII, Apostolic Letter *Orientalium Dignitas* (Nov. 30, 1894); Apostolic Letter *Praeclara Gratulationis* (June 20, 1894), and the documents referred to in note 2 above.

the members of the Eastern rites.[6] To enhance the efficacy of their apostolate, religious and associations of the Latin rite working in Eastern countries or among Eastern faithful are earnestly counseled to found houses or even provinces of the Eastern rite, as far as this can be done.[7]

---

6. Cf. Benedict XV, Motu Proprio *Orientis Catholici* (Oct. 15, 1917); Pius XI, Encyclical Letter *Rerum Orientalium* (Sept. 8, 1928), etc.

7. The practice of the Catholic Church in the time of Pius XI, Pius XII and John XXIII abundantly demonstrates this.

EASTERN RITE PATRIARCHS

7. The patriarchate as an institution has existed in the Church from the earliest times and was recognized by the first ecumenical councils.[8]

By the name "Eastern patriarch" is meant the bishop to whom belongs jurisdiction over all bishops, not excepting metropolitans, clergy and people of his own territory or rite, in accordance with canon law and without prejudice to the primacy of the Roman Pontiff.[9]

Wherever a hierarch of any rite is appointed outside the territorial bounds of the patriarchate, he remains attached to the hierarchy of the patriarchate of that rite in accordance with canon law.

8. Though some of the patriarchates of the Eastern Churches are of earlier and some of later date, nonetheless all are equal in respect of patriarchal dignity without, however, prejudice to the legitimately established precedence of honor.[10]

9. By the most ancient tradition of the Church, the patriarchs of the Eastern Churches are to be accorded special honor, seeing that each is set over his patriarchate as father and head.

This sacred Council, therefore, determines that their rights and privileges should be reestablished in accordance with the ancient tra-

---

8. Cf. First Council of Nicea, can. 6; First Council of Constantinople, can. 2 and 3; Council of Chalcedon, can. 28 and 9; Fourth Council of Constantinople, can. 17 and 21; Fourth Lateran Council, can. 5 and 30; Council of Florence, Decree *Pro Graecis* (July 6, 1439), etc.

9. Cf. First Council of Nicea, can. 6; First Council of Constantinople, can. 3; Fourth Council of Constantinople, can. 17; Pius XII, Motu Proprio *Cleri Sanctitati* (June 2, 1957), can. 216; n. 2, 1.

10. In the ecumenical councils: First Council of Nicea, can. 6; First Council of Constantinople, can. 3; Fourth Council of Constantinople, can. 21; Fourth Lateran Council, can. 5; Council of Florence, Decree *Pro Graecis* (July 6, 1439), n. 9. Cf. Pius XII, Motu Proprio *Cleri Sanctitati* (June 2, 1957), can. 219, etc.

dition of each of the churches and the decrees of the ecumenical councils.[11]

The rights and privileges in question are those that obtained in the time of union between East and West, though they should be adapted somewhat to modern conditions.

The patriarchs with their synods are the highest authority for all business of the patriarchate, including the right of establishing new eparchies and of nominating bishops of their rite within the territorial bounds of the patriarchate, without prejudice to the inalienable right of the Roman Pontiff to intervene in individual cases.

10. What has been said of patriarchs is valid also, in harmony with the canon law, in respect to major archbishops, who rule the whole of some individual church or rite.[12]

11. Seeing that the patriarchal office in the Eastern Church is a traditional form of government, the sacred ecumenical Council ardently desires that new patriarchates should be erected where there is need, to be established either by an ecumenical council or by the Roman Pontiff.[13]

---

11. Cf. above, note 8.

12. Cf. Council of Ephesus, can. 8; Clement VII, *Decet Romanum Pontificem* (Feb. 23, 1596); Pius VII, Apostolic Letter *In Universalis Ecclesiae* (Feb. 22, 1807); Pius XII, Motu Proprio *Cleri Sanctitati* (June 2, 1957), can. 324–327; Council of Carthage (419): can. 17.

13. Council of Carthage (419): can. 17 and 57; Council of Chalcedon (451): can. 12; St. Innocent I, Letter *Et Onus et Honor* (c. 415); *Nam Quid Sciscitaris;* St. Nicholas I, Letter *Ad Consulta Vestra* (Nov. 13, 866); *A Quo Autem;* Innocent III, Letter *Rex Regum* (Feb. 25, 1204); Leo XII, Apostolic Constitution *Petrus Apostolorum Princeps* (Aug. 15, 1824); Leo XIII, Apostolic Letter *Christi Domini* (1895); Pius XII, Motu Proprio *Cleri Sanctitati* (June 2, 1957), can. 159.

THE DISCIPLINE OF THE SACRAMENTS

12. The sacred ecumenical Council confirms and approves the ancient discipline of the sacraments existing in the Oriental Churches, as also the ritual practices connected with their celebration and administration and ardently desires that this should be reestablished if circumstances warrant it.

13. The established practice in respect of the minister of Confirmation that has obtained from most early times in the Eastern Church should be fully restored. Therefore, priests validly confer this sacrament, using chrism blessed by a patriarch or a bishop.[14]

14. All Eastern rite priests, either in conjunction with Baptism or separately from it, can confer this sacrament validly on all the faithful of any rite including the Latin; licitly, however, only if the regulations both of the common and the particular law are observed.[15] Priests also of Latin rite, in accordance with the faculties they enjoy in respect of the administration of this sacrament, validly administer it also to the faithful of Eastern Churches, without prejudice to the rite, observing in regard to licitness the regulations both of the common and of the particular law.[16]

---

14. Cf. Innocent IV, Letter *Sub Catholicae* (March 6, 1254); sec. 3, n. 4; Second Council of Lyons (1274): (profession of faith presented by Michael Palaeologus to Gregory X); Eugene IV, in the Council of Florence, Constitution *Exsultate Deo* (Nov. 22, 1439), sec. 11; Clement VIII, Instruction *Sanctissimus* (Aug. 31,1595); Benedict XIV, Constitution *Etsi Pastoralis* (May 26, 1742), sec. 2, n. 1, sec. 3, n. 1, etc.; Council of Laodicea (347/381): can. 48; Council of Sis of the Armenians (1342); Council of Lebanon of the Maronites (1736), part 2, ch. 3, 2, and other particular councils.

15. Cf. Instruction of the Holy Office to the bishop of Spis (1783); Sacred Congregation for the Propagation of the Faith (for the Copts, March 15, 1790), n. XIII; Decree of Oct. 6, 1863, C, a; Sacred Congregation for the Eastern Church (May 1, 1948); the reply of the Holy Office of April 22, 1896, with the letter of May 19, 1896.

16. *Code of Canon Law,* can. 782, n. 4; Decree of the Sacred Congregation for the Eastern Church, *De Sacramento Confirmationis Administrando Etiam Fidelibus*

15. The faithful are bound to take part on Sundays and feast days in the divine liturgy or, according to the regulations or custom of their own rite, in the celebration of the divine office.[17] That the faithful may be able more easily to fulfill their obligation, it is laid down that the period of time within which the precept should be observed extends from the vespers of the vigil to the end of the Sunday or the feast day.[18] The faithful are earnestly exhorted to receive Holy Communion on these days, and indeed more frequently—yes, even daily.[19]

16. Owing to the fact that the faithful of the different individual churches dwell intermingled with each other in the same area or Eastern territory, the faculties for hearing confessions duly and without restriction given to priests of any rite by their own hierarchs extend to the whole territory of him who grants them and also to the places and faithful of any other rite in the same territory, unless the hierarch of the place has expressly excluded this for places of his rite.[20]

17. In order that the ancient established practice of the sacrament of Orders in the Eastern Churches may flourish again, this sacred Council ardently desires that the office of the permanent diaconate should, where it has fallen into disuse, be restored.[21] The legislative authorities of each individual church should decide about the subdiaconate and the minor orders and the rights and obligations that attach to them.[22]

Orientalibus a Presbyteris Latini Ritus, Qui Hoc Indulto Gaudeant Pro Fidelibus Sui Ritus (May 1, 1948).

17. Cf. Council of Laodicea (347/381): can. 29; St. Nicephorus of Constantinople, ch. 14; Council of Duin of the Armenians (719), can. 31; St. Theodore the Studite, *Sermon* 21; St. Nicholas I, Letter *Ad Consulta Vestra* (Nov. 13, 866): *In Quorum Apostolorum; Nos Cupitis; Quod Interrogatis; Praeterea Consulitis; Si Die Dominico;* and particular councils.

18. This is something new, at least where there is an obligation of assisting at the sacred liturgy; however, it does correspond with the liturgical day among the Orientals.

19. Cf. *Canons of the Apostles*, 8 and 9; Council of Antioch (341): can. 2; Timothy of Alexandria, interrogat. 3; Innocent III, Constitution *Quia Divinae* (Jan. 4, 1215); and many more recent particular councils of the Eastern Churches.

20. While safeguarding the principle of territorial jurisdiction, the canon seeks to provide for the good of souls, for a plurality of jurisdiction in the same territory.

21. Cf. First Council of Nicea, can. 18; Council of Neocaesarea (314/325): can. 12; Council of Sardica (343), can. 8; St. Leo the Great, Letter *Omnium Quidem* (Jan. 13, 444); Council of Chalcedon, can. 6; Fourth Council of Constantinople, can. 23, 26; etc.

22. Among many Eastern Churches, the subdiaconate is considered a minor order, but in the Motu Proprio *Cleri Sanctitati* the obligations of major orders are prescribed to it. The canon proposes a return to the ancient discipline of each of the Churches, in derogation of the common law laid down in *Cleri Sanctitati.*

18. To obviate invalid marriages when Eastern Catholics marry baptized Eastern non-Catholics and in order to promote fidelity in and the sanctity of marriage, as well as peace within the family, the sacred Council determines that the canonical "form" for the celebration of these marriages is of obligation only for liceity; for their validity the presence of a sacred minister is sufficient, provided that other prescriptions of law are observed.[23]

---

23. Cf. Pius XII, Motu Proprio *Crebrae Allatae* (Feb. 22, 1949), can. 32, n. 2, n. 5 (faculty of the patriarchs to dispense from the form); Pius XII, Motu Proprio *Cleri Sanctitati* (June 2, 1957), can. 267 (faculty of the patriarchs concerning *sanatio in radice*); in 1957 the Holy Office and the Sacred Congregation for the Eastern Church granted the power of dispensing from the form and of applying *sanatio* because of defect of the form, for five years: "Outside the patriarchates, to metropolitans and to other local ordinaries…who have no superior beneath the Holy See."

DIVINE WORSHIP

19. It belongs only to an ecumenical council or to the Apostolic See to determine, transfer or suppress feast days common to all the Eastern Churches. On the other hand, to determine, transfer or suppress the feast days of any of the individual churches is within the competence not only of the Apostolic See but also of the patriarchal or archiepiscopal synod, due regard being had to the whole area and the other individual churches.[24]

20. Until such time as all Christians are agreed on a fixed day for the celebration of Easter, with a view meantime to promoting unity among the Christians of the same area or nation, it is left to the patriarchs or supreme authorities of a place to come to an agreement by the unanimous consent and combined counsel of those affected to celebrate the feast of Easter on the same Sunday.[25]

21. Individual faithful dwelling outside the area or territory of their own rite may follow completely the established custom of the place where they live as regards the law of the sacred seasons. In families of mixed rite it is permissible to observe this law according to one and the same rite.[26]

---

24. Cf. St. Leo the Great, Letter *Quod Saepissime* (April 15, 454): *Petitionem autem;* St. Nicephorus of Constantinople, ch. 13; Council of Patriarch Sergius (Sept. 18, 1596); can. 17; Pius VI, Apostolic Letter *Assueto Paterne* (April 8, 1775); etc.

25. Cf. Second Vatican Ecumenical Council, Constitution on the Sacred Liturgy *Sacrosanctum Concilium* (Dec. 4, 1963).

26. Cf. Clement VIII, Instr. *Sanctissimus* (Aug. 31, 1595), n. 6: *Si ipsi graeci;* the Holy Office (June 7, 1673), ad 1 and 3; (March 13, 1727), ad 1; Sacred Congregation for the Propagation of the Faith, *Decree* (Aug. 18, 1913), art. 33; *Decree* (Aug. 14, 1914), art. 27; *Decree* (March 27, 1916), art. 14; Sacred Congregation for the Eastern Church, *Decree* (March 1, 1929), art. 36; *Decree* (May 4, 1930), art. 41.

22. Eastern clerics and religious should celebrate in accordance with the prescriptions and traditions of their own established custom the divine office, which from ancient times has been held in high honor in all Eastern Churches.[27] The faithful too should follow the example of their forebears and assist devoutly as occasion allows at the divine office.

23. It belongs to the patriarch with his synod, or to the supreme authority of each church with the council of the hierarchs, to regulate the use of languages in the sacred liturgical functions and, after reference to the Apostolic See, of approving translations of texts into the vernacular.[28]

---

27. Cf. Council of Laodicea (347/381): can. 18; Council of Mar Issac of the Chaldeans (410): can. 15; St. Nerses Glaien of the Armenians (1166); Innocent IV, Letter *Sub Catholicae* (March 6, 1254), n. 8; Benedict XIV, Constitution *Etsi Pastoralis* (May 26, 1742), n. 7, n. 5; Instruction *Eo Quamvis Tempore* (May 4, 1745), nn. 42 ff.; and recent particular synods: Armenians (1911); Copts (1898); Maronites (1736); Rumanians (1872); Ruthenians (1891); Syrians (1888).

28. From Eastern tradition.

RELATIONS WITH THE BRETHREN
OF THE SEPARATED CHURCHES

24. The Eastern Churches in communion with the Apostolic See of Rome have a special duty of promoting the unity of all Christians, especially Eastern Christians, in accordance with the principles of the decree *About Ecumenism* of this sacred Council, by prayer in the first place, and by the example of their lives, by religious fidelity to the ancient Eastern traditions, by a greater knowledge of each other, by collaboration and a brotherly regard for objects and feelings.[29]

25. If any separated Eastern Christian should, under the guidance of the grace of the Holy Spirit, join himself to the unity of Catholics, no more should be required of him than what a bare profession of the Catholic faith demands. Eastern clerics, seeing that a valid priesthood is preserved among them, are permitted to exercise the Orders they possess on joining the unity of the Catholic Church, in accordance with the regulations established by the competent authority.[30]

26. Common participation in worship *(communicatio in sacris)* which harms the unity of the Church or involves formal acceptance of error or the danger of aberration in the faith, of scandal and indifferentism, is forbidden by divine law.[31] On the other hand, pastoral experience shows clearly that as regards our Eastern brethren, there should be taken into consideration the different cases of individuals, where neither the unity of the Church is hurt nor are verified the dangers that must be avoided, but where the needs of the salvation of souls and their spiritual good are impelling motives. For that reason the Catholic Church has al-

---

29. From the sense of the Bulls of union of the various Eastern Catholic Churches.

30. An obligation established by the Council regarding our separated Eastern brethren and for the orders of every degree of divine and ecclesiastical law.

31. This doctrine is also held in separated Churches.

ways adopted and now adopts rather a mild policy, offering to all the means of salvation and an example of charity among Christians, through participation in the sacraments and in other sacred functions and things. With this in mind, "lest because of the harshness of our judgment we be an obstacle to those seeking salvation" [32] and in order more and more to promote union with the Eastern Churches separated from us, the sacred Council lays down the following policy:

27. Without prejudice to the principles noted earlier, Eastern Christians who are in fact separated in good faith from the Catholic Church, if they ask of their own accord and have the right dispositions, may be admitted to the sacraments of Penance, the Eucharist and the Anointing of the Sick. Further, Catholics may ask for these same sacraments from those non-Catholic ministers whose churches possess valid sacraments, as often as necessity or a genuine spiritual benefit recommends such a course and access to a Catholic priest is physically or morally impossible.[33]

28. Further, given the same principles, common participation by Catholics with their Eastern separated brethren in sacred functions, things and places is allowed for a just cause.[34]

29. This conciliatory policy with regard to *communicatio in sacris* (participation in things sacred) with the brethren of the separated Eastern Churches is put into the care and control of the local hierarchs, in order that by combined counsel among themselves and if need be, after consultation also with the hierarchs of the separated churches, they may by timely and effective regulations and norms direct the relations among Christians.

---

32. St. Basil the Great, *Canonical Letter to Amphilochius: PG* 32, 669 B.

33. The basis for mitigation is considered to be: 1) validity of the sacraments; 2) good faith and disposition; 3) necessity of eternal salvation; 4) absence of one's own priest; 5) exclusion of the dangers to be avoided and of formal adhesion to error.

34. This concerns the so-called "extra-sacramental *communicatio in sacris.*" The Council grants this mitigation while maintaining what should be maintained.

CONCLUSION

30. The sacred Council feels great joy in the fruitful zealous collaboration of the Eastern and the Western Catholic Churches and at the same
time declares: All these directives of law are laid down in view of the
present situation till such time as the Catholic Church and the separated
Eastern Churches come together into complete unity.

Meanwhile, however, all Christians, Eastern as well as Western, are
earnestly asked to pray to God fervently and assiduously, nay, indeed
daily, that with the aid of the most holy Mother of God, all may become
one. Let them pray also that the strength and the consolation of the Holy
Spirit may descend copiously upon all those many Christians of whatsoever church they be who endure suffering and deprivations for their un-
wavering avowal of the name of Christ.

"Love one another with fraternal charity, anticipating one another
with honor" (Rm 12:10).

Each and all these matters which are set forth in this decree have
been favorably voted on by the fathers of the Council. And we, by the
apostolic authority given us by Christ and in union with the fathers, approve, decree and establish them in the Holy Spirit and command that
they be promulgated for the glory of God.

Given in Rome at St. Peter's, November 21, 1964

DECREE ON ECUMENISM

Unitatis Redintegratio

Promulgated by
His Holiness Pope Paul VI
On November 21, 1964

INTRODUCTION

The *Decree on Ecumenism (UR)* exhorts "all the Catholic faithful to recognize the signs of the times and to take an active and intelligent part in the work of ecumenism" (*UR* 4). It expresses the Church's desire to respond to an initiative of the Holy Spirit, whose grace has brought Christians of many communities and confessions to commit themselves to the cause of Christian unity. As such, this commitment constitutes one of the signs of the times through which the Church discerns a call from God.

In this way the Council situates *UR* as the Catholic Church's response to the promptings of the Holy Spirit, already at work in the ecumenical movement among non-Catholics. The purpose is that Catholics "too can respond to this grace and to this divine call" (*UR* 1). The word "too" is significant here. It indicates that in responding to God's will in this matter, the Catholic Church places itself alongside other Christian Churches and ecclesial communities. All stand before God with the dispositions that accompany the "obedience of faith" (*DV* 5).

The stance is conveyed in the title of the first chapter: "Catholic Principles on Ecumenism." Its significance is seen in comparing it to the title of an earlier draft: "Principles of Catholic Ecumenism." The new title indicates that there is only one ecumenical movement with the goal of Christian unity, not two movements, a Catholic and a non-Catholic one. The Catholic Church sees itself as being subject to the Holy Spirit's promptings, just as the other Churches and ecclesial communities are. Fidelity to the movement of the Holy Spirit leading Christians to overcome their divisions is an element of the real though imperfect communion which the decree acknowledges exists among baptized Christians (cf. *UR* 3).

If the Catholic Church places itself alongside other Christian Churches and ecclesial communities in this way, this does not mean that the Catholic Church considers itself just one among many Christian Churches and communities. This is clear in the affirmation of the Catholic understanding of the apostolic nature of the Church (cf. *UR* 2). As *Lumen Gentium* stated: "This Church constituted and organized in the world as a society, subsists in the Catholic Church, which is governed by the Successor of Peter and by the bishops in communion with him, although many elements of sanctification and of truth are found outside of its visible structure" (*LG* 8).

The same attitude of faith that requires the Catholic Church to respond generously to the Holy Spirit's promptings toward full Christian unity requires equally that the Church be faithful to what it knows about itself through divine revelation. The decree rejects as "foreign to the spirit of ecumenism" anything that would compromise the integrity of Catholic doctrine or obscure its meaning (cf. *UR* 11). Article four describes the ultimate goal of ecumenism as the gathering of all Christians "in a common celebration of the Eucharist" which is the efficacious sign of "that unity which Christ bestowed on his Church from the beginning" and which "subsists in the Catholic Church." From the perspective of Catholic faith, full communion has a concrete historical realization and referent, namely, the unity of the Catholic Church (cf. *LG* 8).

The decree calls every member of the Church to contribute to bringing about full communion among Christians (cf. *UR* 5). This is to be a "spiritual ecumenism," which means that a "change of heart and holiness of life, along with public and private prayer for the unity of Christians, should be regarded as the soul of the whole ecumenical movement" (UR 8). Ecumenism cannot be limited to dialogue and agreement among theologians and prelates. Spiritual ecumenism can overcome the frustrations of the past, and provides the basis that will enable theological agreements to bear fruit in realizing full communion.

Though the text does not insinuate it, it would be in keeping with a principle found in *Lumen Gentium* that precisely because the unity of Christ's Church subsists in the Catholic Church, Catholics are more accountable for promoting unity. More will be demanded from the one to whom more has been given (cf. *LG* 14; Lk 12:48). Thus, one could conclude that the Church accepts a greater burden for working toward ecumenism.

UR is the conciliar text which most explicitly and amply develops the theme of the poor, humble Church which is "always in need of being purified" and "always follows the way of penance and renewal" (*LG* 8). The Church must live the humility of Christ (cf. *UR* 4), pray for the grace to be humble (*UR* 7), and humbly seek the forgiveness of God and of our separated brethren (cf. *UR* 7). Humility should also be a mark of theologians contributing to ecumenical dialogue (cf. *UR* 11). It begins by a truthful acceptance of responsibility for the role some of the Church's own sons and daughters played in the great divisions of the past (cf. *UR* 3), the effects of which remain a painful reality for Christians today.

Humility disposes one to rely on God's wisdom, love and power, while acknowledging the gifts one has. The Council speaks of such humility when it states that it "professes its awareness that human powers and capacities cannot achieve this holy objective" of Christian reunification. Consequently, in humility the Council "rests all its hope on the prayer of Christ for the Church, on our Father's love for us, and on the power of the Holy Spirit" (*UR* 24).

UR states that the Holy Spirit is working in the non-Catholic Churches and ecclesial communities and that the Church itself can be edified by these gifts of the Spirit (cf. *UR* 4). This applies to the field of ecumenism an important theme of *Gaudium et Spes,* according to which the Church is conscious of having benefited from the developments of human culture (cf. *GS* 44). A similar statement is found in *AG* 19.

The humility that the Church expresses in this text is based on two things. The first is the movement of the Holy Spirit prompting Christians of many Churches and ecclesial communities to aspire to unity. This desire is a gift of God. A second and fundamental element is the conviction of faith that "God fulfills the desire of all who fear him" (Ps 145:19). God would not give the desire unless he intended to fulfill it. This is the foundation of our hope, a hope like Abraham's who trusted God (cf. Rm 4:18). From a merely human perspective the ecumenical task is overwhelming, but with God all things are possible (cf. Lk 1:37).

The Council does not pretend to fathom the mysterious wisdom of God as to why he permits divisions, and how he will bring good out them. *UR* does not offer a detailed plan for ecumenical activity. It only sets forth general guidelines for the Church's response to the Holy Spirit. Its main purpose is to propose principles that will assure a continued openness and ever more generous response to the Spirit's direction. The hallmark of this response is the call to conversion.

This leads us to the fundamental and distinguishing feature of the decree. The Church's response to the ecumenical movement of the Holy Spirit is to commit itself to renewal through reform or conversion (cf. *UR* 6–7). There are several reasons for this. The first is that the Church does not claim to see the full length of the ecumenical road. It cannot today fathom all that the Lord of unity will ask of it. In this situation, the one thing it can do is respond with a Marian type of fiat at each juncture along the way. A deepening union with Christ through penance and conversion is the best way for the handmaid of the Lord to embrace each new manifestation of the Spirit's movement.

The second reason is that the Church is a sacrament-sign of salvation and unity. Division among Christians compromises the sign-value of the Church and hinders evangelization (cf. *UR* 1; *AG* 6). The Church must show forth the Lord's power by graciously receiving and generously responding to the gift of catholic unity, for such witness contains a power to reach hearts: "The very testimony of their Christian life and good works done in a supernatural spirit have the power to draw men to belief and to God; for the Lord says, 'Even so let your light shine before men in order that they may see your good works and give glory to your Father who is in heaven' (Mt 5:16)" (*AA* 6). So that this power in witness might be increased, the Church can begin by becoming more conscious of its catholic unity, deepening it, and being grateful for it.

Ecumenism hinges on conversion because it goes to the heart of what separates: sin. Calling the members of the Church to this kind of renewal is an implicit recognition of sin on the part of the Church's members (cf. *UR* 3). Pope John Paul II has emphasized this, especially in *Tertio Millennio Adveniente.*

A third element of the ecumenism of conversion is that it makes the Catholic Church an active participant in the ecumenical process. Dialogue is not a polite and patient attitude of "wait until they come back home." In this process, the members of the Church have much to learn as well.

Fourth, if reunion will be based on communion in the essentials, deepening communion with Christ always contributes to ecumenism. From it a genuine *sensus fidei* (cf. *LG* 12) develops by which "there is a growth in the understanding of the realities and the words which have

been handed down" and "a penetrating understanding of the spiritual realities which they experience" (*DV* 8). This light of faith is necessary to
distinguish between the substance of faith and historically conditioned
elements of the Church's life which played a role in misunderstanding
and division among Christians.

UR builds upon the doctrine of *Lumen Gentium,* concretizing and
specifying its implications. While the use of biblical and patristic
sources throughout *LG* can indicate ecumenical influence and openness,
the most important section is article fifteen in chapter two on the People
of God. Especially important is *LG's* teaching that the Catholic Church's
relation to non-Catholic Christians varies, depending on the presence or
absence of apostolic succession and other elements of ecclesial communion (cf. *LG* 15). *UR* shows that the imperfect communion in which
Catholics and non-Catholic Christians are joined admits of various
degrees.

The council fathers had decided to go beyond the terminology of
"membership in the Church," because it contained a kind of "all-or-
nothing" principle: either one is a member of the Church or one is not.
Lumen Gentium describes the conditions for being "fully incorporated"
into the Church (cf. n. 14), and states: "The Church recognizes that in
many ways she is linked with those who, being baptized, are honored
with the name of Christian, though they do not profess the faith in its
entirety or do not preserve unity of communion with the Successor of
Peter (*LG* 15)." This vocabulary of full incorporation and being in some
way joined to the Church develops the final paragraph of *LG* 13, which
concludes from the assertion that all "are called to be part of this catholic unity of the People of God" that all either belong to the Church or are
"related to it in various ways." UR speaks in terms of communion when
considering non-Catholic Christians: those "who believe in Christ and
have been truly baptized are in communion with the Catholic Church
even though this communion is imperfect" (*UR* 3).

Concretely, *LG* translated this call into the necessity of the Church
for salvation, while recognizing that it is possible for people to be outside that Church through no fault of their own, and still be saved. More
directly relevant to ecumenism, *LG* 14 implicitly recognized that it is
possible for a person to know Jesus Christ and yet not see that he has
made the Church necessary for salvation.

The description of faith in *Dei Verbum* brings an illuminating perspective here (cf. *DV* 5). Faith has two dimensions. One is the dimension of entrusting oneself to God through faith. The other is assent to the truths which have been revealed by God and which therefore have his authority behind them. The assent of faith concretely realizes the attitude of entrusting, which it confirms, ratifies and validates. Assent is a particular way of saying "yes" to the God to whose loving care a person has entrusted himself. Just as Abraham said "yes" to God by saying "yes" to the call to journey to Canaan and later to sacrifice Isaac, and as Mary said "yes" to God by saying "yes" to the invitation to conceive and give birth to Jesus, so Christians today say "yes" to God by professing their faith in all that he has revealed.

This faith modeled on that of Abraham and Mary is the bond of communion among separated Christians. The greatest sign of communion in faith is the martyrdom endured by many non-Catholic Christians. Their faith inspired them to prefer death rather than deny the Christian faith. As Pope Paul VI stated, "The witness of Christ borne even to the shedding of blood has become a common inheritance of Catholics, Orthodox, Anglicans and Protestants." Inspired by this, Pope John Paul II has written: "Perhaps the most convincing form of ecumenism is the ecumenism of the saints and of the martyrs. The *communio sanctorum* speaks louder than the things which divide us" (*TMA* 37). God has graciously provided all Christians with this most compelling sign of unity. It constitutes an urgent call to make the witness of unity more perfect and transparent for the world.

UR 4 defines the goal of the ecumenical movement and states: "When individuals wish for full Catholic communion, their preparation and reconciliation is an undertaking which of its nature is distinct from ecumenical action. But there is no opposition between the two, since both proceed from the marvelous ways of God" (*UR* 4). By distinguishing such personal conversions from ecumenical activity, the Council chose to focus on ecumenical dialogue with communities and Churches separated from full communion.

In light of the central place in *UR* of ecumenism through renewal and conversion, the teaching of John Paul II stands out as ecumenically inspired. From his first encyclical through all his other writings, this Pope has interwoven the themes of human dignity, conscience, conversion and awareness of sin. Through revelation God has shown himself as the God who is greater than all evil and who can bring good out of

evil. For John Paul II, authentic ecumenism begins with a serious examination of conscience on the scandal of Christian division. Awareness
of sin constitutes a call to turn to God, who alone can bring good out of
the evil of sin, seek God's mercy, and begin to be converted. This is John
Paul's understanding of how the Church is called to place its hope in
God, who alone can bring unity out of division.

The Catholic Church's commitment to ecumenism is also shown in
the *Directory for the Application of the Principles and Norms on Ecumenism* (1993), the apostolic letter *Orientale Lumen* (1995), and the encyclical *Ut Unum Sint* (1995).

TOPICAL OUTLINE

1. Introduction: Restoration of unity (1)

2. Catholic principles on ecumenism

    A. Unity of the Church (2)

    B. Separated Churches and ecclesial communities (3)

    C. The work of ecumenism (4)

3. The practice of ecumenism

    A. Need for renewal in the Church (5–6)

    B. The call for a change of heart (7)

    C. Worship in common (8)

    D. Dialogue and study of other traditions (9–10)

    E. Clear presentation of the faith (11)

    F. Cooperation among Christians (12)

4. Churches and ecclesial communities separated from the Roman Apostolic See

    A. The special place of the Eastern Churches

        1. Close links between the Eastern and Western Churches (13–14)

        2. Liturgical worship and teaching of the Fathers (15)

        3. Eastern ecclesiastical laws and customs are to be respected (16)

        4. Richness of Eastern theology (17)

        5. Unity respects legitimate diversity (18)

B. Separated Churches and ecclesial communities in the West

    1. Common points and differences (19)

    2. Common faith in Jesus Christ (20)

    3. Love for Sacred Scripture (21)

    4. Baptism as a bond of unity (22)

    5. Prayer and social action (23)

    6. Hope for the future (24)

DECREE ON ECUMENISM

Unitatis Redintegratio

INTRODUCTION

1. The restoration of unity among all Christians is one of the principal concerns of the Second Vatican Council. Christ the Lord founded one Church and one Church only. However, many Christian communions present themselves to men as the true inheritors of Jesus Christ; all indeed profess to be followers of the Lord but differ in mind and go their different ways, as if Christ himself were divided (cf. 1 Cor 1:13). Such division openly contradicts the will of Christ, scandalizes the world and damages the holy cause of preaching the Gospel to every creature.

But the Lord of Ages wisely and patiently follows out the plan of grace on our behalf, sinners that we are. In recent times more than ever before, he has been rousing divided Christians to remorse over their divisions and to a longing for unity. Everywhere large numbers have felt the impulse of this grace, and among our separated brethren also there increases from day to day the movement, fostered by the grace of the Holy Spirit, for the restoration of unity among all Christians. This movement toward unity is called "ecumenical." Those belong to it who invoke the Triune God and confess Jesus as Lord and Savior, doing this not merely as individuals but also as corporate bodies. For almost everyone regards the body in which he has heard the Gospel as his Church and indeed, God's Church. All, however, though in different ways, long for the one visible Church of God, a Church truly universal and sent forth into the world that the world may be converted to the Gospel and so be saved, to the glory of God.

The sacred Council gladly notes all this. It has already declared its teaching on the Church, and now, moved by a desire for the restoration of unity among all the followers of Christ, it wishes to set before all Catholics the ways and means by which they too can respond to this grace and to this divine call.

CHAPTER I

CATHOLIC PRINCIPLES ON ECUMENISM

2. What has revealed the love of God among us is that the Father has sent into the world his only-begotten Son, so that being made man, he might by his redemption give new life to the entire human race and unify it (cf. 1 Jn 4:9; Col 1:18–20; Jn 11:52). Before offering himself up as a spotless victim upon the altar, Christ prayed to his Father for all who believe in him: "that they all may be one; even as you, Father, are in me, and I in you, that they also may be one in us, so that the world may believe that you have sent me" (Jn 17:21). In his Church he instituted the wonderful sacrament of the Eucharist by which the unity of his Church is both signified and made a reality. He gave his followers a new commandment to love one another (cf. Jn 13:34), and promised the Spirit, their Advocate (cf. Jn 16:7), who as Lord and life-giver, should remain with them forever.

After being lifted up on the cross and glorified, the Lord Jesus poured forth his Spirit as he had promised, and through the Spirit he has called and gathered together the people of the New Covenant, who are the Church, into a unity of faith, hope and charity, as the Apostle teaches us: "There is one body and one Spirit, just as you were called to the one hope of your calling; one Lord, one faith, one Baptism" (Eph 4:4–5). For "all you who have been baptized into Christ have put on Christ...for you are all one in Christ Jesus" (Gal 3:27–28). It is the Holy Spirit, dwelling in those who believe and pervading and ruling over the Church as a whole, who brings about that wonderful communion of the faithful. He brings them into intimate union with Christ, so that he is the principle of the Church's unity. The distribution of graces and offices is his work too (cf. 1 Cor 12:4–11), enriching the Church of Jesus Christ with different functions "in order to equip the saints for the work of service, so as to build up the body of Christ" (Eph 4:12).

In order to establish this his holy Church everywhere in the world till the end of time, Christ entrusted to the college of the Twelve the task of teaching, ruling and sanctifying.[1] Among their number he selected Peter, and after his confession of faith determined that on him he would build his Church. Also to Peter he promised the keys of the kingdom of heaven,[2] and after his profession of love, entrusted all his sheep to him to be confirmed in faith (cf. Lk 22:32) and shepherded in perfect unity (cf. Jn 21:15–18). Christ Jesus himself was forever to remain the chief cornerstone (cf. Eph 2:20) and shepherd of our souls.[3]

Jesus Christ, then, willed that the apostles and their successors—the bishops with Peter's successor at their head—should preach the Gospel faithfully, administer the sacraments and rule the Church in love. It is thus, under the action of the Holy Spirit, that Christ wills his people to increase, and he perfects his people's fellowship in unity: in their confessing the one faith, celebrating divine worship in common and keeping the fraternal harmony of the family of God.

The Church, then, is God's only flock; it is like a standard lifted high for the nations to see it (cf. Is 11:10–12), for it serves all mankind through the Gospel of peace[4] as it makes its pilgrim way in hope toward the goal of the fatherland above (cf. 1 Pt 1:3–9).

This is the sacred mystery of the unity of the Church, in Christ and through Christ, the Holy Spirit energizing its various functions. It is a mystery that finds its highest exemplar and source in the unity of the Persons of the Trinity: the Father and the Son in the Holy Spirit, one God.

3. Even in the beginnings of this one and only Church of God, there arose certain rifts (cf. 1 Cor 11:18–19; Gal 1:6–9; 1 Jn 2:18–19) which the Apostle strongly condemned (cf. 1 Cor 1:11 ff., 11:22). But in subsequent centuries much more serious dissensions made their appearance, and quite large communities came to be separated from full communion with the Catholic Church—for which, often enough, men of both sides were to blame. The children who are born into these communities and who grow up believing in Christ cannot be accused of the sin involved

---

1. Cf. Mt 28:18–20, in conjunction with Jn 20:21–23.

2. Cf. Mt 16:18, in conjunction with Mt 18:18.

3. Cf. 1 Pt 2:25; First Vatican Ecumenical Council, Session 4 (1870): Constitution on the Church of Christ *Pastor Aeternus,* Collac 7:482 a.

4. Cf. Eph 2:17–18, in conjunction with Mk 16:15.

in the separation, and the Catholic Church embraces them as brothers, with respect and affection. For men who believe in Christ and have been truly baptized are in communion with the Catholic Church even though this communion is imperfect. The differences that exist in varying degrees between them and the Catholic Church—whether in doctrine and sometimes in discipline, or concerning the structure of the Church—do indeed create many obstacles, sometimes serious ones, to full ecclesiastical communion. The ecumenical movement is striving to overcome these obstacles. But even in spite of them it remains true that all who have been justified by faith in Baptism are members of Christ's body[5] and have a right to be called Christian, and so are correctly accepted as brothers by the children of the Catholic Church.[6]

Moreover, some and even very many of the significant elements and endowments which together go to build up and give life to the Church itself, can exist outside the visible boundaries of the Catholic Church: the written Word of God; the life of grace; faith, hope and charity, with the other interior gifts of the Holy Spirit; and visible elements too. All of these, which come from Christ and lead back to Christ, belong by right to the one Church of Christ.

The brethren divided from us also use many liturgical actions of the Christian religion. These most certainly can truly engender a life of grace in ways that vary according to the condition of each Church or community. These liturgical actions must be regarded as capable of giving access to the community of salvation.

It follows that the separated Churches[7] and communities as such, though we believe them to be deficient in some respects, have been by no means deprived of significance and importance in the mystery of salvation. For the Spirit of Christ has not refrained from using them as means of salvation which derive their efficacy from the very fullness of grace and truth entrusted to the Church.

Nevertheless, our separated brethren, whether considered as individuals or as communities and Churches, are not blessed with that unity

---

5. Cf. Council of Florence, Session 8 (1439): Decree *Exultate Deo:* Mansi 31, 1055 A.

6. Cf. St. Augustine, *In Ps. 32, Enarr.* II, 29: *PL* 36, 299.

7. Cf. Fourth Lateran Council (1215): Constitution IV: Mansi 22, 990; Second Council of Lyons (1274): Profession of faith of Michael Palaeologus: Mansi 24, 71 E; Council of Florence, Session 6 (1439): Definition *Laetentur caeli:* Mansi 31, 1026 E.

which Jesus Christ wished to bestow on all those who through him were born again into one body, and with him quickened to newness of life—that unity which the Holy Scriptures and the ancient Tradition of the Church proclaim. For it is only through Christ's Catholic Church, which is "the all-embracing means of salvation," that they can benefit fully from the means of salvation. We believe that Our Lord entrusted all the blessings of the New Covenant to the apostolic college alone, of which Peter is the head, in order to establish the one body of Christ on earth to which all should be fully incorporated who belong in any way to the People of God. This People of God, though still in its members liable to sin, is ever growing in Christ during its pilgrimage on earth and is guided by God's gentle wisdom, according to his hidden designs, until it shall happily arrive at the fullness of eternal glory in the heavenly Jerusalem.

4. Today, in many parts of the world, under the inspiring grace of the Holy Spirit, many efforts are being made in prayer, word and action to attain that fullness of unity which Jesus Christ desires. The sacred Council exhorts all the Catholic faithful to recognize the signs of the times and to take an active and intelligent part in the work of ecumenism.

The term "ecumenical movement" indicates the initiatives and activities planned and undertaken, according to the various needs of the Church and as opportunities offer, to promote Christian unity. These are: first, every effort to avoid expressions, judgments and actions which do not represent the condition of our separated brethren with truth and fairness and so make mutual relations with them more difficult; then, "dialogue" between competent experts from different Churches and communities. At these meetings, which are organized in a religious spirit, each explains the teaching of his communion in greater depth and brings out clearly its distinctive features. In such dialogue, everyone gains a truer knowledge and more just appreciation of the teaching and religious life of both communions. In addition, the way is prepared for cooperation between them in the duties for the common good of humanity which are demanded by every Christian conscience; and, wherever this is allowed, there is prayer in common. Finally, all are led to examine their own faithfulness to Christ's will for the Church and accordingly to undertake with vigor the task of renewal and reform.

When such actions are undertaken prudently and patiently by the Catholic faithful, with the attentive guidance of their bishops, they promote justice and truth, concord and collaboration, as well as the spirit of brotherly love and unity. This is the way that, when the obstacles to perfect ecclesiastical communion have been gradually overcome, all Christians will at last, in a common celebration of the Eucharist, be gathered into the one and only Church in that unity which Christ bestowed on his Church from the beginning. We believe that this unity subsists in the Catholic Church as something she can never lose, and we hope that it will continue to increase until the end of time.

However, it is evident that when individuals wish for full Catholic communion, their preparation and reconciliation is an undertaking which of its nature is distinct from ecumenical action. But there is no opposition between the two, since both proceed from the marvelous ways of God.

Catholics, in their ecumenical work, must assuredly be concerned for their separated brethren, praying for them, keeping them informed about the Church, making the first approaches toward them. But their primary duty is to make a careful and honest appraisal of whatever needs to be done or renewed in the Catholic household itself, in order that its life may bear witness more clearly and faithfully to the teachings and institutions which have come to it from Christ through the apostles.

For although the Catholic Church has been endowed with all divinely revealed truth and with all means of grace, yet its members fail to live by them with all the fervor that they should, so that the radiance of the Church's image is less clear in the eyes of our separated brethren and of the world at large, and the growth of God's kingdom is delayed. All Catholics must therefore aim at Christian perfection (cf. Jas 1:4; Rm 12:1–2) and, each according to his station, play his part that the Church may daily be more purified and renewed. For the Church must bear in her own body the humility and dying of Jesus (cf. 2 Cor 4:10; Phil 2:5–8), against the day when Christ will present her to himself in all her glory without spot or wrinkle (cf. Eph 5:27).

All in the Church must preserve unity in essentials. But let all, according to the gifts they have received, enjoy a proper freedom in their various forms of spiritual life and discipline, in their different liturgical rites and even in their theological elaborations of revealed truth. In all things let charity prevail. If they are true to this course of action, they will be giving ever better expression to the authentic catholicity and apostolicity of the Church.

On the other hand, Catholics must gladly acknowledge and esteem the truly Christian endowments from our common heritage which are to be found among our separated brethren. It is right and salutary to recognize the riches of Christ and virtuous works in the lives of others who are bearing witness to Christ, sometimes even to the shedding of their blood. For God is always wonderful in his works and worthy of all praise.

Nor should we forget that anything wrought by the grace of the Holy Spirit in the hearts of our separated brethren can be a help to our own edification. Whatever is truly Christian is never contrary to what genuinely belongs to the faith; indeed, it can always bring a deeper realization of the mystery of Christ and the Church.

Nevertheless, the divisions among Christians prevent the Church from attaining the fullness of catholicity proper to her in those of her sons who, though attached to her by Baptism, are yet separated from full communion with her. Furthermore, the Church herself finds it more difficult to express in actual life her full catholicity in all her bearings.

This sacred Council is gratified to note that the participation by the Catholic faithful in ecumenical work is growing daily. It commends this work to the bishops everywhere in the world to be vigorously stimulated by them and guided with prudence.

CHAPTER II

THE PRACTICE OF ECUMENISM

5. The attainment of union is the concern of the whole Church, faithful and shepherds alike. This concern extends to everyone according to his talent, whether it be exercised in his daily Christian life or in his theological and historical research. This concern itself reveals already to some extent the bond of brotherhood between all Christians, and it helps toward that full and perfect unity which God in his kindness wills.

6. Every renewal of the Church[8] is essentially grounded in an increase of fidelity to her own calling. Undoubtedly this is the basis of the movement toward unity.

Christ summons the Church to continual reformation as she sojourns here on earth. The Church is always in need of this, insofar as she is an institution of men here on earth. Thus, if in various times and circumstances, there have been deficiencies in moral conduct or in church discipline, or even in the way that church teaching has been formulated—to be carefully distinguished from the deposit of faith itself—these can and should be set right at the opportune moment.

Church renewal has therefore notable ecumenical importance. Already in various spheres of the Church's life, this renewal is taking place. The biblical and liturgical movements, the preaching of the Word of God and catechetics, the apostolate of the laity, new forms of religious life and the spirituality of married life, and the Church's social teaching and activity—all these should be considered as pledges and signs of the future progress of ecumenism.

7. There can be no ecumenism worthy of the name without a change of heart. For it is from renewal of the inner life of our minds (cf. Eph

---

8. Cf. Fifth Lateran Council, Session 12 (1517): Constitution *Constituti:* Mansi 32, 988 B–C.

4:24), from self-denial and an unstinted love, that desires of unity take their rise and develop in a mature way. We should therefore pray to the Holy Spirit for the grace to be genuinely self-denying, humble, gentle in the service of others, and to have an attitude of brotherly generosity toward them. St. Paul says: "I, therefore, a prisoner for the Lord, beg you to lead a life worthy of the calling to which you have been called, with all humility and meekness, with patience, forbearing one another in love, eager to maintain the unity of the Spirit in the bond of peace" (Eph 4:1–3). This exhortation is directed especially to those raised to sacred Orders precisely that the work of Christ may be continued. He came among us "not to be served but to serve" (Mt 20:28).

The words of St. John hold good about sins against unity: "If we say we have not sinned, we make him a liar, and his word is not in us" (1 Jn 1:10). So we humbly beg pardon of God and of our separated brethren, just as we forgive them that trespass against us.

All the faithful should remember that the more effort they make to live holier lives according to the Gospel, the better will they further Christian unity and put it into practice. For the closer their union with the Father, the Word and the Spirit, the more deeply and easily will they be able to grow in mutual brotherly love.

8. This change of heart and holiness of life, along with public and private prayer for the unity of Christians, should be regarded as the soul of the whole ecumenical movement and merits the name, "spiritual ecumenism."

It is a recognized custom for Catholics to have frequent recourse to that prayer for the unity of the Church which the Savior himself on the eve of his death so fervently appealed to his Father: "That they may all be one" (Jn 17:21).

In certain special circumstances, such as the prescribed prayers "for unity" and during ecumenical gatherings, it is allowable, indeed desirable that Catholics should join in prayer with their separated brethren. Such prayers in common are certainly an effective means of obtaining the grace of unity, and they are a true expression of the ties which still bind Catholics to their separated brethren. "For where two or three are gathered together in my name, there am I in the midst of them" (Mt 18:20).

Yet worship in common *(communicatio in sacris)* is not to be considered as a means to be used indiscriminately for the restoration of

Christian unity. There are two main principles governing the practice of such common worship: first, the bearing witness to the unity of the Church; and second, the sharing in the means of grace. Witness to the unity of the Church very generally forbids common worship to Christians, but the grace to be had from it sometimes commends this practice. The course to be adopted, with due regard to all the circumstances of time, place and persons, is to be decided by local episcopal authority, unless otherwise provided for by the bishops' conference according to its statutes, or by the Holy See.

9. We must get to know the outlook of our separated brethren. To achieve this purpose, study is of necessity required, and this must be pursued with a sense of realism and good will. Catholics who already have a proper grounding need to acquire a more adequate understanding of the respective doctrines of our separated brethren, their history, their spiritual and liturgical life, their religious psychology and general background. Most valuable for this purpose are meetings of the two sides—especially for discussion of theological problems—where each can treat with the other on an equal footing, provided that those who take part in them are truly competent and have the approval of the bishops. From such dialogue will emerge still more clearly what the situation of the Catholic Church really is. In this way, too, the outlook of our separated brethren will be better understood, and our own belief more aptly explained.

10. Sacred theology and other branches of knowledge, especially of a historical nature, must be taught with due regard for the ecumenical point of view, so that they may correspond more exactly with the facts.

It is most important that future shepherds and priests should have mastered a theology that has been carefully worked out in this way and not polemically, especially with regard to those aspects which concern the relations of separated brethren with the Catholic Church.

This importance is the greater because the instruction and spiritual formation of the faithful and of religious depends so largely on the formation which their priests have received.

Moreover, Catholics engaged in missionary work in the same territories as other Christians ought to know, particularly in these times, the problems and the benefits in their apostolate which derive from the ecumenical movement.

11. The way and method in which the Catholic faith is expressed

should never become an obstacle to dialogue with our brethren. It is, of course, essential that the doctrine should be clearly presented in its entirety. Nothing is so foreign to the spirit of ecumenism as a false irenicism, in which the purity of Catholic doctrine suffers loss and its genuine and certain meaning is clouded.

At the same time, the Catholic faith must be explained more profoundly and precisely, in such a way and in such terms as our separated brethren can also really understand.

Moreover, in ecumenical dialogue, Catholic theologians standing fast by the teaching of the Church and investigating the divine mysteries with the separated brethren must proceed with love for the truth, with charity and with humility. When comparing doctrines with one another, they should remember that in Catholic doctrine there exists a "hierarchy" of truths, since they vary in their relation to the fundamental Christian faith. Thus, the way will be opened by which through fraternal rivalry all will be stirred to a deeper understanding and a clearer presentation of the unfathomable riches of Christ (cf. Eph 3:8).

12. Before the whole world let all Christians confess their faith in the triune God, one and three, in the incarnate Son of God, our Redeemer and Lord. United in their efforts, and with mutual respect, let them bear witness to our common hope which does not play us false. In these days when cooperation in social matters is so widespread, all men without exception are called to work together, with much greater reason all those who believe in God, but most of all, all Christians, in that they bear the name of Christ. Cooperation among Christians vividly expresses the relationship which in fact already unites them, and it sets in clearer relief the features of Christ the servant. This cooperation, which has already begun in many countries, should be developed more and more, particularly in regions where a social and technical evolution is taking place, be it in a just evaluation of the dignity of the human person, the establishment of the blessings of peace, the application of Gospel principles to social life, the advancement of the arts and sciences in a truly Christian spirit, or also in the use of various remedies to relieve the afflictions of our times such as famine and natural disasters, illiteracy and poverty, housing shortage and the unequal distribution of wealth. All believers in Christ can, through this cooperation, be led to acquire a better knowledge and appreciation of one another and so pave the way to Christian unity.

CHAPTER III

CHURCHES AND ECCLESIAL COMMUNITIES SEPARATED FROM THE ROMAN APOSTOLIC SEE

13. We now turn our attention to the two chief types of division as they affect the seamless robe of Christ.

The first divisions occurred in the East, when the dogmatic formulae of the Councils of Ephesus and Chalcedon were challenged, and later when ecclesiastical communion between the Eastern Patriarchates and the Roman See was dissolved.

Other divisions arose more than four centuries later in the West, stemming from the events which are usually referred to as "The Reformation." As a result, many communions, national or confessional, were separated from the Roman See. Among those in which Catholic traditions and institutions in part continue to exist, the Anglican communion occupies a special place.

These various divisions differ greatly from one another not only by reason of their origin, place and time, but especially in the nature and seriousness of questions bearing on faith and the structure of the Church. Therefore, without minimizing the differences between the various Christian bodies, and without overlooking the bonds between them which exist in spite of divisions, this holy Council decides to propose the following considerations for prudent ecumenical action.

1. The Special Consideration of the Eastern Churches

14. For many centuries the Church of the East and that of the West each followed their separate ways though linked in a brotherly union of faith and sacramental life; the Roman See by common consent acted as guide when disagreements arose between them over matters of faith or discipline. Among other matters of great importance, it is a pleasure for this Council to remind everyone that there flourish in the East many particular or local Churches, among which the Patriarchal Churches hold

first place, and of these not a few pride themselves in tracing their origins back to the apostles themselves. Hence, a matter of primary concern and care among the Easterns in their local churches has been, and still is, to preserve the family ties of common faith and charity which ought to exist between sister Churches.

Similarly, it must not be forgotten that from the beginning the Churches of the East have had a treasury from which the Western Church has drawn extensively—in liturgical practice, spiritual tradition and law. Nor must we undervalue the fact that it was the ecumenical councils held in the East that defined the basic dogmas of the Christian faith, on the Trinity, on the Word of God who took flesh of the Virgin Mary. To preserve this faith, these Churches have suffered and still suffer much.

However, the heritage handed down by the apostles was received with differences of form and manner, so that from the earliest times of the Church it was explained variously in different places, owing to diversities of genius and conditions of life. All this, quite apart from external causes, prepared the way for decisions arising also from a lack of charity and mutual understanding.

For this reason, the Holy Council urges all, but especially those who intend to devote themselves to the restoration of full communion hoped for between the Churches of the East and the Catholic Church, to give due consideration to this special feature of the origin and growth of the Eastern Churches, and to the character of the relations which obtained between them and the Roman See before separation. They must take full account of all these factors, and where this is done, it will greatly contribute to the dialogue that is looked for.

15. Everyone also knows with what great love the Christians of the East celebrate the sacred liturgy, especially the Eucharistic celebration, source of the Church's life and pledge of future glory, in which the faithful united with their bishop have access to God the Father through the Son, the Word made flesh, who suffered and has been glorified, and so in the outpouring of the Holy Spirit, they enter into communion with the most holy Trinity, being made "sharers of the divine nature" (2 Pt 1:4). Hence, through the celebration of the Holy Eucharist in each of these churches, the Church of God is built up and grows in stature,[9] and

---

9. Cf. St. John Chrysostom, *In Ioannem Homelia XLVI: PG* 59, 260–262.

through concelebration, their communion with one another is made manifest.

In this liturgical worship, the Christians of the East pay high tribute in beautiful hymns of praise to Mary ever Virgin, whom the ecumenical Council of Ephesus solemnly proclaimed to be the holy Mother of God, so that Christ might be acknowledged as being truly Son of God and Son of Man, according to the Scriptures. Many also are the saints whose praise they sing, among them the Fathers of the universal Church.

These Churches, although separated from us, yet possess true sacraments and above all, by apostolic succession, the priesthood and the Eucharist, whereby they are linked with us in closest intimacy. Therefore, some worship in common *(communicatio in sacris)*, given suitable circumstances and the approval of Church authority, is not only possible but to be encouraged.

Moreover, in the East are found the riches of those spiritual traditions which are given expression especially in monastic life. There, from the glorious times of the holy Fathers, monastic spirituality flourished which then later flowed over into the Western world, and there provided the source from which Latin monastic life took its rise and has drawn fresh vigor ever since. Catholics, therefore, are earnestly recommended to avail themselves of the spiritual riches of the Eastern Fathers which lift up the whole man to the contemplation of the divine.

The very rich liturgical and spiritual heritage of the Eastern Churches should be known, venerated, preserved and cherished by all. They must recognize that this is of supreme importance for the faithful preservation of the fullness of Christian tradition, and for bringing about reconciliation between Eastern and Western Christians.

16. Already from the earliest times, the Eastern Churches followed their own forms of ecclesiastical law and custom, which were sanctioned by the approval of the Fathers of the Church, of synods, and even of ecumenical councils. Far from being an obstacle to the Church's unity, a certain diversity of customs and observances only adds to her splendor, and is of great help in carrying out her mission, as has already been stated. To remove, then, all shadow of doubt, this holy Council solemnly declares that the Churches of the East, while remembering the necessary unity of the whole Church, have the power to govern themselves according to the disciplines proper to them, since these are better suited to the character of their faithful and more for the good of their

souls. The perfect observance of this traditional principle, not always indeed carried out in practice, is one of the essential prerequisites for any restoration of unity.

17. What has just been said about the lawful variety that can exist in the Church must also be taken to apply to the differences in theological expression of doctrine. In the study of revelation, East and West have followed different methods, and have developed differently their understanding and confession of God's truth. It is hardly surprising, then, if from time to time one tradition has come nearer to a full appreciation of some aspects of a mystery of revelation than the other, or has expressed it to better advantage. In such cases, these various theological expressions are to be considered often as mutually complementary rather than conflicting. Where the authentic theological traditions of the Eastern Church are concerned, we must recognize the admirable way in which they have their roots in Holy Scripture, and how they are nurtured and given expression in the life of the liturgy. They derive their strength too from the living tradition of the apostles and from the works of the Fathers and spiritual writers of the Eastern Churches. Thus, they promote the right ordering of Christian life, and indeed pave the way to a full vision of Christian truth.

All this heritage of spirituality and liturgy, of discipline and theology, in its various traditions, this holy synod declares to belong to the full Catholic and apostolic character of the Church. We thank God that many Eastern children of the Catholic Church, who preserve this heritage, and wish to express it more faithfully and completely in their lives, are already living in full communion with their brethren who follow the tradition of the West.

18. After taking all these factors into consideration, this sacred Council solemnly repeats the declaration of previous Councils and Roman Pontiffs: that for the restoration or the maintenance of unity and communion it is necessary "to impose no burden beyond what is essential" (Acts 15:28). It is the Council's urgent desire that, in the various organizations and living activities of the Church, every effort should be made toward the gradual realization of this unity, especially by prayer and by fraternal dialogue on points of doctrine and the more pressing pastoral problems of our time. Similarly, the Council commends to the shepherds and faithful of the Catholic Church to develop closer relations with those who are no longer living in the East but are far from home, so

that friendly collaboration with them may increase, in the spirit of love, to the exclusion of all feeling of rivalry or strife. If this cause is whole-heartedly promoted, the Council hopes that the barrier dividing the Eastern Church and Western Church will be removed, and that at last there may be but the one dwelling, firmly established on Christ Jesus the cornerstone, who will make both one.[10]

2. Separated Churches and Ecclesial Communities in the West

19. In the great upheaval which began in the West toward the end of the Middle Ages, and in later times too, Churches and ecclesial communities came to be separated from the Apostolic See of Rome. Yet they have retained a particularly close affinity with the Catholic Church as a result of the long centuries in which all Christendom lived together in ecclesiastical communion.

However, since these Churches and ecclesial communities, on account of their different origins and different teachings in matters of doctrine on the spiritual life, vary considerably not only with us, but also among themselves, the task of describing them at all adequately is extremely difficult; and we have no intention of making such an attempt here.

Although the ecumenical movement and the desire for peace with the Catholic Church have not yet taken hold everywhere, it is our hope that ecumenical feeling and mutual esteem may gradually increase among all men.

It must, however, be admitted that in these Churches and ecclesial communities there exist important differences from the Catholic Church, not only of a historical, sociological, psychological and cultural character, but especially in the interpretation of revealed truth. To make easier the ecumenical dialogue in spite of these differences, we wish to set down some considerations which can and indeed should serve as a basis and encouragement for such dialogue.

20. Our thoughts turn first to those Christians who make open confession of Jesus Christ as God and Lord and as the sole Mediator between God and men, to the glory of the one God, Father, Son and Holy Spirit. We are aware indeed that there exist considerable divergences

10. Cf. Council of Florence, Session 6 (1439): Definition *Laetentur caeli:* Mansi 31, 1026 E.

from the doctrine of the Catholic Church concerning Christ himself, the Word of God made flesh, the work of redemption and consequently, concerning the mystery and ministry of the Church, and the role of Mary in the plan of salvation. But we rejoice to see that our separated brethren look to Christ as the source and center of Church unity. Their longing for union with Christ inspires them to seek an ever closer unity, and also to bear witness to their faith among the peoples of the earth.

21. A love and reverence of Sacred Scripture which might be described as devotion, leads our brethren to a constant meditative study of the sacred text. For the Gospel "is the power of God for salvation to every one who has faith, to the Jew first and then to the Greek" (Rm 1:16).

While invoking the Holy Spirit, they seek in these very Scriptures God as it were speaking to them in Christ, whom the prophets foretold, who is the Word of God made flesh for us. They contemplate in the Scriptures the life of Christ and what the divine Master taught and did for our salvation, especially the mysteries of his death and resurrection.

But while the Christians who are separated from us hold the divine authority of the sacred books, they differ from ours—some in one way, some in another—regarding the relationship between Scripture and the Church. For, according to Catholic belief, the authentic teaching authority of the Church has a special place in the interpretation and preaching of the written Word of God.

But Sacred Scriptures provide for the work of dialogue an instrument of the highest value in the mighty hand of God for the attainment of that unity which the Savior holds out to all.

22. Whenever the sacrament of Baptism is duly administered as Our Lord instituted it and is received with the right dispositions, a person is truly incorporated into the crucified and glorified Christ, and reborn to a sharing of the divine life, as the Apostle says: "You were buried together with him in Baptism, and in him also rose again—through faith in the working of God, who raised him from the dead" (Col 2:12; cf. Rm 6:4).

Baptism therefore establishes a sacramental bond of unity which links all who have been reborn by it. But of itself Baptism is only a beginning, an inauguration wholly directed toward the fullness of life in Christ. Baptism, therefore, envisages a complete profession of faith, complete incorporation in the system of salvation such as Christ willed it to be, and finally complete ingrafting in Eucharistic communion.

Though the ecclesial communities which are separated from us lack the fullness of unity with us flowing from Baptism, and though we believe they have not retained the proper reality of the Eucharistic mystery in its fullness, especially because of the absence of the sacrament of Orders, nevertheless when they commemorate his death and resurrection in the Lord's Supper, they profess that it signifies life in communion with Christ and look forward to his coming in glory. Therefore, the teaching concerning the Lord's Supper, the other sacraments, worship, the ministry of the Church, must be the subject of the dialogue.

23. The daily Christian life of these brethren is nourished by their faith in Christ and strengthened by the grace of Baptism and by hearing the Word of God. This shows itself in their private prayer, their meditation on the Bible, in their Christian family life and in the worship of a community gathered together to praise God. Moreover, their form of worship sometimes displays notable features of the liturgy which they shared with us of old.

Their faith in Christ bears fruit in praise and thanksgiving for the blessings received from the hands of God. Among them, too, is a strong sense of justice and a true charity toward their neighbor. This active faith has been responsible for many organizations for the relief of spiritual and material distress, the furtherance of the education of youth, the improvement of the social conditions of life, and the promotion of peace throughout the world.

While it is true that many Christians understand the moral teaching of the Gospel differently from Catholics, and do not accept the same solutions to the more difficult problems of modern society, nevertheless they share our desire to stand by the words of Christ as the source of Christian virtue, and to obey the command of the Apostle: "And whatever you do, in word or in work, do all in the name of the Lord Jesus Christ, giving thanks to God the Father through him" (Col 3:17). For that reason, an ecumenical dialogue might start with discussion of the application of the Gospel to moral conduct.

24. Now that we have briefly set out the conditions for ecumenical action and the principles by which it is to be directed, we look with confidence to the future. This sacred Council exhorts the faithful to refrain from superficiality and imprudent zeal, which can hinder real progress toward unity. Their ecumenical action must be fully and sincerely Catholic, that is to say, faithful to the truth which we have received from

the apostles and Fathers of the Church, in harmony with the faith which the Catholic Church has always professed, and at the same time directed toward that fullness to which Our Lord wills his body to grow in the course of time.

It is the urgent wish of this holy Council that the measures undertaken by the sons of the Catholic Church should develop in conjunction with those of our separated brethren so that no obstacle be put in the ways of divine Providence and no preconceived judgments impair the future inspirations of the Holy Spirit. The Council moreover professes its awareness that human powers and capacities cannot achieve this holy objective—the reconciling of all Christians in the unity of the one and only Church of Christ. It is because of this that the Council rests all its hope on the prayer of Christ for the Church, on our Father's love for us, and on the power of the Holy Spirit. "And hope does not disappoint, because God's love has been poured into our hearts through the Holy Spirit, who has been given to us" (Rm 5:5).

Each and all these matters which are set forth in this decree have been favorably voted on by the fathers of the Council. And we, by the apostolic authority given us by Christ and in union with the Fathers, approve, decree and establish them in the Holy Spirit and command that they be promulgated for the glory of God.

Given in Rome at St. Peter's, November 21, 1964

DECREE ON THE PASTORAL OFFICE OF BISHOPS IN THE CHURCH

Christus Dominus

Promulgated by
His Holiness Pope Paul VI
On October 28, 1965

ECCLESIAL CLASSICS

INTRODUCTION

The *Decree on the Pastoral Office of Bishops in the Church (CD)* depends greatly on chapter three of *Lumen Gentium*. The relation between the two is a prime example of the pastoral nature of the Council as a whole.

The third chapter of *Lumen Gentium* was one of the most heavily weighed and thoroughly discussed doctrinal parts of all the conciliar texts. It sets forth the Church's faith on collegiality and the primacy of the Pope, and the episcopate as the fullness of the sacrament of Holy Orders. Yet, the bishops' role in the Church is on the level of means. The goal of the Church is the glory of God through the salvation of human persons, while apostolic authority is a divinely instituted means to achieve it.

People often find themselves agreeing about fundamental ends and principles, only to discover that consensus about subordinate matters can be much more complicated. Something similar can be said about the nature, conditions, limits and exercise of episcopal authority in the Church. Faith and divine institution determine the essentials, while the Church's practice, customs and law have decided many particulars in its history.

Lumen Gentium presents the Church's faith on the nature of its apostolic authority, the fullness of which is present and active in the episcopate. *CD* develops the pastoral implications of that teaching. An example of this is the decree's declaration that "all bishops who are members of the episcopal college have the right to be present at an ecumenical council" (*CD* 4). This is derived from the doctrine that the college of bishops is "the subject of supreme and full power over the universal Church" and such power is exercised in an ecumenical council (cf. *LG* 22).

The teaching on collegiality is the foundation for other initiatives, such as the call to reorganize the Roman Curia, including the desire that its personnel reflect the universal nature of the Church (cf. *CD* 9–10). A new institution, the synod of bishops, also flows from this teaching. The synod is a permanent expression of and vehicle for the efficient exercise of hierarchical communion (cf. *CD* 5). Other matters include principles for establishing diocesan boundaries, national episcopal conferences, and within dioceses, the senate or council of priests. These examples suffice to show that the decree contains much legislative material, which would eventually be codified in the 1983 revised *Code of Canon Law.*

Much of this is simply beyond the daily experience of the vast majority of the faithful. But that doesn't mean such matters are unimportant. The decree's directing principle for all matters of organization is this: "The pastoral office of bishops should be so constituted for the governing of dioceses that the good of the Lord's flock is always the supreme consideration" (*CD* 25). Related to this are other reasons given for the establishment and ordering of different ecclesiastical institutions and the ordering of relationships among the clergy and the laity: "For the purpose of duly protecting the freedom of the Church and of promoting more conveniently and efficiently the welfare of the faithful..." (*CD* 20); "In this way the pastoral work in the diocese will be unified and made more effective" (*CD* 30); "In order that the works of the apostolate be carried out harmoniously in individual dioceses and that the unity of diocesan discipline be preserved intact, these principles are established as fundamental" (*CD* 35).

The Council's understanding of "pastoral" is not limited to practical, institutional considerations such as the preceding. Another dimension of its pastoral orientation is the way *CD* goes beyond the *actions* which are required of bishops to fulfill their pastoral office in order to stress the *interior dispositions and attitudes* which should accompany them and from which they should proceed. For example, bishops "should also be mindful of their obligation to give an example of holiness in charity, humility and simplicity of life" (*CD* 15). They are called to esteem and love their coadjutor and auxiliary bishops (*CD* 25).

In the mind of the Council, the effectiveness of the episcopal ministry does not depend only on the good ordering of institutions, but more fundamentally on the bond of charity: "The relationships between the bishop and the diocesan priests should rest most especially upon the bonds of supernatural charity so that the harmony of the will of the priests with that of their bishop will render their pastoral activity more fruitful" (*CD* 25).

This emphasis on interior attitudes and dispositions corresponds to the Council's ecclesiology of communion. The exterior acts and institutions of communion should be the expression, sign and cause of a profound interior and interpersonal communion.

"The bishop is to be considered as the high priest of his flock, from whom the life in Christ of his faithful is in some way derived and dependent" (*SC* 41). The bishops cannot fulfill this function without the assistance of their priests. Because the bishops' service of ministry takes the concrete form of ecclesial communion, it is vital that bishops and their priests exemplify this communion. How can they be the principles of communion if they do not live it themselves? In order for individual bishops to be effective as "the visible principle and foundation of unity in their particular churches" (*LG* 23), they must experience ecclesial unity among themselves and their priests, not just in an institutional manner, but in the most profoundly personal way.

The decree recommends communal life for priests, regular meetings of bishops with their priests, and a presbyteral council or senate of priests. These are all institutional expressions and means of this communion.

Each must do his own part, since this communion first and foremost depends on each individual's communion with God. This explains the decree's emphasis on the bishop's responsibility for the spiritual life and holiness of his priests.

Another element of the bishop's pastoral office is his role as a father with respect to the lay faithful and his priests (cf. *CD* 16, 28; *LG* 28; *PO* 7). The ecclesiological image here is that of the Church as family, underscoring the ministerial or service dimension of the episcopal office. Behind the reality of episcopal authority, the decree calls for the heart of a father. This fatherhood also has a Trinitarian dimension. Jesus said that to see him is to see the Father (cf. Jn 14:9). By exercising their office in the name of Christ and representing him, bishops can make it possible for the faithful to experience the heavenly Father's love.

By episcopal ordination each individual bishop assumes responsibility for the universal Church, and a chief expression of this is his pastoral solicitude for that particular portion of God's people entrusted to him (cf. *CD* 6). The fullness of the sacrament of Holy Orders conferred upon bishops enables them to teach, sanctify and govern in the name and person of Jesus Christ. Even though there are ecclesiastical conditions for the rightful exercise of their pastoral functions, bishops have been entrusted with the care of their flocks through the action of Christ in episcopal consecration (cf. *CD* 11; *LG* 27).

Twenty-five years after Vatican II, the *Catechism of the Catholic Church* underscores the personal responsibility that is an essential element of episcopal and all ecclesial ministry:

> Finally, it belongs to the sacramental nature of ecclesial ministry that it have a *personal character.* Although Christ's ministers act in communion with one another, they also always act in a personal way. Each one is called personally: "You, follow me" (Jn 21:22), in order to be a personal witness within the common mission, to bear personal responsibility before him who gives the mission, acting "in his person" and for other persons: "I baptize you in the name of the Father and of the Son and of the Holy Spirit..."; "I absolve you..." (*CCC* 878).

Recalling that the *Catechism* was written by bishops and was composed first and foremost for bishops, this emphatic statement offers a corrective balance to the enthusiastic and necessary rediscovery and experience of collegiality. Relationships with brother bishops and priests cannot replace the relationship with Jesus Christ established by episcopal consecration.

Personal responsibility means that bishops and clergy are to exercise their pastoral responsibilities knowing they are accountable to God for their actions. Each is to be a man of conscience who knows the difference between prudent consultation with others and the necessity of heeding the voice of God which resounds in the conscience.

Connected to this is the decree's call for each bishop to be a "witness of Christ before all men" (*CD* 11; cf. also 16). In the conciliar documents, "witness" means a total witness of a holy life and verbal proclamation. The actions that flow from this holiness have the power to move people to the goodness of Christ which they see in them. The power in this kind of witness is greater than all the institutional services over which bishops exercise their responsibility.

The decree follows the teaching of *Lumen Gentium* on the ministerial offices of teaching, sanctifying and pastoral care. Concerning the teaching office, "which is conspicuous among the principal duties of bishops" (*CD* 12), they are called to proclaim the Gospel of Christ to all. The ministry of proclaiming the Gospel is seen as a fundamental task of bishops. They are to give special attention to those who have strayed from the truth or have never known it (cf. *CD* 11) and to the poor (cf. *CD* 13). The list of issues mentioned as especially important in our time is not exhaustive or definitive. It is inspired by the main themes of *Gaudium et Spes,* as is the goal given for the catechetical activity for which the bishop is responsible: "to make the faith...a vital, explicit and effective force in the lives of men" (*CD* 14; cf. *GS* 41). In other words, the bishops' ministry of the word is to "activate" the prophetic office of the baptismal priesthood of the faithful. Bishops are also to see that catechists receive proper training, the first element of which is a thorough acquaintance with the doctrine of the Church (cf. *CD* 14).

The goal of the sanctifying office is that the faithful "know and live the Paschal Mystery more deeply through the Eucharist and thus become a firmly knit body in the unity of the charity of Christ" (*CD* 15). Through the ministry of priests the Eucharist is to be the "center and culmination of the whole life of the Christian community" (*CD* 30). Thus, all those committed to their care may exercise their baptismal priesthood through prayer and witness (cf. *CD* 15).

The same pattern is seen in the exercise of the bishop's pastoral office. He is to serve the faithful entrusted to him that they in turn may become Christlike in service by using their gifts and living out their vocation (cf. *CD* 16). Called to be selfless servants, bishops are to "arrange their life in such a way as to accommodate it to the needs of our times" (*CD* 16).

Since bishops fulfill their office of teaching, sanctifying and shepherding through their priests, the decree discusses the pastoral ministry of priests (cf. *CD* 30). Here again we see the pattern: the goal of the ordained priesthood is to serve the baptismal priesthood of the faithful. The faithful are called to be full, conscious and active participants in the life and mission of the Church, to form a holy People of God. They need to be well instructed in the truth of the Gospel, strengthened in faith, and nourished and fortified by God's grace through the sacraments. Strong in hope and living in a communion of charity, they will be fully equipped with gifts from God for the mission Christ has entrusted to the Church. The pastoral office of bishops aims to form the People of God, and this is the measure of all particular pastoral activities and institutions.

The office of bishop is an essential and constitutive element of the Church's life and mission. Vatican II shows this by mentioning the role of bishops in virtually every decree of the Council. Bishops have the responsibility to promote and direct activities regarding the media (cf. *IM* 20), ecumenism (cf. *UR* 4), the missions (cf. *AG* 5, 6, 20, 29), vocations and the formation of priests (cf. *OT* 2, 4), the ministry of priests (cf. *PO* 5–7), and the lay apostolate (*AA* 3, 7, 10, 22). Even when bishops are not explicitly mentioned, it should be kept in mind that the documents of the Council were all written by bishops exercising their solicitude for the universal Church under the guidance of the Holy Spirit.

TOPICAL OUTLINE

1. Introduction (1–3)

2. The relationship of bishops to the universal Church

   A. The role of the bishops in the universal Church

      1. Nature of the episcopal college (4)

      2. Establishment of the synod of bishops (5)

      3. Concern for the universal Church (6–7)

   B. Bishops and the Apostolic See

      1. Bishops have ordinary and immediate authority in exercising their pastoral office (8)

      2. Reorganization of the Roman Curia (9–10)

3. Bishops and their particular churches or dioceses

   A. Diocesan bishops

      1. Role of the diocesan bishop (11)

      2. Proclaiming the Gospel (12–14)

      3. Office of sanctifying (15)

      4. Pastoral office (16)

      5. Apostolic works (17–18)

         a. Relations with civil authorities (19)

         b. Nomination of bishops (20)

      6. Retirement (21)

DECREE ON THE PASTORAL OFFICE OF BISHOPS IN THE CHURCH

Christus Dominus

PREFACE

1. Christ the Lord, Son of the living God, came that he might save his people from their sins (cf. Mt 1:21) and that all men might be sanctified. Just as he himself was sent by the Father, so he also sent his apostles (cf. Jn 20:21). Therefore, he sanctified them, conferring on them the Holy Spirit so that they also might glorify the Father upon earth and save men, "to the building up of the body of Christ" (Eph 4:12), which is the Church.

2. In this Church of Christ, the Roman Pontiff, as the Successor of Peter, to whom Christ entrusted the feeding of his sheep and lambs, enjoys supreme, full, immediate and universal authority over the care of souls by divine institution. Therefore, as pastor of all the faithful, he is sent to provide for the common good of the universal Church and for the good of the individual churches. Hence, he holds a primacy of ordinary power over all the churches.

The bishops themselves, however, having been appointed by the Holy Spirit, are successors of the apostles as pastors of souls.[1] Together with the supreme Pontiff and under his authority they are sent to con-

---

1. Cf. First Vatican Ecumenical Council, Session 4 (1870): Constitution on the Church of Christ *Pastor Aeternus,* c. 3, Denz. 1828 (3061).

tinue throughout the ages the work of Christ, the eternal pastor.[2] Christ gave the apostles and their successors the command and the power to teach all nations, to hallow men in the truth and to feed them. Bishops, therefore, have been made true and authentic teachers of the faith, pontiffs and pastors through the Holy Spirit who has been given to them.[3]

3. Bishops, sharing in the solicitude for all the churches, exercise this episcopal office of theirs, which they have received through episcopal consecration,[4] in communion with and under the authority of the supreme Pontiff. As far as their teaching authority and pastoral government are concerned, all are united in a college or body with respect to the universal Church of God.

They exercise this office individually in reference to the portions of the Lord's flock assigned to them, each one taking care of the particular church committed to him, or sometimes some of them jointly providing for certain common needs of various churches.

This sacred synod, therefore, attentive to the conditions of human association which have brought about a new order of things in our time,[5] intends to determine more exactly the pastoral office of bishops and therefore has decreed the things that follow.

---

2. Cf. First Vatican Ecumenical Council, Session 4 (1870): Constitution on the Church of Christ *Pastor Aeternus,* Introduction, Denz. 1821 (3050).

3. Cf. Second Vatican Ecumenical Council, Dogmatic Constitution on the Church *Lumen Gentium,* 21, 24, 25: *AAS* 57 (1965), 24–25, 29–31.

4. Cf. Second Vatican Ecumenical Council, Dogmatic Constitution on the Church *Lumen Gentium,* 21: *AAS* 57 (1965), 24–25.

5. Cf. John XXIII, Apostolic Constitution *Humanae Salutis* (Dec. 25, 1961): *AAS* 54 (1962), 6.

CHAPTER I

THE RELATIONSHIP OF BISHOPS
TO THE UNIVERSAL CHURCH

1. The Role of the Bishops in the Universal Church

4. By virtue of sacramental consecration and hierarchical communion with the head and members of the college, bishops are constituted as members of the episcopal body.[1] "The order of bishops is the successor to the college of the apostles in teaching and pastoral direction, or rather, in the episcopal order, the apostolic body continues without a break. Together with its head, the Roman Pontiff, and never without this head, it exists as the subject of supreme, plenary power over the universal Church. But this power cannot be exercised except with the agreement of the Roman Pontiff."[2] This power however, "is exercised in a solemn manner in an ecumenical council."[3] Therefore, this sacred synod decrees that all bishops who are members of the episcopal college have the right to be present at an ecumenical council.

"The exercise of this collegiate power in union with the pope is possible, although the bishops are stationed all over the world, provided that the head of the college gives them a call to collegiate action, or at least gives the unified action of the dispersed bishops such approval or such unconstrained acceptance that it becomes truly collegiate action."[4]

5. Bishops chosen from various parts of the world, in ways and manners established or to be established by the Roman Pontiff, render more effective assistance to the supreme pastor of the Church in a deliberative body which will be called by the proper name of *Synod of Bishops*.[5]

---

1. Cf. Second Vatican Ecumenical Council, Dogmatic Constitution on the Church *Lumen Gentium*, 22: *AAS* 57 (1965), 25–27.

2. *Ibid.*

3. *Ibid.*

4. *Ibid.*

5. Cf. Paul VI, Motu Proprio *Apostolica Sollicitudo* (Sept. 15, 1965).

Since it shall be acting in the name of the entire Catholic episcopate, it will at the same time show that all the bishops in hierarchical communion partake of the solicitude for the universal Church.[6]

6. As legitimate successors of the apostles and members of the episcopal college, bishops should realize that they are bound together and should manifest a concern for all the churches. For by divine institution and the rule of the apostolic office, each one together with all the other bishops is responsible for the Church.[7] They should especially be concerned about those parts of the world where the Word of God has not yet been proclaimed or where the faithful, particularly because of the small number of priests, are in danger of departing from the precepts of the Christian life and even of losing the faith itself.

Let bishops, therefore, make every effort to have the faithful actively support and promote works of evangelization and the apostolate. Let them strive, moreover, to see to it that suitable sacred ministers as well as auxiliaries, both religious and lay, be prepared for the missions and other areas suffering from a lack of clergy. They should also see to it as much as possible that some of their own priests go to the above-mentioned missions or dioceses to exercise the sacred ministry there either permanently or for a set period of time.

Bishops should also be mindful, in administering ecclesiastical property, of the needs not only of their own dioceses but also of the other particular churches, for they are also a part of the one Church of Christ. Finally, they should direct their attention, according to their means, to the relief of disasters by which other dioceses and regions are affected.

7. Let them especially embrace in brotherly affection those bishops who for the sake of Christ are plagued with slander and indigence, detained in prisons or held back from their ministry. They should take an active brotherly interest in them so that their sufferings may be assuaged and alleviated through the prayers and good works of their confreres.

---

6. Cf. Second Vatican Ecumenical Council, Dogmatic Constitution on the Church *Lumen Gentium, 23*: *AAS* 57 (1965), 27–28.

7. Cf. Pius XII, Encyclical Letter *Fidei Donum* (April 21, 1957): *AAS* 49 (1957), 27 ff.; cf. also Benedict XV's Apostolic Letter *Maximum Illud* (Nov. 30, 1919): *AAS* 11 (1919), 440; Pius XI's Encyclical Letter *Rerum Ecclesiae* (Feb. 28, 1926): *AAS* 18 (1926), 68.

2. Bishops and the Apostolic See

8. (a) To bishops, as successors of the apostles, in the dioceses entrusted to them there belongs *per se* all the ordinary, proper and immediate authority which is required for the exercise of their pastoral office. But this never in any way infringes upon the power which the Roman Pontiff has, by virtue of his office, of reserving cases to himself or to some other authority.

(b) The general law of the Church grants the faculty to each diocesan bishop to dispense in a particular case the faithful over whom they legally exercise authority, as often as they judge that it contributes to their spiritual welfare, except in those cases which have been especially reserved by the supreme authority of the Church.

9. In exercising supreme, full and immediate power in the universal Church, the Roman Pontiff makes use of the departments of the Roman Curia which, therefore, perform their duties in his name and with his authority for the good of the churches and in the service of the sacred pastors.

The fathers of this sacred Council, however, desire that these departments—which have furnished distinguished assistance to the Roman Pontiff and the pastors of the Church—be reorganized and better adapted to the needs of the times, regions and rites, especially as regards their number, name, competence and peculiar method of procedure, as well as the coordination of work among them.[8] The fathers also desire that in view of the very nature of the pastoral office proper to the bishops, the office of legates of the Roman Pontiff be more precisely determined.

10. Furthermore, since these departments are established for the good of the universal Church, it is desirable that their members, officials and consultors, as well as legates of the Roman Pontiff, be more widely taken from various regions of the Church, insofar as it is possible. In such a way, the offices and central organs of the Catholic Church will exhibit a truly universal character.

It is also desired that some bishops, too—especially diocesan bishops—will be chosen as members of the departments, for they will be

---

8. Cf. Paul VI, *Allocution to the Cardinals, Prelates and Various Officials of the Roman Curia* (Sept. 21, 1963): *AAS* 55 (1963), 793 ff.

able to report more fully to the supreme Pontiff the thinking, the desires and the needs of all the churches.

Finally, the fathers of the Council think it would be most advantageous if these same departments would listen more attentively to laymen who are outstanding for their virtue, knowledge and experience. In such a way they will have an appropriate share in Church affairs.

Chapter II

BISHOPS AND THEIR
PARTICULAR CHURCHES OR DIOCESES

1. Diocesan Bishops

11. A diocese is a portion of the People of God which is entrusted to a bishop to be shepherded by him with the cooperation of the presbytery. Thus, by adhering to its pastor and gathered together by him through the Gospel and the Eucharist in the Holy Spirit, it constitutes a particular church in which the one, holy, catholic and apostolic Church of Christ is truly present and operative.

Individual bishops who have been entrusted with the care of a particular church—under the authority of the supreme Pontiff—feed their sheep in the name of the Lord as their own ordinary and immediate pastors, performing for them the office of teaching, sanctifying and governing. Nevertheless, they should recognize the rights which legitimately belong to patriarchs or other hierarchical authorities.[1]

Bishops should dedicate themselves to their apostolic office as witnesses of Christ before all men. They should not only look after those who already follow the Prince of Pastors but should also wholeheartedly devote themselves to those who have strayed in any way from the path of truth or are ignorant of the Gospel of Christ and his saving mercy, until finally all men walk "in all goodness and justice and truth" (Eph 5:9).

12. In exercising their duty of teaching, which is conspicuous among the principal duties of bishops,[2] they should announce the Gospel of Christ to men, calling them to a faith in the power of the Spirit

---

1. Cf. Second Vatican Ecumenical Council, Decree on the Catholic Churches of the Eastern Rite *Orientalium Ecclesiarum* 7–11: *AAS* 57 (1965), 29 ff.

2. Cf. Council of Trent, Session 5: Decree *De Reform.,* c. 2, Mansi 33, 30; Session 24: Decree *De Reform.,* c. Mansi 33, 159; cf. Second Vatican Ecumenical Council, Dogmatic Constitution on the Church *Lumen Gentium,* 25: *AAS* 57 (1965), 29 ff.

or confirming them in a living faith. They should expound the whole mystery of Christ to them, namely, those truths the ignorance of which is ignorance of Christ. At the same time, they should point out the divinely revealed way to give glory to God and thereby to attain to eternal happiness.[3]

They should show, moreover, that earthly goods and human institutions according to the plan of God the Creator are also disposed for man's salvation and, therefore, can contribute much to the building up of the body of Christ.

Therefore, they should teach, according to the doctrine of the Church, the great value of these things: the human person with his freedom and bodily life, the family and its unity and stability, the procreation and education of children, civil society with its laws and professions, labor and leisure, the arts and technical inventions, poverty and affluence. Finally, they should set forth the ways by which are to be answered the most serious questions concerning the ownership, increase and just distribution of material goods, peace and war, and brotherly relations among all countries.[4]

13. The bishops should present Christian doctrine in a manner adapted to the needs of the times, that is to say, in a manner that will respond to the difficulties and questions by which people are especially burdened and troubled. They should also guard that doctrine, teaching the faithful to defend and propagate it. In propounding this doctrine they should manifest the maternal solicitude of the Church toward all men, whether they be believers or not. With a special affection they should attend upon the poor and the lower classes to whom the Lord sent them to preach the Gospel.

Since it is the mission of the Church to converse with the human society in which it lives,[5] it is especially the duty of bishops to seek out men and both request and promote dialogue with them. These conversations on salvation ought to be noted for clarity of speech as well as humility and mildness, in order that at all times truth may be joined to

---

3. Cf. Second Vatican Ecumenical Council, Dogmatic Constitution on the Church *Lumen Gentium,* 25: *AAS* 57 (1965), 29–31.

4. Cf. John XXIII, Encyclical Letter *Pacem in Terris* (April 11, 1963): *AAS* 55 (1963), 257–304.

5. Cf. Paul VI, Encyclical Letter *Ecclesiam Suam* (Aug. 6, 1964): *AAS* 56 (1964), 639.

charity and understanding with love. Likewise, they should be noted for due prudence joined with trust, which fosters friendship and thus is capable of bringing about a union of minds.[6]

They should also strive to make use of the various media at hand nowadays for proclaiming Christian doctrine, namely, first of all, preaching and catechetical instruction which always hold the first place, then the presentation of this doctrine in schools, academies, conferences and meetings of every kind, and finally its dissemination through public statements at times of outstanding events as well as by the press and various other media of communication, which by all means ought to be used in proclaiming the Gospel of Christ.[7]

14. Bishops should take pains that catechetical instruction—which is intended to make the faith, as illumined by teaching, a vital, explicit and effective force in the lives of men—be given with sedulous care to both children and adolescents, youths and adults. In this instruction a suitable arrangement should be observed as well as a method suited to the matter that is being treated and to the character, ability, age and circumstances of the life of the students. Finally, they should see to it that this instruction is based on Sacred Scripture, Tradition, the liturgy, magisterium and life of the Church.

Moreover, they should take care that catechists be properly trained for their function so that they will be thoroughly acquainted with the doctrine of the Church and will have both a theoretical and a practical knowledge of the laws of psychology and of pedagogical methods.

Bishops should also strive to renew or at least adapt in a better way the instruction of adult catechumens.

15. In exercising their office of sanctifying, bishops should be mindful that they have been taken from among men and appointed their representative before God in order to offer gifts and sacrifices for sins. Bishops enjoy the fullness of the sacrament of Orders, and both presbyters and deacons are dependent upon them in the exercise of their authority. For the presbyters are the prudent fellow workers of the episcopal order and are themselves consecrated as true priests of the New

---

6. Cf. Paul VI, Encyclical Letter *Ecclesiam Suam* (Aug. 6, 1964): *AAS* 56 (1964), 644–645.

7. Cf. Second Vatican Ecumenical Council, Decree on the Media of Social Communication *Inter Mirifica: AAS* 56 (1964), 145–153.

Testament, just as deacons are ordained for the ministry and serve the People of God in communion with the bishop and his presbytery. Therefore, bishops are the principal dispensers of the mysteries of God, as well as being the governors, promoters and guardians of the entire liturgical life in the church committed to them.[8]

They should, therefore, constantly exert themselves to have the faithful know and live the Paschal Mystery more deeply through the Eucharist and thus become a firmly-knit body in the unity of the charity of Christ.[9] "Intent upon prayer and the ministry of the word" (Acts 6:4), they should devote their labor to this end, that all those committed to their care may be of one mind in prayer (cf. Acts 1:14; 2:46) and through the reception of the sacraments may grow in grace and be faithful witnesses to the Lord.

As those who lead others to perfection, bishops should be diligent in fostering holiness among their clerics, religious and laity according to the special vocation of each.[10] They should also be mindful of their obligation to give an example of holiness in charity, humility and simplicity of life. Let them so hallow the churches entrusted to them that the feeling of the universal Church of Christ may shine forth fully in them. For that reason, they should foster priestly and religious vocations as much as possible, and should take a special interest in missionary vocations.

16. In exercising their office of father and pastor, bishops should stand in the midst of their people as those who serve (cf. Lk 22:26–27). Let them be good shepherds who know their sheep and whose sheep know them. Let them be true fathers who excel in the spirit of love and solicitude for all and to whose divinely conferred authority all gratefully submit themselves. Let them so gather and mold the whole family of their flock that everyone, conscious of his own duties, may live and work in the communion of love.

In order effectively to accomplish these things, bishops, "ready for every good work" (2 Tm 2:21) and "enduring all things for the sake of

---

8. Cf. Second Vatican Ecumenical Council, Constitution on the Sacred Liturgy *Sacrosanctum Concilium: AAS* 56 (1964), 97 ff.; Paul VI, Motu Proprio *Sacram Liturgiam* (Jan. 25, 1964): *AAS* 56 (1964), 139 ff.

9. Pius XII, Encyclical Letter *Mediator Dei* (Nov. 20, 1947): *AAS* 39 (1947), 97 ff.; Paul VI, Encyclical Letter *Mysterium Fidei* (Sept. 3, 1965).

10. Cf. Second Vatican Ecumenical Council, Dogmatic Constitution on the Church *Lumen Gentium*, 44, 45: *AAS* 57 (1965), 50–52.

the chosen ones" (2 Tm 2:10), should arrange their life in such a way as to accommodate it to the needs of our times.

Bishops should always embrace priests with a special love since the latter to the best of their ability assume the bishops' anxieties and carry them on day by day so zealously. They should regard the priests as sons and friends (cf. Jn 15:15) and be ready to listen to them. Through their trusting familiarity with their priests, they should strive to promote the whole pastoral work of the entire diocese.

They should be solicitous for the spiritual, intellectual and material welfare of the priests so that the latter can live holy and pious lives and fulfill their ministry faithfully and fruitfully. Therefore, they should encourage institutes and hold special meetings in which priests might gather from time to time both for the performance of longer exercises and the renewal of their spiritual life and for the acquisition of deeper subjects, especially Sacred Scripture and theology, the more important social questions and the new methods of pastoral activity.

With active mercy bishops should pursue priests who are involved in any danger or who have failed in certain respects.

In order to be able to look more closely to the welfare of the faithful according to the condition of each one, bishops should strive to become duly acquainted with their needs in the social circumstances in which they live. Therefore, they ought to employ suitable methods, especially social research. They should manifest their concern for everyone, no matter what their age, condition or nationality, be they natives, strangers or foreigners. In exercising this pastoral care, they should preserve for their faithful the share proper to them in Church affairs; they should also respect their duty and right of actively collaborating in the building up of the Mystical Body of Christ.

They should deal lovingly with the separated brethren, urging the faithful also to conduct themselves with great kindness and charity in their regard and fostering ecumenism as it is understood by the Church.[11] They should also have a place in their hearts for the non-baptized, so that upon them too there may shine the charity of Christ Jesus, to whom the bishops are witnesses before all men.

---

11. Cf. Second Vatican Ecumenical Council, Decree on Ecumenism *Unitatis Redintegratio: AAS* 57 (1965), 90–107.

17. Various forms of the apostolate should be encouraged, and in the whole diocese or in any particular areas of it the coordination and close connection of all apostolic works should be fostered under the direction of the bishop. Thus, all undertakings and organizations, be they catechetical, missionary, charitable, social, familial, educational or anything else pursuing a pastoral aim, should be directed toward harmonious action. Thus, at the same time the unity of the diocese will also be made more evident.

The faithful should be earnestly urged to assume their duty of carrying on the apostolate, each according to his state in life and ability. They should be admonished to participate in and give aid to the various works of the apostolate of the laity, especially Catholic Action. Those associations should also be promoted and supported which either directly or indirectly pursue a supernatural objective, that is, either the attaining of a more perfect life, the spreading of the Gospel of Christ to all men and the promoting of Christian doctrine or the increase of public worship, or the pursuing of social aims or the performing of works of piety and charity.

The forms of the apostolate should be properly adapted to the needs of the present day with regard not only for man's spiritual and moral circumstances, but also for his social, demographic and economic conditions. Religious and social research, through offices of pastoral sociology, contributes much to the efficacious and fruitful attainment of that goal, and it is highly recommended.

18. Special concern should be shown for those among the faithful who, on account of their way of life, cannot sufficiently make use of the common and ordinary pastoral care of parish priests or are quite cut off from it. Among this group are the majority of migrants, exiles and refugees, seafarers, air travelers, gypsies and others of this kind. Suitable pastoral methods should also be promoted to sustain the spiritual life of those who go to other lands for a time for the sake of recreation.

Episcopal conferences, especially national ones, should pay special attention to the very pressing problems concerning the abovementioned groups. Through voluntary agreement and united efforts, they should look to and promote their spiritual care by means of suitable methods and institutions. They should also bear in mind the special rules either already laid down or to be laid down by the Apostolic

See[12] which can be wisely adapted to the circumstances of time, place and persons.

19. In discharging their apostolic office, which concerns the salvation of souls, bishops *per se* enjoy full and perfect freedom and independence from any civil authority. Hence, the exercise of their ecclesiastical office may not be hindered directly or indirectly, nor may they be forbidden to communicate freely with the Apostolic See or ecclesiastical authorities or their subjects.

Assuredly, while sacred pastors devote themselves to the spiritual care of their flock, they also in fact have regard for their social and civil progress and prosperity. According to the nature of their office and as behooves bishops, they collaborate actively with public authorities for this purpose and advocate obedience to just laws and reverence for legitimately constituted authorities.

20. Since the apostolic office of bishops was instituted by Christ the Lord and pursues a spiritual and supernatural purpose, this sacred ecumenical synod declares that the right of nominating and appointing bishops belongs properly, peculiarly and *per se* exclusively to the competent ecclesiastical authority.

Therefore, for the purpose of duly protecting the freedom of the Church and of promoting more conveniently and efficiently the welfare of the faithful, this holy Council desires that in the future no more rights or privileges of election, nomination, presentation or designation for the office of bishop be granted to civil authorities. The civil authorities, on the other hand, whose favorable attitude toward the Church the sacred synod gratefully acknowledges and highly appreciates, are most kindly requested voluntarily to renounce the above-mentioned rights and privileges which they presently enjoy by reason of a treaty or custom, after discussing the matter with the Apostolic See.

21. Since the pastoral office of bishops is so important and weighty, diocesan bishops and others regarded in law as their equals, who have become less capable of fulfilling their duties properly because of the increasing burden of age or some other serious reason, are earnestly

---

12. Cf. St. Pius X, Motu Proprio *Iampridem* (March 19, 1914): *AAS* 6 (1914), 174 ff.; Pius XII, Apostolic Constitution *Exsul Familia* (Aug. 1, 1952): *AAS* 54 (1952), 652 ff.; compiled under the authority of Pius XII, *Regulations for the Apostolate of the Sea* (Nov. 21, 1957): *AAS* 50 (1958), 375 ff.

requested to offer their resignation from office either at their own initiative or upon the invitation of the competent authority. If the competent authority should accept the resignation, it will make provision both for the suitable support of those who have resigned and for special rights to be accorded them.

2. Diocesan Boundaries

22. For a diocese to fulfill its purpose, the nature of the Church must be clearly evident to the People of God who constitute that diocese. To this end also bishops must be able to carry out their pastoral duties effectively among their people. Finally, the welfare of the People of God must be served as perfectly as possible.

All this demands, then, a proper determination of the boundaries of dioceses and a distribution of clergy and resources that is reasonable and in keeping with the needs of the apostolate. All these things will benefit not only the clergy and Christian people involved, but also the entire Catholic Church.

Concerning diocesan boundaries, therefore, this sacred synod decrees that, to the extent required by the good of souls, a fitting revision of diocesan boundaries be undertaken prudently and as soon as possible. This can be done by dividing, dismembering or uniting them, or by changing their boundaries, or by determining a better place for the episcopal see or finally, especially in the case of dioceses having larger cities, by providing them with a new internal organization.

23. In revising diocesan boundaries, first place must be accorded to the organic unity of each diocese, with due regard to the personnel, the offices and institutions which form, as it were, a living body. In individual cases all circumstances should be carefully studied and the general criteria which follow should be kept in mind:

1) In determining a diocesan boundary, as far as possible consideration should be given the variety in composition of the People of God, for this can contribute greatly to a more effective exercise of the pastoral office. At the same time the natural population units of people, together with the civil jurisdictions and social institutions that compose their organic structure, should be preserved as far as possible as units. For this reason, obviously, the territory of each diocese should be continuous.

Attention should also be given, if necessary, to civil boundaries and the special characteristics of regions and peoples, such as their psychological, economic, geographic and historical backgrounds.

2) The extent of the diocese and the number of its inhabitants should generally be such that on the one hand the bishop himself—even though assisted by others—can officiate at pontifical functions, make pastoral visitations, faithfully direct and coordinate all the works of the apostolate in the diocese and know well especially his priests, and also the religious and lay people who are engaged in diocesan projects. On the other hand, an adequate and suitable area should be provided so that bishop and clergy, mindful also of the needs of the universal Church, can usefully devote all their energies to the ministry.

3) Finally, in order that the ministry of salvation be more effectively carried out in each diocese, it should be considered a general rule that each diocese have clergy, in number and qualifications at least sufficient, for the proper care of the People of God; also, there should be no lack of the offices, institutions and organizations which are proper to the particular church and which experience has shown necessary for its efficient government and apostolate; finally, resources for the support of personnel and institutions should be at hand or at least prudently foreseen in prospect.

For this same purpose, where there are faithful of a different rite, the diocesan bishop should provide for their spiritual needs either through priests or parishes of that rite or through an episcopal vicar endowed with the necessary faculties. Wherever it is fitting, the last named should also have episcopal rank. Otherwise the ordinary himself may perform the office of an ordinary of different rites. If for certain reasons, these prescriptions are not applicable in the judgment of the Apostolic See, then a proper hierarchy for the different rites is to be established.[13]

Also, where similar situations exist, provision should be made for the faithful of different language groups, either through priests or parishes of the same language or through an episcopal vicar well versed in the language—and if needs be having the episcopal dignity—or at least in some other more appropriate way.

24. In order to bring about the changes and alterations of dioceses as set forth in numbers 22–23—and leaving untouched the discipline of the Oriental Churches—it is desirable that the competent episcopal conferences examine these matters each for its respective territory. If deemed

---

13. Cf. Second Vatican Ecumenical Council, Decree on the Catholic Churches of the Eastern Rite *Orientalium Ecclesiarum,* 4: *AAS* 57 (1965), 77.

opportune, they may employ a special episcopal commission for this purpose, but always taking into account the opinions of the bishops of the provinces or regions concerned. Finally, they are to propose their recommendations and desires to the Apostolic See.

3. Assistants in the Pastoral Office of the Diocesan Bishops

1. Coadjutor and Auxiliary Bishops

25. The pastoral office of bishops should be so constituted for the governing of dioceses that the good of the Lord's flock is always the supreme consideration. Rightly to achieve this goal, auxiliary bishops will frequently be appointed, because the diocesan bishop cannot personally fulfill all his episcopal duties as the good of souls demands, either because of the vast extent of the diocese or the great number of its inhabitants, or because of the special nature of the apostolate or other reasons of a different nature. Sometimes, in fact, a particular need requires that a coadjutor bishop be appointed to assist the diocesan bishop. Coadjutor and auxiliary bishops should be granted those faculties necessary for rendering their work more effective and safeguarding the dignity proper to bishops. This, of course, should always be accomplished without detriment to the unity of the diocesan administration and the authority of the diocesan bishop.

Furthermore, coadjutor and auxiliary bishops, since they are called to share part of the burden of the diocesan bishops, so should exercise their office that they may proceed in all matters in single-minded agreement with him. In addition, they should always show respect and reverence for the diocesan bishop and he, in turn, should have a fraternal love for coadjutor and auxiliary bishops and hold them in esteem.

26. To the extent that the good of souls demands, the diocesan bishop should not hesitate to ask the competent authority for one or more auxiliaries who will be appointed for the diocese without the right of succession.

If there is no provision for it in the letter of nomination, the diocesan bishop is to appoint his auxiliary or auxiliaries as vicar generals or at least as episcopal vicars. They shall be dependent upon his authority only, and he may wish to consult them in examining questions of major importance, especially of a pastoral nature.

Unless competent authority has otherwise determined, the powers and faculties which auxiliary bishops have by law do not cease when the office of the diocesan bishop comes to an end. It is also desirable that when the see is vacant the office of ruling the diocese—unless some serious reasons persuade otherwise—should be committed to the auxiliary bishop, or when there are more than one, to one of the auxiliaries.

A coadjutor bishop, appointed with the right of succession, must always be named vicar general by the diocesan bishop. In particular cases the competent authority can grant him even more extensive faculties.

In order to provide for the greatest possible present and future good of the diocese, the diocesan bishop and his coadjutor should not fail to consult with each other on matters of great importance.

2. The Diocesan Curia and Commissions

27. The most important office in the diocesan curia is that of vicar general. However, as often as the proper government of the diocese requires it, one or more episcopal vicars can be named by the bishop. These automatically enjoy the same authority which the common law grants the vicar general, but only for a certain part of the diocese, or for a determined type of transaction or for the faithful of a determined rite.

Among the collaborators of the bishop in the government of the diocese are numbered those presbyters who constitute his senate, or council, such as the cathedral chapter, the board of consultors or other committees according to the circumstances or nature of various localities. These institutions, especially the cathedral chapters, should be reorganized wherever necessary in keeping with present-day needs.

Priests and lay people who belong to the diocesan curia should realize that they are making a helpful contribution to the pastoral ministry of the bishop.

The diocesan curia should be so organized that it is an appropriate instrument for the bishop, not only for administering the diocese but also for carrying out the works of the apostolate.

It is greatly desired that in each diocese a pastoral commission will be established over which the diocesan bishop himself will preside and in which specially chosen clergy, religious and lay people will participate. The duty of this commission will be to investigate and weigh pastoral undertakings and to formulate practical conclusions regarding them.

3. The Diocesan Clergy

28. All presbyters, both diocesan and religious, participate in and exercise with the bishop the one priesthood of Christ and are thereby con-stituted prudent cooperators of the episcopal order. In the care of souls, however, the first place is held by diocesan priests who are incardinated or attached to a particular church, for they have fully dedicated themselves in the service of caring for a single portion of the Lord's flock. In consequence, they form one presbytery and one family whose father is the bishop. In order to distribute more equitably and properly the sacred ministries among his priests, the bishop should possess a necessary freedom in bestowing offices and benefices. Therefore, rights or privileges which in any way limit this freedom are to be suppressed.

The relationships between the bishop and the diocesan priests should rest most especially upon the bonds of supernatural charity, so that the harmony of the will of the priests with that of their bishop will render their pastoral activity more fruitful. Wherefore, for the sake of greater service to souls, let the bishop call the priests into dialogue, especially about pastoral matters. This he should do not only on a given occasion but at regularly fixed intervals insofar as this is possible.

Furthermore, all diocesan priests should be united among themselves and so should share a genuine concern for the spiritual welfare of the whole diocese. They should also be mindful that the benefits they receive by reason of their ecclesiastical office are closely bound up with their sacred work. Therefore, they should contribute generously, as the bishop may direct and as their means permit, to the material needs of the diocese.

29. The closer collaborators of the bishop are those priests who are charged with a pastoral office or apostolic organizations of a supra-parochial nature, whether in a certain area of the diocese or among special groups of the faithful or with respect to a specific kind of activity.

Priests assigned by the bishop to various works of the apostolate, whether in schools or in other institutions or associations, contribute an exceedingly valuable assistance. Those priests also who are engaged in supra-diocesan works are commended to the special consideration of the bishop in whose diocese they reside, for they perform outstanding works of the apostolate.

30. Pastors, however, are cooperators of the bishop in a very special way, for as pastors in their own name, they are entrusted with the care of souls in a certain part of the diocese under the bishop's authority.

1) In exercising this care of souls, pastors and their assistants should so fulfill their duty of teaching, sanctifying and governing that the faithful and the parish communities will truly realize that they are members both of the diocese and of the universal Church. For this reason, they should collaborate with other pastors and priests who exercise a pastoral office in the area (such as vicars forane and deans), as well as with those engaged in works of a supra-parochial nature. In this way the pastoral work in the diocese will be unified and made more effective.

Moreover, the care of souls should always be infused with a missionary spirit so that it reaches out as it should to everyone living within the parish boundaries. If the pastor cannot contact certain groups of people, he should seek the assistance of others, even laymen who can assist him in the apostolate.

To render the care of souls more efficacious, community life for priests—especially those attached to the same parish—is highly recommended. This way of living, while it encourages apostolic action, also affords an example of charity and unity to the faithful.

2) In the exercise of their teaching office, it is the duty of pastors to preach God's Word to all the Christian people so that rooted in faith, hope and charity they will grow in Christ, and as a Christian community bear witness to that charity which the Lord commended (cf. Jn 13:35). It is also the duty of pastors to bring the faithful to a full knowledge of the mystery of salvation through a catechetical instruction which is consonant with each one's age. In imparting this instruction, they should seek not only the assistance of religious but also the cooperation of the laity, establishing also the Confraternity of Christian Doctrine.

In discharging their duty of sanctifying their people, pastors should see to it that the celebration of the Eucharistic Sacrifice is the center and culmination of the whole life of the Christian community. They should labor without stint that the faithful are nourished with spiritual food through the devout and frequent reception of the sacraments and through intelligent and active participation in the liturgy. Pastors should also be mindful of how much the sacrament of Penance contributes to developing the Christian life and, therefore, should always make themselves available to hear the confessions of the faithful. If necessary they should invite the assistance of priests who are experienced in various languages.

In fulfilling their office as shepherd, pastors should take pains to know their own flock. Since they are the servants of all the sheep, they should encourage a full Christian life among the individual faithful and also in families, in associations especially dedicated to the apostolate and in the whole parish community. Therefore, they should visit homes and schools to the extent that their pastoral work demands. They should pay special attention to adolescents and youth. They should devote themselves with a paternal love to the poor and the sick. They should have a particular concern for workingmen. Finally, they should encourage the faithful to assist in the works of the apostolate.

3) Assistant pastors, as cooperators with the pastor, make under the authority of the pastor an indispensable and active contribution to the pastoral ministry. Therefore, there should always be fraternal association, mutual charity and reverence between the pastor and his assistants. They should assist one another with counsel, help and example, providing a united will and common zeal in the service of the parish.

31. In forming a judgment on the suitability of a priest for the administration of any parish, the bishop should take into consideration not only his knowledge of doctrine but also his piety, apostolic zeal and other gifts and qualities which are necessary for the proper exercise of the care of souls.

Now, the parish exists solely for the good of souls. Wherefore, the bishop should be able to provide more easily and effectively for vacant pastorates. To this end, all rights whatsoever of presentation, nomination, reservation, excepting the right of religious—and where it exists, the law of concursus whether general or particular—are to be suppressed.

Pastors should enjoy in their respective parishes that stability of office which the good of souls demands. The distinction between removable and irremovable pastors is to be abrogated, and the procedure for transferring and removing pastors is to be reexamined and simplified. In this way the bishop, while observing natural and canonical equity, can better provide for the needs of the good of souls.

Pastors who are unable to fulfill their office properly and fruitfully because of the increasing burden of old age or some other serious reason are urgently requested to tender their resignation voluntarily upon the invitation of the bishop. The bishop should provide suitable support for those who have resigned.

32. Finally, the same concern for souls should be the basis for determining or reconsidering the erection or suppression of parishes and any other changes of this kind which the bishop is empowered to undertake on his own authority.

4. Religious

33. (In all that follows, with religious are included also the members of other institutes who profess the evangelical counsels.) All religious have the duty, each according to his proper vocation, of cooperating zealously and diligently in building up and increasing the whole Mystical Body of Christ and for the good of the particular churches.

It is their first duty to foster these objectives by prayer, works of penance and the example of their own life, for which this sacred synod strongly urges them to increase their esteem and zeal. With due consideration for the character proper to each religious community, they should also enter more vigorously into the external works of the apostolate.

34. Religious priests are by consecration assumed into the responsibilities of the presbyterate so as to become themselves the prudent cooperators of the episcopal order. Today they can be of even greater help to bishops in view of the greater needs of souls. Therefore, they can be said in a real sense to belong to the clergy of the diocese, inasmuch as they share in the care of souls and in carrying out works of the apostolate under the authority of the prelates.

Other members of religious communities, both men and women, also belong in a special way to the diocesan family and offer great assistance to the sacred hierarchy. With the increasing demands of the apostolate, they can and should offer that assistance even more and more.

35. In order that the works of the apostolate be carried out harmoniously in individual dioceses and that the unity of diocesan discipline be preserved intact, these principles are established as fundamental:

1) All religious should always look upon the bishops, as upon successors of the apostles, with devoted respect and reverence. Whenever they are legitimately called upon to undertake works of the apostolate,

they are obliged to discharge their duties as active and obedient helpers of the bishops.[14] Indeed, religious should consider it an honor to respond promptly and faithfully to the requests and desires of the bishops, and in such a way they may assume an even more ample role in the ministry of human salvation. This they should do with due respect for the character of their institute and in keeping with their constitutions which, if need be, should be accommodated to this goal in accord with the principles of this conciliar decree.

Especially in view of the urgent need of souls and the scarcity of diocesan clergy, religious communities which are not dedicated exclusively to the contemplative life can be called upon by the bishops to assist in various pastoral ministries. They should, however, keep in mind the particular character of each community. Superiors should encourage this work to the utmost by accepting parishes, even on a temporary basis.

2) Religious engaged in the active apostolate, however, must always be imbued with the spirit of their religious community and remain faithful to the observance of their rule and spirit of submissiveness due to their own superiors. Bishops should not neglect to impress this obligation upon them.

3) The privilege of exemption, by which religious are called to the service of the supreme Pontiff or other ecclesiastical authority and withdrawn from the jurisdiction of bishops, refers chiefly to the internal order of their communities, so that in them all things may be properly coordinated and the growth and perfection of the religious common life promoted.[15] These communities are also exempt so that the supreme Pontiff can dispose of them for the good of the universal Church[16] and any other competent authority for the good of the churches under its own jurisdiction.

This exemption, however, does not exclude religious in individual dioceses from the jurisdiction of bishops in accordance with the norm of law, insofar as the performance of their pastoral office and the right ordering of the care of souls requires.[17]

---

14. Cf. Pius XII, *Allocution* (Dec. 8, 1950): *AAS* 43 (1951), 28; cf. also Paul VI, *Allocution* (May 23, 1964): *AAS* 56 (1964), 571.

15. Cf. Leo XIII, Apostolic Constitution *Romanos Pontifices* (May 8, 1881): Acts of Leo XIII, vol. 2 (1882), 234.

16. Cf. Paul VI, *Allocution* (May 23, 1964): *AAS* 56 (1965), 570–571.

17. Cf. Pius XII, *Allocution* (Dec. 8, 1950), 1. c.

4) All religious, exempt and non-exempt, are subject to the authority of the local ordinaries in those things which pertain to the public exercise of divine worship—except where differences in rites are concerned—the care of souls, the sacred preaching intended for the people, the religious and moral education of the Christian faithful, especially of the children, catechetical instruction and liturgical formation. They are subject to the local ordinary also in what pertains to the decorum proper to the clerical state as well as in the various works which concern the exercise of the sacred apostolate. Catholic schools conducted by religious are also subject to the authority of the local ordinaries for purposes of general policy-making and vigilance, but the right of religious to direct them remains intact. Religious also are bound to observe all those things which councils or conferences of bishops shall legitimately prescribe for observance by all.

5) A well-ordered cooperation is to be encouraged between various religious communities and between them and the diocesan clergy. There should also be a very close coordination of all apostolic works and activities, which especially depend upon a supernatural attitude of hearts and minds rooted in and founded upon charity. The Apostolic See is competent to supervise this coordination for the universal Church; sacred pastors are competent in their own respective dioceses and patriarchal synods and episcopal conferences in their own territory.

For those works of the apostolate which religious are to undertake, bishops or episcopal conferences, religious superiors or conferences of major religious superiors should take action only after mutual consultations.

6) In order to foster harmonious and fruitful mutual relations between bishops and religious, at stated times and as often as it is deemed opportune, bishops and religious superiors should meet to discuss those affairs which pertain to the apostolate in their territory.

CHAPTER III

CONCERNING BISHOPS COOPERATING FOR THE COMMON GOOD OF MANY CHURCHES

1. Synods, Councils and Especially Episcopal Conferences

36. From the very first centuries of the Church, bishops, as rulers of individual churches, were deeply moved by the communion of fraternal charity and zeal for the universal mission entrusted to the apostles. And so they pooled their abilities and their wills for the common good and for the welfare of the individual churches. Thus came into being synods, provincial councils and plenary councils in which bishops established for various churches the way to be followed in teaching the truths of faith and ordering ecclesiastical discipline.

This sacred ecumenical synod earnestly desires that the venerable institution of synods and councils flourish with fresh vigor. In such a way, faith will be deepened and discipline preserved more fittingly and efficaciously in the various churches as the needs of the times require.

37. In these days especially, bishops frequently are unable to fulfill their office effectively and fruitfully unless they develop a common effort involving constant growth in harmony and closeness of ties with other bishops. Episcopal conferences already established in many nations have furnished outstanding proofs of a more fruitful apostolate. Therefore, this sacred synod considers it to be supremely fitting that everywhere bishops belonging to the same nation or region form an association which would meet at fixed times. Thus, when the insights of prudence and experience have been shared and views exchanged, there will emerge a holy union of energies in the service of the common good of the churches.

Wherefore, this sacred synod decrees the following concerning episcopal conferences:

38. 1) An episcopal conference is, as it were, a council in which the bishops of a given nation or territory jointly exercise their pastoral office

to promote the greater good which the Church offers mankind, especially through the forms and methods of the apostolate fittingly adapted to the circumstances of the age.

2) Members of the episcopal conference are all local ordinaries of every rite—excluding vicar generals—and coadjutors, auxiliaries and other titular bishops who perform a special work entrusted to them by the Apostolic See or the episcopal conferences. Other titular bishops, legates of the Roman Pontiff, because of their exceptional office in the territory are not *de iure* members of the conferences. Local ordinaries and coadjutors hold a deliberative vote. Auxiliaries and other bishops who have a right to attend the conference will hold either a deliberative or a consultative vote, as the statutes of the conference determine.

3) Each episcopal conference is to draft its own statutes for recognition by the Apostolic See. In these statutes, among other things, offices should be established which will aid in achieving its purpose more efficaciously, for example, a permanent board of bishops, episcopal commissions and a general secretariat.

4) Decisions of the episcopal conference, provided they have been approved legitimately and by the votes of at least two-thirds of the prelates who have a deliberative vote in the conference, and have been recognized by the Apostolic See, are to have juridically binding force only in those cases prescribed by the common law or determined by a special mandate of the Apostolic See, given either spontaneously or in response to a petition of the conference itself.

5) Wherever special circumstances require and with the approbation of the Apostolic See, bishops of many nations can establish a single conference.

Communications between episcopal conferences of different nations should be especially encouraged in order to promote and safeguard the common good.

6) It is highly recommended that the prelates of the Oriental Churches, promoting the discipline of their own churches in synods and efficaciously fostering works for the good of religion, should take into account also the common good of the whole territory where many churches of different rites exist. They should exchange views at inter-ritual meetings in keeping with norms to be given by the competent authority.

2. The Boundaries of Ecclesiastical Provinces and the Erection of Ecclesiastical Regions

39. The good of souls requires fitting boundaries not only for dioceses but also for ecclesiastical provinces; indeed, it sometimes counsels the establishment of new ecclesiastical regions. Thus the needs of the apostolate will be better met in keeping with social and local circumstances. Thus, too, the relationships of the bishops with each other and with their metropolitans, and with other bishops of the same nation and even between bishops and civil authorities, will be rendered easier and more fruitful.

40. Therefore, in order to accomplish these aims this sacred synod decrees as follows:

1) The boundaries of ecclesiastical provinces are to be submitted to an early review and the rights and privileges of metropolitans are to be defined by new and suitable norms.

2) As a general rule all dioceses and other territorial divisions that are by law equivalent to dioceses should be attached to an ecclesiastical province. Therefore, dioceses which are now directly subject to the Apostolic See and which are not united to any other are either to be brought together to form a new ecclesiastical province, if that be possible, or else attached to that province which is nearer or more convenient. They are to be made subject to the metropolitan jurisdiction of the bishop, in keeping with the norms of the common law.

3) Wherever advantageous, ecclesiastical provinces should be grouped into ecclesiastical regions for the structure of which juridical provision is to be made.

41. It is fitting that the competent episcopal conferences examine the question of boundaries of such provinces and the establishment of regions in keeping with the norms given with respect to diocesan boundaries in numbers 23–24. They are then to submit their suggestions and desires to the Apostolic See.

3. Bishops Having an Inter-Diocesan Office

42. Since pastoral needs require more and more that some pastoral undertakings be directed and carried forward as joint projects, it is fitting that certain offices be created for the service of all or many dioceses of a determined region or nation. These offices can be filled by bishops.

This sacred synod recommends that between the prelates or bishops serving in these offices and the diocesan bishops and the episcopal conferences, there exist always fraternal association and harmonious cooperation in the expression of pastoral concern.

These relationships should also be clearly defined by common law.

43. Since, because of the unique conditions of their way of life, the spiritual care of military personnel requires special consideration, there should be established in every nation, if possible, a military vicariate. Both the military vicar and the chaplains should devote themselves unsparingly to this difficult work in complete cooperation with the diocesan bishops.[1]

Diocesan bishops should release to the military vicar a sufficient number of priests who are qualified for this serious work. At the same time they should promote all endeavors which will improve the spiritual welfare of military personnel.[2]

General Directive

44. This sacred synod prescribes that in the revision of the code of canon law suitable laws be drawn up in keeping with the principles stated in this decree. Due consideration should also be given the observations made by the commissions and the council fathers.

This sacred synod also prescribes that general directories be prepared treating of the care of souls for the use of both bishops and pastors. Thus they will be provided with certain methods which will help them to discharge their own pastoral office with greater ease and effectiveness.

There should be prepared also a particular directory concerning the pastoral care of special groups of the faithful as the different circumstances of individual nations or regions require. Another directory

---

1. Cf. Consistorial Congregation, *Instruction to Military Ordinariates* (April 23, 1951): *AAS* 43 (1951), 562–565; *Formula Regarding the Conferring of the Status of Military Ordinariates* (Oct. 20, 1956): *AAS* 49 (1957), 150–163; *Decree on* Ad Limina *Visits of Military Ordinariates* (Feb. 28, 1959): *AAS* 51 (1959), 272–274; *Decree on the Granting of Faculties for Confessions to Military Chaplains* (Nov. 27, 1960): *AAS* 53 (1961), 49–50. Cf. also Congregation of Religious, *Instruction on Religious Military Chaplains* (Feb. 2, 1955): *AAS* 47 (1955), 93–97.

2. Cf. Consistorial Congregation, *Letter to the Cardinals, Archbishops and Bishops of Spanish-Speaking Nations* (June 27, 195): *AAS* 43 (1951), 566.

should be composed concerning the catechetical instruction of the Christian people; this directory will consider the fundamental principles of such instruction, its disposition and the composition of books on the subject. In preparing these directories, special attention should be given to the views which have been expressed both by the commissions and the council fathers.

Given in Rome at St. Peter's, October 28, 1965

DECREE ON THE ADAPTATION AND RENEWAL OF RELIGIOUS LIFE

Perfectae Caritatis

Promulgated by
His Holiness Pope Paul VI
On October 28, 1965

INTRODUCTION

The *Decree on the Adaptation and Renewal of Religious Life (PC)* is a pastoral elaboration on Church renewal based on the doctrine of *Lumen Gentium*. *LG* presents the Church as the messianic priestly People of God in which three fundamental groups of members contribute to the life and mission of the Church according to their call, gifts and duties. Chapter three treats the ordained, chapter four concerns the laity, and chapter six speaks of religious. The Church will be renewed through the renewal of each of these groups of the Christian faithful. *PC* thus stands beside the *Decree on the Apostolate of the Laity,* the *Decree on the Pastoral Office of Bishops* and the *Decree on the Ministry and Life of Priests.*

Both *LG* and *PC* call each member of the Church, as well as every distinct group within it, to develop an ecclesial spirituality. This can happen as they become more conscious of what they receive from and contribute to the Church. While *LG* gives a general picture of the role of religious in the Church's life and mission, *PC* specifies the principles that guide the renewal of religious life. This renewal calls religious to live in fidelity to their vocation and thereby more effectively contribute to the overall mission of the Church.

The theological principle underlying a renewed vision of religious life is the role of consecration. Whereas for centuries religious life had been seen primarily in terms of the three vows, the council emphasized consecration as the primary element. Because God is the one who consecrates, this perspective highlights God's initiative in calling persons to this way of life. Consecration comes first and leads to the following of the counsels through vows. Seeing consecration as foundational also focuses on the ultimate goal of consecrated life as the pursuit of charity, and the vows as a means to this holiness.

Vatican II emphasized holiness as the bond of ecclesial communion. This explains the central importance of *LG* chapter five on the universal call to holiness in the Church. This chapter is closely linked to chapter six on religious, and to *PC* itself. *PC* takes up the theme of holiness in its first words: "The perfection of charity." The evangelical counsels are so closely associated with the call to holiness which is charity that every member of the Church is called to live them in the framework of their own vocation. What *LG* only hinted at, Pope John Paul II has made explicit:

> All those reborn in Christ are called to live out, with the strength which is the Spirit's gift, the chastity appropriate to their state of life, obedience to God and to the Church, and a reasonable detachment from material possessions: for all are called to holiness, which consists in perfection of love (cf. *LG* 42) (*VC* 30).

The declaration insists that the genuine renewal of consecrated life cannot remain a merely external reality focused on institutional adaptations. All of the organizational, procedural and institutional changes "will be ineffectual unless they are animated by a renewal of spirit" (*PC* 2). This is due to the nature of consecrated life, in which the counsels are a means to the goal of perfect charity.

In this perspective, the vows themselves are seen more in relation to a total love of God. Formerly, the vows were given a primarily ascetical meaning in which the aspect of renunciation took on great importance. But when they are given their proper place as a means to the pursuit of charity, the vows themselves are seen first of all as oriented to love. "The purpose of religious vows is to scale the heights of love, a complete love, dedicated to Christ under the impulse of the Holy Spirit, and through Christ, offered to the Father" (John Paul II, *General audience* of 10/26/94). For this reason the Council expressly mentions consecrated chastity before the other two vows (cf. *LG* 43; *PC* 12, 13, 14) "because it considers chastity as the determining commitment of the state of consecrated life" (John Paul II, *General audience* of 11/16/94). Consecrated chastity is the wellspring of that dynamism of love by which a person gives him or herself totally over to God. Martyrdom is the supreme witness to such a love for God. In a similar way, religious life is like a bloodless martyrdom, in which virgins, on fire with love for God, give their hearts totally to him.

To facilitate this total gift, *PC* presents two guiding principles for the adaptation and renewal of religious life in the Church. The first is a return to the sources of religious life, and the second is its adaptation to the needs and circumstances of the present time. The first principle includes two criteria: renewal of religious life requires "a return to the sources of all Christian life and to the original spirit of the institutes" (*PC* 2). The text states: "Since the ultimate norm of the religious life is the following of Christ set forth in the Gospels, let this be held by all institutes as the highest rule" (*PC* 2). The Council emphasizes that the following of Christ is the essential source of religious life. This important principle has to guide all renewal efforts.

Along with this, a return to the charism of the founder is essential, so that new riches may be brought forth from the foundational charisms. These charisms are dynamic realities. The gift of the Spirit at work in the charism is expressed in different forms, which can be adapted to new situations and needs. This criterion assures that the renewal envisioned by the Council will be truly Christ-centered and ecclesial.

The call for a return to the original spirit of the founders is to be understood in light of the call for a return to the following of Christ in the Gospel. This is because the gifts and missions of the founders of religious orders are themselves a unique way of living out the Christian life. The particular charisms can only be properly grasped in light of their source, and that source is Christ. Religious founders were striving above all to follow Christ as closely as possible.

These founders first lived the reality of their communion with Christ according to the gift and mission they had received. Only later did they, or their followers, attempt to articulate that life in terms of constitutions and rules. The latter are means to an end, and need to be seen as such. Otherwise, the authentic freedom of the Holy Spirit, which is a reality common to all who follow Christ, can be diminished by a spirit of legalism. This can obscure the Person to whom one is being faithful by observing a rule of life.

For this reason, the Council distinguished between the concrete manifestation and realization of a charism in its original historical context, and its permanent value to the Church. This allows *PC* to state that when an apostolate or service is determined to be "less relevant to the spirit and authentic nature of the community" it is to be abandoned (*PC* 20).

As a gift from God for the sake of the Church's mission of evangelization, holiness, and renewal of the temporal order, institutes of consecrated life correspond to circumstances and needs of the time. *PC* sets forth general criteria for discerning the authenticity of such gifts in teaching that "their necessity or at least the many useful services they promise must be seriously weighed" (*PC* 19). This criterion of utility for the common good is essential for discerning authentic charisms. The text does not assume that God intends every institute to last forever, since some communities and monasteries may "not...possess reasonable hope for further development" and so should not receive novices (cf. *PC* 21). *PC* foresees the possibility of combining such communities with more vibrant ones having a similar identity.

The second principle for the renewal of consecrated life is "adaptation to the changed conditions of our time" (*PC* 2). As full participants in ecclesial life, religious are called upon to take advantage of the work of the Council itself. They must also seek to understand present-day social conditions and the needs of the Church so that they may assist others more effectively (cf. *PC* 2, d). This brings to mind St. Paul's principle: without prejudice to his identity as an apostle, but precisely in fidelity to it and out of its heart, he became all things to all people (cf. 1 Cor 9:19–23).

This adaptation to the times is evident even in the new forms of consecrated life which have sprung up. While the Council referred to religious life, it is clear that it intended to include secular institutes (cf. *PC* 11), which, strictly speaking, are not religious institutes. Between Vatican II and the revision of the Code of Canon Law, the Church came to include both religious and secular institutes in speaking of "life consecrated through profession of the evangelical counsels" (cf. *CIC* 573). The two are distinguished by the presence or absence of public profession and the understanding of how each is present in the world (*PC* 11; *CIC* 607, §3; 710). The most important and fundamental principle of the decree is that religious life is a gift from God (cf. *PC* 1; *LG* chapter 6). In approving religious life, the Church is responding to the initiative of the Holy Spirit and committing itself to remain faithful to God's will.

Another element of the Council's teaching concerns the bond of ecclesial communion which unites religious with all others in the Church. Vatican II desired to stress the common dignity of all the Church's members. By Baptism, they participate in the life and mission of Christ and of his Church. Religious life "constitutes a special consecration, which is deeply rooted in that of Baptism and expresses it more fully" (*PC* 5). In considering the various groups in the Church (such as laity, religious, clergy), Pope John Paul II has developed his teaching in terms of the ecclesiology of communion.

The Council noted the distinctiveness of consecrated life, and that it is an indispensable element of the Church's life of holiness: "Thus, the state which is constituted by the profession of the evangelical counsels, though it does not belong to the hierarchical structure of the Church, nevertheless, undeniably belongs to its life and holiness" (*LG* 44). Consecrated life is not a human construct, but comes from the Lord: "The evangelical counsels of chastity dedicated to God, poverty and obedience are based upon the words and examples of the Lord" (*LG* 43).

In the unity of the Christian life, the various vocations are like so many rays of the one light of Christ, whose radiance "brightens the countenance of the Church" (*LG* 1). By virtue of the secular character of their vocation, the laity reflect the mystery of the incarnate Word particularly insofar as he is the Alpha and the Omega of the world, the foundation and measure of all created things. Sacred ministers, for their part, are living images of Christ the head and shepherd who guides his people during this time of "already and not yet," as they await his coming in glory. The consecrated life shows that the incarnate Son of God is the eschatological goal toward which all things tend, the splendor before which every other light pales, and the infinite beauty which alone can fully satisfy the human heart. The consecrated life is not only a matter of following Christ with one's whole heart, of loving him "more than father or mother, more than son or daughter" (cf. Mt 10:37)—for this is required of every disciple. It concerns living and expressing this by conforming one's whole existence to Christ in an all-encompassing commitment which foreshadows eschatological perfection, to the extent that this is possible in time and in accordance with the different charisms. "By professing the evangelical counsels, consecrated persons not only make Christ the whole meaning of their lives but strive to reproduce in themselves, as far as possible, 'that form of life which he, as the Son of God, accepted in entering this world' (*LG* 44)" (*VC* 16).

Those consecrated by the profession of the evangelical counsels embrace poverty, chastity and obedience in a way which distinguishes them from the laity and clergy. Still, the charity which animates this way of life is common to all. Everyone is called to have the mind of Christ (cf. Phil 2:5), but this mind can be lived out and expressed in more than one way. Concerning celibacy, clearly Jesus was totally consecrated to God, and the most obvious way of reproducing the pattern of his life in our own is to embrace the counsel of celibacy. The same can be said of poverty and obedience.

Behind the Lord's poverty, celibacy and obedience is the will of the Father. Jesus' "yes" to these three counsels was the means he embraced to live according to his Father's will. On the assumption that God calls people to the lay state and to married life and sanctifies them there (cf. *LG* 11, 31), we see that the same adherence to the Father's will that led Jesus to embrace celibacy is found also in those who embrace the lay state and marriage. The laity live the spirit of the evangelical counsels according to their own way of life.

Since the Council, a number of Church documents relating to consecrated life have been issued, including: *Evangelica Testificatio* (Paul VI, 1971), *Religious and Human Promotion* and *The Contemplative Dimension of Religious Life* (1980), *Essential Elements* (1983), *Redemptionis Donum* (John Paul II, 1984) and *Vita Consecrata* (John Paul II, 1996).

TOPICAL OUTLINE

1. Introduction (1)

2. General principles for renewal of religious life

    A. Renewal calls for a return to the sources of Christian life (2)

    B. Adaptation of manner of living (3)

    C. Role of members and competent authorities in renewal (4)

3. Consecration and the following of Christ (5)

4. The love of God, prayer and apostolic service (6)

5. Various types of communities

    A. Contemplative communities (7)

    B. Apostolic communities (8)

    C. The monastic life (9)

    D. Religious life as a state of professing the counsels (10)

    E. Secular institutes (11)

6. The evangelical counsels

    A. Chastity (12)

    B. Poverty (13)

    C. Obedience (14)

7. Particular aspects of renewal

DECREE ON THE ADAPTATION AND RENEWAL OF RELIGIOUS LIFE

Perfectae Caritatis

1. The sacred synod has already shown in the *Constitution on the Church* that the pursuit of perfect charity through the evangelical counsels draws its origin from the doctrine and example of the divine Master and reveals itself as a splendid sign of the heavenly kingdom. Now it intends to treat of the life and discipline of those institutes whose members make profession of chastity, poverty and obedience and to provide for their needs in our time.

Indeed from the very beginning of the Church men and women have set about following Christ with greater freedom and imitating him more closely through the practice of the evangelical counsels, each in his own way leading a life dedicated to God. Many of them, under the inspiration of the Holy Spirit, lived as hermits or founded religious families, which the Church gladly welcomed and approved by her authority. So it is that in accordance with the divine plan a wonderful variety of religious communities has grown up which has made it easier for the Church not only to be equipped for every good work (cf. 2 Tm 3:17) and ready for the work of the ministry—the building up of the body of Christ (cf. Eph 4:12)—but also to appear adorned with the various gifts of her children like a spouse adorned for her husband (cf. Rv 21:2) and for the manifold wisdom of God to be revealed through her (cf. Eph 3:10).

Despite such a great variety of gifts, all those called by God to the practice of the evangelical counsels and who, faithfully responding to the call, undertake to observe the same, bind themselves to the Lord in a special way, following Christ, who chaste and poor (cf. Mt 8:20; Lk 9:58) redeemed and sanctified men through obedience even to the death of the cross (cf. Phil 2:8). Driven by love with which the Holy Spirit floods their hearts (cf. Rm 5:5) they live more and more for Christ and for his body which is the Church (cf. Col 1:24). The more fervently, then, they are joined to Christ by this total lifelong gift of themselves, the richer the life of the Church becomes and the more lively and successful its apostolate.

In order that the great value of a life consecrated by the profession of the counsels and its necessary mission today may yield greater good to the Church, the sacred synod lays down the following prescriptions. They are meant to state only the general principles of the adaptation and renewal of the life and discipline of religious orders and also, without prejudice to their special characteristics, of societies of common life without vows and secular institutes. Particular norms for the proper explanation and application of these principles are to be determined after the council by the authority in question.

2. The adaptation and renewal of the religious life includes both the constant return to the sources of all Christian life and to the original spirit of the institutes and their adaptation to the changed conditions of our time. This renewal, under the inspiration of the Holy Spirit and the guidance of the Church, must be advanced according to the following principles:

a) Since the ultimate norm of the religious life is the following of Christ set forth in the Gospels, let this be held by all institutes as the highest rule.

b) It redounds to the good of the Church that institutes have their own particular characteristics and work. Therefore let their founders' spirit and special aims they set before them as well as their sound traditions—all of which make up the patrimony of each institute—be faithfully held in honor.

c) All institutes should share in the life of the Church, adapting as their own and implementing in accordance with their own characteristics the Church's undertakings and aims in matters biblical, liturgical, dogmatic, pastoral, ecumenical, missionary and social.

d) Institutes should promote among their members an adequate knowledge of the social conditions of the times they live in and of the needs of the Church. In such a way, judging current events wisely in the light of faith and burning with apostolic zeal, they may be able to assist men more effectively.

e) The purpose of the religious life is to help the members follow Christ and be united to God through the profession of the evangelical counsels. It should be constantly kept in mind, therefore, that even the best adjustments made in accordance with the needs of our age will be ineffectual unless they are animated by a renewal of spirit. This must take precedence over even the active ministry.

3. The manner of living, praying and working should be suitably adapted everywhere, but especially in mission territories, to the modern physical and psychological circumstances of the members and also, as required by the nature of each institute, to the necessities of the apostolate, the demands of culture, and social and economic circumstances.

According to the same criteria let the manner of governing the institutes also be examined.

Therefore let constitutions, directories, custom books, books of prayers and ceremonies and such like be suitably re-edited and, obsolete laws being suppressed, be adapted to the decrees of this sacred synod.

4. An effective renewal and adaptation demands the cooperation of all the members of the institute.

However, to establish the norms of adaptation and renewal, to embody it in legislation as well as to make allowance for adequate and prudent experimentation belongs only to the competent authorities, especially to general chapters. The approbation of the Holy See or of the local Ordinary must be obtained where necessary according to law. But superiors should take counsel in an appropriate way and hear the members of the order in those things which concern the future well-being of the whole institute.

For the adaptation and renewal of convents of nuns, suggestions and advice may be obtained also from the meetings of federations or from other assemblies lawfully convoked.

Nevertheless everyone should keep in mind that the hope of renewal lies more in the faithful observance of the rules and constitutions than in multiplying laws.

5. Members of each institute should recall first of all that by professing the evangelical counsels they responded to a divine call so that by being not only dead to sin (cf. Rm 6:11) but also renouncing the world they may live for God alone. They have dedicated their entire lives to his service. This constitutes a special consecration, which is deeply rooted in that of Baptism and expresses it more fully.

Since the Church has accepted their surrender of self they should realize they are also dedicated to its service.

This service of God ought to inspire and foster in them the exercise of the virtues, especially humility, obedience, fortitude and chastity. In such a way they share in Christ's emptying of himself (cf. Phil 2:7) and his life in the Spirit (cf. Rm 8:1–13).

Faithful to their profession then, and leaving all things for the sake of Christ (cf. Mk 10:28), religious are to follow him (cf. Mt 19:21) as the one thing necessary (cf. Lk 10:42), listening to his words (cf. Lk 10:39) and solicitous for the things that are his (cf. 1 Cor 7:32).

It is necessary therefore that the members of every community, seeking God solely and before everything else, should join contemplation, by which they fix their minds and hearts on him, with apostolic love, by which they strive to be associated with the work of redemption and to spread the kingdom of God.

6. Let those who make profession of the evangelical counsels seek and love above all else God who has first loved us (cf. 1 Jn 4:10) and let them strive to foster in all circumstances a life hidden with Christ in God (cf. Col 3:3). This love of God both excites and energizes that love of one's neighbor which contributes to the salvation of the world and the building up of the Church. This love, in addition, quickens and directs the actual practice of the evangelical counsels.

Drawing therefore upon the authentic sources of Christian spirituality, members of religious communities should resolutely cultivate both the spirit and practice of prayer. In the first place they should have recourse daily to the Holy Scriptures in order that, by reading and meditating on Holy Writ, they may learn "the surpassing worth of knowing Jesus Christ" (Phil 3:8). They should celebrate the sacred liturgy, especially the holy sacrifice of the Mass, with both lips and heart as the Church desires and so nourish their spiritual life from this richest of sources.

So refreshed at the table of divine law and the sacred altar of God, they will love Christ's members as brothers, honor and love their pastors as sons should do, and living and thinking ever more in union with the Church, dedicate themselves wholly to its mission.

7. Communities which are entirely dedicated to contemplation, so that their members in solitude and silence, with constant prayer and penance willingly undertaken, occupy themselves with God alone, retain at

all times, no matter how pressing the needs of the active apostolate may be, an honorable place in the Mystical Body of Christ, whose "members do not all have the same function" (Rm 12:4). For these offer to God a sacrifice of praise which is outstanding. Moreover, the manifold results of their holiness lend luster to the People of God which is inspired by their example and which gains new members by their apostolate which is as effective as it is hidden. Thus they are revealed to be a glory of the Church and a wellspring of heavenly graces. Nevertheless, their manner of living should be revised according to the principles and criteria of adaptation and renewal mentioned above. However, their withdrawal from the world and the exercises proper to the contemplative life should be preserved with the utmost care.

8. There are in the Church very many communities, both clerical and lay, which devote themselves to various apostolic tasks. The gifts which these communities possess differ according to the grace which is allotted to them. Administrators have the gift of administration, teachers that of teaching, the gift of stirring speech is given to preachers, liberality to those who exercise charity and cheerfulness to those who help others in distress (cf. Rm 12:5–8). "The gifts are varied, but the Spirit is the same" (1 Cor 12:4).

In these communities apostolic and charitable activity belongs to the very nature of the religious life, seeing that it is a holy service and a work characteristic of love, entrusted to them by the Church to be carried out in its name. Therefore, the whole religious life of their members should be inspired by an apostolic spirit and all their apostolic activity formed by the spirit of religion. Therefore, in order that their members may first correspond to their vocation to follow Christ and serve him in his members, their apostolic activity must spring from intimate union with him. Thus love itself toward God and the neighbor is fostered.

These communities, then, should adjust their rules and customs to fit the demands of the apostolate to which they are dedicated. The fact, however, that apostolic religious life takes on many forms requires that its adaptation and renewal take account of this diversity and provide that the lives of religious dedicated to the service of Christ in these various communities be sustained by special provisions appropriate to each.

9. The monastic life, that venerable institution which in the course of a long history has won for itself notable renown in the Church and in human society, should be preserved with care and its authentic spirit

permitted to shine forth ever more splendidly both in the East and the West. The principal duty of monks is to offer a service to the divine majesty at once humble and noble within the walls of the monastery, whether they dedicate themselves entirely to divine worship in the contemplative life or have legitimately undertaken some apostolate or work of Christian charity. Retaining, therefore, the characteristics of the way of life proper to them, they should revive their ancient traditions of service and so adapt them to the needs of today that monasteries will become institutions dedicated to the edification of the Christian people.

Some religious communities according to their rule or constitutions closely join the apostolic life to choir duty and monastic observances. These should so adapt their manner of life to the demands of the apostolate appropriate to them that they observe faithfully their way of life, since it has been of great service to the Church.

10. The religious life, undertaken by lay people, either men or women, is a state for the profession of the evangelical counsels which is complete in itself. While holding in high esteem, therefore, this way of life so useful to the pastoral mission of the Church in educating youth, caring for the sick and carrying out its other ministries, the sacred synod confirms these religious in their vocation and urges them to adjust their way of life to modern needs.

The sacred synod declares that there is nothing to prevent some members of religious communities of brothers being admitted to Holy Orders by provision of their general chapter in order to meet the need for priestly ministrations in their own houses, provided that the lay character of the community remains unchanged.

11. Secular institutes, although not religious institutes, involve a true and full profession of the evangelical counsels in the world. This profession is recognized by the Church and consecrates to God men and women, lay and clerical, who live in the world. Hence, they should make a total dedication of themselves to God in perfect charity their chief aim, and the institutes themselves should preserve their own proper, i.e., secular character, so that they may be able to carry out effectively everywhere in and, as it were, from the world the apostolate for which they were founded.

It may be taken for granted, however, that so great a task cannot be discharged unless the members be thoroughly trained in matters divine and human so that they are truly a leaven in the world for the strengthening and growth of the body of Christ. Superiors, therefore, should give serious attention especially to the spiritual training to be given members as well as encourage their further formation.

12. The chastity "for the sake of the kingdom of heaven" (Mt 19:12) which religious profess should be counted an outstanding gift of grace. It frees the heart of man in a unique fashion (cf. 1 Cor 7:32–35) so that it may be more inflamed with love for God and for all men. Thus it not only symbolizes in a singular way the heavenly goods but also the most suitable means by which religious dedicate themselves with undivided heart to the service of God and the works of the apostolate. In this way they recall to the minds of all the faithful that wondrous marriage decreed by God and which is to be fully revealed in the future age in which the Church takes Christ as its only spouse.

Religious, therefore, who are striving faithfully to observe the chastity they have professed must have faith in the words of the Lord, and trusting in God's help not overestimate their own strength but practice mortification and custody of the senses. Neither should they neglect the natural means which promote health of mind and body. As a result they will not be influenced by those false doctrines which scorn perfect continence as being impossible or harmful to human development, and they will repudiate by a certain spiritual instinct everything which endangers chastity. In addition let all, especially superiors, remember that chastity is guarded more securely when true brotherly love flourishes in the common life of the community.

Since the observance of perfect continence touches intimately the deepest instincts of human nature, candidates should neither present themselves for nor be admitted to the vow of chastity, unless they have been previously tested sufficiently and have been shown to possess the required psychological and emotional maturity. They should not only be warned about the dangers to chastity which they may meet, but they should be so instructed as to be able to undertake the celibacy which binds them to God in a way which will benefit their entire personality.

13. Religious should diligently practice and if need be express also in new forms that voluntary poverty which is recognized and highly esteemed especially today as an expression of the following of Christ. By

it they share in the poverty of Christ who for our sakes became poor, even though he was rich, so that by his poverty we might become rich (cf. 2 Cor 8:9; Mt 8:20).

With regard to religious poverty, it is not enough to use goods in a way subject to the superior's will, but members must be poor both in fact and in spirit, their treasures being in heaven (cf. Mt 6:20).

Religious should consider themselves in their own assignments to be bound by the common law of labor, and while they procure what is required for their sustenance and works, they should banish all undue solicitude and trust themselves to the provident care of their Father in heaven (cf. Mt 6:25).

Religious congregations by their constitutions can permit their members to renounce inheritances, both those which have been acquired or may be acquired.

Due regard being had for local conditions, religious communities should readily offer a quasi-collective witness to poverty and gladly use their own goods for other needs of the Church and the support of the poor whom all religious should love after the example of Christ (cf. Mt 19:21, 25:34–46 Jas 2:15–16; 1 Jn 3:17). The several provinces and houses of each community should share their temporal goods with one another, so that those who have more help the others who are in need.

Religious communities have the right to possess whatever is required for their temporal life and work, unless this is forbidden by their rules and constitutions. Nevertheless, they should avoid every appearance of luxury, excessive wealth and the accumulation of goods.

14. In professing obedience, religious offer the full surrender of their own will as a sacrifice of themselves to God and so are united permanently and securely to God's salvific will.

After the example of Jesus Christ who came to do the will of the Father (cf. Jn 4:34; 5:30; Heb 10:7; Ps 39:9) and "assuming the nature of a slave" (Phil 2:7) learned obedience in the school of suffering (cf. Heb 5:8), religious under the motion of the Holy Spirit subject themselves in faith to their superiors who hold the place of God. Under their guidance they are led to serve all their brothers in Christ, just as Christ himself in obedience to the Father served his brethren and laid down his life as a ransom for many (cf. Mt 20:28; Jn 10:14–18). So they are closely bound to the service of the Church and strive to attain the measure of the full manhood of Christ (Eph 4:13).

Religious, therefore, in the spirit of faith and love for the divine will should humbly obey their superiors according to their rules and constitutions. Realizing that they are contributing to building up the body of Christ according to God's plan, they should use both the forces of their intellect and will and the gifts of nature and grace to execute the commands and fulfill the duties entrusted to them. In this way religious obedience, far from lessening the dignity of the human person, by extending the freedom of the sons of God, leads it to maturity.

Superiors, as those who are to give an account of the souls entrusted to them (Heb 13:17), should fulfill their office in a way responsive to God's will. They should exercise their authority out of a spirit of service to the brethren, expressing in this way the love with which God loves their subjects. They should govern these as sons of God, respecting their human dignity. In this way they make it easier for them to subordinate their wills. They should be particularly careful to respect their subjects' liberty in the matters of sacramental confession and the direction of conscience. Subjects should be brought to the point where they will cooperate with an active and responsible obedience in undertaking new tasks and in carrying those already undertaken. And so superiors should gladly listen to their subjects and foster harmony among them for the good of the community and the Church, provided that thereby their own authority to decide and command what has to be done is not harmed.

Chapters and deliberative bodies should faithfully discharge the part in ruling entrusted to them, and each should in its own way express that concern for the good of the entire community which all its members share.

15. Common life, fashioned on the model of the early Church where the body of believers was united in heart and soul (cf. Acts 4:32), and given new force by the teaching of the Gospel, the sacred liturgy and especially the Eucharist, should continue to be lived in prayer and communion of the same spirit. As members of Christ living together as brothers, religious should give pride of place in esteem to each other (cf. Rm 12:10) and bear each other's burdens (cf. Gal 6:2). For the community, a true family gathered together in the name of the Lord by God's

love which has flooded the hearts of its members through the Holy Spirit (cf. Rm 5:5), rejoices because he is present among them (cf. Mt 18:20). Moreover, love sums up the whole law (cf. Rm 13:10), binds all together in perfect unity (cf. Col 3:14) and by it we know that we have crossed over from death to life (cf. 1 Jn 3:14). Furthermore, the unity of the brethren is a visible pledge that Christ will return (cf. Jn 13:35; 17:21) and a source of great apostolic energy.

That all the members be more closely knit by the bond of brotherly love, those who are called laybrothers, assistants or some similar name should be drawn closely in to the life and work of the community. Unless conditions really suggest something else, care should be taken that there be only one class of sisters in communities of women. Only that distinction of persons should be retained which corresponds to the diversity of works for which the sisters are destined, either by special vocation from God or by reason of special aptitude.

However, monasteries of men and communities which are not exclusively lay, can, according to their nature and constitutions, admit clerics and lay persons on an equal footing and with equal rights and obligations, excepting those which flow from sacred orders.

16. Papal cloister should be maintained in the case of nuns engaged exclusively in the contemplative life. However, it must be adjusted to conditions of time and place and obsolete practices suppressed. This should be done after due consultation with the monasteries in question. But other nuns applied by rule to apostolic work outside the convent should be exempted from papal cloister in order to enable them better to fulfill the apostolic duties entrusted to them. Nevertheless, cloister is to be maintained according to the prescriptions of their constitutions.

17. The religious habit, an outward mark of consecration to God, should be simple and modest, poor and at the same becoming. In addition it must meet the requirements of health and be suited to the circumstances of time and place and to the needs of the ministry involved. The habits of both men and women religious which do not conform to these norms must be changed.

18. Adaptation and renewal depend greatly on the education of religious. Consequently neither non-clerical religious nor religious women should be assigned to apostolic works immediately after the novitiate. Rather, their religious and apostolic formation, joined with

instruction in arts and science directed toward obtaining appropriate degrees, must be continued as needs require in houses established for those purposes.

In order that the adaptation of religious life to the needs of our time may not be merely external and that those employed by rule in the active apostolate may be equal to their task, religious must be given suitable instruction, depending on their intellectual capacity and personal talent, in the currents and attitudes of sentiment and thought prevalent in social life today. This education must blend its elements together harmoniously so that an integrated life on the part of the religious concerned results.

Religious should strive during the whole course of their lives to perfect the culture they have received in matters spiritual and in arts and sciences. Likewise, superiors must, as far as this is possible, obtain for them the opportunity, equipment and time to do this.

Superiors are also obliged to see to it that directors, spiritual fathers, and professors are carefully chosen and thoroughly trained.

19. When the question of founding new religious communities arises, their necessity or at least the many useful services they promise must be seriously weighed. Otherwise communities may be needlessly brought into being which are useless or which lack sufficient resources. Particularly in those areas where churches have recently been established, those forms of religious life should be promoted and developed which take into account the genius and way of life of the inhabitants and the customs and conditions of the regions.

20. Religious communities should continue to maintain and fulfill the ministries proper to them. In addition, after considering the needs of the universal Church and individual dioceses, they should adapt them to the requirements of time and place, employing appropriate and even new programs and abandoning those works which today are less relevant to the spirit and authentic nature of the community.

The missionary spirit must under all circumstances be preserved in religious communities. It should be adapted accordingly, as the nature of each community permits, to modern conditions so that the preaching of the Gospel may be carried out more effectively in every nation.

21. There may be communities and monasteries which the Holy See, after consulting the interested local ordinaries, will judge not to possess reasonable hope for further development. These should be forbidden to

receive novices in the future. If it is possible, these should be combined with other more flourishing communities and monasteries whose scope and spirit is similar.

22. Independent institutes and monasteries should, when opportune and the Holy See permits, form federations if they can be considered as belonging to the same religious family. Others who have practically identical constitutions and rules and a common spirit should unite, particularly when they have too few members. Finally, those who share the same or a very similar active apostolate should become associated, one to the other.

23. This synod favors conferences or councils of major superiors, established by the Holy See. These can contribute very much to achieve the purpose of each institute; to encourage more effective cooperation for the welfare of the Church; to ensure a more just distribution of ministers of the Gospel in a given area; and finally to conduct affairs of interest to all religious. Suitable coordination and cooperation with episcopal conferences should be established with regard to the exercise of the apostolate.

Similar conferences should also be established for secular institutes.

24. Priests and Christian educators should make serious efforts to foster religious vocations, thereby increasing the strength of the Church, corresponding to its needs. These candidates should be suitably and carefully chosen. In ordinary preaching, the life of the evangelical counsels and the religious state should be treated more frequently. Parents, too, should nurture and protect religious vocations in their children by instilling Christian virtue in their hearts.

Religious communities have the right to make themselves known in order to foster vocations and seek candidates. In doing this, however, they should observe the norms laid down by the Holy See and the local ordinary.

Religious should remember there is no better way than their own example to commend their institutes and gain candidates for the religious life.

25. Religious institutes, for whom these norms of adaptation and renewal have been laid down, should respond generously to the specific vocation God gave them as well as their work in the Church today. The sacred synod highly esteems their way of life in poverty, chastity and obedience, of which Christ the Lord is himself the exemplar. Moreover,

their apostolate, most effective, whether obscure or well known, offers this synod great hope for the future. Let all religious, therefore, rooted in faith and filled with love for God and neighbor, love of the cross and the hope of future glory, spread the good news of Christ throughout the whole world so that their witness may be seen by all and our Father in heaven may be glorified (Mt 5:16). Therefore, let them beseech the Virgin Mary, the gentle Mother of God, "whose life is a model for all" (St. Ambrose, *De Virginitate,* 1, II, c. II, n. 15), that their number may daily increase and their salutary work be more effective.

DECREE ON PRIESTLY TRAINING

Optatam Totius

Promulgated by
His Holiness Pope Paul VI
On October 28, 1965

INTRODUCTION

In the *Decree on Priestly Formation (OT)*, the Council translates its vision and hopes for the renewal of the Church into practical considerations regarding the life, ministry and formation of clergy. The irreplaceable role of priests in the life of the Church, and therefore in the renewal begun by the Council, is recognized in *OT's* opening line: "Animated by the spirit of Christ, this sacred synod is fully aware that the desired renewal of the whole Church depends to a great extent on the ministry of its priests." That ministry, in turn, depends on the education and formation which those preparing for the priesthood receive. They must not only understand the teachings of the Council, but they must be informed by its spirit (cf. *OT,* conclusion).

Another factor connecting priestly formation to the realization of the Council's goals is the lesson of history provided by the implementation of the Council of Trent. The decree states that the Fathers of Vatican II see the directives of *OT* as a continuation of the renewal of priestly life and formation begun at Trent (cf. *OT,* conclusion). However, the historical differences must be kept in mind. Priestly training today has to meet the challenges of the modern world.

The importance of the role of priests is ultimately derived from the ministry of preaching the word and from the central place of the Eucharist in the life of the Church, to which priestly ministry is directed and in which it is perfected. It is also derived from the relation of priests to their bishop. He "is to be considered as the high priest of his flock, from whom the life in Christ of his faithful is in some way derived and dependent" (*SC* 41), and whom priests make present to the faithful (cf. *LG* 28). Since priests represent their bishops, assist them and depend upon them, what the Council teaches about bishops in *Christus Dominus* and about the ministry and life of priests in *Presbyterorum Ordinis* should be read as complements to *OT.*

Vatican II highlights the nature of the priest's relationship with his bishop. "By reason of the gift of the Holy Spirit which is given to priests in Holy Orders, bishops regard them as necessary helpers and counselors in the ministry and in their role of teaching, sanctifying and nourishing the People of God.... On account of this communion in the same priesthood and ministry, bishops should regard priests as their brothers and friends" (*PO* 7). This relationship is a vital component of priestly life and identity and provides a foundation for effective priestly ministry. A significant element of seminary formation is a thorough and faithful ecclesiology which explains the Church's apostolic nature. Seminarians also need sufficient personal interaction with the bishop. It is not realistic to expect priests to play their role as ministers of ecclesial communion if they do not grasp it in its theological reality and experience it in their relationship with their bishop.

Such seminary formation must have a solid foundation upon which to build. Long before a man begins his preparation for the priesthood, he should have embraced the call to holiness and lived according to that faith which imbues every aspect of life. Such faith is ordinarily received, learned and lived in the family. Ideally, vocations to the priesthood begin in the Catholic home, where, among other things, the essential connection between Christian life, the apostolate and service are learned (cf. *AA* 11, 30) and are gradually better understood through catechesis.

The responsibility for promoting vocations, which is shared in different ways by the various members of the Church, is fulfilled "above all by a fully Christian life" (*OT* 2). The first and most important group mentioned in this regard is the family, which the decree calls "a kind of initial seminary." The third article also underscores the importance of the family when it mentions the "proper cooperation of the parents" in developing the daily routine of life in minor seminaries.

A vocation to the priesthood has as its foundation a vibrant faith which ideally develops in the family. A seminary is not a place of initial evangelization or catechesis, but of a specific education and formation for the priestly ministry. This presupposes a mature faith commitment to Christ and his Church as a foundation upon which to build. It would be asking too much of seminaries both to bring faith itself to the necessary stage of maturity, and to provide the essential theological, pastoral and spiritual formation. There would be insufficient time for the latter, which would defeat the purpose of the seminary. It would also fail if seminary formation would be provided without the required foundation of mature faith. The future priest would be unfairly thrust into a pastoral ministry that would not flow from "an intimate companionship" with Christ. The priest needs to develop a genuine friendship with Christ so as to know how to live out his Paschal Mystery (cf. *OT* 8) and grow in love for his Church. The faith of seminarians must continue to develop during their formation years, but an initial level of maturity is required. The decree also emphasizes the development of a profound life of prayer. "They should be taught to seek Christ in the faithful meditation on God's Word, in the active participation in the sacred mysteries of the Church, especially in the Eucharist and in the divine office" (*OT* 8).

The kind of obedience which the spiritual formation of priests intends to foster is one "whereby they accept the authority of superiors from personal conviction, that is to say, from a motive of conscience ...and for supernatural reasons" (*OT* 11). In addition, spiritual formation should prepare them to embrace celibacy as a gift (cf. *OT* 10). Such advanced instructions in the spiritual life presuppose the "school of virtues" which is the family, where respect for God's order in relationships is first learned through the obedience of children to their parents, and where the practice of self-discipline contributes to the virtue of temperance.

When families embrace the life of faith and the call to holiness presented by the Council, young men can be readily attracted to the goodness and fullness of life they perceive in the example of faithful priests. *OT* correlates the role of the family with that of priests. The example of priests' lives should "attract the interest of youths to the priesthood" (*OT* 2). It is up to families to inculcate dispositions in their sons which will help them respond to such examples.

Further, the "human maturity" which seminaries must foster (cf. *OT* 11) and the "humanistic and scientific training" which the decree sees as preparatory to "specifically ecclesiastical subjects" (*OT* 13) can and should begin well before a young man comes to a seminary. Parents can do a great deal both to foster vocations and to provide an appropriate foundation for a future priest's education and formation by securing a genuinely Christian education for their sons (cf. *GE* 2–3).

An important point made in *OT* is the call for "due firmness" in the "process of selecting and testing students." It adds that a shortage of priests should not be a factor in this discernment (cf. *OT* 6). Appropriate screening of candidates is meant for the good of the Church and the individuals involved, to assure that the future priest can embrace his vocation in fidelity and joy. The discernment that a man is not called to the priesthood is not a rejection. It has a positive dimension in that it points to a vocation to the lay apostolate. As the Council teaches, the laity are called by the Lord himself (cf. *LG* 31, *AA* 2). The Council's teaching on the dignity which is rooted in Baptism and is common to all the members of the Church should facilitate this difficult task of discernment.

This call to firmness is grounded in a conviction of faith: "God will not allow his Church to want for ministers if those who are worthy are promoted and those not qualified are, at an early date, guided in a fatherly way to undertake other tasks" (*OT* 6). This firmness in remaining faithful to a set of criteria rounds out the decree's list of the means to foster vocations (cf. *OT* 2): means by which individuals and communities open themselves to God's grace (prayer and penance); means of education about the nature and importance of the priesthood (preaching, catechesis, use of the media); means of organization and coordination of the efforts to foster vocations.

The decree sees all these efforts as the Church's response to God's initiative in providing vocations. Here the ecclesiology of *Lumen Gentium* is evident: Christ continues to guide his Church through the working of the Holy Spirit in the hearts of the faithful. The Church may indeed possess the fullness of the means of sanctification, but it is not self-sufficient or able to complete its mission without God's help. In this light every vocation to the priesthood is evidence of God's fidelity to the people of the New Covenant established by the sacrifice of Christ.

The fifth section on the revision of ecclesiastical studies must be understood in a twofold light: that of the Church's mission and the renewal of Vatican II, and that of the specific ministry of priests. The fundamental concern of Vatican II is to lead the Church to a deeper participation in the life of Christ. A result of this is to revitalize the Church's mission of salvation and each and every ministry, apostolate and service directed to that mission.

The Council recognized the rift between faith and life as one of the greatest challenges to the Church (cf. *GS* 43). So the formation of priests must enable them to exercise their ministry in such a way as to over-come this split. Thus, the theological formation of priests should enable them to "seek the solutions to human problems under the light of revela-tion, to apply the eternal truths of revelation to the changeable condi-tions of human affairs and to communicate them in a way suited to men of our day" (*OT* 16).

To accomplish this, faith and life need to be united in these future priests. To this end, the decree states that theological education aims to impart "a true and intimate formation" and not merely the "communica-tion of ideas" (*OT* 17). Such a formation brings about a personal re-newal of faith by which seminarians enter more deeply into the mystery of Christ. The living faith that gradually penetrates their entire lives will be the source of "a personal dedication and a joyful heart" in fidelity to their vocation (cf. *OT* 14). Through a sound formation they will learn to live Christ's Paschal Mystery, seek him in the many ways he is to be found, and through obedience, simplicity of life and self-denial "con-form themselves to Christ crucified" (*OT* 8–9). Such a formation must begin at the minor seminary where students are prepared "to follow Christ the Redeemer with generosity of spirit and purity of heart" (*OT* 3).

Although St. Thomas Aquinas is the only theologian who is men-tioned by name as the master to be followed in theological studies, the Council wished to recover the wealth of the Church's theological tradi-tion, including the Fathers. St. Thomas enjoys a privileged place due to the Thomistic renewal directed by Pope Leo XIII and carried on most intensely in the first seventy years of this century. This was in continuity with a series of recommendations in prior centuries. The theology of St. Thomas is a perennial theology for the Church because of its clear and principled power of synthesis based on several essential principles of faith and theology. *OT* also mentions the need to study the history of philosophy and especially modern philosophy.

Following *Dei Verbum,* great emphasis is placed on the study of Sa-cred Scripture, described as "the soul of theology." The themes of the "mystery of Christ" and of salvation history are central to priestly for-mation. In addition, the decree calls for the renewal of moral theology in particular, as well as other theological disciplines, which should be "nourished more on the teaching of the Bible" (*OT* 16). This emphasis on the Bible also corresponds to the directives of the *Decree on Ecu-menism,* as does the call that seminarians study about Churches and ecclesial communities which are not in full communion with the Catholic Church.

OT also incorporates the theme of dialogue, developed especially in *Gaudium et Spes* and the *Decree on Ecumenism.* The formation of priests should make them capable of being true mediators between the Church's tradition of faith and the contemporary world. Since the mystery of Christ gives meaning to all history and every human life, the decree's emphasis on intimate, personal contact with this mystery assures this dialogue. Just as the living tradition of the Church can meet the questions of every age, so the priest is to be a man of the Church who represents Christ, as well as a man of his own times, so that he can communicate to others in their own words. This dialogue in charity and truth requires both the ability to acknowledge and build on the goodness and truth present in other systems of thought, and to discern those elements that might be at variance with faith (cf. *OT* 15 and 16).

The Christocentric character of Vatican II is evident in *OT* especially as it indicates that the goal of priestly formation is a "living contact" with the mystery of Christ (cf. *OT* 16). This formation should open students' minds to the mystery of Christ (cf. *OT* 14) and allow them "to adhere to him as friends in an intimate companionship their whole life through" (*OT* 8). The influence of *Lumen Gentium,* especially chapters two, three and four, is manifest where priestly formation is said to aim at equipping priests to exercise the entire pastoral ministry "after the model of our Lord Jesus Christ, teacher, priest and shepherd" (*OT* 4). This threefold ministry of the word, of worship and sanctification, and of service in the parish correspond to the charge of serving the lay faithful by promoting their apostolic activities (cf. *OT* 20; *PO* 9). In this the laity exercise their own baptismal participation in the priestly, prophetic and kingly offices of Jesus Christ.

Like all gifts of grace for serving and building up the Church, the grace of the priesthood is ordered by apostolic authority (cf. *LG* 7). The text mentions the priest's relationship with the Vicar of Christ and with his own bishop. It calls for priestly obedience, seen in the context of following Christ, for whom obedience unto death was the concrete expression of his faithfulness to his Father and his love for the Church.

In synthesis, the goals of priestly formation derive from the Council's understanding of the nature and goal of priestly ministry. The decree describes the vocation to the priesthood in a relational way. Upon being ordained, a priest is established in a new relationship with Christ, in whom he takes on relationships with the Father and the Spirit. The priest is also related to other people: to those he is called to serve after the model of Christ, to the bishop as the one who is charged with ordering his formation and directing his ministry, and with his brother priests. The priest also has a relationship to the Word of God, the tradition and discipline of the Church, and the sacraments. Fidelity to his vocation is the concrete expression and measure of a priest's fidelity to the one who called him and to those he is called to serve.

TOPICAL OUTLINE

1. Introduction: importance of priestly formation

2. The program of priestly training for various countries (1)

3. Urgent need to foster priestly vocations

   A. Vocational work, especially in families (2)

   B. Minor seminaries (3)

4. Major seminaries

   A. Pastoral aim of seminary training (4)

   B. Seminary administrators and teachers (5)

   C. Screening of candidates (6)

   D. Regional seminaries (7)

5. Spiritual formation

   A. Prayer (8)

   B. Witness to unity (9)

   C. Celibacy (10)

   D. Human maturity (11)

   E. Special periods of spiritual formation (12)

6. Program of studies

   A. Necessary foundations (13)

   B. Integration of philosophy and theology (14)

C. Philosophy (15)

D. Program of theological studies (16)

E. Teaching methods and higher studies (17–18)

7. Pastoral training

A. Importance of pastoral concerns (19)

B. Opportunities for pastoral work (20)

8. Training after the course of studies (21)

DECREE ON PRIESTLY TRAINING

Optatam Totius

Animated by the spirit of Christ, this sacred synod is fully aware that the desired renewal of the whole Church depends to a great extent on the ministry of its priests.[1] It proclaims the extreme importance of priestly training and lays down certain basic principles by which those regulations may be strengthened which long use has shown to be sound and by which those new elements can be added which correspond to the constitutions and decrees of this sacred Council and to the changed conditions of our times. Because of the very unity of the Catholic priesthood, this priestly formation is necessary for all priests, diocesan and religious and of every rite. Wherefore, while these prescriptions directly concern the diocesan clergy, they are to be appropriately adapted to all.

---

1. That progress among all the People of God primarily depends on the will of Christ himself and the ministry of priests is clear from the words by which the Lord established his apostles and their successors and cooperators, heralds of the Gospel, leaders of the new chosen people and dispensers of the mysteries of God; it is likewise confirmed by the utterances of the Fathers and saints and repeatedly in documents of the Supreme Pontiffs. Cf. especially St. Pius X, Exhortation to the Clergy *Haerent Animo* (Aug. 4, 1908): Acts of St. Pius X, 237–264; Pius XI, Encyclical Letter *Ad Catholici Sacerdotii* (Dec. 20, 1935): *AAS* 28 (1936), especially 37–52; Pius XII, Apostolic Exhortation *Menti Nostrae* (Sept. 23, 1950): *AAS* 42 (1950), 657–702; John XXIII, Encyclical Letter *Sacerdotii Nostri Primordia* (Aug. 1, 1959): *AAS* 51 (1959), 545–579; Paul VI, Apostolic Letter *Summi Dei Verbum* (Nov. 4, 1963): *AAS* 55 (1963), 979–995.

I. THE PROGRAM OF PRIESTLY TRAINING TO BE UNDERTAKEN BY EACH COUNTRY

1. Since only general laws can be made where there exists a wide variety of nations and regions, a special "program of priestly training" is to be undertaken by each country or rite. It must be set up by the episcopal conferences,[2] revised from time to time and approved by the Apostolic See. In this way will the universal laws be adapted to the particular circumstances of the times and localities so that the priestly training will always be in tune with the pastoral needs of those regions in which the ministry is to be exercised.

---

2. The entire sacerdotal institution—that is, the establishment of a seminary, the spiritual institution, the course of studies, the common life and discipline of students, pastoral practices—all are to be accommodated to the needs of the various localities. This accommodation, especially in its fundamental principles, is to be made according to common norms set down by the episcopal conferences as far as secular priests are concerned, and for suitable reasons by competent superiors in the case of religious clergy. Cf. general statutes attached to the apostolic constitution *Sedes Sapientiae,* article 19.

II. THE URGENT FOSTERING
OF PRIESTLY VOCATIONS

2. The duty of fostering vocations[3] pertains to the whole Christian community, which should exercise it above all by a fully Christian life. The principal contributors to this are the families which, animated by the spirit of faith and love and by the sense of duty, become a kind of initial seminary, and the parishes in whose rich life the young people take part. Teachers and all those who are in any way in charge of the training of boys and young men, especially Catholic associations, should carefully guide the young people entrusted to them so that these will recognize and freely accept a divine vocation. All priests especially are to manifest an apostolic zeal in fostering vocations and are to attract the interest of youths to the priesthood by their own life lived in a humble and industrious manner and in a happy spirit as well as by mutual priestly charity and fraternal sharing of labor.

Bishops, on the other hand, are to encourage their flock to promote vocations and should be concerned with coordinating all forces in a united effort to this end. As fathers, moreover, they must assist without stint those whom they have judged to be called to the Lord's work.

The effective union of the whole people of God in fostering vocations is the proper response to the action of divine Providence which confers the fitting gifts on those men divinely chosen to participate in the hierarchical priesthood of Christ and helps them by his grace. More-

---

3. Among the main afflictions troubling the Church today, the shortage of vocations predominates virtually everywhere. Cf. Pius XII, Apostolic Exhortation *Menti Nostrae:* "...the number of priests both in Catholic regions and mission territories is in most cases insufficient to the growing needs," *AAS* 42 (1950), 682. John XXIII: "The problem of ecclesiastical and religious vocations is the daily preoccupation of the Pope.... It is the yearning of his prayer, the ardent aspiration of his soul." From the allocution to the First International Congress on Vocations to the State of Perfection (Dec. 16, 1961): *L'Osservatore Romano*, (Dec. 17, 1961).

over, this same Providence charges the legitimate ministers of the Church to call forward and to consecrate with the sign of the Holy Spirit to the worship of God and to the service of the Church those candidates whose fitness has been acknowledged and who have sought so great an office with the right intention and with full freedom.[4]

The sacred synod commends first of all the traditional means of common effort such as urgent prayer, Christian penance and a constantly more intensive training of the faithful by preaching, by catechetical instructions or by the many media of social communication that will show forth the need, the nature and the importance of the priestly vocation. The synod moreover orders that the entire pastoral activity of fostering vocations be methodically and coherently planned, and with equal prudence and zeal, fostered by those organizations for promoting vocations which, in accord with the appropriate pontifical documents, have already been or will be set up in the territory of individual dioceses, regions or countries. Also, no opportune aids are to be overlooked which modern psychological and sociological research has brought to light.[5]

The work of fostering vocations should in a spirit of openness transcend the limits of individual dioceses, countries, religious families and rites. Looking to the needs of the universal Church, it should provide aid particularly for those regions in which workers for the Lord's vineyard are being requested more urgently.

3. In minor seminaries erected to develop the seeds of vocations, the students should be prepared by special religious formation, particularly through appropriate spiritual direction, to follow Christ the Redeemer with generosity of spirit and purity of heart. Under the fatherly direction

---

4. Pius XII, Apostolic Constitution *Sedes Sapientiae* (May 31, 1956): *AAS* 48 (1956), 357; Paul VI, Apostolic Letter *Summi Dei Verbum* (Nov. 4, 1963): *AAS* 55 (1963), 984 ff.

5. Cf. especially Pius XII, Motu Proprio *Cum Nobis* (Nov. 4, 1941): *AAS* 33 (1941), 479, concerning the establishment of the Pontifical Society for Priestly Vocations under the direction of the Sacred Congregation of Seminaries and Universities of Studies, with the related norms and statutes promulgated Sept. 8, 1943 by the same Sacred Congregation; Motu Proprio *Cum Supremae* (Feb. 11, 1955): *AAS* 47 (1955), 266, concerning the Pontifical Society for Religious Vocations with the related norms and statutes promulgated by the Sacred Congregation of Religious (*ibid.*, pp. 298–301); Second Vatican Ecumenical Council, Decree on the Adaptation and Renewal of Religious Life *Perfectae Caritatis*, 24; Second Vatican Ecumenical Council, Decree on the Pastoral Office of Bishops in the Church *Christus Dominus*, 15.

of the superiors, and with the proper cooperation of the parents, their daily routine should be in accord with the age, the character and the stage of development of adolescence and fully adapted to the norms of a healthy psychology. Nor should the fitting opportunity be lacking for social and cultural contacts and for contact with one's own family.[6] Moreover, whatever is decreed in the following paragraphs about major seminaries is also to be adapted to the minor seminary to the extent that it is in accord with its purpose and structure. Also, studies undertaken by the students should be so arranged that they can easily continue them elsewhere should they choose a different state of life.

With equal concern the seeds of vocations among adolescents and young men are also to be fostered in those special institutes, which in accord with the local circumstances, serve the purpose of a minor seminary as well as among those who are trained in other schools or by other educational means. Finally, those institutions and other schools initiated for those with a belated vocation are to be carefully developed.

---

6. Cf. Pius XII, Apostolic Exhortation *Menti Nostrae* (Sept. 23, 1950): *AAS* 42 (1950), 685.

III. THE SETTING UP OF MAJOR SEMINARIES

4. Major seminaries are necessary for priestly formation. Here the entire training of the students should be oriented to the formation of true shepherds of souls after the model of our Lord Jesus Christ, teacher, priest and shepherd.[7] They are therefore to be prepared for the ministry of the word: that they might understand ever more perfectly the revealed Word of God, that meditating on it they might possess it more firmly, and that they might express it in words and in example; for the ministry of worship and of sanctification: that through their prayers and their carrying out of the sacred liturgical celebrations they might perfect the work of salvation through the Eucharistic sacrifice and the sacraments; for the ministry of the parish: that they might know how to make Christ present to men, him who did not "come to be served but to serve and to give his life as a ransom for many" (Mk 10:45; cf. Jn 13:12–17), and that having become the servants of all they might win over all the more (cf. 1 Cor 9:19).

Therefore, all the forms of training, spiritual, intellectual, disciplinary, are to be ordered with concerted effort toward this pastoral end, and to attain it all the administrators and teachers are to work zealously and harmoniously together, faithfully obedient to the authority of the bishop.

5. Since the training of students depends both on wise laws and most of all on qualified educators, the administrators and teachers of seminaries are to be selected from the best men,[8] and are to be carefully pre-

---

7. Second Vatican Ecumenical Council, Dogmatic Constitution on the Church *Lumen Gentium,* 28: *AAS* 57 (1965), 34.

8. Pius XI, Encyclical Letter *Ad Catholici Sacerdotii* (Dec. 20, 1935): *AAS* 28 (1936), 37: "Especially diligent must be the selection of moderators and teachers.... Assign to sacred colleges of this kind priests endowed with the highest virtue, and charge them to withdraw from assignments, especially those more burdensome, which cannot be compared with this duty of capital importance, whose place no other can take." This principle

pared in sound doctrine, suitable pastoral experience and special spiritual and pedagogical training. Institutes, therefore, should be set up to attain this end. Or at least courses are to be arranged with a proper program, and the meetings of seminary directors are to take place at specified times.

Administrators, however, and teachers must be keenly aware of how much the success of the students' formation depends on their manner of thinking and acting. Under the rector's leadership they are to form a very closely knit community both in spirit and in activity, and they are to constitute among themselves and with the students that kind of family that will answer to the Lord's prayer: "that they be one" (cf. Jn 17:11) and that will develop in the students a deep joy in their own vocation. The bishop, on the other hand, should, with a constant and loving solicitude, encourage those who labor in the seminary, and prove himself a true father in Christ to the students themselves. Finally, all priests are to look on the seminary as the heart of the diocese and are to offer willingly their own helpful service.[9]

6. With watchful concern for the age of each and for his stage of progress, an inquiry should be made into the candidate's proper intention and freedom of choice, into his spiritual, moral and intellectual qualifications, into his appropriate physical and psychic health—taking into consideration also possible hereditary deficiencies. Also to be considered is the ability of the candidate to bear the priestly burdens and exercise the pastoral offices.[10]

In the entire process of selecting and testing students, however, a due firmness is to be adopted even if a deplorable lack of priests should exist,[11] since God will not allow his Church to want for ministers if those who are worthy are promoted and those not qualified are, at an early

of selecting the best is again inculcated by Pius XII in his apostolic letter to the Ordinaries of Brazil (April 23, 1947): *Discourses and Radio Messages,* vol. IX, 579, 580.

9. Concerning the common duty of supporting zealously the work in seminaries, cf. Paul VI, Apostolic Letter *Summi Dei Verbum* (Nov. 4, 1963): *AAS* 55 (1963), 984.

10. Cf. Pius XII, Apostolic Exhortation *Menti Nostrae* (Sept. 23, 1950): *AAS* 42 (1950), 684; also the Sacred Congregation for the Sacraments, Circular Letter *Magna Equidem* (Dec. 27, 1935), n. 10. For religious, cf. *Statuta Generalia* attached to the Apostolic Constitution *Sedes Sapientiae* (May 31, 1956): *AAS* 48 (1956), art. 33. Paul VI, Apostolic Letter *Summi Dei Verbum* (Nov. 4, 1963): *AAS* 55 (1963), 987 ff.

11. Cf. Pius XI, Encyclical Letter *Ad Catholici Sacerdotii* (Dec. 20, 1935): *AAS* 28 (1936), 41.

date, guided in a fatherly way to undertake other tasks. The latter should also be given sufficient direction so that, conscious of their vocation as Christians, they might eagerly embrace the lay apostolate.

7. Where individual dioceses are unable to institute their own seminaries properly, seminaries for many dioceses or for an entire region or for a country are to be set up and developed so that the sound training of the students, which must be considered the supreme law in this matter, can be taken care of in a more effective manner. These seminaries, if they are regional or national, are to be regulated according to directives set down by the bishops concerned[12] and approved by the Apostolic See.

In these seminaries, however, where there are many students, while retaining a unity of direction and of scientific training, the students should be conveniently divided into smaller groups so that a better provision is had for the personal formation of each.

12. It is established by statute that in determining the statutes of regional or national seminaries all interested bishops take part, despite the prescription of canon 1357, part 4 of the *Code of Canon Law.*

IV. THE CAREFUL DEVELOPMENT
OF THE SPIRITUAL TRAINING

8. The spiritual training should be closely connected with the doctrinal and pastoral, and with the special help of the spiritual director,[13] should be imparted in such a way that the students might learn to live in an intimate and unceasing union with the Father through his Son Jesus Christ in the Holy Spirit. Conformed to Christ the priest through their sacred ordination, they should be accustomed to adhere to him as friends in an intimate companionship their whole life through.[14] They should so live his Paschal Mystery themselves that they can initiate into it the flock committed to them. They should be taught to seek Christ in the faithful meditation on God's Word, in the active participation in the sacred mysteries of the Church, especially in the Eucharist and in the divine office,[15] in the bishop who sends them and in the people to whom they are sent, especially the poor, the children, the sick, the sinners and the unbelievers. They should love and venerate with a filial trust the most Blessed Virgin Mary, who was given as mother to the disciple by Christ Jesus as he was dying on the cross.

---

13. Cf. Pius XII, Apostolic Exhortation *Menti Nostrae* (Sept. 23, 1950): *AAS* 42 (1950), 674; Sacred Congregation of Seminaries and Universities, *The Spiritual Formation of the Candidate for the Priesthood,* Vatican City, 1965.

14. Cf. St. Pius X, Exhortation to the Clergy *Haerent Animo* (Aug. 4, 1908): Acts of St. Pius X, IV, 242, 244; Pius XII, Apostolic Exhortation *Menti Nostrae* (Sept. 23, 1950): *AAS* 42 (1950), 659–661; John XXIII, Encyclical Letter *Sacerdotii Nostri Primordia* (Aug. 1, 1959): *AAS* 51 (1959), 550 ff.

15. Pius XII, Encyclical Letter *Mediator Dei* (Nov. 20, 1947): *AAS* 39 (1947), 547 ff. and 572 ff.; John XXIII, Apostolic Exhortation *Sacrae Laudis* (Jan. 6, 1962): *AAS* 54 (1962), 69; Second Vatican Ecumenical Council, Constitution on the Sacred Liturgy *Sacrosanctum Concilium,* 16, 17; Sacred Congregation of Rites, *Instructio ad Exsecutionem Constitutionis de Sacra Liturgia Recte Ordinandam* (Sept. 26, 1964), nn. 14–17: *AAS* 56 (1954), 880 ff.

Those practices of piety that are commended by the long usage of the Church should be zealously cultivated, but care should be taken lest the spiritual formation consist in them alone or lest it develop only a religious affectation. The students should learn to live according to the Gospel ideal, to be strengthened in faith, hope and charity, so that in the exercise of these practices they may acquire the spirit of prayer,[16] learn to defend and strengthen their vocation, obtain an increase of other virtues and grow in the zeal to gain all men for Christ.

9. The students should be so saturated with the mystery of the Church, especially as described by this sacred synod, that, bound to the Vicar of Christ in a humble and trusting charity, and once ordained priests, adhering to their own bishop as faithful helpers and engaging in a common effort with their fellow-priests, they bear witness to that unity that attracts men to Christ.[17] They should learn to take part with a generous heart in the life of the whole Church in accord with what St. Augustine wrote: "to the extent that one loves the Church of Christ, to that extent does he possess the Holy Spirit."[18] The students should understand most clearly that they are not destined for domination or for honors but are given over totally to the service of God and to the pastoral ministry. With a particular concern should they be so formed in priestly obedience, in a simple way of life and in the spirit of self-denial,[19] that they are accustomed to giving up willingly even those things which are permitted but are not expedient, and to conform themselves to Christ crucified.

The students are to be made clearly aware of the burdens they will be undertaking, and no problem of the priestly life is to be concealed from them. This is to be done, however, not that they should be almost solely concerned with the notion of danger in their future labors, but rather that they might be more readily conformed to a spiritual life that

---

16. Cf. John XXIII, Encyclical Letter *Sacerdotii Nostri Primordia* (Aug. 1, 1959): *AAS* 51 (1959), 559 ff.

17. Second Vatican Ecumenical Council, Dogmatic Constitution on the Church *Lumen Gentium,* 28: *AAS* 57 (1965), 35 ff.

18. St. Augustine, *In Ioannem Tract.* 32, 8: *PL* 35, 1646.

19. Pius XII, Apostolic Exhortation *Menti Nostrae* (Sept. 23, 1950): *AAS* 42 (1950), 626 ff., 685, 690; John XXIII, Encyclical Letter *Sacerdotii Nostri Primordia* (Aug. 1, 1959): *AAS* 51 (1959), 551–553, 556 ff.; Paul VI, Encyclical Letter *Ecclesiam Suam* (Aug. 6, 1964): *AAS* 54 (1964), 634 ff.; Second Vatican Ecumenical Council, Dogmatic Constitution on the Church *Lumen Gentium,* especially n. 8: *AAS* 57 (1965), 12.

more than in any other way is actually strengthened by the very pastoral work they do.

10. Students who follow the venerable tradition of celibacy according to the holy and fixed laws of their own rite are to be educated to this state with great care. For renouncing thereby the companionship of marriage for the sake of the kingdom of heaven (cf. Mt 19:12), they embrace the Lord with an undivided love[20] altogether befitting the New Covenant, bear witness to the resurrection of the world to come (cf. Lk 20:36),[21] and obtain a most suitable aid for the continual exercise of that perfect charity whereby they can become all things to all men in their priestly ministry.[22] Let them deeply realize how gratefully that state ought to be received, not indeed only as commanded by ecclesiastical law, but as a precious gift of God for which they should humbly pray. Through the inspiration and help of the grace of the Holy Spirit, let them freely and generously hasten to respond to this gift.

Students ought rightly to acknowledge the duties and dignity of Christian Matrimony, which is a sign of the love between Christ and the Church. Let them recognize, however, the surpassing excellence of virginity consecrated to Christ,[23] so that with a maturely deliberate and generous choice they may consecrate themselves to the Lord by a complete gift of body and soul.

They are to be warned of the dangers that threaten their chastity especially in present-day society.[24] Aided by suitable safeguards, both divine and human, let them learn to integrate their renunciation of marriage in such a way that they may suffer in their lives and work not only no harm from celibacy, but rather acquire a deeper mastery of soul and body and a fuller maturity and more perfectly receive the blessedness spoken of in the Gospel.

---

20. Cf. Pius XII, Encyclical Letter *Sacra Virginitas* (March 25, 1954): *AAS* 46 (1954), 165 ff.

21. St. Cyprian, *De Habitu Virginum* 22: *PL* 4, 475; St. Ambrose, *De Virginibus,* I, 8, 52: *PL* 16, 202 ff.

22. Pius XII, Apostolic Exhortation *Menti Nostrae* (Sept. 23, 1950): *AAS* 42 (1950), 663.

23. Cf. Pius XII, Encyclical Letter *Sacra Virginitas* (March 25, 1954): *AAS* 46 (1954), 170–174.

24. Pius XII, Apostolic Exhortation *Menti Nostrae* (Sept. 23, 1950): *AAS* 42 (1950), 664, 690 ff.

11. The norms of Christian education are to be religiously observed and properly complemented by the newer findings of sound psychology and pedagogy. Therefore, by a wisely planned training there is also to be developed in the students a due human maturity. This will be made especially evident in stability of mind, in an ability to make weighty decisions, and in a sound evaluation of men and events. The students should be accustomed to work properly at their own development. They are to be formed in strength of character, and in general they are to learn to esteem those virtues which are held in high regard by men and which recommend a minister of Christ.[25] Such virtues are sincerity of mind, a constant concern for justice, fidelity to one's promises, refinement in manners, modesty in speech coupled with charity.

The discipline of seminary life is to be reckoned not only as a strong safeguard of community life and of charity but also as a necessary part of the total whole training formation. For thereby self-mastery is acquired, solid personal maturity is promoted, and the other dispositions of mind are developed which very greatly aid the ordered and fruitful activity of the Church. Seminary discipline should be so maintained, however, that the students acquire an internal attitude whereby they accept the authority of superiors from personal conviction, that is to say, from a motive of conscience (cf. Rm 13:5), and for supernatural reasons. The norms of discipline are to be applied according to the age of the students so that they themselves, as they gradually learn self-mastery, may become accustomed to use freedom wisely, to act spontaneously and energetically,[26] and to work together harmoniously with their fellows and with the laity.

The whole pattern of seminary life, permeated with a desire for piety and silence and a careful concern for mutual help, must be so arranged that it provides, in a certain sense, an initiation into the future life which the priest shall lead.

12. In order that the spiritual training rest upon a more solid basis and that the students embrace their vocation with a fully deliberate choice, it will be the prerogative of the bishops to establish a fitting pe-

---

25. Cf. Paul VI, Apostolic Letter *Summi Dei Verbum* (Nov. 4, 1963): *AAS* 55 (1963), 991.

26. Cf. Pius XII, Apostolic Exhortation *Menti Nostrae* (Sept. 23, 1950): *AAS* 42 (1950), 686.

riod of time for a more intense introduction to the spiritual life. It will also be their charge to determine the opportuneness of providing for a certain interruption in the studies or of establishing a suitable introduction to pastoral work, in order that they may more satisfactorily test the fitness of candidates for the priesthood. In accordance with the conditions of individual regions, it will also be the bishops' responsibility to make a decision about extending the age beyond that demanded at present by common law for the reception of sacred Orders, and of deliberating whether it be opportune to rule that students, at the end of their course in theology, exercise the order of deacon for a fitting period of time before being promoted to the priesthood.

V. THE REVISION OF ECCLESIASTICAL STUDIES

13. Before beginning specifically ecclesiastical subjects, seminarians should be equipped with that humanistic and scientific training which young men in their own countries are wont to have as a foundation for higher studies. Moreover, they are to acquire a knowledge of Latin which will enable them to understand and make use of the sources of so many sciences and of the documents of the Church.[27] The study of the liturgical language proper to each rite should be considered necessary; a suitable knowledge of the languages of the Bible and of Tradition should be greatly encouraged.

14. In revising ecclesiastical studies the aim should first of all be that the philosophical and theological disciplines be more suitably aligned and that they harmoniously work toward opening more and more the minds of the students to the mystery of Christ. For it is this mystery which affects the whole history of the human race, continually influences the Church, and is especially at work in the priestly ministry.[28]

That this vision be communicated to the students from the outset of their training, ecclesiastical studies are to be begun with an introductory course which should last for an appropriate length of time. In this initiation to ecclesiastical studies, the mystery of salvation should be so proposed that the students perceive the meaning, order and pastoral end of their studies. At the same time they should be helped to establish and penetrate their own entire lives with faith and be

---

27. Cf. Paul VI, Apostolic Letter *Summi Dei Verbum* (Nov. 4, 1963): *AAS* 55 (1963), 993.

28. Second Vatican Ecumenical Council, Dogmatic Constitution on the Church *Lumen Gentium,* 7, 28: *AAS* 57 (1965), 9–11, 33 ff.

strengthened in embracing their vocation with a personal dedication and a joyful heart.

15. The philosophical disciplines are to be taught in such a way that the students are first of all led to acquire a solid and coherent knowledge of man, the world, and of God, relying on a philosophical patrimony which is perennially valid[29] and taking into account the philosophical investigations of later ages. This is especially true of those investigations which exercise a greater influence in their own nations. Account should also be taken of the more recent progress of the sciences. The net result should be that the students, correctly understanding the characteristics of the contemporary mind, will be duly prepared for dialogue with men of their time.[30]

The history of philosophy should be so taught that the students, while reaching the ultimate principles of the various systems, will hold on to what is proven to be true therein and will be able to detect the roots of errors and to refute them.

In the very manner of teaching, there should be stirred up in the students a love of rigorously searching for the truth and of maintaining and demonstrating it, together with an honest recognition of the limits of human knowledge. Attention must be carefully drawn to the necessary connection between philosophy and the true problems of life, as well as the questions which preoccupy the minds of the students. Likewise, students should be helped to perceive the links between the subject matter of philosophy and the mysteries of salvation which are considered in theology under the higher light of faith.

16. The theological disciplines, in the light of faith and under the guidance of the Magisterium of the Church,[31] should be so taught that the students will correctly draw out Catholic doctrine from divine rev-

---

29. Cf. Pius XII, Encyclical Letter *Humani Generis* (Aug. 12, 1950): *AAS* 42 (1950), 571–575.

30. Cf. Paul VI, Encyclical Letter *Ecclesiam Suam* (Aug. 6, 1964): *AAS* 54 (1964), 637 ff.

31. Cf. Pius XII, Encyclical Letter *Humani Generis* (Aug. 12, 1950): *AAS* 42 (1950), 567–569; Allocution *Si Diligis* (May 31, 1954): *AAS* 46 (1954), 314 ff.; Paul VI, *Allocution in the Pontifical Gregorian University* (March 12, 1964): *AAS* 56 (1964), 364 ff.; Second Vatican Ecumenical Council, Dogmatic Constitution on the Church *Lumen Gentium*, 25: *AAS* 57 (1965), 29–31.

elation, profoundly penetrate it, make it the food of their own spiritual lives,[32] and be enabled to proclaim, explain and protect it in their priestly ministry.

The students are to be formed with particular care in the study of the Bible, which ought to be, as it were, the soul of all theology.[33] After a suitable introduction, they are to be initiated carefully into the method of exegesis, and they are to see the great themes of divine revelation and to receive from their daily reading of and meditating on the sacred books inspiration and nourishment.[34]

Dogmatic theology should be so arranged that these biblical themes are proposed first of all. Next, there should be opened up to the students what the Fathers of the Eastern and Western Church have contributed to the faithful transmission and development of the individual truths of revelation. The further history of dogma should also be presented, account being taken of its relation to the general history of the Church.[35] Next, in order that they may illumine the mysteries of salvation as completely as possible, the students should learn to penetrate them more deeply with the help of speculation, under the guidance of St. Thomas, and to perceive their interconnections.[36] They should be taught to recog-

---

32. Cf. St. Bonaventure, *Itinerarium Mentis in Deum,* Prol., no. 4: "[No one] believes that reading suffices of itself without unction, speculation without devotion, investigation without wonder, circumspection without exultation, conscientiousness without piety, knowledge without charity, intelligence without humility, zeal without divine grace, observation without wisdom divinely inspired" (St. Bonaventure, *Complete Works* V, ed. Quaracchi, 1891, p. 296).

33. Cf. Leo XIII, Encyclical Letter *Providentissimus Deus* (Nov. 18, 1893): *AAS* 26 (1893–94), 283.

34. Cf. Pontifical Biblical Commission, *Instructio de Sacra Scriptura Recte Docenda* (May 13, 1950): *AAS* 42 (1950), 502.

35. Cf. Pius XII, Encyclical Letter *Humani Generis* (Aug. 12, 1950): *AAS* 42 (1950), 568 ff.: "...sacred disciplines always find rejuvenation in the study of the sacred fonts; while on the other hand that speculation becomes sterile which neglects deeper inquiry into the sacred deposit in order to provide knowledge from experience."

36. Cf. Pius XII, *Address to Seminarians* (June 24, 1939): *AAS* 31 (1939), 247: "Emulation...in seeking and propagating the truth is not suppressed by commending the doctrine of St. Thomas, but rather stimulated and thoroughly directed." Paul VI, *Allocution in the Pontifical Gregorian University* (March 12, 1964): *AAS* 56 (1964), 365: "[Teachers] should reverently listen to the voice of the Church's Doctors, among whom Aquinas holds a special place; such is the power of the Angelic Doctor's genius and such his sincere love of truth; so great his wisdom in investigating the highest truths, in demonstrating and linking them with the most appropriate bonds of unity that as a result his doctrine becomes a most efficacious instrument not only for gathering the fundamental

nize these same mysteries as present and working in liturgical actions[37] and in the entire life of the Church. They should learn to seek the solutions to human problems under the light of revelation, to apply the eternal truths of revelation to the changeable conditions of human affairs and to communicate them in a way suited to men of our day.[38]

Likewise, let the other theological disciplines be renewed through a more living contact with the mystery of Christ and the history of salvation. Special care must be given to the perfecting of moral theology. Its scientific exposition, nourished more on the teaching of the Bible, should shed light on the loftiness of the calling of the faithful in Christ and the obligation that is theirs of bearing fruit in charity for the life of the world. Similarly, the teaching of canon law and of Church history should take into account the mystery of the Church, according to the dogmatic constitution *De Ecclesia* promulgated by this sacred synod. Sacred liturgy, which is to be considered as the primary and indispensable source of the truly Christian spirit, should be taught according to the mind of articles 15 and 16 of the *Constitution on the Sacred Liturgy.*[39]

The circumstances of various regions being duly considered, students are to be brought to a fuller understanding of the churches and ecclesial communities separated from the Apostolic Roman See, so that they may be able to contribute to the work of reestablishing unity among all Christians according to the prescriptions of this holy synod.[40]

Let them also be introduced to a knowledge of other religions which are more widespread in individual regions, so that they may acknowledge more correctly what truth and goodness these religions, in God's

---

aspects of the faith into a unified whole, but also for attaining usefully and securely the fruits of a healthy progression." Cf. also the allocution addressed to the Sixth International Thomistic Congress (Sept. 10, 1965).

37. Cf. Second Vatican Ecumenical Council, Constitution on the Sacred Liturgy *Sacrosanctum Concilium,* 7, 16: *AAS* 56 (1964), 100 ff. and 104 ff.

38. Cf. Paul VI, Encyclical Letter *Ecclesiam Suam* (Aug. 6, 1964): *AAS* 54 (1964), 640 ff.

39. Second Vatican Ecumenical Council, Constitution on the Sacred Liturgy *Sacrosanctum Concilium,* 10, 14, 15, 16; Sacred Congregation of Rites, *Instructio ad Exsecutionem Constitutionis de Sacra Liturgia Recte Ordinandam* (Sept. 26, 1964): nn. 11, 12: *AAS* 56 (1964), 879 ff.

40. Cf. Second Vatican Ecumenical Council, Decree on Ecumenism *Unitatis Redintegratio,* 1, 9, 10: *AAS* 57 (1965), 90, 98 ff.

Providence, possess and so that they may learn to refute their errors and be able to communicate the full light of truth to those who do not have it.

17. But since doctrinal training ought to tend not to a mere communication of ideas but to a true and intimate formation of the students, teaching methods are to be revised both as regards lectures, discussions and seminars and also the development of study on the part of the students, whether done privately or in small groups. Unity and soundness of the entire training is carefully to be provided for by avoiding an excessive multiplication of courses and lectures and by the omission of those questions which scarcely retain any importance or which ought to be referred to higher academic studies.

18. It will be the bishops' concern that young men suited by temperament, virtue, and ability be sent to special institutes, faculties or universities so that priests may be trained at a higher scientific level in the sacred sciences and in other fields which may be judged opportune. Thus they will be able to meet the various needs of the apostolate. The spiritual and pastoral training of these men, however, especially if they are not yet ordained as priests, is in no way to be neglected.

VI. THE PROMOTION OF
STRICTLY PASTORAL TRAINING

19. That pastoral concern which ought to permeate thoroughly the entire training of the students[41] also demands that they be diligently instructed in those matters which are particularly linked to the sacred ministry, especially in catechesis and preaching, in liturgical worship and the administration of the sacraments, in works of charity, in assisting the erring and the unbelieving, and in the other pastoral functions. They are to be carefully instructed in the art of directing souls, whereby they will be able to bring all the sons of the Church first of all to a fully conscious and apostolic Christian life and to the fulfillment of the duties of their state of life. Let them learn to help with equal solicitude religious men and women, that they may persevere in the grace of their vocations and may make progress according to the spirit of their various institutes.[42]

---

41. The ideal of the pastorate can be deduced from documents of recent Pontiffs, which treat distinctly of the life, qualifications and institution of priests; cf. St. Pius X, Exhortation to the Clergy *Haerent Animo* (Aug. 4, 1908): Acts of St. Pius X, 237 ff.; Pius XI, Encyclical Letter *Ad Catholici Sacerdotii* (Dec. 20, 1935): *AAS* 28 (1936), 5 ff.; Pius XII, Apostolic Exhortation *Menti Nostrae* (Sept. 23, 1950): *AAS* 42 (1950), 657 ff.; John XXIII, Encyclical Letter *Sacerdotii Nostri Primordia* (Aug. 1, 1959): *AAS* 51 (1959), 545 ff.; Paul VI, Apostolic Letter *Summi Dei Verbum* (Nov. 4, 1963): *AAS* 55 (1963), 979 ff.

Much concerning pastoral formation can be found also in the encyclicals *Mystici Corporis* (1943); *Mediator Dei* (1947); *Evangelii Praecones* (1951); *Sacra Virginitas* (1954); *Musicae Sacrae Disciplina* (1955); *Princeps Pastorum* (1959) and in the Apostolic Constitution *Sedes Sapientiae* for religious. Pius XII, John XXIII and Paul VI have often illustrated the ideal of the good pastor in their allocutions to seminarians and priests as well.

42. Concerning the importance of the state characterized by the profession of the evangelical counsels, cf. Second Vatican Ecumenical Council, Dogmatic Constitution on the Church *Lumen Gentium,* chapter 6: *AAS* 57 (1965), 49–55; Second Vatican Ecumenical Council, Decree on the Adaptation and Renewal of Religious Life *Perfectae Caritatis.*

In general, those capabilities are to be developed in the students which especially contribute to dialogue with men, such as the ability to listen to others and to open their hearts and minds in the spirit of charity to the various circumstances and needs of men.[43]

20. They should also be taught to use the aids which the disciplines of pedagogy, psychology and sociology can provide,[44] according to correct methodology and the norms of ecclesiastical authority. Likewise, let them be properly instructed in inspiring and fostering the apostolic activity of the laity[45] and in promoting the various and more effective forms of the apostolate. Let them also be imbued with that truly Catholic spirit which will accustom them to transcend the limits of their own diocese, nation or rite, and to help the needs of the whole Church, prepared in spirit to preach the Gospel everywhere.[46]

21. But since it is necessary for the students to learn the art of exercising the apostolate not only theoretically but also practically, and to be able to act both on their own responsibility and in harmonious conjunction with others, they should be initiated into pastoral work, both during their course of studies and also during the time of vacations, by opportune practical projects. These should be carried out in accordance with the age of the students and local conditions, and with the prudent judgment of the bishops, methodically and under the leadership of men skilled in pastoral work, the surpassing power of supernatural means being always remembered.[47]

---

43. Cf. Paul VI Encyclical Letter *Ecclesiam Suam* (Aug. 6, 1964): *AAS* 54 (1964), in several places throughout, especially pp. 635 ff. and 640 ff.

44. Cf. especially John XXIII, Encyclical Letter *Mater et Magistra* (May 15, 1961): *AAS* 53 (1961), 401 ff.

45. Cf. in particular Second Vatican Ecumenical Council, Dogmatic Constitution on the Church *Lumen Gentium,* 33: *AAS* 57 (1965), 39.

46. Cf. Second Vatican Ecumenical Council, Dogmatic Constitution on the Church *Lumen Gentium,* 17: *AAS* 57 (1965), 20 ff.

47. Several pontifical documents warn against the danger in pastoral action of neglecting the supernatural goal and considering supernatural aids of little value at least in practice; cf. especially the documents cited in note 41.

VII. TRAINING TO BE ACHIEVED
AFTER THE COURSE OF STUDIES

22. Since priestly training, because of the circumstances particularly of contemporary society, must be pursued and perfected even after the completion of the course of studies in seminaries,[48] it will be the responsibility of episcopal conferences in individual nations to employ suitable means to this end. Such would be pastoral institutes working together with suitably chosen parishes, meetings held at stated times and appropriate projects whereby the younger clergy would be gradually introduced into the priestly life and apostolic activity under its spiritual, intellectual and pastoral aspects, and would be able, day by day, to renew and foster them more effectively.

---

48. More recent documents of the Holy See urge particular concern for newly ordained priests; especially noteworthy are:

Pius XII, Motu Proprio *Quandoquidem* (April 2, 1949): *AAS* 41 (1949), 165–167; Apostolic Exhortation *Menti Nostrae* (Sept. 23, 1950): *AAS* 42 (1950); Apostolic Constitution *Sedes Sapientiae* (May 31, 1956): *AAS* 48 (1956) and the general statutes attached to it; *Address to the Priests of the* Convictus Barcinonensis (June 14, 1957), *Discourses and Radio Messages,* vol. XIX, 271–273.

Paul VI, *Address to the Priests of the Gian Matteo Giberti Institute of the Diocese of Verona* (March 11, 1964).

CONCLUSION

The fathers of this holy synod have pursued the work begun by the Council of Trent. While they confidently entrust to seminary administrators and teachers the task of forming the future priests of Christ in the spirit of the renewal promoted by this sacred synod, they earnestly exhort those who are preparing for the priestly ministry to realize that the hope of the Church and the salvation of souls is being committed to them. They urge them also to receive the norms of this decree willingly and thus to bring forth most abundant fruit which will always remain.

Given in Rome at St. Peter's, October 28, 1965

DECLARATION ON CHRISTIAN EDUCATION

Gravissimum Educationis

Promulgated by
His Holiness Pope Paul VI
On October 28, 1965

INTRODUCTION

The *Declaration on Christian Education (GE)* is closely associated with the vision of the human person set forth in *Gaudium et Spes* and the *Declaration on Religious Freedom.* According to this vision, the human person is religious by nature, seeking God in seeking the truth. Formal education is the systematic and institutionalized form of this seeking. The right to Christian education is part of the general right of religious freedom, both for the individual and for communities (cf. *DH*).

Similarly, *GE* emphasizes the dignity of the human person and the corresponding desire to participate in culture, society and economic and political life. Education is the process in which the human person participates in order to attain his "cultural and spiritual inheritance" (cf. *GE* intro). It is declared a right (cf. *GE* 1) because it is a necessary means for persons to grow to maturity. The person has a right to education and to everything needed to become complete in one's humanity in order to develop in the way God intends.

GE uses the word "duty" with respect to parents and to the Church. From this duty, which follows on their vocation and their respective responsibility for children, parents and the Church possess the right to the freedom needed to provide this education (cf. *GE* 6, 8).

In the Church's understanding, human dignity is rooted in the person's call to communion with God (cf. *GS* 19). It is inextricably connected to the moral dimension of human existence, especially to the dignity of conscience. Christian education aims to form the entire person, with particular emphasis on moral education and formation of conscience (cf. *GE* 1, 6). Its principal purpose is to introduce the baptized into the knowledge of the mystery of salvation, so that they may lead a fully Christian life and "contribute to the good of the whole society" (cf. *GE* 2).

This kind of education does not prescind from secular education, nor does it exempt the Christian from active involvement in the concerns of the earthly city and its common good. Rather, it results in making one more actively involved in social, economic and political life and in organizations that promote the various aspects of the human good. *Lumen Gentium* 36 and *Gaudium et Spes* (especially 39–40) shed further light on how the Church understands how its members contribute to society.

Christian education should not be seen as a species of education, along with secular education, as if the two could be separated. Christian education is a fully human education and more, insofar as it is directed to the fulfillment of the Christian's calling, which involves a concern for everything human. Just as *Lumen Gentium* recognizes that members of the Church are also citizens of this earth and have duties corresponding to both, while *Gaudium et Spes* unites these in the acting subject, so too Christian education is a unified reality. Christian education is a fully human education in light of the Gospel of Christ.

The primary institution responsible for education is the family, instituted by God. The family's role in Christian education which *GE* elaborates is one of four main discussions of the family in the texts of Vatican II. (The others are *LG* 11, 41; *AA* 11, 30 and *GS* 47–52.) Through the sacrament of marriage, parents and their families are equipped with the gifts needed to fulfill their mission of education. On this, see the further remarks in the introduction to the *Decree on the Apostolate of the Laity.*

Parents are the "first preachers of the faith to their children" (*LG* 11), and because they have been entrusted with the upbringing of their children, parents are the "primary and principal educators" of their children (cf. *GE* 3). A careful reading of the text makes it clear that the declaration sees that this educational responsibility of parents is fulfilled primarily in two ways: through the family (cf. *GE* 3) and through the free choice of schools (cf. *GE* 6).

The declaration beautifully describes the family as the "first school of the social virtues" and the place where children learn respect for God and others. But the family is not normally self-sufficient. It requires and has the right to expect various kinds of support from society and government. This includes education, as well as the right to pursue the education most fitting for children. Parents have the right to expect a similar kind of support from the Church for the Christian education of their children.

The Church in the United States has probably invested more in the various forms of Catholic education than in any other dimension of its mission. The Catholic schools and other programs of religious education are one of the most visible and highly developed aspects of the Church's life.

The declaration calls upon parents and all the faithful "to assist to their utmost in finding suitable methods of education and programs of study and in forming teachers who can give youth a true education" (*GE* 6). To this end, and for the support of schools, they can form associations of parents. It is clear that when the declaration places the responsibility for education on the Church, the operating definition or "model" of the Church is definitely not "just the hierarchy." Certainly, pastors have a grave responsibility to contribute to Christian education (cf. *GE* 2, 9, 10). But here perhaps more than in any other aspect of the Church's mission it is true that "pastors know how much the laity contribute to the welfare of the entire Church. They also know that they were not ordained by Christ to take upon themselves alone the entire salvific mission of the Church toward the world. On the contrary, they understand that it is their noble duty to shepherd the faithful and to recognize their ministries and charisms, so that all according to their proper roles may cooperate in this common undertaking with one mind" *(LG* 30). Since Vatican II, the decline in the number of religious staffing Catholic schools has caused parents to assume a greater responsibility for their children's Christian education.

GE sees education in general, and Christian education in particular, as promoting true human freedom. This freedom corresponds to the increased contemporary awareness of human dignity. Christian education aims at developing a fully mature Christian who can assume responsibility for the common good of both the earthly city and the Church. Parents should provide for their children's education through a love by which they desire to see their children attain their full stature in Christ. In this way, Christian education becomes the means by which parents will be able to say to their children what Christ said to his apostles: "I have called you friends, because I have made known to you everything that I have heard from my Father" (Jn 15:15). Christian education aims to make young people capable of contributing to the common good of society and the Church, so that they will be able to provide that same education to the next generation. Education is a circular reality; it is a receiving in view of giving.

The Council's concern for young people appears in this declaration as it recognizes that "the destiny of society and of the Church itself is intimately linked with the progress of young people pursuing higher studies" (*GE* 10). The notion of education for youth in view of human and Christian maturity implicitly contains a "spirituality for students." It is based on the idea that neither secular society nor the Church place great demands on youth, other than that they use their freedom to become enriched through education. The fundamental contribution youth make to the common good of society and the Church is to freely and energetically embrace this period of formation. For what they can offer later in life to promote the common good will largely depend upon how profoundly they have been formed through their education.

GE takes seriously the universality of the right to Christian education by singling out the poor, reflecting the Council's general solicitude for those who are wanting in material or other goods. Pastors and the faithful are to assist Catholic schools in "caring for the needs of those who are poor in the goods of this world or who are deprived of the assistance and affection of a family or who are strangers to the gift of faith" (*GE* 9). Catholic colleges and universities should not be open only to the elite who can afford them, but students of promise who may lack sufficient resources (cf. *GE* 10).

Because the goal of the Catholic school is "that the knowledge students gradually acquire of the world, life and man is illumined by faith" (*GE* 8), it is clear that much depends on teachers. The school makes possible that wonderful exchange between teacher and student. The school is a community united by the pursuit of knowledge for a fully human and Christian maturity. As the more mature members of the community, teachers bear a special responsibility.

The first prerequisite for teachers is that they be suitably qualified in both secular and religious knowledge. With regard to secular knowledge, *GE* exhibits the generally positive attitude of Vatican II with respect to the use and role of the most recent developments in the human sciences. As the declaration puts it, teachers should possess "pedagogical skill that is in keeping with the findings of the contemporary world"

(*GE* 8). Elsewhere the Council noted that the education of priests, laity and catechists should be assisted by the findings of modern psychology, sociology and pedagogy, and include instruction in them (cf. *OT* 11, 20; *AA* 32; *CD* 14, 17).

Vatican II did not embrace specific schools, theories, practices or trends. Rather, it was concerned that a genuine dialogue with the modern world benefit those involved in the Church's apostolate. The findings of any science, however, must be judged in the light of the Church's faith. The human sciences in particular must be evaluated in light of the Church's understanding of the dignity, freedom and divine calling of the human person. If the secular preparation of teachers is superior in depth and breadth, then it is less likely that faith will be able to hold its own in the dialogue between faith and reason. Since this dialogue is a defining characteristic of the Catholic school, teachers whose own Christian formation has not kept "abreast of their development in secular subjects" (*GE* 7) certainly cannot adequately teach their students. One cannot give what one doesn't have.

Since *GE* was promulgated, additional Church documents have been issued developing aspects of its teaching. Generally, the most recent document will contain references to prior ones, so that in obtaining the most recent text one has access to the titles and dates of others. The Sacred Congregation for Catholic Education has issued *The Catholic School* (March 19, 1977); *Lay Catholics in Schools: Witnesses to Faith* (October 15, 1982) and *The Religious Dimension of Education in a Catholic School* (April 7, 1988). Pope John Paul II has issued *On Ecclesiastical Universities and Faculties (Sapientia Christiana)* on April 29, 1979, and the *Apostolic Constitution on Catholic Universities (Ex Corde Ecclesiae)* on August 15, 1990.

TOPICAL OUTLINE

1. Introduction: the importance of education

2. The meaning of the universal right to an education (1)

3. Christian education (2)

4. Educators (3)

    A. Parents

    B. Civil society and schools

    C. The Church

5. Helps to education (4)

6. The importance of schools (5)

7. The duties and rights of parents (6)

8. Moral and religious education in schools (7)

9. Catholic schools

    A. Mission of the Catholic school (8)

        1. Right of the Church to establish schools

        2. Role of teachers

    B. Various types of Catholic schools

        1. Schools for special needs (9)

        2. Catholic colleges and universities (10)

        3. Faculties of sacred sciences (11)

        4. Collaboration (12)

10. Conclusion

DECLARATION ON CHRISTIAN EDUCATION

Gravissimum Educationis

INTRODUCTION

The sacred ecumenical Council has considered with care how extremely important education is in the life of man and how its influence ever grows in the social progress of this age.[1]

Indeed, the circumstances of our time have made it easier and at once more urgent to educate young people and, what is more, to continue the education of adults. Men are more aware of their own dignity and position; more and more they want to take an active part in social and especially in economic and political life.[2] Enjoying more leisure as

---

1. Among many documents illustrating the importance of education, see above all Benedict XV, Apostolic Letter *Communes Litteras* (April 10, 1919): *AAS* 11 (1919), 172; Pius XI, Apostolic Encyclical *Divini Illius Magistri* (Dec. 31, 1929): *AAS* 22 (1930), 49–86; Pius XII, *Allocution to the Youths of Italian Catholic Action* (April 20, 1946): *Discourses and Radio Messages,* vol. 8, 53–57; *Allocution to Fathers of French Families* (Sept. 18, 1951): *Discourses and Radio Messages,* vol. 13, 241–245; John XXIII, *30th Anniversary Message on the Publication of the Encyclical Letter* Divini Illius Magistri (Dec. 30, 1959): *AAS* 52 (1960), 57–59; Paul VI, *Allocution to Members of Federated Institutes Dependent on Ecclesiastical Authority* (Dec. 30, 1963): *Encyclicals and Discourses of His Holiness Paul VI* (Rome: 1964), 601–603. Above all are to be consulted the *Acts and Documents of the Second Vatican Council* appearing in the first series of the ante-preparatory phase, vol. 3, 363–364; 370–371; 373–374.

2. Cf. John XXIII, Encyclical Letter *Mater et Magistra* (May 15, 1961): *AAS* 53 (1961), 413–415; 417–424; Encyclical Letter *Pacem in Terris* (April 11, 1963): *AAS* 55 (1963), 278 ff.

they sometimes do, men find that the remarkable development of technology and scientific investigation and the new means of communication offer them an opportunity of attaining more easily their cultural and spiritual inheritance and of fulfilling one another in the closer ties between groups and even between peoples.

Consequently, attempts are being made everywhere to promote more education. The rights of men to an education, particularly the primary rights of children and parents, are being proclaimed and recognized in public documents.[3] As the number of pupils rapidly increases schools are multiplied and expanded far and wide, and other educational institutions are established. New experiments are conducted in methods of education and teaching. Mighty attempts are being made to obtain education for all, even though vast numbers of children and young people are still deprived of even rudimentary training, and so many others lack a suitable education in which truth and love are developed together.

To fulfill the mandate she has received from her divine Founder of proclaiming the mystery of salvation to all men and of restoring all things in Christ, holy mother the Church must be concerned with the whole of man's life, even the secular part of it insofar as it has a bearing on his heavenly calling.[4] Therefore, she has a role in the progress and development of education. Hence, this sacred synod declares certain fundamental principles of Christian education especially in schools. These principles will have to be developed at greater length by a special post-conciliar commission and applied by episcopal conferences to varying local situations.

---

3. General Assembly of the United Nations, *Declaration on the Rights of Man* (Dec. 10, 1948); also cf. *Declaration of the Rights of Children* (Nov. 20 1959); *Additional Protocol to the Convention Safeguarding the Rights of Men and Fundamental Liberties,* Paris (March 20, 1952); regarding that universal profession of the character of human laws, cf. John XXIII, Encyclical Letter *Pacem in Terris* (April 11, 1963): *AAS* 55 (1963), 295 ff.

4. Cf. John XXIII, Encyclical Letter *Mater et Magistra* (May 15, 1961): *AAS* 53 (1961), 402; cf. Second Vatican Ecumenical Council, Dogmatic Constitution on the Church *Lumen Gentium,* 17: *AAS* 57 (1965), p. 21, and schema on the Pastoral Constitution on the Church in the Modern World *Gaudium et Spes* (1965).

1. The Meaning of the Universal Right to an Education

All men of every race, condition and age, since they enjoy the dignity of a human being, have an inalienable right to an education[5] that is in keeping with their ultimate goal,[6] their ability, their sex and the culture and tradition of their country, and also in harmony with their fraternal association with other peoples in the fostering of true unity and peace on earth. For a true education aims at the formation of the human person in the pursuit of his ultimate end and of the good of the societies of which as man he is a member, and in whose obligations, as an adult, he will share.

Therefore, children and young people must be helped, with the aid of the latest advances in psychology and the arts and science of teaching, to develop harmoniously their physical, moral and intellectual endowments so that they may gradually acquire a mature sense of responsibility in striving endlessly to form their own lives properly and in pursuing true freedom as they surmount the vicissitudes of life with courage and constancy. Let them be given also as they advance in years a positive and prudent sexual education. Moreover, they should be so trained to take their part in social life that properly instructed in the necessary and opportune skills they can become actively involved in various community organizations, open to discourse with others and willing to do their best to promote the common good.

This sacred synod likewise declares that children and young people have a right to be motivated to appraise moral values with a right conscience, to embrace them with a personal adherence, together with a deeper knowledge and love of God. Consequently, it earnestly entreats all those who hold a position of public authority or who are in charge of education to see to it that youth is never deprived of this sacred right. It further exhorts the sons of the Church to give their attention with generosity to the entire field of education, having especially in mind the need of extending very soon the benefits of a suitable education and training to everyone in all parts of the world.[7]

---

5. Pius XII, *Radio Message* (Dec. 24, 1942): *AAS* 35 (1943), 12–19; John XXIII, Encyclical Letter *Pacem in Terris* (April 11, 1963): *AAS* 55 (1963), 259 ff. Also cf. declaration cited on the rights of man in footnote 3.

6. Cf. Pius XI, Encyclical Letter *Divini Illius Magistri* (Dec. 31, 1929): *AAS* 22 (1930), 50 ff.

7. Cf. John XXIII, Encyclical Letter *Mater et Magistra* (May 15, 1961): *AAS* 53 (1961), 441 ff.

2. Christian Education

Since all Christians have become by rebirth of water and the Holy Spirit a new creature[8] so that they should be called and should be children of God, they have a right to a Christian education. A Christian education does not merely strive for the maturing of a human person as just now described, but has as its principal purpose this goal: that the baptized, while they are gradually introduced to the knowledge of the mystery of salvation, become ever more aware of the gift of faith they have received, and that they learn in addition how to worship God the Father in spirit and truth (cf. Jn 4:23) especially in liturgical action, and be conformed in their personal lives according to the new man created in justice and holiness of truth (Eph 4:22–24); also that they develop into perfect manhood, to the mature measure of the fullness of Christ (cf. Eph 4:13) and strive for the growth of the Mystical Body; moreover, that aware of their calling, they learn not only how to bear witness to the hope that is in them (cf. 1 Pt 3:15) but also how to help in the Christian formation of the world that takes place when natural powers, viewed in the full consideration of man redeemed by Christ, contribute to the good of the whole society.[9] Wherefore, this sacred synod recalls to pastors of souls their most serious obligation to see to it that all the faithful, but especially the youth who are the hope of the Church, enjoy this Christian education.[10]

3. The Authors of Education

Since parents have given children their life, they are bound by the most serious obligation to educate their offspring and therefore must be recognized as the primary and principal educators.[11] This role in educa-

---

8. Cf. Pius XI, Encyclical Letter *Divini Illius Magistri* (Dec. 31, 1929): *AAS* 22 (1930), 1, 83.

9. Cf. Second Vatican Ecumenical Council, Dogmatic Constitution on the Church *Lumen Gentium,* 36: *AAS* 57 (1965), 41 ff.

10. Cf. Second Vatican Ecumenical Council, Decree on the Apostolate of the Laity *Apostolicam Actuositatem* (1965), 12.

11. Cf. Pius XI, Encyclical Letter *Divini Illius Magistri* (Dec. 31, 1929): *AAS* 22 (1930), 1, 59 ff.; Pius XI, Encyclical Letter *Mit Brennender Sorge* (March 14, 1937): *AAS* 29; Pius XII, *Allocution to the First National Congress of the Italian Catholic Teachers' Association* (Sept. 8, 1946): *Discourses and Radio Messages,* vol. 8, 218.

tion is so important that only with difficulty can it be supplied where it is lacking. Parents are the ones who must create a family atmosphere animated by love and respect for God and man, in which the well-rounded personal and social education of children is fostered. Hence, the family is the first school of the social virtues that every society needs. It is particularly in the Christian family, enriched by the grace and office of the sacrament of matrimony, that children should be taught from their early years to have a knowledge of God according to the faith received in Baptism, to worship him and to love their neighbor. Here, too, they find their first experience of a wholesome human society and of the Church. Finally, it is through the family that they are gradually led to a companionship with their fellowmen and with the People of God. Let parents then recognize the inestimable importance a truly Christian family has for the life and progress of God's own people.[12]

The family, which has the primary duty of imparting education, needs the help of the whole community. In addition, therefore, to the rights of parents and others to whom the parents entrust a share in the work of education, certain rights and duties belong indeed to civil society, whose role is to direct what is required for the common temporal good. Its function is to promote the education of youth in many ways, namely: to protect the duties and rights of parents and others who share in education and to give them aid; according to the principle of subsidiarity, when the endeavors of parents and other societies are lacking, to carry out the work of education in accordance with the wishes of the parents; and, moreover, as the common good demands, to build schools and institutions.[13]

Finally, in a special way, the duty of educating belongs to the Church, not merely because she must be recognized as a human society capable of educating, but especially because she has the responsibility of announcing the way of salvation to all men, of communicating the

---

12. Cf. Second Vatican Ecumenical Council, Dogmatic Constitution on the Church *Lumen Gentium*, 11, 35: *AAS* 57 (1965), 16, 40 ff.

13. Cf. Pius XI, Encyclical Letter *Divini Illius Magistri* (Dec. 31, 1929): *AAS* 22 (1930), 1, 63 ff.; Pius XII, *Radio Message* (June 1, 1941): *AAS* 33 (1941), 200; Pius XI, *Allocution to the First National Congress of the Association of Italian Catholic Teachers* (Sept. 8, 1946): *Discourses and Radio Messages,* vol. 8, 218. Regarding the principle of subsidiarity, cf. John XXIII, Encyclical Letter *Pacem in Terris* (April 11, 1963): *AAS* 55 (1963), 294.

life of Christ to those who believe, and in her unfailing solicitude of assisting men to be able to come to the fullness of this life.[14] The Church is bound as a mother to give to these children of hers an education by which their whole life can be imbued with the spirit of Christ and at the same time do all she can to promote for all peoples the complete perfection of the human person, the good of earthly society and the building of a world that is more human.[15]

4. Various Aids to Christian Education

In fulfilling its educational role, the Church, eager to employ all suitable aids, is concerned especially about those which are her very own. Foremost among these is catechetical instruction,[16] which enlightens and strengthens the faith, nourishes life according to the spirit of Christ, leads to intelligent and active participation in the liturgical mystery[17] and gives motivation for apostolic activity. The Church esteems highly and seeks to penetrate and ennoble with her own spirit also other aids which belong to the general heritage of man and which are of great influence in forming souls and molding men, such as the media of communication,[18] various groups for mental and physical development, youth associations and, in particular, schools.

---

14. Cf. Pius XI, Encyclical Letter *Divini Illius Magistri* (Dec. 31, 1929): *AAS* 22 (1930), 1, 53 ff., 56 ff.; Pius XI, Encyclical Letter *Non Abbiamo Bisogno* (June 29, 1931): *AAS* 23 (1931), 311 ff.; Pius XII, *Letter from Secretariat of State to 28th Italian Social Week* (Sept. 20, 1955), *L'Osservatore Romano* (Sept. 29, 1955).

15. The Church praises those local, national and international civic authorities who, conscious of the urgent necessity in these times, expend all their energy so that all peoples may benefit from more education and human culture. Cf. Paul VI, *Allocution to the United Nations General Assembly* (Oct. 4, 1965): *L'Osservatore Romano* (Oct. 6, 1965).

16. Cf. Pius XI, Motu Proprio *Orbem Catholicum* (June 29 1923): *AAS* 15 (1923), 327–329; Pius XI, Decree *Provide Sane* (Jan. 12, 1935): *AAS* 27 (1935), 145–152; Second Vatican Ecumenical Council, Decree on the Pastoral Office of Bishops in the Church *Christus Dominus,* 13–14.

17. Cf. Second Vatican Ecumenical Council, Constitution on the Sacred Liturgy *Sacrosanctum Concilium,* 14: *AAS* 56 (1964), 104.

18. Cf. Second Vatican Ecumenical Council, Decree on the Media of Social Communication *Inter Mirifica,* 13–14: *AAS* 56 (1964), 149 ff.

5. The Importance of Schools

Among all educational instruments the school has a special importance.[19] It is designed not only to develop with special care the intellectual faculties but also to form the ability to judge rightly, to hand on the
cultural legacy of previous generations, to foster a sense of values, to
prepare for professional life. Between pupils of different talents and
backgrounds, it promotes friendly relations and fosters a spirit of mutual
understanding, and it establishes as it were a center whose work and
progress must be shared together by families, teachers, associations of
various types that foster cultural, civic and religious life, as well as by
civil society and the entire human community.

Beautiful indeed and of great importance is the vocation of all those
who aid parents in fulfilling their duties and who, as representatives of
the human community, undertake the task of education in schools. This
vocation demands special qualities of mind and heart, very careful
preparation and continuing readiness to renew and to adapt.

6. The Duties and Rights of Parents

Parents who have the primary and inalienable right and duty to educate their children must enjoy true liberty in their choice of schools.
Consequently, the public power, which has the obligation to protect and
defend the rights of citizens, must see to it, in its concern for distributive
justice, that public subsidies are paid out in such a way that parents are
truly free to choose according to their conscience the schools they want
for their children.[20]

In addition, it is the task of the state to see to it that all citizens are
able to come to a suitable share in culture and are properly prepared to
exercise their civic duties and rights. Therefore, the state must protect
the right of children to an adequate school education, check on the ability of teachers and the excellence of their training, look after the health
of the pupils and in general, promote the whole school project. But it

---

19. Cf. Pius XI, Encyclical Letter *Divini Illius Magistri* (Dec. 31, 1929): *AAS* 22
(1930), 1, 76; Pius XII, *Allocution to Bavarian Association of Catholic Teachers* (Dec.
31, 1956): *Discourses and Radio Messages,* vol. 18, 746.

20. Cf. Third Provincial Council of Cincinnati, 1861: *Collatio Lacensis,* III, col. 1240,
c/d; Pius XI, Encyclical Letter *Divini Illius Magistri* (Dec. 31, 1929): *AAS* 22 (1930), 1,
60, 63 ff.

must always keep in mind the principle of subsidiarity so that there is no kind of school monopoly, for this is opposed to the native rights of the human person, to the development and spread of culture, to the peaceful association of citizens and to the pluralism that exists today in ever so many societies.[21]

Therefore, this sacred synod exhorts the faithful to assist to their utmost in finding suitable methods of education and programs of study and in forming teachers who can give youth a true education. Through the associations of parents in particular they should further with their assistance all the work of the school but especially the moral education it must impart.[22]

7. Moral and Religious Education in All Schools

Feeling very keenly the weighty responsibility of diligently caring for the moral and religious education of all her children, the Church must be present with her own special affection and help for the great number who are being trained in schools that are not Catholic. This is possible by the witness of the lives of those who teach and direct them, by the apostolic action of their fellow students,[23] but especially by the ministry of priests and laymen who give them the doctrine of salvation in a way suited to their age and circumstances and provide spiritual aid in every way the times and conditions allow.

The Church reminds parents of the duty that is theirs to arrange and even demand that their children be able to enjoy these aids and advance in their Christian formation to a degree that is abreast of their development in secular subjects. Therefore, the Church esteems highly those civil authorities and societies, which bearing in mind the pluralism of contemporary society and respecting religious freedom, assist families

21. Cf. Pius XI, Encyclical Letter *Divini Illius Magistri* (Dec. 31, 1929): *AAS* 22 (1930), 1, 63; Pius XI, Encyclical Letter *Non Abbiamo Bisogno* (June 29, 1931): *AAS* 23 (1931), 305; Pius XII, *Letter from the Secretary of State to the 28th Italian Social Week* (Sept. 20, 1955): *L'Osservatore Romano* (Sept. 29, 1955). Paul VI, *Allocution to the Association of Italian Christian Workers* (Oct. 6, 1963): *Encyclicals and Discourses of Paul VI,* vol. 1 (Rome: 1964), 230.

22. Cf. John XXIII, *Message on the 30th anniversary of the Encyclical Letter* Divini Illius Magistri (Dec. 30, 1959): *AAS* 52 (1960), 57.

23. The Church considers it as apostolic action of great worth also when Catholic teachers and associates work in these schools. Cf. Second Vatican Ecumenical Council, Decree on the Apostolate of the Laity *Apostolicam Actuositatem,* 12, 16.

so that the education of their children can be imparted in all schools according to the individual moral and religious principles of the families.[24]

8. Catholic Schools

The influence of the Church in the field of education is shown in a special manner by the Catholic school. No less than other schools does the Catholic school pursue cultural goals and the human formation of youth. But its proper function is to create for the school community a special atmosphere animated by the Gospel spirit of freedom and charity, to help youth grow according to the new creatures they were made through Baptism as they develop their own personalities, and finally to order the whole of human culture to the news of salvation so that the knowledge the students gradually acquire of the world, life and man is illumined by faith.[25] So indeed the Catholic school, while it is open as it must be to the situation of the contemporary world, leads its students to promote efficaciously the good of the earthly city and also prepares them for service in the spread of the kingdom of God, so that by leading an exemplary apostolic life they become as it were a saving leaven in the human community.

Since, therefore, the Catholic school can be such an aid to the fulfillment of the mission of the People of God and to the fostering of the dialogue between the Church and mankind to the benefit of both, it retains even in our present circumstances the utmost importance. Consequently, this sacred synod proclaims anew what has already been taught in several documents of the magisterium,[26] namely, the right of the Church freely to establish and to conduct schools of every type and level. And the Council calls to mind that the exercise of a right of this

---

24. Cf. Second Vatican Ecumenical Council, *Declaration on Religious Freedom Dignitatis Humanae*, 5.

25. Cf. First Provincial Council of Westminster, 1852: *Collatio Lacensis III,* col. 1334, a/b; Pius XI, Encyclical Letter *Divini Illius Magistri,* 1, 77 ff.; Pius XII, *Allocution to the Bavarian Association of Catholic Teachers* (Dec. 31, 1956): *Discourses and Radio Messages,* vol. 18, 746; Paul VI, *Allocution to the Members of Federated Institutes Dependent on Ecclesiastical Authority* (Dec. 30, 1963): *Encyclicals and Discourses of Paul VI,* vol. 1 (Rome: 1964), 602 ff.

26. Cf. especially the document mentioned in the first note; moreover, this law of the Church is proclaimed by many provincial councils and in the most recent declarations of very many of the episcopal conferences.

kind contributes in the highest degree to the protection of freedom of conscience, the rights of parents, as well as to the betterment of culture itself.

But let teachers recognize that the Catholic school depends upon them almost entirely for the accomplishment of its goals and pro-grams.[27] They should therefore be very carefully prepared so that both in secular and religious knowledge they are equipped with suitable qualifications and also with a pedagogical skill that is in keeping with the findings of the contemporary world. Intimately linked in charity to one another and to their students and endowed with an apostolic spirit, may teachers by their life as much as by their instruction bear witness to Christ, the unique teacher. Let them work as partners with parents and together with them in every phase of education give due consideration to the difference of sex and the proper ends divine Providence assigns to each sex in the family and in society. Let them do all they can to stimu-late their students to act for themselves and even after graduation to con-tinue to assist them with advice, friendship and by establishing special associations imbued with the true spirit of the Church. The work of these teachers, this sacred synod declares, is in the real sense of the word an apostolate most suited to and necessary for our times and at once a true service offered to society. The Council also reminds Catholic par-ents of the duty of entrusting their children to Catholic schools wherever and whenever it is possible and of supporting these schools to the best of their ability and of cooperating with them for the education of their children.[28]

9. Different Types of Catholic Schools

To this concept of a Catholic school all schools that are in any way dependent on the Church must conform as far as possible, though the Catholic school is to take on different forms in keeping with local cir-

---

27. Cf. Pius XI, Encyclical Letter *Divini Illius Magistri* (Dec. 31, 1929): *AAS* 22 (1930), 1, 80 ff.; Pius XII, *Allocution to the Catholic Association of Italian Teachers in Secondary Schools* (Jan. 5, 1954): *Discourses and Radio Messages*, vol. 15, 551–55B; John XXIII, *Allocution to the Sixth Congress of the Associations of Catholic Italian Teachers* (Sept. 5, 1959): *Discourses, Messages, Conversations*, vol. 1 (Rome: 1960), 427–431.

28. Cf. Pius XII, *Allocution to the Catholic Association of Italian Teachers in Second-ary Schools* (Jan. 5, 1954), 1, 555.

cumstances.[29] Thus, the Church considers very dear to her heart those Catholic schools, found especially in the areas of the new churches, which are attended also by students who are not Catholics.

Attention should be paid to the needs of today in establishing and directing Catholic schools. Therefore, though primary and secondary schools, the foundation of education, must still be fostered, great importance is to be attached to those which are required in a particular way by contemporary conditions, such as professional[30] and technical schools, centers for educating adults and promoting social welfare or for the retarded in need of special care, and also schools for preparing teachers for religious instruction and other types of education.

This sacred Council of the Church earnestly entreats pastors and all the faithful to spare no sacrifice in helping Catholic schools fulfill their function in a continually more perfect way, and especially in caring for the needs of those who are poor in the goods of this world or who are deprived of the assistance and affection of a family or who are strangers to the gift of faith.

10. Catholic Colleges and Universities

The Church is concerned also with schools of a higher level, especially colleges and universities. In those schools dependent on her, she intends that by their very constitution individual subjects be pursued according to their own principles, method and liberty of scientific inquiry, in such a way that an ever deeper understanding in these fields may be obtained and that, as questions that are new and current are raised and investigations carefully made according to the example of the doctors of the Church and especially of St. Thomas Aquinas,[31] there may be a deeper realization of the harmony of faith and science. Thus, there is accomplished a public, enduring and pervasive influence of the Christian mind in the furtherance of culture, and the students of these institutions are molded into men truly outstanding in their training, ready to

---

29. Cf. Paul VI, *Allocution to the International Office of Catholic Education* (Feb. 25, 1964): *Encyclicals and Discourses of Paul VI,* vol. 2 (Rome: 1964), 232.

30. Cf. Paul VI, *Allocution to the Christian Association of Italian Workers* (Oct. 6, 1963): *Encyclicals and Discourses of Paul VI,* vol. 1 (Rome: 1964), 229.

31. Cf. Paul VI, *Allocution to the International Thomistic Congress* (Sept. 10, 1965): *L'Osservatore Romano* (Sept. 13–14, 1965).

undertake weighty responsibilities in society and witness to the faith in the world.[32]

In Catholic universities where there is no faculty of sacred theology, there should be established an institute or chair of sacred theology in which there should be lectures suited to lay students. Since science advances by means of the investigations peculiar to higher scientific studies, special attention should be given in Catholic universities and colleges to institutes that serve primarily the development of scientific research.

The sacred synod heartily recommends that Catholic colleges and universities be conveniently located in different parts of the world, but in such a way that they are outstanding not for their numbers but for their pursuit of knowledge. Matriculation should be readily available to students of real promise, even though they be of slender means, especially to students from the newly emerging nations.

Since the destiny of society and of the Church itself is intimately linked with the progress of young people pursuing higher studies,[33] the pastors of the Church are to expend their energies not only on the spiritual life of students who attend Catholic universities, but solicitous for the spiritual formation of all their children, they must see to it, after consultations between bishops, that even at universities that are not Catholic there should be associations and university centers under Catholic auspices in which priests, religious and laity, carefully selected and prepared, should give abiding spiritual and intellectual assistance to the youth of the university. Whether in Catholic universities or others, young people of greater ability who seem suited for teaching or research should be specially helped and encouraged to undertake a teaching career.

---

32. Cf. Pius XII, *Allocution to Teachers and Students of French Institutes of Higher Catholic Education* (Sept. 21, 1950): *Discourses and Radio Messages,* vol. 12, 219–221; Pius XII, *Letters to the 22nd Congress of Pax Romana* (Aug. 12, 1952): *Discourses and Radio Messages,* vol. 14, 567–569; John XXIII, *Allocution to the Federation of Catholic Universities* (April 1, 1959): *Discourses, Messages and Conversations,* vol. 1 (Rome: 1960), 226–229; Paul VI, *Allocution to the Academic Senate of the Catholic University of Milan* (April 5, 1964): *Encyclicals and Discourses of Paul VI,* vol, 2 (Rome: 1964), 438–443.

33. Cf. Pius XII, *Allocution to the Academic Senate and Students of the University of Rome* (June 15, 1952): *Discourses and Radio Messages,* vol. 14, 208: "The direction of today's society principally is placed in the mentality and hearts of the universities of today."

11. Faculties of Sacred Sciences

The Church expects much from the zealous endeavors of the faculties of the sacred sciences.[34] For to them she entrusts the very serious responsibility of preparing her own students not only for the priestly ministry, but especially for teaching in the seats of higher ecclesiastical studies or for promoting learning on their own or for undertaking the work of a more rigorous intellectual apostolate. Likewise, it is the role of these very faculties to make more penetrating inquiry into the various aspects of the sacred sciences so that an ever deepening understanding of sacred revelation is obtained, the legacy of Christian wisdom handed down by our forefathers is more fully developed, the dialogue with our separated brethren and with non-Christians is fostered, and answers are given to questions arising from the development of doctrine.[35]

Therefore, ecclesiastical faculties should reappraise their own laws so that they can better promote the sacred sciences and those linked with them and, by employing up-to-date methods and aids, lead their students to more penetrating inquiry.

12. Coordination to Be Fostered in Scholastic Matters

Cooperation is the order of the day. It increases more and more to supply the demand on a diocesan, national and international level. Since it is altogether necessary in scholastic matters, every means should be employed to foster suitable cooperation between Catholic schools, and between these and other schools that collaboration should be developed which the good of all mankind requires.[36] From greater coordination and cooperative endeavor greater fruits will be derived particularly in the area of academic institutions. Therefore, in every university let the various faculties work mutually to this end, insofar as their goal will permit. In addition, let the universities also endeavor to work together by pro-

---

34. Cf. Pius XII, Apostolic Constitution *Deus Scientiarum Dominus* (May 24, 1931): *AAS* 23 (1931), 245–247.

35. Cf. Pius XII, Encyclical Letter *Humani Generis* (Aug. 12, 1950): *AAS* 42 (1950), 568 ff., 578; Paul VI, Encyclical Letter *Ecclesiam Suam,* part III (Aug. 6, 1964): *AAS* 56 (1964), 637–659; Second Vatican Ecumenical Council, Decree on Ecumenism *Unitatis Redintegratio: AAS* 57 (1965), 90–107.

36. Cf. John XXIII, Encyclical Letter *Pacem in Terris* (April 11, 1963): *AAS* 55 (1963), 284 and elsewhere.

moting international gatherings, by sharing scientific inquiries with one another, by communicating their discoveries to one another, by having exchange of professors for a time and by promoting all else that is conducive to greater assistance.

CONCLUSION

The sacred synod earnestly entreats young people themselves to become aware of the importance of the work of education and to prepare themselves to take it up, especially where because of a shortage of teachers the education of youth is in jeopardy. This same sacred synod, while professing its gratitude to priests, religious men and women, and the laity who by their evangelical self-dedication are devoted to the noble work of education and of schools of every type and level, exhorts them to persevere generously in the work they have undertaken and imbuing their students with the spirit of Christ, to strive to excel in pedagogy and the pursuit of knowledge in such a way that they not merely advance the internal renewal of the Church but preserve and enhance its beneficent influence upon today's world, especially the intellectual world.

Given in Rome at St. Peter's, October 28, 1965

DECLARATION ON THE RELATION OF THE CHURCH TO NON-CHRISTIAN RELIGIONS

Nostra Aetate

Promulgated by
His Holiness Pope Paul VI
On October 28, 1965

INTRODUCTION

The shortest of all the texts of Vatican II, *Nostra Aetate (NA)* stresses the positive links that the Church has with non-Christian religions. It complements a line from *Lumen Gentium:* "Those who have not yet received the Gospel are related in various ways to the People of God" (*LG* 16). While *Lumen Gentium* proceeds to enumerate some of the specific links between the Church and various groups of non-Christians, *NA* elaborates the general foundation of these links.

A renewal of the Church's consciousness of itself and of its mission could not help but lead to a reevaluation of its relationship with those who do not profess faith in Jesus Christ. For "the pilgrim Church is missionary by her very nature" (*AG* 2). It is one thing to undertake a renewal that revitalizes missionary charity. It is another thing to reflect on the process of missionary activity and to seek the most effective means to realize the missionary mandate.

Yet *NA* is not part of the *Decree on the Missionary Activity of the Church*. It resembles much more the *Decree on Ecumenism,* especially in its treatment of the Church's attitude to the Jews. However, dialogue with non-Christians is mentioned twice in the context of the Church's missionary activity (cf. *AG* 16, 34). In this light, *NA* can be seen as a complement to and a bridge between the *Decree on Ecumenism* and the *Decree on the Missionary Activity of the Church.*

After recalling that the Church is charged with a mission to promote unity among people, the decree teaches that all people have the same origin and end, namely God. God has created all, and he has made them for the same ultimate purpose of being united with him in the glory of heaven. The decree begins by giving an anthropological development of the unity of human origins in terms of a "question-answer" dynamic. Then, through a rapid and general treatment of the major religions—

Hinduism, Buddhism, Islam and Judaism—the text stresses the ways in which there is a real, though incomplete, union in the final goal of all religion, namely, communion with God.

The third paragraph of the first article then introduces what can be considered a conclusion which follows from this: "Men expect from the various religions answers to the unsolved riddles of the human condition, which today, even as in former times, deeply stir the hearts of men" (*NA* 1). Paul VI had already written: "Wherever men are trying to understand themselves and the world, we can communicate with them" (*ES* 97). "For the lover of truth discussion is always possible" (*ES* 102).

Adherence to religion is an indication of this love for the truth. All religions "try to counter the restlessness of the human heart" (*NA* 2). In other words, all religions, including Christianity, have the same starting point in the human person: "We share with the whole of mankind a common nature, human life with all its gifts and problems. In this primary universal reality we are ready to play our part, to acknowledge the deep-seated claims of its fundamental needs, to applaud the new and sometimes sublime expressions of its genius" (*ES* 97). This led Paul VI to see the Church as possessing that which all seek: "With frank confidence the Church stands upon the path of history and says to all: 'I have that for which you search, that which you lack'" (*ES* 95).

This "question-answer dynamic" was more richly developed in *Gaudium et Spes,* as seen in the following texts:

> To carry out such a task, the Church has always had the duty of scrutinizing the signs of the times and of interpreting them in the light of the Gospel. Thus, in language intelligible to each generation, she can respond to the perennial questions which men ask about this present life and the life to come, and about the relationship of the one to the other (*GS* 4).

> In the face of the modern development of the world, the number constantly swells of the people who raise the most basic questions or recognize them with a new sharpness: What is man? What is this sense of sorrow, of evil, of death, which continues to exist despite so much progress? What purpose have these victories purchased at so high a cost? What can man offer to society; what can he expect from it? What follows this earthly life?
>
> The Church firmly believes that Christ, who died and was raised up for all (cf. 2 Cor 5:15), can through his Spirit offer man the light and the strength to measure up to his supreme destiny. Nor has any other name under the heaven been given to man by which it is fitting for him to be saved (cf. Acts 4:12). She likewise holds that in her most benign

Lord and Master can be found the key, the focal point and the goal of man as well as of all human history (*GS* 10).

The human person is seen as a being who seeks answers to the mysteries about life. Made in God's image, the human person is capable of discovering God's order and is called to do so. But the world is not fully ordered, and neither are persons ordered within themselves. People seek to know who they are and the meaning of their lives by knowing where they came from and where they are headed. They also want to understand the disorder that brings suffering.

This is precisely how Pope John Paul II has interpreted the first article of *NA:*

> In religion man seeks answers to the questions listed above [referring to *NA* 1] and in different ways establishes his own relationship with the "mystery which engulfs our being." Now the various non-Christian religions are above all the expression of this quest on man's part, while the Christian faith is based on revelation on God's part. And here—notwithstanding some similarities with other religions—lies the essential difference with regard to them (*General Audience* of 6/5/85).

> Here we touch on the essential point by which Christianity differs from all the other religions by which man's search for God has been expressed from earliest times. Christianity has its starting point in the Incarnation of the Word. Here it is not simply a case of man seeking God, but of God who comes in person to speak to man of himself and to show him the path by which he may be reached.... The incarnate Word is thus the fulfillment of the yearning present in all the religions of mankind: this fulfillment is brought about by God himself and transcends all human expectations (*TMA* 6).

From the perspective of Christian and Catholic faith, in Jesus Christ people "may find the fullness of religious life" (*NA* 2). This implies that elements of this fullness can be found in other religions. Thus, the Church can "regard with sincere reverence" all that is good and holy in the various religions and consider that these elements "reflect a ray of that truth which enlightens all men" (*NA* 2).

This positive regard for the elements of truth in other religions is based on several assertions found throughout the conciliar texts; first, the understanding of the common foundation for religion found in human nature; second, the belief that God can be known by the light of human reason through creation (cf. *DV* 6); third, the patristic theme of the "seeds of the Word" sown among the peoples of the earth as preparation for receiving the Gospel (cf. *LG* 16; *AG* 11, 18); fourth, the conviction that the Holy Spirit constantly works in human hearts to bring people to faith (cf. *AG* 15; *GS* 41).

In considering the Church's relation to the Jewish people, the Council's vivid awareness of the economy of salvation played a decisive role. Developed in *Dei Verbum* (especially chapter four) and *Lumen Gentium* (especially articles 2–5 and 9), it provides a basis for the decree to stress the historical bonds which join the Church and the people "of Abraham's stock." According to the wisdom of divine pedagogy, the Church sees that its own beginning coincides with the beginning of the chosen people of the Old Covenant.

During a visit to the Jewish community of Rome in April 1986, Pope John Paul II spoke of the special ties that exist between the Church and Judaism: "The Church of Christ discovers her 'bond' with Judaism by 'searching into her own mystery' (*NA* 4). The Jewish religion is not 'extrinsic' to us, but in a certain way is 'intrinsic' to our own religion. With Judaism, therefore, we have a relationship which we do not have with any other religion." The declaration stresses the importance of mutual understanding and respect between Christians and Jews:

> What happened in his [Christ's] passion cannot be charged against all the Jews without distinction then alive, nor against the Jews of today. Although the Church is the new People of God, the Jews should not be presented as rejected or accursed by God, as if this followed from the Holy Scriptures.... Furthermore, in her rejection of every persecution against any man, the Church, mindful of the patrimony she shares with the Jews and moved not by political reasons but by the Gospel's spiritual love, decries hatred, persecutions, displays of antisemitism, directed against Jews at any time and by anyone (*NA* 4).

To foster Jewish-Christian dialogue, after the Council the Holy See established the Commission for Religious Relations with the Jews. A similar office is the Pontifical Council for Interreligious Dialogue, which is concerned with dialogue between Catholics and non-Christian religions such as Hinduism, Buddhism and Islam. This office issued the document *Dialogue and Proclamation* (1991)[1] which discusses the relationship between interreligious dialogue and proclaiming the Gospel.

---

1. This document and others, along with an extensive collection of papal statements on this subject are collected in the book *Interreligious Dialogue: The Official Teaching of the Catholic Church* (Pauline Books & Media, 1997).

TOPICAL OUTLINE

1. Introduction: unity of the human race; universal religious questions (1)

2. Development of various religions (2)

   A. Hinduism

   B. Buddhism

   C. Esteem for the good things found in these religions

3. Islam (3)

4. Judaism (4)

   A. Special bond between the Church and the people of Abraham's stock

   B. Common spiritual patrimony between Christians and Jews

   C. Rejection of all forms of antisemitism

5. Respect for all human persons (5)

DECLARATION ON THE RELATION OF THE CHURCH TO NON-CHRISTIAN RELIGIONS

Nostra Aetate

1. In our time, when day by day mankind is being drawn closer together and the ties between different peoples are becoming stronger, the Church examines more closely her relationship to non-Christian religions. In her task of promoting unity and love among men, indeed among nations, she considers above all in this declaration what men have in common and what draws them to fellowship.

One is the community of all peoples, one their origin, for God made the whole human race to live over the face of the earth (cf. Acts 17:26). One also is their final goal, God. His Providence, his manifestations of goodness, his saving design extend to all men,[1] until that time when the elect will be united in the Holy City, the city ablaze with the glory of God, where the nations will walk in his light (cf. Rv 21:23 ff.).

Men expect from the various religions answers to the unsolved riddles of the human condition, which today even as in former times deeply stir the hearts of men: What is man? What is the meaning, the aim of our life? What is moral good, what sin? Whence suffering and what purpose does it serve? Which is the road to true happiness? What are death, judgment and retribution after death? What, finally, is that ultimate inexpressible mystery which encompasses our existence: Whence do we come, and where are we going?

2. From ancient times down to the present, there is found among various peoples a certain perception of that hidden power which hovers

---

1. Cf. Wis 8:1; Acts 14:17; Rm 2:6–7; 1 Tm 2:4

over the course of things and over the events of human history; at times some indeed have come to the recognition of a Supreme Being, or even of a Father. This perception and recognition penetrates their lives with a profound religious sense.

Religions, however, that are bound up with an advanced culture have struggled to answer the same questions by means of more refined concepts and a more developed language. Thus, in Hinduism men contemplate the divine mystery and express it through an inexhaustible abundance of myths and through searching philosophical inquiry. They seek freedom from the anguish of our human condition either through ascetical practices or profound meditation or a flight to God with love and trust. Again, Buddhism in its various forms realizes the radical insufficiency of this changeable world; it teaches a way by which men in a devout and confident spirit may be able either to acquire the state of perfect liberation, or attain by their own efforts or through higher help, supreme illumination. Likewise, other religions found everywhere try to counter the restlessness of the human heart, each in its own manner, by proposing "ways," comprising teachings, rules of life and sacred rites.

The Catholic Church rejects nothing that is true and holy in these religions. She regards with sincere reverence those ways of conduct and of life, those precepts and teachings which, though differing in many aspects from the ones she holds and sets forth, nonetheless often reflect a ray of that Truth which enlightens all men. Indeed, she proclaims and ever must proclaim Christ "the way, the truth, and the life" (Jn 14:6), in whom men may find the fullness of religious life, in whom God has reconciled all things to himself (cf. 2 Cor 5:18–19).

The Church, therefore, exhorts her sons, that through dialogue and collaboration with the followers of other religions, carried out with prudence and love and in witness to the Christian faith and life, they recognize, preserve and promote the good things, spiritual and moral, as well as the socio-cultural values found among these men.

3. The Church regards with esteem also the Moslems. They adore the one God, living and subsisting in himself, merciful and all-powerful, the Creator of heaven and earth,[2] who has spoken to men; they take

---

2. Cf. St. Gregory VII, *Letter XXI to Anzir (Nacir), King of Mauritania: PL* 148, 450 f.

pains to submit wholeheartedly to even his inscrutable decrees, just as Abraham, with whom the faith of Islam takes pleasure in linking itself, submitted to God. Though they do not acknowledge Jesus as God, they revere him as a prophet. They also honor Mary, his virgin Mother; at times they even call on her with devotion. In addition, they await the day of judgment when God will render their deserts to all those who have been raised up from the dead. Finally, they value the moral life and worship God especially through prayer, almsgiving and fasting.

Since in the course of centuries not a few quarrels and hostilities have arisen between Christians and Moslems, this sacred synod urges all to forget the past and to work sincerely for mutual understanding and to preserve as well as to promote together for the benefit of all mankind social justice and moral welfare, as well as peace and freedom.

4. As the sacred synod searches into the mystery of the Church, it remembers the bond that spiritually ties the people of the New Covenant to Abraham's stock.

Thus, the Church of Christ acknowledges that according to God's saving design, the beginnings of her faith and her election are found already among the patriarchs, Moses and the prophets. She professes that all who believe in Christ—Abraham's sons according to faith (cf. Gal 3:7)—are included in the same patriarch's call, and likewise that the salvation of the Church is mysteriously foreshadowed by the Chosen People's exodus from the land of bondage. The Church, therefore, cannot forget that she received the revelation of the Old Testament through the people with whom God in his inexpressible mercy concluded the ancient covenant. Nor can she forget that she draws sustenance from the root of that well-cultivated olive tree onto which have been grafted the wild shoots, the Gentiles (cf. Rm 11:17–24). Indeed, the Church believes that by his cross Christ, our peace, reconciled Jews and Gentiles, making both one in himself (cf. Eph 2:14–16).

The Church keeps ever in mind the words of the Apostle about his kinsmen: "Theirs is the sonship and the glory and the covenants and the law and the worship and the promises; theirs are the fathers and from them is the Christ according to the flesh" (Rm 9:4–5), the Son of the Virgin Mary. She also recalls that the apostles, the Church's mainstay and pillars, as well as most of the early disciples who proclaimed Christ's Gospel to the world, sprang from the Jewish people.

As Holy Scripture testifies, Jerusalem did not recognize the time of her visitation (cf. Lk 19:44), nor did the Jews in large number accept the Gospel; indeed, not a few opposed its spreading (cf. Rm 11:28). Nevertheless, God holds the Jews most dear for the sake of their Fathers; he does not repent of the gifts he makes or of the calls he issues—such is the witness of the Apostle.[3] In company with the prophets and the same Apostle, the Church awaits that day known to God alone on which all peoples will address the Lord in a single voice and "serve him shoulder to shoulder" (Zep 3:9; cf. Is 66:23; Ps 65:4; Rm 11:11–32).

Since the spiritual patrimony common to Christians and Jews is thus so great, this sacred synod wants to foster and recommend that mutual understanding and respect which is the fruit, above all, of biblical and theological studies as well as of fraternal dialogues.

True, the Jewish authorities and those who followed their lead pressed for the death of Christ (cf. Jn 19:6); still, what happened in his passion cannot be charged against all the Jews without distinction then alive, nor against the Jews of today. Although the Church is the new People of God, the Jews should not be presented as rejected or accursed by God, as if this followed from the Holy Scriptures. All should see to it, then, that in catechetical work or in the preaching of the Word of God they do not teach anything that does not conform to the truth of the Gospel and the spirit of Christ.

Furthermore, in her rejection of every persecution against any man, the Church, mindful of the patrimony she shares with the Jews and moved not by political reasons but by the Gospel's spiritual love, decries hatred, persecutions, displays of anti-Semitism, directed against Jews at any time and by anyone.

Besides, as the Church has always held and holds now, Christ underwent his passion and death freely, because of the sins of men and out of infinite love, in order that all may reach salvation. It is, therefore, the burden of the Church's preaching to proclaim the cross of Christ as the sign of God's all-embracing love and as the fountain from which every grace flows.

5. We cannot truly call on God, the Father of all, if we refuse to treat in a brotherly way any man, created as he is in the image of God. Man's

---

3. Cf. Rm 11:28–29; cf. Second Vatican Ecumenical Council, Dogmatic Constitution on the Church *Lumen Gentium: AAS* 57 (1965), 20.

relation to God the Father and his relation to men his brothers are so linked together that Scripture says: "He who does not love does not know God" (1 Jn 4:8).

No foundation, therefore, remains for any theory or practice that leads to discrimination between man and man or people and people, so far as their human dignity and the rights flowing from it are concerned.

The Church reproves as foreign to the mind of Christ any discrimination against men or harassment of them because of their race, color, condition of life, or religion. On the contrary, following in the footsteps of the holy Apostles Peter and Paul, this sacred synod ardently implores the Christian faithful to "maintain good fellowship among the nations" (1 Pt 2:12), and if possible to live for their part in peace with all men (cf. Rm 12:18), so that they may truly be sons of the Father who is in heaven (cf. Mt 5:45).

DOGMATIC CONSTITUTION ON DIVINE REVELATION

Dei Verbum

Promulgated by
His Holiness Pope Paul VI
On November 18, 1965

INTRODUCTION

The first sentence of *Dei Verbum (DV)* expresses a fundamental theme of this pastoral Council: listening to the Word of God. Authentic renewal begins with listening to God. In outlining the steps of renewal in his first encyclical, *Ecclesiam Suam,* Paul VI used the word "awareness" to describe the goal of this listening. The Church can only become more fully aware of its own identity by listening anew to God's Word, because this identity is not forged by human determination; it is received from God as a gift.

The heightened awareness that the Church is a gift from God will lead to a greater sense of responsibility for it. This sense of responsibility, in turn, will lead to a process of conversion, which Pope Paul VI described in this way: "From this enlightened and effective realization there arises the spontaneous desire to compare the ideal image of the Church...with the actual image which the Church projects today.... Hence there arises the unselfish and almost impatient need for renewal" (*ES* 10, 11).

Renewal as conversion is a form of obedience, the root meaning of which is "to hear." The renewal Vatican II inaugurated is a call to conversion. This leads the Church to make every effort to reflect more perfectly God's will for it. The Church does this by first listening to God's word and then responding to the challenges it presents.

So that this conversion can take place, the Word of God must be approached in prayer: "And let them remember that prayer should accompany the reading of Sacred Scripture, so that God and man may talk together" (*DV* 25). Prayer allows a person to "confront" God's Word "with the reality of our own life" (*CCC* 2723).

Listening to God's Word and responding to it by conversion assures that the renewal is according to God's mind rather than our human mentality. *Dei Verbum* states that the Magisterium is not above God's word, but serves it (cf. *DV* 10). This also applies to the Church as a whole, for the Church is not above the Word of God. God's will, made known through revelation, is the measure of the Church's life and of every historical effort of renewal.

The constitution as a whole is structured according to this dialogical understanding. Chapter one establishes the connection between God's revelation and the response of faith. Chapters two through five consider the gifts God has provided so that his word may be heard and call forth the response of faith throughout the centuries. These gifts are the apostolic tradition and the written Word of God or Sacred Scripture, and the Magisterium. Chapter six sets forth how the Church responds to these gifts by which God's word is communicated to us. The decree calls on the Church as a whole and its various members to nourish themselves on the Word of God and respond in faith.

The first chapter presents faith essentially as the human response to God's revelation (cf. *DV* 5). In revealing himself, God takes an initiative out of love, beginning with creation and climaxing in the mission of Jesus Christ and the sending of the Holy Spirit on Pentecost. Throughout all that he has done, God invites those he has created in his own image to share in his life. Faith is the human reply to this invitation.

The language of this first chapter, especially in articles two and five, emphasizes the interpersonal reality of revelation and faith. God speaks to us as friends and invites us to share in his own nature so as to live in fellowship with him (cf. *DV* 2). According to the text of 1 Jn 1:2–3, from which the constitution takes its direction, the purpose of revelation is fellowship or communion in God. Because Sacred Scripture is the Word of God, through it "the Father who is in heaven meets his children with great love and speaks with them" (*DV* 21).

DV's approach to revelation reflects the great development which had taken place in theology since Vatican I. Formerly, the prevailing notion of revelation saw it primarily in propositional terms, that through revelation God communicated a body of truths. While this is certainly true, Vatican II expanded that notion and placed it in a personalistic context. Revelation was seen in a personal way as God revealing himself through salvation history. Revelation culminated in Jesus Christ, the Word of the Father. As *DV* notes: "Jesus perfected revelation by fulfilling it through his whole work of making himself present and manifesting himself" (*DV* 4).

Faith is presented with a corresponding personalist accent. The "obedience of faith" is not presented as an exclusively intellectual response. Though it includes that aspect, it goes far beyond it. Faith is an act of entrusting oneself to God. It is the acceptance of the gift that God makes of himself in love. Significantly, the text presents the assent of faith as its culmination. Faith as confident trust and faith as assent are complementary. Confident trust would have no meaning without the content attained through assent, and assent can only be directed to God if it is based on the conviction of his trustworthiness.

The text stresses that the response of faith must be freely given. This is made possible by the grace of the Holy Spirit who moves the heart and turns it to God, "giving 'joy and ease to everyone in assenting to the truth'" (*DV* 5). The *Declaration on Religious Freedom* more amply develops the necessity of this freedom.

Karol Cardinal Wojtyla emphasized this definition of faith in *DV* 5, stating that what it teaches about faith "is at the very center of the teaching of Vatican II and contains in a certain manner all that the Council wished to say about the Church, mankind and the world."[1] All of the specific elements of the renewal of Vatican II should be nothing other than various manifestations of the one obedience of faith. The spiritual sacrifices which constitute the object of the common or baptismal priesthood (cf. *LG* 10, 34) are precisely those actions which are accomplished in the obedience of faith.

For Wojtyla, this is not just an interesting theory. Twice in his first encyclical he revealed that he lives by *DV's* definition of faith: he accepted the papal office as a manifestation of God's will in the obedience of faith (cf. *RH* 2, 7). For him, the entire renewal of Vatican II can be seen as the enrichment of this kind of faith.

The structure of *DV* sprang from the Council's desire to respond to the initiatives of the Holy Spirit. The Spirit's initiative results in various "signs of the times" such as the ecumenical movement and the increasing awareness of human dignity. The Spirit is the author of gifts by which the Word of God is transmitted through the Church.

DV is almost a treatise on the Holy Spirit in the life of the Church,

---

1. *Sources of Renewal*, p. 225.

mentioning the Holy Spirit over thirty times. The Spirit's work is accomplished in two spheres. First, he is at work in human hearts. He brings people to faith and deepens their understanding of what God has revealed (cf. *DV* 5, 8).

Corresponding to this is the Holy Spirit's work in the transmission or handing on of divine revelation through Sacred Scripture and Tradition. Both are the result of the Holy Spirit working through human instruments. Sacred Scripture came about through the Spirit's gift of inspiration (cf. *DV* 11), while Sacred Tradition results from other gifts, generically called gifts of assistance, which Christ promised to the apostles and their successors. The Council moved away from seeing Scripture and Tradition as two separate sources of revelation. Instead, they have a common source:

> There exists a close connection and communication between Sacred Tradition and Sacred Scripture. For both of them, flowing from the same divine wellspring, in a certain way merge into a unity and tend toward the same end. For Sacred Scripture is the Word of God inasmuch as it is consigned to writing under the inspiration of the divine Spirit, while Sacred Tradition takes the Word of God entrusted by Christ the Lord and the Holy Spirit to the apostles and hands it on to their successors in its full purity, so that, led by the light of the Spirit of truth, they may in proclaiming it preserve this Word of God faithfully, explain it and make it more widely known. Consequently, it is not from Sacred Scripture alone that the Church draws her certainty about everything which has been revealed. Therefore, both Sacred Tradition and Sacred Scripture are to be accepted and venerated with the same sense of loyalty and reverence (*DV* 9).

The Holy Spirit also provides for authentic interpretation of the Word of God through the apostolic teaching office (cf. *DV* 10). The decree expresses the unity in purpose and complementary coordination of these gifts of the Holy Spirit:

> It is clear, therefore, that Sacred Tradition, Sacred Scripture and the teaching authority of the Church, in accord with God's most wise design, are so linked and joined together that one cannot stand without the others, and that all together and each in its own way under the action of the one Holy Spirit contribute effectively to the salvation of souls (*DV* 10).

The relation of Tradition to Scripture is grounded in the Council's understanding of the revelation that comes to us through and is perfected in Jesus Christ. God's plan of revelation was realized not just through words, but through "deeds and words having an inner unity" (*DV* 2). Christ perfects revelation by fulfilling it "through his whole work of making himself present and manifesting himself" (*DV* 4). The presence and manifestation of Christ cannot be reduced to his words and teachings, but includes his actions and their effects. Similarly, the Word of God continues to be present, active and effective in the Church today. Thus, knowledge of that Word cannot be reduced to knowledge of Scripture alone.

The Bible cannot be isolated from Tradition and the Magisterium. *DV* presents the Bible as one of several gifts of the Holy Spirit. For Scripture to yield all that God intends to communicate through it, it must be complemented by these other gifts of the Spirit. These gifts of the Holy Spirit make it possible for the faith of the Church to be genuinely a faith in God rather than in human beings or the Church. It has been so in all the generations from the time of Christ and the apostles until now.

This understanding of the Holy Spirit's role in the transmission of God's Word is important for interpreting Scripture: "Holy Scripture must be read and interpreted in the sacred spirit in which it was written" (*DV* 12). The Bible is truly the Word of God, and because God is the author of all the books (cf. *DV* 11), they form a fundamental unity. The various books are not simply juxtaposed as if they have no relation to each other. Yet, because the human authors which the Spirit used as instruments were diverse in time, temperament and culture, a wonderful diversity of expression and emphasis is found among the books of the Bible.

There is a parallel here with the catholic unity of the Church, which is a hallmark of the Council's teaching (cf. *LG* 7, 13; *OE; AG*). The parallel extends to the Council's understanding of the Church's nature as including both a divine and a human element, which together form one complex reality (cf. *LG* 8).

Because the Holy Spirit guides the Church, its life is a kind of commentary on Scripture, but not in the sense that the Scriptures are given first and then the Church lives up to them. Instead, the Word of God which is transmitted through the inspired books is also transmitted as it gives life to the Church. Again, God's revelation includes not only his making himself known, but also his communication of himself (cf. *DV* 6). God not only makes his invitation known, but also takes us "into fellowship with himself" (*DV* 2).

The handing on of what God has revealed involves more than just words, written or otherwise. The constitution nearly, if not in fact, identifies Sacred Tradition with the life of the Church itself, describing it as "the Gospel forever whole and alive within the Church" (*DV* 7). It makes Tradition a reality by which the Church "hands on to all generations all that she herself is, all that she believes" (*DV* 8).

Tradition might be thought of as the "culture of the Church." It has been said that culture is the total of one's non-biological inheritance. It both forms persons and is formed by them, for the person contributes to culture and is enriched by it. The culture of the Church is not merely human. It has a transcendent principle, the Holy Spirit, who through various gifts assures that the Church's culture, though it embraces many human cultures, remains faithful to the Word of God which gives it life.

DV was written with the Council's concern about the Church's relationship with all people. Its contribution to ecumenism is seen in the way it acknowledges the importance of trusting confidence for a thorough understanding of faith (cf. *DV* 5). It uses the biblical language of fellowship and communion. It also incorporates the contemporary awareness of the economy of revelation with its Christ-centered character. These are all points of contact for dialogue with non-Catholic Christians. Important too is the assertion that the Church's teaching office is obedient to God's Word and not above it. The decree makes this clear by the way it explains the interrelations among Scripture, Tradition and the Magisterium.

Chapter four treats the Church's understanding of the Old Testament, and so has implications for dialogue with people of Jewish faith (cf. *LG* 16; *NA* 4). The Council's sense of the economy of salvation is evident here, as it is in *LG* 9. The reader must be attentive to the distinction between the Old Covenant and the books of the Old Testament. The books of the Old Testament "show us true divine pedagogy" according to which "the plan of the old covenant was directed...to prepare for the coming of Christ" (*DV* 15). Though the Old Covenant is superseded by the new, the books of the Old Testament "remain permanently valuable" (*DV* 14). They "reveal to all men the knowledge of God and of man and the ways in which God...deals with men" (*DV* 15), and shed light on and explain the New Testament (cf. *DV* 16).

The constitution also speaks of the witness of creation to God's power, goodness and wisdom, along with the assertion that God can be known by the light of human reason. This is a point of connection with people of non-revealed religions (cf. *LG* 16).

Chapter six calls upon all members of the Church—bishops, priests, deacons, all involved in the ministry of the word, religious and laity—to prayerfully read the Word of God. In this way the gift of Scripture may be the "bread of life" that nourishes the life of the entire Church (cf. *DV* 21, 23). When the Council considers the means to holiness (cf. *LG* 42), it first mentions listening to the Word of God. Holiness is the essence of the conciliar renewal.

Particular attention is given to the role of bishops in directing and coordinating the many gifts and responses to the Word of God. They are to see that accurate translations and "necessary and adequate explanations" are provided. They must also give careful attention to the work of exegetes and instruct the faithful on the correct use of Scripture.

All are called to have direct contact with the inspired Word of God, especially theologians and those involved in the ministry of the word. The *Decree on Priestly Training* reflects the teaching of *DV* on reading and interpreting Scripture according to the same spirit in which it was written. It calls on seminarians to seek Christ in Scripture, to prepare for the ministry of the Word, and to make the Bible the soul of their theological studies. They are to study in the Bible the major themes of divine revelation, and then seek to understand these themes as they are found in the life of the Church. This orients the study of the Fathers and the transmission and development of doctrine.

This kind of theological study will provide the Church with wise and faithful clergy, preachers and theologians. They will know how to be faithful to the apostolic tradition and how to express it meaningfully for people today. A theology inspired by the study of Scripture can revitalize evangelization, preaching and catechesis. It will draw life from direct contact with the revealed Word of God presented through Scripture and Tradition, and celebrated in the liturgy. Renewed in this way, the Church will be better able to fulfill its missionary mandate.

In 1993, the Pontifical Biblical Commission issued the document *The Interpretation of the Bible in the Church,* which discusses various approaches to biblical interpretation.

TOPICAL OUTLINE

1. Revelation itself

    A. Through revelation God reveals himself (2)

    B. The plan of salvation (3)

    C. Revelation and Jesus Christ (4)

    D. The response of faith (5)

    E. Revelation and human reason (6)

2. Handing on divine revelation

    A. Role of the apostles and their successors (7)

    B. Sacred Tradition (8)

    C. Relation of Scripture, Tradition and the Church (9–10)

3. Sacred Scripture, its inspiration and divine interpretation

    A. Inspiration of Sacred Scripture (11)

    B. Principles for interpreting Scripture (12–13)

4. The Old Testament

    A. God's covenant with Israel (14)

    B. Value and purpose of the Old Testament (15)

    C. Relation of the two testaments (16)

5. The New Testament

    A. The saving work of Jesus Christ (17)

DOGMATIC CONSTITUTION ON DIVINE REVELATION

Dei Verbum

PREFACE

1. Hearing the Word of God with reverence and proclaiming it with faith, the sacred synod takes its direction from these words of St. John: "We announce to you the eternal life which dwelt with the Father and was made visible to us. What we have seen and heard we announce to you, so that you may have fellowship with us and our common fellowship be with the Father and his Son Jesus Christ" (1 Jn 1:2–3). Therefore, following in the footsteps of the Council of Trent and of the First Vatican Ecumenical Council, this present Council wishes to set forth authentic doctrine on divine revelation and how it is handed on, so that by hearing the message of salvation the whole world may believe, by believing it may hope, and by hoping it may love.[1]

---

1. Cf. St. Augustine, *De Catechizandis Rudibus* 4, 8: *PL* 40, 316.

CHAPTER I

REVELATION ITSELF

2. In his goodness and wisdom God chose to reveal himself and to make known to us the hidden purpose of his will (cf. Eph 1:9) by which through Christ, the Word made flesh, man might in the Holy Spirit have access to the Father and come to share in the divine nature (cf. Eph 2:18; 2 Pt 1:4). Through this revelation, therefore, the invisible God (cf. Col 1:15, 1 Tm 1:17) out of the abundance of his love speaks to men as friends (cf. Ex 33:11; Jn 15:14–15) and lives among them (cf. Bar 3:38), so that he may invite and take them into fellowship with himself. This plan of revelation is realized by deeds and words having an inner unity; the deeds wrought by God in the history of salvation manifest and confirm the teaching and realities signified by the words, while the words proclaim the deeds and clarify the mystery contained in them. By this revelation, then, the deepest truth about God and the salvation of man shines out for our sake in Christ, who is both the mediator and the fullness of all revelation.[2]

3. God, who through the Word creates all things (cf. Jn 1:3) and keeps them in existence, gives men an enduring witness to himself in created realities (cf. Rm 1:19–20). Planning to make known the way of heavenly salvation, he went further and from the start manifested himself to our first parents. Then, after their fall his promise of redemption aroused in them the hope of being saved (cf. Gn 3:15) and from that time on he ceaselessly kept the human race in his care, to give eternal life to those who perseveringly do good in search of salvation (cf. Rm 2:6–7). Then, at the time he had appointed, he called Abraham in order to make of him a great nation (cf. Gn 12:2). Through the patriarchs and after them through Moses and the prophets, he taught this people to ac-

---

2. Cf. Mt 11:27; Jn 1:14, 17; 14:6; 17:1–3; 2 Cor 3:16, 4:6; Eph 1:3–14.

knowledge himself the one living and true God, provident Father and just judge, and to wait for the Savior promised by him, and in this manner prepared the way for the Gospel down through the centuries.

4. Then, after speaking in many and varied ways through the prophets, "now at last in these days God has spoken to us in his Son" (Heb 1:1–2). For he sent his Son, the eternal Word who enlightens all men, so that he might dwell among men and tell them of the innermost being of God (cf. Jn 1:1–18). Jesus Christ, therefore, the Word made flesh, was sent as "a man to men."[3] He "speaks the words of God" (Jn 3:34) and completes the work of salvation which his Father gave him to do (cf. Jn 5:36; 17:4). To see Jesus is to see his Father (Jn 14:9). For this reason Jesus perfected revelation by fulfilling it through his whole work of making himself present and manifesting himself: through his words and deeds, his signs and wonders, but especially through his death and glorious resurrection from the dead and final sending of the Spirit of truth. Moreover, he confirmed with divine testimony what revelation proclaimed, that God is with us to free us from the darkness of sin and death, and to raise us up to life eternal.

The Christian dispensation, therefore, as the new and definitive covenant, will never pass away and we now await no further new public revelation before the glorious manifestation of our Lord Jesus Christ (cf. 1 Tm 6:14 and Ti 2:13).

5. "The obedience of faith" (Rm 16:26; cf. Rm 1:5; 2 Cor 10:5–6) "is to be given to God who reveals, an obedience by which man commits his whole self freely to God, offering the full submission of intellect and will to God who reveals,"[4] and freely assenting to the truth revealed by him. To make this act of faith, the grace of God and the interior help of the Holy Spirit must precede and assist, moving the heart and turning it to God, opening the eyes of the mind and giving "joy and ease to everyone in assenting to the truth and believing it."[5] To bring about an ever deeper understanding of revelation, the same Holy Spirit constantly brings faith to completion by his gifts.

---

3. *Epistle to Diognetus,* 7, 4: Funk, *Apostolic Fathers,* I, 403.

4. First Vatican Ecumenical Council, Dogmatic Constitution on the Catholic Faith *Dei Filius,* ch. 3, "On Faith": Denz. 1789 (3008).

5. Second Council of Orange, Canon 7: Denz. 180 (377); First Vatican Ecumenical Council, Dogmatic Constitution on the Catholic Faith *Dei Filius,* ch. 3, "On Faith": Denz. 1791 (3010).

6. Through divine revelation, God chose to show forth and communicate himself and the eternal decisions of his will regarding the salvation of men. That is to say, he chose to share with them those divine treasures which totally transcend the understanding of the human mind.[6]

As a sacred synod has affirmed, God, the beginning and end of all things, can be known with certainty from created reality by the light of human reason (cf. Rm 1:20), but teaches that it is through his revelation that those religious truths which are by their nature accessible to human reason can be known by all men with ease, with solid certitude and with no trace of error, even in this present state of the human race.[7]

---

6. First Vatican Ecumenical Council, Dogmatic Constitution on the Catholic Faith *Dei Filius,* ch. 2, "On Revelation": Denz. 1786 (3005).

7. First Vatican Ecumenical Council, Dogmatic Constitution on the Catholic Faith *Dei Filius*, ch. 2, "On Revelation": Denz. 1785 and 1786 (3004 and 3005).

CHAPTER II

HANDING ON DIVINE REVELATION

7. In his gracious goodness, God has seen to it that what he had re-vealed for the salvation of all nations would abide perpetually in its full integrity and be handed on to all generations. Therefore, Christ the Lord in whom the full revelation of the supreme God is brought to completion (cf. 1 Cor 1:20; 3:13; 4:6), commissioned the apostles to preach to all men that Gospel which is the source of all saving truth and moral teach-ing,[1] and to impart to them heavenly gifts. This Gospel had been prom-ised in former times through the prophets, and Christ himself had fulfilled it and promulgated it with his lips. This commission was faith-fully fulfilled by the apostles, who by their oral preaching, by example and by observances handed on what they had received from the lips of Christ, from living with him and from what he did, or what they had learned through the prompting of the Holy Spirit. The commission was fulfilled, too, by those apostles and apostolic men, who under the inspi-ration of the same Holy Spirit, committed the message of salvation to writing.[2]

But in order to keep the Gospel forever whole and alive within the Church, the apostles left bishops as their successors, "handing over" to them "the authority to teach in their own place."[3] This Sacred Tradition, therefore, and Sacred Scripture of both the Old and New Testaments are like a mirror in which the pilgrim Church on earth looks at God, from whom she has received everything, until she is brought finally to see him as he is, face to face (cf. 1 Jn 3:2).

---

1. Cf. Mt 28:19–20; Mk 16:15; Council of Trent, Session 4, *Decree on Scriptural Can-ons:* Denz. 783 (1501).

2. Cf. Council of Trent, Session 4, *Decree on Scriptural Canons:* Denz. 783 (1501); First Vatican Ecumenical Council, Session 3, Dogmatic Constitution on the Catholic Faith *Dei Filius,* ch. 2, "On Revelation": Denz. 1787 (3005).

3. St. Irenaeus, *Against Heretics* III, 3, 1: *PG* 7, 848; Harvey, 2, 9.

8. And so the apostolic preaching, which is expressed in a special way in the inspired books, was to be preserved by an unending succession of preachers until the end of time. Therefore, the apostles, handing on what they themselves had received, warn the faithful to hold fast to the traditions which they have learned either by word of mouth or by letter (cf. 2 Thes 2:15), and to fight in defense of the faith handed on once and for all (cf. Jude 1:3).[4] Now, what was handed on by the apostles includes everything which contributes toward the holiness of life and increase in faith of the People of God; and so the Church, in her teaching, life and worship, perpetuates and hands on to all generations all that she herself is, all that she believes.

This Tradition which comes from the apostles develops in the Church with the help of the Holy Spirit.[5] For there is a growth in the understanding of the realities and the words which have been handed down. This happens through the contemplation and study made by believers, who treasure these things in their hearts (cf. Lk 2:19, 51) through a penetrating understanding of the spiritual realities which they experience, and through the preaching of those who have received through episcopal succession the sure gift of truth. For as the centuries succeed one another, the Church constantly moves forward toward the fullness of divine truth until the words of God reach their complete fulfillment in her.

The words of the holy Fathers witness to the presence of this living Tradition, whose wealth is poured into the practice and life of the believing and praying Church. Through the same Tradition, the Church's full canon of the sacred books is known, and the sacred writings themselves are more profoundly understood and unceasingly made active in her; and thus God, who spoke of old, uninterruptedly converses with the bride of his beloved Son; and the Holy Spirit, through whom the living voice of the Gospel resounds in the Church and through her in the world, leads unto all truth those who believe, and makes the word of Christ dwell abundantly in them (cf. Col 3:16).

---

4. Cf. Second Council of Nicea: Denz. 303 (602); Fourth Council of Constantinople, Session 10, Canon 1: Denz. 336 (650–652).

5. Cf. First Vatican Ecumenical Council, Dogmatic Constitution on the Catholic Faith *Dei Filius,* ch. 4, "On Faith and Reason": Denz. 1800 (3020).

9. Hence, there exists a close connection and communication between Sacred Tradition and Sacred Scripture. For both of them, flowing from the same divine wellspring, in a certain way merge into a unity and tend toward the same end. For Sacred Scripture is the Word of God inasmuch as it is consigned to writing under the inspiration of the divine Spirit, while Sacred Tradition takes the Word of God entrusted by Christ the Lord and the Holy Spirit to the apostles and hands it on to their successors in its full purity, so that, led by the light of the Spirit of truth, they may in proclaiming it preserve this Word of God faithfully, explain it and make it more widely known. Consequently, it is not from Sacred Scripture alone that the Church draws her certainty about everything which has been revealed. Therefore, both Sacred Tradition and Sacred Scripture are to be accepted and venerated with the same sense of loyalty and reverence.[6]

10. Sacred Tradition and Sacred Scripture form one sacred deposit of the Word of God, committed to the Church. Holding fast to this deposit, the entire holy people united with their shepherds remain always steadfast in the teaching of the apostles, in the common life, in the breaking of the bread and in prayers (cf. Acts 2:42, Greek text), so that holding to, practicing and professing the heritage of the faith, it becomes on the part of the bishops and faithful a single common effort.[7]

But the task of authentically interpreting the Word of God, whether written or handed on,[8] has been entrusted exclusively to the living teaching office of the Church,[9] whose authority is exercised in the name of Jesus Christ. This teaching office is not above the Word of God but serves it, teaching only what has been handed on, listening to it devoutly, guarding it scrupulously and explaining it faithfully in accord with a divine commission and with the help of the Holy Spirit; it draws from this one deposit of faith everything which it presents for belief as divinely revealed.

---

6. Cf. Council of Trent, Session 4, *Decree on Scriptural Canons:* Denz. 783 (1501).

7. Cf. Pius XII, Apostolic Constitution *Munificentissimus Deus* (Nov. 1, 1950): *AAS* 42 (1950), 756; *Collected Writings of St. Cyprian, Letter 66,* 8: Hartel, III, B, p. 733: "The Church [is] the people united with the priest and the pastor together with his flock."

8. Cf. First Vatican Ecumenical Council, Dogmatic Constitution on the Catholic Faith *Dei Filius,* ch. 3, "On Faith": Denz. 1792 (3011).

9. Cf. Pius XII, Encyclical Letter *Humani Generis* (Aug. 12, 1950): *AAS* 42 (1950), 568–69: Denz. 2314 (3886).

It is clear, therefore, that Sacred Tradition, Sacred Scripture and the teaching authority of the Church, in accord with God's most wise design, are so linked and joined together that one cannot stand without the others, and that all together and each in its own way under the action of the one Holy Spirit contribute effectively to the salvation of souls.

CHAPTER III

SACRED SCRIPTURE, ITS INSPIRATION AND DIVINE INTERPRETATION

11. Those divinely revealed realities which are contained and presented in Sacred Scripture have been committed to writing under the inspiration of the Holy Spirit. For holy mother Church, relying on the belief of the apostles (cf. Jn 20:31; 2 Tm 3:16; 2 Pt 1:19–20; 3:15–16), holds that the books of both the Old and New Testaments in their entirety, with all their parts, are sacred and canonical because, written under the inspiration of the Holy Spirit, they have God as their author and have been handed on as such to the Church herself.[1] In composing the sacred books, God chose men and while employed by him[2] they made use of their powers and abilities, so that with him acting in them and through them,[3] they, as true authors, consigned to writing everything and only those things which he wanted.[4]

Therefore, since everything asserted by the inspired authors or sacred writers must be held to be asserted by the Holy Spirit, it follows that the books of Scripture must be acknowledged as teaching solidly, faithfully and without error that truth which God wanted put into sacred writings[5] for the sake of salvation. Therefore, "all Scripture is divinely

---

1. Cf. First Vatican Ecumenical Council, Dogmatic Constitution on the Catholic Faith *Dei Filius,* ch. 2, "On Revelation": Denz. 1787 (3006); Biblical Commission, *Decree* (June 18, 1915): Denz. 2180 (3629): *EB* 420; Holy Office, *Letter* (Dec. 22, 1923): *EB* 499.

2. Cf. Pius XII, Encyclical Letter *Divino Afflante Spiritu* (Sept. 30, 1943): *AAS* 35 (1943), 314; *EB* 556.

3. "In" and "for" man: cf. Heb 1:1, 4:7; ("in"): 2 Sm 23:2; Mt 1:22 and various places; ("for"): First Vatican Ecumenical Council, *Schema on Catholic Doctrine,* note 9: Coll. Lac. VII, 522.

4. Leo XIII, Encyclical Letter *Providentissimus Deus* (Nov. 18, 1893): Denz. 1952 (3293); *EB* 125.

5. Cf. St. Augustine, *Gen. ad Litt.,* 2, 9, 20: *PL* 34, 270–271; *Epistle* 82, 3: *PL* 33, 277: *CSEL* 34, 2, p. 354; St. Thomas, *On Truth,* q. 12, a. 2, c.; Council of Trent, Session 4,

inspired and has its use for teaching the truth and refuting error, for reformation of manners and discipline in right living, so that the man who belongs to God may be efficient and equipped for good work of every kind" (2 Tm 3:16–17, Greek text).

12. However, since God speaks in Sacred Scripture through men in human fashion,[6] the interpreter of Sacred Scripture, in order to see clearly what God wanted to communicate to us, should carefully investigate what meaning the sacred writers really intended, and what God wanted to manifest by means of their words.

To search out the intention of the sacred writers, attention should be given, among other things, to "literary forms." For truth is set forth and expressed differently in texts which are variously historical, prophetic, poetic or of other forms of discourse. The interpreter must investigate what meaning the sacred writer intended to express and actually expressed in particular circumstances by using contemporary literary forms in accordance with the situation of his own time and culture.[7] For the correct understanding of what the sacred author wanted to assert, due attention must be paid to the customary and characteristic styles of feeling, speaking and narrating which prevailed at the time of the sacred writer and to the patterns men normally employed at that period in their everyday dealings with one another.[8]

But since Holy Scripture must be read and interpreted in the same spirit in which it was written,[9] no less serious attention must be given to the content and unity of the whole of Scripture if the meaning of the sacred texts is to be correctly worked out. The living Tradition of the whole Church must be taken into account along with the harmony which exists between elements of the faith. It is the task of exegetes to work according to these rules toward a better understanding and explanation of the meaning of Sacred Scripture, so that through preparatory study

---

Scriptural Canons: Denz. 783 (1501); Leo XIII, Encyclical Letter *Providentissimus Deus* (Nov. 18, 1893): *EB* 121, 124, 126–127; Pius XII, Encyclical Letter *Divino Afflante Spiritu* (Sept. 30, 1943); *EB* 539.

6. St. Augustine, *City of God,* XVII, 6, 2: *PL* 41, 537: *CSEL* XL, 2, 228.

7. St. Augustine, *On Christian Doctrine,* III, 18, 26; *PL* 34, 75–76.

8. Pius XII, Encyclical Letter *Divino Afflante Spiritu* (Sept. 30, 1943): Denz. 2294 (3829–3830); *EB* 557–562.

9. Cf. Benedict XV, Encyclical Letter *Spiritus Paraclitus* (Sept. 15, 1920): *EB* 469; St. Jerome, *In Galatians* 5, 19–20: *PL* 26, 417 A.

the judgment of the Church may mature. For all of what has been said about the way of interpreting Scripture is subject finally to the judgment of the Church, which carries out the divine commission and ministry of guarding and interpreting the Word of God.[10]

13. In Sacred Scripture, therefore, while the truth and holiness of God always remains intact, the marvelous "condescension" of eternal wisdom is clearly shown, "that we may learn the gentle kindness of God, which words cannot express, and how far he has gone in adapting his language with thoughtful concern for our weak human nature."[11] For the words of God expressed in human language have been made like human discourse, just as the Word of the eternal Father, when he took to himself the flesh of human weakness, was in every way made like men.

---

10. Cf. First Vatican Ecumenical Council, Dogmatic Constitution on the Catholic Faith *Dei Filius,* ch. 2, "On Revelation": Denz. 1788 (3007).

11. St. John Chrysostom *In Genesis* 3, 8 (Homily 17, 1): *PG* 53, 134; *attemperatio* [in English "suitable adjustment"], in Greek *synkatábasis.*

CHAPTER IV

THE OLD TESTAMENT

14. In carefully planning and preparing the salvation of the whole human race, the God of infinite love, by a special dispensation, chose for himself a people to whom he would entrust his promises. First he entered into a covenant with Abraham (cf. Gn 15:18) and, through Moses, with the people of Israel (cf. Ex 24:8). To this people which he had acquired for himself, he so manifested himself through words and deeds as the one true and living God, that Israel came to know by experience the ways of God with men. Then too, when God himself spoke to them through the mouth of the prophets, Israel daily gained a deeper and clearer understanding of his ways and made them more widely known among the nations (cf. Ps 21:29; 95:1–3; Is 2:1–5; Jer 3:17). The plan of salvation foretold by the sacred authors, recounted and explained by them, is found as the true Word of God in the books of the Old Testament; these books, therefore, written under divine inspiration, remain permanently valuable. "For all that was written for our instruction, so that by steadfastness and the encouragement of the Scriptures we might have hope" (Rm 15:4).

15. The principal purpose to which the plan of the Old Covenant was directed was to prepare for the coming of Christ, the Redeemer of all and of the messianic kingdom, to announce this coming by prophecy (cf. Lk 24:44; Jn 5:39; 1 Pt 1:10), and to indicate its meaning through various types (cf. 1 Cor 10:12). Now the books of the Old Testament, in accordance with the state of mankind before the time of salvation established by Christ, reveal to all men the knowledge of God and of man and the ways in which God, just and merciful, deals with men. These books, though they also contain some things which are incomplete and temporary, nevertheless show us true divine pedagogy.[1] These same books,

---

1. Pius XI, Encyclical Letter *Mit Brennender Sorge* (March 14, 1937): *AAS* 29 (1937), 51.

then, give expression to a lively sense of God, contain a store of sublime teachings about God, sound wisdom about human life, and a wonderful treasury of prayers, and in them the mystery of our salvation is present in a hidden way. Christians should receive them with reverence.

16. God, the inspirer and author of both Testaments, wisely arranged that the New Testament be hidden in the Old and the Old be made manifest in the New.[2] For, though Christ established the New Covenant in his blood (cf. Lk 22:20; 1 Cor 11:25), still the books of the Old Testament with all their parts, caught up into the proclamation of the Gospel,[3] acquire and show forth their full meaning in the New Testament (cf. Mt 5:17; Lk 24:27; Rm 16:25–26; 2 Cor 14:16) and in turn shed light on it and explain it.

---

2. St. Augustine, *Quest. in hept.* 2, 73: *PL* 34, 623.

3. St. Irenaeus, *Against Heretics* III, 21, 3: *PG* 7, 950; (same as 25, 1: Harvey, 2, p. 115); St. Cyril of Jerusalem, *Catech.* 4, 35; *PG* 33, 497. Theodore of Mopsuestia, *In Soph.* 1, 4–6: *PG* 66, 452D–453A.

CHAPTER V

THE NEW TESTAMENT

17. The Word of God, which is the power of God for the salvation of all who believe (cf. Rm 1:16), is set forth and shows its power in a most excellent way in the writings of the New Testament. For when the fullness of time arrived (cf. Gal 4:4), the Word was made flesh and dwelt among us in his fullness of grace and truth (cf. Jn 1:14). Christ established the kingdom of God on earth, manifested his Father and himself by deeds and words, and completed his work by his death, resurrection and glorious ascension and by the sending of the Holy Spirit. Having been lifted up from the earth, he draws all men to himself (cf. Jn 12:32, Greek text), he who alone has the words of eternal life (cf. Jn 6:68). This mystery had not been manifested to other generations as it was now revealed to his holy apostles and prophets in the Holy Spirit (cf. Eph 3:4–6, Greek text), so that they might preach the Gospel, stir up faith in Jesus, Christ and Lord, and gather together the Church. Now the writings of the New Testament stand as a perpetual and divine witness to these realities.

18. It is common knowledge that among all the Scriptures, even those of the New Testament, the Gospels have a special preeminence, and rightly so, for they are the principal witness for the life and teaching of the incarnate Word, our Savior.

The Church has always and everywhere held and continues to hold that the four Gospels are of apostolic origin. For what the apostles preached in fulfillment of the commission of Christ, afterward they themselves and apostolic men, under the inspiration of the divine Spirit, handed on to us in writing: the foundation of faith, namely, the fourfold Gospel, according to Matthew, Mark, Luke and John.[1]

---

1. Cf. St. Irenaeus, *Against Heretics* III, 11; 8: *PG* 7, 885, Sagnard Edition, p. 194.

19. Holy mother Church has firmly and with absolute constancy held and continues to hold that the four Gospels just named, whose historical character the Church unhesitatingly asserts, faithfully hand on what Jesus Christ, while living among men, really did and taught for their eternal salvation until the day he was taken up into heaven (cf. Acts 1:1). Indeed, after the ascension of the Lord the apostles handed on to their hearers what he had said and done. This they did with that clearer understanding which they enjoyed (Jn 2:22; 12:16; cf. 14:26; 16:12–13; 7:39) after they had been instructed by the glorious events of Christ's life and taught by the light of the Spirit of truth (cf. Jn 14:26; 16:13). The sacred authors wrote the four Gospels, selecting some things from the many which had been handed on by word of mouth or in writing, reducing some of them to a synthesis, explaining some things in view of the situation of their churches, and preserving the form of proclamation, but always in such fashion that they told us the honest truth about Jesus.[2] For their intention in writing was that either from their own memory and recollections or from the witness of those who "themselves from the beginning were eyewitnesses and ministers of the Word," we might know "the truth" concerning those matters about which we have been instructed (cf. Lk 1:2–4).

20. Besides the four Gospels, the canon of the New Testament also contains the epistles of St. Paul and other apostolic writings, composed under the inspiration of the Holy Spirit, by which, according to the wise plan of God, those matters which concern Christ the Lord are confirmed; his true teaching is more and more fully stated; the saving power of the divine work of Christ is preached; the story is told of the beginnings of the Church and its marvelous growth; and its glorious fulfillment is foretold.

For the Lord Jesus was with his apostles as he had promised (cf. Mt 28:20) and sent them the advocate Spirit who would lead them into the fullness of truth (cf. Jn 16:13).

---

2. Cf. Pontifical Biblical Commission, Instruction *Holy Mother Church: AAS* 56 (1964), 715.

CHAPTER VI

SACRED SCRIPTURE
IN THE LIFE OF THE CHURCH

21. The Church has always venerated the divine Scriptures just as she venerates the Body of the Lord, since, especially in the sacred liturgy, she unceasingly receives and offers to the faithful the bread of life from the table both of God's Word and of Christ's Body. She has always maintained them and continues to do so, together with Sacred Tradition, as the supreme rule of faith, since as inspired by God and committed once and for all to writing, they impart the Word of God himself without change, and make the voice of the Holy Spirit resound in the words of the prophets and apostles. Therefore, like the Christian religion itself, all the preaching of the Church must be nourished and regulated by Sacred Scripture. For in the sacred books, the Father who is in heaven meets his children with great love and speaks with them; and the force and power in the Word of God is so great that it stands as the support and energy of the Church, the strength of faith for her sons, the food of the soul, the pure and everlasting source of spiritual life. Consequently, these words are perfectly applicable to Sacred Scripture: "For the Word of God is living and active" (Heb 4:12) and "it has power to build you up and give you your heritage among all those who are sanctified" (Acts 20:32; cf. 1 Thes 2:13).

22. Easy access to Sacred Scripture should be provided for all the Christian faithful. That is why the Church from the very beginning accepted as her own that very ancient Greek translation of the Old Testament which is called the Septuagint, and she has always given a place of honor to other Eastern translations and Latin ones, especially the Latin translation known as the Vulgate. But since the Word of God should be accessible at all times, the Church, by her authority and with maternal concern, sees to it that suitable and correct translations are made into different languages, especially from the original texts of the sacred books. And should the opportunity arise and the Church au-

thorities approve, if these translations are produced in cooperation with the separated brethren as well, all Christians will be able to use them.

23. The bride of the incarnate Word, the Church taught by the Holy Spirit, is concerned to move ahead toward a deeper understanding of the Sacred Scriptures so that she may increasingly feed her sons with the divine words. Therefore, she also encourages the study of the holy Fathers of both East and West and of sacred liturgies. Catholic exegetes then and other students of sacred theology, working diligently together and using appropriate means, should devote their energies, under the watchful care of the sacred teaching office of the Church, to an exploration and exposition of the divine writings. This should be so done that as many ministers of the divine word as possible will be able effectively to provide the nourishment of the Scriptures for the People of God, to enlighten their minds, strengthen their wills and set men's hearts on fire with the love of God.[1] The sacred synod encourages the sons of the Church and biblical scholars to continue energetically, following the mind of the Church, with the work they have so well begun, with a constant renewal of vigor.[2]

24. Sacred theology rests on the written Word of God, together with sacred Tradition, as its primary and perpetual foundation. By scrutinizing in the light of faith all truth stored up in the mystery of Christ, theology is most powerfully strengthened and constantly rejuvenated by that word. For the Sacred Scriptures contain the Word of God and since they are inspired, really are the Word of God, and so the study of the sacred page is, as it were, the soul of sacred theology.[3] By the same Word of Scripture the ministry of the word also, that is, pastoral preaching, catechetics and all Christian instruction, in which the liturgical homily must hold the foremost place, is nourished in a healthy way and flourishes in a holy way.

---

1. Cf. Pius XII, Encyclical Letter *Divino Afflante Spiritu* (Sept. 30, 1943): *EB* 551, 553, 567; Pontifical Biblical Commission, *Instruction on Proper Teaching of Sacred Scripture in Seminaries and Religious Colleges* (May 13, 1950): *AAS* 42 (1950), 495–505.

2. Cf. Pius XII, Encyclical Letter *Divino Afflante Spiritu* (Sept. 30, 1943): *EB* 569.

3. Cf. Leo XIII, Encyclical Letter *Providentissimus Deus*: *EB* 114; Benedict XV, Encyclical Letter *Spiritus Paraclitus*: *EB* 483.

25. Therefore, all the clergy must hold fast to the Sacred Scriptures through diligent sacred reading and careful study, especially the priests of Christ and others, such as deacons and catechists, who are legitimately active in the ministry of the word. This is to be done so that none of them will become "an empty preacher of the Word of God outwardly, who is not a listener to it inwardly"[4] since they must share the abundant wealth of the divine word with the faithful committed to them, especially in the sacred liturgy. The sacred synod also earnestly and especially urges all the Christian faithful, especially religious, to learn by frequent reading of the divine Scriptures the "excellent knowledge of Jesus Christ" (Phil 3:8). "For ignorance of the Scriptures is ignorance of Christ."[5] Therefore, they should gladly put themselves in touch with the sacred text itself, whether it be through the liturgy, rich in the divine word, or through devotional reading, or through instructions suitable for the purpose and other aids which, in our time, with approval and active support of the shepherds of the Church, are commendably spread everywhere. And let them remember that prayer should accompany the reading of Sacred Scripture, so that God and man may talk together; for "we speak to him when we pray; we hear him when we read the divine saying."[6]

It devolves on sacred bishops "who have the apostolic teaching"[7] to give the faithful entrusted to them suitable instruction in the right use of the divine books, especially the New Testament and above all the Gospels. This can be done through translations of the sacred texts, which are to be provided with the necessary and really adequate explanations so that the children of the Church may safely and profitably become conversant with the Sacred Scriptures and be penetrated with their spirit.

Furthermore, editions of the Sacred Scriptures, provided with suitable footnotes, should be prepared also for the use of non-Christians and adapted to their situation. Both pastors of souls and Christians generally should see to the wise distribution of these in one way or another.

---

4. St. Augustine, *Sermons,* 179, 1: *PL* 38, 966.

5. St. Jerome, *Commentary on Isaiah,* Prol. *PL* 24, 17. Cf. Benedict XV, Encyclical Letter *Spiritus Paraclitus: EB* 475–480; Pius XII, Encyclical Letter *Divino Afflante Spiritu* (Sept. 30, 1943): *EB* 544.

6. St. Ambrose, *On the Duties of Ministers,* I, 20, 88: *PL* l6, 50.

7. St. Irenaeus, *Against Heretics* IV, 32, 1: *PG* 7, 1071; (same as 49, 2: Harvey, 2, p. 255).

26. In this way, therefore, through the reading and study of the sacred books "the Word of God may spread rapidly and be glorified" (2 Thes 3:1) and the treasure of revelation entrusted to the Church may more and more fill the hearts of men. Just as the life of the Church is strengthened through more frequent celebration of the Eucharistic mystery, similarly we may hope for a new stimulus for the life of the Spirit from a growing reverence for the Word of God, which "lasts forever" (Is 40:8; cf. 1 Pt 1:23–25).

Given in Rome at St. Peter's, November 18, 1965

DECREE ON THE APOSTOLATE OF THE LAITY

Apostolicam Actuositatem

Promulgated by
His Holiness Pope Paul VI
On November 18, 1965

INTRODUCTION

A pastoral council dedicated to "imparting an ever increasing vigor to the Christian life of the faithful" (*SC* 1) through a renewal based on conversion and the universal call to holiness (cf. *LG* 39–42), could not fail to address specifically the numerically largest group in the Church, the laity. Further, a pastoral council conscious of the Church's relation to the world and concerned to be more effective in its mission could hardly overlook the laity. As Pope Pius XII had acknowledged in 1946, they are "on the front lines of the Church's life" and they "ought to have an ever clearer consciousness not only of belonging to the Church, but of being the Church."

At the end of the introductory article this decree mentions "the unmistakable work being done today by the Holy Spirit in making the laity ever more conscious of their own responsibility." This situates *Apostolicam Actuositatem (AA)* as another element of the Church's response to the initiative of the Holy Spirit. In the language of *Gaudium et Spes,* this initiative is seen as one of the "signs of the times" (*GS* 4) through which God's will for the Church is discerned.

The decree should be understood as an effort on the part of the conciliar bishops to make a judgment regarding the movements and gifts of the Holy Spirit in order "not to extinguish the Spirit but to test all things and hold for what is good (cf. 1 Thes 5:12, 19, 21)" (*AA* 3). It expresses the Council's goal of making the Church a more effective instrument in the hands of God for completing its mission. Reminiscent of the formula the apostles used in stating their decision at the Council of Jerusalem— "for it has seemed good to the Holy Spirit and to us..." (Acts 15:28)— the decree's final words include: "Through this holy synod, the Lord renews his invitation to all the laity to come closer to him every day... to associate themselves with him in his saving mission" (*AA* 33).

This Christocentric emphasis is also clear early in the text. The laity are described as participating in the Church's mission because they participate in the priestly, prophetic and royal offices of Christ and thereby bear witness to Christ in all that they do. Their apostolate, and their right and duty to exercise it, are grounded in their union with Christ who appoints them to the apostolate.

The text stresses that "the success of the lay apostolate depends upon the laity's living union with Christ," especially "active participation in the sacred liturgy" (AA 4). The decree enumerates the gifts by which this living union is maintained, emphasizing above all faith, hope and charity. Various means for developing this union with Christ are set forth, including the sacraments, meditating on the Word of God, using gifts received from God, and imitating Mary, the Mother of God.

Mary is presented as the "perfect example of this type of spiritual and apostolic life" (AA 4). She led an ordinary life among the people of her time, but maintained through it all a vital union with her Son that made her whole life a great cooperation in his saving work. This is one of several instances in which the decree underscores the challenge of uniting faith and life (cf. AA 13, 18, 28). This emphasis corresponds to the Council's concern that "This split between the faith which many profess and their daily lives deserves to be counted among the more serious errors of our age" (GS 43), so that what is needed is a faith that "prove[s] its fruitfulness by penetrating the believer's entire life, including its worldly dimensions" (GS 21).

Though the laity can exercise their apostolate in the Church as well as in the world, the special challenge of the laity is precisely the "penetrating and perfecting of the temporal order through the spirit of the Gospel" (AA 2), which is their "special obligation" (AA 7) and "can never be performed properly by others" (AA 13).

AA is thus linked to chapter four of Lumen Gentium which situated the laity within the essential makeup of the Church as the messianic People of God who continue Christ's mission as prophet, priest and king. It taught that the laity participate in the saving mission of the Church by consecrating the world to God. God calls them to "seek the kingdom of God by engaging in temporal affairs and by ordering them according to the plan of God" (LG 31).

Since Vatican II, a tremendous growth has taken place in the numbers of lay people serving the Church in visible, stable and often paid positions. Many lay people serve as coordinators of religious education, directors for youth programs, and in other offices on both the diocesan and parish levels. In addition, they serve as members of diocesan and parish pastoral and finance councils, as lectors and as extraordinary ministers of the Eucharist.

As important, useful and irreplaceable as such services are, it would be contrary to the mind of the Council to define the lay apostolate primarily with respect to them. If that is adopted, the result could be a kind of two-class laity: those who are truly active and involved in the Church, and those who are not. But the vast majority of the lay faithful exercise their apostolate through the consecration of the world to God by infusing "a Christian spirit into the mentality, customs, laws and structures of the community" (*AA* 13). This is the consecration of the world the Council calls for (cf. *LG* 34).

The vocation to consecrate the world to God carries a special challenge: to bring a faith perspective to the many secular activities which the laity have in common with their contemporaries. Of course, the witness of the laity will stand out more when their actions contrast with those around them. This happens when in fidelity to the Gospel they take stands that appear "counter-cultural."

It might be considered more difficult for the laity to live out their faith when such differences are not so visible and Christian motives for acting have to be elaborated from within. For example, Catholics may work with non-Christians in efforts to care for the poor. For "Catholics should try to cooperate with all men and women of good will to promote whatever is true, whatever just, whatever holy, whatever lovable (cf. Phil 4:8)" (*AA* 14; cf. 7, 8, 11). However, while non-Christians might be motivated by a genuine spirit of humanitarianism, Catholics see "the image of [the Church's] poor and suffering Founder" (*LG* 8) and show mercy to others because they have experienced God's mercy toward themselves. This kind of interior elaboration can happen only through faith, hope and charity. Often mentioned in the decree, these virtues can "attract all to the love of the true and the good," thus preparing hearts "for the workings of saving grace" which can eventually lead them to Christ and his Church (*AA* 13). The witness of the laity makes the Church present in all the temporal activities lay people engage in (*AA* 29).

An attentive reading of the decree reveals many parallels between its fourth article and chapter five of *Lumen Gentium* on the universal call to holiness. This is significant because it shows that the same things which bring about holiness are also principles of the apostolate. *Lumen Gentium* had stressed that each group in the Church—clergy, religious, laity, married persons, workers, the suffering—can pursue holiness by fulfilling their duties and seeking God's will in the circumstances of their lives. In this decree virtually the same thing is said about the apostolate, so that by "performing their work according to God's will, they grow in that union [with Christ]" (*AA* 4).

Clearly, apostolate or function within the Church and union with God or holiness are inseparable. The implicit principle here is that action follows upon being. What a thing does depends on what it is. There are actions which are characteristic of Christians because by grace they really are sanctified and share in God's life. "It is no longer I who live, but it is Christ who lives in me" (Gal 2:20). Thus, the decree goes into specifics about formation for the apostolate only after setting forth the principles of preserving communion with Christ, apart from whom no one can bear fruit (cf. Jn 15:4–5).

While new life in Christ is ordered to action, these actions flow from the new being that comes with grace. Thus, technical and practical knowledge and experience are necessary but not sufficient for the apostolate. This is why the document sets forth a genuine spirituality for the apostolate that includes a constant return to the sources of grace, the Word of God and the sacraments.

This order must be respected if the renewal of Vatican II is to become a reality for the laity. The Church does not offer opportunities for people to "feel" that they belong by performing a task. The Church imparts to people a new way of being, from which flows a participation in the mission of Christ and of the Church, and thus new ways of acting.

The lay apostolate includes a fully developed theology of work, sketched out in *AA* (n. 7). Work includes the vast spheres of productive activity which unleashes the potential of created goods to serve humanity. When it conforms to the moral order, all work serves humanity. Because created things and human society have God as their origin they "enjoy their own laws and values which must be gradually deciphered, put to use, and regulated." When people respect the "stability, truth, goodness, proper laws and order" of creation, whether they are conscious of it or not, they are "being led by the hand of God" (*GS* 36). By the many forms of human work which occupy the laity, the natural goodness of all that God has created serves the human person and is thereby ennobled (cf. *AA* 7). Knowing this in faith, the laity are by no means "unconscious collaborators with God's will," but are fully conscious of the dignity of being "'God's fellow workers' and co-workers for his kingdom" (*CCC* 307).

The decree stresses an important point when it teaches that the apostolate is received from the Lord himself (*AA* 3). This call to the apostolate is brought about through Baptism and Confirmation. For its accomplishment, God provides the Eucharist and a variety of gifts: sanctifying gifts of faith, hope and charity, the gift of participation in Christ's offices of prophet, priest and king, and other gifts more specific to the various apostolates.

The laity have the right and duty to exercise their gifts for the apostolate, since it is received from the Lord (*AA* 3). The decree presents a balanced understanding of the laity's apostolic activity. In the sphere of their secular activity the laity are free and responsible to take initiatives without a prior mandate or directive from the hierarchy. Yet at times some apostolates require such a mandate or greater direction and supervision.

In general, because the apostolate, its actions and its principles are received from God, they must be exercised according to his order (cf. *AA* 23–27). Essentially this means exercising the apostolate in communion with the Church. This has two fundamental dimensions: communion with sacred pastors, and coordination of gifts and activities within the apostolate of the Church. Communion with sacred pastors requires following the doctrine and discipline of the Church, as well as being attentive to those who are charged with this responsibility (cf. *AA* 19, 24). While the Spirit subjects those gifted with charisms to apostolic authority (cf. *LG* 7), history shows that new developments are not always welcomed by Church officials. The lives of the saints indicate how much patience is often required before a genuine charism is recognized. In addition, the laity are to respond generously to the pastoral initiatives of their shepherds (*AA* 9). In a short passage which has a parallel in the *Decree on the Renewal and Adaptation of Religious Life,* the decree states that dispersion of efforts should be avoided with respect to new associations and projects (cf. *AA* 19; *PC* 19).

No rivalry need exist among the specific apostolates, except perhaps in St. Paul's sense of striving to outdo one another in doing good. Instead there should be a genuine sense of the common good of the Church and the valuable contribution of the many gifts and apostolates. This spirit of unity and mutual esteem (cf. *AA* 16) will be easily developed if the faithful remember that apostolic associations are not ends in themselves but means for advancing the Church's mission (cf. *AA* 19). The sign of a healthy apostolate is a greater concern about the Church itself than about the continuation and growth of the particular work, for the goal supersedes the means. It cannot be concluded even from abundant fruit that God intends a given mission or apostolic association to endure forever. It can happen that an association attains its goals, or that its methods are no longer adequate, or that the needs it was designed to serve no longer exist (cf. *AA* 19). The supreme rule of the apostolate is service, not self-perpetuation.

Such service is sometimes referred to as "ministry," and the widespread use of this term has led to some confusion. The decree does not use the term "ministry" with respect to the laity. The Council used that term to refer to the sanctifying and teaching functions of the ordained. However, restriction of ministry to the ordained or those who are very closely associated with activities of the ordained ministry in no way denigrates the dignity of the laity. Both *LG* and *AA* explicitly assert this dignity. In *The Lay Members of Christ's Faithful People,* issued after the 1987 Synod of Bishops on the laity, John Paul II clarifies this question. First he notes the difference between the ministerial priesthood and the laity's participation in Christ's priesthood through Baptism: "The ordained ministries, apart from the persons who receive them, are a grace for the entire Church. These ministries express and realize a participation in the priesthood of Jesus Christ that is different, not simply in degree but in essence, from the participation given to all the lay faithful through Baptism and Confirmation."

Their baptismal consecration gives the laity an important role to play in the Church. The new awareness of this which the Council fostered, along with a shortage of priests in many areas, has led to increased lay participation:

> The pastors, therefore, ought to acknowledge and foster the ministries, the offices and roles of the lay faithful that find their foundation in the sacraments of Baptism and Confirmation, indeed, for a good many of them, in the sacrament of Matrimony.
>
> When necessity and expediency in the Church require it, the pastors, according to established norms from universal law, can entrust to

the lay faithful certain offices and roles that are connected to their pastoral ministry but do not require the character of Orders.... However, the exercise of such tasks does not make the lay faithful pastors: in fact, a person is not a minister simply in performing a task, but through sacramental ordination. Only the sacrament of Orders gives the ordained minister a particular participation in the office of Christ, the shepherd and head, and in his eternal priesthood. The task exercised in virtue of supply takes its legitimacy formally and immediately from the official deputation given by the pastors, as well as from its concrete exercise under the guidance of ecclesiastical authority... (*CL* 23).

The Pope then mentions that during the 1987 Synod of Bishops, a concern was expressed about "a too-indiscriminate use of the word 'ministry,'" and "the confusion and the equating of the common priesthood and the ministerial priesthood."

The Synod then went on to stress "the necessity to express with greater clarity, and with a more precise terminology, both the unity of the Church's mission in which all the baptized participate, and the substantial diversity of the ministry of pastors which is rooted in the sacrament of Orders, all the while respecting the other ministries, offices and roles in the Church, which are rooted in the sacraments of Baptism and Confirmation" (*CL* 22–23). These principles provide the theological basis for the role of the laity in the Church.

The concluding chapter of the decree underscores the respect that God shows for our freedom and the responsibility we must exercise in responding to his gifts. "The apostolate can attain its maximum effectiveness only through a diversified and thorough formation" (*AA* 28). Echoing this, but with even greater force, the *General Catechetical Directory* states: "Any pastoral activity for the carrying out of which there are not at hand persons with the right formation and preparation will necessarily come to nothing" (n. 108).

Apostolic activities require adequate training and preparation. Because the lay apostolate has a secular character, this formation must include specific, accurate and even technical knowledge in the various fields in which it is exercised. Because the lay apostolate is a participation in the mission of Christ and the Church, it also requires a formation in doctrine and spirituality.

The decree mentions in particular the apostolate specific to married persons and the family, identifying it as having a "unique importance for the Church and civil society" (*AA* 11; cf. 30). This passage is one of four main considerations of the family in the texts of Vatican II. (The others are *LG* 11; *GE* 3, 6; *GS* 47–52.)

A novelty of the conciliar teaching on the family which has been little noticed (due, at least in part, to imprecise translations) is that Vatican II applied the word "ordo" to marriage (cf. *LG* 11; *GS* 52). "By reason of their state and rank *(ordine)* in life they have their own special gift among the People of God" (*LG* 11). This indicates that the Council spoke of the married as a visible, identifiable group, constituted by a specific function and the gifts and graces to accomplish it that come through the sacrament of Matrimony. A specific way of life and a corresponding set of virtues and spirituality distinguish the family, resulting in a genuine "order of those who are married."

Mission or apostolate and the gifts to accomplish it can be distinguished from sanctifying grace and faith, hope and charity. Nevertheless, the Christian virtues should direct the use of the gifts or charisms for the sake of the apostolate; otherwise, a person resembles St. Paul's description of the one who speaks the language of angels, moves mountains and divests himself of all things, but gains nothing and is nothing without charity (cf. 1 Cor 13:1–13). Once again we see that holiness is to be sought in the activities by which one fulfills the duties and functions of his state in life and vocation (cf. *LG* 39–42).

A final theme of the decree is its repeated insistence on the need for explicit verbal proclamation and witness to Christ as a complement to the witness of a holy life (cf. *AA* 6, 13, 16). This should be seen as developing and applying to the laity the ecclesiology of *Lumen Gentium,* according to which the Church is a sacrament or sign through which God works (cf. *LG* 35). The ultimate source for this theme is *Dei Verbum* and its understanding of Christ bringing revelation to completion and perfection through his words and actions (cf. *DV* 2). In fidelity to the wisdom of God revealed in Jesus Christ and the reality of how grace makes his disciples real sharers in his life and mission, *AA* applies this principle to the lay apostolate.

TOPICAL OUTLINE

1. Introduction: importance of the laity (1)

2. The vocation of the laity to the apostolate

   A. The laity share in the mission of the Church (2)

   B. The laity's mission is rooted in Baptism and sustained by gifts of the Spirit (3)

   C. Union with Christ in faith, hope and charity (4)

3. Objectives

   A. Renewal of the temporal order (5)

   B. Witness and proclamation (6)

   C. Directing the temporal order to God through Christ (7)

   D. The works of love (8)

4. The various fields of the apostolate

   A. Church communities such as the parish and diocese (9–10)

   B. The family (11)

   C. Young people (12)

   D. Wider society (13)

   E. National and international levels (14)

5. The various forms of the apostolate

   A. The Christian witness of individual persons (15–17)

DECREE ON THE APOSTOLATE OF THE LAITY

Apostolicam Actuositatem

INTRODUCTION

1. To intensify the apostolic activity of the People of God,[1] the most holy synod earnestly addresses itself to the laity, whose proper and indispensable role in the mission of the Church has already been dealt with in other documents.[2] The apostolate of the laity derives from their Christian vocation, and the Church can never be without it. Sacred Scripture clearly shows how spontaneous and fruitful such activity was at the very beginning of the Church (cf. Acts 11:19–21; 18:26; Rm 16:1–16; Phil 4:3).

---

1. Cf. John XXIII, Apostolic Constitution *Humani Salutis* (Dec. 25, 1961): *AAS* 54 (1962), 7–10.

2. Cf. Second Vatican Ecumenical Council, Dogmatic Constitution on the Church *Lumen Gentium*, 33 ff.: *AAS* 57 (1965), 39 ff.; cf. Second Vatican Ecumenical Council, Constitution on the Sacred Liturgy *Sacrosanctum Concilium*, 26–40: *AAS* 56 (1964), 107–111; cf. Second Vatican Ecumenical Council, Decree on the Media of Social Communication *Inter Mirifica: AAS* 56 (1964), 145–158; cf. Second Vatican Ecumenical Council, Decree on Ecumenism *Unitatis Redintegratio: AAS* 57 (1965), 90–107; cf. Second Vatican Ecumenical Council, Decree on the Pastoral Office of Bishops in the Church *Christus Dominus*, 16–18; cf. Second Vatican Ecumenical Council, Declaration on Christian Education *Gravissimum Educationis*, 3, 5, 7; cf. Second Vatican Ecumenical Council, Decree on the Mission Activity of the Church *Ad Gentes*, 15, 21, 41; cf. Second Vatican Ecumenical Council, Decree on the Ministry and Life of Priests *Presbyterorum Ordinis*, 9.

Our own times require of the laity no less zeal; in fact, modern conditions demand that their apostolate be broadened and intensified. With a constantly increasing population, continual progress in science and technology, and closer interpersonal relationships, the areas for the lay apostolate have been immensely widened particularly in fields that have been for the most part open to the laity alone. These factors have also occasioned new problems which demand their expert attention and study. This apostolate becomes more imperative in view of the fact that many areas of human life have become increasingly autonomous. This is as it should be, but it sometimes involves a degree of departure from the ethical and religious order and a serious danger to Christian life. Besides, in many places where priests are very few, or in some instances deprived of due freedom for priestly work, the Church could scarcely exist and function without the activity of the laity.

An indication of this manifold and pressing need is the unmistakable work being done today by the Holy Spirit in making the laity ever more conscious of their own responsibility and encouraging them to serve Christ and the Church in all circumstances.[3]

In this decree the Council seeks to describe the nature, character and diversity of the lay apostolate, to state its basic principles and to give pastoral directives for its more effective exercise. All these should be regarded as norms when the canon law, as it pertains to the lay apostolate, is revised.

---

3. Cf. Pius XII, *Allocution to Cardinals* (Feb. 18, 1946): *AAS* 38 (1946), 101–102; cf. Pius XII, *Sermon to Young Catholic Workers* (Aug. 25, 1957): *AAS* 49 (1957), 843.

CHAPTER I

THE VOCATION OF THE LAITY
TO THE APOSTOLATE

2. The Church was founded for the purpose of spreading the kingdom of Christ throughout the earth for the glory of God the Father, to enable all men to share in his saving redemption,[1] and that through them the whole world might enter into a relationship with Christ. All activity of the Mystical Body directed to the attainment of this goal is called the apostolate, which the Church carries on in various ways through all her members. For the Christian vocation by its very nature is also a vocation to the apostolate. No part of the structure of a living body is merely passive but has a share in the functions as well as life of the body; so, too, in the body of Christ, which is the Church, "the whole body...in keeping with the proper activity of each part, derives its increase from its own internal development" (Eph 4:16).

Indeed, the organic union in this body and the structure of the members are so compact that the member who fails to make his proper contribution to the development of the Church must be said to be useful neither to the Church nor to himself.

In the Church there is a diversity of ministry but a oneness of mission. Christ conferred on the apostles and their successors the duty of teaching, sanctifying, and ruling in his name and power. But the laity likewise share in the priestly, prophetic and royal office of Christ and therefore have their own share in the mission of the whole People of God in the Church and in the world.[2]

They exercise the apostolate in fact by their activity directed to the evangelization and sanctification of men and to the penetrating and perfecting of the temporal order through the spirit of the Gospel. In this

---

1. Cf. Pius XI, Encyclical Letter *Rerum Ecclesiae* (Feb. 28, 1926): *AAS* 18 (1926), 65.
2. Cf. Second Vatican Ecumenical Council, Dogmatic Constitution on the Church *Lumen Gentium,* 31: *AAS* 57 (1965), 37.

way, their temporal activity openly bears witness to Christ and promotes the salvation of men. Since the laity, in accordance with their state of life, live in the midst of the world and its concerns, they are called by God to exercise their apostolate in the world like leaven, with the ardor of the spirit of Christ.

3. The laity derive the right and duty to the apostolate from their union with Christ the head; incorporated into Christ's Mystical Body through Baptism and strengthened by the power of the Holy Spirit through Confirmation, they are assigned to the apostolate by the Lord himself. They are consecrated for the royal priesthood and the holy people (cf. 1 Pt 2:4–10) not only that they may offer spiritual sacrifices in everything they do but also that they may witness to Christ throughout the world. The sacraments, however, especially the most holy Eucharist, communicate and nourish that charity which is the soul of the entire apostolate.[3]

One engages in the apostolate through the faith, hope and charity which the Holy Spirit diffuses in the hearts of all members of the Church. Indeed, by the precept of charity, which is the Lord's greatest commandment, all the faithful are impelled to promote the glory of God through the coming of his kingdom and to obtain eternal life for all men—that they may know the only true God and him whom he sent, Jesus Christ (cf. Jn 17:3). On all Christians, therefore, is laid the preeminent responsibility of working to make the divine message of salvation known and accepted by all men throughout the world.

For the exercise of this apostolate, the Holy Spirit who sanctifies the People of God through ministry and the sacraments gives the faithful special gifts also (cf. 1 Cor 12:7), "allotting them to everyone according as he wills" (1 Cor 12:11) in order that individuals, administering grace to others just as they have received it, may also be "good stewards of the manifold grace of God" (1 Pt 4:10), to build up the whole body in charity (cf. Eph 4:16). From the acceptance of these charisms, including those which are more elementary, there arise for each believer the right and duty to use them in the Church and in the world for the good of men and the building up of the Church, in the freedom of the Holy Spirit who "breathes where he wills" (Jn 3:8). This should be done by the laity in

---

3. Cf. Second Vatican Ecumenical Council, Dogmatic Constitution on the Church *Lumen Gentium,* 33: *AAS* 57 (1965), 39; cf. also *ibid.,* 10, *AAS* 57 (1965), 14.

communion with their brothers in Christ, especially with their pastors who must make a judgment about the true nature and proper use of these gifts, not to extinguish the Spirit but to test all things and hold for what is good (cf. 1 Thes 5:12, 19, 21).[4]

4. Since Christ, sent by the Father, is the source and origin of the whole apostolate of the Church, the success of the lay apostolate depends upon the laity's living union with Christ, in keeping with the Lord's words, "He who abides in me, and I in him, bears much fruit, for without me you can do nothing" (Jn 15:5). This life of intimate union with Christ in the Church is nourished by spiritual aids which are common to all the faithful, especially active participation in the sacred liturgy.[5] These are to be used by the laity in such a way that while correctly fulfilling their secular duties in the ordinary conditions of life, they do not separate union with Christ from their life, but rather, performing their work according to God's will, they grow in that union. In this way the laity must make progress in holiness in a happy and ready spirit, trying prudently and patiently to overcome difficulties.[6] Neither family concerns nor other secular affairs should be irrelevant to their spiritual life, in keeping with the words of the Apostle, "Whatever you do in word or work, do all in the name of the Lord Jesus Christ, giving thanks to God the Father through him" (Col 3:17).

Such a life requires a continual exercise of faith, hope and charity. Only by the light of faith and by meditation on the Word of God can one always and everywhere recognize God in whom "we live and move and have our being" (Acts 17:28), seek his will in every event, see Christ in everyone whether he be a relative or a stranger, and make correct judgments about the true meaning and value of temporal things both in themselves and in their relation to man's final goal.

They who have this faith live in the hope of the revelation of the sons of God and keep in mind the cross and resurrection of the Lord. In the pilgrimage of this life, hidden with Christ in God and free from en-

---

4. Second Vatican Ecumenical Council, Dogmatic Constitution on the Church *Lumen Gentium,* 12: *AAS* 57 (1965), 16.

5. Cf. Second Vatican Ecumenical Council, Constitution on the Sacred Liturgy *Sacrosanctum Concilium,* 11: *AAS* 56 (1964), 102–103.

6. Cf. Second Vatican Ecumenical Council, Dogmatic Constitution on the Church *Lumen Gentium,* 32: *AAS* 57 (1965), 38; cf. also *ibid.* 40–41: *AAS* 57 (1965), 45–47.

slavement to wealth, they aspire to those riches which remain forever and generously dedicate themselves wholly to the advancement of the kingdom of God and to the reform and improvement of the temporal order in a Christian spirit. Among the trials of this life they find strength in hope, convinced that "the sufferings of the present time are not worthy to be compared with the glory to come that will be revealed in us" (Rm 8:18).

Impelled by divine charity, they do good to all men, especially to those of the household of the faith (cf. Gal 6:10), laying aside "all malice and all deceit and pretense, and envy and all slander" (1 Pt 2:1), and thereby they draw men to Christ. This charity of God, "which is poured forth in our hearts by the Holy Spirit who has been given to us" (Rm 5:5), enables the laity really to express the spirit of the beatitudes in their lives. Following Jesus in his poverty, they are neither depressed by the lack of temporal goods nor inflated by their abundance; imitating Christ in his humility, they have no obsession for empty honors (cf. Gal 5:26) but seek to please God rather than men, ever ready to leave all things for Christ's sake (cf. Lk 14:26) and to suffer persecution for justice sake (cf. Mt 5:10), as they remember the words of the Lord, "If anyone wishes to come after me, let him deny himself and take up his cross and follow me" (Mt 16:24). Promoting Christian friendship among themselves, they help one another in every need whatsoever.

This plan for the spiritual life of the laity should take its particular character from their married or family state or their single or widowed state, from their state of health and from their professional and social activity. They should not cease to develop earnestly the qualities and talents bestowed on them in accord with these conditions of life, and they should make use of the gifts which they have received from the Holy Spirit.

Furthermore, the laity who have followed their vocation and have become members of one of the associations or institutes approved by the Church try faithfully to adopt the special characteristics of the spiritual life which are proper to them as well. They should also hold in high esteem professional skill, family and civic spirit, and the virtues relating to social customs, namely, honesty, justice, sincerity, kindness and courage, without which no true Christian life can exist.

The perfect example of this type of spiritual and apostolic life is the most Blessed Virgin Mary, queen of apostles, who while leading the life common to all here on earth, one filled with family concerns and labors, was always intimately united with her Son and in an entirely unique way cooperated in the work of the Savior. Having now been assumed into heaven, with her maternal charity she cares for these brothers of her Son who are still on their earthly pilgrimage and remain involved in dangers and difficulties until they are led into the happy fatherland.[7] All should devoutly venerate her and commend their life and apostolate to her maternal care.

---

7. Second Vatican Ecumenical Council, Dogmatic Constitution on the Church *Lumen Gentium,* 62: *AAS* 57 (1965), 63; cf. also *ibid.* 65: *AAS* 57 (1965), 64–65.

CHAPTER II

OBJECTIVES

5. Christ's redemptive work, while essentially concerned with the salvation of men, includes also the renewal of the whole temporal order. Hence, the mission of the Church is not only to bring the message and grace of Christ to men but also to penetrate and perfect the temporal order with the spirit of the Gospel. In fulfilling this mission of the Church, the Christian laity exercise their apostolate both in the Church and in the world, in both the spiritual and the temporal orders. These orders, although distinct, are so connected in the singular plan of God that he himself intends to raise up the whole world again in Christ and to make it a new creation, initially on earth and completely on the last day. In both orders the layman, being simultaneously a believer and a citizen, should be continuously led by the same Christian conscience.

6. The mission of the Church pertains to the salvation of men, which is to be achieved by belief in Christ and by his grace. The apostolate of the Church and of all its members is primarily designed to manifest Christ's message by words and deeds and to communicate his grace to the world. This is done mainly through the ministry of the Word and the sacraments, entrusted in a special way to the clergy, wherein the laity also have their very important roles to fulfill if they are to be "fellow workers for the truth" (3 Jn 8). It is especially on this level that the apostolate of the laity and the pastoral ministry are mutually complementary.

There are innumerable opportunities open to the laity for the exercise of their apostolate of evangelization and sanctification. The very testimony of their Christian life and good works done in a supernatural spirit have the power to draw men to belief and to God; for the Lord says, "Even so let your light shine before men in order that they may see your good works and give glory to your Father who is in heaven" (Mt 5:16).

However, an apostolate of this kind does not consist only in the witness of one's way of life; a true apostle looks for opportunities to announce Christ by words addressed either to non-believers with a view to leading them to faith, or to the faithful with a view to instructing, strengthening and encouraging them to a more fervent life. "For the charity of Christ impels us" (2 Cor 5:14). The words of the Apostle should echo in all hearts, "Woe to me if I do not preach the Gospel" (1 Cor 9:16).[1]

Since in our own times new problems are arising and very serious errors are circulating which tend to undermine the foundations of religion, the moral order and human society itself, this sacred synod earnestly exhorts laymen—each according to his own gifts of intelligence and learning—to be more diligent in doing what they can to explain, defend and properly apply Christian principles to the problems of our era in accordance with the mind of the Church.

7. God's plan for the world is that men should work together to renew and constantly perfect the temporal order.

All those things which make up the temporal order namely, the good things of life and the prosperity of the family, culture, economic matters, the arts and professions, the laws of the political community, international relations and other matters of this kind, as well as their development and progress—not only aid in the attainment of man's ultimate goal but also possess their own intrinsic value. This value has been established in them by God, whether they are considered in themselves or as parts of the whole temporal order. "God saw that all he had made was very good" (Gn 1:31). This natural goodness of theirs takes on a special dignity as a result of their relation to the human person, for whose service they were created. It has pleased God to unite all things, both natural and supernatural, in Christ Jesus "so that in all things he may have the first place" (Col 1:18). This destination, however, not only does not deprive the temporal order of its independence, its proper goals, laws, supports and significance for human welfare but rather perfects the temporal order in its own intrinsic strength and worth and puts it on a level with man's whole vocation upon earth.

---

1. Cf. Pius XI, Encyclical Letter *Ubi Arcano* (Dec. 23, 1922): *AAS* 14 (1922), 659; Pius XII, Encyclical Letter *Summi Pontificatus* (Oct. 20, 1939): *AAS* 31 (1939), 442–443.

In the course of history, the use of temporal things has been marred by serious vices. Affected by original sin, men have frequently fallen into many errors concerning the true God, the nature of man and the principles of the moral law. This has led to the corruption of morals and human institutions and not rarely to contempt for the human person himself. In our own time, moreover, those who have trusted excessively in the progress of the natural sciences and the technical arts have fallen into an idolatry of temporal things and have become their slaves rather than their masters.

The whole Church must work vigorously in order that men may become capable of rectifying the distortion of the temporal order and directing it to God through Christ. Pastors must clearly state the principles concerning the purpose of creation and the use of temporal things and must offer the moral and spiritual aids by which the temporal order may be renewed in Christ.

The laity must take up the renewal of the temporal order as their own special obligation. Led by the light of the Gospel and the mind of the Church and motivated by Christian charity, they must act directly and in a definite way in the temporal sphere. As citizens they must cooperate with other citizens with their own particular skill and on their own responsibility. Everywhere and in all things they must seek the justice of God's kingdom. The temporal order must be renewed in such a way that, without detriment to its own proper laws, it may be brought into conformity with the higher principles of the Christian life and adapted to the shifting circumstances of time, place and peoples. Preeminent among the works of this type of apostolate is that of Christian social action which the sacred synod desires to see extended to the whole temporal sphere, including culture.[2]

8. While every exercise of the apostolate should be motivated by charity, some works by their very nature can become specially vivid expressions of this charity. Christ the Lord wanted these works to be signs of his messianic mission (cf. Mt 11:4–5).

The greatest commandment in the law is to love God with one's whole heart and one's neighbor as oneself (cf. Mt 22:37–40). Christ

---

2. Cf. Leo XIII, Encyclical Letter *Rerum Novarum* (May 15, 1891): *AAS* 23 (1890–91), 47; Pius XI Encyclical Letter *Quadragesimo Anno* (May 15, 1931): *AAS* 23 (1931), 190; Pius XII, *Radio Message* (June 1, 1941): *AAS* 33 (1941), 207.

made this commandment of love of neighbor his own and enriched it with a new meaning. For he wanted to equate himself with his brethren as the object of this love when he said, "As long as you did it for one of these, the least of my brethren, you did it for me" (Mt 25:40). Assuming human nature, he bound the whole human race to himself as a family through a certain supernatural solidarity and established charity as the mark of his disciples, saying, "By this will all men know that you are my disciples, if you have love for one another" (Jn 13:35).

In her very early days, the holy Church added the agape to the Eucharistic Supper and thus showed itself to be wholly united around Christ by the bond of charity. So, too, in every era it is recognized by this sign of love, and while it rejoices in the undertakings of others, it claims works of charity as its own inalienable duty and right. For this reason, pity for the needy and the sick and works of charity and mutual aid intended to relieve human needs of every kind are held in highest honor by the Church.[3]

At the present time, with the development of more rapid facilities for communication, with the barrier of distance separating men greatly reduced, with the inhabitants of the entire globe becoming one great family, these charitable activities and works have become more urgent and universal. These charitable enterprises can and should reach out to all persons and all needs. Wherever there are people in need of food and drink, clothing, housing, medicine, employment, education; wherever men lack the facilities necessary for living a truly human life or are afflicted with serious distress or illness or suffer exile or imprisonment, there Christian charity should seek them out and find them, console them with great solicitude and help them with appropriate relief. This obligation is imposed above all upon every prosperous nation and person.[4]

In order that the exercise of charity on this scale may be unexceptionable in appearance as well as in fact, it is altogether necessary that one should consider in one's neighbor the image of God in which he has been created, and also Christ the Lord to whom is really offered whatever is given to a needy person. It is imperative also that the freedom and dignity of the person being helped be respected with the utmost con-

---

3. Cf. John XXIII, Encyclical Letter *Mater et Magistra* (May 15, 1961): *AAS* 53 (1961), 402.

4. Cf. John XXIII, Encyclical Letter *Mater et Magistra* (May 15, 1961): *AAS* 53 (1961), 440–441.

sideration, that the purity of one's charitable intentions be not stained by seeking one's own advantage or by striving for domination,[5] and especially that the demands of justice be satisfied lest the giving of what is due in justice be represented as the offering of a charitable gift. Not only the effects but also the causes of these ills must be removed and the help be given in such a way that the recipients may gradually be freed from dependence on outsiders and become self-sufficient.

Therefore, the laity should hold in high esteem and, according to their ability, aid the works of charity and projects for social assistance, whether public or private, including international programs whereby effective help is given to needy individuals and peoples. In so doing, they should cooperate with all men of good will.[6]

---

5. Cf. John XXIII, Encyclical Letter *Mater et Magistra* (May 15, 1961): *AAS* 53 (1961), 442–443.

6. Cf. Pius XII, *Allocution to Pax Romana* (April 25, 1957): *AAS* 49 (1957), 298–299; and especially John XXIII, *Ad Conventum Consilii,* Food and Agriculture Organization (Nov. 10, 1959): *AAS* 51 (1959), 856–866.

Chapter III

THE VARIOUS FIELDS OF THE APOSTOLATE

9. The laity carry out their manifold apostolate both in the Church and in the world. In both areas there are various opportunities for apostolic activity. We wish to list here the more important fields of action, namely, church communities, the family, youth, the social milieu and national and international levels. Since in our times women have an ever more active share in the whole life of society, it is very important that they participate more widely also in the various fields of the Church's apostolate.

10. As sharers in the role of Christ as priest, prophet and king, the laity have their work cut out for them in the life and activity of the Church. Their activity is so necessary within the Church communities that without it the apostolate of the pastors is often unable to achieve its full effectiveness. In the manner of the men and women who helped Paul in spreading the Gospel (cf. Acts 18:18, 26; Rm 16:3), the laity with the right apostolic attitude supply what is lacking to their brethren and refresh the spirit of pastors and of the rest of the faithful (cf. 1 Cor 16:17–18). Strengthened by active participation in the liturgical life of their community, they are eager to do their share of the apostolic works of that community. They bring to the Church people who perhaps are far removed from it, earnestly cooperate in presenting the Word of God especially by means of catechetical instruction, and offer their special skills to make the care of souls and the administration of the temporalities of the Church more efficient and effective.

The parish offers an obvious example of the apostolate on the community level inasmuch as it brings together the many human differences within its boundaries and merges them into the universality of the Church.[1] The laity should accustom themselves to working in the parish

---

1. Cf. St. Pius X, Apostolic Letter *Creationis Duarum Novarum Paroeciarum* (June 1,

in union with their priests,[2] bringing to the Church community their own and the world's problems as well as questions concerning human salvation, all of which they should examine and resolve by deliberating in common. As far as possible the laity ought to provide helpful collaboration for every apostolic and missionary undertaking sponsored by their local parish.

They should develop an ever-increasing appreciation of their own diocese, of which the parish is a kind of cell, ever ready at their pastor's invitation to participate in diocesan projects. Indeed, to fulfill the needs of cities and rural areas,[3] they should not limit their cooperation to the parochial or diocesan boundaries but strive to extend it to interparochial, interdiocesan, national and international fields. This is constantly becoming all the more necessary because the daily increase in mobility of populations, reciprocal relationships and means of communication no longer allow any sector of society to remain closed in upon itself. Thus, they should be concerned about the needs of the People of God dispersed throughout the world. They should especially make missionary activity their own by giving material or even personal assistance. It is a duty and honor for Christians to return to God a part of the good things that they receive from him.

11. Since the Creator of all things has established conjugal society as the beginning and basis of human society and by his grace has made it a great mystery in Christ and the Church (cf. Eph 5:32), the apostolate of married persons and families is of unique importance for the Church and civil society.

Christian husbands and wives are cooperators in grace and witnesses of faith for each other, their children and all others in their household. They are the first to communicate the faith to their children and to educate them by word and example for the Christian and apostolic life.

1905): *AAS* 38 (1905), 65–67; Pius XII, *Allocution to the Faithful of the Parish of St. Saba* (Jan. 11, 1953): *Discourses and Radio Messages of His Holiness Pius XII,* 14 (1952–53), 449–454; John XXIII, *Allocution to the Clergy and Faithful of the Suburbicarian Diocese of Albano, Ad Arcem Gandulfi Habita* (Aug. 26, 1962): *AAS* 54 (1962), 656–660.

2. Cf. Leo XIII, *Allocution* (Jan. 28, 1894): Acts of Leo XIII, 14 (1894), 424–425.

3. Cf. Pius XII, *Allocution to Pastors, etc.* (Feb. 6, 1951): *Discourses and Radio Messages of His Holiness Pius XII,* 12 (1950–51), 437–443; 852: *ibid.,* 14 (1952–53), 5–10; *Allocution* (March 27, 1953): *ibid.,* 15 (1953–54), 27–35; *Allocution* (Feb. 28, 1954): *ibid.,* 585–590.

They prudently help them in the choice of their vocation and carefully promote any sacred vocation which they may discern in them.

It has always been the duty of Christian married partners, but today it is the greatest part of their apostolate, to manifest and prove by their own way of life the indissolubility and sacredness of the marriage bond, strenuously to affirm the right and duty of parents and guardians to educate children in a Christian manner, and to defend the dignity and lawful autonomy of the family. They and the rest of the faithful, therefore, should cooperate with men of good will to ensure the preservation of these rights in civil legislation and to make sure that governments give due attention to the needs of the family regarding housing, the education of children, working conditions, social security and taxes, and that in policy decisions affecting migrants their right to live together as a family should be safeguarded.[4]

This mission—to be the first and vital cell of society—the family has received from God. It will fulfill this mission if it appears as the domestic sanctuary of the Church by reason of the mutual affection of its members and the prayer that they offer to God in common, if the whole family makes itself a part of the liturgical worship of the Church, and if it provides active hospitality and promotes justice and other good works for the service of all the brethren in need. Among the various activities of the family apostolate may be enumerated the following: the adoption of abandoned infants, hospitality to strangers, assistance in the operation of schools, helpful advice and material assistance for adolescents, help to engaged couples in preparing themselves better for marriage, catechetical work, support of married couples and families involved in material and moral crises, help for the aged not only by providing them with the necessities of life but also by obtaining for them a fair share of the benefits of an expanding economy.

At all times and places but particularly in areas where the first seeds of the Gospel are being sown or where the Church is just beginning or is

---

4. Cf. Pius XI, Encyclical Letter *Casti Connubii* (Dec. 31, 1930): *AAS* 22 (1930), 554; Pius XII, *Radio Message* (Jan. 1, 1941): *AAS* 33 (1941), 203; *Radio Message to Delegates of the Convention of the Members of the International Union to Protect the Rights of Families* (Sept. 20, 1949): *AAS* 41 (1949), 552; *Radio Message* to *Heads of Families on Pilgrimage from France to Rome* (Sept. 18, 1951): *AAS* 43 (1951), 731, *Christmas Radio Message of 1952*: *AAS* 45 (1953), 41; John XXIII, Encyclical Letter *Mater et Magistra* (May 15, 1961): *AAS* 53 (1961), 429, 439.

involved in some serious difficulty, Christian families can give effective testimony to Christ before the world by remaining faithful to the Gospel and by providing a model of Christian marriage through their whole way of life.[5]

To facilitate the attainment of the goals of their apostolate, it can be useful for families to be brought together into groups.[6]

12. Young persons exert a very important influence in modern society.[7] There has been a radical change in the circumstances of their lives, their mental attitudes and their relationships with their own families. Frequently they move too quickly into a new social and economic status. While their social and even their political importance is growing from day to day, they seem to be unable to cope adequately with their new responsibilities.

Their heightened influence in society demands of them a proportionate apostolic activity, but their natural qualities also fit them for this activity. As they become more conscious of their own personalities, they are impelled by a zest for life and a ready eagerness to assume their own responsibility, and they yearn to play their part in social and cultural life. If this zeal is imbued with the spirit of Christ and is inspired by obedience and love for the Church, it can be expected to be very fruitful. They should become the first to carry on the apostolate directly to other young persons, concentrating their apostolic efforts within their own circle, according to the needs of the social environment in which they live.[8]

Adults ought to engage in such friendly discussion with young people that both age groups, overcoming the age barrier, may become better acquainted and share the special benefits each generation can offer the other. Adults should stimulate young persons first by good example to take part in the apostolate and, if the opportunity presents itself, by offering them effective advice and willing assistance. By the

---

5. Cf. Pius XII, Encyclical Letter *Evangelii Praecones* (June 2, 1951): *AAS* 43 (1951), 514.

6. Cf. Pius XII, *To Delegates to the Convention of Members of the International Union for the Defense of Family Rights* (Sept. 20, 1949): *AAS* 41 (1949), 552.

7. Cf. St. Pius X, *Allocution to Association of French Catholic Youth on Piety, Knowledge and Action* (Sept. 25, 1904): *AAS* 37 (1904–05), 296–300.

8. Cf. Pius XII, Letter *Dans Quelques Semaines* to Archbishop of Montreal, Canada, to be relayed to the Assemblies of Canadian Young Christian Workers (May 24, 1947): *AAS* 39 (1947), 257; *Radio Message to Young Christian Workers, Brussels* (Sept. 3, 1950): *AAS* 42 (1950), 640–641.

same token young people should cultivate toward adults respect and trust, and although they are naturally attracted to novelties, they should duly appreciate praiseworthy traditions.

13. The apostolate in the social milieu, that is, the effort to infuse a Christian spirit into the mentality, customs, laws and structures of the community in which one lives, is so much the duty and responsibility of the laity that it can never be performed properly by others. In this area the laity can exercise the apostolate of like toward like. It is here that they complement the testimony of life with the testimony of the word.[9] It is here, where they work or practice their profession, study, reside, spend their leisure time or have their companionship, that they are more capable of helping their brethren.

The laity fulfill this mission of the Church in the world especially by conforming their lives to their faith so that they become the light of the world as well as by practicing honesty in all their dealings so that they attract all to the love of the true and the good and finally to the Church and to Christ. They fulfill their mission also by fraternal charity which presses them to share in the living conditions, labors, sorrows and aspirations of their brethren with the result that the hearts of all about them are quietly prepared for the workings of saving grace. Another requisite for the accomplishment of their task is a full consciousness of their role in building up society, whereby they strive to perform their domestic, social and professional duties with such Christian generosity that their manner of acting should gradually penetrate the whole world of life and labor.

This apostolate should reach out to all wherever they may be encountered; it should not exclude any spiritual or temporal benefit which they have the ability to confer. True apostles, however, are not content with this activity alone but endeavor to announce Christ to their neighbors by means of the spoken word as well. For there are many persons who can hear the Gospel and recognize Christ only through the laity who live near them.

Children also have their own apostolic work to do. According to their ability, they are true living witnesses of Christ among their companions.

---

9. Cf. Pius XI, Encyclical Letter *Quadragesimo Anno* (May 15, 1931): *AAS* 23 (1931), 225–226.

14. A vast field for the apostolate has opened up on the national and international levels where the laity especially assist with their Christian wisdom. In loyalty to their country and in faithful fulfillment of their civic obligations, Catholics should feel themselves obliged to promote the true common good. Thus, they should make the weight of their opinion felt in order that the civil authority may act with justice and that legislation may conform to moral precepts and the common good. Catholics skilled in public affairs and adequately enlightened in faith and Christian doctrine should not refuse to administer public affairs since by doing this in a worthy manner they can both further the common good and at the same time prepare the way for the Gospel.

Catholics should try to cooperate with all men and women of good will to promote whatever is true, whatever just, whatever holy, whatever lovable (cf. Phil 4:8). They should hold discussions with them, treat them with prudence and courtesy, and initiate research on social and public practices which should be improved in line with the spirit of the Gospel.

Among the signs of our times, the irresistibly increasing sense of the solidarity of all peoples is especially noteworthy. It is a function of the lay apostolate sedulously to promote this awareness and to transform it into a sincere and genuine love of brotherhood. Furthermore, the laity should be aware of the international field and of the questions and solutions, doctrinal as well as practical, which arise in this field, with special reverence to developing nations.[10]

All who work in or give help to foreign nations must remember that relations among peoples should be a genuine fraternal exchange in which each party is at the same time a giver and a receiver. Travelers, whether their interest is international affairs, business or leisure, should remember that they are itinerant heralds of Christ wherever they go and should act accordingly.

---

10. Cf. John XXIII, Encyclical Letter *Mater et Magistra* (May 15, 1961): *AAS* 53 (1961), 448–450.

CHAPTER IV

THE VARIOUS FORMS OF THE APOSTOLATE

15. The laity can engage in their apostolic activity either as individuals or together as members of various groups or associations.

16. The individual apostolate, flowing generously from its source in a truly Christian life (cf. Jn 4:14), is the origin and condition of the whole lay apostolate, even of the organized type, and it admits of no substitute.

Regardless of status, all lay persons (including those who have no opportunity or possibility for collaboration in associations) are called to this type of apostolate and obliged to engage in it. This type of apostolate is useful at all times and places, but in certain circumstances it is the only one appropriate and feasible.

There are many forms of the apostolate whereby the laity build up the Church, sanctify the world and give it life in Christ. A particular form of the individual apostolate as well as a sign specially suited to our times is the testimony of the whole lay life arising from faith, hope and charity. It manifests Christ living in those who believe in him. Then by the apostolate of the spoken and written word, which is utterly necessary under certain circumstances, lay people announce Christ, explain and spread his teaching in accordance with one's status and ability, and faithfully profess it.

Furthermore, in collaborating as citizens of this world, in whatever pertains to the upbuilding and conducting of the temporal order, the laity must seek in the light of faith loftier motives of action in their family, professional, cultural and social life and make them known to others when the occasion arises. Doing this, they should be aware of the fact that they are cooperating with God the Creator, Redeemer and Sanctifier and are giving praise to him.

Finally, the laity should vivify their life with charity and express it as best they can in their works.

They should all remember that they can reach all men and contribute to the salvation of the whole world by public worship and prayer as well as by penance and voluntary acceptance of the labors and hardships of life whereby they become like the suffering Christ (cf. 2 Cor 4:10; Col 1:24).

17. There is a very urgent need for this individual apostolate in those regions where the freedom of the Church is seriously infringed. In these trying circumstances, the laity do what they can to take the place of priests, risking their freedom and sometimes their life to teach Christian doctrine to those around them, training them in a religious way of life and a Catholic way of thinking, leading them to receive the sacraments frequently and developing in them piety, especially Eucharistic devotion.[1] While the sacred synod heartily thanks God for continuing also in our times to raise up lay persons of heroic fortitude in the midst of persecutions, it embraces them with fatherly affection and gratitude.

The individual apostolate has a special field in areas where Catholics are few in number and widely dispersed. Here the laity who engage in the apostolate only as individuals, whether for the reasons already mentioned or for special reasons including those deriving also from their own professional activity, usefully gather into smaller groups for serious conversation without any more formal kind of establishment or organization, so that an indication of the community of the Church is always apparent to others as a true witness of love. In this way, by giving spiritual help to one another through friendship and the communicating of the benefit of their experience, they are trained to overcome the disadvantages of an excessively isolated life and activity and to make their apostolate more productive.

18. The faithful are called to engage in the apostolate as individuals in the varying circumstances of their life. They should remember, nevertheless, that man is naturally social and that it has pleased God to unite those who believe in Christ into the People of God (cf. 1 Pt 2:5–10) and into one body (cf. 1 Cor 12:12). The group apostolate of Christian believers then happily corresponds to a human and Christian need and at the same time signifies the communion and unity of the Church in Christ, who said, "Where two or three are gathered together in my name, there am I in the midst of them" (Mt 18:20).

---

1. Cf. Pius XII, *Allocution to the First Convention of Laymen Representing All Nations on the Promotion of the Apostolate* (Oct. 15, 1951): *AAS* 43 (1951), 788.

For this reason, the faithful should participate in the apostolate by way of united effort.[2] They should be apostles both in their family communities and in their parishes and dioceses, which themselves express the community nature of the apostolate, as well as in the informal groups which they decide to form among themselves.

The group apostolate is very important also because the apostolate must often be performed by way of common activity in both the Church communities and the various spheres. For the associations established for carrying on the apostolate in common sustain their members, form them for the apostolate, and rightly organize and regulate their apostolic work so that much better results can be expected than if each member were to act on his own.

In the present circumstances, it is quite necessary that in the area of lay activity the united and organized form of the apostolate be strengthened. In fact, only the pooling of resources is capable of fully achieving all the aims of the modern apostolate and firmly protecting its interests.[3] Here it is important that the apostolate encompass even the common attitudes and social conditions of those for whom it is designed. Otherwise, those engaged in the apostolate are often unable to bear up under the pressure of public opinion or of social institutions.

19. There is a great variety of associations in the apostolate.[4] Some set before themselves the broad apostolic purpose of the Church; others aim to evangelize and sanctify in a special way. Some work to infuse a Christian spirit into the temporal order; others bear witness to Christ in a special way through works of mercy and charity.

Among these associations, those which promote and encourage closer unity between the concrete life of the members and their faith must be given primary consideration. Associations are not ends unto themselves; rather, they should serve the mission of the Church to the world. Their apostolic dynamism depends on their conformity with the goals of the Church as well as on the Christian witness and evangelical spirit of every member and of the whole association.

---

2. Cf. Pius XII, *Allocution to the First Convention of Laymen Representing All Nations on the Promotion of the Apostolate* (Oct. 15, 1951): *AAS* 43 (1951), 787–788.

3. Cf. Pius XII, Encyclical Letter *Le Pelerinage de Lourdes* (July 2, 1957): *AAS* 49 (1957), 615.

4. Cf. Pius XII, *Allocution to the Assembly of the International Federation of Catholic Men* (Dec. 8, 1956): *AAS* 49 (1957), 26–27

Now, in view of the progress of social institutions and the fast-moving pace of modern society, the global nature of the Church's mission requires that apostolic enterprises of Catholics should more and more develop organized forms in the international sphere. Catholic international organizations will more effectively achieve their purpose if the groups comprising them, as well as their members, are more closely united to these international organizations.

Maintaining the proper relationship to Church authorities,[5] the laity have the right to found and control such associations[6] and to join those already existing. Yet the dispersion of efforts must be avoided. This happens when new associations and projects are promoted without a sufficient reason, or if antiquated associations or methods are retained beyond their period of usefulness. Nor is it always fitting to transfer indiscriminately forms of the apostolates that have been used in one nation to other nations.[7]

20. Many decades ago the laity in many nations began to dedicate themselves increasingly to the apostolate. They grouped themselves into various kinds of activities and societies which, while maintaining a closer union with the hierarchy, pursued and continue to pursue goals which are properly apostolic. Of these associations, or even among similar and older institutions, those are specially noteworthy which followed different methods of operation and yet produced excellent results for Christ's kingdom. These societies were deservedly recommended and promoted by the Popes and many bishops, from whom they received the title of "Catholic Action" and were often described as the collaboration of the laity in the apostolate of the hierarchy.[8]

Whether these forms of the apostolate have the name of "Catholic Action" or some other title, they exercise an apostolate of great value for our times and consist in the combination and simultaneous possession of the following characteristics:

---

5. Cf. below, ch. 5, no. 24.

6. Cf. Sacred Congregation of the Council, Decree *Concerning the Dissolution of the Corrientes Diocese in Argentina* (Nov. 13, 1920): *AAS* 13 (1921), 139.

7. Cf. John XXIII, Encyclical Letter *Princeps Pastorum* (Dec. 10, 1959): *AAS* 51 (1959), 856.

8. Cf. Pius XI, Letter *Quae Nobis* to Cardinal Bertram (Nov. 13, 1928): *AAS* 20 (1928), 385. Cf. also Pius XII, *Allocution to Italian Catholic Action* (Sept. 4, 1940): *AAS* 32 (1940), 362.

a) The immediate aim of organizations of this kind is the Church's apostolic aim, that is, the evangelization and sanctification of men and the formation of a Christian conscience among them so that they can infuse the spirit of the Gospel into various communities and departments of life.

b) Cooperating with the hierarchy in their own way, the laity contribute the benefit of their experience to, and assume responsibility for, the direction of these organizations, the consideration of the conditions in which the pastoral activity of the Church is to be conducted, and the elaboration and execution of the plan of things to be done.

c) The laity act together in the manner of an organic body so that the community of the Church is more fittingly symbolized and the apostolate rendered more effective.

d) Whether they offer themselves spontaneously or are invited to action and direct cooperation with the apostolate of the hierarchy, the laity function under the higher direction of the hierarchy itself, and the latter can sanction this cooperation by an explicit mandate.

Organizations in which, in the opinion of the hierarchy, the ensemble of these characteristics is realized, must be considered to be Catholic Action even though they take on various forms and titles because of the needs of different regions and peoples.

The most holy Council earnestly recommends these associations, which surely answer the needs of the apostolate of the Church among many peoples and countries, and invites the clergy and laity working in them to develop the above-mentioned characteristics to an ever greater degree and to cooperate at all times with all other forms of the apostolate in a fraternal manner in the Church.

21. All associations of the apostolate must be given due appreciation. Those, however, which the hierarchy have praised or recommended as responsive to the needs of time and place, or have ordered to be established as particularly urgent, must be held in highest esteem by priests, religious and laity and promoted according to each one's ability. Among these associations, moreover, international associations or groups of Catholics must be specially appreciated at the present time.

22. Deserving of special honor and commendation in the Church are those lay people, single or married, who devote themselves with professional experience, either permanently or temporarily, to the service of associations and their activities. There is a source of great joy for the

Church in the fact that there is a daily increase in the number of lay persons who offer their personal service to apostolic associations and activities, either within the limits of their own nation or in the international field or especially in Catholic mission communities and in regions where the Church has only recently been implanted.

The pastors of the Church should gladly and gratefully welcome these lay persons and make sure that the demands of justice, equity and charity relative to their status be satisfied to the fullest extent, particularly as regards proper support for them and their families. They should also take care to provide for these lay people the necessary formation, spiritual consolation and incentive.

CHAPTER V

EXTERNAL RELATIONSHIPS

23. Whether the lay apostolate is exercised by the faithful as individuals or as members of organizations, it should be incorporated into the apostolate of the whole Church according to a right system of relationships. Indeed, union with those whom the Holy Spirit has assigned to rule his Church (cf. Acts 20:28) is an essential element of the Christian apostolate. No less necessary is cooperation among various projects of the apostolate which must be suitably directed by the hierarchy.

Indeed, the spirit of unity should be promoted in order that fraternal charity may be resplendent in the whole apostolate of the Church, common goals may be attained and destructive rivalries avoided. For this there is need for mutual esteem among all the forms of the apostolate in the Church and, with due respect for the particular character of each organization, proper coordination.[1] This is most fitting since a particular activity in the Church requires harmony and apostolic cooperation on the part of both branches of the clergy, the religious and the laity.

24. The hierarchy should promote the apostolate of the laity, provide it with spiritual principles and support, direct the conduct of this apostolate to the common good of the Church and attend to the preservation of doctrine and order.

Indeed, the lay apostolate admits of different types of relationships with the hierarchy in accordance with the various forms and objects of this apostolate. For in the Church there are many apostolic undertakings which are established by the free choice of the laity and regulated by their prudent judgment. The mission of the Church can be better accom-

---

1. Cf. Pius XI, Encyclical Letter *Quamvis Nostra* (April 30, 1936): *AAS* 28 (1936), 160–161.

plished in certain circumstances by undertakings of this kind, and therefore they are frequently praised or recommended by the hierarchy.[2] No project, however, may claim the name "Catholic" unless it has obtained the consent of the lawful Church authority.

Certain forms of the apostolate of the laity are given explicit recognition by the hierarchy, though in various ways.

Because of the demands of the common good of the Church, moreover, ecclesiastical authority can select and promote in a particular way some of the apostolic associations and projects which have an immediately spiritual purpose, thereby assuming in them a special responsibility. Thus, making various dispositions of the apostolate according to circumstances, the hierarchy joins some particular form of it more closely with its own apostolic function. Yet the proper nature and distinctiveness of each apostolate must be preserved, and the laity must not be deprived of the possibility of acting on their own accord. In various Church documents this procedure of the hierarchy is called a mandate.

Finally, the hierarchy entrusts to the laity certain functions which are more closely connected with pastoral duties, such as the teaching of Christian doctrine, certain liturgical actions and the care of souls. By virtue of this mission, the laity are fully subject to higher ecclesiastical control in the performance of this work.

As regards works and institutions in the temporal order, the role of the ecclesiastical hierarchy is to teach and authentically interpret the moral principles to be followed in temporal affairs. Furthermore, they have the right to judge, after careful consideration of all related matters and consultation with experts, whether or not such works and institutions conform to moral principles, and the right to decide what is required for the protection and promotion of values of the supernatural order.

25. Bishops, pastors of parishes and other priests of both branches of the clergy should keep in mind that the right and duty to exercise this apostolate is common to all the faithful, both clergy and laity, and that the laity also have their own roles in building up the Church.[3] For this

---

2. Cf. Sacred Congregation of the Council, Decree *Concerning the Dissolution of the Corrientes Diocese in Argentina* (Nov. 13, 1920): *AAS* 13 (1921), 137–140.

3. Cf. Pius XII, *Allocution to the Second Convention of Laymen Representing All Nations on the Promotion of the Apostolate* (Oct. 5, 1957): *AAS* 49 (1957), 927.

reason they should work fraternally with the laity in and for the Church and take special care of the lay persons in these apostolic works.[4]

Special care should be taken to select priests who are capable of promoting particular forms of the apostolate of the laity and are properly trained.[5] Those who are engaged in this ministry represent the hierarchy in their pastoral activity by virtue of the mission they receive from the hierarchy. Always adhering faithfully to the spirit and teaching of the Church, they should promote proper relations between laity and hierarchy. They should devote themselves to nourishing the spiritual life and an apostolic attitude in the Catholic societies entrusted to them; they should contribute their wise counsel to the apostolic activity of these associations and promote their undertakings. Through continuous dialogue with the laity, these priests should carefully investigate which forms make apostolic activity more fruitful. They should promote the spirit of unity within the association as well as between it and others.

Finally, in keeping with the spirit and norms of their societies, religious brothers and sisters should value the apostolic works of the laity and willingly devote themselves to promoting lay enterprises.[6] They should also strive to support, uphold and fulfill priestly functions.

26. In dioceses, insofar as possible, there should be councils which assist the apostolic work of the Church either in the field of evangelization and sanctification or in the charitable, social or other spheres, and here it is fitting that the clergy and religious should cooperate with the laity. While preserving the proper character and autonomy of each organization, these councils will be able to promote the mutual coordination of various lay associations and enterprises.[7]

Councils of this type should be established as far as possible also on the parochial, interparochial and interdiocesan level as well as in the national or international sphere.[8]

---

4. Cf. Second Vatican Ecumenical Council, Dogmatic Constitution on the Church *Lumen Gentium, 37: AAS* 57 (1965), 442–443.

5. Cf. Pius XII, Apostolic Exhortation *Menti Nostrae* (Sept. 23 1950): *AAS* 42 (1950), 660.

6. Cf. Second Vatican Ecumenical Council, Decree on the Adaptation and Renewal of Religious Life *Perfectae Caritatis, 8.*

7. Cf. Benedict XIV, *On the Diocesan Synod,* I, 3, ch. 9, no. 7.

8. Cf. Pius XI, Encyclical Letter *Quamvis Nostra* (April 30, 1936): *AAS* 28 (1936), 160–161.

A special secretariat, moreover, should be established at the Holy See for the service and promotion of the lay apostolate. It can serve as a well-equipped center for communicating information about the various apostolic programs of the laity, promoting research into modern problems arising in this field, and assisting the hierarchy and laity in their apostolic works with its advice. The various movements and projects of the apostolate of the laity throughout the world should also be represented in this secretariat, and here clergy and religious also are to cooperate with the laity.

27. The quasi-common heritage of the Gospel and the common duty of Christian witness resulting from it recommend and frequently require the cooperation of Catholics with other Christians, on the part of individuals and communities within the Church, either in activities or in associations, in the national or international field.[9]

Likewise, common human values not infrequently call for cooperation between Christians pursuing apostolic aims and those who do not profess Christ's name but acknowledge these values.

By this dynamic and prudent cooperation,[10] which is of special importance in temporal activities, the laity bear witness to Christ, the Savior of the world, as well as to the unity of the human family.

---

9. Cf. John XXIII, Encyclical Letter *Mater et Magistra* (May 15, 1961): *AAS* 53 (1961), 456–457; cf. Second Vatican Ecumenical Council, Decree on Ecumenism *Unitatis Redintegratio,* 12: *AAS* 57 (1965), 99–100.

10. Cf. Second Vatican Ecumenical Council, Decree on Ecumenism *Unitatis Redintegratio,* 12: *AAS* 57 (1965), 100. Cf. also Second Vatican Ecumenical Council, Dogmatic Constitution on the Church *Lumen Gentium,* 15: *AAS* 57 (1965), 19–20.

Chapter VI

FORMATION FOR THE APOSTOLATE

28. The apostolate can attain its maximum effectiveness only through a diversified and thorough formation. This is demanded not only by the continuous spiritual and doctrinal progress of the lay person himself but also by the accommodation of his activity to circumstances varying according to the affairs, persons and duties involved. This formation for the apostolate should rest upon those bases which have been stated and proclaimed by this most holy Council in other documents.[1] In addition to the formation which is common for all Christians, many forms of the apostolate demand also a specific and particular formation because of the variety of persons and circumstances.

29. Since the laity share in their own way in the mission of the Church, their apostolic formation is specially characterized by the distinctively secular and particular quality of the lay state and by its own form of the spiritual life.

The formation for the apostolate presupposes a certain human and well-rounded formation adapted to the natural abilities and conditions of each lay person. Well-informed about the modern world, the lay person should be a member of his own community and adjusted to its culture.

However, the lay person should learn especially how to perform the mission of Christ and the Church by basing his life on belief in the divine mystery of creation and redemption and by being sensitive to the movement of the Holy Spirit who gives life to the People of God and who urges all to love God the Father as well as the world and men in

---

1. Cf. Second Vatican Ecumenical Council, Dogmatic Constitution on the Church *Lumen Gentium,* chs. 2, 4 and 5: *AAS* 57 (1965), 12–21, 37–49; cf. also Second Vatican Ecumenical Council, Decree on Ecumenism *Unitatis Redintegratio,* 4, 6, 7, 12: *AAS* 57 (1965), 94, 96–97, 99–100; cf. also above, no. 4.

him. This formation should be deemed the basis and condition for every successful apostolate.

In addition to spiritual formation, a solid doctrinal instruction in theology, ethics and philosophy adjusted to differences of age, status and natural talents, is required. The importance of general culture along with practical and technical formation should also be kept in mind.

To cultivate good human relations, truly human values must be fostered, especially the art of living fraternally and cooperating with others and of striking up friendly conversation with them.

Since formation for the apostolate cannot consist in merely theoretical instruction, from the beginning of their formation the laity should gradually and prudently learn how to view, judge and do all things in the light of faith, as well as to develop and improve themselves along with others through doing, thereby entering into active service to the Church.[2] This formation, always in need of improvement because of the increasing maturity of the human person and the proliferation of problems, requires an ever-deeper knowledge and planned activity. In the fulfillment of all the demands of formation, the unity and integrity of the human person must be kept in mind at all times so that his harmony and balance may be safeguarded and enhanced.

In this way the lay person engages himself wholly and actively in the reality of the temporal order and effectively assumes his role in conducting the affairs of this order. At the same time, as a living member and witness of the Church, he renders the Church present and active in the midst of temporal affairs.[3]

30. The training for the apostolate should start with the children's earliest education. In a special way, however, adolescents and young persons should be initiated into the apostolate and imbued with its spirit. This formation must be perfected throughout their whole life in keeping with the demands of new responsibilities. It is evident, therefore, that those who have the obligation to provide a Christian education also have the duty of providing formation for the apostolate.

---

2. Cf. Pius XII, *Allocution to the First International Boy Scouts Congress* (June 6, 1952): *AAS* 44 (1952), 579–580; John XXIII, Encyclical Letter *Mater et Magistra* (May 15, 1961): *AAS* 53 (1961), 456.

3. Cf. Second Vatican Ecumenical Council, Dogmatic Constitution on the Church *Lumen Gentium,* 33: *AAS* 57 (1965), 39.

In the family parents have the task of training their children from childhood on to recognize God's love for all men. By example especially they should teach them little by little to be solicitous for the material and spiritual needs of their neighbor. The whole family in its common life, then, should be a sort of apprenticeship for the apostolate. Children must be educated, too, in such fashion that transcending the family circle, they may open their minds to both ecclesiastical and temporal communities. They should be so involved in the local community of the parish that they will acquire a consciousness of being living and active members of the People of God. Priests should focus their attention on the formation of the laity for the apostolate in their catechetics, their ministry of the word, their direction of souls and in their other pastoral services.

Schools, colleges, and other Catholic educational institutions also have the duty to develop a Catholic sense and apostolic activity in young persons. If young people lack this formation either because they do not attend these schools or because of any other reason, all the more should parents, pastors of souls, and apostolic organizations attend to it. Teachers and educators on the other hand, who carry on a distinguished form of the apostolate of the laity by their vocation and office, should be equipped with that learning and pedagogical skill that are needed for imparting such education effectively.

Likewise, lay groups and associations dedicated to the apostolate or other supernatural goals, should carefully and assiduously promote formation for the apostolate in keeping with their purpose and condition.[4] Frequently these groups are the ordinary vehicle for harmonious formation for the apostolate inasmuch as they provide doctrinal, spiritual and practical formation. Their members meet in small groups with their associates or friends, examine the methods and results of their apostolic activity, and compare their daily way of life with the Gospel.

Formation of this type must be so organized that it takes into account the whole lay apostolate, which must be carried on not only among the organized groups themselves but also in all circumstances throughout one's whole life, especially one's professional and social life. Indeed, everyone should diligently prepare himself for the apos-

---

4. Cf. John XXIII, Encyclical Letter *Mater et Magistra* (May 15, 1961): *AAS* 53 (1961), 455.

tolate, this preparation being the more urgent in adulthood. For the advance of age brings with it a more open mind, enabling each person to detect more readily the talents with which God has enriched his soul and to exercise more effectively those charisms which the Holy Spirit has bestowed on him for the good of his brethren.

31. Various types of the apostolate demand also a specially suitable formation.

a) In regard to the apostolate for evangelizing and sanctifying men, the laity must be specially formed to engage in conversation with others, believers or non-believers, in order to manifest Christ's message to all men.[5]

Since in our times different forms of materialism are spread far and wide even among Catholics, the laity should not only learn doctrine more diligently, especially those main points which are the subjects of controversy, but should also exhibit the witness of an evangelical life in contrast to all forms of materialism.

b) In regard to the Christian renewal of the temporal order, the laity should be instructed in the true meaning and value of temporal things, both in themselves and in relation to all the aims of the human person. They should be trained in the right use of things and the organization of institutions, attentive always to the common good in line with the principles of the moral and social teaching of the Church. Laymen should above all learn the principles and conclusions of the social doctrine so as to become capable of working for the development of this doctrine to the best of their ability and of rightly applying these same principles and conclusions to individual cases.[6]

c) Since the works of charity and mercy express the most striking testimony of the Christian life, apostolic formation should lead also to the performance of these works so that the faithful may learn from childhood on to have compassion for their brethren and to be generous in helping those in need.[7]

---

5. Cf. Pius XII, Encyclical Letter *Sertum Laetitiae* (Nov. 1, 1939): *AAS* 31 (1939), 653–654; cf. Pius XII, *To Graduates of Italian Catholic Action* (May 24, 1953).

6. Cf. Pius XII, *Allocution to the Universal Congress of the World Federation of Young Catholic Women* (April 18, 1952): *AAS* 42 (1952), 414–419; cf. Pius XII, *Allocution to the Christian Association of Italian Workers* (May 1, 1955): *AAS* 47 (1955), 403–404.

7. Cf. Pius XII, *To Delegates of the Assembly of Charity Associations* (April 27,1952), 470–471.

32. There are many aids for lay persons devoted to the apostolate, namely, study sessions, congresses, periods of recollection, spiritual exercises, frequent meetings, conferences, books and periodicals directed toward the acquisition of a deeper knowledge of Sacred Scripture and Catholic doctrine, the nourishment of spiritual life, the discernment of world conditions, and the discovery and development of suitable methods.[8]

These aids in formation take into consideration the various types of the apostolate in the milieu where it is exercised.

For this purpose also centers or higher institutes have been erected, and they have already proved highly successful.

The most holy Council rejoices over projects of this kind which are already flourishing in certain areas, and it desires that they may be promoted also in other areas where they may be needed. Furthermore, centers of documentation and study not only in theology but also in anthropology, psychology, sociology and methodology should be established for all fields of the apostolate for the better development of the natural capacities of the laity—men and women, young persons and adults.

---

8. Cf. John XXIII, Encyclical Letter *Mater et Magistra* (May 15, 1961): *AAS* 53 (1961), 454.

EXHORTATION

33. The most holy Council, then, earnestly entreats all the laity in the Lord to answer gladly, nobly and promptly the more urgent invitation of Christ in this hour, and the impulse of the Holy Spirit. Younger persons should feel that this call has been directed to them especially and they should respond to it eagerly and generously. Through this holy synod, the Lord renews his invitation to all the laity to come closer to him every day, recognizing that what is his is also their own (Phil 2:5), to associate themselves with him in his saving mission. Once again he sends them into every town and place where he will come (cf. Lk 10:1) so that they may show that they are co-workers in the various forms and modes of the one apostolate of the Church, which must be constantly adapted to the new needs of our times. Ever productive as they should be in the work of the Lord, they know that their labor in him is not in vain (cf. 1 Cor 15:58).

Given in Rome at St. Peter's, November 18, 1965

DECLARATION ON RELIGIOUS FREEDOM

Dignitatis Humanae

Promulgated by
His Holiness Pope Paul VI
On December 7, 1965

INTRODUCTION

The *Declaration on Religious Freedom (DH)* is a concrete example of a principle contained in *Gaudium et Spes*. The Church "goes forward together with humanity and experiences the same earthly lot which the world does" in such a way that "the earthly and the heavenly city penetrate each other." The Church believes that this is according to the wisdom of God, and so views it with the eyes of faith. In that light the Church is convinced that it "can be abundantly and variously helped by the world in the matter of preparing the ground for the Gospel" (*GS* 40).

The declaration states that the growing consciousness of people today with regard to their own dignity helps the Church in its mission. *DH* is the Church's response to this "sign of the times" in view of making its own mission more effective. This response has two basic elements. First, it affirms the harmony between the Church's understanding of human nature and the act of faith. Second, it involves the Church's claim to the freedom to pursue its mission. The growing awareness of people today in regard to their dignity has led to an increased emphasis on their need to be free from coercion.

Though elsewhere the Church credits itself with having a "healing and elevating impact on the dignity of the person," thus contributing "greatly toward making the family of man and its history more human" (*GS* 40), such credit is not expressed in *DH*. At one point *DH* confesses the failure of the Church's members to live up to the doctrine of religious freedom. "In the life of the People of God, as it has made its pilgrim way through the vicissitudes of human history, there has at times appeared a way of acting that was hardly in accord with the spirit of the Gospel, or even opposed to it" (*DH* 12).

Vatican II was a pastoral council of renewal based on conversion (cf. *ES*), and it openly admitted the need for constant penance and purification (cf. *LG* 8). This text of *DH* acknowledges actual historical failures. The Church appears in a humble state as the Council presents a doctrine about which it has great conviction, but which its members have not always lived up to.

Pope John Paul II has inserted this "spirit of repentance" into a general schema for preparation for the third millennium that involves examination of conscience and conversion.

> Another painful chapter of history to which the sons and daughters of the Church must return with a spirit of repentance is that of the acquiescence given, especially in certain centuries, to intolerance and even the use of violence in the service of truth.
>
> It is true that an accurate historical judgment cannot prescind from careful study of the cultural conditioning of the times, as a result of which many people may have held in good faith that an authentic witness to the truth could include suppressing the opinions of others or at least paying no attention to them. Many factors frequently converged to create assumptions which justified intolerance and fostered an emotional climate from which only great spirits, truly free and filled with God, were in some way able to break free. Yet the consideration of mitigating factors does not exonerate the Church from the obligation to express profound regret for the weaknesses of so many of her sons and daughters who sullied her face, preventing her from fully mirroring the image of her crucified Lord, the supreme witness of patient love and of humble meekness. From these painful moments of the past a lesson can be drawn for the future, leading all Christians to adhere fully to the sublime principle stated by the Council: "The truth cannot impose itself except by virtue of its own truth, as it wins over the mind with both gentleness and power" (*TMA* 35, quoting *DH* 1).

The doctrine of religious freedom has been held "throughout the ages" and "has always stood firm." Yet now, assisted by this great sign of the times—an increased awareness of human dignity and the right to religious freedom—the Church can articulate it more clearly.

We might say that this declaration reveals the Church's profound confidence in what it believes about itself. The Church professes the faith that there is one true religion and only one Church of Christ. Based on this faith, the Church claims a "sacred freedom" "because the only-begotten Son endowed with it the Church which he purchased with his blood" (*DH* 13). However, the Church cannot expect those outside the

Catholic faith to accept this. So it takes its place among the religions of the world, claiming for itself the rights inherent in human nature and the creative plan of God which are common to all.

The declaration affirms: "The freedom of the Church is the fundamental principle in what concerns the relations between the Church and governments and the whole civil order" (*DH* 13). The Church does not trust in any status which might accrue to it because of unique historical circumstances. Instead, it seeks to ground the freedom it needs in a reality which is not subject to historical and cultural vicissitudes. Although concordats and agreements with political authorities may continue to play an important role, the foundation of the Church's freedom is not established by human agreement. Rather, it is grounded in the nature and dignity of the human person (cf. *DH* 2). Since human beings are social by nature, this right to freedom from coercion extends to religious communities as well (cf. *DH* 4). As Pope John Paul II has stated:

> I appeal in the name of all believers throughout the world to those on whom the organization of social and public life in some way depends, earnestly requesting them to respect the rights of religion and of the Church's activity. No privilege is asked for, but only respect for an elementary right. Actuation of this right is one of the fundamental tests of man's authentic progress in any regime, in any society, system or milieu (*RH* 17).

The declaration is constructed on a series of correlative terms: truth-conscience, dignity-freedom, rights-duties. Especially in article three, *DH* is one of three main texts which develop the Council's teaching on conscience. *Gaudium et Spes* 16 gives conscience its anthropological context in terms of human dignity. *Lumen Gentium* 16 speaks of conscience in terms of God's universal salvific will, the Church's role in this salvation and the invitation extended to everyone to belong to the Church. *DH* treats conscience as the key element of the Church's understanding of rights and duties which determine fundamental relationships between individuals and God, among individuals themselves, and between individuals and groups, such as governments and other groups.

This declaration is based on the dignity of the human person and the consequent rights of conscience. *DH* states that "the exercise of religion, of its very nature, consists before all else in those internal, voluntary and free acts whereby man sets the course of his life directly toward God" (*DH* 3). These are precisely acts of conscience. Seeking the truth honestly, assenting to it and following it without compromise constitutes the highest sort of human goodness. It is the greatest testimony and affirmation of human dignity.

Human dignity is defined in terms of the human person's ability to transcend himself and know and love God (cf. *GS* 19). When the declaration teaches that the right to religious freedom "has its foundation in the very dignity of the human person" (*DH* 2), it teaches that no power on earth can interfere with the person's duty to seek God in seeking the truth. By his nature, the human person is made for the truth. In seeking the truth he fulfills himself and is led into a right relationship with God. This is why *DH* can say: "In all his activity a man is bound to follow his conscience, in order that he may come to God, the end and purpose of life" (*DH* 3).

This declaration lays the foundation of what could be called the Council's theocentric anthropology, or conversely, anthropocentric theology. It does this by defining human dignity in terms of communion with God, and defining conscience in terms of seeking the truth which leads to God. John Paul II commented on this in his encyclical *Redemptor Hominis:*

> The *Declaration on Religious Freedom* shows us convincingly that, when Christ and, after him, his apostles proclaimed the truth that comes not from men but from God…they preserved, while acting with their full force of spirit, a deep esteem for man, for his intellect, his will, his conscience and his freedom. Thus, the human person's dignity itself becomes part of the content of that proclamation, being included not necessarily in words but by an attitude toward it. This attitude seems to fit the special needs of our times. Since man's true freedom is not found in everything that the various systems and individuals see and propagate as freedom, the Church, because of her divine mission, becomes all the more the guardian of this freedom, which is the condition and basis for the human person's true dignity (*RH* 12).

The declaration pairs duties with rights, for duties are prior to rights. "Every man has the duty, and therefore the right, to seek the truth" (*DH* 3). The duty is to the truth and to God, while the rights concern relations among people. The right to religious freedom is a necessary means for persons "to fulfill their duty to worship God" (*DH* 1). It is the right to be free of coercion that would interfere with seeking religious truth and expressing and communicating it. It means not being forced to perform actions contrary to one's religious beliefs and convictions.

The declaration distinguishes between the right of religious freedom and its exercise. The right is absolute, but it must be exercised "within due limits" (*DH* 2). This means that it cannot be exercised in a way that threatens the "just public order" (*DH* 2, 3, 4). The just public order, or the common good, embraces the personal or private good of each individual in such a way that the two cannot be placed in opposition.

Religious freedom does not result in individualism which would exempt persons from fulfilling their duties as citizens. These duties include the obligation in conscience to obey lawful authority exercised in harmony with God's laws (cf. *GS* 74). Those who seek religious truth make good citizens because they strive to live according to God's plan. However, "society has the right to defend itself against possible abuses committed on the pretext of freedom of religion" (*DH* 7). If individuals cannot use religious freedom as a pretext, neither can government use its responsibility for the common good as a pretext to suppress the right to religious freedom (cf. *DH* 7).

The right to religious freedom is a means to the goal of human fulfillment, which is directed to two ends. The first and the highest is the truth which is God himself. The other, which is subordinate to the first, is the just order of society. Though the declaration does not use this vocabulary, it finds a confirmation of this in Acts 5:29: "It is necessary to obey God rather than men" (*DH* 11). It immediately adds that obeying God first can call forth martyrs when governments attempt to coerce people to act contrary to the will of God.

This shows the seriousness of the duty to seek religious truth, to accept it and to live it out. Religious freedom involves respecting the human person's rights of conscience in pursuing religious truth. It does not mean that one is free of the moral obligation to seek and accept the truth.

The theme of witness is closely related to this. Witness is a form of communication which testifies to the truth while respecting others' freedom to accept it or not. Witness allows the truth to work in virtue of its own truth (cf. *DH* 1; *CCC* 559), and makes the goodness of the truth shine out through fidelity to it under trial. Martyrs give the ultimate witness.

Respect for human freedom marks the dialogue of salvation in which God has revealed himself. As in all things, Jesus is the model of this respect for the condition of faith itself. To the points made in the declaration, we might add that Jesus, who is eternal and divine love incarnate, watched as the rich young man walked away sad (cf. Mt 19:22), and as many of his disciples left him (cf. Jn 6:66). Clearly he respected human freedom and did not coerce people; even more, he died for all.

The Council's general solicitude for the poor is expressed in article four which labels coercion as especially reprehensible when it involves taking advantage of the poor or uneducated. This can be compared to the call in *Ad Gentes* 13 to test the motives of converts to the faith. Not only does the Church foreswear using any manipulation in its work, but it makes every effort to confirm the necessary freedom on the part of catechumens.

In many respects, *DH* is a landmark document that shows a significant development in the Church's attitude toward the question of religious freedom. It recognizes the reality of the modern world, in which people of varying religious beliefs live together. Besides this, the growing awareness of the dignity of the human person has fostered a climate in which religious liberty is a fundamental concern of the Church and society.

TOPICAL OUTLINE

1. General principles concerning religious freedom

    A. Introduction

        1. Increased awareness of the dignity of the person

        2. All are bound to seek the truth

        3. Role of the Church (1)

    B. The right to religious freedom

        1. Dignity of the person and duty to seek the truth (2)

        2. Role of conscience

        3. Governments cannot interfere (3)

        4. Rights of religious communities (4)

        5. Rights of the family (5)

        6. Governments must protect religious freedom (6)

        7. Religious freedom requires responsibility (7–8)

2. Religious freedom and divine revelation

    A. Dignity of the person

        1. Religious freedom is rooted in human dignity (9)

        2. The act of faith is a free act (10)

    B. The Church and freedom

        1. The example of Jesus and the apostles (11)

        2. The Church upholds religious freedom despite its failures (12)

        3. The Church requires freedom to act (13)

        4. The Church as the teacher of truth (14)

        5. Plea that freedom be respected by all (15)

DECLARATION ON RELIGIOUS FREEDOM

Dignitatis Humanae

ON THE RIGHT OF THE PERSON AND OF COMMUNITIES TO SOCIAL AND CIVIL FREEDOM IN MATTERS RELIGIOUS

1. A sense of the dignity of the human person has been impressing itself more and more deeply on the consciousness of contemporary man,[1] and the demand is increasingly made that men should act on their own judgment, enjoying and making use of a responsible freedom, not driven by coercion but motivated by a sense of duty. The demand is likewise made that constitutional limits should be set to the powers of government, in order that there may be no encroachment on the rightful freedom of the person and of associations. This demand for freedom in human society chiefly regards the quest for the values proper to the human spirit. It regards, in the first place, the free exercise of religion in society. This Vatican Council takes careful note of these desires in the minds of men. It proposes to declare them to be greatly in accord with truth and justice. To this end, it searches into the sacred Tradition and doctrine of the Church—the treasury out of which the Church continually brings forth new things that are in harmony with the things that are old.

---

1. Cf. John XXIII, Encyclical Letter *Pacem in Terris* (April 11, 1963): *AAS* 55 (1963), 279, 265; Pius XII, *Radio Message* (Dec. 24, 1944): *AAS* 37 (1945), 14.

First, the Council professes its belief that God himself has made known to mankind the way in which men are to serve him, and thus be saved in Christ and come to blessedness. We believe that this one true religion subsists in the Catholic and Apostolic Church, to which the Lord Jesus committed the duty of spreading it abroad among all men. Thus he spoke to the apostles: "Go, therefore, and make disciples of all nations, baptizing them in the name of the Father and of the Son and of the Holy Spirit, teaching them to observe all things whatsoever I have enjoined upon you" (Mt 28:19–20). On their part, all men are bound to seek the truth, especially in what concerns God and his Church, and to embrace the truth they come to know, and to hold fast to it.

This Vatican Council likewise professes its belief that it is upon the human conscience that these obligations fall and exert their binding force. The truth cannot impose itself except by virtue of its own truth, as it makes its entrance into the mind at once quietly and with power.

Religious freedom, in turn, which men demand as necessary to fulfill their duty to worship God, has to do with immunity from coercion in civil society. Therefore, it leaves untouched traditional Catholic doctrine on the moral duty of men and societies toward the true religion and toward the one Church of Christ.

Over and above all this, the Council intends to develop the doctrine of recent popes on the inviolable rights of the human person and the constitutional order of society.

2. This Vatican Council declares that the human person has a right to religious freedom. This freedom means that all men are to be immune from coercion on the part of individuals or of social groups and of any human power, in such wise that no one is to be forced to act in a manner contrary to his own beliefs, whether privately or publicly, whether alone or in association with others, within due limits.

The Council further declares that the right to religious freedom has its foundation in the very dignity of the human person, as this dignity is known through the revealed Word of God and by reason itself.[2] This

---

2. Cf. John XXIII, Encyclical Letter *Pacem in Terris* (April 11, 1963): *AAS* 55 (1963), 260–261; Pius XII, *Radio Message* (Dec. 24, 1942): *AAS* 35 (1943), 19; Pius XI, Encyclical Letter *Mit Brennender Sorge* (March 14, 1937): *AAS* 29 (1937), 160; Leo XIII, Encyclical Letter *Libertas Praestantissimum* (June 20, 1888): Acts of Leo XIII, 8 (1888), 237–238.

right of the human person to religious freedom is to be recognized in the constitutional law whereby society is governed, and thus it is to become a civil right.

It is in accordance with their dignity as persons—that is, beings endowed with reason and free will and therefore privileged to bear personal responsibility—that all men should be at once impelled by nature and also bound by a moral obligation to seek the truth, especially religious truth. They are also bound to adhere to the truth, once it is known, and to order their whole lives in accord with the demands of truth. However, men cannot discharge these obligations in a manner in keeping with their own nature unless they enjoy immunity from external coercion as well as psychological freedom. Therefore, the right to religious freedom has its foundation not in the subjective disposition of the person, but in his very nature. In consequence, the right to this immunity continues to exist even in those who do not live up to their obligation of seeking the truth and adhering to it, and the exercise of this right is not to be impeded, provided that just public order be observed.

3. Further light is shed on the subject if one considers that the highest norm of human life is the divine law—eternal, objective and universal—whereby God orders, directs and governs the entire universe and all the ways of the human community by a plan conceived in wisdom and love. Man has been made by God to participate in this law, with the result that, under the gentle disposition of divine Providence, he can come to perceive ever more fully the truth that is unchanging. Wherefore every man has the duty, and therefore the right, to seek the truth in matters religious in order that he may with prudence form for himself right and true judgments of conscience, under use of all suitable means.

Truth, however, is to be sought after in a manner proper to the dignity of the human person and his social nature. The inquiry is to be free, carried on with the aid of teaching or instruction, communication and dialogue, in the course of which men explain to one another the truth they have discovered, or think they have discovered, in order thus to assist one another in the quest for truth.

Moreover, as the truth is discovered, it is by a personal assent that men are to adhere to it.

On his part, man perceives and acknowledges the imperatives of the divine law through the mediation of conscience. In all his activity a man is bound to follow his conscience in order that he may come to God, the end and purpose of life. It follows that he is not to be forced to act in a manner contrary to his conscience. Nor, on the other hand, is he to be restrained from acting in accordance with his conscience, especially in matters religious. The reason is that the exercise of religion, of its very nature, consists before all else in those internal, voluntary and free acts whereby man sets the course of his life directly toward God. No merely human power can either command or prohibit acts of this kind.[3] The social nature of man, however, itself requires that he should give external expression to his internal acts of religion: that he should share with others in matters religious; that he should profess his religion in community. Injury, therefore, is done to the human person and to the very order established by God for human life, if the free exercise of religion is denied in society, provided just public order is observed.

There is a further consideration. The religious acts whereby men, in private and in public and out of a sense of personal conviction, direct their lives to God transcend by their very nature the order of terrestrial and temporal affairs. Government therefore ought indeed to take account of the religious life of the citizenry and show it favor, since the function of government is to make provision for the common welfare. However, it would clearly transgress the limits set to its power were it to presume to command or inhibit acts that are religious.

4. The freedom or immunity from coercion in matters religious, which is the endowment of persons as individuals, is also to be recognized as their right when they act in community. Religious communities are a requirement of the social nature both of man and of religion itself.

Provided the just demands of public order are observed, religious communities rightfully claim freedom in order that they may govern themselves according to their own norms, honor the Supreme Being in public worship, assist their members in the practice of the religious life, strengthen them by instruction, and promote institutions in which they may join together for the purpose of ordering their own lives in accordance with their religious principles.

Religious communities also have the right not to be hindered, either by legal measures or by administrative action on the part of government,

3. Cf. John XXIII, Encyclical Letter *Pacem in Terris* (April 11, 1963): *AAS* 55 (1963), 270; Paul VI, *Radio Message* (Dec. 22, 1964): *AAS* 57 (1965), 181–182.

in the selection, training, appointment, and transferral of their own ministers, in communicating with religious authorities and communities abroad, in erecting buildings for religious purposes, and in the acquisition and use of suitable funds or properties.

Religious communities also have the right not to be hindered in their public teaching and witness to their faith, whether by the spoken or by the written word. However, in spreading religious faith and in introducing religious practices, everyone ought at all times to refrain from any manner of action which might seem to carry a hint of coercion or of a kind of persuasion that would be dishonorable or unworthy, especially when dealing with poor or uneducated people. Such a manner of action would have to be considered an abuse of one's right and a violation of the right of others.

In addition, it comes within the meaning of religious freedom that religious communities should not be prohibited from freely undertaking to show the special value of their doctrine in what concerns the organization of society and the inspiration of the whole of human activity. Finally, the social nature of man and the very nature of religion afford the foundation of the right of men freely to hold meetings and to establish educational, cultural, charitable and social organizations, under the impulse of their own religious sense.

5. The family, since it is a society in its own original right, has the right freely to live its own domestic religious life under the guidance of parents. Parents, moreover, have the right to determine, in accordance with their own religious beliefs, the kind of religious education that their children are to receive. Government, in consequence, must acknowledge the right of parents to make a genuinely free choice of schools and of other means of education, and the use of this freedom of choice is not to be made a reason for imposing unjust burdens on parents, whether directly or indirectly. Besides, the rights of parents are violated if their children are forced to attend lessons or instructions which are not in agreement with their religious beliefs, or if a single system of education, from which all religious formation is excluded, is imposed upon all.

6. Since the common welfare of society consists in the entirety of those conditions of social life under which men enjoy the possibility of achieving their own perfection in a certain fullness of measure and also with some relative ease, it chiefly consists in the protection of the rights

and in the performance of the duties of the human person.[4] Therefore, the care of the right to religious freedom devolves upon the whole citizenry, upon social groups, upon government, and upon the Church and other religious communities, in virtue of the duty of all toward the common welfare, and in the manner proper to each.

The protection and promotion of the inviolable rights of man rank among the essential duties of government.[5] Therefore government is to assume the safeguard of the religious freedom of all its citizens, in an effective manner, by just laws and by other appropriate means.

Government is also to help create conditions favorable to the fostering of religious life in order that the people may be truly enabled to exercise their religious rights and to fulfill their religious duties, and also in order that society itself may profit by the moral qualities of justice and peace which have their origin in men's faithfulness to God and to his holy will.[6]

If, in view of peculiar circumstances obtaining among peoples, special civil recognition is given to one religious community in the constitutional order of society, it is at the same time imperative that the right of all citizens and religious communities to religious freedom should be recognized and made effective in practice.

Finally, government is to see to it that equality of citizens before the law, which is itself an element of the common good, is never violated, whether openly or covertly, for religious reasons. Nor is there to be discrimination among citizens.

It follows that a wrong is done when government imposes upon its people, by force or fear or other means, the profession or repudiation of any religion, or when it hinders men from joining or leaving a religious community. All the more is it a violation of the will of God and of the sacred rights of the person and the family of nations when force is brought to bear in any way in order to destroy or repress religion, either in the whole of mankind or in a particular country or in a definite community.

---

4. Cf. John XXIII, Encyclical Letter *Mater et Magistra* (May 15, 1961): *AAS* 53 (1961), 417; *idem,* Encyclical Letter *Pacem in Terris* (April 11, 1963): *AAS* 55 (1963), 273.

5. Cf. John XXIII, Encyclical Letter *Pacem in Terris* (April 11, 1963): *AAS* 55 (1963), 273–274; Pius XII, *Radio Message* (June 1, 1941): *AAS* 33 (1941), 200.

6. Cf. Leo XIII, Encyclical Letter *Immortale Dei* (Nov. 1, 1885): *AAS* 18 (1885), 161.

7. The right to religious freedom is exercised in human society: hence its exercise is subject to certain regulatory norms. In the use of all freedoms, the moral principle of personal and social responsibility is to be observed. In the exercise of their rights, individual men and social groups are bound by the moral law to have respect both for the rights of others and for their own duties toward others and for the common welfare of all. Men are to deal with their fellows in justice and civility.

Furthermore, society has the right to defend itself against possible abuses committed on the pretext of freedom of religion. It is the special duty of government to provide this protection. However, government is not to act in an arbitrary fashion or in an unfair spirit of partisanship. Its action is to be controlled by juridical norms which are in conformity with the objective moral order. These norms arise out of the need for the effective safeguard of the rights of all citizens and for the peaceful settlement of conflicts of rights, also out of the need for an adequate care of genuine public peace, which comes about when men live together in good order and in true justice, and finally out of the need for a proper guardianship of public morality.

These matters constitute the basic component of the common welfare; they are what is meant by public order. For the rest, the usages of society are to be the usages of freedom in their full range: that is, the freedom of man is to be respected as far as possible and is not to be curtailed except when and insofar as necessary.

8. Many pressures are brought to bear upon the men of our day, to the point where the danger arises lest they lose the possibility of acting on their own judgment. On the other hand, not a few can be found who seem inclined to use the name of freedom as the pretext for refusing to submit to authority and for making light of the duty of obedience. Wherefore this Vatican Council urges everyone, especially those who are charged with the task of educating others, to do their utmost to form men who on the one hand will respect the moral order and be obedient to lawful authority, and on the other hand will be lovers of true freedom—men, in other words, who will come to decisions on their own judgment and in the light of truth, govern their activities with a sense of responsibility, and strive after what is true and right, willing always to join with others in cooperative effort.

Religious freedom therefore ought to have this further purpose and aim: namely, that men may come to act with greater responsibility in fulfilling their duties in community life.

9. The declaration of this Vatican Council on the right of man to religious freedom has its foundation in the dignity of the person, whose exigencies have come to be more fully known to human reason through centuries of experience. What is more, this doctrine of freedom has roots in divine revelation, and for this reason Christians are bound to respect it all the more conscientiously. Revelation does not indeed affirm in so many words the right of man to immunity from external coercion in matters religious. It does, however, disclose the dignity of the human person in its full dimensions. It gives evidence of the respect which Christ showed toward the freedom with which man is to fulfill his duty of belief in the Word of God, and it gives us lessons in the spirit which disciples of such a Master ought to adopt and continually follow. Thus, further light is cast upon the general principles upon which the doctrine of this declaration on religious freedom is based. In particular, religious freedom in society is entirely consonant with the freedom of the act of Christian faith.

10. It is one of the major tenets of Catholic doctrine that man's response to God in faith must be free; no one therefore is to be forced to embrace the Christian faith against his own will.[7] This doctrine is contained in the Word of God and it was constantly proclaimed by the Fathers of the Church.[8] The act of faith is of its very nature a free act. Man, redeemed by Christ the Savior and through Christ Jesus called to be God's adopted son (cf. Eph 1:5), cannot give his adherence to God revealing himself, unless under the drawing of the Father (cf. Jn 6:44), he offers to God the reasonable and free submission of faith. It is therefore

---

7. Cf. *Code of Canon Law,* can. 1351; Pius XII, *Allocution to Prelate Auditors and Other Officials and Administrators of the Tribune of the Holy Roman Rota* (Oct. 6, 1946): *AAS* 38 (1946), 394; *idem,* Encyclical Letter *Mystici Corporis* (June 29, 1943): *AAS* (1943), 243.

8. Cf. Lactantius, *Divinarum Institutionum,* Book V, 19: *CSEL* 19, 463–464, 465: *PL* 6, 614, 616 (ch. 20); St. Ambrose, *Epistola ad Valentianum Imp., Letter 21: PL* 16, 1005; St. Augustine, *Contra Litteras Petiliani,* Book II, ch. 83: *CSEL* 52, 112: *PL* 43, 315; cf. C. 23, q. 5, c. 33, ed. Friedberg, col. 939; *idem, Letter 23: PL* 33, 98; *idem, Letter 34: PL* 33, 132; *idem, Letter 35: PL* 33, 135; St. Gregory the Great, *Epistola ad Virgilium et Theodorum Episcopos Massiliae Galliarum,* Register of Letters I, 45: *MGH Letter 1,* p. 72: *PL* 77, 510–511 (Book I, Letter 47); *idem, Epistola ad Johannem Episcopum Constantinopolitanum,* Register of Letters, III, 52: *MGH Letter* 1, p. 210: *PL* 77, 649 (Book III, Letter 53); cf. D. 45, c. 1, ed. Friedberg, col. 160; Fourth Council of Toledo, c. 57: Mansi 10, 633; cf. D. 45, c. 5, ed. Friedberg, col. 161–162; Clement III: X, V, 6, 9, ed. Friedberg, col. 774; Innocent III, *Epistola ad Arelatensem Archiepiscopum,* X, III, 42, 3, ed. Friedberg, col. 646.

completely in accord with the nature of faith that in matters religious every manner of coercion on the part of men should be excluded. In consequence, the principle of religious freedom makes no small contribution to the creation of an environment in which men can without hindrance be invited to the Christian faith, embrace it of their own free will, and profess it effectively in their whole manner of life.

11. God calls men to serve him in spirit and in truth; hence they are bound in conscience but they stand under no compulsion. God has regard for the dignity of the human person, whom he himself created, and man is to be guided by his own judgment, and he is to enjoy freedom. This truth appears at its height in Christ Jesus, in whom God manifested himself and his ways with men. Christ is at once our Master and our Lord (cf. Jn 13:13) and also meek and humble of heart (cf. Mt 11:29). In attracting and inviting his disciples, he used patience (cf. Mt 11:28–30; Jn 6:67–68). He wrought miracles to illuminate his teaching and to establish its truth, but his intention was to rouse faith in his hearers and to confirm them in faith, not to exert coercion upon them.[9] He did indeed denounce the unbelief of some who listened to him, but he left vengeance to God in expectation of the day of judgment (cf. Mt 11:20–24; Rm 12:19–20; 2 Thes 1:8). When he sent his apostles into the world, he said to them: "He who believes and is baptized will be saved. He who does not believe will be condemned" (Mk 16:16). But he himself, noting that the cockle had been sown amid the wheat, gave orders that both should be allowed to grow until the harvest time, which will come at the end of the world (cf. Mt 13:30, 40–42). He refused to be a political messiah, ruling by force (cf. Mt 4:8–10; Jn 6:15). He preferred to call himself the Son of Man, who came "to serve and to give his life as a ransom for the many" (Mk 10:45). He showed himself the perfect servant of God (cf. Is 42:1–4), who "does not break the bruised reed nor extinguish the smoking flax" (Mt 12:20).

He acknowledged the power of government and its rights when he commanded that tribute be given to Caesar, but he gave clear warning that the higher rights of God are to be kept inviolate: "Render to Caesar the things that are Caesar's and to God the things that are God's" (Mt 22:21). In the end, when he completed on the cross the work of redemption, whereby he achieved salvation and true freedom for men, he

---

9. Cf. Mt 9:28–29; Mk 9:23–24; 6:5–6; Paul VI, Encyclical Letter *Ecclesiam Suam* (Aug. 6, 1964): *AAS* 56 (1964), 642–643.

brought his revelation to completion. For he bore witness to the truth (cf. Jn 18:37), but he refused to impose the truth by force on those who spoke against it. Not by force of blows does his rule assert its claims (cf. Mt 26:51–53; Jn 18:36). It is established by witnessing to the truth and by hearing the truth, and it extends its dominion by the love whereby Christ, lifted up on the cross, draws all men to himself (cf. Jn 12:32).

Taught by the word and example of Christ, the apostles followed the same way. From the very origins of the Church, the disciples of Christ strove to convert men to faith in Christ as the Lord, not, however, by the use of coercion or of devices unworthy of the Gospel, but by the power, above all, of the Word of God (cf. 1 Cor 2:3–5; 1 Thes 2:3–5). Steadfastly they proclaimed to all the plan of God our Savior, "who wills that all men should be saved and come to the acknowledgment of the truth" (1 Tm 2:4). At the same time, however, they showed respect for those of weaker stuff even though they were in error, and thus they made it plain that "each one of us is to render to God an account of himself" (Rm 14:12; cf. Rm 14:1–23; 1 Cor 8:9–13; 10:23–33) and for that reason is bound to obey his conscience. Like Christ himself, the apostles were unceasingly bent upon bearing witness to the truth of God, and they showed the fullest measure of boldness in "speaking the word with confidence" (Acts 4:31; cf. Eph 6:19–20) before the people and their rulers. With a firm faith, they held that the Gospel is indeed the power of God unto salvation for all who believe (cf. Rm 1:16). Therefore they rejected all "carnal weapons" (cf. 2 Cor 10:4; 1 Thes 5:8–9); they followed the example of the gentleness and respectfulness of Christ, and they preached the Word of God in the full confidence that there was resident in this word itself a divine power able to destroy all the forces arrayed against God (cf. Eph 6:11–17) and bring men to faith in Christ and to his service (cf. 2 Cor 10:3–5). As the Master, so too the apostles recognized legitimate civil authority. "For there is no power except from God," the Apostle teaches, and thereafter commands: "Let everyone be subject to higher authorities.... He who resists authority resists God's ordinance" (Rm 13:1–5; cf. 1 Pt 2:13–17). At the same time, however, they did not hesitate to speak out against governing powers which set themselves in opposition to the holy will of God: "It is necessary to obey God rather than men" (Acts 5:29; cf. Acts 4:19–20). This is the way along which the martyrs and other faithful have walked through all ages and over all the earth.

12. In faithfulness, therefore, to the truth of the Gospel, the Church is

following the way of Christ and the apostles when she recognizes and gives support to the principle of religious freedom as befitting the dignity of man and as being in accord with divine revelation. Throughout the ages the Church has kept safe and handed on the doctrine received from the Master and from the apostles. In the life of the People of God, as it has made its pilgrim way through the vicissitudes of human history, there has at times appeared a way of acting that was hardly in accord with the spirit of the Gospel, or even opposed to it. Nevertheless, the doctrine of the Church that no one is to be coerced into faith has always stood firm.

Thus, the leaven of the Gospel has long been about its quiet work in the minds of men, and to it is due in great measure the fact that in the course of time men have come more widely to recognize their dignity as persons, and the conviction has grown stronger that the person in society is to be kept free from all manner of coercion in matters religious.

13. Among the things that concern the good of the Church and indeed the welfare of society here on earth—things therefore that are always and everywhere to be kept secure and defended against all injury—this certainly is preeminent, namely, that the Church should enjoy that full measure of freedom which her care for the salvation of men requires.[10] This is a sacred freedom, because the only-begotten Son endowed with it the Church which he purchased with his blood. Indeed, it is so much the property of the Church that to act against it is to act against the will of God. The freedom of the Church is the fundamental principle in what concerns the relations between the Church and governments and the whole civil order.

In human society and in the face of government, the Church claims freedom for herself in her character as a spiritual authority, established by Christ the Lord, upon which there rests by divine mandate the duty of going out into the whole world and preaching the Gospel to every creature.[11] The Church also claims freedom for herself in her character as a society of men who have the right to live in society in accordance with the precepts of the Christian faith.[12]

---

10. Cf. Leo XIII, Encyclical Letter *Officio Sanctissimo* (Dec. 22, 1887): *AAS* 20 (1887), 269; *idem,* Encyclical Letter *Ex Litteris* (April 7 1887): *AAS* 19 (1886), 465.

11. Cf. Mk 16:15; Mt 28:18–20, Pius XII, Encyclical Letter *Summi Pontificatus* (Oct. 20, 1939): *AAS* 31 (1939), 445–446.

12. Cf. Pius XI, Encyclical Letter *Firmissiman Constantiam* (March 28, 1937): *AAS* 29 (1937), 196.

In turn, where the principle of religious freedom is not only proclaimed in words or simply incorporated in law but also given sincere and practical application, there the Church succeeds in achieving a stable situation of right as well as of fact and the independence which is necessary for the fulfillment of her divine mission.

This independence is precisely what the authorities of the Church claim in society.[13] At the same time, the Christian faithful, in common with all other men, possess the civil right not to be hindered in leading their lives in accordance with their consciences. Therefore, a harmony exists between the freedom of the Church and the religious freedom which is to be recognized as the right of all men and communities and sanctioned by constitutional law.

14. In order to be faithful to the divine command, "teach all nations" (Mt 28:19–20), the Catholic Church must work with all urgency and concern "that the Word of God be spread abroad and glorified" (2 Thes 3:1). Hence, the Church earnestly begs of its children that "first of all, supplications, prayers, petitions, acts of thanksgiving be made for all men.... For this is good and agreeable in the sight of God our Savior, who wills that all men be saved and come to the knowledge of the truth" (1 Tm 2:1–4). In the formation of their consciences, the Christian faithful ought carefully to attend to the sacred and certain doctrine of the Church.[14] For the Church is, by the will of Christ, the teacher of the truth. It is her duty to give utterance to and authoritatively to teach that truth which is Christ himself, and also to declare and confirm by her authority those principles of the moral order which have their origins in human nature itself. Furthermore, let Christians walk in wisdom in the face of those outside, "in the Holy Spirit, in unaffected love, in the word of truth" (2 Cor 6:6–7), and let them be about their task of spreading the light of life with all confidence (cf. Acts 4:29) and apostolic courage, even to the shedding of their blood.

The disciple is bound by a grave obligation toward Christ his Master ever more fully to understand the truth received from him, faithfully to proclaim it, and vigorously to defend it, never—be it understood—having recourse to means that are incompatible with the spirit of the Gospel. At the same time, the charity of Christ urges him to love and have prudence

---

13. Cf. Pius XII, Allocution *Ci Riesce* (Dec. 6, 1953): *AAS* 45 (1953), 802.
14. Cf. Pius XII, *Radio Message* (March 23, 1952): *AAS* 44 (1952): 270–278.

and patience in his dealings with those who are in error or in ignorance with regard to the faith.[15] All is to be taken into account: the Christian duty to Christ, the life-giving word which must be proclaimed, the rights of the human person, and the measure of grace granted by God through Christ to men who are invited freely to accept and profess the faith.

15. The fact is that men of the present day want to be able freely to profess their religion in private and in public. Indeed, religious freedom has already been declared to be a civil right in most constitutions, and it is solemnly recognized in international documents.[16] The further fact is that forms of government still exist under which, even though freedom of religious worship receives constitutional recognition, the powers of government are engaged in the effort to deter citizens from the profession of religion and to make life very difficult and dangerous for religious communities.

This Council greets with joy the first of these two facts as among the signs of the times. With sorrow, however, it denounces the other fact, as only to be deplored. The Council exhorts Catholics, and it directs a plea to all men, most carefully to consider how greatly necessary religious freedom is, especially in the present condition of the human family. All nations are coming into even closer unity. Men of different cultures and religions are being brought together in closer relationships. There is a growing consciousness of the personal responsibility that every man has. All this is evident. Consequently, in order that relationships of peace and harmony be established and maintained within the whole of mankind, it is necessary that religious freedom be everywhere provided with an effective constitutional guarantee and that respect be shown for the high duty and right of man freely to lead his religious life in society.

May the God and Father of all grant that the human family, through careful observance of the principle of religious freedom in society, may be brought by the grace of Christ and the power of the Holy Spirit to the sublime and unending and "glorious freedom of the sons of God" (Rm 8:21).

Given in Rome at St. Peter's, December 7, 1965

---

15. Cf. John XXIII, Encyclical Letter *Pacem in Terris* (April 11, 1963): *AAS* 55 (1963), 299–300.

16. Cf. John XXIII, Encyclical Letter *Pacem in Terris* (April 11, 1963): *AAS* 55 (1963), 295–296.

DECREE ON THE MISSION ACTIVITY OF THE CHURCH

Ad Gentes

Promulgated by
His Holiness Pope Paul VI
On December 7, 1965

INTRODUCTION

No other document draws so abundantly on other conciliar texts as does the *Decree on the Mission Activity of the Church (AG)*. It depends most on *Lumen Gentium,* as seen in its title, *Ad Gentes* ("to the nations"), and by developing the theme of the Church as a sacrament. Its opening sentence states: "Divinely sent *to the nations* of the world to be...'a universal sacrament of salvation....'" The Church is sent to the nations because it is the sacrament of Christ's mission of salvation and unity, and Christ is the light of the nations (cf. *LG* 1).

AG also draws heavily from *LG* 17 on the Church's missionary character. Besides these obvious connections, *AG* incorporates the overall understanding of ecclesiology set forth in *LG,* especially the sacramental nature of the Church by which the mystery of the saving presence of the Trinity is made a reality on earth. Whereas *LG* begins with three articles on the roles of the Father, Son and Holy Spirit in salvation history, culminating in the Church, *AG* teaches that the missionary character of the Church derives from the fact that it finds its origin in the mission of the Son and the Holy Spirit, according to the decree of God the Father (cf. *AG* 2). Thus, *AG* emphasizes the trinitarian foundation of mission.

AG is, so to speak, the Council's final word, the culmination of a reflection on what it means to be the Church of Christ in the world today: "The pilgrim Church is missionary by her very nature" (*AG* 2). As the final word, *AG* corresponds to Pope Paul VI's outline for renewal in *Ecclesiam Suam (ES),* where missionary dialogue follows on and is the fruit of the renewal of the Church. This is a vital point for *AG* and for the entire Council. The ultimate beneficiaries of the renewal of Vatican II are those who have not yet learned of the mystery of Christ. Like Christ, the Church does not exist to be served, but to give its life in service to others. The more it becomes like Christ through renewal, the more this law of love directs its every activity.

AG attests to the most important and all-embracing principle of renewal: that the Church will be renewed primarily through deepening its life in Christ. Both the actions of renewal and the actions that will result from it have the same root: the life of Christ within us. If the Church is the sacrament of salvation and unity by reason of its union with Christ (cf. *LG* 1; *AG* 5), then to become more perfectly what it is called to be, the Church must deepen this union.

The decree applies the principle to missionary activity: "Since the whole Church is missionary, and the work of evangelization is a basic duty of the People of God, this sacred synod invites all to a deep interior renewal" (*AG* 35).

This renewal will result in "a vivid awareness of their own responsibility for spreading the Gospel," which will in turn result in the appropriate actions by which all "may do their share in missionary work among the nations" (*AG* 35). The "deep interior renewal" and "vivid awareness of responsibility" make it possible for the Church to discover that obedience to the mandate of Christ to evangelize flows from "the inner necessity of [the Church's] own catholicity" (*AG* 1). True renewal results in the missionary mandate being seen as springing from the nature of the Church. Renewal in the mystery of Christ brings about that identification with Christ which transcends the dichotomy between being faithful to self and being faithful to God: in Christ, the two become one and the same. "Whence the duty that lies on the Church of spreading the faith and the salvation of Christ [is hers] not only in virtue of the express command...but also in virtue of that life which flows from Christ into his members" (*AG* 5).

That life comes to us through the cross. "The Paschal Mystery is also the wellspring of the Church's missionary nature" (*VC* 25). The mystery of the cross always marks the Church's mission. "For thus did all the apostles walk in hope, and by many trials and sufferings they filled up those things wanting to the passion of Christ for his body which is the Church (cf. Col 1:24). For often, the blood of Christians was like a seed" (*AG* 5).

The starting point of missionary activity is missionary charity, which derives from a profound appreciation for the gift of redemption in Jesus Christ. Missionary activity increases when this gift is fully appreciated as the pearl of great price. It is absolutely necessary that the members of the Church experience Christ's love so intently that they burn with the desire that others might share it too. Authentic renewal will bring about this increasingly profound experience of the mystery of Christ.

Having been called to participate in God's life in Christ, the Church walks alongside Christ as "God's co-workers," (*AG* 15), collaborating with him to bring his life to as many as possible. Holiness is not a static reality (cf. *LG* 5), but is missionary by nature. The classic expression *bonum diffusivum sui* means that the good is diffusive of itself. By its very nature it communicates itself to others and enriches them. St. Augustine put it this way: "Any good thing which can be shared is not properly possessed unless it is being shared" *(On Christian Doctrine)*. We only possess God's life to the extent that we see it as a common good which holds the promise of happiness for others.

St. Augustine also held that charity leads us to love everyone as a friend. Some are loved as actual friends because we already share with them the new life in Christ, while others are loved as potential friends. God communicates his life to the Church in such a way that the Church becomes an agent of communicating that life to others. Christ loved us in this way and called us to be his friends (cf. Jn 15:13–15). The Church is called to love in the same way, communicating God's life in such a way that those who receive it become true friends, fellow-workers (cf. 1 Cor 3:9) in continuing the mission of unity through salvation.

In this light, the Church's missionary activity has a circular character. It begins with missionary charity as its motive and achieves its ultimate goal only when such missionary charity is operative in the new Church which resulted from the mission. *AG* recognizes that young churches do not come of age until they have an indigenous clergy, laity who collaborate with them, and sufficient gifts to be self-sustaining. However, *AG* is not content to describe ecclesial maturity in merely institutional terms. Full possession of the mystery of Christ is evidenced by bringing Christ to others.

All Christians are called to possess this missionary charity, though only some are called to dedicate their whole lives to mission work. This is similar to the teaching of *LG* 42 on martyrdom. All are called to the perfection of charity which would dispose one to be a martyr if the circumstances called for it, though not all receive the gift. Similarly, the perfection of charity is common to all and for some this entails embracing the evangelical vows of chastity, poverty and obedience.

Authentic missionary work must flow from this sharing in the mystery of Christ. Nonetheless, it requires a call from God and specific gifts. Yet, gifts are not identical with the Giver, to whom we must be attached above all things. Fidelity to the Giver of gifts means receiving them gladly and gratefully, and developing them to the best of one's ability. The decree teaches that missionary gifts should be exercised from the motive of charity by which one seeks God's glory through human salvation.

AG stresses the importance of preparation, education, specific training and spiritual formation for those who possess missionary gifts, if the Church is to be a good steward of missionary gifts and graces. The decree states that such training, education and formation are the Church's response to God's initiative. This systematic training should join practical experience to theological and spiritual formation. The mission to proclaim Christ is based on the doctrine he revealed, and must also be adapted to the culture in which it is presented. Much depends on the witness of the missionary, which in turn depends on holiness of life.

Coordination of missionary training and activity requires cooperation among all the members of the Church whose various gifts contribute to missionary work. While special attention is given to bishops and to the office of the Holy See directly responsible for missionary activity, the Congregation for the Evangelization of Peoples, all members of the Church are addressed: priests, religious and laity. The decree calls for planning and coordination on three levels: that of the universal Church, regional and national groupings, and the diocese. The decree recognizes the uniquely important role of the local church (cf. *AG* 19–22).

Bishops are to discern and order the missionary gifts and the work of various organizations and institutions. Planning and coordinating must be done in a way which preserves and fosters the gifts themselves. A principle from the *Decree on the Apostolate of the Laity* applies here. Bishops "must make a judgment about the true nature and proper use of these gifts, not to extinguish the Spirit but to test all things and hold for what is good (cf. 1 Thes 5:12, 19, 21)" (*AA* 3).

The result is that the Church's missionary activity is both human and divine, as is the Church itself. The initiative is God's, in calling missionaries to their work and in equipping them with every necessary gift. One element of the human response is knowing how to integrate faith with culture. Without using the expression, *AG* calls for a full inculturation of faith. *Gaudium et Spes* 53–62 should be read as background for this. Especially important is *GS* 58, where the Council acknowledges the role of culture in the economy of revelation. In addition, Pope Paul VI's apostolic exhortation *Evangelii Nuntiandi* (especially articles 18–20) is essential reading on this subject.

Faith must enter into the fabric of culture because culture is so essential to the human person's social nature: "Man comes to a true and full humanity only through culture" (*GS* 53). Culture is formed by and gives expression to the values of the people who participate in it; it also forms values, passing them on through a variety of cultural components: customs, education, entertainment, media, etc. Through culture faith comes into contact with the daily lives of believers. Vatican II stated: "This split between the faith which many profess and their daily lives deserves to be counted among the more serious errors of our age" (*GS* 43). Paul VI would rephrase this in terms of culture: "The split between the Gospel and culture is without a doubt the drama of our time" (*EN* 21).

Evangelization "always takes the person as one's starting point" (*EN* 20) and seeks to root the Church's faith in culture through the renewal of individual persons. It brings about a purification, assimilation and elevation of culture. The inculturation of the Church's faith comes about through the conversion of "the personal and collective consciences of people" by "upsetting...mankind's criteria of judgment, determining values, points of interest, lines of thought, sources of inspiration and models of life, which are in contrast with the Word of God and the plan of salvation" (*EN* 18–19).

To the extent that these values are compatible with the Church's understanding of the dignity of the human person and the Gospel, they are good and can be "healed, uplifted and perfected for the glory of God" (*AG* 9; cf. *LG* 13), thus adding to the richness of the Church's catholic unity through a "mutual exchange" (*AG* 19). For this exchange between the particular church and the universal Church to take place, a prior exchange between the particular church and its own culture must occur (cf. *AG* 22).

The decree shows that such exchanges require that theological reflection "submit to a new scrutiny the words and deeds which God has revealed, and which have been set down in Sacred Scripture and explained by the Fathers and by the magisterium" (*AG* 22). Paul VI has already written that missionary dialogue requires "forcing our reasoning process out of the worn paths and...obliging it to deepen its research, to find fresh expressions." Dialogue "does not bind itself to ineffectual theories and does not cling to hard and fast forms when these have lost their power to speak to men and move them" (*ES* 83–85).

Such statements reveal the confidence the Church has in the ability of the Gospel message to respond to, fulfill and surpass the "spiritual expectations" of those who hear it proclaimed (*AG* 13). "But the Church knows that it is the seed, the leaven, the salt and light of the world. It sees clearly enough the astounding newness of modern times, but with frank confidence it stands upon the path of history and says to men: 'I have that for which you search, that which you lack'" (*ES* 95). In the dialogue with new individuals and new cultures and peoples, the Church has much to learn and to gain.

The decree emphasizes the role of personal witness in evangelization. This is greatly developed in the post-conciliar magisterium, especially in Paul VI's *Evangelii Nuntiandi* (n. 21), and John Paul II's *Redemptoris Missio*. Witness awakens in human hearts a desire which can only be fulfilled in the Gospel revelation of love, thus "gradually opening up a fuller approach to God" (*AG* 12). "Through this wordless witness these Christians stir up irresistible questions in the hearts of those who see how they live" (*EN* 21). With the help of God's grace, such questions can lead to the conversion of faith that discovers in Christ God's definitive answer to humanity's most profound questions.

The essence of evangelization, however, is preaching the Word of God so as to bring about conversion (cf. *AG* 13), which springs from the grace of the Holy Spirit which accompanies the missionary proclamation. Evangelization is a breathing together of God's word into human hearts, for faith comes from hearing and from the Holy Spirit who opens hearts.

To facilitate the process of conversion and the working of God's grace, catechumens need a good preparation for their full initiation into the Paschal Mystery of Christ. To this end, *AG* speaks of the importance of the catechumenate. It also recommends a restoration of the Lenten liturgy to help catechumens prepare for the solemn celebration of Easter (cf. *AG* 14; *CD* 14; *SC* 64–66). As a result, A revised *Rite of Christian Initiation of Adults* was produced in 1988.

In line with the Council's invitation for a deeper study of missiology, this study has been developing since Vatican II. The document *Attitude of the Church toward Followers of Other Religions* by the Secretariat for Non-Christians (now the Pontifical Council for Interreligious Dialogue) has summarized some of this important theological work. The document states that mission includes five distinct elements: presence and witness, development and human promotion, worship and liturgical life, interreligious dialogue, and proclamation and catechesis. Integrating all these elements provides a more comprehensive view of the nature of mission, which is also treated in Paul VI's *Evangelii Nuntiandi* and John Paul II's *Redemptoris Missio*.

TOPICAL OUTLINE

1. Preface: The Church is sent to the nations (1)

2. Doctrinal principles

    A. Trinitarian foundation of mission (2)

    B. Jesus Christ in the plan of salvation (3)

    C. The Holy Spirit's work in the Church (4)

    D. The apostles and the Church's missionary mandate (5)

    E. Missions and particular churches (6)

    F. Importance of mission for human salvation (7–9)

3. Mission work itself

    A. Urgency of the task (10)

    B. Christian witness

        1. Witness and dialogue (11)

        2. Collaboration in social and economic affairs (12)

    C. Preaching the Gospel

        1. Proclamation and new converts (13)

        2. The catechumenate (14)

    D. Forming the Christian community

        1. Importance of the laity and various ministries (15)

        2. Formation of priests from the young churches (16)

DECREE ON THE MISSION ACTIVITY OF THE CHURCH

Ad Gentes

PREFACE

1. Divinely sent to the nations of the world to be unto them "a universal sacrament of salvation,"[1] the Church, driven by the inner necessity of her own catholicity, and obeying the mandate of her Founder (cf. Mk 16:16), strives ever to proclaim the Gospel to all men. The apostles themselves, on whom the Church was founded, following in the footsteps of Christ, "preached the word of truth and begot churches."[2] It is the duty of their successors to make this task endure "so that the Word of God may run and be glorified" (2 Thes 3:1) and the kingdom of God be proclaimed and established throughout the world.

In the present state of affairs, out of which there is arising a new situation for mankind, the Church, being the salt of the earth and the light of the world (cf. Mt 5:13–14), is more urgently called upon to save and renew every creature, that all things may be restored in Christ and all men may constitute one family in him and one People of God.

Therefore, this sacred synod, while rendering thanks to God for the excellent results that have been achieved through the whole Church's

---

1. Second Vatican Ecumenical Council, Dogmatic Constitution on the Church *Lumen Gentium,* 48.

2. St. Augustine, *Exposition on Psalm 44,* 23: *PL* 36, 508; *CChr* 38, 510.

great-hearted endeavor, desires to sketch the principles of missionary activity and to rally the forces of all the faithful in order that the People of God, marching along the narrow way of the cross, may spread everywhere the reign of Christ, Lord and overseer of the ages (cf. Eccl 36:19), and may prepare the way for his coming.

CHAPTER I

PRINCIPLES OF DOCTRINE

2. The pilgrim Church is missionary by her very nature, since it is from the mission of the Son and the mission of the Holy Spirit that she draws her origin, in accordance with the decree of God the Father.[1]

This decree, however, flows from the "fount-like love" or charity of God the Father, who being the "principle without principle" from whom the Son is begotten and the Holy Spirit proceeds through the Son, freely creating us on account of his surpassing and merciful kindness and graciously calling us moreover to share with him his life and his glory, has generously poured out, and does not cease to pour out still, his divine goodness. Thus he who created all things may at last be "all in all" (1 Cor 15:28), bringing about at one and the same time his own glory and our happiness. But it pleased God to call men to share his life, not just singly, apart from any mutual bond, but rather to mold them into a people in which his sons, once scattered abroad, might be gathered together (cf. Jn 11:52).

3. This universal design of God for the salvation of the human race is carried out not only, as it were, secretly in the soul of a man, or by the attempts (even religious ones) by which in diverse ways it seeks after God, if perchance it may contact him or find him, though he be not far from any one of us (cf. Acts 17:27). For these attempts need to be enlightened and healed, even though, through the kindly workings of divine Providence, they may sometimes serve as leading strings toward God, or as a preparation for the Gospel.[2] Now God, in order to establish

---

1. Cf. Second Vatican Ecumenical Council, Dogmatic Constitution on the Church *Lumen Gentium,* 1.

2. Cf. St. Irenaeus, *Against Heretics* III, 18, 1: "The Word existing in the presence of God, through whom all things were made, and who always is present to the human race...": *PG* 7, 932; *idem,* IV, 6, 7: "From the beginning even the Son, being present in

peace or the communion of sinful human beings with himself, as well as to fashion them into a fraternal community, did ordain to intervene in human history in a way both new and final by sending his Son, clothed in our flesh, in order that through him he might snatch men from the power of darkness and Satan (cf. Col 1:13; Acts 10:38) and reconcile the world to himself in him (cf. 2 Cor 5:19). Him, then, by whom he made the world,[3] he appointed heir of all things, that in him he might restore all (cf. Eph 1:10).

For Jesus Christ was sent into the world as a real mediator between God and men. Since he is God, all divine fullness dwells bodily in him (Col 2:9). According to his human nature, on the other hand, he is the new Adam, made head of a renewed humanity, and full of grace and of truth (Jn 1:14). Therefore, the Son of God walked the ways of a true Incarnation that he might make men sharers in the nature of God: made poor for our sakes, though he had been rich, in order that his poverty might enrich us (2 Cor 8:9). The Son of Man came not that he might be served, but that he might be a servant, and give his life as a ransom for the many—that is, for all (cf. Mk 10:45). The Fathers of the Church proclaim without hesitation that what has not been taken up by Christ is not made whole.[4] Now, what he took up was our entire human nature such as it is found among us poor wretches, save only sin (cf. Heb 4:15; 9:28). For Christ said concerning himself, he whom the Father sanctified and sent into the world (cf. Jn 10:36): "The Spirit of the Lord is upon me, because he anointed me; to bring good news to the poor he sent me,

---

his creation, reveals the Father to all to whom he wills and when he wills, and insofar as the Father wills it" (*ibid.,* 990); cf. IV, 20, 6 and 7 (*ibid.,* 1037); *Demonstration No. 34* (Eastern Fathers, XII, 773; *Sources Chretiennes,* 62, Paris, 1958, p. 87); Clement of Alexandria, *Protrept.* 112, 1 (*GCS* Clement I, 79); *Strom.* VI, 6, 44, 1 (*GCS* Clement II, 453), 13, 106, 3 and 4 (*ibid.,* 485). For the doctrine itself, cf. Pius XII, *Radio Message* (Dec. 31, 1952); Dogmatic Constitution on the Church *Lumen Gentium,* 16.

3. Cf. Heb 1:2; Jn 1:3, 10; 1 Cor 8:6; Col 1:16.

4. Cf. St. Athanasius, *Letter to Epictetus* 7: *PG* 26, 1060; St. Cyril of Jerusalem, *Catech.* 4, 9: *PG* 33, 465; Marius Victorinus, *Against Arius* 3, 3: *PL* 8, 1101; St. Basil, *Letter 261,* 2: *PG* 32, 969; St. Gregory Nazianzen, *Letter 101: PG* 37, 181; St. Gregory of Nyssa, *Antirrheticus, Against Apollin.* 17: *PG* 45, 1156; St. Ambrose, *Letter 48, 5: PL* 16, 1153; St. Augustine, *On John's Gospel,* tract XXIII, 6: *PL* 35, 1585; *CChr* 36, 236; above all in this way it is evident that the Holy Spirit has not redeemed us, since he has not become flesh: *On the Agony of Christ* 22, 24: *PL* 40, 309; St. Cyril of Alexandria, *Against Nestorius* I, 1: *PG* 76, 20; St. Fulgentius, *Letter 17, 3, 5: PL* 65, 454; *Ad Trasimundum* III, 21: *PL* 65, 284: on sorrow and fear.

to heal the brokenhearted, to proclaim to the captives release, and sight to the blind" (Lk 4:18). And again: "The Son of Man has come to seek and to save what was lost" (Lk 19:10).

But what the Lord preached that one time, or what was wrought in him for the saving of the human race, must be spread abroad and published to the ends of the earth (Acts 1:8), beginning from Jerusalem (cf. Lk 24:27), so that what he accomplished at that one time for the salvation of all, may in the course of time come to achieve its effect in all.

4. To accomplish this, Christ sent from the Father his Holy Spirit, who was to carry on inwardly his saving work and prompt the Church to spread out. Doubtless, the Holy Spirit was already at work in the world before Christ was glorified.[5] Yet on the day of Pentecost, he came down upon the disciples to remain with them forever (cf. Jn 14:16). The Church was publicly displayed to the multitude; the Gospel began to spread among the nations by means of preaching, and there was presaged that union of all peoples in the catholicity of the faith by means of the Church of the New Covenant, a Church which speaks all tongues, understands and accepts all tongues in her love, and so supersedes the divisiveness of Babel.[6] For it was from Pentecost that the "Acts of the Apostles" took origin, just as Christ was conceived when the Holy Spirit

---

5. It is the Spirit who has spoken through the prophets: Creed of Constantinople: *DS* 150; St. Leo the Great, *Sermon 76: PL* 54, 405–406: "When on the day of Pentecost the Holy Spirit filled the disciples of the Lord, it was not so much the beginning of a gift as it was the completion of one already bountifully possessed: because the patriarchs, the prophets, the priests and all the holy men who preceded them were already quickened by the life of the same Spirit...although they did not possess his gifts to the same degree." Also *Sermon 77, 1: PL* 54, 412; Leo XIII, Encyclical Letter *Divinum Illud* (May 9, 1897): *AAS* (1897), 650–651. Also St. John Chrysostom, where he insists on the newness of the Holy Spirit's mission on Pentecost, *On Eph.,* ch. 4, *Homily 10,* 1: *PG* 62, 75.

6. The holy Fathers often speak of Babel and Pentecost: Origen, *On Genesis,* ch. 1: *PG* 12, 112; St. Gregory Naz., *Oration* 41, 16: *PG* 36, 449; St. John Chrysostom, *Homily 2 on Pentecost* 2: *PG* 50, 467; *On the Acts of the Apostles: PG* 44; St. Augustine, *Narration on Psalm 54,* 11: *PL* 36, 636; *CChr* 39, 664 ff., *Sermon 271: PL* 38, 1245; St. Cyril of Alexandria, *Glaphyra on Genesis* II: *PG* 69, 79; St. Gregory the Great, *Homily on the Gospels,* Book 2, *Homily 30,* 4: *PL* 76, 1222; St. Bede, *On Hexaeum,* Book 3: *PL* 91, 125. See above all the images in St. Mark's Basilica in Venice.

The Church speaks all languages, and thus gathers all in the catholicity of the faith: St. Augustine, *Sermons* 267, 268, 269: *PL* 38, 1225–1237, *Sermon 175,* 3: *PL* 38, 946; St. John Chrysostom, *On the First Epistle to the Corinthians, Homily 35: PG* 61 296; St. Cyril of Alexandria, *Fragment on the Acts: PG* 74, 758; St. Fulgentius, *Sermon 8,* 2–3: *PL* 6, 743–744.

Concerning Pentecost as the consecration of the apostles to their mission, cf. J. A. Cramer, *Catena on the Acts of the Apostles,* Oxford, 1838, p. 24 ff.

came upon the Virgin Mary, and just as Christ was impelled to the work of his ministry by the same Holy Spirit descending upon him while he prayed.[7]

Now, the Lord Jesus, before freely giving his life for the world, did so arrange the apostles' ministry and promise to send the Holy Spirit that both they and the Spirit might be associated in effecting the work of salvation always and everywhere.[8] Throughout all ages, the Holy Spirit makes the entire Church "one in communion and in ministering; he equips her with various gifts of a hierarchical and charismatic nature,"[9] giving life, soul-like, to ecclesiastical institutions[10] and instilling into the hearts of the faithful the same mission spirit which impelled Christ himself. Sometimes he even visibly anticipates the apostles' acting,[11] just as he unceasingly accompanies and directs it in different ways.[12]

5. From the very beginning, the Lord Jesus "called to himself those whom he wished; and he caused twelve of them to be with him; and to be sent out preaching" (Mk 3:13; cf. Mt 10:1–42). Thus the apostles were the first budding-forth of the New Israel and at the same time the beginning of the sacred hierarchy. Then, when he had by his death and his resurrection completed once for all in himself the mysteries of our salvation and the renewal of all things, the Lord, having now received all power in heaven and on earth (cf. Mt 28:18), before he was taken up into heaven (cf. Acts 1:11), founded his Church as the sacrament of salvation and sent his apostles into all the world just as he himself had been sent by his Father (cf. Jn 20:21), commanding them: "Go, therefore, and make disciples of all nations, baptizing them in the name of the Father and of the Son and of the Holy Spirit; teaching them to observe all that I have commanded you" (Mt 28:19 ff.). "Go into the whole world, preach the Gospel to every creature. He who believes and is baptized shall be

---

7. Cf. Lk 3:22; 4:1; Acts 10:38.

8. Cf. Jn ch. 14–17; Paul VI, *Allocution during the Council* (Sept. 14, 1964): *AAS* (1964), 807.

9. Cf. Second Vatican Ecumenical Council, Dogmatic Constitution on the Church *Lumen Gentium,* 4.

10. St. Augustine, *Sermon 267,* 4: *PL* 38, 1231: "The Holy Spirit does in the whole Church what the soul does in all the members of one body." Cf. *Lumen Gentium,* 7 (together with note 8).

11. Cf. Acts 10:44–47; 11:15; 15:8.

12. Cf. Acts 4:8; 5:32; 8:26, 29, 39; 9:31; 10; 11:24–28; 13:2, 4, 9; 16:6–7; 20:22–23; 21:11; etc.

saved; but he who does not believe, shall be condemned" (Mk 16:15 ff.). Whence the duty that lies on the Church of spreading the faith and the salvation of Christ, not only in virtue of the express command which was inherited from the apostles by the order of bishops, assisted by the priests, together with the Successor of Peter and supreme shepherd of the Church, but also in virtue of that life which flows from Christ into his members: "From him the whole body, being closely joined and knit together through every joint of the system, according to the functioning in due measure of each single part, derives its increase to the building up of itself in love" (Eph 4:16). The mission of the Church, therefore, is fulfilled by that activity which makes her, obeying the command of Christ and influenced by the grace and love of the Holy Spirit, fully present to all men or nations, in order that by the example of her life and by her preaching, by the sacraments and other means of grace, she may lead them to the faith, the freedom and the peace of Christ, that thus there may lie open before them a firm and free road to full participation in the mystery of Christ.

Since this mission goes on and in the course of history unfolds the mission of Christ himself, who was sent to preach the Gospel to the poor, the Church, prompted by the Holy Spirit, must walk in the same path on which Christ walked: a path of poverty and obedience, of service and self-sacrifice to the death, from which death he came forth a victor by his resurrection. For thus did all the apostles walk in hope, and by many trials and sufferings they filled up those things wanting to the passion of Christ for his body which is the Church (cf. Col 1:24). For often, the blood of Christians was like a seed.[13]

6. This duty, to be fulfilled by the order of bishops, under the Successor of Peter and with the prayers and help of the whole Church, is one and the same everywhere and in every condition, even though it may be carried out differently according to circumstances. Hence, the differences recognizable in this, the Church's activity, are not due to the inner nature of the mission itself, but rather to the circumstances in which this mission is exercised.

These circumstances in turn depend sometimes on the Church, sometimes on the peoples or groups or men to whom the mission is directed. For the Church, although of itself including the totality or full-

---

13. Tertullian, *Apologeticum* 50, 13: *PL* 1, 534; *CChr* 1, 171.

ness of the means of salvation, does not and cannot always and instantly bring them all into action. Rather, she experiences beginnings and degrees in that action by which she strives to make God's plan a reality. In fact, there are times when, after a happy beginning, she must again lament a setback, or at least must linger in a certain state of unfinished insufficiency. As for the men, groups and peoples concerned, only by degrees does she touch and pervade them, and thus take them up into full catholicity. The right sort of means and actions must be suited to any state or situation.

"Missions" is the term usually given to those particular undertakings by which the heralds of the Gospel, sent out by the Church and going forth into the whole world, carry out the task of preaching the Gospel and planting the Church among peoples or groups who do not yet believe in Christ. These undertakings are brought to completion by missionary activity and are mostly exercised in certain territories recognized by the Holy See. The proper purpose of this missionary activity is evangelization, and the planting of the Church among those peoples and groups where it has not yet taken root.[14] Thus from the seed which is the Word of God, particular autochthonous churches should be sufficiently established and should grow up all over the world, endowed with their own maturity and vital forces. Under a hierarchy of their own, together with the faithful people, and adequately fitted out with requisites for living a full Christian life, they should make their contribution to the good of the whole Church. The chief means of the planting referred to is the

---

14. Already St. Thomas Aquinas speaks of the apostolic duty of "planting" the Church, cf. *Sent.* Book I, dist. 16, q. 1, 2 *ad* 2 and *ad* 4; a. 3 sol.; *Summa Theol.,* 1, q. 43, a.7 *ad* 6; I–II, q. 106, a. 4 *ad* 4. Cf. Benedict XV, Encyclical Letter *Maximum Illud* (Nov. 30, 1919): *AAS* (1919), 445 and 453; Pius XI, Encyclical Letter *Rerum Ecclesiae* (Feb. 28, 1926): *AAS* (1926), 74; Pius XII, April 30, 1939, to the directors of the Pontifical Missionary Societies; *idem,* June 24, 1944, to the directors of the Pontifical Missionary Societies: *AAS* (1944), 210, again in *AAS* (1950), 727 and 1951, 508; *idem,* June 29, 1948, to the native clergy: *AAS* (1948), 374; *idem,* Encyclical Letter *Evangelii Praecones* (June 2, 1951): *AAS* (1951), 507; *idem,* Encyclical Letter *Fidei Donum* (Jan. 15, 1957): *AAS* (1957), 236; John XXIII, Encyclical Letter *Princeps Pastorum* (Nov. 28, 1959): *AAS* (1959), 835; Paul VI, *Homily* (Oct. 18, 1964): *AAS* (1964), 911.

Both the supreme Pontiffs and the Fathers and scholastics have spoken of the expansion of the Church: St. Thomas Aquinas, *Commentary on Mt 16:28;* Leo XIII, Encyclical Letter *Sancta Dei Civitas* (Dec. 3, 1880): *AAS* (1880), 241; Benedict XV, Encyclical Letter *Maximum Illud* (Nov. 30, 1919): *AAS* (1919), 442; Pius XI, Encyclical Letter *Rerum Ecclesiae* (Feb. 28, 1926): *AAS* (1926), 65.

preaching of the Gospel of Jesus Christ. To preach this Gospel, the Lord sent forth his disciples into the whole world, that being reborn by the Word of God (cf. 1 Pt 1:23), men might be joined to the Church through Baptism—that Church which, as the body of the Word Incarnate, is nourished and lives by the Word of God and by the Eucharistic bread (cf. Acts 2:42).

In this missionary activity of the Church various stages sometimes are found side by side: first, that of the beginning or planting, then, that of newness or youth. When these have passed, the Church's missionary activity does not cease, but there lies upon the particular churches already set up the duty of continuing this activity and of preaching the Gospel to those still outside.

Moreover, the groups among which the Church dwells are often radically changed, for one reason or other, so that an entirely new set of circumstances may arise. Then the Church must deliberate whether these conditions might again call for her missionary activity. Besides, circumstances are sometimes such that, for the time being, there is no possibility of expounding the Gospel directly and forthwith. Then, of course, missionaries can and must at least bear witness to Christ by charity and by works of mercy, with all patience, prudence and great confidence. Thus, they will prepare the way for the Lord and make him somehow present.

Thus it is plain that missionary activity wells up from the Church's inner nature and spreads abroad her saving faith. It perfects her Catholic unity by this expansion. It is sustained by her apostolicity. It exercises the collegial spirit of her hierarchy. It bears witness to her sanctity while spreading and promoting it. Thus, missionary activity among the nations differs from pastoral activity exercised among the faithful as well as from undertakings aimed at restoring unity among Christians. And yet these two ends are most closely connected with the missionary zeal,[15] because the division among Christians damages the most holy cause of

---

15. In this notion of missionary activity, as is evident, according to the circumstances, even those parts of Latin America are included in which there is neither a hierarchy proper to the region nor maturity of Christian life, nor sufficient preaching of the Gospel. Whether or not such territory *de facto* is recognized as missionary by the Holy See does not depend on this council. Therefore, regarding the connection between the notion of missionary activity and a certain territory, it is wise to say that this activity "in the majority of cases" is exercised in certain territories recognized by the Holy See.

preaching the Gospel to every creature[16] and blocks the way to the faith for many. Hence, by the very necessity of mission, all the baptized are called to gather into one flock, and thus they will be able to bear unanimous witness before the nations to Christ their Lord. And if they are not yet capable of bearing witness to the same faith, they should at least be animated by mutual love and esteem.

7. This missionary activity derives its reason from the will of God, "who wishes all men to be saved and to come to the knowledge of the truth. For there is one God, and one mediator between God and men, himself a man, Jesus Christ, who gave himself as a ransom for all" (1 Tm 2:4–5), "neither is there salvation in any other" (Acts 4:12). Therefore, all must be converted to him, made known by the Church's preaching, and all must be incorporated into him by Baptism and into the Church which is his body. For Christ himself "by stressing in express language the necessity of faith and Baptism (cf. Mk 16:16; Jn 3:5), at the same time confirmed the necessity of the Church, into which men enter by baptism, as by a door. Therefore, those men cannot be saved, who though aware that God, through Jesus Christ, founded the Church as something necessary, still do not wish to enter into it or to persevere in it."[17] Therefore, though God in ways known to himself can lead those inculpably ignorant of the Gospel to find that faith without which it is impossible to please him (Heb 11:6), yet a necessity lies upon the Church (1 Cor 9:16), and at the same time a sacred duty, to preach the Gospel. And hence missionary activity today as always retains its power and necessity.

By means of this activity, the Mystical Body of Christ unceasingly gathers and directs its forces toward its own growth (cf. Eph 4:11–16). The members of the Church are impelled to carry on such missionary activity by reason of the love with which they love God and by which they desire to share with all men the spiritual goods of both this life and the life to come.

Finally, by means of this missionary activity, God is fully glorified, provided that men fully and consciously accept his work of salvation,

---

16. Second Vatican Ecumenical Council, Decree on Ecumenism *Unitatis Redintegratio*, 1.

17. Cf. Second Vatican Ecumenical Council, Dogmatic Constitution on the Church *Lumen Gentium*, 14.

which he has accomplished in Christ. In this way and by this means, the plan of God is fulfilled—that plan to which Christ conformed with loving obedience for the glory of the Father who sent him,[18] that the whole human race might form one People of God and be built up into one temple of the Holy Spirit which, being the expression of brotherly harmony, corresponds with the inmost wishes of all men. And so at last, there will be realized the plan of our Creator who formed man to his own image and likeness, when all who share one human nature, regenerated in Christ through the Holy Spirit and beholding the glory of God, will be able to say with one accord: "Our Father."[19]

8. Missionary activity is closely bound up even with human nature itself and its aspirations. For by manifesting Christ, the Church reveals to men the real truth about their condition and their whole calling, since Christ is the source and model of that redeemed humanity, imbued with brotherly love, sincerity and a peaceful spirit, to which they all aspire. Christ and the Church, which bears witness to him by preaching the Gospel, transcend every peculiarity of race or nation and therefore cannot be considered foreign anywhere or to anybody.[20] Christ himself is

---

18. Cf. Jn 7:18; 8:30, 44; 8:50; 17:1.

19. On this synthetic idea, see the teaching of St. Irenaeus, *De Recapitulatione.* Cf. also Hippolytus, *De Antichristo* 3: "Wishing all, and desiring to save all, wishing all the excellence of God's children and calling all the saints in one perfect man...": *PG* 10, 732; *GCS* Hippolyt. I, 2 p. 6; *Benedictiones Iacob,* 7: T.U., 38–1 p. 18, lin 4 ff.; Origen, *In Ioann.,* tom. I, n. 16: "When there will be one action of knowing God on the part of all those who have attained to God, under the leadership of the Word who is with God, that thus all sons may be correctly instructed in the knowledge of the Father, as now only the Son knows the Father": *PG* 14, 49; *GCS* Origen IV, 20; St. Augustine, *De Sermone Domini in Monte,* I, 41: "Let us love what can lead us to that kingdom where no one says, 'My Father,' but all say to the one God: 'Our Father'": *PL* 34, 120; St. Cyril of Alexandria, *In Joann.* I: "For we are all in Christ, and the common person of humanity comes back to life in him. That is why he is also called the New Adam.... For he dwelt among us, who by nature is the Son of God and therefore in his Spirit we cry out: Abba, Father! But the Word dwells in all, in one temple, namely that which he assumed for us and from us, that having us, all in himself, he might, as Paul says, reconcile all in one body to the Father": *PG* 73, 161–164.

20. Benedict XV, Encyclical Letter *Maximum Illud* (Nov. 30, 1919): *AAS* (1919): "For as the Church of God is Catholic and is foreign to no people or nation...." Cf. John XXIII, Encyclical Letter *Mater et Magistra* (May 15, 1961): *AAS* 53 (1961): "By divine right the Church belongs to all nations...since she has, as it were transfused her energy into the veins of a people, she neither is nor considers herself an institution imposed on that people from without.... And hence whatever seems to her good and noble they confirm and perfect" (namely those reborn in Christ).

the way and the truth, which the preaching of the Gospel opens to all in proclaiming in the hearing of all these words of Christ: "Repent, and believe the Gospel" (Mk 1:15). Now, since he who does not believe is already judged (cf. Jn 3:18), the words of Christ are at one and the same time words of judgment and of grace, of death and of life. For it is only by putting to death what is old that we are able to approach the newness of life. This is true first of all about persons, but it holds also for the various goods of this world which bear the mark both of man's sin and of God's blessing: "For all have sinned and have need of the glory of God" (Rm 3:23). No one is freed from sin by himself and by his own power; no one is raised above himself; no one is completely rid of his sickness or his solitude or his servitude.[21] On the contrary, all stand in need of Christ, their model, their mentor, their liberator, their Savior, their source of life. The Gospel has truly been a leaven of liberty and progress in human history, even in the temporal sphere, and always proves itself a leaven of brotherhood, of unity and of peace. Not without cause is Christ hailed by the faithful as "the expected of the nations, and their Savior."[22]

9. And so the time for missionary activity extends between the first coming of the Lord and the second, in which latter the Church will be gathered from the four winds like a harvest into the kingdom of God.[23] For the Gospel must be preached to all nations before the Lord shall come (cf. Mk 13:10).

Missionary activity is nothing else and nothing less than an epiphany, or a manifesting of God's decree, and its fulfillment in the world and in world history, in the course of which God, by means of mission, manifestly works out the history of salvation. By the preaching of the word and by the celebration of the sacraments, the center and summit of which is the most holy Eucharist, he brings about the presence of Christ, the author of salvation. But whatever truth and grace are to be found among the nations, as a sort of secret presence of God, he frees from all taint of evil and restores to Christ its maker, who overthrows the devil's domain and wards off the manifold malice of vice. And so, whatever

---

21. Cf. Irenaeus, *Against Heretics* III, 15, 3: *PG* 7, 919: "They were preachers of truth and apostles of liberty."

22. "O Antiphon" for Dec. 23.

23. Cf. Mt 24:31; *Didache* 10, 5, ed. F. X. Funk, I, p. 32.

good is found to be sown in the hearts and minds of men, or in the rites and cultures peculiar to various peoples, not only is not lost, but is healed, uplifted, and perfected for the glory of God, the shame of the demon, and the bliss of men.[24] Thus, missionary activity tends toward eschatological fullness.[25] For by it the people of God is increased to that measure and time which the Father has fixed in his power (cf. Acts 1:7). To this people it was said in prophecy: "Enlarge the space for your tent, and spread out your tent cloths unsparingly" (Is 54:2).[26] By missionary activity, the Mystical Body grows to the mature measure of the fullness of Christ (cf. Eph 4:13); and the spiritual temple, where God is adored in spirit and in truth (cf. Jn 4:23), grows and is built up upon the foundation of the apostles and prophets, Christ Jesus himself being the supreme corner stone (Eph 2:20).

---

24. Second Vatican Ecumenical Council, Dogmatic Constitution on the Church *Lumen Gentium,* 17; St. Augustine 7, *City of God,* 19, 17: *PL* 41, 646. Instr. S.C.P.F. (Collectanea I, n. 35, p. 42).

25. According to Origen, the Gospel must be preached before the end of this world: *Homily on Luke* XXI (*GCS,* Origen IX, 136, 21 ff.), *Comm. On Matthew* 39 (XI 75, 25 ff., 76, 4 ff.) *Homily on Jeremiah* III, 2 (VIII 308, 29 ff.); St. Thomas, *Summa Theol.,* I–II, q. 106, a. 4 *ad* 4.

26. Hilary of Poitiers, *On the Psalms* 14: *PL* 9, 301; Eusebius of Caesarea, *On Isaiah* 54, 2–3: *PG* 24, 462–463; Cyril of Alexandria, *On Isaiah* V, ch. 54, 1–3: *PG* 70, 1193.

CHAPTER II

MISSION WORK ITSELF

10. The Church, sent by Christ to reveal and to communicate the love of God to all men and nations, is aware that there still remains a gigantic missionary task for her to accomplish. For the Gospel message has not yet, or hardly yet, been heard by two billion human beings (and their number is increasing daily), who are formed into large and distinct groups by permanent cultural ties, by ancient religious traditions, and by firm bonds of social necessity. Some of these men are followers of one of the great religions, but others remain strangers to the very knowledge of God, while still others expressly deny his existence, and sometimes even attack it. The Church, in order to be able to offer all of them the mystery of salvation and the life brought by God, must implant herself into these groups for the same motive which led Christ to bind himself, in virtue of his Incarnation, to certain social and cultural conditions of those human beings among whom he dwelt.

Article 1: Christian Witness

11. The Church must be present in these groups through her children, who dwell among them or who are sent to them. For all Christians, wherever they live, are bound to show forth, by the example of their lives and by the witness of the word, that new man put on at Baptism and that power of the Holy Spirit by which they have been strengthened at Confirmation. Thus other men, observing their good works, can glorify the Father (cf. Mt 5:16) and can perceive more fully the real meaning of human life and the universal bond of the community of mankind.

In order that they may be able to bear more fruitful witness to Christ, let them be joined to those men by esteem and love; let them acknowledge themselves to be members of the group of men among whom they live; let them share in cultural and social life by the various undertakings and enterprises of human living; let them be familiar with their national and religious traditions; let them gladly and reverently lay bare the seeds of the Word which lie hidden among their fellows. At the same time, however, let them look to the profound changes which are taking place among nations, and let them exert themselves to keep modern man, intent as he is on the science and technology of today's world from becoming a stranger to things divine; rather, let them awaken in him a yearning for that truth and charity which God has revealed. Even as Christ himself searched the hearts of men and led them to divine light, so also his disciples, profoundly penetrated by the Spirit of Christ, should know the people among whom they live and should converse with them, that they themselves may learn by sincere and patient dialogue what treasures a generous God has distributed among the nations of the earth. But at the same time, let them try to furbish these treasures, set them free, and bring them under the dominion of God their Savior.

12. The presence of the Christian faithful in these human groups should be inspired by that charity with which God has loved us, and with which he wills that we should love one another (cf. 1 Jn 4:11). Christian charity truly extends to all, without distinction of race, creed, or social condition: it looks for neither gain nor gratitude. For as God loved us with an unselfish love, so also the faithful should in their charity care for the human person himself, loving him with the same affection with which God sought out man. Just as Christ, then, went about all the towns and villages, curing every kind of disease and infirmity as a sign that the kingdom of God had come (cf. Mt 9:35 ff; Acts 10:38), so also the Church, through her children, is one with men of every condition, but especially with the poor and the afflicted. For them she gladly spends and is spent (cf. 2 Cor 12:15), sharing in their joys and sorrows, knowing of their longings and problems, suffering with them in death's anxieties. To those in quest of peace, she wishes to answer in fraternal dialogue, bearing them the peace and the light of the Gospel.

Let Christians labor and collaborate with others in rightly regulating the affairs of social and economic life. With special care let them devote themselves to the education of children and young people by means of different kinds of schools, which should be considered not only as the most excellent means of forming and developing Christian youth, but also as a valuable public service, especially in the developing nations, working toward the uplifting of human dignity and toward better living conditions. Furthermore, let them take part in the strivings of those peoples who, waging war on famine, ignorance, and disease, are struggling to better their way of life and to secure peace in the world. In this activity the faithful should be eager to offer prudent aid to projects sponsored by public and private organizations, by governments, by various Christian communities, and even by non-Christian religions.

However, the Church has no desire at all to intrude itself into the government of the earthly city. It claims no other authority than that of ministering to men with the help of God, in a spirit of charity and faithful service (cf. Mt 20:26; 23:11).[1]

Closely united with men in their life and work, Christ's disciples hope to render to others true witness of Christ and to work for their salvation, even where they are not able to announce Christ fully. For they are not seeking a mere material progress and prosperity for men, but are promoting their dignity and brotherly union, teaching those religious and moral truths which Christ illumined with his light, and in this way they are gradually opening up a fuller approach to God. Thus, they help men to attain to salvation by love for God and neighbor, and the mystery of Christ begins to shine forth, in which there appears the new man, created according to God (cf. Eph 4:24), and in which the charity of God is revealed.

Article 2: Preaching the Gospel and Gathering Together the People of God

13. Wherever God opens a door of speech for proclaiming the mystery of Christ (cf. Col 4:3), there is announced to all men (cf. Mk 16:15; 1 Cor 9:15; Rm 10:14) with confidence and constancy (cf. Acts 4:13, 29, 31; 9:27, 28; 13:46; 14:3; 19:8; 26:26; 28:31; 1 Thes 2:2; 2 Cor 3:12; 7:4; Phil 1:20; Eph 3:12; 6:19, 20) the living God, and he whom he has sent for the salvation of all, Jesus Christ (cf. 1 Thes 1:9–10; 1 Cor 1:18–21; Gal 1:31; Acts 14:15–17, 17:22–31), in order that non-Christians, when the Holy Spirit opens their heart (cf. Acts 16:14), may believe and be freely converted to the Lord, that they may cleave sincerely to him who, being the "way, the truth, and the life" (Jn 14:6), fulfills all their spiritual expectations and even infinitely surpasses them.

---

1. Cf. Paul VI, *Allocution in the Council* (Nov. 21, 1964): *AAS* (1964), 1013.

This conversion must be taken as an initial one, yet sufficient to make a man realize that he has been snatched away from sin and led into the mystery of God's love, who called him to enter into a personal relationship with him in Christ. For by the workings of divine grace, the new convert sets out on a spiritual journey by means of which, already sharing through faith in the mystery of Christ's death and resurrection, he passes from the old man to the new one, perfected in Christ (cf. Col 3:5–10; Eph 4:20–24). This bringing with it a progressive change of outlook and morals, must become evident with its social consequences and must be gradually developed during the time of the catechumenate. Since the Lord he believes in is a sign of contradiction (cf. Lk 2:34; Mt 10:34–39), the convert often experiences an abrupt breaking off of human ties, but he also tastes the joy which God gives without measure (cf. 1 Thes 1:6).

The Church strictly forbids forcing anyone to embrace the faith, or alluring or enticing people by worrisome wiles. By the same token, she also strongly insists on this right, that no one be frightened away from the faith by unjust vexations on the part of others.[2]

In accord with the Church's ancient custom, the convert's motives should be looked into, and if necessary, purified.

14. Those who, through the Church, have accepted from God a belief in Christ[3] are admitted to the catechumenate by liturgical rites. The catechumenate is not a mere expounding of doctrines and precepts, but a training period in the whole Christian life and an apprenticeship duty drawn out, during which disciples are joined to Christ their teacher. Therefore, catechumens should be properly instructed in the mystery of salvation and in the practice of Gospel morality, and by sacred rites which are to be held at successive intervals,[4] they should be introduced into the life of faith, of liturgy, and of love, which is led by the People of God.

---

2. Cf. Second Vatican Ecumenical Council, Declaration on Religious Liberty *Dignitatis Humanae,* 2, 4, 10; Dogmatic Constitution on the Church *Lumen Gentium;* Pastoral Constitution on the Church in the Modern World *Gaudium et Spes.*

3. Cf. Second Vatican Ecumenical Council, Dogmatic Constitution on the Church *Lumen Gentium,* 17.

4. Cf. Second Vatican Ecumenical Council, Constitution on the Sacred Liturgy *Sacrosanctum Concilium,* 64–65.

Then, when the sacraments of Christian initiation have freed them from the power of darkness (cf. Col 1:13),[5] having died with Christ, been buried with him and risen together with him (cf. Rm 6:4–11; Col 2:12–13; 1 Pt 3:21–22; Mk 16:16), they receive the Spirit (cf. 1 Thes 3:5–7; Acts 8:14–17) of adoption of sons and celebrate the remembrance of the Lord's death and resurrection together with the whole People of God.

It is to be desired that the liturgy of the Lenten and paschal seasons should be restored in such a way as to dispose the hearts of the catechumens to celebrate the Easter mystery at whose solemn ceremonies they are reborn to Christ through Baptism.

But this Christian initiation in the catechumenate should be taken care of not only by catechists or priests, but by the entire community of the faithful, so that right from the outset the catechumens may feel that they belong to the People of God. And since the life of the Church is an apostolic one, the catechumens also should learn to cooperate wholeheartedly, by the witness of their lives and by the profession of their faith, in the spread of the Gospel and in the building up of the Church.

Finally, the juridic status of catechumens should be clearly defined in the new code of canon law. For since they are joined to the Church,[6] they are already of the household of Christ,[7] and not seldom they are already leading a life of faith, hope and charity.

Article 3: Forming a Christian Community

15. The Holy Spirit, who calls all men to Christ by the seeds of the word and by the preaching of the Gospel, stirs up in their hearts a submission to the faith. When in the womb of the baptismal font, he begets to a new life those who believe in Christ, he gathers them into the one People of God which is "a chosen race, a royal priesthood, a holy nation, a purchased people" (1 Pt 2:9).[8]

---

5. Concerning this liberation from demons and the powers of darkness, in the Gospel, cf. Mt 12:28; Jn 8:44; 12:31. (Cf. 1 Jn 3:8; Eph 2:1–2). On the liturgy of Baptism, cf. *Roman Ritual.*

6. Cf. Second Vatican Ecumenical Council, Dogmatic Constitution on the Church *Lumen Gentium,* 14.

7. Cf. St. Augustine, *Tract on John* 11, 4: *PL* 35, 1476.

8. Cf. Second Vatican Ecumenical Council, Dogmatic Constitution on the Church *Lumen Gentium,* 9.

Therefore, let the missionaries, God's co-workers, (cf. 1 Cor 3:9), raise up congregations of the faithful such that, walking worthy of the vocation to which they have been called (cf. Eph 4:1), they may exercise the priestly, prophetic and royal office which God has entrusted to them. In this way the Christian community will be a sign of God's presence in the world: for by reason of the Eucharistic Sacrifice, this community is ceaselessly on the way with Christ to the Father;[9] carefully nourished on the Word of God[10] it bears witness to Christ;[11] and finally, it walks in charity and is fervent with the apostolic spirit.[12]

The Christian community should from the very start be so formed that it can provide for its own necessities insofar as this is possible.

This congregation of the faithful, endowed with the riches of its own nation's culture, should be deeply rooted in the people. Let families flourish which are imbued with the spirit of the Gospel,[13] and let them be assisted by good schools; let associations and groups be organized by means of which the lay apostolate will be able to permeate the whole of society with the spirit of the Gospel. Lastly, let charity shine out between Catholics of different rites.[14]

The ecumenical spirit should be nurtured in the neophytes, who should take into account that the brethren who believe in Christ are Christ's disciples, reborn in Baptism, sharers with the People of God in very many good things. Insofar as religious conditions allow, ecumenical activity should be furthered in such a way that, excluding any appearance of indifference or confusion on the one hand, or of unhealthy rivalry on the other, Catholics should cooperate in a brotherly spirit with their separated brethren, according to the norms of the *Decree on Ecumenism,* making before the nations a common profession of faith,

---

9. Cf. Cf. Second Vatican Ecumenical Council, Dogmatic Constitution on the Church *Lumen Gentium,* 10, 11, 34.

10. Cf. Second Vatican Ecumenical Council, Dogmatic Constitution on Divine Revelation *Dei Verbum,* 21.

11. Cf. Second Vatican Ecumenical Council, Dogmatic Constitution on the Church *Lumen Gentium,* 12, 35.

12. Cf. Second Vatican Ecumenical Council, Dogmatic Constitution on the Church *Lumen Gentium,* 23, 36.

13. Cf. Second Vatican Ecumenical Council, Dogmatic Constitution on the Church *Lumen Gentium,* 11, 35, 41.

14. Cf. Second Vatican Ecumenical Council, Decree on the Catholic Churches of the Eastern Rite *Orientalium Ecclesiarum,* 30.

insofar as their beliefs are common, in God and in Jesus Christ, and co-operating in social and in technical projects as well as in cultural and religious ones. Let them cooperate especially for the sake of Christ, their common Lord; let his name be the bond that unites them! This cooperation should be undertaken not only among private persons, but also, subject to approval by the local ordinary, among churches or ecclesial communities and their works.

The Christian faithful gathered together out of all nations into the Church "are not marked off from the rest of men by their government, nor by their language, nor by their political institutions,"[15] and so they should live for God and Christ in a respectable way of their own national life. As good citizens, they should be true and effective patriots, altogether avoiding racial prejudice and hypernationalism, and should foster a universal love for man.

To obtain all these things, the most important and therefore worthy of special attention are the Christian laity: namely, those who have been incorporated into Christ and live in the world. For it is up to them, imbued with the Spirit of Christ, to be a leaven working on the temporal order from within, to dispose it always in accordance with Christ.[16]

But it is not enough that the Christian people be present and be organized in a given nation, nor is it enough to carry out an apostolate by way of example. They are organized for this purpose; they are present for this: to announce Christ to their non-Christian fellow-citizens by word and example, and to aid them toward the full reception of Christ.

Now, in order to plant the Church and to make the Christian community grow, various ministries are needed, which are raised up by divine calling from the midst of the faithful congregation, and are to be carefully fostered and tended to by all. Among these are the offices of priests, of deacons, and of catechists, and Catholic action. Religious men and women likewise, by their prayers and by their active work, play an indispensable role in rooting and strengthening the kingdom of Christ in souls and in causing it to be spread.

---

15. *Epistle to Diognetus* 5: *PG* 2, 1173; cf. Second Vatican Ecumenical Council, Dogmatic Constitution on the Church *Lumen Gentium,* 38.

16. Cf. Second Vatican Ecumenical Council, Dogmatic Constitution on the Church *Lumen Gentium,* 32; Second Vatican Ecumenical Council, Decree on the Apostolate of the Laity *Apostolicam Actuositatem.*

16. Joyfully the Church gives thanks for the priceless gift of the priestly calling which God has granted to so many youths among those nations but recently converted to Christ. For the Church drives deeper roots in any given sector of the human family when the various faithful communities all have, from among their members, their own ministers of salvation in the order of bishops, priests and deacons serving their own brethren, so that the young churches gradually acquire a diocesan structure with their own clergy.

What this Council has decreed concerning priestly vocations and formation should be religiously observed where the Church is first planted, and among the young churches. Of great importance are the things which are said about closely joining spiritual formation with the doctrinal and pastoral, about living a life patterned after the Gospel without looking out for one's own comfort or that of one's family, about cultivating a deep appreciation of the mystery of the Church. From all this, they will be well taught to dedicate themselves wholly to the service of the body of Christ and to the work of the Gospel, to cleave to their own bishop as his faithful co-workers, and to cooperate with their colleagues.[17]

To attain this general end, the whole training of the students should be planned in the light of the mystery of salvation as it is revealed in the Scriptures. This mystery of Christ and of man's salvation they can discover and live in the liturgy.[18]

These common requirements of priestly training, including the pastoral and practical ones prescribed by the Council[19] should be combined with an attempt to make contact with their own particular national way of thinking and acting. Therefore, let the minds of the students be kept open and attuned to an acquaintance and an appreciation of their own nation's culture. In their philosophical and theological studies, let them consider the points of contact which mediate between the traditions and religion of their homeland on the one hand and the Christian religion on

---

17. Cf. Second Vatican Ecumenical Council, Decree on Priestly Training *Optatam Totius,* 4, 8, 9.

18. Cf. Second Vatican Ecumenical Council, Constitution on the Sacred Liturgy *Sacrosanctum Concilium,* 17.

19. Cf. Second Vatican Ecumenical Council, Decree on Priestly Training *Optatam Totius,* 1.

the other.[20] Likewise, priestly training should have an eye to the pastoral needs of that region, and the students should learn the history, aim and method of the Church's missionary activity, and the special social, economic and cultural conditions of their own people. Let them be educated in the ecumenical spirit and duly prepared for fraternal dialogue with non-Christians.[21] All this demands that studies for the priesthood be undertaken, so far as possible, in association and living together with their own people.[22] Finally, let care be taken that students are trained in ordinary ecclesiastical and financial administration.

Moreover, suitable priests should be chosen, after a little pastoral practice, to pursue higher studies in universities, even abroad and especially in Rome, as well as in other institutes of learning. In this way the young churches will have at hand men from among the local clergy equipped with the learning and skill needed for discharging more difficult ecclesiastical duties.

Where episcopal conferences deem it opportune, the order of the diaconate should be restored as a permanent state of life according to the norms of the Constitution *De Ecclesia*.[23] For there are men who actually carry out the functions of the deacon's office: either preaching the Word of God as catechists, or presiding over scattered Christian communities in the name of the pastor and the bishop, or practicing charity in social or relief work. It is only right to strengthen them by the imposition of hands which has come down from the apostles, and to bind them more closely to the altar, that they may carry out their ministry more effectively because of the sacramental grace of the diaconate.

17. Likewise worthy of praise are the ranks of men and women catechists, well deserving of missionary work to the nations. Imbued with the apostolic spirit, they labor much to make an outstanding and altogether necessary contribution to the spread of the faith and of the Church.

---

20. Cf. John XXIII, *Princeps Pastorum* (Nov. 28, 1959): *AAS* (1959), 843–844).

21. Cf. Second Vatican Ecumenical Council, Decree on Ecumenism *Unitatis Redintegratio*, 4.

22. Cf. John XXIII, Encyclical Letter *Princeps Pastorum* (Nov. 28, 1959): *AAS* (1959), 842.

23. Cf. Second Vatican Ecumenical Council, Dogmatic Constitution on the Church *Lumen Gentium*, 29.

In our time, when there are so few clerics to preach the Gospel to such great numbers and to exercise the pastoral ministry, the position of catechists is of great importance. Therefore, their training must be so accomplished and so adapted to advances on the cultural level that as reliable co-workers of the priestly order, they may perform their task well, though it be weighed down with new and greater burdens.

There should therefore be an increase in the number of schools, both on the diocesan and on the regional levels, wherein future catechists may study Catholic doctrine, especially in the fields of Scripture and the liturgy, as well as catechetical method and pastoral practice; schools wherein they can develop in themselves a Christian character,[24] and wherein they can devote themselves tirelessly to cultivating piety and sanctity of life. Moreover, conventions or courses should be held in which at certain times catechists could be refreshed in the disciplines and skills useful for their ministry and in which their spiritual life could be nourished and strengthened. In addition, for those who devote themselves entirely to this work, a decent standard of living should be provided, and social security, by paying them a just wage.[25]

It would be desirable for the Sacred Congregation for the Propagation of the Faith to provide special funds for the due training and support of catechists. If it seems necessary and fitting, let a special *Opus pro Catechists* be founded.

Moreover, the churches should gratefully acknowledge the noble work being done by auxiliary catechists, whose help they will need. These preside over the prayers in their communities and teach sacred doctrine. Something suitable should be done for their doctrinal and spiritual training. Besides, it is to be hoped that, where it seems opportune, catechists who are duly trained should receive a *missio canonica* in a publicly celebrated liturgical ceremony, so that in the eyes of the people they may serve the faith with greater authority.

18. Right from the planting stage of the Church, the religious life should be carefully fostered. This not only offers precious and absolutely necessary assistance to missionary activity, but by a more inward

---

24. Cf. John XXIII, Encyclical Letter *Princeps Pastorum* (Nov. 28, 1959): *AAS* (1959), 855.

25. The reference is to expressions of this kind: *catechistes a plein temps,* "full time catechists."

consecration made to God in the Church, it also clearly manifests and signifies the inner nature of the Christian calling.[26]

Religious institutes, working to plant the Church, and thoroughly imbued with mystic treasures with which the Church's religious tradition is adorned, should strive to give expression to them and to hand them on, according to the nature and the genius of each nation. Let them reflect attentively on how Christian religious life might be able to assimilate the ascetic and contemplative traditions, whose seeds were sometimes planted by God in ancient cultures already prior to the preaching of the Gospel.

Various forms of religious life are to be cultivated in the young churches, in order that they may display various aspects of the mission of Christ and of the life of the Church, and may devote themselves to various pastoral works, and prepare their members to exercise them rightly. On the other hand, the bishops in their conference should see to it that congregations pursuing the same apostolic aims are not multiplied to the detriment of the religious life and of the apostolate.

Worthy of special mention are the various projects for causing the contemplative life to take root. There are those who in such an attempt have kept the essential element of a monastic institution and are bent on implanting the rich tradition of their order; there are others again who are returning to the simpler forms of ancient monasticism. But all are studiously looking for a genuine adaptation to local conditions. Since the contemplative life belongs to the fullness of the Church's presence, let it be put into effect everywhere.

---

26. Cf. Second Vatican Ecumenical Council, Dogmatic Constitution on the Church *Lumen Gentium,* 31, 44.

CHAPTER III

PARTICULAR CHURCHES

19. The work of planting the Church in a given human community reaches a certain goal when the congregation of the faithful, already rooted in social life and somewhat conformed to the local culture, enjoys a certain firmness and stability. That is to say, it is already equipped with its own supply (perhaps still insufficient) of local priests, religious, and laymen, and is endowed with these institutions and ministries which are necessary for leading and expanding the life of the People of God under the guidance of their own bishop.

In such new churches, the life of the People of God must mature in all those fields of Christian life which are to be reformed by the norms of this Council. The congregations of the faithful become daily more aware of their status as communities of faith, liturgy and love. The laity strive by their civic and apostolic activity to set up a public order based on justice and love. The means of social communication are put to wise use at the opportune time. By a truly Christian life, families become seedbeds of the lay apostolate and of vocations to the priesthood and the religious life. Finally, the faith is taught by an adequate catechesis; it is celebrated in a liturgy in harmony with the genius of the people, and by suitable canonical legislation, it is introduced into upright institutions and local customs.

The bishops, in turn, each one together with his own college of priests, being more and more imbued with the mind of Christ and of the Church, feel and live along with the universal Church. Let the young church keep up an intimate communion with the whole Church, whose tradition they should link to their own culture, in order to increase, by a certain mutual exchange of forces, the life of the Mystical Body.[1] Hence,

---

1. Cf. John XXIII, Encyclical Letter *Princeps Pastorum* (Nov. 28, 1959): *AAS* (1959), 838.

stress should be laid on those theological, psychological, and human elements which can contribute to fostering this sense of communion with the universal Church.

But these churches, very often located in the poorer portions of the globe, are mostly suffering from a very serious lack of priests and of material support. Therefore, they are badly in need of the continued missionary activity of the whole Church to furnish them with those subsidies which serve for the growth of the local church, and above all for the maturity of Christian life. This mission action should also furnish help to those churches, founded long since, which are in a certain state of regression or weakness.

Yet these churches should launch a common pastoral effort and suitable works to increase the number of vocations to the diocesan clergy and to religious institutes, to discern them more readily, and to train them more efficiently,[2] so that little by little these churches may be able to provide for themselves and to bring aid to others.

20. Since the particular church is bound to represent the universal Church as perfectly as possible, let it realize that it has been sent to those also who are living in the same territory with it, and who do not yet believe in Christ. By the life witness of each one of the faithful and of the whole community, let the particular church be a sign which points out Christ to others.

Furthermore, there is need of the ministry of the word, so that the Gospel may reach all. The bishop should be first and foremost a herald of the faith, who leads new disciples to Christ.[3] In order that he may properly fulfill this noble task, let him thoroughly study both the conditions of his flock and the private opinions of his countrymen concerning God, taking careful note also of those changes which urbanization, migrations and religious indifferentism have introduced.

The local priests in the young churches should zealously address themselves to the work of spreading the Gospel, and join forces with the foreign missionaries who form with them one college of priests, united under the authority of the bishop. They should do this not only with a

---

2. Cf. Second Vatican Ecumenical Council, Decree on the Ministry and Life of Priests *Presbyterorum Ordinis,* 11; Decree on Priestly Training *Optatam Totius,* 2.

3. Cf. Second Vatican Ecumenical Council, Dogmatic Constitution on the Church *Lumen Gentium,* 25.

view to the feeding the faithful flock and to the celebrating of divine worship, but also to the preaching of the Gospel to those outside. Let them show themselves ready, and when the occasion presents itself, let them with a willing heart offer the bishop their services for missionary work in distant and forsaken areas of their own diocese or of other dioceses.

Let religious men and women, and the laity too, show the same fervent zeal toward their countrymen, especially toward the poor.

Episcopal conferences should see to it that biblical, theological, spiritual and pastoral refresher courses are held at stated intervals with this intention, that amid all vicissitudes and changes the clergy may acquire a fuller knowledge of the theological sciences and of pastoral methods.

For the rest, those things which this Council has laid down, particularly in the *Decree on the Life and Work of Priests,* should be religiously observed.

In order that this missionary work of the particular church may be performed, there is need of qualified ministers, who are to be prepared in due time in a way suited to the conditions of each church. Now, since men are more and more banding together into associations, it is very fitting that episcopal conferences should form a common plan concerning the dialogue to be held with such associations. But if perchance in certain regions, groups of men are to be found who are kept away from embracing the Catholic faith because they cannot adapt themselves to the peculiar form which the Church has taken on there, it is hoped that this condition will be provided for in a special way,[4] until such time as all Christians can gather together in one community. Let individual bishops call to their dioceses the missionaries whom the Holy See may have on hand for this purpose, or let them receive such missionaries gladly, and support their undertakings effectively.

In order that this missionary zeal may flourish among those in their own homeland, it is very fitting that the young churches should participate as soon as possible in the universal missionary work of the Church,

---

4. Cf. Second Vatican Ecumenical Council, Decree on the Ministry and Life of Priests *Presbyterorum Ordinis,* 10, where in order to render particular pastoral labors easier for various social groups, provision is made for the establishment of personal prelacies, insofar as needs of the apostolate demand it.

and send their own missionaries to proclaim the Gospel all over the world, even though they themselves are suffering from a shortage of clergy. For their communion with the universal Church will be somehow brought to perfection when they themselves take an active part in missionary zeal toward other nations.

21. The Church has not been really founded and is not yet fully alive, nor is it a perfect sign of Christ among men, unless there is a laity worthy of the name working along with the hierarchy. For the Gospel cannot be deeply grounded in the abilities, life and work of any people without the active presence of laymen. Therefore, even at the very founding of a church, great attention is to be paid to establishing a mature, Christian laity.

For the lay faithful fully belong at one and the same time both to the People of God and to civil society; they belong to the nation in which they were born; they have begun to share in its cultural treasures by means of their education; they are joined to its life by manifold social ties; they are cooperating in its progress by their efforts, each in his own profession; they feel its problems to be their very own, and they are trying to solve them. They also belong to Christ, because they were regenerated in the Church by faith and by Baptism, so that they are Christ's in newness of life and work (cf. 1 Cor 15:23), in order that in Christ, all things may be made subject to God, and finally God will be all in all (cf. 1 Cor 15:28).

Their main duty, whether they are men or women, is the witness which they are bound to bear to Christ by their life and works in the home, in their social milieu, and in their own professional circle. In them there must appear the new man created according to God in justice and true holiness (cf. Eph 4:24). But they must give expression to this newness of life in the social and cultural framework of their own homeland, according to their own national traditions. They must be acquainted with this culture; they must heal it and preserve it; they must develop it in accordance with modern conditions, and finally perfect it in Christ, so that the faith of Christ and the life of the Church are no longer foreign to the society in which they live, but begin to permeate and to transform it. Let them be one with their fellow countrymen in sincere charity, so that there appears in their way of life a new bond of unity and of universal solidarity, which is drawn from the mystery of Christ. Let them also spread the faith of Christ among those with whom they live or have professional connections—an obligation which is all the more urgent, because very many men can hear of Christ and of the Gospel only by means of the laity who are their neighbors. In fact, wherever possible, the laity should be prepared, in more immediate cooperation with the hierarchy, to fulfill a special mission of proclaiming the Gospel and communicating Christian teachings, so that they may add vigor to the nascent Church.

Let the clergy highly esteem the arduous apostolate of the laity. Let them train the laity to become conscious of the responsibility which they as members of Christ have for all men; let them instruct them deeply in the mystery of Christ, introduce them to practical methods, and be at their side in difficulties, according to the tenor of the Constitution *Lumen Gentium* and the Decree *Apostolicam Actuositatem*.

While pastors and laymen, then, each retain their own state of life and their own responsibilities, let the whole young church render one firm and vital witness to Christ, and become a shining beacon of the salvation which comes to us in Christ.

22. The seed which is the Word of God, watered by divine dew, sprouts from the good ground and draws from thence its moisture, which it transforms and assimilates into itself, and finally bears much fruit. In harmony with the economy of the Incarnation, the young churches, rooted in Christ and built up on the foundation of the apostles, take to themselves in a wonderful exchange all the riches of the nations which were given to Christ as an inheritance (cf. Ps 2:8). They borrow from the customs and traditions of their people, from their wisdom and their learning, from their arts and disciplines, all those things which can contribute to the glory of their Creator, or enhance the grace of their Savior, or dispose Christian life the way it should be.[5]

To achieve this goal, it is necessary that in each major socio-cultural area such theological speculation should be encouraged, in the light of the universal Church's tradition, as may submit to a new scrutiny the words and deeds which God has revealed, and which have been set down in Sacred Scripture and explained by the Fathers and by the magisterium.

---

5. Cf. Second Vatican Ecumenical Council, Dogmatic Constitution on the Church *Lumen Gentium,* 13.

Thus it will be more clearly seen in what ways faith may seek for understanding, with due regard for the philosophy and wisdom of these peoples; it will be seen in what ways their customs, views on life, and social order can be reconciled with the manner of living taught by divine revelation. From here the way will be opened to a more profound adaptation in the whole area of Christian life. By this manner of acting, every appearance of syncretism and of false particularism will be excluded, and Christian life will be accommodated to the genius and the dispositions of each culture.[6] Particular traditions, together with the peculiar patrimony of each family of nations, illumined by the light of the Gospel, can then be taken up into Catholic unity. Finally, the young particular churches, adorned with their own traditions, will have their own place in the ecclesiastical communion, saving always the primacy of Peter's See, which presides over the entire assembly of charity.[7]

And so it is to be hoped that episcopal conferences within the limits of each major socio-cultural territory will so coordinate their efforts that they may be able to pursue this proposal of adaptation with one mind and with a common plan.

---

6. Cf. Paul VI, *Allocution at the Canonization of the Uganda Martyrs: AAS* (1964), 908.

7. Cf. Second Vatican Ecumenical Council, Dogmatic Constitution on the Church *Lumen Gentium,* 13.

CHAPTER IV

MISSIONARIES

23. Although every disciple of Christ, as far in him lies, has the duty of spreading the faith,[1] Christ the Lord always calls whomever he will from among the number of his disciples, to be with him and to be sent by him to preach to the nations (cf. Mk 3:13). Therefore, by the Holy Spirit, who distributes the charismata as he wills for the common good (1 Cor 12:11), he inspires the missionary vocation in the hearts of individuals, and at the same time he raises up in the Church certain institutes[2] which take as their own special task the duty of preaching the Gospel, a duty belonging to the whole Church.

They are assigned with a special vocation who, being endowed with a suitable natural temperament and being fit as regards talent and other qualities, have been trained to undertake mission work;[3] or be they autochthonous or be they foreigners: priests, religious or laymen. Sent by legitimate authority, they go out in faith and obedience to those who are far from Christ. They are set apart for the work for which they have been taken up (cf. Acts 13:2), as ministers of the Gospel, "that the offering up of the Gentiles may become acceptable, being sanctified by the Holy Spirit" (Rm 15:16).

24. Yet man must respond to God who calls, and that in such a way that without taking counsel with flesh and blood (Gal 1:16), he devotes himself wholly to the work of the Gospel. This response, however, can

---

1. Second Vatican Ecumenical Council, Dogmatic Constitution on the Church *Lumen Gentium*, 17.

2. "Institutes" refer to orders, congregations, institutions and associations which work in the missions.

3. Cf. Pius XI, Encyclical Letter *Rerum Ecclesiae* (Feb. 28, 1926): *AAS* (1926), 69–71; Pius XII, Encyclical Letter *Saeculo Exeunte* (June 13, 1940): *AAS* (1940), 140, 256; Pius XII, Encyclical Letter *Evangelii Praecones* (June 2, 1951): *AAS* (1951), 191, 506.

only be given when the Holy Spirit gives his inspiration and his power. For he who is sent enters upon the life and mission of him who "emptied himself, taking the nature of a slave" (Phil 2:7). Therefore, he must be ready to stay at his vocation for an entire lifetime, and to renounce himself and all those whom he thus far considered as his own, and instead to "make himself all things to all men" (1 Cor 9:22).

Announcing the Gospel to all nations, he confidently makes known the mystery of Christ, whose ambassador he is, so that in him he dares to speak as he ought (cf. Eph 6:19; Acts 4:31), not being ashamed of the scandal of the cross. Following in his Master's footsteps, meek and humble of heart, he proves that his yoke is easy and his burden light (Mt 11:29 ff.). By a truly evangelical life,[4] in much patience, in long-suffering, in kindness, in unaffected love (cf. 2 Cor 6:4 ff.), he bears witness to his Lord, if need be to the shedding of his blood. He will ask of God the power and strength, that he may know that there is an overflowing of joy amid much testing of tribulation and deep poverty (2 Cor 8:2). Let him be convinced that obedience is the hallmark of the servant of Christ, who redeemed the human race by his obedience.

The heralds of the Gospel, lest they neglect the grace which is in them, should be renewed day by day in the spirit of their mind (cf. 1 Tm 4:14; Eph 4:23; 2 Cor 4:16). Their ordinaries and superiors should gather the missionaries together from time to time, that they be strengthened in the hope of their calling and may be renewed in the apostolic ministry, even in houses expressly set up for this purpose.

25. For such an exalted task, the future missionary is to be prepared by a special spiritual and moral training.[5] For he must have the spirit of initiative in beginning, as well as that of constancy in carrying through what he has begun; he must be persevering in difficulties, patient and strong of heart in bearing with solitude, fatigue and fruitless labor. he will encounter men with an open mind and a wide heart; he will gladly take up the duties which are entrusted to him; he will with a noble spirit

---

4. Cf. Benedict XV, Encyclical Letter *Maximum Illud* (Nov. 30, 1919): *AAS* (1919), 449–450.

5. Cf. Benedict XV, Encyclical Letter *Maximum Illud* (Nov. 30, 1919): *AAS* (1919), 448–449; Pius XII, Encyclical Letter *Evangelii Praecones* (June 2, 1951): *AAS* (1951), 507. In the formation of priests to be missionaries, consideration is to be given to these things established by statute in the decree *On Priestly Training* of the Second Vatican Council.

adapt himself to the people's foreign way of doing things and to changing circumstances; while in the spirit of harmony and mutual charity, he will cooperate with his brethren and all who dedicate themselves to the same task, so that together with the faithful, they will be one heart and one soul (cf. Acts 2:42; 4:32) in imitation of the apostolic community.

These habits of mind should be earnestly exercised already in his time of training; they should be cultivated and should be upliftcd and nourished by the spiritual life. Imbued with a living faith and a hope that never fails, the missionary should be a man of prayer. Let him have an ardent spirit of power and of love and of prudence (cf. 2 Tm 1:7). Let him learn to be self-sufficing in whatever circumstances (Phil 4:11), always bearing about in himself the dying of Jesus, so that the life of Jesus may work in those to whom he is sent (2 Cor 4:10 ff.); out of zeal of souls, let him gladly spend all and be spent himself for souls (cf. 2 Cor 12:15 ff.), so that "by the daily practice of his duty he may grow in the love of God and neighbor."[6] Thus obedient to the will of the Father together with Christ, he will continue his mission under the hierarchical authority of the Church.

26. Those who are sent to different nations in order to be good ministers of Christ should he nourished with the "words of faith and with good doctrine" (1 Tm 4:6), which they should draw principally from the Sacred Scriptures, studying the mystery of Christ, whose heralds and witnesses they will be.

Therefore, all missionaries—priests, brothers, sisters and lay folk— each according to their own state, should be prepared and trained, lest they be found unequal to the demands of their future work.[7] From the very beginning, their doctrinal training should be so planned that it takes in both the universality of the Church and the diversity of the world's nations. This holds for all of their studies, by which they are prepared for the exercise of the ministry, as also for the other studies which it would be useful for them to learn, that they may have a general knowledge of the peoples, cultures and religions: not only a knowledge that looks to the past, but one that considers the present time. For anyone

---

6. Second Vatican Ecumenical Council, Dogmatic Constitution on the Church *Lumen Gentium,* 41.

7. Cf. Benedict XV, Encyclical Letter *Maximum Illud* (Nov. 30, 1919): *AAS* (1919), 440; Pius XII, Encyclical Letter *Evangelii Praecones* (June 2, 1951): *AAS* (1951), 507.

who is going to encounter another people should have a great esteem for their patrimony and their language and their customs. It is very necessary for the future missionary to devote himself to missiological studies: that is, to know the teachings and norms of the Church concerning missionary activity, to know along what roads the heralds of the Gospel have run in the course of the centuries, and also what is the present condition of the missions, and what methods are considered more effective at the present time.[8]

But even though this entire training program is imbued with pastoral solicitude, a special and organized apostolic training ought to be given, by means of both teaching and practical exercises.[9]

Brothers and sisters, in great numbers, should be well instructed and prepared in the catechetical art, that they may collaborate still better in the apostolate.

Even those who take part in missionary activity only for a time have to be given a training which is suited to their condition.

All these different kinds of formation should be completed in the lands to which they are sent, so that the missionaries may have a more thorough knowledge of the history, social structures, and customs of the people; that they may have an insight into their moral order and their religious precepts, and into the secret notions which, according to their sacred tradition, they have formed concerning God, the world and man.[10] Let the missionaries learn the languages to such a degree that they can use them in a fluent and polished manner, and so find more easy access to the minds and the hearts of men.[11] Furthermore, they should be properly introduced into special pastoral problems.

Some should be more thoroughly prepared in missiological institutes or in other faculties or universities, so that they may be able to

---

8. Benedict XV, Encyclical Letter *Maximum Illud* (Nov. 30, 1919): *AAS* (1919), 448; Decree S.C.P.F., (May 20, 1923): *AAS* (1923), 369–370; Pius XII Encyclical Letter *Saeculo Exeunte* (June 13, 1940): *AAS* (1940), 256; Encyclical Letter *Evangelii Praecones* (June 2, 1951): *AAS* (1951), 507; John XXIII, Encyclical Letter *Princeps Pastorum* (Nov. 28, 1959): *AAS* (1959), 843–844.

9. Second Vatican Ecumenical Council, Decree on Priestly Training *Optatam Totius,* 19–21; Apostolic Constitution *Sedes Sapientiae,* with general statutes.

10. Pius XII, Encyclical Letter *Evangelii Praecones* (June 2, 1951): *AAS* (1951), 523–524.

11. Benedict XV, Encyclical Letter *Maximum Illud* (Nov. 30, 1919): *AAS* (1919), 448; Pius XII, Encyclical Letter *Evangelii Praecones* (June 2, 1951): *AAS* (1951), 507.

discharge special duties more effectively[12] and be a help, by their learning, to other missionaries in carrying on the mission work, which especially in our time presents so many difficulties and opportunities. It is, moreover, highly desirable that the regional episcopal conferences should have available an abundance of such experts, and that they should make fruitful use of their knowledge and experience in the necessities of their office. Nor should there be wanting some who are perfectly skilled in the use of practical instruments and the means of social communication, the importance of which should be highly appreciated by all.

27. All these things, though necessary for everyone who is sent to the nations, can scarcely be attained to in reality by individual missionaries. Since even mission work itself, as experience teaches, cannot be accomplished by lone individuals, a common calling has gathered these individuals together into institutes, in which, with united efforts, they are properly trained and might carry out this work in the name of the Church and under the direction of the hierarchy. For many centuries these institutes have borne the burden of the day and the heat, devoting themselves to missionary labor either entirely or in part. Often vast territories were committed to them by the Holy See for evangelization, and there they gathered together a new people for God, a local church clinging to their own shepherds. With their zeal and experience, they will serve, by fraternal cooperation, either in the care of souls or in rendering special services for the common good, those churches which were founded at the cost of their sweat and even of their blood.

Sometimes, throughout the entire extent of some region, they will take certain tasks upon themselves: e.g., the evangelization of groups of peoples who perhaps for special reasons have not yet accepted the Gospel message, or who have thus far resisted it.[13]

If need be, let them be on hand to help and train, out of their own experience, those who will devote themselves to missionary activity for a time.

For these reasons, and since there are still many nations to be led to Christ, the institutes remain extremely necessary.

---

12. Cf. Pius XII, Encyclical Letter *Fidei Donum* (Jan. 15, 1957): *AAS* (1957), 234.

13. Cf. Second Vatican Ecumenical Council, Decree on the Ministry and Life of Priests *Presbyterorum Ordinis,* 10, where it refers to dioceses and personal prelatures and the like.

CHAPTER V

PLANNING MISSIONARY ACTIVITY

28. The Christian faithful, having different gifts (cf. Rm 12:6), according to each one's opportunity, ability, charisms and ministry (cf. 1 Cor 3:10), must all cooperate in the Gospel. Hence, all alike, those who sow and those who reap (cf. Jn 4:37), those who plant and those who irrigate, must be one (cf. 1 Cor 3:8), so that "in a free and orderly fashion cooperating toward the same end,"[1] they may spend their forces harmoniously for the building up of the Church.

Wherefore, the labors of the Gospel heralds and the help given by the rest of the Christian faithful must be so directed and intertwined that "all may be done in order" (1 Cor 14:40) in all fields of missionary activity and cooperation.

29. Since the charge of proclaiming the Gospel in the whole world falls primarily on the body of bishops,[2] the synod of bishops or that "stable council of bishops for the entire Church,"[3] among the affairs of general concern,[4] should give special consideration to missionary activity, which is the greatest and holiest task of the Church.[5]

For all missions and for the whole of missionary activity, there should be only one competent office, namely that of the "Propagation of the Faith," which should direct and coordinate throughout the world

---

1. Cf. Second Vatican Ecumenical Council, Dogmatic Constitution on the Church *Lumen Gentium,* 18.

2. Cf. Second Vatican Ecumenical Council, Dogmatic Constitution on the Church *Lumen Gentium,* 23.

3. Cf. Paul VI, Motu Proprio *Apostolica Sollicitudo* (Sept. 15, 1965).

4. Cf. Paul VI, *Allocution in the Council* (Nov. 21, 1964): *AAS* (1964).

5. Cf. Benedict XV, Encyclical Letter *Maximum Illud* (Nov. 30, 1919): *AAS* (1919), 39–40.

both missionary work itself and missionary cooperation. However, the law of the Oriental Churches is to remain untouched.[6]

Although the Holy Spirit in diverse manners arouses the mission spirit in the Church of God, and oft times anticipates the action of those whose task it is to rule the life of the Church, yet for its part, this office should promote missionary vocations and missionary spirituality, zeal and prayer for the missions, and should put out authentic and adequate reports about them. Let it raise up missionaries and distribute them according to the more urgent needs of various areas. Let it arrange for an orderly plan of action, issue directives and principles adapted to evangelization, and give the impetus. Let it take care of stimulating and coordinating an effective collection of funds, which are to be distributed according to reasons of necessity and usefulness, the extent of the territory in question, the number of believers and non-believers, of undertakings and institutes, of ministers and missionaries.

In coordination with the Secretariat for Promoting Christian Unity, let it search out ways and means for bringing about and directing fraternal cooperation as well as harmonious living, with missionary undertakings of other Christian communities, that as far as possible the scandal of division may be removed.

Therefore, this office must be both an instrument of administration and an organ of dynamic direction, which makes use of scientific methods and means suited to the conditions of modern times, always taking into consideration present-day research in matters of theology, of methodology and missionary pastoral procedure.

In the direction of this office, an active role with a deliberative vote should be had by selected representatives of all those who cooperate in missionary work: that is, the bishops of the whole world (the episcopal conferences should be heard from in this regard), as well as the moderators of pontifical institutes and works, in ways and under conditions to be fixed by the Roman Pontiff. All these, being called together at stated times, will exercise supreme control of all mission work under the authority of the supreme Pontiff. This office should

---

6. If these missions for special reasons are made subject to other ecclesiastical jurisdictions for a time, it is fitting that this ecclesiastic jurisdiction establish relations with the Sacred Congregation for the Propagation of the Faith so that in ordering and directing all these missions, a regular and uniform pattern can be realized.

have available a permanent group of expert consultors, of proven knowledge and experience, whose duty it will be, among other things, to gather pertinent information about local conditions in various regions, and about the thinking of various groups of men, as well as about the means of evangelization to be used. They will then propose scientifically based conclusions for mission work and cooperation.

Institutes of religious women, regional undertakings for the mission cause, and organizations of laymen (especially international ones) should be suitably represented.

30. In order that the proper goals and results may be obtained, all missionary workers should have but "one heart and one soul" (Acts 4:32) in the actual carrying out of mission work itself.

It is the bishop's role, as the ruler and center of unity in the diocesan apostolate, to promote missionary activity, to direct it and to coordinate it, but always in such a way that the zeal and spontaneity of those who share in the work may be preserved and fostered. All missionaries, even exempt religious, are subject to his power in the various works which refer to the exercise of the sacred apostolate.[7] To improve coordination, let the bishop set up, insofar as possible, a pastoral council in which clergy, religious and laity may have a part, through the medium of selected delegates. Moreover, let them take care that apostolic activity be not limited to those only who have already been converted. A fair proportion of personnel and funds should be assigned to the evangelization of non-Christians.

31. Episcopal conferences should take common counsel to deal with weightier questions and urgent problems, without, however, neglecting local differences.[8] Lest the already insufficient supply of men and means be further dissipated, or lest projects be multiplied without necessity, it is recommended that they pool their resources to found projects which will serve the good of all: as for instance, seminaries; technical schools and schools of higher learning; pastoral, catechetical, and liturgical centers; as well as the means of social communication.

Such cooperation, when indicated, should also be initiated between several different episcopal conferences.

---

7. Cf. Second Vatican Ecumenical Council, Decree on the Pastoral Office of Bishops in the Church *Christus Dominus,* 35, 4.

8. Cf. Second Vatican Ecumenical Council, Decree on the Pastoral Office of Bishops in the Church *Christus Dominus,* 36–38.

32. It would also be good to coordinate the activities which are being carried on by ecclesiastical institutes and associations. All these, of whatever kind, should defer to the local ordinary in all that concerns missionary activity itself. Therefore, it will be very helpful to draw up contracts to regulate relations between local ordinaries and the moderator of the institute.

When a territory has been committed to a certain institute, both the ecclesiastical superior and the institute will be concerned to direct everything to this end, that the new Christian community may grow into a local church, which in due time will be governed by its own pastor with his clergy.

When the commission of a certain territory expires, a new state of affairs begins. Then the episcopal conference and the institutes in joint deliberation should lay down norms governing the relations between local ordinaries and the institutes.[9] It will be the role of the Holy See to outline the general principles according to which regional and even particular contracts are to be drawn up.

Although the institutes will be prepared to continue the work which they have begun, cooperating in the ordinary ministry of the care of souls, yet when the local clergy grows numerous, it will be provided that the institute, insofar as this is in agreement with its purpose, should remain faithful to the diocese, generously taking over special works or some area in it.

33. The institutes engaged in missionary activity in the same territory should find ways and means of coordinating their work. Therefore, it will be very useful to have conferences of religious men and unions of religious women, in which institutes of the same country or region should take part. These conferences should ask what things can be done by combined efforts, and they should be in close touch with the episcopal conferences.

All these things, with equal reason, should be extended to include the cooperation of missionary institutes in the home lands, so that questions and joint projects can be settled with less expense: as for instance, the formation of future missionaries, as well as courses for missionaries,

---

9. Cf. Second Vatican Ecumenical Council, Decree on the Pastoral Office of Bishops in the Church *Christus Dominus,* 35, 5–6.

relations with public authorities and with international or supranational organizations.

34. Since the right and methodical exercise of missionary activity requires that those who labor for the Gospel should be scientifically prepared for their task, and especially for dialogue with non-Christian religions and cultures, and also that they should be effectively assisted in the carrying out of this task, it is desired that for the sake of the missions, there should be fraternal and generous collaboration on the part of scientific institutes which specialize in missiology and in other arts and disciplines useful for the missions, such as ethnology and linguistics, the history and science of religions, sociology, pastoral skills and the like.

CHAPTER VI

COOPERATION

35. Since the whole Church is missionary, and the work of evangelization is a basic duty of the People of God, this sacred synod invites all to a deep interior renewal; so that, having a vivid awareness of their own responsibility for spreading the Gospel, they may do their share in missionary work among the nations.

36. As members of the living Christ, incorporated into him and made like unto him through Baptism and through Confirmation and the Eucharist, all the faithful are duty-bound to cooperate in the expansion and spreading out of his body, to bring it to fullness as soon as may be (Eph 4:13).

Therefore, all sons of the Church should have a lively awareness of their responsibility to the world; they should foster in themselves a truly catholic spirit; they should spend their forces in the work of evangelization. And yet, let everyone know that their first and most important obligation for the spread of the faith is this: to lead a profoundly Christian life. For their fervor in the service of God and their charity toward others will cause a new spiritual wind to blow for the whole Church, which will then appear as a sign lifted up among the nations (cf. Is 11:12), "the light of the world" (Mt 5:14) and "the salt of the earth" (Mt 5:13). This testimony of a good life will more easily have its effect if it is given in unison with other Christian communities, according to the norms of the *Decree on Ecumenism,* 12.[1] From this renewed spirit, prayer and works of penance will be spontaneously offered to God that he may fructify the missionaries' work with his grace; and then there will be missionary vocations, and the material subsidies which the missions need will be forthcoming.

---

1. Cf. Second Vatican Ecumenical Council, Decree on Ecumenism *Unitatis Redintegratio,* 12.

But in order that each and every one of the Christian faithful may be fully acquainted with the present condition of the Church in the world and may hear the voice of the multitudes who cry "help us!" (cf. Acts 16:9), modern means of social communication should be used to furnish such mission information that the faithful may feel this mission work to be their very own, and may open their hearts to such vast and profound human needs, and may come to their assistance.

It is also necessary to coordinate the information and to cooperate with national and international agencies.

37. But since the People of God live in communities, especially in dioceses and parishes, and become somehow visible in them, it is also up to these to witness Christ before the nations.

The grace of renewal cannot grow in communities unless each of these extends the range of its charity to the ends of the earth, and devotes the same care to those afar off as it does to those who are its own members.

Thus the whole community prays, works together and exercises its activity among the nations through those of its sons whom God has chosen for this most excellent task.

It will be very useful, provided the universal scope of mission work is not thereby neglected, to keep in contact with missionaries who are from one's own community, or with some parish or diocese in the missions, so that the communion between the communities may be made visible and serve for their mutual edification.

38. All bishops, as members of the body of bishops succeeding to the college of apostles, are consecrated not just for some one diocese, but for the salvation of the entire world. The mandate of Christ to preach the Gospel to every creature (Mk 16:15) primarily and immediately concerns them, with Peter and under Peter. Whence there arises that communion and cooperation of churches which is so necessary today for carrying on the work of evangelization. In virtue of this communion, the individual churches bear the burden of care for them all, and make their necessities known to one another, and exchange mutual communications regarding their affairs, since the extension of the body of Christ is the duty of the whole college of bishops.[2]

---

2. Cf. Second Vatican Ecumenical Council, Dogmatic Constitution on the Church *Lumen Gentium*, 23–24.

In his own diocese, with which he constitutes one unit, the bishop, stimulating, promoting and directing the work for the missions, makes the mission spirit and zeal of the People of God present and as it were visible, so that the whole diocese becomes missionary.

It will be the bishop's task to raise up from among his own people, especially the sick and those oppressed by hardship, some souls to offer prayers and penance to God with a wide open heart for the evangelization of the world. The bishop will also gladly encourage youths and clerics who have vocations to mission institutes, accepting it with a grateful spirit if God should call some of them to be employed in the missionary activity of the Church. The bishop will exhort and help the diocesan congregations to play a role of their own in the missions; he will promote the works of mission institutes among his own faithful, but most especially the papal mission works. For it is only right to give these works pride of place, since they are the means of imbuing Catholics from their very infancy with a real universal and missionary outlook; and they are also the means of making an effective collection of funds to subsidize all missions, each according to its needs.[3]

But since the need for workers in the vineyard of the Lord is growing from day to day, and diocesan priests have expressed the wish to play an ever greater part in the evangelization of the world, this sacred synod desires that the bishops, considering the very serious dearth of priests which is hindering the evangelization of many areas, should send some of their better priests, who offer themselves for mission work and have received a suitable preparation, to those dioceses which are lacking in clergy, where at least for a time they will exercise their missionary ministry in a spirit of service.[4]

But in order that the missionary activity of the bishops may be exercised more effectively for the good of the whole Church, it would be expedient for the episcopal conferences to take charge of those affairs which concern the orderly cooperation of their own region.

In their own conference, the bishops should deliberate about dedi-

---

3. Cf. Benedict XI, Encyclical Letter *Maximum Illud* (Nov. 30, 1919): *AAS* (1919), 453–454); Pius XI, Encyclical Letter *Rerum Ecclesiae* (Feb. 28, 1926): *AAS* (1926), 71–73; Pius XII, Encyclical Letter *Evangelii Praecones* (June 2, 1951): *AAS* (1951), 525–526; *idem,* Encyclical Letter *Fidei Donum* (Jan. 15, 1957): *AAS* (1957), 241.

4. Cf. Pius XII, Encyclical Letter *Fidei Donum* (Jan. 15, 1957): *AAS* (1957), 245–246.

cating to the evangelization of the nations some priests from among the diocesan clergy; they should decide what definite offering each diocese should be obliged to set aside annually for the work of the missions, in proportion to its own budget;[5] they should consider how to direct and control the ways and means by which the missions receive direct help; they should deal with assisting and, if need be, founding missionary institutes and seminaries for diocesan mission clergy, and the promoting of closer relations between such institutes and the dioceses.

It also pertains to the episcopal conferences to found and promote works for the brotherly reception and due pastoral care of those who immigrate from mission lands for the sake of studying or finding work. For through them, far-away peoples are sometimes made near; and an excellent opportunity is offered to communities which have long been Christian to converse with nations which have not yet heard the Gospel, and to show them in their own dutiful love and aid, the genuine face of Christ.[6]

39. Priests personally represent Christ and are collaborators of the order of bishops in that threefold sacred task which by its very nature belongs to the mission of the Church.[7] Therefore, they should fully understand that their life is also consecrated to the service of the missions. Now, because by means of their own ministry—which consists principally in the Eucharist which perfects the Church—they are in communion with Christ the head and are leading others to this communion, they cannot help but feel how much is yet wanting to the fullness of that body, and how much therefore must be done that it may grow from day to day. They shall therefore plan their pastoral care in such a way that it will serve to spread the Gospel among non-Christians.

In their pastoral activities, priests should stir up and preserve amid the faithful a zeal for the evangelization of the world, by instructing them in sermons and in Christian doctrine courses about the Church's task of announcing Christ to all nations, by enlightening Christian families about the necessity and the honor of fostering missionary vocations

---

5. Second Vatican Ecumenical Council, Decree on the Pastoral Office of Bishops in the Church *Christus Dominus,* 6.

6. Cf. Pius XII, Encyclical Letter *Fidei Donum* (Jan. 15, 1957): *AAS* (1957), 245.

7. Cf. Second Vatican Ecumenical Council, Dogmatic Constitution on the Church *Lumen Gentium,* 28.

among their own sons and daughters, by promoting mission fervor in young people from the schools and Catholic associations so that among them there may arise future heralds of the Gospel. Let priests teach the faithful to pray for the missions, and let them not be ashamed to ask alms of them for this purpose, becoming like beggars for Christ and for the salvation of souls.[8]

Professors in seminaries and universities will teach young people the true state of the world and of the Church, so that the necessity of a more intense evangelization of non-Christians will become clear to them and will nurture their zeal. In teaching the dogmatic, biblical, moral and historical branches, they should focus attention on the missionary elements therein contained, so that in this way a missionary awareness may be formed in future priests.

40. Religious institutes of the contemplative and of the active life have so far played, and still do play, the main role in the evangelization of the world. This sacred synod gladly acknowledges their merits and thanks God for all that they have expended for the glory of God and the service of souls, while exhorting them to go on untiringly in the work which they have begun, since they know that the virtue of charity, which by reason of their vocation they are bound to practice with greater perfection, obliges and impels them to a truly catholic spirit and work.[9]

Institutes of the contemplative life, by their prayers, sufferings, and works of penance, have a very great importance in the conversion of souls, because it is God who sends workers into his harvest when he is asked to do so (cf. Mt 9:38), God who opens the minds of non-Christians to hear the Gospel (cf. Acts 16:14), and God who fructifies the word of salvation in their hearts (cf. 1 Cor 3:7). In fact, these institutes are asked to found houses in mission areas, as not a few of them have already done, so that there, living out their lives in a way accommodated to the truly religious traditions of the people, they can bear excellent witness among non-Christians to the majesty and love of God, as well as to our union in Christ.

Institutes of the active life, whether they pursue a strictly mission ideal or not, should ask themselves sincerely in the presence of God

---

8. Cf. Pius XI, Encyclical Letter *Rerum Ecclesiae* (Feb. 28, 1926): *AAS* (1926), 72.

9. Cf. Second Vatican Ecumenical Council, Dogmatic Constitution on the Church *Lumen Gentium*, 44.

whether they would not be able to extend their activity for the expansion of the kingdom of God among the nations; whether they could possibly leave certain ministries to others so that they themselves could expend their forces for the missions; whether they could possibly undertake activity in the missions, adapting their constitutions if necessary, but according to the spirit of their founder; whether their members are involved as totally as possible in the mission effort; and whether their type of life is a witness to the Gospel accommodated to the character and condition of the people.

Now, since under the inspiration of the Holy Spirit, secular institutes are daily increasing in the Church, their activity, under the authority of the bishop, could be fruitful in the missions in many ways as a sign of complete dedication to the evangelization of the world.

41. Laymen cooperate in the Church's work of evangelization; as witnesses and at the same time as living instruments, they share in her saving mission,[10] especially if they have been called by God and have been accepted by the bishop for this work.

In those lands which are already Christian, laymen cooperate in the work of evangelization by nurturing in themselves and in others a knowledge and love of the missions; by stimulating vocations in their own family, in Catholic associations, and in the schools; by offering subsidies of every kind, that they may offer to others that gift of faith which they have received gratis.

But in mission lands, let laymen, whether foreigners or autochthonous, teach in schools, administer temporal goods, cooperate in parish and diocesan activities and organize and promote various forms of the lay apostolate, in order that the faithful of the young churches may be able to take part as soon as possible in the life of the Church.[11]

Lastly, let laymen gladly offer socio-economic cooperation to peoples on the way of development. This cooperation is all the more to be praised the more it concerns itself with founding institutes which touch on the basic structures of social life, or which are oriented to the training of those who bear the responsibility for the government.

---

10. Cf. Second Vatican Ecumenical Council, Dogmatic Constitution on the Church *Lumen Gentium,* 33, 35.

11. Cf. Pius XII, Encyclical Letter *Evangelii Praecones* (June 2, 1951): *AAS* (1951), 510, 514); John XXIII, Encyclical Letter *Princeps Pastorum* (Nov. 28, 1959): *AAS* (1959), 851–852).

Worthy of special praise are those laymen who, in universities or in scientific institutes, promote by their historical and scientific religious research the knowledge of peoples and of religions, thus helping the heralds of the Gospel and preparing for the dialogue with non-Christians.

They should cooperate in a brotherly spirit with other Christians, with non-Christians and with members of international organizations, always having before their eyes the fact that "the building up of the earthly city should have its foundation in the Lord, and should be directed toward him."[12]

To be equal to all these tasks, laymen need the necessary technical and spiritual preparation, which should be given in institutes destined for this, so that their lives may be a witness for Christ among non-Christians, according to the words of the Apostle: "Do not be a stumbling block to Jews and Greeks and to the Church of God, even as I myself in all things please all men, not seeking what is profitable to myself but to the many, that they may be saved" (1 Cor 10:32–33).

---

12. Cf. Second Vatican Ecumenical Council, Dogmatic Constitution on the Church *Lumen Gentium,* 46.

CONCLUSION

42. The council fathers together with the Roman Pontiff, feeling deeply their duty to spread everywhere the kingdom of God, lovingly salute all heralds of the Gospel, and especially those who suffer persecution for the name of Christ, being made partakers of their sufferings.[13]

They are afire with that same love with which Christ burned toward men. But aware that it is God who brings it about that his kingdom should come on earth, they pour forth their prayers together with all the Christian faithful, that through the intercession of the Virgin Mary, queen of the apostles, the nations may soon be led to the knowledge of the truth (1 Tm 2:4) and the glory of God which shines on the face of Jesus Christ may shine upon all men through the Holy Spirit (2 Cor 4:6).

Given in Rome at St. Peter's, December 7, 1965

---

13. Cf. Pius XII, Encyclical Letter *Evangelii Praecones* (June 2, 1951): *AAS* (1951), 527); John XXIII, Encyclical Letter *Princeps Pastorum* (Nov. 28, 1959): *AAS* (1959), 864.

DECREE ON THE MINISTRY AND LIFE OF PRIESTS

Presbyterorum Ordinis

Promulgated by
His Holiness Pope Paul VI
On December 7, 1965

INTRODUCTION

The introductory paragraph of the *Decree on the Ministry and Life of Priests (PO)* manifests its pastoral character. Though the role of priests in the life and mission of the Church had been treated in *Lumen Gentium* and *Christus Dominus,* and their formation in *Optatam Totius,* the Council deemed a lengthier treatment necessary because of the irreplaceable role of priests in the renewal of the Church. Its pastoral provisions are intended that the ministry of priests "be carried on more effectively and their lives be better provided for" (*PO* 1).

The decree can be seen in relation to the Church's understanding of its own apostolic nature. Its foundation is the conciliar teaching that by episcopal consecration bishops receive the fullness of the sacrament of Holy Orders and are, in Christ, made high priests (*LG* 21). So important is the role of the episcopate and of each individual bishop that the council could declare: "The bishop is to be considered as the high priest of his flock from whom the life in Christ of his faithful is in some way derived and upon whom it in some way depends" (*SC* 41). "The individual bishops, however, are the visible principle and foundation of unity in their particular churches" (*LG* 23). Communion with Christ in the Eucharist, and communion with the whole Church through the college of bishops, is expressed and realized through the ministry of bishops. The importance of priestly ministry derives from the importance of the ministry of bishops.

Formerly, the presbyterate was seen as the fundamental order of the priesthood, and the episcopate as something added only by way of jurisdiction. The Council stated that the episcopate is the fullness of the sacrament, in which the presbyterate participates. Because of this shift in emphasis, increased efforts are necessary if the faithful are to both understand and experience this role of bishops. One difficulty here is the infrequency of direct, personal encounters between the faithful and their bishops. Another is an insufficient understanding of the role of priests, particularly the inseparability of the sacraments and apostolic succession, especially as regards the Eucharist, and their relationship of communion with their bishop. Most commonly, the faithful experience the apostolicity of the Church primarily through the ministry of priests, who "participate in the office of the apostles" (*PO* 2).

While it is up to the bishops to "arrange their life in such a way as to accommodate it to the needs of our time" (*CD* 16), the spiritual renewal of the priesthood and the directives set forth in *PO* represent the best hope of giving the faithful an experience of the apostolic ministry that corresponds to the teaching of the Council.

Lumen Gentium and *PO* describe priests as the bishops' co-workers, assistants, helpers and cooperators. As the Council elsewhere noted: "But because it is impossible for the bishop always and everywhere to preside over the whole flock in his Church, he cannot do other than establish smaller groupings of the faithful. Among these the parishes set up locally under a pastor who takes the place of the bishop are the most important" (*SC* 42). Bound to their bishop and dependent on him for "the exercise of their power" (*LG* 28), priests "in a certain way...make him present in every congregation" (*PO* 5).

The Council spoke of the priestly ministry in terms of the threefold office of prophet, priest and king. Since the Council of Trent, there had been an emphasis on the priesthood's relation to worship, and specifically the Eucharist. Vatican II balanced the three elements, giving a certain priority to the ministry of the word: "Priests...have the primary duty of proclaiming the Gospel of God to all." This recovery of the importance of the ministry of the word is extremely significant. John Paul II elaborated on this in the exhortation *I Will Give You Shepherds*:

> The priest is first of all a minister of the word of God. He is consecrated and sent forth to proclaim the good news of the kingdom to all, calling every person to the obedience of faith and leading believers to an ever increasing knowledge of and communion in the mystery of God, as revealed and communicated to us in Christ (*PDV* 26).

The sacramental ministry retains its importance, and the decree notes that the Eucharist is "the source and the apex of the whole work of preaching the Gospel" (*PO* 5); it is the fulfillment of the community's priestly self offering (cf. *PO* 5); it is the "basis and center" of all service and the exercise of gifts by which the community is unified (*PO* 6). *PO* says the priestly ministry is directed to and perfected in making the spiritual sacrifices of the faithful complete by uniting them with the sacrifice of Christ (cf. *PO* 2).

Concelebration of the Eucharist, "whereby the unity of the priesthood is appropriately manifested" (*SC* 57), especially with the bishop, is the most excellent expression of the communion of priests with their bishop and with one another (cf. *PO* 7).

The decree also speaks of the office of shepherd or pastor: "Exercising the office of Christ, the shepherd and head, and according to their share of his authority, priests, in the name of the bishop, gather the family of God together" (*PO* 6). This pastoral ministry demands great kindness in dealing with people, and calls for special attention to the poor, youth, married people and parents. The decree situates this ministry in a universal perspective: "The office of pastor is not confined to the care of the faithful as individuals, but also in a true sense is extended to the formation of a genuine Christian community. Yet the spirit of the community should be so fostered as to embrace not only the local church, but also the universal Church" (*PO* 6).

The decree began by acknowledging the irreplaceable role of priests in effecting Church renewal. In *PO* 12, the thought returns; however, here it incorporates the most basic principle of Vatican II: renewal of the Church comes about through its members' growth in holiness. For this reason, the following assertion can be considered the most fundamental declaration of the decree:

> Hence, this holy Council, to fulfill its pastoral desires of an internal renewal of the Church, of the spread of the Gospel in every land and of a dialogue with the world of today, strongly urges all priests that they strive always for that growth in holiness by which they will become consistently better instruments in the service of the whole People of God, using for this purpose those means which the Church has approved (*PO* 12).

Holiness "does much for priests in carrying on a fruitful ministry" (*PO* 12) and for the renewal undertaken by the Council. For this reason "above all upon the bishops rests the heavy responsibility for the sanctity of their priests" (*PO* 7).

Here we encounter the second meaning of the pastoral orientation of Vatican II. It can refer to the practical, juridical, organizational directives intended to translate the Council's teaching into ecclesial life. Or it can mean going beyond the externals of the Church's structure and the actions of her members, to consider the spiritual reality which these are meant to signify, facilitate and express.

The Council's most basic principle is its emphasis on personal communion with Jesus Christ in charity. This is derived from the Church's faith-awareness that it is what it is—the sacrament of salvation and unity—only by reason of its union with Christ (cf. *LG* 1). The same is true of the Church's unity, which is a participation in the unity of the Trinity (cf. *LG* 4), and its holiness (cf. *LG* 39). From this, Vatican II derived the principle that the Church can only fulfill its vocation by deepening its union with Christ. This union is essentially the bond of supernatural charity, by which the Church possesses a real participation in the holiness of God. This is why chapter five on the universal call to holiness is the key to *Lumen Gentium*. Because this is the central document of the Council, it can be said that its chapter five is the key to the Council's entire plan for renewal.

In this light, the section of *PO* on the vocation of priests to holiness (articles 12–14) can be seen as the key to the Council's teaching on the priesthood. In keeping with *Lumen Gentium's* treatment of the holiness of priests (cf. *LG* 41), the decree emphasizes the unbreakable connection between priestly holiness and ministerial activity. The work of priestly ministry is related to union with Christ as fruit to a tree, as action to being.

By the sacrament of Holy Orders priests are "made living instruments of Christ" and are able to act "in place of Christ himself" (*PO* 12). God does not use people as instruments the way people use hammers and saws. When God calls a member of the Church to a specific function and service, he does not envision only the common good of the Church at the expense of the one called. Rather, through his vocation a priest will also find happiness and personal fulfillment. The sacrament of Holy Orders confers the graces a priest requires for holiness precisely through performing the duties of priestly ministry (cf. *PO* 13), which indicate God's will for the priest.

Fulfilling this ministry is a concrete way for the priest to say "yes" to God. In Mary we find the example of a faith that discerns God's will in all things, embraces a mission from God, and carries it out faithfully (cf. *PO* 18). She said "yes" to God by accepting his will to be the mother of his Son. In this, she said "yes" to every detail of his life and mission. In her fiat she said "yes" to the journey to Egypt, to the loss of Jesus for three days, to the wedding at Cana, and especially to Jesus' death.

Such Marian faith can help priests integrate spirituality and life, between vocation as service and as personal fulfillment. It will help them see in every demand placed upon them and every challenge of the ministry an event to which they had already said "yes" at the time of their ordination. Just as Mary ratified her fiat in every act of obedience that would come with her association in her Son's mission, so priests can, in faith, see in every circumstance and person that comes to them as a result of their priestly ministry, a manifestation of God's will and an event to which they have already said "yes."

Since holiness means union with Christ, the decree proceeds to apply this principle to each of the three priestly offices. By teaching, priests are "brought closer to Christ the teacher"; in administering the sacraments, especially the Eucharist, they "share in the love of him who gives himself as food" and "are united with the intention and love of Christ"; in their service as shepherds they reproduce the example of Christ in giving their lives for their sheep (*PO* 13).

Since holiness and union with Christ become reality in charity, *PO* underscores that "in the very exercise of their pastoral charity they will discover a bond of priestly perfection" and that this pastoral charity is "the root and center of the whole life of a priest" (*PO* 14).

In this light we can appreciate that the decree situates the ministry and life of priests within the ecclesiology elaborated by the Council, which is fundamentally an ecclesiology of communion. Concretely, this means that it is an ecclesiology of relationships, both with God and with others. On being ordained, a priest is established in a new relationship with Christ, in whom he takes on relationships with the Trinity, with those he is called to serve after the model of Christ, with his brother priests and with the bishop, who is charged with ordering his formation and directing his ministry.

The priest's relationship with his bishop is crucial. The gift of the priesthood, like all gifts, must be lived out in relation to apostolic authority (cf. *LG* 7). The decree presents obedience as a reality within a more fundamental one, that of brotherhood, trust, collaboration and friendship. The bishop should conduct himself as a father toward his priests, and priests respect him as a father. The obedience required by good order in the Church is a necessary means, but only a means. This priestly obedience is an element of priestly pastoral charity. Obedience corresponds to the fullness of responsibility which the bishop holds as the principle of the unity and the life of his Church.

The kind of obedience the decree envisions must contribute to mature freedom, and calls for taking initiatives. Above all, by it priests are conformed to Christ (cf. *PO* 15). The Council had envisioned that seminary formation should prepare students to "accept the authority of superiors from personal conviction, that is to say, from a motive of conscience...and for supernatural reasons" (*OT* 11; cf. *PO* 7).

The communion between bishop and presbyterate is so important because these ministers are the principles of the unity of the Church. This communion is to be expressed and fostered in an institution envisioned by the Council, a presbyteral council or senate (cf. *PO* 7).

Though the text does not go further in establishing the foundation of this communion, it does suggest an avenue for development when it states that Christ has entrusted priests with the charge of being "co-workers of the episcopal order" (*PO* 2). Such entrusting was first experienced by St. Peter when he was "commissioned in humility to be the head of the Church of sinners" (St. Thomas). Filled with that love for the Lord which was the fruit of his conversion, Peter was worthy of this entrustment and was so filled with the love of God that he could make Christ's love present in the Church. Even better, Christ's love could reach through Peter to those he would serve.

This is the pastoral charity which animates the priestly ministry, the fruit of priests making their own what they celebrate on the altar (cf. *PO* 14). That mystery is the mystery of God's merciful love for sinners. This kind of charity makes it possible for priests to have a special solicitude for the poor (cf. *PO* 6, 17, 20).

Communion in priestly ministry is above all a communion in this kind of pastoral charity. Collaboration with brother priests and assistance to a priest's bishop can be seen as acts of genuine friendship in which true friends work together to communicate to others the good which they possess. Every brother priest is a helpful associate whose gifts and labors can contribute to satisfying a love that would embrace everyone in need.

Bishops, too, should look upon their priests as genuine friends, mature in Christ and worthy of being entrusted with a share in the pastoral care of Christ's flock. This is why bishops must exercise the greatest solicitude over their priests' education and spiritual formation, and see to it that these continue after ordination and throughout the years of priestly service. So much depends on growing in that maturity in Christ which enables a person to freely place his energies at the service of others, and the priestly ministry is above all this kind of service motivated by pastoral charity.

Celibacy is a gift from God well suited to express and foster this pastoral charity (cf. *PO* 16). Celibacy is a sign of total consecration to the service of God through the priestly ministry. "Perfect and perpetual continence for the sake of the kingdom of heaven, commended by Christ the Lord...is held by the Church to be of great value in a special manner for the priestly life. It is at the same time a sign and a stimulus for pastoral charity and a special source of spiritual fecundity in the world" (*PO* 16).

Just as the goal of the episcopal ministry is the full maturation of the baptismal priesthood for the most effective carrying out of the Church's mission, so it is for the priestly ministry. The ministerial priesthood exists to promote the baptismal priesthood of the Messianic People of God so that the Church can more effectively fulfill its mission to be the sacrament of salvation and unity, for human salvation and the glory of God.

TOPICAL OUTLINE

1. Introduction: importance of the priestly ministry (1)

2. The priesthood in the ministry of the Church

   A. Place of the priesthood in the Church (2)

   B. Priests are set apart for the Gospel but must be close to those they serve (3)

3. The ministry of priests

   A. The role of the priest

      1. Ministry of the word (4)

      2. Sacramental ministry (5)

      3. Pastoral ministry (6)

   B. Priests' relationships with others

      1. Bishops (7)

      2. Fellow priests (8)

      3. The laity (9)

   C. The distribution of priests, and vocations to the priesthood

      1. Equitable distribution of priests (10)

      2. Vocational work (11)

4. The life of priests

   A. Priests are called to holiness

      1. Importance of holiness for the priestly ministry (12)

      2. The priestly ministry itself leads to holiness (13)

3. Union with Christ (14)

B. Special spiritual requirements in the life of a priest

1. Obedience (15)

2. Celibacy (16)

3. Spirit of poverty (17)

C. Helps to the priestly life

1. Prayer and other means of nourishing the spiritual life (18)

2. Study and pastoral knowledge (19)

3. Equitable remuneration for priests (20–21)

5. Conclusion (22)

DECREE ON THE MINISTRY AND LIFE OF PRIESTS

Presbyterorum Ordinis

PREFACE

1. The excellence of the order of priests in the Church has already been recalled to the minds of all by this sacred synod.[1] Since, however, in the renewal of Christ's Church tasks of the greatest importance and of ever increasing difficulty are being given to this order, it was deemed most useful to treat of the subject of priests at greater length and with more depth. What is said here applies to all priests, especially those devoted to the care of souls, with suitable adaptations being made for priests who are religious. Priests by sacred ordination and mission which they receive from the bishops are promoted to the service of Christ the teacher, priest and king. They share in his ministry, a ministry whereby the Church here on earth is unceasingly built up into the People of God, the body of Christ and the temple of the Holy Spirit. Therefore, in order that their ministry be carried on more effectively and their lives be better provided for in pastoral and human circumstances which very often change so profoundly, this sacred synod declares and decrees as follows.

---

1. Second Vatican Ecumenical Council, Constitution on the Sacred Liturgy *Sacrosanctum Concilium* (Dec. 4, 1963): *AAS* 56 (1964), 97 ff.; Second Vatican Ecumenical Council, Dogmatic Constitution on the Church *Lumen Gentium* (Nov. 21, 1964): *AAS* 57 (1965), 5 ff.; Second Vatican Ecumenical Council, Decree on the Pastoral Office of Bishops in the Church *Christus Dominus* (Oct. 28, 1965); Second Vatican Ecumenical Council, Decree on Priestly Training *Optatam Totius* (Oct. 28, 1965).

CHAPTER I

THE PRIESTHOOD
IN THE MINISTRY OF THE CHURCH

2. The Lord Jesus, "whom the Father has sent into the world" (Jn 10:36) has made his whole Mystical Body a sharer in the anointing of the Spirit with which he himself is anointed (cf. Mt 3:16; Lk 4:18; Acts 4:27, 10:38). In him all the faithful are made a holy and royal priesthood; they offer spiritual sacrifices to God through Jesus Christ, and they proclaim the perfections of him who has called them out of darkness into his marvelous light (cf. 1 Pt 2:5, 9). Therefore, there is no member who does not have a part in the mission of the whole body; but each one ought to hallow Jesus in his heart (cf. 1 Pt 3:15) and in the spirit of prophecy bear witness to Jesus.[1]

The same Lord, however, has established ministers among his faithful to unite them together in one body in which "not all the members have the same function" (Rm 12:4). These ministers in the society of the faithful are able by the sacred power of Orders to offer sacrifice and to forgive sins,[2] and they perform their priestly office publicly for men in the name of Christ. Therefore, having sent the apostles just as he himself had been sent by the Father,[3] Christ, through the apostles themselves, made their successors, the bishops,[4] sharers in his consecration and mission. The office of their ministry has been handed down, in a lesser degree indeed, to the priests.[5] Established in the order of the priesthood,

---

1. Second Vatican Ecumenical Council, Dogmatic Constitution on the Church *Lumen Gentium* (Nov. 21, 1964), 35: *AAS* 57 (1965), 40–41.

2. Council of Trent, Session 23, ch. 1, canon 1: Denz. 957 and 961 (1764 and 1771).

3. Second Vatican Ecumenical Council, Dogmatic Constitution on the Church *Lumen Gentium* (Nov. 21, 1964), 22: *AAS* 57 (1965), 21–28.

4. Cf. Second Vatican Ecumenical Council, Dogmatic Constitution on the Church *Lumen Gentium* (Nov. 21, 1964), 22: *AAS* 57 (1965), 33–36.

5. Cf. Second Vatican Ecumenical Council, Dogmatic Constitution on the Church *Lumen Gentium* (Nov. 21, 1964), 22: *AAS* 57 (1965), 33–36 .

they can be co-workers of the episcopal order for the proper fulfillment of the apostolic mission entrusted to priests by Christ.[6]

The office of priests, since it is connected with the episcopal order, also in its own degree shares the authority by which Christ builds up, sanctifies and rules his body. Wherefore the priesthood, while indeed it presupposes the sacraments of Christian initiation, is conferred by that special sacrament; through it priests, by the anointing of the Holy Spirit, are signed with a special character and are conformed to Christ the priest in such a way that they can act in the person of Christ the head.[7]

In the measure in which they participate in the office of the apostles, God gives priests a special grace to be ministers of Christ among the people. They perform the sacred duty of preaching the Gospel, so that the offering of the people can be made acceptable and sanctified by the Holy Spirit (cf. Rm 15:16—Greek text). Through the apostolic proclamation of the Gospel, the People of God are called together and assembled. All belonging to this people, since they have been sanctified by the Holy Spirit, can offer themselves as "a sacrifice, living, holy, pleasing to God" (Rm 12:1). Through the ministry of the priests, the spiritual sacrifice of the faithful is made perfect in union with the sacrifice of Christ. He is the only mediator who in the name of the whole Church is offered sacramentally in the Eucharist and in an unbloody manner until the Lord himself comes (cf. 1 Cor 11:26) The ministry of priests is directed to this goal and is perfected in it. Their ministry, which begins with the evangelical proclamation, derives its power and force from the sacrifice of Christ. Its aim is that "the entire commonwealth of the redeemed and the society of the saints be offered to God through the high priest who offered himself also for us in his passion that we might be the body of so great a head."[8]

The purpose, therefore, which priests pursue in their ministry and by their life is to procure the glory of God the Father in Christ. That glory

---

6. Cf. Roman Pontifical Ordination of a Priest, preface. These words are already found in the *Verona Sacramentary,* ed. L. C. Mohlberg (Rome: 1956), p. 122; also in the *Frankish Missal,* ed. L. C. Mohlberg (Rome: 1957), p. 9 and in the *Book of Sacramentaries of the Roman Church,* ed. L. C. Mohlberg (Rome: 1960), p. 25 and *Roman-German Pontificals,* ed. Vogel-Elze (Vatican City: 1963), vol. I, p. 34.

7. Cf. Second Vatican Ecumenical Council, Dogmatic Constitution on the Church *Lumen Gentium* (Nov. 21, 1964), 10: *AAS* 57 (1965), 14–15.

8. St. Augustine, *De Civitate Dei* 10, 6: *PL* 41, 284.

consists in this—that men working freely and with a grateful spirit receive the work of God made perfect in Christ and then manifest it in their whole lives. Hence, priests, while engaging in prayer and adoration, or preaching the Word, or offering the Eucharistic sacrifice and administering the other sacraments, or performing other works of the ministry for men, devote all this energy to the increase of the glory of God and to man's progress in the divine life. All of this, since it comes from the Pasch of Christ, will be crowned by the glorious coming of the same Lord, when he hands over the kingdom to God the Father (cf. 1 Cor 15:24).

3. Priests, who are taken from among men and ordained for men in the things that belong to God in order to offer gifts and sacrifices for sins, (cf. Heb 5:1), nevertheless live on earth with other men as brothers. The Lord Jesus, the Son of God, a man sent by the Father to men, dwelt among us and willed to become like his brethren in all things except sin (cf. Heb 2:17; 4:15). The holy apostles imitated him. Blessed Paul, the doctor of the Gentiles, "set apart for the Gospel of God" (Rm 1:1), declares that he became all things to all men that he might save all (cf. 1 Cor 9:19–23—Vg.). Priests of the New Testament, by their vocation and ordination, are in a certain sense set apart in the bosom of the People of God. However, they are not to be separated from the People of God or from any person, but they are to be totally dedicated to the work for which the Lord has chosen them (cf. Acts 13:2). They cannot be ministers of Christ unless they be witnesses and dispensers of a life other than earthly life. But they cannot be of service to men if they remain strangers to the life and conditions of men.[9] Their ministry itself by a special title forbids that they be conformed to this world (cf. Rm 12:2), yet at the same time it requires that they live in this world among men. They are to live as good shepherds who know their sheep, and they are to seek to lead those who are not of this sheepfold that they, too, may hear the voice of Christ, so that there might be one fold and one shepherd (cf. Jn 10:14–16). To achieve this aim, certain virtues which in human affairs are deservedly esteemed contribute a great deal, such as goodness of heart, sincerity, strength and constancy of mind, zealous pursuit of jus-

---

9. Paul VI, Encyclical Letter *Ecclesiam Suam* (Aug. 6, 1964): *AAS* 56 (1964), 627–638.

tice, affability and others. The Apostle Paul commends them saying: "Whatever things are true, whatever honorable, whatever just, whatever holy, whatever loving, whatever of good repute, if there be any virtue, if anything is worthy of praise, think upon these things" (Phil 4:8).[10]

---

10. Cf. St. Polycarp, *Epist. ad Philippenses* 6, 1, ed. F. X. Funk, *Apostolic Fathers,* I, p. 303.

CHAPTER II

THE MINISTRY OF PRIESTS

Section 1: Priests' Functions

4. The People of God are joined together primarily by the Word of the living God.[1] And rightfully they expect this from their priests (cf. Mal 2:7; 1 Tm 4:11–13; 1 Tm 1:9). Since no one can be saved who does not first believe (cf. Mk 16:16), priests, as co-workers with their bishops, have the primary duty of proclaiming the Gospel of God to all.[2] In this way they fulfill the command of the Lord: "Going therefore into the whole world preach the Gospel to every creature" (Mk 16:15),[3] and they establish and build up the People of God. Through the saving word the spark of faith is lit in the hearts of unbelievers and fed in the hearts of the faithful. This is the way that the congregation of faithful is started and grows, just as the Apostle describes: "Faith comes from hearing, and hearing through the word of Christ" (Rm 10:17).

To all men, therefore, priests are debtors that the truth of the Gospel

---

1. Cf. 1 Pt 1:23; Acts 6:7; 12:24. "[The apostles] preached the word of truth and founded Churches"; St. Augustine, *On Psalms* 44, 23: *PL* 36, 508.

2. Cf. 2 Cor 11:7. All that has been said regarding bishops also applies to priests inasmuch as they are cooperators of the bishops. Cf. *Statuta Ecclesiae Antiqua,* c. 3 ed. Ch. Munier (Paris: 1960), p. 79; Decree of Gratian, ch. 6, D. 88, ed. Friedberg, 1, 307; Council of Trent, Session 5, Decree *De Reform.,* c. 2, n. 9 (*Ecumenical Council Decrees,* ed. Herder, Rome: 1963, p 645); Session 24, c. 4, (p. 739); Second Vatican Ecumenical Council, Dogmatic Constitution on the Church *Lumen Gentium,* 25.

3. Cf. *Constitutiones Apostolorum* II, 26, 7: "[Priests] are teachers of sacred science as the Lord himself commanded when he said: 'Going, therefore, teach, etc.,'" ed. F. X. Funk, *Didascalia and Constitutions of the Apostles,* I (Paderborn: 1905), p. 105; *Leonine Sacramentary* and other sacramentaries up to the *Roman Pontifical,* preface of the ordination of priests: "By this Providence, Lord, you have added to the apostles of your Son fellow teachers of the faith through whom the apostles have filled the whole world with their teaching." *Ordo Book of the Mozarabic Liturgy,* preface to the ordination of priests: "Teacher of peoples and ruler of subjects, he keeps intact the Catholic faith and announces true salvation to all," ed. M. Ferotin (Paris: 1904), col. 55.

(cf. Gal 2:5) which they have may be given to others. And so, whether by entering into profitable dialogue they bring people to the worship of God (cf. 1 Pt 2:12), whether by openly preaching they proclaim the mystery of Christ, or whether in the light of Christ they treat contemporary problems, they are relying not on their own wisdom for it is the word of Christ they teach, and it is to conversion and holiness that they exhort all men.[4] But priestly preaching is often very difficult in the circumstances of the modern world. In order that it might more effectively move men's minds, the Word of God ought not to be explained in a general and abstract way, but rather by applying the lasting truth of the Gospel to the particular circumstances of life.

The ministry of the word is carried out in many ways, according to the various needs of those who hear and the special gifts of those who preach. In areas or communities of non-Christians, the proclaiming of the Gospel draws men to faith and to the sacraments of salvation.[5] In the Christian community, especially among those who seem to understand and believe little of what they practice, the preaching of the word is needed for the very ministering of the sacraments. They are precisely sacraments of faith, a faith which is born of and nourished by the word.[6] This is especially true of the Liturgy of the Word in the celebration of Mass, in which the proclaiming of the death and resurrection of Christ is inseparably joined to the response of the people who hear, and to the very offering whereby Christ ratified the New Testament in his blood. In this offering the faithful are united both by their dispositions and by their discernment of the sacrament.[7]

---

4. Cf. Rite of priestly ordination in the Alexandrian Jacobite Church: "...Gather your people to the word of doctrine like a foster-mother who nourishes her children" (H. Denzinger, *Oriental Rites,* Book II, Wurzburg 1863, 14).

5. Tertullian, *On Baptism* 14, 2 (The Body of Christians, Latin Series, I, p. 289, 11–13); St. Athanasius, *Against the Arians* 2, 42: *PG* 26, 237; St. Jerome, *On Matthew* 28, 19: *PL* 26, 218 BC: "First let them teach all nations, and then pour water on those who have learned. It cannot be that the body receive the sacrament of Baptism unless the soul first has received the truth of faith"; St. Thomas, *Exposition of the First Decretal,* n 1: "Sending his disciples to preach, our Savior enjoined on them three things: first, that they teach the faith; second, that they confer the sacraments on believers....," ed. Marietti, Opuscula Theologica (Turin-Rome: 1954), 1138.

6. Cf. Second Vatican Ecumenical Council, Constitution on the Sacred Liturgy *Sacrosanctum Concilium* (Dec. 4, 1963), 35, 2: *AAS* 56 (1964), 109.

7. Cf. Second Vatican Ecumenical Council, Constitution on the Sacred Liturgy *Sacrosanctum Concilium* (Dec. 4, 1963), 33, 35, 48, 52: *AAS* 56 (1964), 108–9, 113–4.

5. God, who alone is holy and who alone bestows holiness, willed to take as his companions and helpers men who would humbly dedicate themselves to the work of sanctification. Hence, through the ministry of the bishop, God consecrates priests, that being made sharers by special title in the priesthood of Christ, they might act as his ministers in performing sacred functions. In the liturgy they continue to carry on his priestly office by the action of his Spirit.[8] By Baptism men are truly brought into the People of God; by the sacrament of Penance sinners are reconciled to God and his Church; by the Anointing of the Sick, the ill are given solace; and especially by the celebration of Mass they offer sacramentally the sacrifice of Christ. In administering all sacraments, as St. Ignatius Martyr[9] has borne witness from the early days of the Church, priests by various titles are bound together hierarchically with the bishop. And so in a certain way they make him present in every congregation.[10]

The other sacraments, as well as with every ministry of the Church and every work of the apostolate, are tied together with the Eucharist and are directed toward it.[11] The Most Blessed Eucharist contains the entire spiritual boon of the Church,[12] that is, Christ himself, our Pasch and living bread, by the action of the Holy Spirit through his very flesh vital and vitalizing, giving life to men who are thus invited and encouraged to offer themselves, their labors and all created things together with him. In this light the Eucharist shows itself as the source and the apex of the whole work of preaching the Gospel. Those under instruction are introduced by stages to a sharing in the Eucharist, and the faithful, already marked with the seal of Baptism and Confirmation, are through the reception of the Eucharist fully joined to the Body of Christ.

---

8. Cf. Second Vatican Ecumenical Council, Constitution on the Sacred Liturgy *Sacrosanctum Concilium* (Dec. 4, 1963), 7: *AAS* 56 (1964), 100–101; Pius XII, Encyclical Letter *Mystici Corporis* (June 29, 1943): *AAS* 35 (1943), 230.

9. St. Ignatius Martyr, *Smyrn.* 8, 1–2, ed. F. X. Funk, p. 282, 6–15; *Constitutions of the Apostles,* VIII, 12, 3, ed. F. X. Funk, p. 496; VIII, 29, 2, p. 532.

10. Cf. Second Vatican Ecumenical Council, Dogmatic Constitution on the Church *Lumen Gentium* (Nov. 21, 1964), 28: *AAS* 57 (1965), 33–36.

11. "The Eucharist indeed is a quasi consummation of the spiritual life and the goal of all the sacraments": St. Thomas, *Summa Theol.,* III, q. 73, a. 3 c; cf. *Summa Theol.,* III, q. 65, a. 3.

12. Cf. St. Thomas, *Summa Theol.,* III, q. 65, a. 3 *ad* 1; q. 79, a. 1 c., *ad* 1.

Thus, the Eucharistic action over which the priest presides is the very heart of the congregation. So priests must instruct their people to offer to God the Father the divine victim in the sacrifice of the Mass, and to join to it the offering of their own lives. In the spirit of Christ the shepherd, they must prompt their people to confess their sins with a contrite heart in the sacrament of Penance, so that mindful of his words "Repent for the kingdom of God is at hand" (Mt 4:17), they are drawn closer to the Lord more and more each day. Priests likewise must instruct their people to participate in the celebrations of the sacred liturgy in such a way that they become proficient in genuine prayer. They must coax their people on to an ever more perfect and constant spirit of prayer for every grace and need. They must gently persuade everyone to the fulfillment of the duties of his state of life, and to greater progress in responding in a sensible way to the evangelical counsels. Finally, they must train the faithful to sing hymns and spiritual songs in their hearts to the Lord, always giving thanks to God the Father for all things in the name of our Lord Jesus Christ (cf. Eph 5:19–20).

Priests themselves extend to the other hours of the day the praise and thanksgiving of the Eucharistic celebration in praying the divine office, offered in the name of the Church for all the people entrusted to their care, and indeed for the whole world.

The house of prayer in which the most holy Eucharist is celebrated and reserved, where the faithful gather and where the presence of the Son of God, our Savior, offered for us on the altar of sacrifice bestows strength and blessings on the faithful, must be spotless and suitable for prayer and sacred functions.[13] There pastors and the faithful are called to acknowledge with grateful heart the gift of him who through his humanity constantly pours divine life into the members of his body.[14] Let priests take care so to foster a knowledge of and facility in the liturgy, that by their own liturgical ministry Christian communities entrusted to their care may ever more perfectly give praise to God, the Father and Son and Holy Spirit.

6. Exercising the office of Christ, the shepherd and head, and according to their share of his authority, priests, in the name of the bishop,

---

13. Cf. St. Jerome, *Epistles* 114, 2: *PL* 22, 934: cf. Second Vatican Ecumenical Council, Constitution on the Sacred Liturgy *Sacrosanctum Concilium,* 122–127.

14. Paul VI, Encyclical Letter *Mysterium Fidei* (Sept. 3, 1965): *AAS* 57 (1965), 771.

gather the family of God together as a brotherhood enlivened by one spirit. Through Christ they lead them in the Holy Spirit to God the Father.[15] For the exercise of this ministry, as for the other priestly duties, spiritual power is conferred upon them for the building up of the Church (cf. 2 Cor 10:8; 13:10). In building up the Church, priests must treat all with exceptional kindness in imitation of the Lord. They should act toward men not as seeking to please them (cf. Gal 1:10), but in accord with the demands of Christian doctrine and life. They should teach them and admonish them as beloved sons (cf. 1 Cor 4:14), according to the words of the Apostle: "Be urgent in season, out of season; reprove, entreat, rebuke in all patience and doctrine" (2 Tm 4:2).[16]

Priests, therefore, as educators in the faith must see to it either by themselves or through others that the faithful are led individually in the Holy Spirit to a development of their own vocation according to the Gospel, to a sincere and practical charity and to that freedom with which Christ has made us free (cf. Gal 4:3; 5:1, 13). Ceremonies, however beautiful, or associations, however flourishing, will be of little value if they are not directed toward the education of men to Christian maturity.[17] In furthering this priests should help men to see what is required and what is God's will in the important and unimportant events of life. Also, Christians should be taught that they live not only for themselves but according to the demands of the new law of charity; as every man has received grace, he must administer the same to others (cf. 1 Pt 4:10 ff.). In this way all will discharge in a Christian manner their duties in the community of men.

Although they have obligations toward all men, priests have a special obligation to the poor and weak entrusted to them, for our Lord himself showed that he was united to them (cf. Mt 25:34–45), and their evangelization is mentioned as a sign of messianic activity (cf. Lk 4:18). With special diligence, attention should be given to youth and also to married people and parents. It is desirable that these join together in friendly meetings for mutual aid in leading more easily and fully and in

---

15. Cf. Second Vatican Ecumenical Council, Dogmatic Constitution on the Church *Lumen Gentium* (Nov. 21, 1964), 28: *AAS* 57 (1965), 33–36.

16. Cf. *Didascalia,* II, 34, 3; II, 46, 6; II, 47, 1; *Constitutions of the Apostles,* II, 47, 1, ed. F. X. Funk, *Didascalia and Constitutions of the Apostles,* I, pp. 116, 142, 143.

17. Cf. St. Jerome, *Epistles* 58, 7: *PL* 22, 584.

a Christian manner a life that is often difficult. Priests should remember that all religious, both men and women, who certainly have a distinguished place in the house of the Lord, deserve special care in their spiritual progress for the good of the whole Church. Finally, and above all, priests must be solicitous for the sick and the dying, visiting them and strengthening them in the Lord.[18]

The office of pastor is not confined to the care of the faithful as individuals, but also in a true sense is extended to the formation of a genuine Christian community. Yet the spirit of the community should be so fostered as to embrace not only the local church, but also the universal Church. The local community should promote not only the care of its own faithful, but filled with a missionary zeal it should prepare also the way to Christ for all men. In a special way, catechumens and the newly-baptized who must be educated gradually to know and to live the Christian life are entrusted to his care.

No Christian community, however, is built up unless it has its basis and center in the celebration of the most holy Eucharist; from this, therefore, all education to the spirit of community must take its origin.[19] This celebration, if it is to be genuine and complete, should lead to various works of charity and mutual help, as well as to missionary activity and to different forms of Christian witness.

The ecclesial community by prayer, example and works of penance, exercises a true motherhood toward souls who are to be led to Christ. The Christian community forms an effective instrument by which the path to Christ and his Church is pointed out and made smooth for non-believers. It is an effective instrument also for arousing, nourishing and strengthening the faithful for their spiritual combat.

In building the Christian community, priests are never to put themselves at the service of some human faction or ideology, but as heralds of the Gospel and shepherds of the Church, they are to spend themselves for the spiritual growth of the body of Christ.

---

18. Other categories could be named, e.g. migrants, nomads, etc.: cf. Second Vatican Ecumenical Council, Decree on the Pastoral Office of Bishops in the Church *Christus Dominus* (Oct. 28, 1965).

19. Cf. *Didascalia,* II, 59, 1–3, ed. F. X. Funk, I, p. 170; Paul VI, *Allocution to Italian Clergy Present at the 13th Week-long Congress at Orvieto on Pastoral Aggiornamento* (Sept. 6, 1963): *AAS* 55 (1963), 750 ff.

Section 2: Priests' Relationships with Others

7. All priests, in union with bishops, so share in one and the same priesthood and ministry of Christ that the very unity of their consecration and mission requires their hierarchical communion with the order of bishops.[20] At times in an excellent manner they manifest this communion in liturgical concelebration as joined with the bishop when they celebrate the Eucharistic sacrifice.[21] Therefore, by reason of the gift of the Holy Spirit which is given to priests in Holy Orders, bishops regard them as necessary helpers and counselors in the ministry and in their role of teaching, sanctifying and nourishing the People of God.[22] Already in the ancient ages of the Church we find liturgical texts proclaiming this with insistence, as when they solemnly call upon God to pour out upon the candidate for priestly ordination "the spirit of grace and counsel, so that with a pure heart he may help and govern the People of God,"[23] just as in the desert the spirit of Moses was spread abroad in the minds of the seventy prudent men (cf. Nm 11:16–25), "and using them as helpers among the people, he easily governed countless multitudes."[24]

---

20. Cf. Second Vatican Ecumenical Council, Dogmatic Constitution on the Church *Lumen Gentium* (Nov. 21, 1964), 28: *AAS* 57 (1965), 35.

21. Cf. cited *Constitutions of the Apostles*, XVIII, ed. Th. Schermann, *Die allgemeine Kirchenordnung*, I (Paderborn: 1914), p. 26; A. Harnack, T. u. U., II, 4, p. 13, nn. 18 and 19; Pseudo-Jerome, *The Seven Orders of the Church*, ed. A. W. Kalff (Wurzburg: 1937), p. 45; St. Isidore of Seville, *Ecclesiastical Offices*, c. VII: *PL* 83, 787.

22. Cf. *Didascalia*, II, 28, 4, ed. F. X. Funk, p. 108; *Constitutions of the Apostles*, II, 28, 4; II, 34, 3 (*ibid.*, pp. 109 and 117).

23. *Constitutions of the Apostles*, VIII, 16, 4, ed. F. X. Funk, 1, p. 522, 13; cf. *Epitome of the Constitutions of the Apostles*, VI (*ibid.*, II, p. 80, 3–4); *Testamentum Domini,* (trans., I. E. Rahmani Moguntiae: 1899, p. 69). Also in *Trad. Apost.*, (ed. B. Botte, *La Tradition Apostolique, Munster*, i. W. 1963, p. 20).

24. *Roman Pontifical* on the ordination of a priest, preface; these words are also found in the *Leonine Sacramentary*, the *Gelasian Sacramentary* and the *Gregorian Sacramentary*. Similar words can be found in the Oriental liturgies: cf. *Trad Apost.* (ancient Latin version of Verona, ed. B. Botte, *La Tradition Apostolique de St. Hippolyte. Essai de reconstruction,* Munster i. W. 1963, p. 20); *Constitutions of the Apostles*, VIII, 16, 4, ed. F. X. Funk, I, p. 522, 16–17; *Epitome on the Constitutions of the Apostles*, 6, ed. F. X. Funk, II, p. 20, 5–7; *Testamentum Domini,* (trans., I. E. Rahmani Moguntiae: 1899, p. 69); *Euchologium Serapionis*, XXVII, ed. F. X. Funk, *Didascalia and Constitutions*, II, p. 190, lines 1–7; *Maronite Rite of Ordination*, trans., H. Denzinger, *Rites of the Orientals,* II (Wurzburg: 1863), p. 161. Among the Fathers can be cited: Theodore of Mopsuestia, *On First Timothy* 3, 8, ed. Swete, II, pp. 119–121; Theodoretus, *Questions on Numbers*, XVIII: *PG* 80, 372 b.

Therefore, on account of this communion in the same priesthood and ministry, bishops should regard priests as their brothers and friends[25] and be concerned as far as they are able for their material and especially for their spiritual well-being. For above all upon the bishops rests the heavy responsibility for the sanctity of their priests.[26] Therefore, they should exercise the greatest care in the continual formation of their priests.[27] They should gladly listen to their priests, indeed consult them and engage in dialogue with them in those matters which concern the necessities of pastoral work and welfare of the diocese. In order to put this into effect, there should be—in a manner suited to today's conditions and necessities,[28] and with a structure and norms to be determined by law—a body or senate[29] of priests representing all the priests. This representative body by its advice will be able to give the bishop effective assistance in the administration of the diocese.

Priests, never losing sight of the fullness of the priesthood which the bishops enjoy, must respect in them the authority of Christ, the supreme shepherd. They must therefore stand by their bishops in sincere charity and obedience.[30] This priestly obedience, imbued with a spirit of coop-

---

25. Cf. Second Vatican Ecumenical Council, Dogmatic Constitution on the Church *Lumen Gentium* (Nov. 21, 1964), 28: *AAS* 57 (1965), 35.

26. Cf. John XXIII, Encyclical Letter *Sacerdotii Nostri Primordia* (Aug. 1, 1959): *AAS* 51 (1959), 576; St. Pius X, Exhortation to the Clergy *Haerent Animo* (Aug. 4, 1908): *Acts of St. Pius X,* vol. IV (1908), 237 ff.

27. Cf. Second Vatican Ecumenical Council, Decree on the Pastoral Office of Bishops in the Church *Christus Dominus* (Oct. 28, 1956), 15–16.

28. The Cathedral Chapter is already found in established law, as the "senate and assembly" of the bishop (*Code of Canon Law,* c. 391), or if there is not one, an assembly of diocesan consultors (cf. *Code of Canon Law,* cc. 423–428). It is our desire to give recognition to such institutions so that modern circumstances and necessities might better be provided for. As is evident, this synod of priests forms the pastoral consilium spoken of in the *Decree on the Pastoral Office of Bishops* of Oct. 28, 1965 (n. 27), of which the laity can also be members, and whose function is mainly to map out a plan of action for pastoral work. Concerning priests as counselors of the bishops, one might refer to the *Didascalia,* II, 28, 4, ed. F. X. Funk, II, p. 108; also *Constitutions of the Apostles,* II 28, 4, ed. F. X. Funk, I, p. 109; St. Ignatius Martyr, *Magn.* 6, 1, ed. F. X. Funk, p. 234, 10–16; *Trall.* 3, 1, ed. F. X. Funk, p. 244, 10–12; Origen, *Against Celsus,* 3, 30: "Priests are counselors or *'bouleytai'*": (*PG* 11, 957 d–960 a).

29. St. Ignatius Martyr, *Magn.* 6, 1, ed. F. X. Funk, p. 234, 10–13; St. Ignatius Martyr, *Trall.* 3, 1, (*ibid.,* p. 244, 10–12); St. Jerome, *On Isaiah,* II, 3: *PL* 24, 61 A.

30. Cf. Paul VI, *Allocution to the Family Heads of Rome and Lenten Speakers* (March 1, 1965): *AAS* 57 (1965), 326.

eration, is based on the very sharing in the episcopal ministry which is conferred on priests both through the sacrament of Orders and the canonical mission.[31]

This union of priests with their bishops is all the more necessary today since in our present age, for various reasons, apostolic undertakings must necessarily not only take on many forms but frequently extend even beyond the boundaries of one parish or diocese. No priest, therefore, can on his own accomplish his mission in a satisfactory way. He can do so only by joining forces with other priests under the direction of the Church authorities.

8. Priests by virtue of their ordination to the priesthood are united among themselves in an intimate sacramental brotherhood. In individual dioceses priests form one priesthood under their own bishop. Even though priests are assigned to different duties, nevertheless they carry on one priestly ministry for men. All priests are sent as co-workers in the same apostolate, whether they engage in parochial or extra-parochial ministry. This is true whether they devote their efforts to scientific research or teaching, or whether by manual labor they share in the lot of the workers themselves—if there is need for this and competent authority approves—or finally whether they fulfill some other apostolic tasks or labor designed for the apostolate. All, indeed, are united in the building up of the body of Christ which especially in our times requires manifold duties and new methods. It is very important that all priests, whether diocesan or religious, help one another always to be fellow workers in the truth (cf. 3 Jn 8). Each one, therefore, is united in special bonds of apostolic charity, ministry and brotherhood with the other members of this priesthood. This has been manifested from ancient times in the liturgy, when the priests present at an ordination are invited to impose hands together with the ordaining bishop on the new candidate and with united hearts concelebrate the sacred Eucharist. Each and every priest, therefore, is united with his fellow priests in a bond of charity, prayer and total cooperation. In this manner they manifest that unity which Christ willed, namely, that his own be perfected in one so that the world might know that the Son was sent by the Father (cf. Jn 17:23).

---

31. Cf. *Constitutions of the Apostles*, VIII, 47, 39, ed. F. X. Funk, p. 577.

Older priests, therefore, should receive younger priests as true brothers and help them in their first undertakings and priestly duties. The older ones should likewise endeavor to understand the mentality of younger priests, even though it be different from their own, and follow their projects with good will. By the same token, young priests should respect the age and experience of their seniors; they should seek their advice and willingly cooperate with them in everything that pertains to the care of souls. In a fraternal spirit, priests should extend hospitality (cf. Heb 13:1–2), cultivate kindliness and share their goods in common (cf. Heb 13:16). They should be particularly solicitous for the sick, the afflicted, those overburdened with work, the lonely, those exiled from their homeland and those who suffer persecution (cf. Mt 5:10). They should gladly and joyfully gather together for recreation, remembering Christ's invitation to the weary apostles: "Come aside to a desert place and rest awhile" (Mk 6:31). And further, in order that priests may find mutual assistance in the development of their spiritual and intellectual life, that they may be able to cooperate more effectively in their ministry and be saved from the dangers of loneliness which may arise, it is necessary that some kind of common life or some sharing of common life be encouraged among priests. This, however, may take many forms according to different personal or pastoral needs, such as living together where this is possible, or having a common table, or at least by frequent and periodic meetings. One should hold also in high regard and eagerly promote those associations which, having been recognized by competent ecclesiastical authority, encourage priestly holiness in the ministry by the use of an appropriate and duly approved rule of life and by fraternal aid, intending thus to do service to the whole order of priests.

Finally, by reason of the same communion in the priesthood, priests should realize that they are obliged in a special manner toward those priests who labor under certain difficulties. They should give them timely help and also, if necessary, admonish them discreetly. Moreover, they should always treat with fraternal charity and magnanimity those who have failed in some matters, offer urgent prayers to God for them and continually show themselves as true brothers and friends.

9. Though priests of the New Testament, in virtue of the sacrament of Orders, exercise the most outstanding and necessary office of father and teacher among and for the People of God, they are nevertheless, together with all Christ's faithful, disciples of the Lord, made sharers in

his kingdom by the grace of God's call (cf. 1 Thes 2:12; Col 1:13). For priests are brothers among brothers[32] with all those who have been reborn at the baptismal font. They are all members of one and the same body of Christ, the building up of which is required of everyone.[33]

Priests, therefore, must take the lead in seeking the things of Jesus Christ, not the things that are their own (cf. Phil 2:21). They must work together with the lay faithful and conduct themselves in their midst after the example of their Master, who among men "came not to be ministered unto, but to minister, and to give his life as redemption for many" (Mt 20:28). Priests must sincerely acknowledge and promote the dignity of the laity and the part proper to them in the mission of the Church. And they should hold in high honor that just freedom which is due to everyone in the earthly city. They must willingly listen to the laity, consider their wants in a fraternal spirit, recognize their experience and competence in the different areas of human activity, so that together with them they will be able to recognize the signs of the times. While trying the spirits to see if they be of God (cf. 1 Jn 4:1), priests should uncover with a sense of faith, acknowledge with joy and foster with diligence the various humble and exalted charisms of the laity. Among the other gifts of God, which are found in abundance among the laity, those are worthy of special mention by which not a few of the laity are attracted to a higher spiritual life. Likewise, they should confidently entrust to the laity duties in the service of the Church, allowing them freedom and room for action; in fact, they should invite them on suitable occasions to undertake works on their own initiative.[34]

Finally, priests have been placed in the midst of the laity to lead them to the unity of charity, "loving one another with fraternal love, eager to give one another precedence" (Rm 12:10). It is their task, therefore, to reconcile differences of mentality in such a way that no one need feel himself a stranger in the community of the faithful. They are defenders of the common good, with which they are charged in the name of the bishop. At the same time, they are strenuous assertors of the truth,

---

32. Cf. Paul VI, Encyclical Letter *Ecclesiam Suam* (Aug. 6, 1964): *AAS* 58 (1964), 647.

33. *Constitutions of the Apostles,* VIII, 1, 20, ed. F. X. Funk, I, p. 467.

34. Cf. Second Vatican Ecumenical Council, Dogmatic Constitution on the Church *Lumen Gentium* (Nov. 21, 1964), 37: *AAS* 57 (1965), 42–43.

lest the faithful be carried about by every wind of doctrine (cf. Eph 4:14). They are united by a special solicitude with those who have fallen away from the use of the sacraments, or perhaps even from the faith. Indeed, as good shepherds, they should not cease from going out to them.

Mindful of the prescripts on ecumenism,[35] let them not forget their brothers who do not enjoy full ecclesiastical communion with us.

Finally, they have entrusted to them all those who do not recognize Christ as their Savior.

The Christian faithful, for their part, should realize their obligations to their priests, and with filial love they should follow them as their pastors and fathers. In like manner, sharing their cares, they should help their priests by prayer and work insofar as possible so that their priests might more readily overcome difficulties and be able to fulfill their duties more fruitfully.[36]

Section 3: The Distribution of Priests, and Vocations to the Priesthood

10. The spiritual gift which priests receive at their ordination prepared them not for a sort of limited and narrow mission but for the widest possible and universal mission of salvation "even to the ends of the earth" (Acts 1:8), for every priestly ministry shares in the universality of the mission Christ entrusted to his apostles. The priesthood of Christ, in which all priests really share, is necessarily intended for all peoples and all times, and it knows no limits of blood, nationality or time, since it is already mysteriously prefigured in the person of Melchisedech (cf. Heb 7:3). Let priests remember, therefore, that the care of all churches must be their intimate concern. Hence, priests of such dioceses as are rich in vocations should show themselves willing and ready, with the permission of their own ordinaries (bishops), to volunteer for work in other regions, missions or endeavors which are poor in numbers of clergy.

Present norms of incardination and excardination should be so revised that, while this ancient institution still remains intact, they will

---

35. Cf. Second Vatican Ecumenical Council, Decree on Ecumenism *Unitatis Redintegratio* (Nov. 21, 1964): *AAS* 57 (1965), 90 ff.

36. Cf. Second Vatican Ecumenical Council, Dogmatic Constitution on the Church *Lumen Gentium* (Nov. 21, 1964), 37: *AAS* 57 (1965), 42–43.

better correspond to today's pastoral needs. Where a real apostolic spirit requires it, not only should a better distribution of priests be brought about but there should also be favored such particular pastoral works as are necessary in any region or nation anywhere on earth. To accomplish this purpose, there should be set up international seminaries, special personal dioceses or prelatures (vicariates) and so forth, by means of which, according to their particular statutes and always saving the right of bishops, priests may be trained and incardinated for the good of the whole Church.

Priests should not be sent singly to a new field of labor, especially to one where they are not completely familiar with the language and customs; rather, after the example of the disciples of Christ (cf. Lk 10:1), they should be sent two or three together so that they may be mutually helpful to one another. Likewise, thoughtful care should be given to their spiritual life as well as their mental and bodily welfare, and so far as is possible, the circumstances and conditions of labor should be adapted to individual needs and capabilities. At the same time it will be quite advantageous if those priests who go to work in a nation new to them not only know well the language of that place but also the psychological and social milieu peculiar to the people they go to serve, so that they may communicate with them easily, thus following the example of Paul the Apostle who could say of himself: "For when I was free of all I made myself the servant of all, that I might win over many. Among Jews I was a Jew that I might win over the Jews" (1 Cor 9:19–20).

11. The shepherd and bishop of our souls (cf. 1 Pt 2:25) so constituted his Church that the people whom he chose and acquired by his blood (cf. Acts 20:28) would have its priests to the end of time, and that Christians would never be like sheep without a shepherd (cf. Mt 9:36). Recognizing Christ's desire, and at the inspiration of the Holy Spirit, the apostles considered it their duty to select men "who will be capable of teaching others" (2 Tm 2:2). This duty, then, is a part of the priestly mission by which every priest becomes a sharer in the care of the whole Church, lest ministers be ever lacking for the People of God on earth. Since, however, there is common cause between the captain of a ship and the sailors,[37] let all Christian people be taught that it is their duty to

---

37. *Roman Pontifical*, "Ordination of a Priest."

cooperate in one way or another, by constant prayer and other means at their disposal,[38] that the Church will always have a sufficient number of priests to carry out her divine mission. In the first place, therefore, it is the duty of priests, by the ministry of the word and by the example of their own lives, showing forth the spirit of service and the paschal joy, to demonstrate to the faithful the excellence and necessity of the priesthood; then they should see to it that young men and adults whom they judge worthy of such ministry should be called by their bishops to ordination, sparing no effort or inconvenience in helping them to prepare for this call, always saving their internal and external freedom of action. In this effort diligent and prudent spiritual direction is of the greatest value. Parents and teachers and all who are engaged in any way in the education of boys and young men should so prepare them that they will recognize the solicitude of our Lord for his flock, will consider the needs of the Church and will be prepared to respond generously to our Lord when he calls, saying: "Here I am Lord, send me" (Is 6:8). This voice of the Lord calling, however, is never to be expected as something which in an extraordinary manner will be heard by the ears of the future priest. It is rather to be known and understood in the manner in which the will of God is daily made known to prudent Christians. These indications should be carefully noted by priests.[39]

Works favoring vocations, therefore, whether diocesan or national, are highly recommended to the consideration of priests.[40] In sermons, in catechetical instructions, and written articles, priests should set forth the needs of the Church both locally and universally, putting into vivid light the nature and excellence of the priestly ministry, which balances heavy burdens with great joys, and in which in a special way, as the Fathers of the Church point out, the greatest love of Christ can be shown.[41]

---

38. Cf. Second Vatican Ecumenical Council, Decree on Priestly Training *Optatam Totius* (Oct. 28, 1965), 2.

39. Paul VI, *Allocution* (May 5, 1965), *L'Osservatore Romano* (May 5, 1965), 1.

40. Cf. Second Vatican Ecumenical Council, Decree on Priestly Training *Optatam Totius* (Oct. 28, 1965), 2.

41. The Fathers teach this in their explanations of Christ's words to Peter: "Do you love me?... Feed my sheep" (Jn 21:17); thus St. John Chrysostom, *On the Priesthood,* II, 1–2: *PG* 47–48, 633; St. Gregory the Great, *Reg. Past. Liber,* P. I. c. 5: *PL* 77, 19 a.

Chapter III

THE LIFE OF PRIESTS

Section 1: The Vocation of Priests to the Life of Perfection

12. Priests are made in the likeness of Christ the priest by the sacrament of Orders, so that they may, in collaboration with their bishops, work for the building up and care of the Church which is the whole body of Christ, acting as ministers of him who is the head. Like all other Christians they have received in the sacrament of Baptism the symbol and gift of such a calling and such grace that even in human weakness (cf. 2 Cor 12:9), they can and must seek for perfection, according to the exhortation of Christ: "Be you therefore perfect, as your heavenly Father is perfect" (Mt 5:48). Priests are bound, however, to acquire that perfection in special fashion. They have been consecrated by God in a new manner at their ordination and made living instruments of Christ the eternal priest that they may be able to carry on in time his marvelous work whereby the entire family of man is again made whole by power from above.[1] Since, therefore, every priest in his own fashion acts in place of Christ himself, he is enriched by a special grace, so that as he serves the flock committed to him and the entire People of God, he may the better grow in the grace of him whose tasks he performs, because to the weakness of our flesh there is brought the holiness of him who for us was made a high priest "holy, guiltless, undefiled, not reckoned among us sinners" (Heb 7:26).

Christ, whom the Father sanctified, consecrated and sent into the world (cf. Jn 10:36) "gave himself for us that he might redeem us from all iniquity and cleanse for himself an acceptable people, pursuing good

---

1. Cf. Pius XI, Encyclical Letter *Ad Catholici Sacerdotii* (Dec. 20, 1935), 10: *AAS* 28 (1936).

works" (Ti 2:14), and thus through suffering entered into his glory (Lk 24:26). In like fashion, priests consecrated by the anointing of the Holy Spirit and sent by Christ must mortify the works of the flesh in themselves and give themselves entirely to the service of men. It is in this way that they can go forward in that holiness with which Christ endows them, to become the perfect man (cf. Eph 4:13).

Hence, those who exercise the ministry of the spirit and of justice (cf. 2 Cor 3:8–9) will be confirmed in the life of the spirit, so long as they are open to the Spirit of Christ, who gives them life and direction. By the sacred actions which are theirs daily as well as by their entire ministry, which they share with the bishop and their fellow priests, they are directed to perfection in their lives. Holiness does much for priests in carrying on a fruitful ministry. Although divine grace could use unworthy ministers to effect the work of salvation, yet for the most part God chooses, to show forth his wonders, those who are more open to the power and direction of the Holy Spirit, and who can by reason of their close union with Christ and their holiness of life say with St. Paul: "And yet I am alive; or rather, not I; it is Christ who lives in me" (Gal 2:20).

Hence, this holy Council, to fulfill its pastoral desires of an internal renewal of the Church, of the spread of the Gospel in every land and of a dialogue with the world of today, strongly urges all priests that they strive always for that growth in holiness by which they will become consistently better instruments in the service of the whole People of God, using for this purpose those means which the Church has approved.[2]

13. Priests who perform their duties sincerely and indefatigably in the Spirit of Christ arrive at holiness by this very fact.

Since they are ministers of God's word, each day they read and hear the Word of God, which it is their task to teach others. If at the same time they are ready to receive the word themselves, they will grow daily into more perfect followers of the Lord. As St. Paul wrote to Timothy,

---

2. Cf. among others: St. Pius X, Exhortation to the Clergy *Haerent Animo* (Aug. 4, 1908): *AAS* 4 (1908), 237 ff.; Pius XI, Encyclical Letter *Ad Catholici Sacerdotii* (Dec. 20, 1935): *AAS* 28 (1936); Pius XII, Apostolic Exhortation *Menti Nostrae* (Sept. 23, 1950): *AAS* (1950), 657 ff.; John XXIII, Encyclical Letter *Sacerdoti Nostri Primordia* (Aug. 1, 1959): *AAS* 51 (1959), 545 ff.

"Let this be your study, these your employments, so that all may see how well you do. Two things claim your attention, yourself and the teaching of the faith; spend your care on them, so will you and those who listen to you achieve salvation" (1 Tm 4:15–16). As they seek how they may better teach others what they have learned,[3] they will better understand "the unfathomable riches of Christ" (Eph 3:8) and the manifold wisdom of God (cf. Heb 3:9–10). If they keep in mind that it is God who opens hearts (cf. Acts 16:14), and that power comes not from themselves but from the might of God (cf. 2 Cor 4:7), in the very fact of teaching God's word they will be brought closer to Christ the teacher and led by his Spirit. Thus those who commune with Christ share in God's love, the mystery of which, kept hidden from the beginning of time (cf. Eph 3:9), is revealed in Christ.

Priests act especially in the person of Christ as ministers of holy things, particularly in the sacrifice of the Mass, the sacrifice of Christ who gave himself for the sanctification of men. Hence, they are asked to take example from that with which they deal, and inasmuch as they celebrate the mystery of the Lord's death, they should keep their bodies free of wantonness and lusts.[4] In the mystery of the Eucharistic Sacrifice, in which priests fulfill their greatest task, the work of our redemption is being constantly carried on;[5] and hence, the daily celebration of Mass is strongly urged, since even if there cannot be present a number of the faithful, it is still an act of Christ and of the Church.[6] Thus, when priests join in the act of Christ the priest, they offer themselves entirely to God, and when they are nourished with the Body of Christ they profoundly share in the love of him who gives himself as food to the faithful. In like fashion they are united with the intention and love of Christ when they administer the sacraments. This is true in a special way when in the performance of their duty in the sacrament of Penance they show themselves altogether and always ready whenever the sacrament is reasonably sought by the faithful. In the recitation of the divine office, they offer the voice of the Church which perseveres in

---

3. Cf. St. Thomas, *Summa Theol.,* II–II, q. 188, a. 7.

4. Cf. *Roman Pontifical,* "Ordination of a Priest."

5. Cf. Roman Missal, Prayer over the offerings of the Ninth Sunday after Pentecost.

6. Paul VI, Encyclical Letter *Mysterium Fidei* (Sept. 3, 1965): *AAS* 57 (1965), 761–762. Cf. Second Vatican Ecumenical Council, Constitution on the Sacred Liturgy *Sacrosanctum Concilium* (Dec. 4, 1963), 26–27: *AAS* 56 (1964), 107.

prayer in the name of the whole human race, together with Christ who "lives on still to make intercession on our behalf."

As they direct and nourish the People of God, may they be aroused by the example of the good shepherd that they may give their life for their sheep (cf. Jn 10:11), ready for the supreme sacrifice following the example of priests who, even in our own day, have not shrunk from giving their lives. As they are leaders in the faith and as they "enter the sanctuary with confidence through the blood of Christ" (Heb 10:19), they approach God "with sincere hearts in the full assurance of the faith" (Heb 10:22); they set up a sure hope for their faithful (cf. 2 Cor 1:7), that they may comfort those who are depressed, by the same consolation wherewith God consoles them (cf. 2 Cor 1:4). As leaders of the community, they cultivate an asceticism becoming to a shepherd of souls, renouncing their personal convenience, seeking not what is useful to themselves but to many for their salvation (cf. 1 Cor 10:33), always making further progress to do their pastoral work better, and where needful, prepared to enter into new pastoral ways under the direction of the Spirit of love, which breathes where it will (cf. Jn 3:8).

14. In the world of today, when people are so burdened with duties and their problems, which oftentimes have to be solved with great haste and range through so many fields, there is considerable danger of dissipating their energy. Priests, too, involved and constrained by so many obligations of their office, certainly have reason to wonder how they can coordinate and balance their interior life with feverish outward activity. Neither the mere external performance of the works of the ministry, nor the exclusive engagement in pious devotion, although very helpful, can bring about this necessary coordination. Priests can arrive at this only by following the example of Christ our Lord in their ministry. His food was to follow the will of him who had sent him to accomplish his work (cf. Jn 4:34).

In order to continue doing the will of his Father in the world, Christ works unceasingly through the Church. He operates through his ministers, and hence he remains always the source and wellspring of the unity of their lives. Priests then can achieve this coordination and unity of life by joining themselves with Christ to acknowledge the will of the Father. For them this means a complete gift of themselves to the flock committed to them (cf. 1 Jn 3:16). Hence, as they fulfill the role of the good shepherd, in the very exercise of their pastoral charity they will discover a bond of priestly perfection which draws their life and activity to unity and coordination. This pastoral charity[7] flows out in a very special way from the Eucharistic Sacrifice. This stands as the root and center of the whole life of a priest. What takes place on the altar of sacrifice, the priestly heart must make his own. This cannot be done unless priests through prayer continue to penetrate more deeply into the mystery of Christ.

In order to measure and verify this coordination of life in a concrete way, let priests examine all their works and projects to see what is the will of God (cf. Rm 12:2), namely, to see how their endeavors compare with the goals of the gospel mission of the Church. Fidelity to Christ cannot be separated from faithfulness to his Church. Pastoral charity requires that priests avoid operating in a vacuum (cf. Gal 2:2) and that they work in a strong bond of union with their bishops and brother priests. If this be their program, priests will find the coordination and unity of their own life in the oneness of the Church's mission. They will be joined with the Lord and through him with the Father in the Holy Spirit. This will bring them great satisfaction and a full measure of happiness (cf. 2 Cor 7:4).

Section 2: Special Spiritual Requirements in the Life of a Priest

15. Among the virtues that priests must possess for their sacred ministry, none is so important as a frame of mind and soul whereby they are always ready to know and do the will of him who sent them and not their own will (cf. Jn 4:34; 5:30; 6:38). The divine task that they are called by the Holy Spirit to fulfill (cf. Acts 13:2) surpasses all human wisdom and human ability. "God chooses the weak things of the world to confound the strong" (1 Cor 1:27). Aware of his own weakness, the true minister of Christ works in humility trying to do what is pleasing to God (cf. Eph 5:10). Filled with the Holy Spirit (cf. Acts 20:22), he is guided by him who desires the salvation of all men. He understands this desire of God and follows it in the ordinary circumstances of his everyday life. With humble disposition he waits upon all whom God has sent him to serve in the work assigned to him and in the multiple experiences of his life.

---

7. "May it be a duty of love to feed the Lord's flock": St. Augustine, *Tract on John* 123, 5: *PL* 35, 1967.

However, the priestly ministry, since it is the ministry of the Church itself, can only function in the hierarchical union of the whole body. Pastoral charity, therefore, urges priests, as they operate in the framework of this union, to dedicate their own will by obedience to the service of God and their fellow men. In a great spirit of faith, let them receive and execute whatever orders the Holy Father, their own bishop or other superiors give or recommend.

With a willing heart let them spend and even exhaust themselves (cf. 2 Cor 12:15) in whatever task they are given, even though it be menial and unrecognized. They must preserve and strengthen a necessary oneness with their brothers in the ministry, especially with those whom God has selected as visible rulers of his Church. For in this way they are laboring to build the body of Christ which grows "through every gesture of service" (cf. Eph 4:11–16). This obedience is designed to promote the mature freedom of the children of God; by its very nature it postulates that in the carrying out of their work, spurred on by charity, they develop new approaches and methods for the greater good of the Church. With enthusiasm and courage, let priests propose new projects and strive to satisfy the needs of their flocks. Of course, they must be ready to submit to the decisions of those who rule the Church of God.

By this humility and by willing responsible obedience, priests conform themselves to Christ. They make their own the sentiments of Jesus Christ who "emptied himself, taking on the form of a servant," becoming obedient even to death (Phil 2:7–9). By this obedience he conquered and made up for the disobedience of Adam, as the Apostle testifies, "for as by the disobedience of one man, many were made sinners, so also by the obedience of one, many shall be made just" (Rm 5:19).

16. (Celibacy is to be embraced and esteemed as a gift.) Perfect and perpetual continence for the sake of the kingdom of heaven, commended by Christ the Lord (cf. Mt 19:22) and through the course of time as well as in our own days freely accepted and observed in a praiseworthy manner by many of the faithful, is held by the Church to be of great value in a special manner for the priestly life. It is at the same time a sign and a stimulus for pastoral charity and a special source of spiritual fecundity in the world.[8] Indeed, it is not demanded by the very nature of

---

8. Cf. Second Vatican Ecumenical Council, Dogmatic Constitution on the Church *Lumen Gentium* (Nov. 21, 1964), 42: *AAS* 57 (1965), 47–49.

the priesthood, as is apparent from the practice of the early Church (cf. 1 Tm 3:2–5: Ti 1:6), and from the traditions of the Eastern Churches, where besides those who with all the bishops, by a gift of grace, choose to observe celibacy, there are also married priests of highest merit. This holy synod, while it commends ecclesiastical celibacy, in no way intends to alter that different discipline which legitimately flourishes in the Eastern Churches. It permanently exhorts all those who have received the priesthood and marriage to persevere in their holy vocation so that they may fully and generously continue to expend themselves for the sake of the flock commended to them.[9]

Indeed, celibacy has a many-faceted suitability for the priesthood. For the whole priestly mission is dedicated to the service of a new humanity which Christ, the victor over death, has aroused through his Spirit in the world and which has its origin "not of blood, nor of the will of the flesh, nor of the will of man but of God" (Jn 1:13). Through virginity, then, or celibacy observed for the kingdom of heaven (cf. Mt 19:12), priests are consecrated to Christ by a new and exceptional reason. They adhere to him more easily with an undivided heart (cf. 1 Cor 7:32–34), they dedicate themselves more freely in him and through him to the service of God and men, and they more expeditiously minister to his kingdom and the work of heavenly regeneration, and thus they are apt to accept, in a broad sense, paternity in Christ. In this way they profess themselves before men as willing to be dedicated to the office committed to them—namely, to commit the faithful to one man and to present them as a chaste virgin to Christ (cf. 2 Cor 11:2) and thus to evoke the mysterious marriage established by Christ and fully to be manifested in the future, in which the Church has Christ as her only spouse.[10] They give, moreover, a living sign of the world to come, by a faith and charity already made present, in which the children of the resurrection neither marry nor take wives.[11]

---

9. Cf. Pius XI, Encyclical Letter *Ad Catholici Sacerdotii* (Dec. 30, 1935): *AAS* 28 (1936), 28.

10. Cf. Second Vatican Ecumenical Council, Dogmatic Constitution on the Church *Lumen Gentium* (Nov. 21, 1964), 42, 44: *AAS* 57 (1965), 47–49, 50–51; Second Vatican Ecumenical Council, Decree on the Adaptation and Renewal of Religious Life *Perfectae Caritatis* (Oct. 18, 1965), 12.

11. Pius XI, Encyclical Letter *Ad Catholici Sacerdotii* (Dec. 20, 1935): *AAS* 28 (1936), 24–28; Pius XII, Encyclical Letter *Sacra Virginitas* (March 25, 1954), 169–172: *AAS* 46 (1954).

For these reasons, based on the mystery of Christ and his mission, celibacy, which first was recommended to priests, later in the Latin Church was imposed upon all who were to be promoted to sacred Orders. This legislation, pertaining to those who are destined for the priesthood, this holy synod again approves and confirms, fully trusting this gift of the Spirit so fitting for the priesthood of the New Testament, freely given by the Father, provided that those who participate in the priesthood of Christ through the sacrament of Orders—and also the whole Church—humbly and fervently pray for it. This sacred synod also exhorts all priests who in following the example of Christ freely receive sacred celibacy as a grace of God, that they magnanimously and whole-heartedly adhere to it, and that persevering faithfully in it, they may acknowledge this outstanding gift of the Father which is so openly praised and extolled by the Lord (cf. Mt 19:11). Let them keep before their eyes the great mysteries signified by it and fulfilled in it. Insofar as perfect continence is thought by many men to be impossible in our times, to that extent priests should all the more humbly and steadfastly pray with the Church for that grace of fidelity, which is never denied those who seek it, and use all the supernatural and natural aids available. They should especially seek, lest they omit them, the ascetical norms which have been proved by the experience of the Church and which are scarcely less necessary in the contemporary world. This holy synod asks not only priests but all the faithful that they might receive this precious gift of priestly celibacy in their hearts and ask of God that he will always bestow this gift upon his Church.

17. (Relationship to the world and temporal goods, and voluntary poverty.) In their friendly and brotherly dealings with one another and with other men, priests are able to learn and appreciate human values and esteem created goods as gifts of God. By living in the world, let priests know how not to be of the world, according to the word of our Lord and master (cf. Jn 17:14–16). By using the world as those who do not use it (cf. 1 Cor 7:31), let them achieve that freedom whereby they are free from every inordinate concern and become docile to the voice of God in their daily life. From this freedom and docility grows spiritual discretion in which is found the right relationship to the world and earthly goods. Such a right relationship is of great importance to priests, because the mission of the Church is fulfilled in the midst of the world, and because created goods are altogether necessary for the personal de-

velopment of man. Let them be grateful, therefore, for all that the heavenly Father has given them to lead a full life rightly, but let them see in the light of faith all that comes to them, so that they might correctly use goods in response to the will of God and reject those which are harmful to their mission.

For priests who have the Lord as their "portion and heritage" (Nm 18:20), temporal goods should be used only toward ends which are licit according to the doctrine of Christ and the direction of the Church.

Ecclesiastical goods, properly so called, according to their nature and ecclesiastical law, should be administered by priests with the help of capable laymen as far as possible and should always be employed for those purposes in the pursuit of which it is licit for the Church to possess temporal goods, namely, for the carrying out of divine worship, for the procuring of honest sustenance for the clergy and for the exercise of the works of the holy apostolate or works of charity, especially in behalf of the needy.[12] Those goods which priests and bishops receive for the exercise of their ecclesiastical office should be used for adequate support and the fulfillment of their office and status, excepting those governed by particular laws.[13] That which is in excess they should be willing to set aside for the good of the Church or for works of charity. Thus, they are not to seek ecclesiastical office or the benefits of it for the increase of their own family wealth.[14] Therefore, in no way placing their heart in treasures (cf. Ps 62:11), they should avoid all greediness and carefully abstain from every appearance of business.

Priests, moreover, are invited to embrace voluntary poverty by which they are more manifestly conformed to Christ and become eager in the sacred ministry. For Christ, though he was rich, became poor on account of us, that by his need we might become rich (cf. 2 Cor 8:9). And by their example the apostles witnessed that a free gift of God is to be freely given (cf. Acts 8:18–25) with the knowledge of how to sustain both abundance and need (cf. Phil 4:12). A certain common use of

---

12. Council of Antioch, canon 25: Mansi 2, 1328; *Decree of Gratian,* ch. 23, C. 12 q. 1, ed. Friedberg, 1, pp. 684–685.

13. This is to be understood especially with regard to the laws and customs prevailing in the Eastern Churches.

14. Council of Paris, a. 829, can. 15: M. G. H., sect. III, *Concilia,* t. 2, par. 6, 622; Council of Trent, Session 25, *De Reform.,* ch. 1.

goods, similar to the common possession of goods in the history of the primitive Church (cf. Acts 2:42–47), furnishes an excellent means of pastoral charity. By living this form of life, priests can laudably reduce to practice that spirit of poverty commended by Christ.

Led by the Spirit of the Lord, who anointed the Savior and sent him to evangelize the poor (cf. Lk 4:18), priests, therefore, and also bishops, should avoid everything which in any way could turn the poor away. Before the other followers of Christ, let priests set aside every appearance of vanity in their possessions. Let them arrange their homes so that they might not appear unapproachable to anyone, lest anyone, even the most humble, fear to visit them.

Section 3: Aids to the Life of Priests

18. (Aids to encourage the spiritual life.) In order that in all conditions of life they may be able to grow in union with Christ, priests, besides the exercise of their conscious ministry, enjoy the common and particular means, old and new, which the Spirit never ceases to arouse in the People of God and which the Church commends and sometimes commands[15] for the sanctification of her members. Outstanding among all these spiritual aids are those acts by which the faithful are nourished in the Word of God at the double table of Sacred Scripture and the Eucharist.[16] The importance of frequent use of these for the sanctification of priests is obvious to all. The ministers of sacramental grace are intimately united to Christ our Savior and pastor through the fruitful reception of the sacraments, especially sacramental Penance, in which, prepared by the daily examination of conscience, the necessary conversion of heart and love for the Father of mercy is greatly deepened. Nourished by spiritual reading, under the light of faith, they can more diligently seek signs of God's will and impulses of his grace in the various events of life, and so from day to day become more docile to the mission they have assumed in the Holy Spirit. They will always find a wonderful example of such docility in the Blessed Virgin Mary, who was led by the Holy Spirit to dedicate herself totally to the mystery of man's redemp-

---

15. Cf. *Code of Canon Law,* 125 ff.

16. Cf. Second Vatican Ecumenical Council, Decree on the Adaptation and Renewal of Religious Life *Perfectae Caritatis* (Oct. 18, 1965), 6; Second Vatican Ecumenical Council, Dogmatic Constitution on Divine Revelation *Dei Verbum* (Nov. 18, 1965), 21.

tion.[17] Let priests love and venerate with filial devotion and veneration this mother of the eternal high priest, queen of apostles and protector of their own ministry.

In the fulfillment of their ministry with fidelity to the daily colloquy with Christ, a visit to and veneration of the most holy Eucharist, spiritual retreats and spiritual direction are of great worth. In many ways, but especially through mental prayer and the vocal prayers which they freely choose, priests seek and fervently pray that God will grant them the spirit of true adoration whereby they themselves, along with the people committed to them, may intimately unite themselves with Christ, the Mediator of the New Testament, and so as adopted children of God may be able to call out "Abba, Father" (Rm 8:15).

19. (Study and pastoral knowledge.) Priests are admonished by their bishop in the sacred rite of ordination that they "be mature in knowledge" and that their doctrine be "spiritual medicine for the People of God."[18] The knowledge of the sacred minister ought to be sacred because it is drawn from the sacred source and directed to a sacred goal. Especially is it drawn from reading and meditating on the Sacred Scriptures,[19] and it is equally nourished by the study of the holy Fathers and other doctors and monuments of Tradition. In order, moreover, that they may give apt answers to questions posed by men of this age, it is necessary for priests to know well the doctrines of the magisterium and the councils and documents of the Roman Pontiffs and to consult the best of prudent writers of theological science.

Since human culture and also sacred science has progressed in our times, priests are urged to suitably and without interruption perfect their knowledge of divine things and human affairs and so prepare themselves to enter more opportunely into conversation with their contemporaries.

Therefore, let priests more readily study and effectively learn the methods of evangelization and the apostolate. Let opportune aids be prepared with all care, such as the institution of courses and meetings ac-

---

17. Cf. Second Vatican Ecumenical Council, Dogmatic Constitution on the Church *Lumen Gentium* (Nov. 21, 1964), 65: *AAS* 57 (1965), 64–65.

18. *Roman Pontifical,* "Ordination of a Priest."

19. Cf. Second Vatican Ecumenical Council, Dogmatic Constitution on Divine Revelation *Dei Verbum* (Nov. 18, 1965), 25.

cording to territorial conditions, the erection of centers of pastoral studies, the establishment of libraries and the qualified supervision of studies by suitable persons. Moreover, let bishops, either individually or united in groups, see to it that all their priests at established intervals, especially a few years after their ordination,[20] may be able to frequent courses in which they will be given the opportunity to acquire a fuller knowledge of pastoral methods and theological science, both in order that they may strengthen their spiritual life and mutually communicate their apostolic experiences with their brothers.[21] New pastors and those who have newly begun pastoral work, as well as those who are sent to other dioceses or nations, should be helped by these and other suitable means with special care.

Finally, the bishops will be solicitous that there will be some who dedicate themselves to a deeper study of theology, that there will not be lacking suitable teachers for the formation of clerics, that the rest of the priests and the faithful will be helped to acquire the doctrine they need, and that healthy progress will be encouraged in the sacred disciplines, so necessary for the Church.

20. (Providing equitable remuneration for priests.) As those dedicated to the service of God and the fulfillment of the office entrusted to them, priests deserve to receive an equitable remuneration, because "the laborer is worthy of his hire" (Lk 10:7; cf. Mt 10:10; 1 Cor 9:7; 1 Tm 5:18), and "the Lord directed that those who preach the Gospel should have their living from the Gospel" (1 Cor 9:14). Wherefore, insofar as an equitable remuneration of the priests would not be provided otherwise, the faithful themselves—that is, those in whose behalf the priest labors—are truly obliged to see to it that they can provide what help is necessary for the honorable and worthy life of the priests. The bishops, however, should admonish the faithful concerning this obligation of theirs. And they should see to it—whether each individual for his own diocese or, more aptly, several together for their common territory—that norms are established according to which suitable support is rightly provided for those who do fulfill or have fulfilled a special office in the ser-

---

20. This course is not the same as the pastoral course which is to be undertaken immediately after ordination, spoken of in the *Decree on Priestly Training* (Oct. 28, 1965), 22.

21. Second Vatican Ecumenical Council, Decree on the Pastoral Office of Bishops in the Church *Christus Dominus* (Oct. 28, 1965), 16.

vice of the People of God. The remuneration received by each one, in accord with his office and the conditions of time and place, should be fundamentally the same for all in the same circumstances and befitting his station. Moreover, those who have dedicated themselves to the service of the priesthood, by reason of the remuneration they receive, should not only be able to honorably provide for themselves but also themselves be provided with some means of helping the needy. For the ministry to the poor has always been held in great honor in the Church from its beginnings. Furthermore, this remuneration should be such that it will permit priests each year to take a suitable and sufficient vacation, something which indeed the bishops should see that their priests are able to have.

Special importance ought to be given to the office fulfilled by sacred ministers. Therefore, the so-called system of benefices should be relinquished or at least so reformed that the place of the benefits, or the right to revenue from the endowment attached to an office, would be held as secondary, and the first place in law would be given to the ecclesiastical office itself. From this it should be understood that whatever office is conferred in a stable manner is to be exercised for a spiritual purpose.

21. (On setting up common funds and establishing a system of social assistance for priests.) We should always keep before our eyes the example of the faithful of the early Church in Jerusalem, who "held all things in common" (Acts 4:32) "and distribution was made to each according to each one's need" (Acts 4:35). So it is supremely fitting, at least in regions where the support of the clergy completely or largely depends on the offerings of the faithful, that their offerings for this purpose be collected by a particular diocesan institution, which the bishop administers with the help of priests and, when useful, of laymen who are expert in financial matters. Further it is hoped that insofar as is possible in individual dioceses or regions there be established a common fund enabling bishops to satisfy obligations to other deserving persons and meet the needs of various dioceses. This would also enable wealthier dioceses to help the poorer, that the need of the latter might be supplemented by the abundance of the former (cf. 2 Cor 8:14). These common funds, even though they should be principally made up of the offerings of the faithful, also should be provided for by other duly established sources.

Moreover, in nations where social security for the clergy is not yet aptly established, let the episcopal conferences see to it that—in accord with ecclesiastical and civil laws—there may be either diocesan institutes, whether federated with one another or established for various dioceses together, or territorial associations, which under the vigilance of the hierarchy would make sufficient and suitable provision for a program of preventive medicine, and the necessary support of priests who suffer from sickness, invalid conditions or old age. Let priests share in this established institute, prompted by a spirit of solidarity with their brothers to take part in their tribulations (cf. Phil 4:14), while at the same time being freed from an anxious concern for their own future so that they can cultivate evangelical poverty more readily and give themselves fully to the salvation of souls. Let those in charge of this act to bring together the institutes of various nations in order that their strength be more firmly achieved and more broadly based.

CONCLUSION AND EXHORTATION

22. Having before our eyes the joys of the priestly life, this holy synod cannot at the same time overlook the difficulties which priests experience in the circumstances of contemporary life. For we know how much economic and social conditions are transformed, and even more how much the customs of men are changed, how much the scale of values is changed in the estimation of men. As a result, the ministers of the Church and sometimes the faithful themselves feel like strangers in this world, anxiously looking for the ways and words with which to communicate with it. For there are new obstacles which have arisen to the faith: the seeming unproductivity of work done, and also the bitter loneliness which men experience can lead them to the danger of becoming spiritually depressed.

The world which today is entrusted to the loving ministry of the pastors of the Church is that which God so loved that he would give his only Son for it (cf. Jn 3:16). Truly this world, indeed weighed down with many sins but also endowed with many talents, provides the Church with the living stones (cf. 1 Pt 2:5) which are built up into the dwelling place of God in the Spirit (cf. Eph 2:22). This same Holy Spirit, while impelling the Church to open new ways to go to the world of today, suggests and favors the growth of fitting adaptations in the ministry of priests.

Priests should remember that in performing their office they are never alone, but strengthened by the power of Almighty God, and believing in Christ who called them to share in his priesthood, they should devote themselves to their ministry with complete trust, knowing that God can cause charity to grow in them.[1] Let them be mindful of their

---

1. Cf. *Roman Pontifical,* "Ordination of a Priest."

brothers in the priesthood as well, and also of the faithful of the entire world who are associated with them. For all priests cooperate in carrying out the saving plan of God (cf. Eph 3:9), that is, the mystery of Christ, the sacrament hidden from the ages in God, which is only brought to fulfillment little by little through the collaboration of many ministries in building up the body of Christ until it grows to the fullness of time. All this, hidden with Christ in God (cf. Col 3:3) can be uniquely perceived by faith. For the leaders of the People of God must walk by faith, following the example of faithful Abraham, who in faith "obeyed by going out into a place which he was to receive for an inheritance; and he went out not knowing where he was going" (Heb 11:8). Indeed, the dispenser of the mysteries of God can see himself in the man who sowed his field, of whom the Lord said that he should: "then sleep and rise, night and day, and the seed should sprout without his knowing" (Mk 4:27). As for the rest, the Lord Jesus, who said: "Take courage, I have overcome the world" (Jn 16:33), did not by these words promise his Church a perfect victory in this world. Certainly this holy synod rejoices that the earth has been sown with the seed of the Gospel which now bears fruit in many places, under the direction of the Holy Spirit who fills the whole earth and who has stirred up a missionary spirit in the hearts of many priests and faithful. Concerning all this, this holy synod gives fervent thanks to the priests of the entire world. "Now to him who is able to accomplish all things in a measure far beyond what we ask or conceive in keeping with the power that is at work in us—to him be glory in the Church and in Christ Jesus" (Eph 3:20–21).

Given in Rome at St. Peter's, December 7, 1965

PASTORAL CONSTITUTION ON THE CHURCH IN THE MODERN WORLD

Gaudium et Spes

Promulgated by
His Holiness Pope Paul VI
On December 7, 1965

INTRODUCTION

Gaudium et Spes (GS) has a unique place among the documents of Vatican II. The Council adopted a generally pastoral orientation and this is the only document with the word "pastoral" in its title. *GS* is the most comprehensive development of this pastoral concern, taking an in-depth look at the role of the Church in the modern world.

In reading the constitution it is apparent that "pastoral" is not opposed to "doctrinal." In the texts of the Council, "pastoral" can mean two things. First, it concerns translating doctrine into practical, juridical and institutional directives. This sense of "pastoral" is well attested to in documents such as *Christus Dominus* and *Presbyterorum Ordinis,* which anticipated the revision of the Code of Canon Law, completed in 1983.

In a second sense, "pastoral" means focusing on the interior, grace-filled, spiritual dimension of the Church's life. This is the fundamental principle of renewal, which seeks to overcome the split between faith and life. This sense is found in virtually every document of the Council and constitutes the main characteristic of Vatican II: the renewal of the Church will come about through a recentering in Christ and a growth in holiness. This second sense is certainly found in *GS,* especially articles 43 and 76.

However, in *GS* this second sense is incorporated into a larger pastoral schema of dialogue with the modern world. *GS* is unique in that it considers subjects that are important to non-Christians as well as Christians and Catholics, things such as human dignity, the family, culture, economic and political activity, and war and peace.

The Church is not an expert in these matters in a technical sense. But as Paul VI said, the Church is "an expert in humanity." In Christ, the Church knows the full truth about the human person: his or her dignity, capacity to know and love God, social nature and fulfillment in love. This expertise guides all that the constitution teaches.

Since this anthropology is the foundation of the document, it will be the second of two main considerations of this introduction. First, however, it is important to understand the overall framework in which this anthropology is situated.

GS could be described as a pastoral statement of the relationship between the Church and the world. In this respect, it is a masterpiece. It treats creation and its order as a patrimony common to both believers and unbelievers, and acknowledges the legitimate autonomy of the secular order. On the level of knowledge, faith is not opposed to human acquired wisdom. Some of the things known by faith and taught by the Church (existence of God, precepts of natural law) can be known by reason alone, unaided by faith. However, faith confirms these things which reason can discover, and integrates them into a higher order known by God's revelation. Similarly, one's duties to promote the common good as a citizen are in harmony with one's duties as a member of the Church. The orientation to the kingdom of heaven which comes with grace and faith does not do away with the order of creation. This order retains its "own stability, truth, goodness, proper laws and order" (*GS* 36). It is precisely here that the Church comes into contact with and can carry on a dialogue with the world.

An example of this is *GS's* treatment of sin. After summarizing biblical revelation on sin, the text states: "What divine revelation makes known to us agrees with experience" (*GS* 13). The text then goes on to describe this in language not dependent on faith. This procedure shows the real genius of *GS*. If the Church exists to serve human persons (cf. *GS* 3), it must understand not only who they are in their essence, but also their situation. For love is concrete, not abstract, and the actions of love must be directed to people in their actual, existential condition. The Church cannot have too much knowledge about the circumstances and opportunities of people today, as well as those things which threaten them, if it is to serve them effectively. Thus, a careful analysis is required, which *GS* provides.

In addition, this approach can bring credibility to the Church. If through the perspective of faith the Church expresses the human situation in a manner which people find compelling in its accuracy, this can dispose them positively toward the content of the faith. In light of this, the human situation is seen more clearly. It is hoped that modern people will discover that the truth about themselves is linked to the truth about God, which the Church holds in faith.

GS presents God as being at work in the world. For this reason it can state that whoever "labors to penetrate the secrets of reality with a humble and steady mind, even though he is unaware of the fact, is nevertheless being led by the hand of God, who holds all things in existence and gives them their identity" (*GS* 36). The same principle applies to human action. Those who, though ignorant of God, work to complete the goods of creation, to perfect its harmony for their own good and that of their neighbors while respecting their "stability, truth, goodness, proper laws and order" (*GS* 36), are "unconscious collaborators with God" (*CCC* 307). Such rightly ordered activity is according to God's will and can lead such persons to a certain communion with him. Since this is the same God with whom believers are in communion, the Church is aware of a profound solidarity which unites its children and their destiny with that of the other men and women of the contemporary world.

The basic questions that arise from human experience are common to all people, believers and unbelievers alike. People experience goodness, grandeur, triumph, advancement and hope, as well as evil, suffering, fear and anxiety. Such experiences raise fundamental questions about the meaning of life, death, justice, injustice, truth, suffering and guilt (cf. *GS* 10). "To this questioning only God fully and most certainly provides an answer as he summons man to higher knowledge and humbler probing" (*GS* 21). "Through Christ and in Christ, the riddles of sorrow and death grow meaningful. Apart from his Gospel, they overwhelm us" (*GS* 22). Christians ask the same questions as other people, and through faith have discovered that "By love, God has revealed himself and given himself to man. He has thus provided the definitive, superabundant answer to the questions that man asks himself about the meaning and purpose of his life" (*CCC* 68).

The Church is called to dialogue with contemporary people, strive to understand their questions and anxieties, and offer the answer it has discovered in faith. The *Decree on the Mission Activity of the Church* takes up this theme, which has also played a pivotal role in Pope John Paul II's teaching.

Thus, *GS* presents the Church as intimately involved in and concerned with the questions which people today are asking. One of the signs of the times is that people are especially conscious of their own dignity. For this reason, *GS* opens with an extraordinary chapter on the dignity of the human person in the light of revelation. It ends with the assertion that only in Christ can people know the full truth about themselves, their happiness, their call to communion with God, and their social nature, that they are made for love (cf. *GS* 22, 24).

This anthropology is seen throughout the document. The specific questions taken up in the second part are considered in light of the full truth about the human person and his dignity. An essential constituent of this dignity is freedom, which the constitution acknowledges as highly esteemed by contemporary people, but also misunderstood (cf. *GS* 17; *Veritatis Splendor* 35–53). The misconception of freedom poses a serious threat, since when misunderstood it can destroy itself and bring slavery. Freedom, as dignity itself, must be defined in terms of truth.

The quest for truth is the first fundamental expression of human dignity. Especially in seeking moral truth, persons can transcend themselves in the direction of God. This brings up the topic of conscience. *GS* contains one of three important passages in which the Council presents its teaching on conscience. (The other two are *DH* 3 and *LG* 16.) First it describes the action of conscience as "summoning [the person] to love good and avoid evil" *GS* 16). Then it states that the voice of conscience makes known God's law, and that human dignity consists in obeying that law known by conscience.

The reference to God's voice connects conscience to God, as does another conciliar text: "In all his activity a man is bound to follow his conscience in order that he may come to God, the end and purpose of life" (*DH* 3). The first demand of conscience is that the truth be honestly sought. The text does not discuss technical considerations of the obligatory nature of an erroneous conscience, though it does affirm that when it is in error despite an honest search for the truth (invincible ignorance), conscience does not lose its dignity. That dignity is lost, however, when the error is due to neglect or sin.

It is worth recalling that human dignity is defined in terms of communion with God (cf. *GS* 19). So according to this anthropology, an essential link exists between seeking truth, assenting to it and patterning one's life on it, and one's relationship with God. This is why *GS* 16 connects judgment to its treatment on conscience, and why *LG* 16 describes in terms of conscience the possibility of salvation for those who do not know Christ or God.

Pope John Paul II has made this link between dignity and conscience a hallmark of his teaching, which links the human person and conscience. This is to look at the person as God does. He searches the heart and by grace brings conversion through the purification of conscience (cf. Heb 9:14; *DViv* 42–45).

A consequence of this outlook leads to an astounding statement. As egregious as violations of human dignity are—such as murder, genocide, abortion, euthanasia and exploiting people for profit—they "do more harm to those who practice them than those who suffer from the injury" (*GS* 27). Implicitly, the Council here is making a significant distinction between the rights which follow upon human dignity and the essence of dignity itself. In terms of the person's relationship with God, no created thing external to him can separate him from God's love (cf. Rm 8:38–39). The only thing that can separate a person from God is sin, which is always an act opposed to the dictate of conscience. That this vision of the human person confirms what can be known apart from faith is seen in Socrates, a "natural martyr" for the truth, who held that he would rather be the victim of an injustice than commit an injustice.

The 20th century has seen tragic crimes committed against humanity. In response the Church has called her sons and daughters to build social, legal, cultural, political and economic structures which promote respect for human rights. Yet the Church addresses a deeper appeal to the heart, for all human actions originate from the inner world of the heart and conscience. These are directly related to God. The Church's fundamental mission is to proclaim the Good News of God's love in order to bring about the conversion of hearts and direct people to God. All other relationships derive their proper order from this transcendent relationship with God in the truth. The Church penetrates the temporal order through the actions of her members which proceed from a heart renewed by the truth and love of God. This is the Church's unique contribution to the world. In this way her mission of salvation is simultaneously a mission for renewing the temporal order.

The second manifestation of human dignity which is central to *GS* is the social nature of the human person, by which one enters into relationships of communion through love. The constitution describes living in love as making a sincere gift of self (*GS* 24). Here it is important to distinguish between the person entering into communion with God, and entering into communion with other people. Human beings are made for both, but the two are so ordered that one's relationships with other persons depend on one's relationship with God.

The constitution refers to the common good on several occasions. It is "the sum of those conditions of social life which allow social groups and their individual members relatively thorough and ready access to their own fulfillment" (*GS* 26). All people are called to promote the common good, and this provides another contact point between the Church and the world. The common good, however, is not a pure product of human creativity. It has an objective content of justice based on the anthropology developed in *GS,* for human fulfillment can only be understood in terms of human nature.

The constant reference to human rights throughout *GS* must be understood in this light. Rights correspond to the duty to seek self-fulfillment, and they and the institutions designed to protect them are an essential component of the common good. The Council also spoke of rights in other documents, notably *DH* and *GE.*

But to say that the common good depends upon anthropology is to say that it depends upon God, who is the author of human nature and its fulfillment. In its treatment of marriage, culture, economic and political activity, the duties of citizens, war and peace, *GS* often refers to the common good, which is defined with a double reference to the human person and to God. Otherwise, human activity, which is intended to bring fulfillment, cannot achieve its purpose, but can become a force of destruction. The human person, human actions, institutions and the common good itself cannot be fully known except in reference to God: "For without the Creator the creature would disappear" (*GS* 36).

The determination to define the person always in reference to God is the real key to *GS,* as Pope John Paul II has made clear:

> The more the Church's mission is centered upon man—the more it is, so to speak, anthropocentric—the more it must be confirmed and actualized theocentrically, that is to say, be directed in Jesus Christ to the Father. While the various currents of human thought both in the past and at the present have tended and still tend to separate theocentrism and anthropocentrism, and even to set them in opposition to each other, the Church, following Christ, seeks to link them up in human history in a deep and organic way. And this is also one of the basic principles, perhaps the most important one, of the teaching of the last Council (*Dives in Misericordia* 1).

TOPICAL OUTLINE

Preface: the Church's interest in the world of today (1–3)

Introductory statement: the current world situation (4–10)

Part One: The Church and humanity

1. The dignity of the human person

   A. Nature of the human person; the problem of evil (12–15)

   B. Conscience and freedom (16–17)

   C. The mystery of death (18)

   D. The problem of atheism (19–21)

   E. The mystery of Christ illuminates the mystery of the human person (22)

2. The human community

   A. Interdependence and the social nature of the human person (23–25)

   B. Dignity of the human person and consequent rights (26)

   C. Practical consequences of this

   1. Condemnation of various crimes (27)

   2. Respect for all (28–29)

   3. Social obligations according to justice and love (30)

   4. Social life (31–32)

A. Importance of culture (53)

B. Culture in the world today (54–56)

C. Principles for the proper development of culture (57–59)

D. Duties of Christians in regard to culture (60–62)

3. Economic and social life

A. Economic life today (63)

B. Economic development (64–66)

C. Principles governing socio-economic life as a whole

1. Role of labor (67–68)

2. Property and the just distribution of goods (69)

3. Investments (70)

4. Private property and the common good (71)

5. Work for justice and peace (72)

4. The life of the political community

A. Concerns about political life today (73)

B. Nature and purpose of the political community (74)

C. Participation of citizens (75)

D. Relation of the political community and the Church (76)

5. Fostering peace and promoting a community of nations

A. Meaning and importance of peace (77–78)

B. Avoiding war

1. The horrors of war; nuclear weapons (79–80)

2. The arms race (81)

3. Efforts to insure peace (82)

C. Setting up an international community

1. The causes of war (83)

2. International organizations (84)

PASTORAL CONSTITUTION ON THE CHURCH IN THE MODERN WORLD

Gaudium et Spes

PREFACE[1]

1. The joys and the hopes, the griefs and the anxieties of the men of this age, especially those who are poor or in any way afflicted, are the joys and hopes, the griefs and anxieties of the followers of Christ. Indeed, nothing genuinely human fails to raise an echo in their hearts. For theirs is a community composed of men. United in Christ, they are led by the Holy Spirit in their journey to the kingdom of their Father, and they have welcomed the news of salvation which is meant for every

---

1. The *Pastoral Constitution on the Church in the Modern World* is made up of two parts, yet it constitutes an organic unity.

By way of explanation: the constitution is called "pastoral" because, while resting on doctrinal principles, it seeks to express the relation of the Church to the world and modern mankind. The result is that, on the one hand, a pastoral slant is present in the first part, and on the other hand, a doctrinal slant is present in the second part.

In the first part, the Church develops her teaching on man, on the world which is the enveloping context of man's existence and on man's relations to his fellow men. In part two, the Church gives closer consideration to various aspects of modern life and human society; special consideration is given to those questions and problems which, in this general area, seem to have a greater urgency in our day. As a result, in part two the subject matter which is viewed in the light of doctrinal principles is made up of diverse elements. Some elements have a permanent value; others only a transitory one.

Consequently, the constitution must be interpreted according to the general norms of theological interpretation. Interpreters must bear in mind—especially in part two—the changeable circumstances which the subject matter, by its very nature, involves.

man. That is why this community realizes that it is truly linked with mankind and its history by the deepest bonds.

2. Hence this Second Vatican Council, having probed more profoundly into the mystery of the Church, now addresses itself without hesitation not only to the sons of the Church and to all who invoke the name of Christ, but to the whole of humanity. For the Council yearns to explain to everyone how it conceives of the presence and activity of the Church in the world of today.

Therefore, the Council focuses its attention on the world of men, the whole human family, along with the sum of those realities in the midst of which it lives; that world which is the theater of man's history and the heir of his energies, his tragedies and his triumphs; that world which the Christian sees as created and sustained by its Maker's love, fallen indeed into the bondage of sin yet emancipated now by Christ, who was crucified and rose again to break the stranglehold of personified evil, so that the world might be fashioned anew according to God's design and reach its fulfillment.

3. Though mankind is stricken with wonder at its own discoveries and its power, it often raises anxious questions about the current trend of the world, about the place and role of man in the universe, about the meaning of its individual and collective strivings and about the ultimate destiny of reality and of humanity. Hence, giving witness and voice to the faith of the whole People of God gathered together by Christ, this Council can provide no more eloquent proof of its solidarity with, as well as its respect and love for the entire human family with which it is bound up, than by engaging with it in conversation about these various problems. The Council brings to mankind light kindled from the Gospel, and puts at its disposal those saving resources which the Church herself, under the guidance of the Holy Spirit, receives from her Founder. For the human person deserves to be preserved; human society deserves to be renewed. Hence, the focal point of our total presentation will be man himself, whole and entire, body and soul, heart and conscience, mind and will.

Therefore, this sacred synod, proclaiming the noble destiny of man and championing the Godlike seed which has been sown in him, offers to mankind the honest assistance of the Church in fostering that brotherhood of all men which corresponds to this destiny of theirs. Inspired by no earthly ambition, the Church seeks but a solitary goal: to carry forward the work of Christ under the lead of the befriending Spirit. And Christ entered this world to give witness to the truth, to rescue and not to sit in judgment, to serve and not to be served (cf. Jn 18:37; Mt 20:28; Mk 10:45).

Introductory Statement

The Situation of Men in the Modern World

4. To carry out such a task, the Church has always had the duty of scrutinizing the signs of the times and of interpreting them in the light of the Gospel. Thus, in language intelligible to each generation, she can respond to the perennial questions which men ask about this present life and the life to come, and about the relationship of the one to the other. We must therefore recognize and understand the world in which we live, its explanations, its longings, and its often dramatic characteristics. Some of the main features of the modern world can be sketched as follows.

Today, the human race is involved in a new stage of history. Profound and rapid changes are spreading by degrees around the whole world. Triggered by the intelligence and creative energies of man, these changes recoil upon him, upon his decisions and desires, both individual and collective, and upon his manner of thinking and acting with respect to things and to people. Hence, we can already speak of a true cultural and social transformation, one which has repercussions on man's religious life as well.

As happens in any crisis of growth, this transformation has brought serious difficulties in its wake. Thus, while man extends his power in every direction, he does not always succeed in subjecting it to his own welfare. Striving to probe more profoundly into the deeper recesses of his own mind, he frequently appears more unsure of himself. Gradually and more precisely he lays bare the laws of society, only to be paralyzed by uncertainty about the direction to give it.

Never has the human race enjoyed such an abundance of wealth, resources and economic power, and yet a huge proportion of the world's citizens are still tormented by hunger and poverty, while countless numbers suffer from total illiteracy. Never before has man had so keen an understanding of freedom, yet at the same time new forms of social and psychological slavery make their appearance. Although the world of today has a very vivid awareness of its unity and of how one man depends on another in needful solidarity, it is most grievously torn into opposing camps by conflicting forces. For political, social, economic, racial and ideological disputes still continue bitterly, and with them the peril of a war which would reduce everything to ashes. True, there is a growing exchange of ideas, but the very words by which key concepts are expressed take on quite different meanings in diverse ideological systems. Finally, man painstakingly searches for a better world, without a corresponding spiritual advancement.

Influenced by such a variety of complexities, many of our contemporaries are kept from accurately identifying permanent values and adjusting them properly to fresh discoveries. As a result, buffeted between hope and anxiety and pressing one another with questions about the present course of events, they are burdened down with uneasiness. This same course of events leads men to look for answers; indeed, it forces them to do so.

5. Today's spiritual agitation and the changing conditions of life are part of a broader and deeper revolution. As a result of the latter, intellectual formation is ever increasingly based on the mathematical and natural sciences and on those dealing with man himself, while in the practical order the technology which stems from these sciences takes on mounting importance.

This scientific spirit has a new kind of impact on the cultural sphere and on modes of thought. Technology is now transforming the face of the earth and is already trying to master outer space. To a certain extent, the human intellect is also broadening its dominion over time: over the past by means of historical knowledge, over the future by the art of projecting and by planning.

Advances in biology, psychology and the social sciences not only bring men hope of improved self-knowledge; in conjunction with technical methods, they are helping men exert direct influence on the life of social groups.

At the same time, the human race is giving steadily increasing thought to forecasting and regulating its own population growth. History itself speeds along on so rapid a course that an individual person can scarcely keep abreast of it. The destiny of the human community has become all of a piece, where once the various groups of men had a kind of private history of their own.

Thus, the human race has passed from a rather static concept of reality to a more dynamic, evolutionary one. In consequence, there has arisen a new series of problems, a series as numerous as can be, calling for efforts of analysis and synthesis.

6. By this very circumstance, the traditional local communities such as families, clans, tribes, villages, various groups and associations stemming from social contacts experience more thorough changes every day.

The industrial type of society is gradually being spread, leading some nations to economic affluence and radically transforming ideas and social conditions established for centuries.

Likewise, the cult and pursuit of city living has grown, either because of a multiplication of cities and their inhabitants or by a transplantation of city life to rural settings.

New and more efficient media of social communication are contributing to the knowledge of events; by setting off chain reactions, they are giving the swiftest and widest possible circulation to styles of thought and feeling.

It is also noteworthy how many men are being induced to migrate on various counts and are thereby changing their manner of life. Thus, a man's ties with his fellows are constantly being multiplied, and at the same time "socialization" brings further ties, without, however, always promoting appropriate personal development and truly personal relationships.

This kind of evolution can be seen more clearly in those nations which already enjoy the conveniences of economic and technological progress, though it is also astir among peoples still striving for such progress and eager to secure for themselves the advantages of an industrialized and urbanized society. These peoples, especially those among them who are attached to older traditions, are simultaneously undergoing a movement toward more mature and personal exercise of liberty.

7. A change in attitudes and in human structures frequently calls accepted values into question, especially among young people, who have grown impatient on more than one occasion, and indeed become rebels in their distress. Aware of their own influence in the life of society, they want a part in it sooner. This frequently causes parents and educators to experience greater difficulties day by day in discharging their tasks. The institutions, laws and modes of thinking and feeling as handed down from previous generations do not always seem to be well adapted to the

contemporary state of affairs; hence arises an upheaval in the manner and even the norms of behavior.

Finally, these new conditions have their impact on religion. On the one hand, a more critical ability to distinguish religion from a magical view of the world and from the superstitions which still circulate purifies it and exacts day by day a more personal and explicit adherence to faith. As a result many persons are achieving a more vivid sense of God. On the other hand, growing numbers of people are abandoning religion in practice. Unlike former days, the denial of God or of religion, or the abandonment of them, are no longer unusual and individual occurrences. For today it is not rare for such things to be presented as requirements of scientific progress or of a certain new humanism. In numerous places these views are voiced not only in the teachings of philosophers, but on every side they influence literature, the arts, the interpretation of the humanities and of history and civil laws themselves. As a consequence, many people are shaken.

8. This development, coming so rapidly and often in a disorderly fashion, combined with keener awareness itself of the inequalities in the world, begets or intensifies contradictions and imbalances.

Within the individual person there develops rather frequently an imbalance between an intellect which is modern in practical matters and a theoretical system of thought which can neither master the sum total of its ideas, nor arrange them adequately into a synthesis. Likewise, an imbalance arises between a concern for practicality and efficiency and the demands of moral conscience; also very often between the conditions of collective existence and the requisites of personal thought and even of contemplation. At length there develops an imbalance between specialized human activity and a comprehensive view of reality.

As for the family, discord results from population, economic and social pressures, or from difficulties which arise between succeeding generations, or from new social relationships between men and women.

Differences crop up too between races and between various kinds of social orders; between wealthy nations and those which are less influential or are needy; finally, between international institutions born of the popular desire for peace, and the ambition to propagate one's own ideology, as well as collective greeds existing in nations or other groups.

What results is mutual distrust, enmities, conflicts and hardships. Of such is man at once the cause and the victim.

9. Meanwhile, the conviction grows not only that humanity can and should increasingly consolidate its control over creation, but even more that it devolves on humanity to establish a political, social and economic order which will growingly serve man and help individuals as well as groups to affirm and develop the dignity proper to them.

As a result, many persons are quite aggressively demanding those benefits of which with vivid awareness they judge themselves to be deprived, either through injustice or unequal distribution. Nations on the road to progress, like those recently made independent, desire to participate in the goods of modern civilization, not only in the political field but also economically, and to play their part freely on the world scene. Still, they continually fall behind, while very often their economic and other dependence on wealthier nations advances more rapidly.

People hounded by hunger call upon those better off. Where they have not yet won it, women claim for themselves an equity with men before the law and in fact. Laborers and farmers seek not only to provide for the necessities of life, but to develop the gifts of their personality by their labors and indeed to take part in regulating economic, social, political and cultural life. Now, for the first time in human history, all people are convinced that the benefits of culture ought to be and actually can be extended to everyone.

Still, beneath all these demands lies a deeper and more widespread longing: persons and societies thirst for a full and free life worthy of man, one in which they can subject to their own welfare all that the modern world can offer them so abundantly. In addition, nations try harder every day to bring about a kind of universal community.

Since all these things are so, the modern world shows itself at once powerful and weak, capable of the noblest deeds or the foulest; before it lies the path to freedom or to slavery, to progress or retreat, to brotherhood or hatred. Moreover, man is becoming aware that it is his responsibility to guide aright the forces which he has unleashed and which can enslave him or minister to him. That is why he is putting questions to himself.

10. The truth is that the imbalances under which the modern world labors are linked with that more basic imbalance which is rooted in the heart of man. For in man himself many elements wrestle with one another. Thus, on the one hand, as a creature he experiences his limitations in a multitude of ways; on the other he feels himself to be boundless in

his desires and summoned to a higher life. Pulled by manifold attractions he is constantly forced to choose among them and renounce some. Indeed, as a weak and sinful being, he often does what he would not, and fails to do what he would (cf. Rm 7:14 ff.). Hence, he suffers from internal divisions and from these flow so many and such great discords in society. No doubt, many whose lives are infected with a practical materialism are blinded against any sharp insight into this kind of dramatic situation, or else weighed down by unhappiness, they are prevented from giving the matter any thought. Thinking they have found serenity in an interpretation of reality everywhere proposed these days, many look forward to a genuine and total emancipation of humanity wrought solely by human effort; they are convinced that the future rule of man over the earth will satisfy every desire of his heart. Nor are there lacking men who despair of any meaning to life, and praise the boldness of those who think that human existence is devoid of any inherent significance and strive to confer a total meaning on it by their own ingenuity alone.

Nevertheless, in the face of the modern development of the world, the number constantly swells of the people who raise the most basic questions or recognize them with a new sharpness: What is man? What is this sense of sorrow, of evil, of death, which continues to exist despite so much progress? What purpose have these victories purchased at so high a cost? What can man offer to society; what can he expect from it? What follows this earthly life?

The Church firmly believes that Christ, who died and was raised up for all (cf. 2 Cor 5:15), can through his Spirit offer man the light and the strength to measure up to his supreme destiny. Nor has any other name under the heaven been given to man by which it is fitting for him to be saved (cf. Acts 4:12). She likewise holds that in her most benign Lord and Master can be found the key, the focal point and the goal of man as well as of all human history. The Church also maintains that beneath all changes there are many realities which do not change and which have their ultimate foundation in Christ, who is the same yesterday and today, yes and forever (cf. Heb 13:8). Hence, under the light of Christ, the image of the unseen God, the firstborn of every creature (cf. Col 1:15), the Council wishes to speak to all men in order to shed light on the mystery of man and to cooperate in finding the solution to the outstanding problems of our time.

PART I

THE CHURCH AND MAN'S CALLING

11. The People of God believes that it is led by the Lord's Spirit, who fills the earth. Motivated by this faith, it labors to decipher authentic signs of God's presence and purpose in the happenings, needs and desires in which this people has a part along with other men of our age. For faith throws a new light on everything, manifests God's design for man's total vocation and thus directs the mind to solutions which are fully human.

This Council, first of all, wishes to assess in this light those values which are most highly prized today and to relate them to their divine source. Insofar as they stem from endowments conferred by God on man, these values are exceedingly good. Yet they are often wrenched from their rightful function by the taint in man's heart, and hence stand in need of purification.

What does the Church think of man? What needs to be recommended for the upbuilding of contemporary society? What is the ultimate significance of human activity throughout the world? People are waiting for an answer to these questions. From the answers it will be increasingly clear that the People of God and the human race in whose midst it lives render service to each other. Thus, the mission of the Church will show its religious, and by that very fact its supremely human character.

CHAPTER I

THE DIGNITY OF THE HUMAN PERSON

12. According to the almost unanimous opinion of believers and unbelievers alike, all things on earth should be related to man as their center and crown.

But what is man? About himself he has expressed and continues to express many divergent and even contradictory opinions. In these he often exalts himself as the absolute measure of all things or debases himself to the point of despair. The result is doubt and anxiety. The Church certainly understands these problems. Endowed with light from God, she can offer solutions to them, so that man's true situation can be portrayed and his defects explained, while at the same time his dignity and destiny are justly acknowledged.

For Sacred Scripture teaches that man was created "to the image of God," is capable of knowing and loving his Creator, and was appointed by him as master of all earthly creatures (cf. Gn 1:26, Wis 2:23) that he might subdue them and use them to God's glory (cf. Sir 17:3–10). "What is man that you should care for him? You have made him little less than the angels, and crowned him with glory and honor. You have given him rule over the works of your hands, putting all things under his feet" (Ps 8:5–7).

But God did not create man as a solitary, for from the beginning "male and female he created them" (Gn 1:27). Their companionship produces the primary form of interpersonal communion. For by his innermost nature man is a social being, and unless he relates himself to others he can neither live nor develop his potential.

Therefore, as we read elsewhere in Holy Scripture, God saw "all that he had made, and it was very good" (Gn 1:31).

13. Although he was made by God in a state of holiness, from the very onset of his history man abused his liberty at the urging of the Evil One. Man set himself against God and sought to attain his goal apart

from God. Although they knew God, they did not glorify him as God, but their senseless minds were darkened, and they served the creature rather than the Creator (cf. Rm 1:21–25). What divine revelation makes known to us agrees with experience. Examining his heart, man finds that he has inclinations toward evil, too, and is engulfed by manifold ills which cannot come from his good Creator. Often refusing to acknowledge God as his beginning, man has disrupted also his proper relationship to his own ultimate goal as well as his whole relationship toward himself and others and all created things.

Therefore, man is split within himself. As a result all of human life, whether individual or collective, shows itself to be a dramatic struggle between good and evil, between light and darkness. Indeed, man finds that by himself he is incapable of battling the assaults of evil successfully, so that everyone feels as though he is bound by chains. But the Lord himself came to free and strengthen man, renewing him inwardly and casting out that "prince of this world" (Jn 12:31) who held him in the bondage of sin (cf. Jn 8:34). For sin has diminished man, blocking his path to fulfillment.

The call to grandeur and the depths of misery, both of which are a part of human experience, find their ultimate and simultaneous explanation in the light of this revelation.

14. Though made of body and soul, man is one. Through his bodily composition he gathers to himself the elements of the material world; thus they reach their crown through him and through him raise their voice in free praise of the Creator (cf. Dn 3:57–90). For this reason man is not allowed to despise his bodily life; rather, he is obliged to regard his body as good and honorable since God has created it and will raise it up on the last day. Nevertheless, wounded by sin, man experiences rebellious stirrings in his body. But the very dignity of man postulates that man glorify God in his body (cf. 1 Cor 6:13–20) and forbid it to serve the evil inclinations of his heart.

Now, man is not wrong when he regards himself as superior to bodily concerns, and as more than a speck of nature or a nameless constituent of the city of man. For by his interior qualities he outstrips the whole sum of mere things. He plunges into the depths of reality whenever he enters into his own heart; God, who probes the heart (cf. 1 Kgs 16:7; Jer 17:10) awaits him there; there he discerns his proper destiny beneath the eyes of God. Thus, when he recognizes in himself a spiritual and immortal soul, he is not being mocked by a fantasy born only of physical or social influences, but is rather laying hold of the proper truth of the matter.

15. Man judges rightly that by his intellect he surpasses the material universe, for he shares in the light of the divine mind. By relentlessly employing his talents through the ages, he has indeed made progress in the practical sciences and in technology and the liberal arts. In our times he has won superlative victories, especially in his probing of the material world and in subjecting it to himself. Still, he has always searched for more penetrating truths, and finds them. For his intelligence is not confined to observable data alone, but can with genuine certitude attain to reality itself as knowable, though in consequence of sin that certitude is partly obscured and weakened.

The intellectual nature of the human person is perfected by wisdom and needs to be, for wisdom gently attracts the mind of man to a quest and a love for what is true and good. Steeped in wisdom, man passes through visible realities to those which are unseen.

Our era, more than bygone ages, needs such wisdom if the discoveries made by man are to be further humanized. For the future of the world stands in peril unless wiser men are forthcoming. It should also be pointed out that many nations, poorer in economic goods, are quite rich in wisdom and can offer noteworthy advantages to others.

It is, finally, through the gift of the Holy Spirit that man comes by faith to the contemplation and appreciation of the divine plan (cf. Sir 17:7–8).

16. In the depths of his conscience, man detects a law which he does not impose upon himself, but which holds him to obedience. Always summoning him to love good and avoid evil, the voice of conscience when necessary speaks to his heart: do this, shun that. For man has in his heart a law written by God; to obey it is the very dignity of man; according to it he will be judged (cf. Rm 2:15–16). Conscience is the most secret core and sanctuary of a man. There he is alone with God, whose voice echoes in his depths.[1] In a wonderful manner, conscience reveals that law which is fulfilled by love of God and neighbor (cf. Mt 22:37–40; Gal 5:14). In fidelity to conscience, Christians are joined with the

---

1. Cf. Pius XII, *Radio Address on the Correct Formation of a Christian Conscience in the Young* (March 23, 1952): *AAS* (1952), 271.

rest of men in the search for truth, and for the genuine solution to the numerous problems which arise in the life of individuals from social relationships. Hence, the more right conscience holds sway, the more persons and groups turn aside from blind choice and strive to be guided by the objective norms of morality. Conscience frequently errs from invincible ignorance without losing its dignity. The same cannot be said for a man who cares but little for truth and goodness, or for a conscience which by degrees grows practically sightless as a result of habitual sin.

17. Only in freedom can man direct himself toward goodness. Our contemporaries make much of this freedom and pursue it eagerly, and rightly to be sure. Often, however, they foster it perversely as a license for doing whatever pleases them, even if it is evil. For its part, authentic freedom is an exceptional sign of the divine image within man. For God has willed that man remain "under the control of his own decisions" (cf. Sir 15:14) so that he can seek his Creator spontaneously, and come freely to utter and blissful perfection through loyalty to him. Hence, man's dignity demands that he act according to a knowing and free choice that is personally motivated and prompted from within, not under blind internal impulse nor by mere external pressure. Man achieves such dignity when, emancipating himself from all captivity to passion, he pursues his goal in a spontaneous choice of what is good, and procures for himself through effective and skillful action, apt helps to that end. Since man's freedom has been damaged by sin, only by the aid of God's grace can he bring such a relationship with God into full flower. Before the judgment seat of God each man must render an account of his own life, whether he has done good or evil (cf. 2 Cor 5:10).

18. It is in the face of death that the riddle of human existence grows most acute. Not only is man tormented by pain and by the advancing deterioration of his body, but even more so by a dread of perpetual extinction. He rightly follows the intuition of his heart when he abhors and repudiates the utter ruin and total disappearance of his own person. He rebels against death because he bears in himself an eternal seed which cannot be reduced to sheer matter. All the endeavors of technology, though useful in the extreme, cannot calm his anxiety, for prolongation of biological life is unable to satisfy that desire for higher life which is inescapably lodged in his breast.

Although the mystery of death utterly beggars the imagination, the Church has been taught by divine revelation and firmly teaches that man has been created by God for a blissful purpose beyond the reach of earthly misery. In addition, that bodily death from which man would have been immune had he not sinned (cf. Wis 1:13; 2:23–24; Rm 5:21; 6:23; Jas 1:15) will be vanquished, according to the Christian faith, when man who was ruined by his own doing is restored to wholeness by an almighty and merciful Savior. For God has called man and still calls him so that with his entire being he might be joined to him in an endless sharing of a divine life beyond all corruption. Christ won this victory when he rose to life, for by his death he freed man from death (cf. 1 Cor 15:56–57). Hence, to every thoughtful man a solidly established faith provides the answer to his anxiety about what the future holds for him. At the same time, faith gives him the power to be united in Christ with his loved ones who have already been snatched away by death; faith arouses the hope that they have found true life with God.

19. The root reason for human dignity lies in man's call to communion with God. From the very circumstance of his origin, man is already invited to converse with God. For man would not exist were he not created by God's love and constantly preserved by it, and he cannot live fully according to truth unless he freely acknowledges that love and devotes himself to his Creator. Still, many of our contemporaries have never recognized this intimate and vital link with God or have explicitly rejected it. Thus, atheism must be accounted among the most serious problems of this age and is deserving of closer examination.

The word atheism is applied to phenomena which are quite distinct from one another. For while God is expressly denied by some, others believe that man can assert absolutely nothing about him. Still others use such a method to scrutinize the question of God as to make it seem devoid of meaning. Many, unduly transgressing the limits of the positive sciences, contend that everything can be explained by this kind of scientific reasoning alone, or by contrast they altogether disallow that there is any absolute truth. Some laud man so extravagantly that their faith in God lapses into a kind of anemia, though they seem more inclined to affirm man than to deny God. Again, some form for themselves such a fallacious idea of God that when they repudiate this figment they are by no means rejecting the God of the Gospel. Some never get to the point of raising questions about God, since they seem to experience no religious stirrings nor do they see why they should trouble themselves about religion. Moreover, atheism results not rarely from a violent protest against the evil in this world, or from the absolute character with which certain human values are unduly invested, and which thereby already accords them the stature of God. Modern civilization itself often complicates the approach to God not for any essential reason but because it is so heavily engrossed in earthly affairs.

Undeniably, those who willfully shut out God from their hearts and try to dodge religious questions are not following the dictates of their consciences, and hence are not free of blame; yet believers themselves frequently bear some responsibility for this situation. For, taken as a whole, atheism is not a spontaneous development but stems from a variety of causes, including a critical reaction against religious beliefs and in some places against the Christian religion in particular. Hence, believers can have more than a little to do with the birth of atheism. To the extent that they neglect their own training in the faith, or teach erroneous doctrine, or are deficient in their religious, moral or social life, they must be said to conceal rather than reveal the authentic face of God and religion.

20. Modern atheism often takes on a systematic expression, which in addition to other causes, stretches the desires for human independence to such a point that it poses difficulties against any kind of dependence on God. Those who profess atheism of this sort maintain that it gives man freedom to be an end unto himself, the sole artisan and creator of his own history. They claim that this freedom cannot be reconciled with the affirmation of a Lord who is author and purpose of all things, or at least that this freedom makes such an affirmation altogether superfluous. Favoring this doctrine can be the sense of power which modern technical progress generates in man.

Not to be overlooked among the forms of modern atheism is that which anticipates the liberation of man especially through his economic and social emancipation. This form argues that by its nature religion thwarts this liberation by arousing man's hope for a deceptive future life, thereby diverting him from constructing the earthly city. Consequently, when the proponents of this doctrine gain governmental power, they vigorously fight against religion and promote atheism by using, especially in the education of youth, those means of pressure which public power has at its disposal.

21. In her loyal devotion to God and men, the Church has already repudiated[2] and cannot cease repudiating, sorrowfully but as firmly as possible, those poisonous doctrines and actions which contradict reason and the common experience of humanity and dethrone man from his native excellence.

Still, she strives to detect in the atheistic mind the hidden causes for the denial of God; conscious of how weighty are the questions which atheism raises, and motivated by love for all men, she believes these questions ought to be examined seriously and more profoundly.

The Church holds that the recognition of God is in no way hostile to man's dignity, since this dignity is rooted and perfected in God. For man was made an intelligent and free member of society by God who created him, but even more important, he is called as a son to commune with God and share in his happiness. She further teaches that a hope related to the end of time does not diminish the importance of intervening duties but rather undergirds the acquittal of them with fresh incentives. By contrast, when a divine instruction and the hope of life eternal are wanting, man's dignity is most grievously lacerated, as current events often attest; riddles of life and death, of guilt and of grief go unsolved with the frequent result that men succumb to despair.

Meanwhile, every man remains to himself an unsolved puzzle, however obscurely he may perceive it. For on certain occasions no one can entirely escape the kind of self-questioning mentioned earlier, especially when life's major events take place. To this questioning only God fully and most certainly provides an answer as he summons man to higher knowledge and humbler probing.

The remedy which must be applied to atheism, however, is to be sought in a proper presentation of the Church's teaching as well as in the integral life of the Church and her members. For it is the function of the Church, led by the Holy Spirit who renews and purifies her ceaselessly,[3] to make God the Father and his incarnate Son present and in a sense

---

2. Cf. Pius XI, Encyclical Letter *Divini Redemptoris* (March 19, 1937): *AAS* 29 (1937), 65–106; Pius XII, Encyclical Letter *Ad Apostolorum Principis* (June 29, 1958): *AAS* 50 (1958), 601–614; John XXIII, Encyclical Letter *Mater et Magistra* (May 15, 1961): *AAS* 53 (1961), 451–453; Paul VI, Encyclical Letter *Ecclesiam Suam* (Aug. 6, 1964): *AAS* 56 (1964), 651–653.

3. Cf. Second Vatican Ecumenical Council, Dogmatic Constitution on the Church *Lumen Gentium,* 8: *AAS* 57 (1965), 12.

visible. This result is achieved chiefly by the witness of a living and mature faith, namely, one trained to see difficulties clearly and to master them. Many martyrs have given luminous witness to this faith and continue to do so. This faith needs to prove its fruitfulness by penetrating the believer's entire life, including its worldly dimensions, and by activating him toward justice and love, especially regarding the needy. What does the most to reveal God's presence, however, is the brotherly charity of the faithful who are united in spirit as they work together for the faith of the Gospel (cf. Phil 1:27) and who prove themselves a sign of unity.

While rejecting atheism, root and branch, the Church sincerely professes that all men, believers and unbelievers alike, ought to work for the rightful betterment of this world in which all alike live; such an ideal cannot be realized, however, apart from sincere and prudent dialogue. Hence, the Church protests against the distinction which some state authorities make between believers and unbelievers, with prejudice to the fundamental rights of the human person. The Church calls for the active liberty of believers to build up in this world God's temple, too. She courteously invites atheists to examine the Gospel of Christ with an open mind.

Above all, the Church knows that her message is in harmony with the most secret desires of the human heart when she champions the dignity of the human vocation, restoring hope to those who have already despaired of anything higher than their present lot. Far from diminishing man, her message brings to his development light, life and freedom. Apart from this message nothing will avail to fill up the heart of man: "Thou hast made us for thyself," O Lord, "and our hearts are restless till they rest in Thee."[4]

22. The truth is that only in the mystery of the incarnate Word does the mystery of man take on light. For Adam, the first man, was a figure of him who was to come,[5] namely Christ the Lord. Christ, the final Adam, by the revelation of the mystery of the Father and his love, fully reveals man to man himself and makes his supreme calling clear. It is

---

4. St. Augustine, *Confessions* I, 1: *PL* 32, 661.

5. Cf. Rm 5:14; cf. also Tertullian, *De carnis resurrectione* 6: "The shape that the slime of the earth was given was intended with a view to Christ, the future man": *PL* 2, 282; *CSEL* 47, 33, 1, 12–13.

not surprising, then, that in him all the aforementioned truths find their root and attain their crown.

He who is "the image of the invisible God" (Col 1:15; cf. 2 Cor 4:4), is himself the perfect man. To the sons of Adam he restores the divine likeness which had been disfigured from the first sin onward. Since human nature as he assumed it was not annulled,[6] by that very fact it has been raised up to a divine dignity in our respect, too. For by his Incarnation the Son of God has united himself in some fashion with every man. He worked with human hands, he thought with a human mind, acted by human choice[7] and loved with a human heart. Born of the Virgin Mary, he has truly been made one of us, like us in all things except sin (cf. Heb 4:15).

As an innocent lamb he merited life for us by the free shedding of his own blood. In him God reconciled us (cf. 2 Cor 5:18–19; Col 1:20–22) to himself and among ourselves; from bondage to the devil and sin he delivered us, so that each one of us can say with the Apostle: The Son of God "loved me and gave himself up for me" (Gal 2:20). By suffering for us he not only provided us with an example for our imitation (cf. 1 Pt 2:21; Mt 16:24; Lk 14:27), he blazed a trail, and if we follow it, life and death are made holy and take on a new meaning.

The Christian man, conformed to the likeness of that Son who is the firstborn of many brothers (cf. Rm 8:29; Col 3:10–14), received "the first-fruits of the Spirit" (Rm 8:23) by which he becomes capable of discharging the new law of love (cf. Rm 8:1–11) Through this Spirit, who is "the pledge of our inheritance" (Eph 1:14), the whole man is renewed from within, even to the achievement of "the redemption of the body" (Rm 8:23): "If the Spirit of him who raised Jesus from the death dwells in you, then he who raised Jesus Christ from the dead will also bring to life your mortal bodies because of his Spirit who dwells in you" (Rm

---

6. Cf. Second Council of Constantinople, canon 7: "The divine Word was not changed into a human nature, nor was a human nature absorbed by the Word": Denz. 219 (428); cf. also Third Council of Constantinople: "For just as his most holy and immaculate human nature, though deified, was not destroyed *(theotheisa ouk anerethe),* but rather remained in its proper state and mode of being": Denz. 291 (556); cf. Council of Chalcedon: "to be acknowledged in two natures, without confusion, change, division or separation": Denz. 148 (302).

7. Cf. Third Council of Constantinople: "and so his human will, though deified, is not destroyed": Denz. 291 (556).

8:11; cf. 2 Cor 4:14). Pressing upon the Christian, to be sure, are the need and the duty to battle against evil through manifold tribulations and even to suffer death. But, linked with the Paschal Mystery and patterned on the dying Christ, he will hasten forward to resurrection in the strength which comes from hope (cf. Phil 3:19; Rm 8:17).

All this holds true not only for Christians, but for all men of good will in whose hearts grace works in an unseen way.[8] For, since Christ died for all men (cf. Rm 8:32), and since the ultimate vocation of man is in fact one and divine, we ought to believe that the Holy Spirit in a manner known only to God offers to every man the possibility of being associated with this Paschal Mystery.

Such is the mystery of man, and it is a great one, as seen by believers in the light of Christian revelation. Through Christ and in Christ, the riddles of sorrow and death grow meaningful. Apart from his Gospel, they overwhelm us. Christ has risen, destroying death by his death; he has lavished life upon us[9] so that, as sons in the Son, we can cry out in the Spirit: Abba, Father (cf. Rm 8:15; Gal 4:6; Jn 1:22; 3:1–2).

---

8. Cf. Second Vatican Ecumenical Council, Dogmatic Constitution on the Church *Lumen Gentium*, 16: *AAS* 57 (1965), 20.

9. Cf. the Byzantine Easter Liturgy.

CHAPTER II

THE COMMUNITY OF MANKIND

23. One of the salient features of the modern world is the growing interdependence of men one on the other, a development promoted chiefly by modern technical advances. Nevertheless, brotherly dialogue among men does not reach its perfection on the level of technical progress, but on the deeper level of interpersonal relationships. These demand a mutual respect for the full spiritual dignity of the person. Christian revelation contributes greatly to the promotion of this communion between persons, and at the same time leads us to a deeper understanding of the laws of social life which the Creator has written into man's moral and spiritual nature.

Since rather recent documents of the Church's teaching authority have dealt at considerable length with Christian doctrine about human society,[1] this Council is merely going to call to mind some of the more basic truths, treating their foundations under the light of revelation. Then, it will dwell more at length on certain of their implications having special significance for our day.

24. God, who has fatherly concern for everyone, has willed that all men should constitute one family and treat one another in a spirit of brotherhood. For having been created in the image of God, who "from one man has created the whole human race and made them live all over the face of the earth" (Acts 17:26), all men are called to one and the same goal, namely God himself.

For this reason, love for God and neighbor is the first and greatest commandment. Sacred Scripture, however, teaches us that the love of

---

1. Cf. John XXIII, Encyclical Letter *Mater et Magistra* (May 15, 1961): *AAS* 53 (1961), 401–464; Encyclical Letter *Pacem in Terris* (April 11, 1963): *AAS* 55 (1963), 257–304; Paul VI, Encyclical Letter *Ecclesiam Suam* (Aug. 6, 1964): *AAS* 54 (1964), 609–659.

God cannot be separated from love of neighbor: "If there is any other commandment, it is summed up in this saying: Thou shalt love thy neighbor as thyself.... Love therefore is the fulfillment of the Law" (Rm 13:9–10; cf. 1 Jn 4:20). To men growing daily more dependent on one another, and to a world becoming more unified every day, this truth proves to be of paramount importance.

Indeed, the Lord Jesus, when he prayed to the Father, "that all may be one...as we are one" (Jn 17:21–22) opened up vistas closed to human reason, for he implied a certain likeness between the union of the divine Persons, and the unity of God's sons in truth and charity. This likeness reveals that man, who is the only creature on earth which God willed for itself, cannot fully find himself except through a sincere gift of himself (cf. Lk 17:33).

25. Man's social nature makes it evident that the progress of the human person and the advance of society itself hinge on one another. For the beginning, the subject and the goal of all social institutions is and must be the human person, which for its part and by its very nature stands completely in need of social life.[2] Since this social life is not something added on to man, through his dealings with others, through reciprocal duties and through fraternal dialogue, he develops all his gifts and is able to rise to his destiny.

Among those social ties which man needs for his development, some, like the family and political community, relate with greater immediacy to his innermost nature; others originate rather from his free decision. In our era, for various reasons, reciprocal ties and mutual dependencies increase day by day and give rise to a variety of associations and organizations, both public and private. This development, which is called socialization, while certainly not without its dangers, brings with it many advantages with respect to consolidating and increasing the qualities of the human person, and safeguarding his rights.[3]

But if by this social life the human person is greatly aided in responding to his destiny, even in its religious dimensions, it cannot be denied that men are often diverted from doing good and spurred toward

---

2. Cf. St. Thomas, 1 *Ethica Lect.,* 1.

3. Cf. John XXIII, Encyclical Letter *Mater et Magistra* (May 15, 1961): *AAS* 53 (1961), 418; cf. also Pius XI, Encyclical Letter *Quadragesimo Anno* (May 15, 1931): *AAS* 23 (1931), 222 ff.

evil by the social circumstances in which they live and are immersed from their birth. To be sure, the disturbances which so frequently occur in the social order result in part from the natural tensions of economic, political and social forms. But at a deeper level they flow from man's pride and selfishness, which contaminate even the social sphere. When the structure of affairs is flawed by the consequences of sin, man, already born with a bent toward evil, finds there new inducements to sin, which cannot be overcome without strenuous efforts and the assistance of grace.

26. Every day human interdependence grows more tightly drawn and spreads by degrees over the whole world. As a result the common good, that is, the sum of those conditions of social life which allow social groups and their individual members relatively thorough and ready access to their own fulfillment, today takes on an increasingly universal complexion and consequently involves rights and duties with respect to the whole human race. Every social group must take account of the needs and legitimate aspirations of other groups, and even of the general welfare of the entire human family.[4]

At the same time, however, there is a growing awareness of the exalted dignity proper to the human person, since he stands above all things, and his rights and duties are universal and inviolable. Therefore, there must be made available to all men everything necessary for leading a life truly human: such as food, clothing and shelter, the right to choose a state of life freely and to found a family, the right to education, to employment, to a good reputation, to respect, to appropriate information, to activity in accord with the upright norm of one's own conscience, to protection of privacy and rightful freedom, even in matters religious.

Hence, the social order and its development must invariably work to the benefit of the human person if the disposition of affairs is to be subordinate to the personal realm and not contrariwise, as the Lord indicated when he said that the Sabbath was made for man, and not man for the Sabbath (Mk 2:27).

This social order requires constant improvement. It must be founded on truth, built on justice and animated by love; in freedom it should

---

4. Cf. John XXIII, Encyclical Letter *Mater et Magistra* (May 15, 1961): *AAS* 53 (1961).

grow every day toward a more humane balance.[5] An improvement in attitudes and abundant changes in society will have to take place if these objectives are to be gained.

God's Spirit, who with a marvelous Providence directs the unfolding of time and renews the face of the earth, is not absent from this development. The ferment of the Gospel too has aroused and continues to arouse in man's heart the irresistible requirements of his dignity.

27. Coming down to practical and particularly urgent consequences, this Council lays stress on reverence for man; everyone must consider his every neighbor without exception as another self, taking into account first of all his life and the means necessary to living it with dignity (cf. Jas 2:15–16), so as not to imitate the rich man who had no concern for the poor man Lazarus (cf. Lk 16:18–31).

In our times a special obligation binds us to make ourselves the neighbor of every person without exception. and of actively helping him when he comes across our path, whether he be an old person abandoned by all, a foreign laborer unjustly looked down upon, a refugee, a child born of an unlawful union and wrongly suffering for a sin he did not commit, or a hungry person who disturbs our conscience by recalling the voice of the Lord, "As long as you did it for one of these the least of my brethren, you did it for me" (Mt 25:40).

Furthermore, whatever is opposed to life itself, such as any type of murder, genocide, abortion, euthanasia or willful self-destruction; whatever violates the integrity of the human person, such as mutilation, torments inflicted on body or mind, attempts to coerce the will itself; whatever insults human dignity, such as subhuman living conditions, arbitrary imprisonment, deportation, slavery, prostitution, the selling of women and children; as well as disgraceful working conditions, where men are treated as mere tools for profit, rather than as free and responsible persons; all these things and others of their like are infamies indeed. They poison human society, but they do more harm to those who practice them than those who suffer from the injury. Moreover, they are a supreme dishonor to the Creator.

28. Respect and love ought to be extended also to those who think or act differently than we do in social, political and even religious matters.

---

5. Cf. John XXIII, Encyclical Letter *Pacem in Terris* (April 11, 1963): *AAS* 55 (1963), 266.

In fact, the more deeply we come to understand their ways of thinking through such courtesy and love, the more easily will we be able to enter into dialogue with them.

This love and good will, to be sure, must in no way render us indifferent to truth and goodness. Indeed, love itself impels the disciples of Christ to speak the saving truth to all men. But it is necessary to distinguish between error, which always merits repudiation, and the person in error, who never loses the dignity of being a person even when he is flawed by false or inadequate religious notions.[6] God alone is the judge and searcher of hearts; for that reason he forbids us to make judgments about the internal guilt of anyone (cf. Lk 6:37–38; Mt 7:1–2; Rm 2:1–11; 14:10–12).

The teaching of Christ even requires that we forgive injuries (cf. Mt 5:43–47) and extends the law of love to include every enemy, according to the command of the New Law: "You have heard that it was said: Thou shalt love thy neighbor and hate thy enemy. But I say to you: love your enemies, do good to those who hate you, and pray for those who persecute and calumniate you" (Mt 5:43–44).

29. Since all men possess a rational soul and are created in God's likeness, since they have the same nature and origin, have been redeemed by Christ and enjoy the same divine calling and destiny, the basic equality of all must receive increasingly greater recognition.

True, all men are not alike from the point of view of varying physical power and the diversity of intellectual and moral resources. Nevertheless, with respect to the fundamental rights of the person, every type of discrimination, whether social or cultural, whether based on sex, race, color, social condition, language or religion, is to be overcome and eradicated as contrary to God's intent. For in truth it must still be regretted that fundamental personal rights are still not being universally honored. Such is the case of a woman who is denied the right to choose a husband freely, to embrace a state of life or to acquire an education or cultural benefits equal to those recognized for men.

Therefore, although rightful differences exist between men, the equal dignity of persons demands that a more humane and just condition

---

6. Cf. John XXIII, Encyclical Letter *Pacem in Terris* (April 11, 1963): *AAS* 55 (1963), 299–300.

of life be brought about. For excessive economic and social differences between the members of the one human family or population groups cause scandal and militate against social justice, equity, the dignity of the human person, as well as social and international peace.

Human institutions, both private and public, must labor to minister to the dignity and purpose of man. At the same time, let them put up a stubborn fight against any kind of slavery, whether social or political, and safeguard the basic rights of man under every political system. Indeed, human institutions themselves must be accommodated by degrees to the highest of all realities, spiritual ones, even though, meanwhile, a long enough time will be required before they arrive at the desired goal.

30. Profound and rapid changes make it more necessary that no one, ignoring the trend of events or drugged by laziness, content himself with a merely individualistic morality. It grows increasingly true that the obligations of justice and love are fulfilled only if each person, contributing to the common good, according to his own abilities and the needs of others, also promotes and assists the public and private institutions dedicated to bettering the conditions of human life. Yet there are those who, while possessing grand and rather noble sentiments, nevertheless in reality live always as if they cared nothing for the needs of society. Many in various places even make light of social laws and precepts, and do not hesitate to resort to various frauds and deceptions in avoiding just taxes or other debts due to society. Others think little of certain norms of social life, for example those designed for the protection of health, or laws establishing speed limits; they do not even avert to the fact that by such indifference they imperil their own life and that of others.

Let everyone consider it his sacred obligation to esteem and observe social necessities as belonging to the primary duties of modern man. For the more unified the world becomes, the more plainly do the offices of men extend beyond particular groups and spread by degrees to the whole world. But this development cannot occur unless individual men and their associations cultivate in themselves the moral and social virtues and promote them in society; thus, with the needed help of divine grace, men who are truly new and artisans of a new humanity can be forthcoming.

31. In order for individual men to discharge with greater exactness the obligations of their conscience toward themselves and the various group to which they belong, they must be carefully educated to a higher

degree of culture through the use of the immense resources available today to the human race. Above all, the education of youth from every social background has to be undertaken, so that there can be produced not only men and women of refined talents, but those great-souled persons who are so desperately required by our times.

Now a man can scarcely arrive at the needed sense of responsibility unless his living conditions allow him to become conscious of his dignity, and to rise to his destiny by spending himself for God and for others. But human freedom is often crippled when a man encounters extreme poverty, just as it withers when he indulges in too many of life's comforts and imprisons himself in a kind of splendid isolation. Freedom acquires new strength, by contrast, when a man consents to the unavoidable requirements of social life, takes on the manifold demands of human partnership and commits himself to the service of the human community.

Hence, the will to play one's role in common endeavors should be everywhere encouraged. Praise is due to those national procedures which allow the largest possible number of citizens to participate in public affairs with genuine freedom. Account must be taken, to be sure, of the actual conditions of each people and the decisiveness required by public authority. If every citizen is to feel inclined to take part in the activities of the various groups which make up the social body, these must offer advantages which will attract members and dispose them to serve others. We can justly consider that the future of humanity lies in the hands of those who are strong enough to provide coming generations with reasons for living and hoping.

32. As God did not create man for life in isolation, but for the formation of social unity, so also "it has pleased God to make men holy and save them not merely as individuals, without bond or link between them, but by making them into a single people, a people which acknowledges him in truth and serves him in holiness."[7] So from the beginning of salvation history, he has chosen men not just as individuals but as members of a certain community. Revealing his mind to them, God called these chosen ones "his people" (Ex 3:7–12), and even made a covenant with them on Sinai (cf. Ex 24:1–8).

---

7. Cf. Second Vatican Ecumenical Council, Dogmatic Constitution on the Church *Lumen Gentium,* 9: *AAS* 57 (1965), 12–13.

This communitarian character is developed and consummated in the work of Jesus Christ. For the very Word made flesh willed to share in the human fellowship. He was present at the wedding of Cana, visited the house of Zacchaeus, ate with publicans and sinners. He revealed the love of the Father and the sublime vocation of man in terms of the most common of social realities and by making use of the speech and the imagery of plain everyday life. Willingly obeying the laws of his country, he sanctified those human ties, especially family ones, which are the source of social structures. He chose to lead the life proper to an artisan of his time and place.

In his preaching he clearly taught the sons of God to treat one another as brothers. In his prayers he pleaded that all his disciples might be "one." Indeed, as the Redeemer of all, he offered himself for all even to point of death. "Greater love than this no one has, that one lay down his life for his friends" (Jn 15:13). He commanded his apostles to preach to all peoples the Gospel's message that the human race was to become the family of God, in which the fullness of the Law would be love.

As the firstborn of many brethren and by the giving of his Spirit, he founded after his death and resurrection a new brotherly community composed of all those who receive him in faith and in love. This he did through his body, which is the Church. There everyone, as members one of the other, would render mutual service according to the different gifts bestowed on each.

This solidarity must be constantly increased until that day on which it will be brought to perfection. Then, saved by grace, men will offer flawless glory to God as a family beloved of God and of Christ their brother.

CHAPTER III

MAN'S ACTIVITY THROUGHOUT THE WORLD

33. Through his labors and his native endowments, man has ceaselessly striven to better his life. Today, however, especially with the help of science and technology, he has extended his mastery over nearly the whole of nature and continues to do so. Thanks to increased opportunities for many kinds of social contact among nations, a human family is gradually recognizing that it comprises a single world community and is making itself so. Hence, many benefits once looked for, especially from heavenly powers, man has now enterprisingly procured for himself.

In the face of these immense efforts which already preoccupy the whole human race, men agitate numerous questions among themselves. What is the meaning and value of this feverish activity? How should all these things be used? To the achievement of what goal are the strivings of individuals and societies heading? The Church guards the heritage of God's word and draws from it moral and religious principles without always having at hand the solution to particular problems. As such, she desires to add the light of revealed truth to mankind's store of experience so that the path which humanity has taken in recent times will not be a dark one.

34. Throughout the course of the centuries, men have labored to better the circumstances of their lives through a monumental amount of individual and collective effort. To believers, this point is settled: considered in itself, this human activity accords with God's will. For man, created to God's image, received a mandate to subject to himself the earth and all it contains, and to govern the world with justice and holiness (cf. Gn 1:26–27; 9:2–3; Wis 9:2–3), a mandate to relate himself and the totality of things to him who was to be acknowledged as the Lord and Creator of all. Thus, by the subjection of all things to man, the name of God would be wonderful in all the earth (cf. Ps 8:7 and 10).

This mandate concerns the whole of everyday activity as well. For while providing the substance of life for themselves and their families, men and women are performing their activities in a way which appropriately benefits society. They can justly consider that by their labor they are unfolding the Creator's work, consulting the advantages of their fellow men, and are contributing by their personal industry to the realization in history of the divine plan.[1]

Thus, far from thinking that works produced by man's own talent and energy are in opposition to God's power, and that the rational creature exists as a kind of rival to the Creator, Christians are convinced that the triumphs of the human race are a sign of God's grace and the flowering of his own mysterious design. For the greater man's power becomes, the farther his individual and community responsibility extends. Hence, it is clear that men are not deterred by the Christian message from building up the world, or impelled to neglect the welfare of their fellows, but that they are rather more stringently bound to do these very things.[2]

35. Human activity, to be sure, takes its significance from its relationship to man. Just as it proceeds from man, so it is ordered toward man. For when a man works, he not only alters things and society, he develops himself as well. He learns much, he cultivates his resources, he goes outside of himself and beyond himself. Rightly understood, this kind of growth is of greater value than any external riches which can be garnered. A man is more precious for what he is than for what he has.[3] Similarly, all that men do to obtain greater justice, wider brotherhood, a more humane disposition of social relationships, has greater worth than technical advances. For these advances can supply the material for human progress, but of themselves alone they can never actually bring it about.

Hence, the norm of human activity is this: that in accord with the divine plan and will, it harmonize with the genuine good of the human race, and that it allow men as individuals and as members of society to pursue their total vocation and fulfill it.

---

1. Cf. John XXIII, Encyclical Letter *Pacem in Terris* (April 11, 1963): *AAS* 55 (1963), 297.

2. Cf. *Message to All Mankind Sent By the Fathers at the Beginning of the Second Vatican Council* (Oct. 20, 1962): *AAS* 54 (1962), 823.

3. Cf. Paul VI, *Address to the Diplomatic Corps* (Jan. 7, 1965): *AAS* 57 (1965), 232.

36. Now many of our contemporaries seem to fear that a closer bond between human activity and religion will work against the independence of men, of societies or of the sciences.

If by the autonomy of earthly affairs we mean that created things and societies themselves enjoy their own laws and values which must be gradually deciphered, put to use, and regulated by men, then it is entirely right to demand that autonomy. Such is not merely required by modern man, but harmonizes also with the will of the Creator. For by the very circumstance of their having been created, all things are endowed with their own stability, truth, goodness, proper laws and order. Man must respect these as he isolates them by the appropriate methods of the individual sciences or arts. Therefore, if methodical investigation within every branch of learning is carried out in a genuinely scientific manner and in accord with moral norms, it never truly conflicts with faith, for earthly matters and the concerns of faith derive from the same God.[4] Indeed, whoever labors to penetrate the secrets of reality with a humble and steady mind, even though he is unaware of the fact, is nevertheless being led by the hand of God, who holds all things in existence and gives them their identity. Consequently, we cannot but deplore certain habits of mind, which are sometimes found too among Christians, which do not sufficiently attend to the rightful independence of science and which, from the arguments and controversies they spark, lead many minds to conclude that faith and science are mutually opposed.[5]

But if the expression "the independence of temporal affairs" is taken to mean that created things do not depend on God, and that man can use them without any reference to their Creator, anyone who acknowledges God will see how false such a meaning is. For without the Creator the creature would disappear. For their part, however, all believers of whatever religion always hear his revealing voice in the discourse of creatures. When God is forgotten, however, the creature itself grows unintelligible.

37. Sacred Scripture teaches the human family what the experience of the ages confirms: that while human progress is a great advantage to man, it brings with it a strong temptation. For when the order of values

---

4. Cf. First Vatican Council, Dogmatic Constitution on the Catholic Faith *Dei Filius,* ch. 3: Denz. 1785–1186 (3004–3005).

5. Cf. Msgr. Pio Paschini, *Vita e opere di Galileo Galilei,* 2 vols. (Vatican Press: 1964).

is jumbled and bad is mixed with the good, individuals and groups pay heed solely to their own interests and not to those of others. Thus it happens that the world ceases to be a place of true brotherhood. In our own day, the magnified power of humanity threatens to destroy the race itself.

For a monumental struggle against the powers of darkness pervades the whole history of man. The battle was joined from the very origins of the world and will continue until the last day, as the Lord has attested (cf. Mt 24:13; 13:24–30, 36–43). Caught in this conflict, man is obliged to wrestle constantly if he is to cling to what is good, nor can he achieve his own integrity without great efforts and the help of God's grace.

That is why Christ's Church, trusting in the design of the Creator, acknowledges that human progress can serve man's true happiness, yet she cannot help echoing the Apostle's warning: "Be not conformed to this world" (Rm 12:2). Here by "the world" is meant that spirit of vanity and malice which transforms into an instrument of sin those human energies intended for the service of God and man.

Hence, if anyone wants to know how this unhappy situation can be overcome, Christians will tell him that all human activity, constantly imperiled by man's pride and deranged self-love, must be purified and perfected by the power of Christ's cross and resurrection. For redeemed by Christ and made a new creature in the Holy Spirit, man is able to love the things themselves created by God, and ought to do so. He can receive them from God and respect and reverence them as flowing constantly from the hand of God. Grateful to his benefactor for these creatures, using and enjoying them in detachment and liberty of spirit, man is led forward into a true possession of them, as having nothing, yet possessing all things (cf. 2 Cor 6:10). "All are yours, and you are Christ's, and Christ is God's" (1 Cor 3:22–23).

38. For God's Word, through whom all things were made, was himself made flesh and dwelt on the earth of men (cf. Jn 1:3, 14). Thus he entered the world's history as a perfect man, taking that history up into himself and summarizing it (cf. Eph 1:10). He himself revealed to us that "God is love" (1 Jn 4:8) and at the same time taught us that the new command of love was the basic law of human perfection and hence of the world's transformation.

To those, therefore, who believe in divine love, he gives assurance that the way of love lies open to men and that the effort to establish a universal brotherhood is not a hopeless one. He cautions them at the same time that this charity is not something to be reserved for important matters, but must be pursued chiefly in the ordinary circumstances of life. Undergoing death itself for all of us sinners (cf. Jn 3:16; Rm 5:8), he taught us by example that we too must shoulder that cross which the world and the flesh inflict upon those who search after peace and justice. Appointed Lord by his resurrection and given plenary power in heaven and on earth (cf. Acts 2:36; Mt 28:18), Christ is now at work in the hearts of men through the energy of his Holy Spirit, arousing not only a desire for the age to come, but by that very fact animating, purifying and strengthening those noble longings too by which the human family makes its life more human and strives to render the whole earth submissive to this goal.

Now, the gifts of the Spirit are diverse; while he calls some to give clear witness to the desire for a heavenly home and to keep that desire green among the human family, he summons others to dedicate themselves to the earthly service of men and to make ready the material of the celestial realm by this ministry of theirs. Yet he frees all of them so that by putting aside love of self and bringing all earthly resources into the service of human life, they can devote themselves to that future when humanity itself will become an offering accepted by God (cf. Rm 15:16).

The Lord left behind a pledge of this hope and strength for life's journey in that sacrament of faith where natural elements refined by man are changed into his glorified Body and Blood, providing a meal of brotherly solidarity and a foretaste of the heavenly banquet.

39. We do not know the time for the consummation of the earth and of humanity (cf. Acts 1:7), nor do we know how all things will be transformed. As deformed by sin, the shape of this world will pass away;[6] but we are taught that God is preparing a new dwelling place and a new earth where justice will abide (cf. 2 Cor 5:2; 2 Pt 3:13) and whose blessedness will answer and surpass all the longings for peace which spring up in the human heart (cf. 1 Cor 2:9; Rv 21:4–5). Then, with death overcome, the sons of God will be raised up in Christ, and what was sown in weakness and corruption will be invested with incorruptibility (cf. 1 Cor 15:42, 53). Enduring with charity and its fruits (cf. 1 Cor 13:8; 3:14), all

---

6. Cf. 1 Cor 7:31; St. Irenaeus, *Against Heretics* V, 36: *PG* VIII, 1221.

that creation (cf. Rm 8:19–21) which God made on man's account will be unchained from the bondage of vanity.

Therefore, while we are warned that it profits a man nothing if he gain the whole world and lose himself (cf. Lk 9:25), the expectation of a new earth must not weaken but rather stimulate our concern for cultivating this one. For here grows the body of a new human family, a body which even now is able to give some kind of foreshadowing of the new age.

Hence, while earthly progress must be carefully distinguished from the growth of Christ's kingdom, to the extent that the former can contribute to the better ordering of human society, it is of vital concern to the kingdom of God.[7]

For after we have obeyed the Lord, and in his Spirit nurtured on earth the values of human dignity, brotherhood and freedom, and indeed all the good fruits of our nature and enterprise, we will find them again, but freed of stain, burnished and transfigured, when Christ hands over to the Father: "a kingdom eternal and universal, a kingdom of truth and life, of holiness and grace, of justice, love and peace."[8] On this earth that kingdom is already present in mystery. When the Lord returns it will be brought into full flower.

---

7. Cf. Pius XI, Encyclical Letter *Quadragesimo Anno* (May 15, 1931): *AAS* 23 (1931), 207.

8. Preface of the Feast of Christ the King.

CHAPTER IV

THE ROLE OF THE CHURCH
IN THE MODERN WORLD

40. Everything we have said about the dignity of the human person and about the human community and the profound meaning of human activity, lays the foundation for the relationship between the Church and the world, and provides the basis for dialogue between them.[1] In this chapter, presupposing everything which has already been said by this Council concerning the mystery of the Church, we must now consider this same Church inasmuch as she exists in the world, living and acting with it.

Coming forth from the eternal Father's love,[2] founded in time by Christ the Redeemer and made one in the Holy Spirit (cf. Eph 1:3; 5:6, 13–14, 23), the Church has a saving and an eschatological purpose which can be fully attained only in the future world. But she is already present in this world and is composed of men, that is, of members of the earthly city who have a call to form the family of God's children during the present history of the human race, and to keep increasing it until the Lord returns. United on behalf of heavenly values and enriched by them, this family has been "constituted and structured as a society in this world"[3] by Christ, and is equipped "by appropriate means for visible and social union."[4] Thus, the Church, at once "a visible association and a spiritual community,"[5] goes forward together with humanity and experi-

---

1. Cf. Paul VI, Encyclical Letter *Ecclesiam Suam*, III, (Aug. 6, 1964): *AAS* 54 (1964), 637–659.

2. Cf. Ti 3:4: "love of mankind."

3. Second Vatican Ecumenical Council, Dogmatic Constitution on the Church *Lumen Gentium*, 8: *AAS* 57 (1965), 12.

4. Second Vatican Ecumenical Council, Dogmatic Constitution on the Church *Lumen Gentium*, 9: *AAS* 57 (1965), 14; cf. n. 8: *AAS loc. cit.*, 11.

5. Second Vatican Ecumenical Council, Dogmatic Constitution on the Church *Lumen Gentium*, 8: *AAS* 57 (1965), 11.

ences the same earthly lot which the world does. She serves as a leaven and as a kind of soul for human society[6] as it is to be renewed in Christ and transformed into God's family.

That the earthly and the heavenly city penetrate each other is a fact accessible to faith alone; it remains a mystery of human history, which sin will keep in great disarray until the splendor of God's sons is fully revealed. Pursuing the saving purpose which is proper to her, the Church does not only communicate divine life to men, but in some way casts the reflected light of that life over the entire earth, most of all by its healing and elevating impact on the dignity of the person, by the way in which it strengthens the seams of human society and imbues the everyday activity of men with a deeper meaning and importance. Thus, through her individual members and her whole community, the Church believes she can contribute greatly toward making the family of man and its history more human.

In addition, the Catholic Church gladly holds in high esteem the things which other Christian Churches and ecclesial communities have done or are doing cooperatively by way of achieving the same goal. At the same time, she is convinced that she can be abundantly and variously helped by the world in the matter of preparing the ground for the Gospel. This help she gains from the talents and industry of individuals and from human society as a whole. The Council now sets forth certain general principles for the proper fostering of this mutual exchange and assistance in concerns which are in some way common to the world and the Church.

41. Modern man is on the road to a more thorough development of his own personality and to a growing discovery and vindication of his own rights. Since it has been entrusted to the Church to reveal the mystery of God, who is the ultimate goal of man, she opens up to man at the same time the meaning of his own existence, that is, the innermost truth about himself. The Church truly knows that only God, whom she serves, meets the deepest longings of the human heart, which is never fully satisfied by what this world has to offer.

She also knows that man is constantly worked upon by God's Spirit, and hence can never be altogether indifferent to the problems of reli-

---

6. Cf. Second Vatican Ecumenical Council, Dogmatic Constitution on the Church *Lumen Gentium,* 38: *AAS* 57 (1965), 43, with note 120.

gion. The experience of past ages proves this, as do numerous indications in our own times. For man will always yearn to know, at least in an obscure way, what is the meaning of his life, of his activity, of his death. The very presence of the Church recalls these problems to his mind. But only God, who created man to his own image and ransomed him from sin, provides the most adequate answer to the questions, and this he does through what he has revealed in Christ his Son, who became man. Whoever follows after Christ, the perfect man, becomes himself more of a man. For by his Incarnation, the Father's Word assumed and sanctified through his cross and resurrection the whole of man, body and soul, and through that totality the whole of nature created by God for man's use.

Thanks to this belief, the Church can anchor the dignity of human nature against all tides of opinion, for example those which undervalue the human body or idolize it. By no human law can the personal dignity and liberty of man be so aptly safeguarded as by the Gospel of Christ which has been entrusted to the Church. For this Gospel announces and proclaims the freedom of the sons of God, and repudiates all the bondage which ultimately results from sin (cf. Rm 8:14–17); it has a sacred reverence for the dignity of conscience and its freedom of choice, constantly advises that all human talents be employed in God's service and men's, and finally commends all to the charity of all (cf. Mt 22:39).

This agrees with the basic law of the Christian dispensation. For though the same God is Savior and Creator, Lord of human history as well as of salvation history, in the divine arrangement itself, the rightful autonomy of the creature and particularly of man is not withdrawn, but is rather reestablished in its own dignity and strengthened in it.

The Church, therefore, by virtue of the Gospel committed to her, proclaims the rights of man; she acknowledges and greatly esteems the dynamic movements of today by which these rights are everywhere fostered. Yet these movements must be penetrated by the spirit of the Gospel and protected against any kind of false autonomy. For we are tempted to think that our personal rights are fully ensured only when we are exempt from every requirement of divine law. But this way lies not the maintenance of the dignity of the human person, but its annihilation.

42. The union of the human family is greatly fortified and fulfilled by the unity, founded on Christ,[7] of the family of God's sons.

Christ, to be sure, gave his Church no proper mission in the political, economic or social order. The purpose which he set before her is a religious one.[8] But out of this religious mission itself come a function, a light and an energy which can serve to structure and consolidate the human community according to the divine law. As a matter of fact, when circumstances of time and place produce the need, she can and indeed should initiate activities on behalf of all men, especially those designed for the needy, such as the works of mercy and similar undertakings.

The Church recognizes that worthy elements are found in today's social movements, especially an evolution toward unity, a process of wholesome socialization and of association in civic and economic realms. The promotion of unity belongs to the innermost nature of the Church, for she is, "thanks to her relationship with Christ, a sacramental sign and an instrument of intimate union with God, and of the unity of the whole human race."[9] Thus, she shows the world that an authentic union, social and external, results from a union of minds and hearts, namely from that faith and charity by which her own unity is unbreakably rooted in the Holy Spirit. For the force which the Church can inject into the modern society of man consists in that faith and charity put into vital practice, not in any external dominion exercised by merely human means.

Moreover, since in virtue of her mission and nature she is bound to no particular form of human culture, nor to any political, economic or social system, the Church by her very universality can be a very close bond between diverse human communities and nations, provided these trust her and truly acknowledge her right to true freedom in fulfilling her

---

7. Second Vatican Ecumenical Council, Dogmatic Constitution on the Church *Lumen Gentium,* 9: *AAS* 57 (1965), 12–14.

8. Cf. Pius XII, *Address to the International Union of Institutes of Archeology, History and History of Art* (March 9, 1956): *AAS* 48 (1965), 212: "Its divine Founder, Jesus Christ, has not given it any mandate or fixed any end of the cultural order. The goal which Christ assigns to it is strictly religious.... The Church must lead men to God, in order that they may be given over to him without reserve.... The Church can never lose sight of the strictly religious, supernatural goal. The meaning of all its activities, down to the last canon of its Code, can only cooperate directly or indirectly in this goal."

9. Second Vatican Ecumenical Council, Dogmatic Constitution on the Church *Lumen Gentium,* 1: *AAS* 57 (1965), 5.

mission. For this reason, the Church admonishes her own sons, but also humanity as a whole, to overcome all strife between nations and race in this family spirit of God's children, and in the same way, to give internal strength to human associations which are just.

With great respect, therefore, this Council regards all the true, good and just elements inherent in the very wide variety of institutions which the human race has established for itself and constantly continues to establish. The Council affirms, moreover, that the Church is willing to assist and promote all these institutions to the extent that such a service depends on her and can be associated with her mission. She has no fiercer desire than that in pursuit of the welfare of all she may be able to develop herself freely under any kind of government which grants recognition to the basic rights of person and family, to the demands of the common good and to the free exercise of her own mission.

43. This Council exhorts Christians, as citizens of two cities, to strive to discharge their earthly duties conscientiously and in response to the Gospel spirit. They are mistaken who, knowing that we have here no abiding city but seek one which is to come (cf. Heb 13:14), think that they may therefore shirk their earthly responsibilities. For they are forgetting that by the faith itself they are more obliged than ever to measure up to these duties, each according to his proper vocation (cf. 2 Thes 3:6–13; Eph 4:28). Nor, on the contrary, are they any less wide of the mark who think that religion consists in acts of worship alone and in the discharge of certain moral obligations, and who imagine they can plunge themselves into earthly affairs in such a way as to imply that these are altogether divorced from the religious life. This split between the faith which many profess and their daily lives deserves to be counted among the more serious errors of our age. Long since, the prophets of the Old Testament fought vehemently against this scandal (cf. Is 58: 1–12), and even more so did Jesus Christ himself in the New Testament threaten it with grave punishments (cf. Mt 23:3–23; Mk 7: 10–13). Therefore, let there be no false opposition between professional and social activities on the one part and religious life on the other. The Christian who neglects his temporal duties, neglects his duties toward his neighbor and even God, and jeopardizes his eternal salvation. Christians should rather rejoice, that following the example of Christ who worked as an artisan, they are free to give proper exercise to all their earthly activities and to their humane, domestic, professional, social and technical enterprises by

gathering them into one vital synthesis with religious values, under whose supreme direction all things are harmonized unto God's glory.

Secular duties and activities belong properly although not exclusively to laymen. Therefore, acting as citizens in the world, whether individually or socially, they will keep the laws proper to each discipline and labor to equip themselves with a genuine expertise in their various fields. They will gladly work with men seeking the same goals. Acknowledging the demands of faith and endowed with its force, they will unhesitatingly devise new enterprises where they are appropriate, and put them into action. Laymen should also know that it is generally the function of their well-formed Christian conscience to see that the divine law is inscribed in the life of the earthly city; from priests they may look for spiritual light and nourishment. Let the layman not imagine that his pastors are always such experts, that to every problem which arises, however complicated, they can readily give him a concrete solution, or even that such is their mission. Rather, enlightened by Christian wisdom and giving close attention to the teaching authority of the Church,[10] let the layman take on his own distinctive role.

Often enough, the Christian view of things will itself suggest some specific solution in certain circumstances. Yet it happens rather frequently, and legitimately so, that with equal sincerity some of the faithful will disagree with others on a given matter. Even against the intentions of their proponents, however, solutions proposed on one side or another may be easily confused by many people with the Gospel message. Hence, it is necessary for people to remember that no one is allowed in the aforementioned situations to appropriate the Church's authority for his opinion. They should always try to enlighten one another through honest discussion, preserving mutual charity and caring above all for the common good.

Since they have an active role to play in the whole life of the Church, laymen are not only bound to penetrate the world with a Christian spirit, but are also called to be witnesses to Christ in all things in the midst of human society.

Bishops, to whom is assigned the task of ruling the Church of God, should together with their priests so preach the news of Christ that all

---

10. Cf. John XXIII, Encyclical Letter *Mater et Magistra* IV, (May 15, 1961): *AAS* 53 (1961), 456–457; cf. I: *AAS loc. cit.,* 407, 410–411.

the earthly activities of the faithful will be bathed in the light of the Gospel. All pastors should remember too that by their daily conduct and concern[11] they are revealing the face of the Church to the world, and men will judge the power and truth of the Christian message thereby. By their lives and speech, in union with religious and their faithful, may they demonstrate that even now the Church by her presence alone and by all the gifts which she contains, is an unspent fountain of those virtues which the modern world needs the most.

By unremitting study they should fit themselves to do their part in establishing dialogue with the world and with men of all shades of opinion. Above all, let them take to heart the words which this Council has spoken: "Since humanity today increasingly moves toward civil, economic and social unity, it is more than ever necessary that priests, with joint concern and energy, and under the guidance of the bishops and the Supreme Pontiff, erase every cause of division so that the whole human race may be led to the unity of God's family."[12]

Although by the power of the Holy Spirit the Church will remain the faithful spouse of her Lord and will never cease to be the sign of salvation on earth, still she is very well aware that among her members,[13] both clerical and lay, some have been unfaithful to the Spirit of God during the course of many centuries; in the present age, too, it does not escape the Church how great a distance lies between the message she offers and the human failings of those to whom the Gospel is entrusted. Whatever be the judgment of history on these defects, we ought to be conscious of them, and struggle against them energetically, lest they inflict harm on spread of the Gospel. The Church also realizes that in working out her relationship with the world she always has great need of the ripening which comes with the experience of the centuries. Led by the Holy Spirit, mother Church unceasingly exhorts her sons "to purify and renew themselves so that the sign of Christ can shine more brightly on the face of the Church."[14]

---

11. Cf. Second Vatican Ecumenical Council, Dogmatic Constitution on the Church *Lumen Gentium,* 28: *AAS* 57 (1965), 35.

12. Second Vatican Ecumenical Council, Dogmatic Constitution on the Church *Lumen Gentium,* 28: *AAS loc. cit.,* 35–36.

13. Cf. St. Ambrose, *De Virginitate* VIII, 48: *PL* 16, 278.

14. Cf. Second Vatican Ecumenical Council, Dogmatic Constitution on the Church *Lumen Gentium,* 15: *AAS* 57 (1965), 20.

44. Just as it is in the world's interest to acknowledge the Church as an historical reality and to recognize her good influence, so the Church herself knows how richly she has profited by the history and development of humanity.

The experience of past ages, the progress of the sciences and the treasures hidden in the various forms of human culture, by all of which the nature of man himself is more clearly revealed and new roads to truth are opened, profit the Church, too. For from the beginning of her history, she has learned to express the message of Christ with the help of the ideas and terminology of various philosophers, and has tried to clarify it with their wisdom, too. Her purpose has been to adapt the Gospel to the grasp of all as well as to the needs of the learned, insofar as such was appropriate. Indeed, this accommodated preaching of the revealed word ought to remain the law of all evangelization. For thus the ability to express Christ's message in its own way is developed in each nation, and at the same time there is fostered a living exchange between the Church and the diverse cultures of people.[15] To promote such exchange especially in our days, the Church requires the special help of those who live in the world, are versed in different institutions and specialties, and grasp their innermost significance in the eyes of both believers and unbelievers. With the help of the Holy Spirit, it is the task of the entire People of God, especially pastors and theologians, to hear, distinguish and interpret the many voices of our age, and to judge them in the light of the divine word, so that revealed truth can always be more deeply penetrated, better understood and set forth to greater advantage.

Since the Church has a visible and social structure as a sign of her unity in Christ, she can and ought to be enriched by the development of human social life; not that there is any lack in the constitution given her by Christ, but that she can understand it more penetratingly, express it better and adjust it more successfully to our times. Moreover, she gratefully understands that in her community life no less than in her individual sons, she receives a variety of helps from men of every rank and condition; for whoever promotes the human community at the family level, culturally, in its economic, social and political dimensions, both

---

15. Cf. Second Vatican Ecumenical Council, Dogmatic Constitution on the Church *Lumen Gentium,* 13: *AAS* 57 (1965), 17.

nationally and internationally—such a one, according to God's design, is contributing greatly to the Church as well, to the extent that she depends on things outside herself. Indeed, the Church admits that she has greatly profited and still profits from the antagonism of those who oppose or who persecute her.[16]

45. While helping the world and receiving many benefits from it, the Church has a single intention: that God's kingdom may come, and that the salvation of the whole human race may come to pass. For every benefit which the People of God during its earthly pilgrimage can offer to the human family stems from the fact that the Church is "the universal sacrament of salvation,"[17] simultaneously manifesting and exercising the mystery of God's love.

For God's Word, by whom all things were made, was himself made flesh so that as perfect man he might save all men and sum up all things in himself. The Lord is the goal of human history, the focal point of the longings of history and of civilization, the center of the human race, the joy of every heart and the answer to all its yearnings.[18] He it is whom the Father raised from the dead, lifted on high and stationed at his right hand, making him judge of the living and the dead. Enlivened and united in his Spirit, we journey toward the consummation of human history, one which fully accords with the counsel of God's love: "To re-establish all things in Christ, both those in the heavens and those on the earth" (Eph 11:10).

The Lord himself speaks: "Behold I come quickly! And my reward is with me, to render to each one according to his works. I am the Alpha and the Omega, the first and the last, the beginning and the end" (Rv 22: 12–13).

---

16. Cf. Justin, *Dialogue with Trypho,* ch. 110: *PG* 6, 729, ed. Otto, 1897, 391–393: "...but the greater the number of persecutions which are inflicted upon us, so much the greater the number of other men who become devout believers through the name of Jesus." Cf. Tertullian, *Apologeticus,* ch. 50, 13: "Every time you mow us down like grass, we increase in number: the blood of Christians is a seed!" Cf. Second Vatican Ecumenical Council, Dogmatic Constitution on the Church *Lumen Gentium,* 9: *AAS* 57 (1965), 14.

17. Cf. Second Vatican Ecumenical Council, Dogmatic Constitution on the Church *Lumen Gentium,* 15: *AAS* 57 (1965), 20.

18. Cf. Paul VI, *Address* (Feb. 3, 1965).

PART II

SOME PROBLEMS OF SPECIAL URGENCY

46. This Council has set forth the dignity of the human person, and the work which men have been destined to undertake throughout the world, both as individuals and as members of society. There are a number of particularly urgent needs characterizing the present age, needs which go to the roots of the human race. To a consideration of these in the light of the Gospel and of human experience, the Council would now direct the attention of all.

Of the many subjects arousing universal concern today, it may be helpful to concentrate on these: marriage and the family, human progress, life in its economic, social and political dimensions, the bonds between the family of nations, and peace. On each of these may there shine the radiant ideals proclaimed by Christ. By these ideals may Christians be led, and all mankind enlightened, as they search for answers to questions of such complexity.

CHAPTER I

FOSTERING THE NOBILITY
OF MARRIAGE AND THE FAMILY

47. The well-being of the individual person and of human and Christian society is intimately linked with the healthy condition of that community produced by marriage and family. Hence, Christians and all men who hold this community in high esteem sincerely rejoice in the various ways by which men today find help in fostering this community of love and perfecting its life, and by which parents are assisted in their lofty calling. Those who rejoice in such aids look for additional benefits from them and labor to bring them about.

Yet the excellence of this institution is not everywhere reflected with equal brilliance, since polygamy, the plague of divorce, so-called free love and other disfigurements have an obscuring effect. In addition, married love is too often profaned by excessive self-love, the worship of pleasure and illicit practices against human generation. Moreover, serious disturbances are caused in families by modern economic conditions, by influences at once social and psychological, and by the demands of civil society. Finally, in certain parts of the world, problems resulting from population growth are generating concern.

All these situations have produced anxiety of consciences. Yet the power and strength of the institution of marriage and family can also be seen in the fact that time and again, despite the difficulties produced, the profound changes in modern society reveal the true character of this institution in one way or another.

Therefore, by presenting certain key points of Church doctrine in a clearer light, this sacred synod wishes to offer guidance and support to those Christians and other men who are trying to preserve the holiness and to foster the natural dignity of the married state and its superlative value.

48. The intimate partnership of married life and love has been established by the Creator and qualified by his laws, and is rooted in the conjugal covenant of irrevocable personal consent. Hence, by that human

act whereby spouses mutually bestow and accept each other, a relationship arises which by divine will and in the eyes of society too is a lasting one. For the good of the spouses and their offspring as well as of society, the existence of the sacred bond no longer depends on human decisions alone. For God himself is the author of matrimony, endowed as it is with various benefits and purposes.[1] All of these have a very decisive bearing on the continuation of the human race, on the personal development and eternal destiny of the individual members of a family, and on the dignity, stability, peace and prosperity of the family itself and of human society as a whole. By their very nature, the institution of matrimony itself and conjugal love are ordained for the procreation and education of children, and find in them their ultimate crown. Thus, a man and a woman who by their compact of conjugal love "are no longer two, but one flesh" (Mt 19:6 ff.), render mutual help and service to each other through an intimate union of their persons and of their actions. Through this union they experience the meaning of their oneness and attain to it with growing perfection day by day. As a mutual gift of two persons, this intimate union and the good of the children impose total fidelity on the spouses and argue for an unbreakable oneness between them.[2]

Christ the Lord abundantly blessed this many-faceted love, welling up as it does from the fountain of divine love and structured as it is on the model of his union with his Church. For as God of old made himself present[3] to his people through a covenant of love and fidelity, so now the Savior of men and the spouse[4] of the Church comes into the lives of married Christians through the sacrament of Matrimony. He abides with them thereafter so that just as he loved the Church and handed himself over on her behalf (cf. Eph 5:25), the spouses may love each other with perpetual fidelity through mutual self-bestowal.

Authentic married love is caught up into divine love and is governed and enriched by Christ's redeeming power and the saving activity of the

---

1. Cf. St. Augustine, *De Bene Coniugali: PL* 40, 375–376 and 394; St. Thomas, *Summa Theol.,* Suppl., q. 49, a. 3 *ad* 1; *Decretum pro Armenis: DS* 1327; Pius XI, Encyclical Letter *Casti Connubii: AAS* 22 (1930), 547–548; *DS* 3703–3714.

2. Cf. Pius XI, Encyclical Letter *Casti Connubii* (Dec. 31, 1930): *AAS* 22 (1930), 546–547; *DS* 3706.

3. Cf. Hos 2; Jer 3:6–13; Ez 16, 23; Is 54.

4. Cf. Mt 9:15; Mk 2:19–20; Lk 5:34–35; Jn 3:29; cf. also 2 Cor 11:2; Eph 5:27; Rv 19:7–8; 21:2, 9.

Church, so that this love may lead the spouses to God with powerful effect and may aid and strengthen them in the sublime office of being a father or a mother.[5] For this reason Christian spouses have a special sacrament by which they are fortified and receive a kind of consecration in the duties and dignity of their state.[6] By virtue of this sacrament, as spouses fulfill their conjugal and family obligation, they are penetrated with the spirit of Christ, which suffuses their whole lives with faith, hope and charity. Thus, they increasingly advance the perfection of their own personalities as well as their mutual sanctification, and hence contribute jointly to the glory of God.

As a result, with their parents leading the way by example and family prayer, children and indeed everyone gathered around the family hearth will find a readier path to human maturity, salvation and holiness. Graced with the dignity and office of fatherhood and motherhood, parents will energetically acquit themselves of a duty which devolves primarily on them, namely education and especially religious education.

As living members of the family, children contribute in their own way to making their parents holy. For they will respond to the kindness of their parents with sentiments of gratitude, with love and trust. They will stand by them as children should when hardships overtake their parents and old age brings its loneliness. Widowhood, accepted bravely as a continuation of the marriage vocation, should be esteemed by all (cf. 1 Tm 5:3). Families, too, will share their spiritual riches generously with other families. Thus the Christian family, which springs from marriage as a reflection of the loving covenant uniting Christ with the Church (cf. Eph 5:32), and as a participation in that covenant, will manifest to all men Christ's living presence in the world and the genuine nature of the Church. This the family will do by the mutual love of the spouses, by their generous fruitfulness, their solidarity and faithfulness, and by the loving way in which all members of the family assist one another.

49. The biblical Word of God several times urges the betrothed and the married to nourish and develop their wedlock by pure conjugal love and undivided affection.[7] Many men of our own age also highly regard

---

5. Cf. Second Vatican Ecumenical Council, Dogmatic Constitution on the Church *Lumen Gentium: AAS* 57 (1965), 15–16; 40–41; 47.

6. Pius XI, Encyclical Letter *Casti Connubii* (Dec. 31, 1930): *AAS* 22 (1930), 583.

7. Cf. Gn 2:22–24, Prv 5:15–20, 31:10–31; Tb 8:4–8; Cant 1:2–3; 1:16; 4:16; 5:1; 7:8–14; 1 Cor 7:3–6; Eph 5:25–33.

true love between husband and wife as it manifests itself in a variety of ways, depending on the worthy customs of various peoples and times.

This love is an eminently human one since it is directed from one person to another through an affection of the will; it involves the good of the whole person, and therefore can enrich the expressions of body and mind with a unique dignity, ennobling these expressions as special ingredients and signs of the friendship distinctive of marriage. This love God has judged worthy of special gifts: healing, perfecting and exalting gifts of grace and of charity. Such love, merging the human with the divine, leads the spouses to a free and mutual gift of themselves, a gift providing itself by gentle affection and by deed; such love pervades the whole of their lives;[8] indeed by its busy generosity it grows better and grows greater. Therefore, it far excels mere erotic inclination, which selfishly pursued, soon enough fades wretchedly away.

This love is uniquely expressed and perfected through the appropriate enterprise of matrimony. The actions within marriage by which the couple are united intimately and chastely are noble and worthy ones. Expressed in a manner which is truly human, these actions promote that mutual self-giving by which spouses enrich each other with a joyful and a ready will. Sealed by mutual faithfulness and hallowed above all by Christ's sacrament, this love remains steadfastly true in body and in mind, in bright days or dark. It will never be profaned by adultery or divorce. Firmly established by the Lord, the unity of marriage will radiate from the equal personal dignity of wife and husband, a dignity acknowledged by mutual and total love. The constant fulfillment of the duties of this Christian vocation demands notable virtue. For this reason, strengthened by grace for holiness of life, the couple will painstakingly cultivate and pray for steadiness of love, large-heartedness and the spirit of sacrifice.

Authentic conjugal love will be more highly prized, and wholesome public opinion created about it, if Christian couples give outstanding witness to faithfulness and harmony in their love, and to their concern for educating their children, also if they do their part in bringing about the needed cultural, psychological and social renewal on behalf of marriage and the family. Especially in the heart of their own families,

---

8. Cf. Pius XI, Encyclical Letter *Casti Connubii* (Dec. 31, 1930): *AAS* 22 (1930), 547 and 548; *DS* 3707.

young people should be aptly and seasonably instructed in the dignity, duty and work of married love. Trained thus in the cultivation of chastity, they will be able at a suitable age to enter a marriage of their own after an honorable courtship.

50. Marriage and conjugal love are by their nature ordained toward the begetting and educating of children. Children are really the supreme gift of marriage and contribute very substantially to the welfare of their parents. The God himself who said, "It is not good for man to be alone" (Gn 2:18) and "who made man from the beginning male and female" (Mt 19:4), wishing to share with man a certain special participation in his own creative work, blessed male and female, saying: "Increase and multiply" (Gn 1:28). Hence, while not making the other purposes of matrimony of less account, the true practice of conjugal love and the whole meaning of the family life which results from it have this aim: that the couple be ready with stout hearts to cooperate with the love of the Creator and the Savior, who through them will enlarge and enrich his own family day by day.

Parents should regard as their proper mission the task of transmitting human life and educating those to whom it has been transmitted. They should realize that they are thereby cooperators with the love of God the Creator and are, so to speak, the interpreters of that love. Thus, they will fulfill their task with human and Christian responsibility, and with docile reverence toward God, will make decisions by common counsel and effort. Let them thoughtfully take into account both their own welfare and that of their children, those already born and those which the future may bring. For this accounting they need to reckon with both the material and the spiritual conditions of the times as well as of their state in life. Finally, they should consult the interests of the family group, of temporal society and of the Church herself. The parents themselves and no one else should ultimately make this judgment in the sight of God. But in their manner of acting, spouses should be aware that they cannot proceed arbitrarily, but must always be governed according to a conscience dutifully conformed to the divine law itself, and should be submissive toward the Church's teaching office, which authentically interprets that law in the light of the Gospel. That divine law reveals and protects the integral meaning of conjugal love and impels it toward a truly human fulfillment. Thus, trusting in divine Providence and refining the spirit of sacrifice (cf. 1 Cor 7:5), married Christians glorify the Creator and strive toward fulfillment in Christ when with a generous human and Christian sense of responsibility they acquit themselves of the duty to procreate. Among the couples who fulfill their God-given task in this way, those merit special mention who with a gallant heart and with wise and common deliberation, undertake to bring up suitably even a relatively large family.[9]

Marriage, to be sure, is not instituted solely for procreation; rather, its very nature as an unbreakable compact between persons, and the welfare of the children, both demand that the mutual love of the spouses be embodied in a rightly ordered manner, that it grow and ripen. Therefore, marriage persists as a whole manner and communion of life, and maintains its value and indissolubility even when, despite the often intense desire of the couple, offspring are lacking.

51. This Council realizes that certain modern conditions often keep couples from arranging their married lives harmoniously, and that they find themselves in circumstances where at least temporarily the size of their families should not be increased. As a result, the faithful exercise of love and the full intimacy of their lives is hard to maintain. But where the intimacy of married life is broken off, its faithfulness can sometimes be imperiled and its quality of fruitfulness ruined, for then the upbringing of the children and the courage to accept new ones are both endangered.

To these problems there are those who presume to offer dishonorable solutions; indeed they do not recoil even from the taking of life. But the Church issues the reminder that a true contradiction cannot exist between the divine laws pertaining to the transmission of life and those pertaining to authentic conjugal love.

For God, the Lord of life, has conferred on men the surpassing ministry of safeguarding life in a manner which is worthy of man. Therefore, from the moment of its conception life must be guarded with the greatest care, while abortion and infanticide are unspeakable crimes. The sexual characteristics of man and the human faculty of reproduction wonderfully exceed the dispositions of lower forms of life. Hence, the acts themselves which are proper to conjugal love and which are exercised in accord with genuine human dignity must be honored with great reverence. Hence, when there is question of harmonizing conjugal love

---

9. Cf. Pius XII, Address *Tra le veritá* (Jan. 20, 1958): *AAS* 50 (1958), 91.

with the responsible transmission of life, the moral aspects of any procedure does not depend solely on sincere intentions or on an evaluation of motives, but must be determined by objective standards. These, based on the nature of the human person and his acts, preserve the full sense of mutual self-giving and human procreation in the context of true love. Such a goal cannot be achieved unless the virtue of conjugal chastity is sincerely practiced. Relying on these principles, sons of the Church may not undertake methods of birth control which are found blameworthy by the teaching authority of the Church in its unfolding of the divine law.[10]

All should be persuaded that human life and the task of transmitting it are not realities bound up with this world alone. Hence, they cannot be measured or perceived only in terms of it, but always have a bearing on the eternal destiny of men.

52. The family is a kind of school of deeper humanity. But if it is to achieve the full flowering of its life and mission, it needs the kindly communion of minds and the joint deliberation of spouses, as well as the painstaking cooperation of parents in the education of their children. The active presence of the father is highly beneficial to their formation. The children, especially the younger among them, need the care of their mother at home. This domestic role of hers must be safely preserved, though the legitimate social progress of women should not be underrated on that account.

Children should be so educated that as adults they can follow their vocation, including a religious one, with a mature sense of responsibility and can choose their state of life; if they marry, they can thereby establish their family in favorable moral, social and economic conditions. Parents or guardians should by prudent advice provide guidance to their young with respect to founding a family, and the young ought to listen gladly. At the same time no pressure, direct or indirect, should be put on the young to make them enter marriage or choose a specific partner.

---

10. Cf. Pius XI, Encyclical Letter *Casti Connubii* (Dec. 31, 1930): *AAS* 22 (1930); *DS* 3716–3718; Pius XII, *Allocution to the Congress of Italian Midwives* (Oct. 29, 1951): *AAS* 43 (1951), 835–854; Paul VI, *Allocution to the Cardinals* (June 23, 1964): *AAS* 56 (1964), 581–589. Certain questions which need further and more careful investigation have been handed over, at the command of the Supreme Pontiff, to a commission for the study of population, family and births, in order that after it fulfills its function, the Supreme Pontiff may pass judgment. With the doctrine of the magisterium in this state, this holy synod does not intend to propose immediately concrete solutions.

Thus the family, in which the various generations come together and help one another grow wiser and harmonize personal rights with the other requirements of social life, is the foundation of society. All those, therefore, who exercise influence over communities and social groups should work efficiently for the welfare of marriage and the family. Public authority should regard it as a sacred duty to recognize, protect and promote their authentic nature, to shield public morality and to favor the prosperity of home life. The right of parents to beget and educate their children in the bosom of the family must be safeguarded. Children, too, who unhappily lack the blessing of a family should be protected by prudent legislation and various undertakings and assisted by the help they need.

Christians, redeeming the present time (cf. Eph 5:16; Col 4:5) and distinguishing eternal realities from their changing expressions, should actively promote the values of marriage and the family, both by the examples of their own lives and by cooperation with other men of good will. Thus, when difficulties arise, Christians will provide on behalf of family life, those necessities and helps which are suitably modern. To this end, the Christian instincts of the faithful, the upright moral consciences of men and the wisdom and experience of persons versed in the sacred sciences will have much to contribute.

Those too who are skilled in other sciences, notably the medical, biological, social and psychological, can considerably advance the welfare of marriage and the family along with peace of conscience if by pooling their efforts they labor to explain more thoroughly the various conditions favoring a proper regulation of births.

It devolves on priests duly trained about family matters to nurture the vocation of spouses by a variety of pastoral means, by preaching God's word, by liturgical worship and by other spiritual aids to conjugal and family life, to sustain them sympathetically and patiently in difficulties and to make them courageous through love, so that families which are truly illustrious can be formed.

Various organizations, especially family associations, should try by their programs of instruction and action to strengthen young people and spouses themselves, particularly those recently wed, and to train them for family, social and apostolic life.

Finally, let the spouses themselves, made to the image of the living God and enjoying the authentic dignity of persons, be joined to one another[11] in equal affection, harmony of mind and the work of mutual sanctification. Thus, following Christ who is the principle of life (cf. Rm 5:15, 18; 6:5–11; Gal 2:20), by the sacrifices and joys of their vocation and through their faithful love, married people can become witnesses of the mystery of love which the Lord revealed to the world by his dying and his rising up to life again (cf. Eph 5:25–27).

---

11. Cf. *Sacramentarium Gregorianum: PL* 78, 262.

CHAPTER II

THE PROPER DEVELOPMENT OF CULTURE

53. Man comes to a true and full humanity only through culture, that is, through the cultivation of the goods and values of nature. Wherever human life is involved, therefore, nature and culture are quite intimately connected one with the other.

The word "culture" in its general sense indicates everything whereby man develops and perfects his many bodily and spiritual qualities; he strives by his knowledge and his labor to bring the world itself under his control. He renders social life more human both in the family and the civic community, through improvement of customs and institutions. Throughout the course of time he expresses, communicates and conserves in his works great spiritual experiences and desires, that they might be of advantage to the progress of many, even of the whole human family.

Thence, it follows that human culture has necessarily a historical and social aspect, and the word "culture" also often assumes a sociological and ethnological sense. According to this sense, we speak of a plurality of cultures. Different styles of life and multiple scales of values arise from the diverse manner of using things, of laboring, of expressing oneself, of practicing religion, of forming customs, of establishing laws and juridic institutions, of cultivating the sciences, the arts and beauty. Thus, the customs handed down to it form the patrimony proper to each human community. It is also in this way that there is formed the definite historical milieu which enfolds the man of every nation and age and from which he draws the values which permit him to promote civilization.

Section 1: The Circumstances of Culture in the World Today

54. The circumstances of the life of modern man have been so profoundly changed in their social and cultural aspects, that we can speak

of a new age of human history.[1] New ways are open, therefore, for the perfection and the further extension of culture. These ways have been prepared by the enormous growth of natural, human and social sciences, by technical progress and advances in developing and organizing means whereby men can communicate with one another. Hence, the culture of today possesses particular characteristics: sciences which are called exact greatly develop critical judgment; the more recent psychological studies more profoundly explain human activity; historical studies make it much easier to see things in their mutable and evolutionary aspects; customs and usages are becoming more and more uniform; industrialization, urbanization and other causes which promote community living create a mass-culture from which are born new ways of thinking, acting and making use of leisure. The increase of commerce between the various nations and human groups opens more widely to all the treasures of different civilizations, and thus little by little there develops a more universal form of human culture, which better promotes and expresses the unity of the human race to the degree that it preserves the particular aspects of the different civilizations.

55. From day to day, in every group or nation, there is an increase in the number of men and women who are conscious that they themselves are the authors and the artisans of the culture of their community. Throughout the whole world there is a mounting increase in the sense of autonomy as well as of responsibility. This is of paramount importance for the spiritual and moral maturity of the human race. This becomes more clear if we consider the unification of the world and the duty which is imposed upon us, that we build a better world based upon truth and justice. Thus, we are witnesses of the birth of a new humanism, one in which man is defined first of all by this responsibility to his brothers and to history.

56. In these conditions it is no cause of wonder that man, who senses his responsibility for the progress of culture, nourishes a high hope but also looks with anxiety upon many contradictory things which he must resolve:

What is to be done to prevent the increased exchanges between cultures, which should lead to a true and fruitful dialogue between groups

---

1. Cf. Introductory statement of this constitution, n. 4 ff.

and nations, from disturbing the life of communities, from destroying the wisdom received from ancestors, or from placing in danger the character proper to each people?

How is the dynamism and expansion of a new culture to be fostered without losing a living fidelity to the heritage of tradition? This question is of particular urgency when a culture which arises from the enormous progress of science and technology must be harmonized with a culture nourished by classical studies according to various traditions.

How can we quickly and progressively harmonize the proliferation of particular branches of study with the necessity of forming a synthesis of them, and of preserving among men the faculties of contemplation and observation which lead to wisdom?

What can be done to make all men partakers of cultural values in the world, when the human culture of those who are more competent is constantly becoming more refined and more complex?

Finally, how is the autonomy which culture claims for itself to be recognized as legitimate without generating a notion of humanism which is merely terrestrial, and even contrary to religion itself?

In the midst of these conflicting requirements, human culture must evolve today in such a way that it can both develop the whole human person and aid man in those duties to whose fulfillment all are called, especially Christians fraternally united in one human family.

Section 2: Some Principles for the Proper Development of Culture

57. Christians, on pilgrimage toward the heavenly city, should seek and think of these things which are above (cf. Col 3:2). This duty in no way decreases, rather it increases, the importance of their obligation to work with all men in the building of a more human world. Indeed, the mystery of the Christian faith furnishes them with an excellent stimulant and aid to fulfill this duty more courageously and especially to uncover the full meaning of this activity, one which gives to human culture its eminent place in the integral vocation of man.

When man develops the earth by the work of his hands or with the aid of technology, in order that it might bear fruit and become a dwelling worthy of the whole human family, and when he consciously takes part in the life of social groups, he carries out the design of God manifested at the beginning of time: that he should subdue the earth (cf. Gn 1:28), perfect creation and develop himself. At the same time he obeys the commandment of Christ that he place himself at the service of his brethren.

Furthermore, when man gives himself to the various disciplines of philosophy, history and of mathematical and natural science, and when he cultivates the arts, he can do very much to elevate the human family to a more sublime understanding of truth, goodness and beauty, and to the formation of considered opinions which have universal value. Thus, mankind may be more clearly enlightened by that marvelous Wisdom which was with God from all eternity, composing all things with him, rejoicing in the earth, delighting in the sons of men (cf. Prv 8:30–31).

In this way the human spirit, being less subjected to material things, can be more easily drawn to the worship and contemplation of the Creator. Moreover, by the impulse of grace, he is disposed to acknowledge the Word of God, who before he became flesh in order to save all and to sum up all in himself was already "in the world" as "the true light which enlightens every man" (Jn 1:9–10).[2]

Indeed, today's progress in science and technology can foster a certain exclusive emphasis on observable data and an agnosticism about everything else. For the methods of investigation which these sciences use can be wrongly considered as the supreme rule of seeking the whole truth. By virtue of their methods, these sciences cannot penetrate to the intimate notion of things. Indeed, the danger is present that man, confiding too much in the discoveries of today, may think that he is sufficient unto himself and no longer seek the higher things.

Those unfortunate results, however, do not necessarily follow from the culture of today, nor should they lead us into the temptation of not acknowledging its positive values. Among these values are included: scientific study and fidelity toward truth in scientific inquiries, the necessity of working together with others in technical groups, a sense of international solidarity, a clearer awareness of the responsibility of experts to aid and even to protect men, the desire to make the conditions of life more favorable for all, especially for those who are poor in culture or who are deprived of the opportunity to exercise responsibility. All of these provide some preparation for the acceptance of the message of the

---

2. Cf. St. Irenaeus, *Against Heretics,* III, 11, 8, ed. Sagnard, p. 200; cf. *ibid.,* 16, 6: 290–292; 21, 10–22: pp. 370–372; 22, 3: p. 378; etc.

Gospel, a preparation which can be animated by divine charity through him who has come to save the world.

58. There are many ties between the message of salvation and human culture. For God, revealing himself to his people to the extent of a full manifestation of himself in his incarnate Son, has spoken according to the culture proper to each epoch.

Likewise, the Church, living in various circumstances in the course of time, has used the discoveries of different cultures so that in her preaching she might spread and explain the message of Christ to all nations, that she might examine it and more deeply understand it, that she might give it better expression in liturgical celebration and in the varied life of the community of the faithful.

But at the same time, the Church, sent to all peoples of every time and place, is not bound exclusively and indissolubly to any race or nation, any particular way of life or any customary way of life recent or ancient. Faithful to her own tradition and at the same time conscious of her universal mission, she can enter into communion with the various civilizations, to their enrichment and the enrichment of the Church herself.

The Gospel of Christ constantly renews the life and culture of fallen man; it combats and removes the errors and evils resulting from the permanent allurement of sin. It never ceases to purify and elevate the morality of peoples. By riches coming from above, it makes fruitful, as it were from within, the spiritual qualities and traditions of every people and of every age. It strengthens, perfects and restores (cf. Eph 1:10) them in Christ. Thus the Church, in the very fulfillment of her own function,[3] stimulates and advances human and civic culture; by her action, also by her liturgy, she leads them toward interior liberty.

59. For the above reasons, the Church recalls to the mind of all that culture is to be subordinated to the integral perfection of the human person, to the good of the community and of the whole society. Therefore, it is necessary to develop the human faculties in such a way that there results a growth of the faculty of admiration, of intuition, of contemplation, of making personal judgment, of developing a religious, moral and social sense.

---

3. Cf. the words of Pius XI to Father M. D. Roland-Gosselin: "It is necessary never to lose sight of the fact that the objective of the Church is to evangelize, not to civilize. If it civilizes, it is for the sake of evangelization" (Semaines sociales de France, Versailles, 1936, 461–462).

Culture, because it flows immediately from the spiritual and social character of man, has constant need of a just liberty in order to develop; it needs also the legitimate possibility of exercising its autonomy according to its own principles. It therefore rightly demands respect and enjoys a certain inviolability within the limits of the common good, as long, of course, as it preserves the rights of the individual and the community, whether particular or universal.

This sacred synod, therefore, recalling the teaching of the first Vatican Council, declares that there are "two orders of knowledge" which are distinct, namely faith and reason; and that the Church does not forbid that "the human arts and disciplines use their own principles and their proper method, each in its own domain"; therefore, "acknowledging this just liberty," this sacred synod affirms the legitimate autonomy of human culture and especially of the sciences.[4]

All this supposes that within the limits of morality and the common utility, man can freely search for the truth, express his opinion and publish it; that he can practice any art he chooses; that finally, he can avail himself of true information concerning events of a public nature.[5]

As for public authority, it is not its function to determine the character of the civilization, but rather to establish the conditions and to use the means which are capable of fostering the life of culture among all, even within the minorities of a nation.[6] It is necessary to do everything possible to prevent culture from being turned away from its proper end and made to serve as an instrument of political or economic power.

Section 3: Some More Urgent Duties of Christians in Regard to Culture

60. It is now possible to free most of humanity from the misery of ignorance. Therefore, the duty most consonant with our times, especially for Christians, is that of working diligently for fundamental deci-

---

4. First Vatican Ecumenical Council, Constitution on the Catholic Faith *Dei Filius:* Denz. 1795, 1799 (3015, 3019). Cf. Pius XI, Encyclical Letter *Quadragesimo Anno* (May 15, 1931): *AAS* 23 (1931), 190.

5. Cf. John XXIII, Encyclical Letter *Pacem in Terris* (April 11, 1963): *AAS* 55 (1963), 260.

6. Cf. John XXIII, Encyclical Letter *Pacem in Terris* (April 11, 1963): *AAS* 55 (1963), 283; Pius XII, *Radio Address* (Dec. 24, 1941): *AAS* 34 (1942), 16–17.

sions to be taken in economic and political affairs, both on the national and international level, which will everywhere recognize and satisfy the right of all to a human and social culture in conformity with the dignity of the human person without any discrimination of race, sex, nation, religion or social condition. Therefore, it is necessary to provide all with a sufficient quantity of cultural benefits, especially of those which constitute the so-called fundamental culture, lest very many be prevented from cooperating in the promotion of the common good in a truly human manner because of illiteracy and a lack of responsible activity.

We must strive to provide for those men who are gifted the possibility of pursuing higher studies; and in such a way that, as far as possible, they may occupy in society those duties, offices and services which are in harmony with their natural aptitude and the competence they have acquired.[7] Thus, each man and the social groups of every people will be able to attain the full development of their culture in conformity with their qualities and traditions.

Everything must be done to make everyone conscious of the right to culture and the duty he has of developing himself culturally and of helping others. Sometimes there exist conditions of life and of work which impede the cultural striving of men and destroy in them the eagerness for culture. This is especially true of farmers and workers. It is necessary to provide for them those working conditions which will not impede their human culture but rather favor it. Women now work in almost all spheres. It is fitting that they are able to assume their proper role in accordance with their own nature. It will belong to all to acknowledge and favor the proper and necessary participation of women in the cultural life.

61. Today it is more difficult to form a synthesis of the various disciplines of knowledge and the arts than it was formerly. For while the mass and the diversity of cultural factors are increasing, there is a decrease in each man's faculty of perceiving and unifying these things, so that the image of "universal man" is being lost sight of more and more. Nevertheless, it remains each man's duty to retain an understanding of the whole human person in which the values of intellect, will, conscience and fraternity are preeminent. These values are all rooted in God the Creator and have been wonderfully restored and elevated in Christ.

---

7. John XXIII, Encyclical Letter *Pacem in Terris* (April 11, 1963): *AAS* 55 (1963), 260.

The family is, as it were, the primary mother and nurse of this education. There, the children, in an atmosphere of love, more easily learn the correct order of things, while proper norms of human culture impress themselves in an almost unconscious manner upon the mind of the developing adolescent.

Opportunities for the same education are to be found also in the societies of today, due especially to the increased circulation of books and to the new means of cultural and social communication which can foster a universal culture. With the more or less generalized reduction of working hours, the leisure time of most men has increased. May this leisure be used properly to relax, to fortify the health of soul and body through spontaneous study and activity, through tourism which refines man's character and enriches him with understanding of others, through sports activity which helps to preserve equilibrium of spirit even in the community, and to establish fraternal relations among men of all conditions, nations and races. Let Christians cooperate so that the cultural manifestations and collective activity characteristic of our time may be imbued with a human and a Christian spirit.

All these leisure activities, however, are not able to bring man to a full cultural development unless there is at the same time a profound inquiry into the meaning of culture and science for the human person.

62. Although the Church has contributed much to the development of culture, experience shows that, for circumstantial reasons, it is sometimes difficult to harmonize culture with Christian teaching. These difficulties do not necessarily harm the life of faith; rather, they can stimulate the mind to a deeper and more accurate understanding of the faith. The recent studies and findings of science, history and philosophy raise new questions which affect life and which demand new theological investigations. Furthermore, theologians, within the requirements and methods proper to theology, are invited to seek continually for more suitable ways of communicating doctrine to the men of their times; for the deposit of faith or the truths are one thing, and the manner in which they are enunciated, in the same meaning and understanding, is another.[8] In pastoral care, sufficient use must be made not only of theological

---

8. Cf. John XXIII, *Prayer Delivered at the Beginning of the Council* (Oct. 11, 1962): *AAS* 54 (1962), 792.

principles, but also of the findings of the secular sciences, especially of psychology and sociology, so that the faithful may be brought to a more adequate and mature life of faith.

Literature and the arts are also, in their own way, of great importance to the life of the Church. They strive to make known the proper nature of man, his problems and his experiences in trying to know and perfect both himself and the world. They have much to do with revealing man's place in history and in the world, with illustrating the miseries and joys, the needs and strengths of man and with foreshadowing a better life for him. Thus, they are able to elevate human life, expressed in multifold forms according to various times and regions.

Efforts must be made so that those who foster these arts feel that the Church recognizes their activity and so that, enjoying orderly liberty, they may initiate more friendly relations with the Christian community. The Church acknowledges also new forms of art which are adapted to our age and are in keeping with the characteristics of various nations and regions. They may be brought into the sanctuary since they raise the mind to God, once the manner of expression is adapted and they are conformed to liturgical requirements.[9]

Thus, the knowledge of God is better manifested, and the preaching of the Gospel becomes clearer to human intelligence and shows itself to be relevant to man's actual conditions of life.

May the faithful, therefore, live in very close union with the other men of their time and may they strive to understand perfectly their way of thinking and judging, as expressed in their culture. Let them blend new sciences and theories and the understanding of the most recent discoveries with Christian morality and the teaching of Christian doctrine, so that their religious culture and morality may keep pace with scientific knowledge and with the constantly progressing technology. Thus, they will be able to interpret and evaluate all things in a truly Christian spirit.

Let those who teach theology in seminaries and universities strive to collaborate with men versed in the other sciences through a sharing of their resources and points of view. Theological inquiry should pursue a profound understanding of revealed truth; at the same time it should not

---

9. Cf. Second Vatican Ecumenical Council, Constitution on the Sacred Liturgy *Sacrosanctum Concilium,* 131; Paul VI, *Discourse to the Artists of Rome: AAS* 56 (1964), 439–442.

neglect close contact with its own time, that it may be able to help these men skilled in various disciplines to attain to a better understanding of the faith. This common effort will greatly aid the formation of priests, who will be able to present to our contemporaries the doctrine of the Church concerning God, man and the world, in a manner more adapted to them so that they may receive it more willingly.[10] Furthermore, it is to be hoped that many of the laity will receive a sufficient formation in the sacred sciences and that some will dedicate themselves professionally to these studies, developing and deepening them by their own labors. In order that they may fulfill their function, let it be recognized that all the faithful, whether clerics or laity, possess a lawful freedom of inquiry, freedom of thought and of expressing their mind with humility and fortitude in those matters on which they enjoy competence.[11]

---

10. Cf. Second Vatican Ecumenical Council, Decree on Priestly Training *Optatam Totius* and Declaration on Christian Education *Gravissimum Educationis*.

11. Cf. Second Vatican Ecumenical Council, Dogmatic Constitution on the Church *Lumen Gentium,* 37: *AAS* 57 (1965), 42–43.

CHAPTER III

ECONOMIC AND SOCIAL LIFE

63. In the economic and social realms, too, the dignity and complete vocation of the human person and the welfare of society as a whole are to be respected and promoted. For man is the source, the center and the purpose of all economic and social life.

Like other areas of social life, the economy of today is marked by man's increasing domination over nature, by closer and more intense relationships between citizens, groups and countries and their mutual dependence, and by the increased intervention of the state. At the same time progress in the methods of production and in the exchange of goods and services has made the economy an instrument capable of better meeting the intensified needs of the human family.

Reasons for anxiety, however, are not lacking. Many people, especially in economically advanced areas, seem, as it were, to be ruled by economics, so that almost their entire personal and social life is permeated with a certain economic way of thinking. Such is true both of nations that favor a collective economy and of others. At the very time when the development of economic life could mitigate social inequalities (provided that it be guided and coordinated in a reasonable and human way), it is often made to embitter them; or in some places it even results in a decline of the social status of the underprivileged and in contempt for the poor. While an immense number of people still lack the absolute necessities of life, some, even in less advanced areas, live in luxury or squander wealth. Extravagance and wretchedness exist side by side. While a few enjoy very great power of choice, the majority are deprived of almost all possibility of acting on their own initiative and responsibility, and often subsist in living and working conditions unworthy of the human person.

A similar lack of economic and social balance is to be noticed between agriculture, industry and the services, and also between different parts of one and the same country. The contrast between the economically more advanced countries and other countries is becoming more serious day by day, and the very peace of the world can be jeopardized thereby.

Our contemporaries are coming to feel these inequalities with an ever sharper awareness, since they are thoroughly convinced that the ampler technical and economic possibilities which the world of today enjoys can and should correct this unhappy state of affairs. Hence, many reforms in the socio-economic realm and a change of mentality and attitude are required of all. For this reason, the Church down through the centuries and in the light of the Gospel has worked out the principles of justice and equity demanded by right reason both for individual and social life and for international life, and she has proclaimed them especially in recent times. This sacred Council intends to strengthen these principles according to the circumstances of this age and to set forth certain guidelines, especially with regard to the requirements of economic development.[1]

Section 1: Economic Development

64. Today more than ever before, attention is rightly given to the increase of the production of agricultural and industrial goods and of the rendering of services, for the purpose of making provision for the growth of population and of satisfying the increasing desires of the human race. Therefore, technical progress, an inventive spirit, an eagerness to create and to expand enterprises, the application of methods of production, and the strenuous efforts of all who engage in production—in a word, all the elements making for such development—must be promoted. The fundamental finality of this production is not the mere increase of products nor profit or control but rather the service of man, and indeed of the whole man with regard for the full range of his material needs and the demands of his intellectual, moral, spiritual and religious life; this applies to every man whatsoever and to every group of men, of every race and of every part of the world. Consequently, economic activity is to be carried on according to its own methods and laws within

---

1. Cf. Pius XII, *Address* (March 23, 1952): *AAS* 44 (1953), 273; John XXIII, *Allocution to the Catholic Association of Italian Workers* (May 1, 1959): *AAS* 51 (1959), 358.

the limits of the moral order,[2] so that God's plan for mankind may be realized.[3]

65. Economic development must remain under man's determination and must not be left to the judgment of a few men or groups possessing too much economic power, or of the political community alone, or of certain more powerful nations. It is necessary, on the contrary, that at every level the largest possible number of people, and when it is a question of international relations, all nations have an active share in directing that development. There is need as well of the coordination and fitting and harmonious combination of the spontaneous efforts of individuals and of free groups with the undertakings of public authorities.

Growth is not to be left solely to a kind of mechanical course of the economic activity of individuals, nor to the authority of government. For this reason, doctrines which obstruct the necessary reforms under the guise of a false liberty, and those which subordinate the basic rights of individual persons and groups to the collective organization of production must be shown to be erroneous.[4]

Citizens, on the other hand, should remember that it is their right and duty, which is also to be recognized by the civil authority, to contribute to the true progress of their own community according to their ability. Especially in underdeveloped areas, where all resources must urgently be employed, those who hold back their unproductive resources or who deprive their community of the material or spiritual aid that it needs— saving the personal right of migration—gravely endanger the common good.

66. To satisfy the demands of justice and equity, strenuous efforts must be made, without disregarding the rights of persons or the natural qualities of each country, to remove as quickly as possible the immense

2. Cf. Pius XI, Encyclical Letter *Quadragesimo Anno* (May 15, 1931): *AAS* 23 (1931), 190 ff; Pius XII, *Address* (March 23, 1952): *AAS* 44 (1952), 276 ff.; John XXIII, Encyclical Letter *Mater et Magistra* (May 15, 1961): *AAS* 53 (1961), 450; Second Vatican Ecumenical Council, Decree on the Media of Social Communication *Inter Mirifica,* 6: *AAS* 56 (1964), 147.

3. Cf. Mt 16:26, Lk 16:1–31, Col 3:17.

4. Cf. Leo XIII, Encyclical Letter *Libertas,* Acts of Leo XIII, t. VIII, p. 220 ff.; Pius XI, Encyclical Letter *Quadragesimo Anno* (May 15, 1931): *AAS* 23 (1931), 191 ff.; Pius XI, Encyclical Letter *Divini Redemptoris* (March 19, 1937): *AAS* 39 (1937), 65 ff.; Pius XII, *Nuntius Natalicius* (1941): *AAS* 34 (1942), 10 ff.: John XXIII, Encyclical Letter *Mater et Magistra* (May 15, 1961): *AAS* 53 (1961), 401–464.

economic inequalities which now exist and in many cases are growing, and which are connected with individual and social discrimination. Likewise, in many areas, in view of the special difficulties of agriculture relative to the raising and selling of produce, country people must be helped both to increase and to market what they produce, and to introduce the necessary development and renewal and also obtain a fair income. Otherwise, as too often happens, they will remain in the condition of lower-class citizens. Let farmers themselves, especially young ones, apply themselves to perfecting their professional skill, for without it, there can be no agricultural advance.[5]

Justice and equity likewise require that the mobility which is necessary in a developing economy be regulated in such a way as to keep the life of individuals and their families from becoming insecure and precarious. When workers come from another country or district and contribute to the economic advancement of a nation or region by their labor, all discrimination as regards wages and working conditions must be carefully avoided. All the people, moreover, above all the public authorities, must treat them not as mere tools of production but as persons, and must help them to bring their families to live with them and to provide themselves with a decent dwelling; they must also see to it that these workers are incorporated into the social life of the country or region that receives them. Employment opportunities, however, should be created in their own areas as far as possible.

In economic affairs which today are subject to change, as in the new forms of industrial society in which automation, for example, is advancing, care must be taken that sufficient and suitable work and the possibility of the appropriate technical and professional formation are furnished. The livelihood and the human dignity especially of those who are in very difficult conditions because of illness or old age must be guaranteed.

Section 2: Certain Principles Governing Socio-Economic Life As a Whole

67. Human labor which is expended in the production and exchange of goods or in the performance of economic services is superior to the

---

5. In reference to agricultural problems cf. especially John XXIII, Encyclical Letter *Mater et Magistra* (May 15, 1961): *AAS* 53 (1961).

other elements of economic life, for the latter have only the nature of tools.

This labor, whether it is engaged in independently or hired by someone else, comes immediately from the person, who as it were stamps the things of nature with his seal and subdues them to his will. By his labor a man ordinarily supports himself and his family, is joined to his fellow men and serves them, and can exercise genuine charity and be a partner in the work of bringing divine creation to perfection. Indeed, we hold that through labor offered to God man is associated with the redemptive work of Jesus Christ, who conferred an eminent dignity on labor when at Nazareth he worked with his own hands. From this there follows for every man the duty of working faithfully and also the right to work. It is the duty of society, moreover, according to the circumstances prevailing in it and in keeping with its role, to help the citizens to find sufficient employment. Finally, remuneration for labor is to be such that man may be furnished the means to cultivate worthily his own material, social, cultural and spiritual life and that of his dependents, in view of the function and productiveness of each one, the conditions of the factory or workshop, and the common good.[6]

Since economic activity for the most part implies the associated work of human beings, any way of organizing and directing it which may be detrimental to any working men and women would be wrong and inhuman. It happens too often, however, even in our days, that workers are reduced to the level of being slaves to their own work. This is by no means justified by the so-called economic laws. The entire process of productive work, therefore, must be adapted to the needs of the person and to his way of life, above all to his domestic life, especially in respect to mothers of families, always with due regard for sex and age. The opportunity, moreover, should be granted to workers to unfold their own abilities and personality through the performance of their work. Applying their time and strength to their employment with a due sense

---

6. Cf. Leo XIII, Encyclical Letter *Rerum Novarum* (May 15, 1891): *AAS* 23 (1890–91), 649, 662; Pius XI, Encyclical Letter *Quadragesimo Anno* (May 15, 1931): *AAS* 23 (1931), 200–201; Pius XI, Encyclical Letter *Divini Redemptoris* (March 19, 1937): *AAS* 29 (1937), 92; Pius XII, *Radio Address on Christmas Eve* (1942): *AAS* 35 (1943), 20; Pius XII, *Allocution* (June 13, 1943): *AAS* 35 (1943), 172; Pius XII, *Radio Address to the Workers of Spain* (March 11, 1951): *AAS* 43 (1951), 215; John XXIII, Encyclical Letter *Mater et Magistra* (May 15, 1961): *AAS* 53 (1961), 419.

of responsibility, they should also all enjoy sufficient rest and leisure to cultivate their familial, cultural, social and religious life. They should also have the opportunity freely to develop the energies and potentialities which perhaps they cannot bring to much fruition in their professional work.

68. In economic enterprises it is persons who are joined together, that is, free and independent human beings created to the image of God. Therefore, with attention to the functions of each—owners or employers, management or labor—and without doing harm to the necessary unity of management, the active sharing of all in the administration and profits of these enterprises in ways to be properly determined is to be promoted.[7] Since more often, however, decisions concerning economic and social conditions, on which the future lot of the workers and of their children depends, are made not within the business itself but by institutions on a higher level, the workers themselves should have a share also in determining these conditions—in person or through freely elected delegates.

Among the basic rights of the human person is to be numbered the right of freely founding unions for working people. These should be able truly to represent them and to contribute to the organizing of economic life in the right way. Included is the right of freely taking part in the activity of these unions without risk of reprisal. Through this orderly participation joined to progressive economic and social formation, all will grow day by day in the awareness of their own function and responsibility, and thus they will be brought to feel that they are comrades in the whole task of economic development and in the attainment of the universal common good according to their capacities and aptitudes.

When, however, socio-economic disputes arise, efforts must be made to come to a peaceful settlement. Although recourse must always be had first to a sincere dialogue between the parties, a strike, nevertheless, can remain even in present-day circumstances a necessary though ultimate aid for the defense of the workers' own rights and the ful-

---

7. Cf. John XXIII, Encyclical Letter *Mater et Magistra* (May 15, 1961): *AAS* 53 (1961), 408, 424, 427; however, the word "curatione" has been taken from the Latin text of the Encyclical Letter *Quadragesimo Anno* (May 15, 1931): *AAS* 23 (1931), 199. Under the aspect of the evolution of the question cf. also: Pius XII, *Allocution* (June 3, 1950): *AAS* 42 (1950), 485–488; Paul VI, *Allocution* (June 8, 1964): *AAS* 56 (1964), 573–579.

fillment of their just desires. As soon as possible, however, ways should be sought to resume negotiation and the discussion of reconciliation.

69. God intended the earth with everything contained in it for the use of all human beings and peoples. Thus, under the leadership of justice and in the company of charity, created goods should be in abundance for all in like manner.[8] Whatever the forms of property may be, as adapted to the legitimate institutions of peoples according to diverse and changeable circumstances, attention must always be paid to this universal destination of earthly goods. In using them, therefore, man should regard the external things that he legitimately possesses not only as his own but also as common in the sense that they should be able to benefit not only him but also others.[9] On the other hand, the right of having a share of earthly goods sufficient for oneself and one's family belongs to everyone. The Fathers and Doctors of the Church held this opinion, teaching that men are obliged to come to the relief of the poor and to do so not merely out of their superfluous goods.[10] If one is in extreme necessity, he has the right to procure for himself what he needs out of the riches of others.[11] Since there are so many people prostrate with hunger

---

8. Cf. Pius XII, Encyclical Letter *Sertum Laetitiae* (Nov. 1, 1939): *AAS* 31 (1939), 642; John XXIII, *Consistorial Allocution: AAS* 52 (1960), 5–11; John XXIII, Encyclical Letter *Mater et Magistra* (May 15, 1961): *AAS* 53 (1961), 411.

9. Cf. St. Thomas, *Summa Theol.,* II–II, q. 32, a. 5 *ad* 2; *ibid.* q. 66, a. 2; cf. explanation in Leo XIII, Encyclical Letter *Rerum Novarum* (May 15, 1891): *AAS* 23 (1890–91), 651; cf. also Pius XII, *Allocution* (June 1, 1941): *AAS* 33 (1941), 199; Pius XII, *Birthday Radio Address* (1954): *AAS* 47 (1955), 27.

10. Cf. St. Basil, *Hom. in Illud Lucae,* "Destruam horrea mea," 2: *PG* 31, 263; Lactantius, *Divinarum Institutionum,* Book V on justice: *PL* 6, 565 B; St. Augustine, *In Ioann. Ev. Tr.,* 50, 6: *PL* 35, 1760; St. Augustine, *Enarratio in Ps.* CXLVII, 12: *PL* 37, 192); St. Gregory the Great, *Homiliae in Ev.,* hom. 20: *PL* 76, 1165; St. Gregory the Great, *The Pastoral Rule* 3, 21: *PL* 77, 87; St. Bonaventure, *In III Sent.,* d. 33, dub. 1, ed. Quaracchi, III, 728; St. Bonaventure, *In IV Sent.,* d. 15, p. 11, a. 2, q. 1 (ed. cit. IV, 371 b); q. *De Superfluo* (ms. *Assisi Bibl. Commun.* 186 ff. 112a–113a); St. Albert the Great, *In III Sent.,* d. 33, a.3, sol. 1 (ed. Borgnet XXVIII, 611); *idem, In IV Sent.,* d. 15, a. 1 (ed. cit. XXIX, 494–497). As for the determination of what is superfluous in our day and age, cf. John XXIII, *Radio-television Message* (Sept. 11, 1962): *AAS* 54 (1962), 682: "The obligation of every man, the urgent obligation of the Christian man, is to reckon what is superfluous by the measure of the needs of others, and to see to it that the administration and the distribution of created goods serve the common good."

11. In that case, the old principle holds true: "In extreme necessity all goods are common, that is, all goods are to be shared." On the other hand, for the order, extension, and manner by which the principle is applied in the proposed text, besides the modern authors: cf. St. Thomas, *Summa Theol.,* II–II, q. 66, a. 7. Obviously, for the correct application of the principle, all the conditions that are morally required must be met.

in the world, this sacred Council urges all, both individuals and governments, to remember the aphorism of the Fathers, "Feed the man dying of hunger, because if you have not fed him, you have killed him,"[12] and really to share and employ their earthly goods, according to the ability of each, especially by supporting individuals or peoples with the aid by which they may be able to help and develop themselves.

In economically less advanced societies, the common destination of earthly goods is partly satisfied by means of the customs and traditions proper to the community, by which the absolutely necessary things are furnished to each member. An effort must be made, however, to avoid regarding certain customs as altogether unchangeable if they no longer answer the new needs of this age. On the other hand, imprudent action should not be taken against respectable customs which, provided they are suitably adapted to present-day circumstances, do not cease to be very useful. Similarly, in highly developed nations, a body of social institutions dealing with protection and security can, for its own part, bring to reality the common destination of earthly goods. Family and social services, especially those that provide for culture and education, should be further promoted. When all these things are being organized, vigilance is necessary to prevent the citizens from being led into a certain inactivity vis-a-vis society or from rejecting the burden of taking up office or from refusing to serve.

70. Investments, for their part, must be directed toward procuring employment and sufficient income for the people both now and in the future. Whoever makes decisions concerning these investments and the planning of the economy—whether they be individuals or groups of public authorities—are bound to keep these objectives in mind and to recognize their serious obligation of watching, on the one hand, that provision be made for the necessities required for a decent life both of individuals and of the whole community and, on the other, of looking out for the future and of establishing a right balance between the needs of present-day consumption, both individual and collective, and the demands of investing for the generation to come. They should also always bear in mind the urgent needs of underdeveloped countries or regions. In monetary matters they should beware of hurting the welfare of their own

---

12. Cf. Gratian, *Decretum,* C. 21, dist. LXXXVI, ed. Friedberg I, 302. This axiom is also found already in *PL* 54, 591 A and *PL* 56, 1132 b; cf. in *Antonianum* 27 (1952), 349–366.

country or of other countries. Care should also be taken lest the economically weak countries unjustly suffer any loss from a change in the value of money.

71. Since property and other forms of private ownership of external goods contribute to the expression of the personality, and since, moreover, they furnish one an occasion to exercise his function in society and in the economy, it is very important that the access of both individuals and communities to some ownership of external goods be fostered.

Private property or some ownership of external goods confers on everyone a sphere wholly necessary for the autonomy of the person and the family, and it should be regarded as an extension of human freedom. Lastly, since it adds incentives for carrying on one's function and charge, it constitutes one of the conditions for civil liberties.[13]

The forms of such ownership or property are varied today and are becoming increasingly diversified. They all remain, however, a cause of security not to be underestimated, in spite of social funds, rights and services provided by society. This is true not only of material property but also of immaterial things such as professional capacities.

The right of private ownership, however, is not opposed to the right inherent in various forms of public property. Goods can be transferred to the public domain only by the competent authority, according to the demands and within the limits of the common good, and with fair compensation. Furthermore, it is the right of public authority to prevent anyone from abusing his private property to the detriment of the common good.[14]

By its very nature private property has a social quality which is based on the law of the common destination of earthly goods.[15] If this social quality is overlooked, property often becomes an occasion of pas-

---

13. Cf. Leo XIII, Encyclical Letter *Rerum Novarum* (May 15, 1891): *AAS* 23 (1890–91), 643–646, Pius XI, Encyclical Letter *Quadragesimo Anno* (May 15, 1931): *AAS* 23 (1931), 191; Pius XII, *Radio Message* (June 1, 1941): *AAS* 33 (1941), 199; Pius XII, *Radio Message on Christmas Eve* (1942): *AAS* 35 (1943), 17; Pius XII, *Radio Message* (Sept. 1, 1944): *AAS* 36 (1944), 253; John XXIII, Encyclical Letter *Mater et Magistra* (May 15, 1961): *AAS* 53 (1961), 428–429.

14. Cf. Pius XI, Encyclical Letter *Quadragesimo Anno* (May 15, 1931): *AAS* 23 (1931), 214; John XXIII, Encyclical Letter *Mater et Magistra* (May 15, 1961): *AAS* 53 (1961), 429.

15. Cf. Pius XII, *Radio Message of Pentecost* (1941): *AAS* 44 (1941), 199; John XXIII, Encyclical Letter *Mater et Magistra* (May 15, 1961): *AAS* 53 (1961), 430.

sionate desires for wealth and serious disturbances, so that a pretext is given to the attackers for calling the right itself into question.

In many underdeveloped regions there are large or even extensive rural estates which are only slightly cultivated or lie completely idle for the sake of profit, while the majority of the people either are without land or have only very small fields, and on the other hand, it is evidently urgent to increase the productivity of the fields. Not infrequently those who are hired to work for the landowners or who till a portion of the land as tenants receive a wage or income unworthy of a human being, lack decent housing and are exploited by middlemen. Deprived of all security, they live under such personal servitude that almost every opportunity of acting on their own initiative and responsibility is denied to them and all advancement in human culture and all sharing in social and political life is forbidden to them. According to the different cases, therefore, reforms are necessary: that income may grow, working conditions should be improved, security in employment increased and an incentive to working on one's own initiative given. Indeed, insufficiently cultivated estates should be distributed to those who can make these lands fruitful; in this case the necessary things and means, especially educational aids and the right facilities for cooperative organization, must be supplied. Whenever, nevertheless, the common good requires expropriation, compensation must be reckoned in equity after all the circumstances have been weighed.

72. Christians who take an active part in present-day socio-economic development and fight for justice and charity should be convinced that they can make a great contribution to the prosperity of mankind and to the peace of the world. In these activities let them, either as individuals or as members of groups, give a shining example. Having acquired the absolutely necessary skill and experience, they should observe the right order in their earthly activities in faithfulness to Christ and his Gospel. Thus, their whole life, both individual and social, will be permeated with the spirit of the beatitudes, notably with a spirit of poverty.

Whoever in obedience to Christ seeks first the kingdom of God, takes therefrom a stronger and purer love for helping all his brethren and for perfecting the work of justice under the inspiration of charity.[16]

---

16. For the right use of goods according to the doctrine of the New Testament, cf. Lk 3:11; 10:30 ff.; 11:41; 1 Pt 5:3; Mk 8:36; 12:39–41; Jas 5:1–6; 1 Tm 6:8; Eph 4:28; 2 Cor 8:13; 1 Jn 3:17 ff.

CHAPTER IV

THE LIFE OF THE POLITICAL COMMUNITY

73. In our day, profound changes are apparent also in the structure and institutions of peoples. These result from their cultural, economic and social evolution. Such changes have a great influence on the life of the political community, especially regarding the rights and duties of all in the exercise of civil freedom and in the attainment of the common good, and in organizing the relations of citizens among themselves and with respect to public authority.

The present keener sense of human dignity has given rise in many parts of the world to attempts to bring about a politico-juridical order which will give better protection to the rights of the person in public life. These include the right freely to meet and form associations, the right to express one's own opinion and to profess one's religion both publicly and privately. The protection of the rights of a person is indeed a necessary condition so that citizens, individually or collectively, can take an active part in the life and government of the state.

Along with cultural, economic and social development, there is a growing desire among many people to play a greater part in organizing the life of the political community. In the conscience of many arises an increasing concern that the rights of minorities be recognized, without any neglect for their duties toward the political community. In addition, there is a steadily growing respect for men of other opinions or other religions. At the same time, there is wider cooperation to guarantee the actual exercise of personal rights to all citizens and not only to a few privileged individuals.

However, those political systems prevailing in some parts of the world are to be reproved which hamper civic or religious freedom, victimize large numbers through avarice and political crimes, and divert the exercise of authority from the service of the common good to the interests of one or another faction or of the rulers themselves.

There is no better way to establish political life on a truly human basis than by fostering an inward sense of justice and kindliness and of service to the common good, and by strengthening basic convictions as to the true nature of the political community and the aim, right exercise and sphere of action of public authority.

74. Men, families and the various groups which make up the civil community are aware that they cannot achieve a truly human life by their own unaided efforts. They see the need for a wider community, within which each one makes his specific contribution every day toward an ever broader realization of the common good.[1] For this purpose they set up a political community according to various forms. The political community exists, consequently, for the sake of the common good, in which it finds its full justification and significance, and the source of its inherent legitimacy. Indeed, the common good embraces the sum of those conditions of the social life whereby men, families and associations more adequately and readily may attain their own perfection.[2]

Yet the people who come together in the political community are many and diverse, and they have every right to prefer divergent solutions. If the political community is not to be torn apart while everyone follows his own opinion, there must be an authority to direct the energies of all citizens toward the common good, not in a mechanical or despotic fashion, but by acting above all as a moral force which appeals to each one's freedom and sense of responsibility.

It is clear, therefore, that the political community and public authority are founded on human nature and hence belong to the order designed by God, even though the choice of a political regime and the appointment of rulers are left to the free will of citizens (cf. Rm 13:1–5).

It follows also that political authority, both in the community as such and in the representative bodies of the state, must always be exercised within the limits of the moral order and directed toward the common good—with a dynamic concept of that good—according to the juridical order legitimately established or due to be established. When authority is so exercised, citizens are bound in conscience to obey (cf. Rm 13:5). Accordingly, the responsibility, dignity and importance of leaders are indeed clear.

---

1. Cf. John XXIII, Encyclical Letter *Mater et Magistra* (May 15, 1961): *AAS* 53 (1961), 417.

2. *Ibid.*

But where citizens are oppressed by a public authority overstepping its competence, they should not protest against those things which are objectively required for the common good; but it is legitimate for them to defend their own rights and the rights of their fellow citizens against the abuse of this authority, while keeping within those limits drawn by the natural law and the Gospels.

According to the character of different peoples and their historic development, the political community can, however, adopt a variety of concrete solutions in its structures and the organization of public authority. For the benefit of the whole human family, these solutions must always contribute to the formation of a type of man who will be cultivated, peace-loving and well-disposed toward all his fellow men.

75. It is in full conformity with human nature that there should be juridico-political structures providing all citizens, in an ever better fashion and without any discrimination, the practical possibility of freely and actively taking part in the establishment of the juridical foundations of the political community and in the direction of public affairs, in fixing the terms of reference of the various public bodies and in the election of political leaders.[3] All citizens, therefore, should be mindful of the right and also the duty to use their free vote to further the common good. The Church praises and esteems the work of those who for the good of men devote themselves to the service of the state and take on the burdens of this office.

If the citizens' responsible cooperation is to produce the good results which may be expected in the normal course of political life, there must be a statute of positive law providing for a suitable division of the functions and bodies of authority and an efficient and independent system for the protection of rights. The rights of all persons, families and groups, and their practical application, must be recognized, respected and furthered, together with the duties binding on all citizens.[4] Among the latter it will be well to recall the duty of rendering the political community such material and personal services as are required by the common good. Rulers must be careful not to hamper the development of

---

3. Cf. Pius XII, *Radio Message* (Dec. 24, 1942): *AAS* 35 (1943), 9–24; *Radio Message* (Dec. 24, 1944): *AAS* 37 (1945), 11–17; John XXIII, Encyclical Letter *Pacem in Terris* (April 11, 1963): *AAS* 55 (1963), 263, 271, 277, 278.

4. Cf. Pius XII, *Radio Message* (June 7, 1941): *AAS* 33 (1941), 200: John XXIII, Encyclical Letter *Pacem in Terris* (April 11, 1963): *AAS* 55 (1963), 273–274.

family, social or cultural groups, nor that of intermediate bodies or organizations, and not to deprive them of opportunities for legitimate and constructive activity; they should willingly seek, rather, to promote the orderly pursuit of such activity. Citizens, for their part, either individually or collectively, must be careful not to attribute excessive power to public authority, not to make exaggerated and untimely demands upon it in their own interests, les-sening in this way the responsible role of persons, families and social groups.

The complex circumstances of our day make it necessary for public authority to intervene more often in social, economic and cultural matters in order to bring about favorable conditions which will give more effective help to citizens and groups in their free pursuit of man's total well-being. The relations, however, between socialization[5] and the autonomy and development of the person can be understood in different ways according to various regions and the evolution of peoples. But when the exercise of rights is restricted temporarily for the common good, freedom should be restored immediately upon change of circumstances. Moreover, it is inhuman for public authority to fall back on dictatorial systems or totalitarian methods which violate the rights of the person or social groups.

Citizens must cultivate a generous and loyal spirit of patriotism, but without being narrow minded. This means that they will always direct their attention to the good of the whole human family, united by the different ties which bind together races, people and nations.

All Christians must be aware of their own specific vocation within the political community. It is for them to give an example by their sense of responsibility and their service of the common good. In this way they are to demonstrate concretely how authority can be compatible with freedom, personal initiative with the solidarity of the whole social organism, and the advantages of unity with fruitful diversity. They must recognize the legitimacy of different opinions with regard to temporal solutions and respect citizens who, even as a group, defend their points of view by honest methods. Political parties, for their part, must promote those things which in their judgment are required for the common good; it is never allowable to give their interests priority over the common good.

---

5. Cf. John XXIII, Encyclical Letter *Mater et Magistra* (May 15, 1961): *AAS* 53 (1961), 416.

Great care must be taken about civic and political formation, which is of the utmost necessity today for the population as a whole, and especially for youth, so that all citizens can play their part in the life of the political community. Those who are suited or can become suited should prepare themselves for the difficult, but at the same time, the very noble art of politics,[6] and should seek to practice this art without regard for their own interests or for material advantages. With integrity and wisdom, they must take action against any form of injustice and tyranny, against arbitrary domination by an individual or a political party and any intolerance. They should dedicate themselves to the service of all with sincerity and fairness, indeed, with the charity and fortitude demanded by political life.

76. It is very important, especially where a pluralistic society prevails, that there be a correct notion of the relationship between the political community and the Church, and a clear distinction between the tasks which Christians undertake, individually or as a group, on their own responsibility as citizens guided by the dictates of a Christian conscience, and the activities which, in union with their pastors, they carry out in the name of the Church.

The Church, by reason of her role and competence, is not identified in any way with the political community nor bound to any political system. She is at once a sign and a safeguard of the transcendent character of the human person.

The Church and the political community in their own fields are autonomous and independent from each other. Yet both, under different titles, are devoted to the personal and social vocation of the same men. The more that both foster sounder cooperation between themselves with due consideration for the circumstances of time and place, the more effective will their service be exercised for the good of all. For man's horizons are not limited only to the temporal order; while living in the context of human history, he preserves intact his eternal vocation. The Church, for her part, founded on the love of the Redeemer, contributes toward the reign of justice and charity within the borders of a nation and between nations. By preaching the truths of the Gospel, and bringing to bear on all fields of human endeavor the light of her doctrine and of a

---

6. Pius XI, *Allocution to the Directors of the Catholic University Federation: Discorsi di Pio XI,* ed. Bertetto, vol. 1 (Turin: 1960), 743.

Christian witness, she respects and fosters the political freedom and responsibility of citizens.

The apostles, their successors and those who cooperate with them are sent to announce to mankind Christ, the Savior. Their apostolate is based on the power of God, who very often shows forth the strength of the Gospel on the weakness of its witnesses. All those dedicated to the ministry of God's word must use the ways and means proper to the Gospel, which in a great many respects differ from the means proper to the earthly city.

There are, indeed, close links between earthly things and those elements of man's condition which transcend the world. The Church herself makes use of temporal things insofar as her own mission requires it. She, for her part, does not place her trust in the privileges offered by civil authority. She will even give up the exercise of certain rights which have been legitimately acquired if it becomes clear that their use will cast doubt on the sincerity of her witness, or that new ways of life demand new methods. It is only right, however, that at all times and in all places, the Church should have true freedom to preach the faith, to teach her social doctrine, to exercise her role freely among men and also to pass moral judgment in those matters which regard public order when the fundamental rights of a person or the salvation of souls require it. In this, she should make use of all the means—but only those—which accord with the Gospel and which correspond to the general good according to the diversity of times and circumstances.

While faithfully adhering to the Gospel and fulfilling her mission to the world, the Church, whose duty it is to foster and elevate[7] all that is found to be true, good and beautiful in the human community, strengthens peace among men for the glory of God (cf. Lk 2:14).

---

7. Cf. Second Vatican Ecumenical Council, Dogmatic Constitution on the Church *Lumen Gentium,* 13: *AAS* 57 (1965), 17.

CHAPTER V

THE FOSTERING OF PEACE AND THE PROMOTION OF A COMMUNITY OF NATIONS

77. In our generation when men continue to be afflicted by acute hardships and anxieties arising from the ravages of war or the threat of it, the whole human family faces an hour of supreme crisis in its advance toward maturity. Moving gradually together and everywhere more conscious already of its unity, this family cannot accomplish its task of constructing for all men everywhere a world more genuinely human unless each person devotes himself to the cause of peace with renewed vigor. Thus, it happens that the Gospel message, which is in harmony with the loftier strivings and aspirations of the human race, takes on a new luster in our day as it declares that the artisans of peace are blessed "because they will be called the sons of God" (Mt 5:9).

Consequently, as it points out the authentic and noble meaning of peace and condemns the frightfulness of war, the Council wishes passionately to summon Christians to cooperate, under the help of Christ the author of peace, with all men in securing among themselves a peace based on justice and love and in setting up the instruments of peace.

78. Peace is not merely the absence of war, nor can it be reduced solely to the maintenance of a balance of power between enemies, nor is it brought about by dictatorship. Instead, it is rightly and appropriately called an enterprise of justice. Peace results from that order structured into human society by its divine Founder, and actualized by men as they thirst after ever greater justice. The common good of humanity finds its ultimate meaning in the eternal law. But since the concrete demands of this common good are constantly changing as time goes on, peace is never attained once and for all, but must be built up ceaselessly. Moreover, since the human will is unsteady and wounded by sin, the achievement of peace requires a constant mastering of passions and the vigilance of lawful authority.

But this is not enough. This peace on earth cannot be obtained unless personal well-being is safeguarded and men freely and trustingly share with one another the riches of their inner spirits and their talents. A firm determination to respect other men and peoples and their dignity, as well as the studied practice of brotherhood, are absolutely necessary for the establishment of peace. Hence, peace is likewise the fruit of love, which goes beyond what justice can provide.

That earthly peace which arises from love of neighbor symbolizes and results from the peace of Christ which radiates from God the Father. For by the cross the incarnate Son, the prince of peace, reconciled all men with God. By thus restoring all men to the unity of one people and one body, he slew hatred in his own flesh, and after being lifted on high by his resurrection, he poured forth the spirit of love into the hearts of men.

For this reason, all Christians are urgently summoned to do in love what the truth requires, and to join with all true peacemakers in pleading for peace and bringing it about.

Motivated by this same spirit, we cannot fail to praise those who renounce the use of violence in the vindication of their rights and who resort to methods of defense which are otherwise available to weaker parties too, provided this can be done without injury to the rights and duties of others or of the community itself.

Insofar as men are sinful, the threat of war hangs over them, and hang over them it will until the return of Christ. But insofar as men vanquish sin by a union of love, they will vanquish violence as well and make these words come true: "They shall turn their swords into ploughshares, and their spears into sickles. Nation shall not lift up sword against nation; neither shall they learn war any more" (Is 2:4).

Section 1: The Avoidance of War

79. Even though recent wars have wrought physical and moral havoc on our world, the devastation of battle still goes on day by day in some part of the world. Indeed, now that every kind of weapon produced by modern science is used in war, the fierce character of warfare threatens to lead the combatants to a savagery far surpassing that of the past. Furthermore, the complexity of the modern world and the intricacy of international relations allow guerrilla warfare to be drawn out by new methods of deceit and subversion. In many causes the use of terrorism is regarded as a new way to wage war.

Contemplating this melancholy state of humanity, the Council wishes, above all things else, to recall the permanent binding force of universal natural law and its all-embracing principles. Man's conscience itself gives ever more emphatic voice to these principles. Therefore, actions which deliberately conflict with these same principles, as well as orders commanding such actions, are criminal, and blind obedience cannot excuse those who yield to them. The most infamous among these are actions designed for the methodical extermination of an entire people, nation or ethnic minority. Such actions must be vehemently condemned as horrendous crimes. The courage of those who fearlessly and openly resist those who issue such commands merits supreme commendation.

On the subject of war, quite a large number of nations have subscribed to international agreements aimed at making military activity and its consequences less inhuman. Their stipulations deal with such matters as the treatment of wounded soldiers and prisoners. Agreements of this sort must be honored. Indeed, they should be improved upon so that the frightfulness of war can be better and more workably held in check. All men, especially government officials and experts in these matters, are bound to do everything they can to effect these improvements. Moreover, it seems right that laws make humane provisions for the case of those who for reasons of conscience refuse to bear arms, provided, however, that they agree to serve the human community in some other way.

Certainly, war has not been rooted out of human affairs. As long as the danger of war remains and there is no competent and sufficiently powerful authority at the international level, governments cannot be denied the right to legitimate defense once every means of peaceful settlement has been exhausted. State authorities and others who share public responsibility have the duty to conduct such grave matters soberly and to protect the welfare of the people entrusted to their care. But it is one thing to undertake military action for the just defense of the people, and something else again to seek the subjugation of other nations. Nor, by the same token, does the mere fact that war has unhappily begun mean that all is fair between the warring parties.

Those, too, who devote themselves to the military service of their country should regard themselves as the agents of security and freedom of peoples. As long as they fulfill this role properly, they are making a genuine contribution to the establishment of peace.

80. The horror and perversity of war is immensely magnified by the addition of scientific weapons. For acts of war involving these weapons can inflict massive and indiscriminate destruction, thus going far beyond the bounds of legitimate defense. Indeed, if the kind of instruments which can now be found in the armories of the great nations were to be employed to their fullest, an almost total and altogether reciprocal slaughter of each side by the other would follow, not to mention the widespread devastation that would take place in the world and the deadly aftereffects that would be spawned by the use of weapons of this kind.

All these considerations compel us to undertake an evaluation of war with an entirely new attitude.[1] The men of our time must realize that they will have to give a somber reckoning of their deeds of war, for the course of the future will depend greatly on the decisions they make today.

With these truths in mind, this most holy synod makes its own the condemnations of total war, already pronounced by recent Popes,[2] and issues the following declaration.

Any act of war aimed indiscriminately at the destruction of entire cities or extensive areas along with their population is a crime against God and man himself. It merits unequivocal and unhesitating condemnation.

The unique hazard of modern warfare consists in this: it provides those who possess modern scientific weapons with a kind of occasion for perpetrating just such abominations; moreover, through a certain inexorable chain of events, it can catapult men into the most atrocious decisions. That such may never truly happen in the future, the bishops of the whole world gathered together beg all men, especially government officials and military leaders, to give unremitting thought to their gigantic responsibility before God and the entire human race.

81. To be sure, scientific weapons are not amassed solely for use in war. Since the defensive strength of any nation is considered to be dependent upon its capacity for immediate retaliation, this accumulation

---

1. Cf. John XXIII, Encyclical Letter *Pacem in Terris* (April 11, 1963): *AAS* 55 (1963), 291: "Therefore, in this age of ours which prides itself on its atomic power, it is irrational to believe that war is still an apt means of vindicating violated rights."

2. Cf. Pius XII, *Allocution* (Sept. 30, 1954): *AAS* 46 (1954), 589; *Radio Message* (Dec. 24, 1954): *AAS* 47 (1955), 15 ff., John XXIII, Encyclical Letter *Pacem in Terris* (April 11, 1963): *AAS* 55 (1963), 286–291; Paul VI, *Allocution to the United Nations* (Oct. 4, 1965).

of arms, which increases each year, likewise serves, in a way heretofore unknown, as deterrent to possible enemy attack. Many regard this procedure as the most effective way by which peace of a sort can be maintained between nations at the present time.

Whatever be the facts about this method of deterrence, men should be convinced that the arms race in which an already considerable number of countries are engaged is not a safe way to preserve a steady peace, nor is the so-called balance resulting from this race a sure and authentic peace. Rather than being eliminated thereby, the causes of war are in danger of being gradually aggravated. While extravagant sums are being spent for the furnishing of ever new weapons, an adequate remedy cannot be provided for the multiple miseries afflicting the whole modern world. Disagreements between nations are not really and radically healed; on the contrary, they spread the infection to other parts of the earth. New approaches based on reformed attitudes must be taken to remove this trap and to emancipate the world from its crushing anxiety through the restoration of genuine peace.

Therefore, we say it again: the arms race is an utterly treacherous trap for humanity, and one which ensnares the poor to an intolerable degree. It is much to be feared that if this race persists, it will eventually spawn all the lethal ruin whose path it is now making ready. Warned by the calamities which the human race has made possible, let us make use of the interlude granted us from above and for which we are thankful, to become more conscious of our own responsibility and to find means for resolving our disputes in a manner more worthy of man. Divine Providence urgently demands of us that we free ourselves from the age-old slavery of war. If we refuse to make this effort, we do not know where we will be led by the evil road we have set upon.

It is our clear duty, therefore, to strain every muscle in working for the time when all war can be completely outlawed by international consent. This goal undoubtedly requires the establishment of some universal public authority acknowledged as such by all and endowed with the power to safeguard on the behalf of all, security, regard for justice and respect for rights. But before this hoped for authority can be set up, the highest existing international centers must devote themselves vigorously to the pursuit of better means for obtaining common security. Since peace must be born of mutual trust between nations and not be imposed on them through a fear of the available weapons, everyone must labor to put an end at last to the arms race and to make a true beginning of disarmament, not unilaterally, indeed, but proceeding at an equal pace according to agreement, and backed up by true and workable safeguards.[3]

82. In the meantime, efforts which have already been made and are still underway to eliminate the danger of war are not to be underrated. On the contrary, support should be given to the good will of the very many leaders who work hard to do away with war, which they abominate. These men, although burdened by the extremely weighty preoccupations of their high office, are nonetheless moved by the very grave peacemaking task to which they are bound, even if they cannot ignore the complexity of matters as they stand. We should fervently ask God to give these men the strength to go forward perseveringly and to follow through courageously on this work of building peace with vigor. It is a work of supreme love for mankind. Today it certainly demands that they extend their thoughts and their spirit beyond the confines of their own nation, that they put aside national selfishness and ambition to dominate other nations, and that they nourish a profound reverence for the whole of humanity, which is already making its way so laboriously toward greater unity.

The problems of peace and of disarmament have already been the subject of extensive, strenuous and constant examination. Together with in-ternational meetings dealing with these problems, such studies should be regarded as the first steps toward solving these serious questions, and should be promoted with even greater urgency by way of yielding concrete results in the future.

Nevertheless, men should take heed not to entrust themselves only to the efforts of some, while not caring about their own attitudes. For government officials, who must at one and the same time guarantee the good of their own people and promote the universal good, are very greatly dependent on public opinion and feeling. It does them no good to work for peace as long as feelings of hostility, contempt and distrust, as well as racial hatred and unbending ideologies, continue to divide men and place them in opposing camps. Consequently, there is above all a pressing need for a renewed education of attitudes and for new inspira-

---

3. Cf. John XXIII, Encyclical Letter *Pacem in Terris* (April 11, 1963): *AAS* 55 (1963), 287 (where reduction of arms is mentioned).

tion in public opinion. Those who are dedicated to the work of education, particularly of the young, or who mold public opinion, should consider it their most weighty task to instruct all in fresh sentiments of peace. Indeed, we all need a change of heart as we regard the entire world and those tasks which we can perform in unison for the betterment of our race.

But we should not let false hope deceive us. For unless enmities and hatred are put away and firm, honest agreements concerning world peace are reached in the future, humanity, which already is in the middle of a grave crisis, even though it is endowed with remarkable knowledge, will perhaps be brought to that dismal hour in which it will experience no peace other than the dreadful peace of death. But while we say this, the Church of Christ, present in the midst of the anxiety of this age, does not cease to hope most firmly. She intends to propose to our age over and over again, in season and out of season, this apostolic message: "Behold, now is the acceptable time" for a change of heart; "behold, now is the day of salvation" (2 Cor 2:6).

Section 2: Setting up an International Community

83. In order to build up peace above all, the causes of discord among men, especially injustice, which foment wars must be rooted out. Not a few of these causes come from excessive economic inequalities and from putting off the steps needed to remedy them. Other causes of discord, however, have their source in the desire to dominate and in a contempt for persons. And if we look for deeper causes, we find them in human envy, distrust, pride and other egotistical passions. Man cannot bear so many ruptures in the harmony of things. Consequently, the world is constantly beset by strife and violence between men even when no war is being waged. Besides, since these same evils are present in the relations between various nations as well, in order to overcome or forestall them and to keep violence once unleashed within limits, it is absolutely necessary for countries to cooperate more advantageously and more closely together and to organize together international bodies and to work tirelessly for the creation of organizations which will foster peace.

84. In view of the increasingly close ties of mutual dependence today between all the inhabitants and peoples of the earth, the apt pursuit and efficacious attainment of the universal common good now require of the community of nations that it organize itself in a manner suited to

its present responsibilities, especially toward the many parts of the world which are still suffering from unbearable want.

To reach this goal, organizations of the international community, for their part, must make provision for men's different needs, both in the fields of social life—such as food supplies, health, education, labor— and also in certain special circumstances which can crop up here and there, e.g., the need to promote the general improvement of developing countries, or to alleviate the distressing conditions in which refugees dispersed throughout the world find themselves, or also to assist migrants and their families.

Already existing international and regional organizations are certainly well-deserving of the human race. These are the first efforts at laying the foundations on an international level for a community of all men to work for the solution to the serious problems of our times, to encourage progress everywhere and to obviate wars of whatever kind. In all of these activities, the Church takes joy in the spirit of true brotherhood flourishing between Christians and non-Christians as it strives to make ever more strenuous efforts to relieve abundant misery.

85. The present solidarity of mankind also calls for a revival of greater international cooperation in the economic field. Although nearly all peoples have become autonomous, they are far from being free of every form of undue dependence, and far from escaping all danger of serious internal difficulties.

The development of a nation depends on human and financial aids. The citizens of each country must be prepared by education and professional training to discharge the various tasks of economic and social life. But this in turn requires the aid of foreign specialists, who when they give aid will not act as overlords, but as helpers and fellow-workers. Developing nations will not be able to procure material assistance unless radical changes are made in the established procedures of modern world commerce. Other aid should be provided as well by advanced nations in the form of gifts, loans or financial investments. Such help should be accorded with generosity and without greed on the one side and received with complete honesty on the other side.

If an authentic economic order is to be established on a worldwide basis, an end will have to be put to profiteering, to national ambitions, to the appetite for political supremacy, to militaristic calculations and to machinations for the sake of spreading and imposing ideologies.

86. The following norms seem useful for such cooperation:

a) Developing nations should take great pains to seek, as the object for progress, to express and secure the total human fulfillment of their citizens. They should bear in mind that progress arises and grows above all out of the labor and genius of the nations themselves because it has to be based not only on foreign aid, but especially on the full utilization of their own resources and on the development of their own culture and traditions. Those who exert the greatest influence on others should be outstanding in this respect.

b) On the other hand, it is a very important duty of the advanced nations to help the developing nations in discharging their above-mentioned responsibilities. They should, therefore, gladly carry out on their own home front those spiritual and material readjustments that are required for the realization of this universal cooperation.

Consequently, in business dealings with weaker and poorer nations, they should be careful to respect their profit, for these countries need the income they receive on the sale of their homemade products to support themselves.

c) It is the role of the international community to coordinate and promote development, but in such a way that the resources earmarked for this purpose will be allocated as effectively as possible and with complete equity. It is likewise this community's duty, with due regard for the principle of subsidiarity, so to regulate economic relations throughout the world that these will be carried out in accordance with the norms of justice.

Suitable organizations should be set up to foster and regulate international business affairs, particularly with the underdeveloped countries, and to compensate for losses resulting from an excessive inequality of power among the various nations. This type of organization, in unison with technical, cultural and financial aid, should provide the help which developing nations need so that they can advantageously pursue their own economic advancement.

d) In many cases there is an urgent need to revamp economic and social structures. But one must guard against proposals of technical solutions that are untimely. This is particularly true of those solutions providing man with material conveniences, but nevertheless contrary to man's spiritual nature and advancement. For "not by bread alone does man live, but by every word which proceeds from the mouth of God"

(Mt 4:4). Every sector of the family of man carries within itself and in its best traditions some portion of the spiritual treasure entrusted by God to humanity, even though many may not be aware of the source from which it comes.

87. International cooperation is needed today especially for those peoples who, besides facing so many other difficulties, likewise undergo pressures due to a rapid increase in population. There is an urgent need to explore, with the full and intense cooperation of all, and especially of the wealthier nations, ways whereby the human necessities of food and a suitable education can be furnished and shared with the entire human community. But some peoples could greatly improve upon the conditions of their life if they would change over from antiquated methods of farming to the new technical methods, applying them with needed prudence according to their own circumstances. Their life would likewise be improved by the establishment of a better social order and by a fairer system for the distribution of land ownership.

Governments undoubtedly have rights and duties, within the limits of their proper competency, regarding the population problem in their respective countries, for instance, in the line of social and family life legislation, or regarding the migration of country dwellers to the cities, or with respect to information concerning the condition and needs of the country. Since men today are giving thought to this problem and are so greatly disturbed over it, it is desirable in addition that Catholic specialists, especially in the universities, skillfully pursue and develop studies and projects on all these matters.

But there are many today who maintain that the increase in world population, or at least the population increase in some countries, must be radically curbed by every means possible and by any kind of intervention on the part of public authority. In view of this contention, the Council urges everyone to guard against solutions, whether publicly or privately supported or at times even imposed, which are contrary to the moral law. For in keeping with man's inalienable right to marry and generate children, a decision concerning the number of children they will have depends on the right judgment of the parents, and it cannot in any way be left to the judgment of public authority. But since the judgment of the parents presupposes a rightly formed conscience, it is of the utmost importance that the way be open for everyone to develop a correct and genuinely human responsibility which respects the divine law and takes into consideration the circumstances of the situation and the time. But sometimes this requires an improvement in educational and social conditions and, above all, formation in religion or at least a complete moral training. Men should discreetly be informed, furthermore, of scientific advances in exploring methods whereby spouses can be helped in regulating the number of their children and whose safeness has been well proven and whose harmony with the moral order has been ascertained.

88. Christians should cooperate willingly and wholeheartedly in establishing an international order that includes a genuine respect for all freedoms and amicable brotherhood between all. This is all the more pressing since the greater part of the world is still suffering from so much poverty that it is as if Christ himself were crying out in these poor to beg the charity of the disciples. Do not let men, then, be scandalized because some countries with a majority of citizens who are counted as Christians have an abundance of wealth, whereas others are deprived of the necessities of life and are tormented with hunger, disease and every kind of misery. The spirit of poverty and charity are the glory and witness of the Church of Christ.

Those Christians are to be praised and supported, therefore, who volunteer their services to help other men and nations. Indeed, it is the duty of the whole People of God, following the word and example of the bishops, to alleviate as far as they are able the sufferings of the modern age. They should do this, too, as was the ancient custom in the Church, out of the substance of their goods and not only out of what is superfluous.

The procedure of collecting and distributing aids, without being inflexible and completely uniform, should nevertheless be carried on in an orderly fashion in dioceses, nations and throughout the entire world. Wherever it seems convenient, this activity of Catholics should be carried on in unison with other Christian brothers. For the spirit of charity does not forbid but, on the contrary, commands that charitable activity be carried out in a careful and orderly manner. Therefore, it is essential for those who intend to dedicate themselves to the services of the developing nations to be properly trained in appropriate institutes.

89. Since in virtue of her mission received from God, the Church preaches the Gospel to all men and dispenses the treasures of grace, she contributes to the ensuring of peace everywhere on earth and to the plac-

ing of the fraternal exchange between men on solid ground by imparting knowledge of the divine and natural law. Therefore, to encourage and stimulate cooperation among men, the Church must be clearly present in the midst of the community of nations both through her official channels and through the full and sincere collaboration of all Christians—a collaboration motivated solely by the desire to be of service to all.

This will come about more effectively if the faithful themselves, conscious of their responsibility as men and as Christians, will exert their influence in their own milieu to arouse a ready willingness to cooperate with the international community. Special care must be given, in both religious and civil education, to the formation of youth in this regard.

90. An outstanding form of international activity on the part of Christians is found in the joint efforts which, both as individuals and in groups, they contribute to institutes already established or to be established for the encouragement of cooperation among nations. There are also various Catholic associations on an international level which can contribute in many ways to the building up of a peaceful and fraternal community of nations. These should be strengthened by augmenting in them the number of well qualified collaborators, by increasing needed resources and by advantageously fortifying the coordination of their energies. For today both effective action and the need for dialogue demand joint projects. Moreover, such associations contribute much to the development of a universal outlook—something certainly appropriate for Catholics. They also help to form an awareness of genuine universal solidarity and responsibility.

Finally, it is very much to be desired that Catholics, in order to fulfill their role properly in the international community, will seek to cooperate actively and in a positive manner both with their separated brothers, who together with them profess the Gospel of charity and with all men thirsting for true peace.

The Council, considering the immensity of the hardships which still afflict the greater part of mankind today, regards it as most opportune that an organism of the universal Church be set up in order that both the justice and love of Christ toward the poor might be developed everywhere. The role of such an organism would be to stimulate the Catholic community to promote progress in needy regions and international social justice.

91. Drawn from the treasures of Church teaching, the proposals of this sacred synod look to the assistance of every man of our time, whether he believes in God or does not explicitly recognize him. If adopted, they will promote among men a sharper insight into their full destiny, and thereby lead them to fashion the world more to man's surpassing dignity, to search for a brotherhood which is universal and more deeply rooted, and to meet the urgencies of our ages with a gallant and unified effort born of love.

Undeniably this conciliar program is but a general one in several of its parts, and deliberately so, given the immense variety of situations and forms of human culture in the world. Indeed, while it presents teaching already accepted in the Church, the program will have to be followed up and amplified since it sometimes deals with matters in a constant state of development. Still, we have relied on the Word of God and the spirit of the Gospel. Hence, we entertain the hope that many of our proposals will prove to be of substantial benefit to everyone, especially after they have been adapted to individual nations and mentalities by the faithful, under the guidance of their pastors.

92. By virtue of her mission to shed on the whole world the radiance of the Gospel message, and to unify under one Spirit all men of whatever nation, race or culture, the Church stands forth as a sign of that brotherhood which allows honest dialogue and gives it vigor.

Such a mission requires in the first place that we foster within the Church herself mutual esteem, reverence and harmony through the full recognition of lawful diversity. Thus, all those who compose the one People of God, both pastors and the general faithful, can engage in dialogue with ever abounding fruitfulness. For the bonds which unite the faithful are mightier than anything dividing them. Hence, let there be unity in what is necessary, freedom in what is unsettled, and charity in any case.

Our hearts embrace also those brothers and communities not yet living with us in full communion; to them we are linked, nonetheless, by our profession of the Father and the Son and the Holy Spirit, and by the bond of charity. We do not forget that the unity of Christians is today awaited and desired by many, too, who do not believe in Christ; for the farther it advances toward truth and love under the powerful impulse of the Holy Spirit, the more this unity will be a harbinger of unity and peace for the world at large. Therefore, by common effort and in ways which are today increasingly appropriate for seeking this splendid goal effectively, let us take pains to pattern ourselves after the Gospel more exactly every day, and thus work as brothers in rendering service to the human family. For in Christ Jesus this family is called to the family of the sons of God.

We think cordially, too, of all who acknowledge God and who preserve in their traditions precious elements of religion and humanity. We want frank conversation to compel us all to receive the impulses of the Spirit faithfully and to act on them energetically.

For our part, the desire for such dialogue, which can lead to truth through love alone, excludes no one, though an appropriate measure of prudence must undoubtedly be exercised. We include those who cultivate outstanding qualities of the human spirit, but do not yet acknowledge the Source of these qualities. We include those who oppress the Church and harass her in manifold ways. Since God the Father is the origin and purpose of all men, we are all called to be brothers. Therefore, if we have been summoned to the same destiny, human and divine, we can and we should work together without violence and deceit in order to build up the world in genuine peace.

93. Mindful of the Lord's saying: "By this will all men know that you are my disciples, if you have love for one another" (Jn 13:35), Christians cannot yearn for anything more ardently than to serve the men of the modern world with mounting generosity and success. Therefore, by holding faithfully to the Gospel and benefiting from its resources, by joining with every man who loves and practices justice, Christians have shouldered a gigantic task for fulfillment in this world, a task concerning which they must give a reckoning to him who will judge every man on the last of days.

Not everyone who cries, "Lord, Lord," will enter into the kingdom of heaven, but those who do the Father's will by taking a strong grip on the work at hand. Now, the Father wills that in all men we recognize Christ our brother and love him effectively, in word and in deed. By thus giving witness to the truth, we will share with others the mystery of the heavenly Father's love. As a consequence, men throughout the world will be aroused to a lively hope—the gift of the Holy Spirit—that some day at last they will be caught up in peace and utter happiness in that fatherland radiant with the glory of the Lord.

Now to him who is able to accomplish all things in a measure far beyond what we ask or conceive, in keeping with the power that is at work in us—to him be glory in the Church and in Christ Jesus, down through all the ages of time without end. Amen (Eph 3:20–21).

Given in Rome at St. Peter's, December 7, 1965

INDEX

B

Pauline
BOOKS & MEDIA

The Daughters of St. Paul operate book and media centers at the following addresses. Visit, call or write the one nearest you today, or find us on the World Wide Web, www.pauline.org

California
3908 Sepulveda Blvd., Culver City, CA 90230; 310-397-8676
5945 Balboa Ave., San Diego, CA 92111; 619-565-9181
46 Geary Street, San Francisco, CA 94108; 415-781-5180

Florida
145 S.W. 107th Ave., Miami, FL 33174; 305-559-6715

Hawaii
1143 Bishop Street, Honolulu, HI 96813; 808-521-2731
Neighbor Islands call: 800-259-8463

Illinois
172 North Michigan Ave., Chicago, IL 60601; 312-346-4228

Louisiana
4403 Veterans Memorial Blvd., Metairie, LA 70006; 504-887-7631

Massachusetts
Rte. 1, 885 Providence Hwy., Dedham, MA 02026; 781-326-5385

Missouri
9804 Watson Rd., St. Louis, MO 63126; 314-965-3512

New Jersey
561 U.S. Route 1, Wick Plaza, Edison, NJ 08817; 732-572-1200

New York
150 East 52nd Street, New York, NY 10022; 212-754-1110
78 Fort Place, Staten Island, NY 10301; 718-447-5071

Ohio
2105 Ontario Street, Cleveland, OH 44115; 216-621-9427

Pennsylvania
9171-A Roosevelt Blvd., Philadelphia, PA 19114; 215-676-9494

South Carolina
243 King Street, Charleston, SC 29401; 843-577-0175

Tennessee
4811 Poplar Ave., Memphis, TN 38117; 901-761-2987

Texas
114 Main Plaza, San Antonio, TX 78205; 210-224-8101

Virginia
1025 King Street, Alexandria, VA 22314; 703-549-3806

Canada
3022 Dufferin Street, Toronto, Ontario, Canada M6B 3T5; 416-781-9131
1155 Yonge Street, Toronto, Ontario, Canada M4T 1W2; 416-934-3440

¡También somos su fuente para libros, videos y música en español!